Urban Land Use Planning

Urban Land Use Planning

Second Edition

by F. Stuart Chapin, Jr.

Professor of Planning
University of North Carolina

University of Illinois Press, Urbana, 1965

Second Printing, 1965

SECOND EDITION

© 1965 by the Board of Trustees of the University of Illinois.
Manufactured in the United States of America.
Library of Congress Catalog Card No. 64-18666.

Foreword

Not so long ago social historians were alerting Americans to dramatic changes in the urban way of life to be expected from the rise of industrialism. The changes have been vastly more far-reaching and complex than anything anticipated. The mechanization of agriculture and the phenomenal developments in transportation and communications had a profound effect in redistributing populations of entire regions and concentrating them in rapidly developing new centers of commerce and industry. Then came the countermovements of population within these centers. The automobile and the quest for better living conditions meant the rise of suburbia, leaving a legacy in the center of congestion, an obsolete physical plant, and an ever-widening expanse of "gray areas." With suburban development came a Balkanization of local government and a shift in the main strength of the revenue base from the central city to the fringe. Concomitantly the center became the receiving area for the poor, the destitute, and the outcast. Even as metropolitan areas have been caught up in the complexities of these changes, new breakthroughs in science and technology have set in motion a train of events which are certain to have more far-reaching effects on cities than anything yet encountered.

The city planning profession came into being fifty years ago with the first great wave of urban growth and has been caught up in a tactical situation ever since. As the pressures have mounted there has been a growing realization that a purely pragmatic approach to the increasing complexities of urban change could not continue without a much firmer strategic underpinning. So we see in progress today some promising realignments in emphases. Without any diminished effort going into the tactical aspects of city planning practice, there has been a steady and significant growth in fundamental research in the field, and there has been an alertness among planning agencies to bring the latest and the best of these developments into the fray.

Since the first edition of this book appeared there have been several particularly noteworthy trends in the practice of planning which the new edition endeavors to reflect. First, there has been an increasing interest and sense of responsibility among planning agencies in bringing plans into closer harmony with the basic currents of economic development in the metropolitan area. Growth and development are being seen as phenomena closely allied to economic policy, requiring much more sophisticated methods of analysis than were in common use earlier. Along with this new emphasis, there has been a growing concern with the relation that urban form has to human behavior and the opportunities for making the structure and form of cities more responsive to activity patterns of people and their attitudes and values. There has also been a growing awareness of the importance of integrating planning more directly with policy formulation in the political process. Each of these lines of development is given special attention in this new edition. A new chapter on developments in theory and a section on the use of models in planning have been introduced; the chapter on economic analysis has been extended; a new chapter on urban activity systems has been added; and the policy orientation of the first edition has been extended, with the technical process made more integral with policy formulation.

While introducing these new emphases, the new edition continues to stress the basic orientation introduced initially. Essentially the many and diverse forces noted above as they create pressures for growth and renewal in the physical form of the urban environment remain a central concern. With this concern in view, city planning may be regarded as a means for systematically anticipating and achieving adjustment in the physical environment of a city consistent with social and economic trends and sound principles of civic design. It involves a continuing process of deriving, organizing, and presenting a broad and comprehensive program for urban development and renewal. It is designed to fulfill local objectives of social, economic, and physical well-being, considering both immediate needs and those of the forseeable future. It examines the economic basis for an urban center existing in the first place; it investigates its cultural, political, economic, and physical characteristics both as an independent entity and as a component of a whole cluster of urban centers in a given region; and it attempts to design a physical environment which brings these elements into the soundest and most harmonious plan for the development and renewal of the urban area as a whole.

Land use planning is a part of this larger process of city planning. While taking into account its interrelatedness with transportation and utility planning, land use planning is basically concerned with the location, intensity, and amount of land development required for the various space-using functions of city life—industry, wholesaling, business, housing, recreation, education, and the religious and cultural activities of the people. Fundamentally, the land use plan as a part of an overall plan embodies a proposal as to how land should be used as expansion and renewal proceed in the future.

Besides being limited to one element of comprehensive planning, this book treats only limited aspects of the land use planning process. It is primarily focused on theory and methods, with special attention given to the techniques required in making analyses of land use, in measuring trends, and in estimating present and future requirements for the uses of land. In short, in the pages which follow, an attempt is made to bring together in one book the theoretical background for land use planning and to summarize techniques the city planner employs in diagnosing the ills and needs of land development. Those aspects concerned with the legal basis of planning, its legislative controls, and its administrative organization are specifically excluded from detailed treatment.

In so defining the scope of this book, the author is fully cognizant of the difficulty and the temerity of outlining the theoretical basis of land use planning and of setting down techniques in a field which is changing so swiftly from year to year. He is cognizant of the incomplete and, in some respects, tentative character of the theory he attempts to introduce. Moreover, he is fully aware of the imbalance in the degree to which techniques are developed and the imbalance in the relative utility of the different methods described herein. Some will be found to be too crude and others too refined for the purposes for which they are used. Many of the techniques will be found to be too recent in development to have been tested for reliability, accuracy, and general adaptability for any extensive use. These are all inherent difficulties in a field so young and one which is changing so rapidly. Yet the author is firmly convinced that, if nothing more is accomplished, a useful purpose is served simply by bringing this material together where it can be subject to more critical examination and provide a stimulus for research and experimentation so sorely needed.

The material in this book is organized in three parts. Part I brings together theoretical work which has relevance to land use planning. Part II is concerned with "tooling-up" studies which, though basic to all city planning inquiries, are treated with special attention to the needs of land use planning. Finally, Part III covers the land use planning process itself, presenting in sequence techniques for the development of the land use plan.

This introduction would be incomplete without acknowledgement of the encouragement and critical suggestions from the many who have experimented with methods in planning offices, from university colleagues, and from students over a number of years. Their comments have contributed much to the first edition and particularly to this revised edition.

F. STUART CHAPIN, JR.

Chapel Hill, N.C.
September, 1964

Contents

Tables

Figures

Part I

Land Use
Determinants

URBAN LAND USE is a term used in at least three ways in contemporary planning literature. In some of the writing, it means the spatial distribution of city functions—its residential areas, its industrial, commercial, and retail business districts, and the spaces set aside for institutional and leisure-time functions. In some of the literature, it means a two-part framework for visualizing urban areas: first, in terms of activity patterns of people in the urban setting and their institutions as they require space (for example, activities involved in earning a living, shopping, following leisure-time pursuits), and second, in terms of physical facilities or improvements to the land in the urban setting which are made to accommodate these activity patterns (that is, the functional use patterns identified above). In still other parts of the literature, land use involves still another level of exploration and study. In addition to focusing on the activity-use relationships involved in the two-part framework, attention is also devoted to the role that value systems of people play as they regulate space-using activities and thence the use patterns which emerge.

There is an ascending order of complexity implied in these three ways of viewing urban land use, and, as we will presently see, the analytical aspects of land use planning (as distinguished from the design aspects) must go to a form of systems analysis to handle these complexities. These developments will be covered in Parts II and III. In Part I we will be mainly concerned with the theoretical bases of these ways of viewing urban land use and indicating how the beginnings of theoretical research in planning are seeking to synthesize relevant work from a variety of city planning–related fields such as anthropology, architecture, economics, geography, human ecology, social psychology, sociology, and others. Depending upon the interests and background of the writer and the research traditions of his field, some of this work is subjective and speculative, some of it is documentary and descriptive, and some of it is mathematical and experimental, adhering closely to the maxims of the scientific method.

Perhaps the earliest attempts in this country at a systematic theoretical explanation of land use come out of the work of such people as Burgess, Hoyt, McKenzie, Harris and Ullman, and Firey.[1] In retrospect, we can see an evolutionary sequence to the work of these people which undoubtedly

[1] Ernest W. Burgess, "The Growth of the City," in R. E. Park *et al.* (eds.), *The City*, Chicago: University of Chicago Press, 1925; Homer Hoyt, *The Structure and Growth of Residential Neighborhoods in American Cities*, Washington: Federal Housing Administration, 1939; Arthur M. Weimer and Homer Hoyt, *Principles of Real Estate*, New York: The Ronald Press Company, 1960; R. D. McKenzie, *The Metropolitan Community*, New York: McGraw-Hill Book Company, Inc., 1933; Chauncy D. Harris and Edward L. Ullman, "The Nature of Cities," *The Annals of the American Academy of Political and Social Science*, November, 1945; Walter Firey, *Land Use in Central Boston*, Cambridge: Harvard University Press, 1947; and Sidney M. Willhelm, *Urban Zoning and Land-Use Theory*, New York: The Free Press of Glencoe and The Macmillan Company, 1962.

has had some influence on one or more of the three above-cited ways of viewing urban land use. Burgess was concerned with the very general tendencies in the patterning of land uses and the growth of a metropolitan area. In the work of Hoyt, land use is explained in terms of the economic behavior of land users or their agents in the marketplace. There is a predisposition in his work to seek explanations of city structure and its land use configuration in terms of universal economic forces which tend to govern the makeup and change in this configuration. In McKenzie's work on the national patterns of metropolitan dominance, and in Harris and Ullman's conceptualization in the more localized setting, the emphasis shifts to multiple centers of activity. In Firey's work, land use arrangements are interpreted in terms of values and attitudes by city residents and the resultant actions in the selection of locations to satisfy these values and attitudes. Both in Burgess' concentric zone concept and in Hoyt's sector theory and to a less extent in the Harris-Ullman multiple nuclei hypothesis, heavy emphasis is placed on economic determinism of land use, with the implication that human value systems and group action are self-regulating and contained by dominant economic forces. When Firey challenged this deterministic view of land-using activities and land use patterns and argued that culturally rooted values and social behavior in the city were influential to an important degree, he was unknowingly ushering in a new and broadened tradition to research in land use, pointing the way to the kind of work that Willhelm and others have since undertaken to interpret the role of values in shaping land use decisions.

As these explanations of land use have developed, each in a theoretical system of its own, city planning, in slowly maturing as a professional field, has been more directly concerned with the applied aspects of land use arrangements. Due perhaps in part to this practical orientation, in part to the great variety of fields it draws upon, and in part to the process of "coming of age," it has had little occasion until recently to engage in fundamental research, particularly of a kind aimed at defining a theoretical frame of reference for urban planning. Such a theoretical framework is urgently needed, and work of the above order in related fields has much to contribute toward accomplishing this objective. While such work has been largely undisciplinary in orientation with understandable emphasis on the concepts which predominate within these respective fields, obviously city planning as a field cutting across many different disciplines cannot very well overlook this significant work.

The emerging work on the structural organization and form of urban areas, what is called "urban spatial structure," has been ranging freely across discipline lines. While it also clearly reflects a disposition to develop into what may be thought of as an urban science with a standing in its own right, some of the new effort links up theoretical work from social science disciplines in ways which would have been improbable had these fields been left to their own devices. Accordingly, it seems fitting to begin the study of urban land use planning by examining some of its conceptual origins from related fields. Chapter 1 aims to supply a common base line in this respect, and Chapter 2 comes to focus on theoretical work more centrally concerned with urban land use planning.

In effect, the chapters of Part I thus supply some of the conceptual bases of urban land use planning methods and techniques set forth in Parts II and III. As fundamental research begins to supply systematic foundation theory to guide the planning practitioner in land use planning, the concepts presented in these two chapters may be altered and will certainly become considerably more refined and less fragmentary in the future. Directed as it is toward the city planning practitioner, this summary aims to bring together only those concepts which have direct present or potential application to the land use planning procedure.

Chapter 1

Land Use Perspectives

Since the beginnings of the Industrial Revolution, the city has increasingly occupied men's minds as an object of study, and undoubtedly as cities and metropolitan complexes continue to expand, urban phenomena will receive more and more attention. Such fields as anthropology, economics, geography, political science, and sociology have shown new interest in the metropolitan community as a focus of investigation. In one sense, if urban society in the American scene is construed to be synonymous today with human society, this seemingly new interest in urban phenomena is nothing more than a semantic adaptation to the mainstream of study that has been going on for some time in these fields. However, in another sense it represents an important new emphasis. When these investigations see urban concentrations and industrialization molding human behavior into certain patterns, with these in turn bearing some relation to urban spatial structure, this interest is new indeed and possesses some relevance for the work of city planners. While the urban-related developments in these fields are too numerous to cite in detail, the work which has particular significance for theory in urban spatial structure is taken up below. In the first section, attention is devoted to economic perspectives of land development. This is followed by a section on socially rooted determinants of land use, and a third focuses on the public interest as a determinant of land development. Finally, a fourth section brings these perspectives together and examines some of the interrelationships among them which have meaning for city planning.

Economic Determinants of Land Use

The economic explanations of the urban land use pattern begin with forces extending far beyond the immediate environs of any particular urban center of interest, and involve considerations of the structure and functioning of the urban economy as it fits into the larger economy of the region and the nation. Implicit in this way of approaching the economic basis of land use is a rationale that both regional and localized forces interact to shape the urban land use pattern, or, more specifically, that external forces affecting the makeup and vitality of the economy act upon internally focused processes of the urban land market to determine the location of urban functions on the land. To an important degree these regional forces influence how much and at what rate land goes into development.

While we acknowledge at the outset the role that these external forces play in determining land use in a given urban center, discussion of regional considerations is postponed until Chapter 3 in which the urban economy in the context of the region is examined in fuller detail. This section of the present chapter will concern itself primarily with the intraurban workings of the land market, maintaining a rough parallelism in approach followed in the second and third sections below. Considered here are first the factors influencing the use of the individual parcel of land, then an examination of the total configuration of land uses in the urban center, and finally a discussion of the application of land economics theory to land use planning.

Use of the Individual Land Parcel

The land economist views land use in terms of economic theory, with the use of each land parcel determined in what he calls "the urban land market." He looks upon land (real éstate in the generic sense) as a commodity traded in this market subject to the forces of supply and demand. According to classical equilibrium theory, price then becomes both a function of the costs of making land productive (in the sense of providing valuable services) and a function of the net income or return realizable by the development of that land. All land is viewed as being in the market competing for the consumer's money, and decisions to buy or sell are prompted by the opportunities for maximizing return from a transaction in the market. It is beyond the scope of this discussion to go into the intricacies of the operation of forces of supply and demand, except to note that in the process of interacting in the market, these forces are viewed as the final determinants of the uses to which urban land is put.

Urban land is considered to have value because of its potential to produce income in the future. This value is based on what developers would be economically justified in paying for it according to an assumed plan for its use and development. As considered in this assumed plan, "the value of land is the sum of all the net land incomes that will accrue in perpetuity discounted for the period of time that will elapse before they are received. Since incomes due one hundred years in the future have only a negligible value today, the valuation of land involves a prophecy as to the net income of the land for the next thirty or forty years." [1]

Economic value of land approaches the selling price under conditions of perfect competition in the market. "It may deviate from price and often does, especially since value is often identified with specific purposes, such as value for mortgage-lending purposes, for tax purposes, for insurance purposes, for estate settlement, for condemnation, for quick sale in a current market, and for many others." [2] Since the developer is seeking the most favorable return, the market value to him or the price he is willing to pay is the net worth that his development would have based on his anticipated profits. "If he assumes that so many dollars must be invested in the buildings and land improvements, then the calculated net worth less this sum will represent what he would be justified in paying for the land. But if he assumes an acquisition cost for the land, then the balance of the net worth after deducting land cost will represent what he would be justified in paying for building and improvements. His decision to proceed with the investment in the enterprise will depend upon the relationship of the hypothetical initial net worth of the proposed land development and the necessary or actual total capital cost of acquiring the land and erecting the buildings." [3]

The market value of land varies, among other things, according to the functional type of area in which it is located in the overall pattern of land uses and with respect to other sites within one particular type of use area.

Each parcel of land occupies a unique physical relationship with every other parcel of land. Because in every community there exists a variety of land uses, each parcel is the focus of a complex but singular set of space relationships with the social and economic activities that are centered on all other parcels. To each combination of space relationships, the market attaches a special evaluation, which largely determines the amount of the bid for that site which is the focus of the combination. Thus certain locations are more highly valued for residential use than other sites because of the greater convenience to shops, schools, centers of employment, and recreational facilities. Corner locations command a higher price for certain types of retail use because of greater convenience to streams of pedestrian traffic. [4]

Thus to the economist, land is pressed into use by the existence of a value as established by the alternatives of land development, and the use of a particular parcel is finally determined in the operations of market forces

[1] Homer Hoyt, *One Hundred Years of Land Values in Chicago,* Chicago: University of Chicago Press, 1933, p. 449.

[2] Arthur M. Weimer and Homer Hoyt, *Principles of Real Estate,* New York: The Ronald Press Company, 1960, p. 114.

[3] Richard U. Ratcliff, *Urban Land Economics,* New York: McGraw-Hill Book Company, Inc., 1949, p. 356.

[4] *Ibid.,* pp. 283–284.

by the price paid and the decision as to what alternative will yield the highest return.

The Total Land Use Pattern

The foregoing view of the way in which the individual parcel obtains a value and is priced in the market cannot be separated from the aggregate view of all parcels and how their values are established. So, next it is useful to view the structure of land values as a whole and examine the relationships between land values and land uses in the aggregate. Here we find some new and suggestive perspectives. The land economist still looks to classical rent theory and equilibrium models for the analysis of supply and demand relationships and the pricing of land in the marketplace, but he sees the total pattern of land use as the cumulative result of the sorting process of many marketplace decisions over a long period of time of the kind we have noted above for the individual parcel. The very complexity of market transactions of this magnitude and longitudinal character suggests that future theoretical research more and more will involve the use of models which are geared to the use of the high-speed computer.

The generalized model sets forth the nature of the relationships that must be recognized in these more advanced models. The typical model states that the value of land is the expected aggregate net annual return on the land expressed as a percentage of the annual rate at which the total investment is estimated to be amortized annually. Expressing the expected net annual return as the difference between gross revenue and expected costs, Wendt has stated the general model as follows:[5]

$$\text{Land Value} = \frac{(\text{Aggregate Gross Revenues}) \text{ minus } (\text{Total Expected Costs})}{\text{Capitalization Rate}}$$

In using such a model, Wendt stresses the importance of distinguishing between factors which affect the aggregate of land values and those which operate on the individual site. Thus there may be variations in land value stemming from changes in economic conditions, and there may be variations due to conditions inherent in particular locations or districts, for example, differential conditions of growth or decline. In the above model, Wendt indicates the variables of the revenues component in the numerator to be (1) investors' expectation of the size of the market, (2) the income spent for various urban services within the market, (3) the urban area's competitive pull, (4) the supply of competitive urban land, and (5) the prospective investment in public improvements. The expected cost component

---

[5] Paul F. Wendt, "Theory of Urban Land Values," *Land Economics*, August, 1957.

in the numerator he gives as the sum of (1) local property taxes, (2) operating costs, (3) interest on capital invested in present and future improvements, and (4) depreciation allowances for these improvements. Wendt lists the variables affecting the capitalization rate in the denominator as (1) interest rates, (2) allowances for anticipated risk, and (3) expectations concerning capital gains.

According to land economics theory, these factors are taken into account in the marketplace. Here users of land bid for sites in accordance with what will maximize their profits and minimize their costs. Land users in retail business and services tend to bid for space at the highest prices, and land best suited for these activities shows the highest value. For this type of use the revenue component in the above formulation of land value is based on the volume of sales expected at alternative sites, and the cost component is based on the costs of doing business to obtain these sales at these sites. Similarly, for industrial users, the revenue component is based on product sales potentials at different competing sites, and the cost component is based on costs of production at those sites. For households the revenue component is based on the dollar value placed on benefits anticipated from alternative sites, with costs being measured in terms of commuting expenses, taxes, improvement costs, and so on at each such alternative site.

How the structure of values varies spatially in the city in accordance with site use potential has been shown for the small city by Knos in his study of Topeka (see Figure 1).[6] In the relatively simple representation of the structure of land values to be found in the small city, the central business district towers above everything else. Since it is a focus for employment, business transactions, and shopping, and the alternative sites for these uses have been largely confined to this location (at least until recent time), values are high and there is more intensive use of space. Industrial concentrations and outlying business appear as hills, with residential areas assuming more intensive patterns of use on the slopes of the central peak and the hills. However, intensity of space use rapidly falls off as the less accessible outer sections of the city are reached.

In his study of Topeka, Knos tested the relationship between land values and several commonly assumed characteristics of land use. Where he postulated that land values would vary inversely with the distance from the center of the city, he found that they varied inversely with the reciprocal of the distance. Similarly he found that land values also varied inversely with the reciprocal of the distance from the major radial thoroughfares converging on this center.

---

[6] Duane S. Knos, *Distribution of Land Values in Topeka, Kansas,* Lawrence: Center for Research in Business, The University of Kansas, May, 1962.

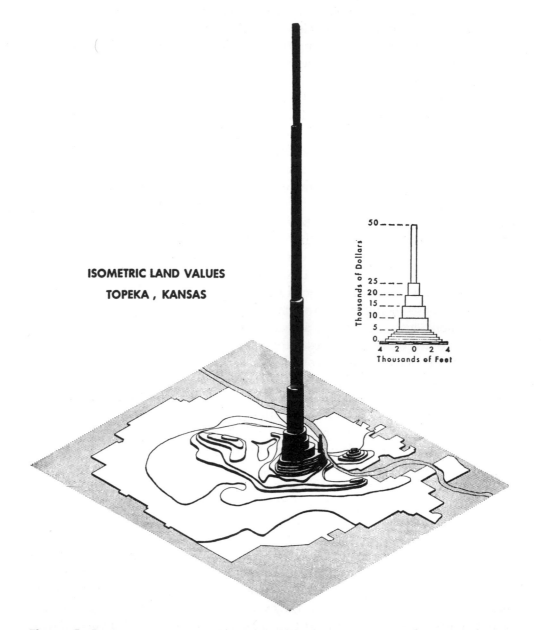

Figure 1. Representation of the Structure of Urban Land Values. (*Source:* Duane S. Knos, *Distribution of Land Values in Topeka, Kansas,* Lawrence: Center for Research in Business, The University of Kansas, May, 1962.)

As cities become larger than Topeka, as they assume metropolitan proportions, and as urban regions begin to develop, the above three-dimensional view of land values assumes a greater and greater complexity. Hoyt gives a vivid picture of values that developed in the large metropolitan centers during the post–World War I period of urban growth:

If the land values in Chicago were shown in the form of a relief map, in which the elevations represented high land value, a picture of startling contrasts would be disclosed. In the center would be the Himalaya Mountain peaks of the Loop, but on all sides except along a high ridge running north along the lake there would be a descent into the deep valleys of the blighted areas. Gradually, as one went farther from the center, the elevation would begin to rise. Along the lake, both north and south, would be a high ridge which slopes down sharply as one goes west. Beginning 5 or 6 miles from the center of the city, there would be a plateau several miles wide encircling the city that is uptilted toward the lake, on top of which would be high ridges a mile apart that culminated in towering pinnacles at each intersection.[7]

While such spatial variations in land values have long been recognized and accepted, Hoyt's work provided the first systematic empirical demonstration that these variations and the "topography" of the entire pattern bear a close relationship to the land use configuration of the city. His study confirmed another long-accepted relationship, namely, that as the patterns of values change in time, use patterns change, and conversely, as the patterns of uses change, the patterns of values change in time.

Knos's study provides empirical evidence of a second relationship which is widely accepted, namely, that land values influence the intensity of land use. This study and Hoyt's earlier work suggest that intensity, too, will change in time as land values change and that there are complex feedback relations from intensity of use to the structure of land values. Indeed, it is clear that the patterns of uses, intensities, and values are all three strongly intercorrelated. While these interrelationships seem apparent, there are many other factors bound up in the social and economic history of the community, the effects of which defy clear-cut differentiation. As simulation models are perfected, we can expect to learn more about these forces.

Meanwhile, as Hoyt reminds us, we can get some insights about the changing structure of land values from history. In this respect, transportation can be seen to be a major influence in the twentieth century. From the earliest development of cities in this country, there was a logical tendency for them to grow in tightly knit patterns. The highly centralized pattern followed the mass transportation lines, persisting through the 'twenties. Then in the 'thirties the ever-increasing use of the automobile,

---

[7] Hoyt, *One Hundred Years of Land Values in Chicago*, p. 297.

coupled with the widespread influence of the depression-born FHA program of home-financing guarantees, produced a shift to a more dispersed pattern. In the immediate post–World War II period, this outward expansion picked up momentum, producing first what frequently has been called "sprawl" and then, with expressway developments and the merchandising systems of modern shopping centers, what has come to be called "scatteration." In turn these scatter patterns have given rise in the more urbanized parts of the country to urban regions, great belts of coalescing metropolitan areas. In reviewing the implications of these changes for the structure of land values, Hoyt sees fewer spectacular peaks developing in the future, suggesting that the creation of new values is more likely to be found in connection with the trend toward large-scale Levittown-type developments.[8] Some see this prospect as a natural extension of the current big business phenomenon, with the structure of future land values controlled to a greater extent by a relatively few very large developments.

CONCENTRIC ZONE CONCEPT

1. Central Business District
2. Zone of Transition
3. Zone of Workingmen's Homes
4. Zone of Better Residences
5. Commuters' Zone

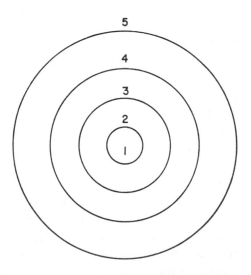

Figure 2. Generalized Explanations of the Land Use Patterns of Cities. (*Source:* Chauncy D. Harris and Edward L. Ullman, "The Nature of Cities," *The Annals of the American Academy of Political and Social Science*, November, 1945.)

---

[8] Homer Hoyt, "Changing Patterns of Land Values," *Land Economics,* May, 1960.

Space Organization Concepts

With this general view of the pattern to the distribution of land values in urban areas before us, it is useful to consider some of the conceptual systems which have been offered in explanation of these patterns and their changes over time. Apart from economic theory noted at the outset, three explanations have been advanced: one known as the concentric zone concept, a second referred to as the sector concept, and the third, the multiple nuclei concept (see Figure 2). The first and last descriptions deal with the entire pattern of use areas, whereas the sector system of explanation was developed primarily to explain the structure of residential areas. The zonal and sector theories are used to describe changes in the basic arrangements of land use patterns, whereas the multiple nuclei approach is primarily an observation of the structural form of the urban land use pattern at a particular point in time.

SECTOR CONCEPT

1. Central Business District
2. Wholesale Light Manufacturing
3. Low-Class Residential
4. Medium-Class Residential
5. High-Class Residential

MULTIPLE NUCLEI CONCEPT

6. Heavy Manufacturing
7. Outlying Business District
8. Residential Suburb
9. Industrial Suburb

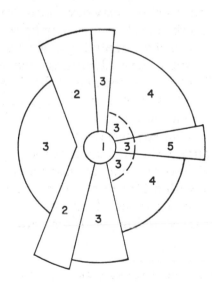

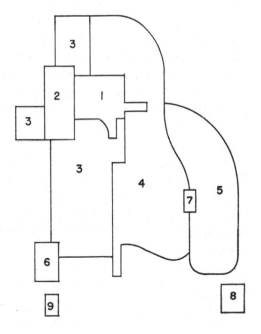

Concentric Zone Concept

Early land economists frequently used Burgess' conventionalized diagram to explain the composite effect of market forces upon land use arrangements.[9] Developed in the early 'twenties to explain ecological processes in the city, Burgess conceived the city as a series of five concentric zones. At the core is his "loop" district with its shopping areas, its theater districts, its hotels, its office buildings, its banking houses, and the other businesses which seek a central location. In small communities these business functions intermingle; in large cities they form more or less distinct subdistricts.

Adjoining the "loop" and fanning out into the next zone are the city's commercial functions. Here the market districts and the older wholesale districts and warehouse areas are located. When the city is situated on the edge of a body of water, its port functions in most cases are interspersed with these functions. Usually industries which do not require much ground area also locate here. Cutting across this and the remaining outer zones along railroad rights of way and forming long wedge-like areas are the larger industrial sections of the city.

His second zone is the area which has been termed "the zone of transition." It is easily identified by the variety and changing character of uses. Here the residential areas commence. In one portion of the zone, there may be an island-like cluster of "first-citizen" homes persisting behind brick walls and iron fences, clinging tenaciously to the respectability that once marked the entire area. In some sections such structures may have been supplanted by large apartment houses. In others the old structures may be still standing, but there are antique shop or tearoom signs signifying a new use. In some locations the now shabby homes display signs advertising "rooms to let" or "light-housekeeping apartments." Often other sections of the zone, particularly those adjoining the industrial wedges, contain residential slum areas. The second zone blends into a third zone consisting largely of workingmen's homes—homes of factory workers, laborers, and so on.

Next is his fourth zone, containing the large residential areas of the city. This is the area where the white-collar workers and middle-class families are found. Later, Burgess dealt more fully with a fifth ring, a commuters' zone.[10] In this ring are the suburban communities found along the arteries of transportation. This is where the middle-class and upper-income groups reside.

---

[9] Ernest W. Burgess, "The Growth of the City," in R. E. Park *et al.* (eds.), *The City*, Chicago: University of Chicago Press, 1925.

[10] Ernest W. Burgess, "Urban Areas," in T. V. Smith and L. D. White (eds.), *Chicago: An Experiment in Social Science Research*, Chicago: University of Chicago Press, 1929.

As growth occurs, each inner zone of the generalized diagram (and Burgess propounded it only as a diagram to explain observable tendencies in the internal structure of the city) tends to invade the next outer zone following what the human ecologist refers to as a sequence of "invasion-succession" (see the next section). The rate of progression of this rippling tendency depends on economic expansion in the city and rate of population growth. In contrast, when urban areas are decreasing in population, the outer zones tend to remain stationary, but the inner fringe of the transitional zone tends to recede into the commercial district. In this connection the accompanying contraction of the commercial district, and a consequent expansion of the transitional area (which in reality is no longer transitional), is frequently interpreted to mean the creation of "permanent" commercial as well as residential slums.

As a theoretical explanation of the positioning of the major functional areas of land use in a city and how they change over the years, the elemental simplicity of this approach has had considerable appeal. While it is a useful and pictorial way of describing broad and general tendencies at work in the patterning of urban land uses, in many respects it is an oversimplification. More recent work relating to the sector and multiple nuclei approaches, as described below, seeks theoretical explanations of land use patterns which take into account irregularities that tend to develop in use patterns.

Sector Concept

Following Burgess' work about a decade later, Homer Hoyt's well-known study of residential areas in the United States provided some new insights into the patterning of land uses and led to a theoretical explanation of residential land uses in terms of wedge-shaped sectors radial to the city's center along established lines of transportation. This theory holds that the different income group classes of a city tend to be found in distinct areas describable in terms of sectors of a circle centered on the central business district. The high-rent or high-price residential areas can be identified in particular sectors, and "there is a gradation of rentals downward from these high rental areas in all directions. Intermediate rental areas, or those ranking next to the highest rental areas, adjoin the high-rent area on one or more sides, and tend to be located in the same sectors as the high rental areas. Low-rent areas occupy other entire sectors of the city from the center to the periphery." [11]

---

[11] Homer Hoyt, *The Structure and Growth of Residential Neighborhoods in American Cities,* Washington: Federal Housing Administration, 1939, p. 76.

Viewed in the context of change, the theory holds that similar types of use originating near the center of the city tend to migrate within the same sector and away from the center. High-rent areas (and high-price areas) are conceived as having a dominant influence on the direction of residential area growth, and exhibit the following growth characteristics:

1. High-grade residential growth tends to proceed from the given point of origin, along established lines of travel or toward another existing nucleus of buildings or trading centers.
2. The zone of high-rent areas tends to progress toward high ground which is free from the risk of floods and to spread along lake, bay, river, and ocean fronts, where such waterfronts are not used for industry.
3. High-rent residential districts tend to grow toward the section of the city which has free, open country beyond the edges and away from "dead end" sections which are limited by natural or artificial barriers to expansion.
4. The higher-priced residential neighborhood tends to grow toward the homes of the leaders of the community.
5. Trends of movement of office buildings, banks, and stores pull the higher-priced residential neighborhoods in the same general direction.
6. High-grade residential areas tend to develop along the fastest existing transportation lines.
7. The growth of high-rent neighborhoods continues in the same direction for a long period of time.
8. De luxe high-rent apartment areas tend to be established near the business center in old residential areas.
9. Real estate promoters may bend the direction of high-grade residential growth.[12]

The operations of these characteristics are observable in the way in which old fashionable close-in boulevard developments have been left for the more recent exclusive outlying subdivisions—a move attributed to the modern automobile. With some exceptions, these moves have been found to occur in the same sectors. The abandoned homes, often too expensive to maintain for succeeding groups of lower income level, become areas of small housekeeping apartments, with a few institutions taking over properties here and there. Parts of these areas may be cleared later to make way for the exclusive high-rent apartment developments.

In the same way that the high-rent or high-price residential areas move radially outward, it is noted that where "a certain sector develops originally as a low-rent or low-price area, the balance of that sector is likely to be occupied by low-rent or low-price residences as expansion proceeds outward. The same tendency is typical of intermediate-rent or -price sectors."[13]

The sector theory thus provides a more detailed explanation of residential

---

[12] *Ibid.*, pp. 117–119.
[13] Weimer and Hoyt, *Principles of Real Estate*, p. 351.

patterns of land use than that set forth in the concentric zone formulation, particularly in the more discriminating way in which it deals with the dynamics of growth processes. It has received criticisms, but these and the stream of commentary that have followed the publication of Hoyt's study clearly indicate the profound effect the sector theory has had in stimulating awareness of the need for a theory of urban land use to which all fields can subscribe.[14]

Multiple Nuclei Concept

First suggested by McKenzie, the multiple nuclei hypothesis is built around the observation that frequently there are a series of nuclei in the patterning of the urban land uses rather than the single central core used in the other two theories.[15] In expanding on this concept in an essay on the nature of cities, Harris and Ullman observed that sometimes these were distinct centers in the origins of the metropolitan area, persisting as centers as growth has filled in the areas between them, and sometimes they have emerged as new centers as urbanization has proceeded.[16]

Harris and Ullman note that the number and the function of each nucleus vary from one metropolitan area to another. The central business district clearly serves as one nucleus. Others may appear in the form of industrial or wholesaling centers where specialized economic activities of similar or complementing character have gravitated together. Still others may emerge in the guise of a major outlying retail center or a university center. Finally, the suburban center and the more distant satellite community for commuters are mentioned as nuclei to be recognized in this conception of the urban land use configuration.

In discussing the multiple nuclei hypothesis, Harris and Ullman identify

---

[14] See Walter Firey, *Land Use in Central Boston,* Cambridge: Harvard University Press, 1947, pp. 41–86. In a critique of the exceptions Firey has taken to the theory that relate largely to what Firey considers to be errors of omission with respect to the determinism of group values and social action in land use, Lloyd Rodwin gives the theory a clean bill of health on these grounds, but goes on to discuss what he considers to be other defects which he summarizes as follows: (a) the ambiguous formulation and use of the sector concept; (b) its oversimplified version of class structure; (c) its distorted dependence on upper-class "attractions" as a basis for interpreting shifts in residential location; (d) the inaccuracy of some of the empirical generalizations; (e) its potentially misleading reliance on nineteenth-century free market residential trends; and (f) the narrow perspectives resulting from the essential purpose of the inquiry. For this critique, see Lloyd Rodwin, "The Theory of Residential Growth and Structure," *The Appraisal Journal,* July, 1950, pp. 295–317, and for rejoinders by Hoyt and Firey, see *The Appraisal Journal,* October, 1950.

[15] R. D. McKenzie, *The Metropolitan Community,* New York: McGraw-Hill Book Company, Inc., 1933, pp. 197–198.

[16] Chauncy D. Harris and Edward L. Ullman, "The Nature of Cities," *The Annals of the American Academy of Political and Social Sciences,* November, 1945. See also Ullman's later comments in "The Nature of Cities Reconsidered," *Papers and Proceedings of the Regional Science Association,* IX, Philadelphia: University of Pennsylvania, 1962.

four factors that tend to account for the emergence of separate nuclei in urban land use patterns. One is the interdependency of certain types of activities and their need for close physical proximity to one another. A second is a natural clustering tendency among certain types of activities which find it mutually profitable to congregate together, as evidenced in retail centers, medical centers to some extent, and outlying office building centers. A third is the converse of the last—the appearance of centers to accommodate activities that may have no particular affinity for one another, but which are inimical to other uses by virtue of the traffic they generate, the extensive railroad or truck-loading facilities they require, and so on. Finally, there is the related factor of high rents or high land costs which have the effect of attracting or repelling uses in the process of nucleation.

As a hypothesis, the multiple nuclei concept appears to recognize many of the realities of contemporary metropolitan area land use patterns. At the same time, it needs elaboration, and probably modification, on the basis of empirical investigations of the kind undertaken by Hoyt before it can become an operationally useful theory of urban land use, and it requires clearer differentiation between factors explaining the structure and dynamics of change. For example, some nuclei recognized in the concept probably find their explanation primarily in terms of "natural" market forces; others in terms of overcoming the "friction of space" made possible by the automobile, the development of electric power, and other technological advances; and still others in terms of community values and legalistic controls such as zoning. Some may be sluggish, and some may be volatile in their response to forces of change. Some may affect surrounding patterns of land use in one way, and some may affect them in quite another way.

The above theoretical explanations of the patterning of urban land uses serve a useful purpose in securing a picture of the effects of the economic forces which the land economist tells us are fundamental in shaping these patterns. If his view is accepted, and if land use patterns, by whatever structure theory they are described, are the aggregate result of the interplay of the forces of supply and demand acting on the sum total of all land parcels in the urban area, then some nexus, some intermediate set of operational generalizations that recognize these forces, is needed to serve as a guide in making the transition from economic theory to land use planning principles. In Chapter 2 we examine some of the significant steps being taken in this direction. In the process we will see direct tiebacks to the concepts of land economics we have been reviewing here.

The purpose of the foregoing summary has been to sketch out economic explanations of urban land use with relevance for the land use planning

process. Although presented separately, the economic are constantly interacting with the social determinants which are taken up next. Broadly, the
economic explanation of land use has its roots in the structure and functioning of the urban economy and in the forces of external origin reacting
on this economy. Studies of the urban economy presented in a later chapter
give us a clue as to how much land is going into development for various
purposes, the amount being a function of economic expansion and resultant
population growth. In turn, the vitality of the local economy, also discussed
later, provides an indication of the rate at which land goes into development. Finally, supply and demand forces of the urban land market activated
by these primary considerations operate to determine the location of various
functional use areas and the siting of specific land uses in the urban area.

Socially Rooted Determinants of Land Use

Another series of influences affecting the location and arrangement of land
use are those with social origins—what are referred to here as socially
rooted determinants of urban land use. These are less understood and
frequently confused with the economic determinants discussed in the previous section. Most research in this aspect of urban development lacks an
operational slant and has not progressed sufficiently so that it is possible
to make an entirely satisfactory differentiation between social and economic
determinants. Probably for this reason, there is a strong predisposition in
much of the writing on the subject to equate social influences with the economic, and social motivations of people and groups with economic motivations. While unquestionably both kinds of influences are constantly in
interaction and complexly interrelated so as to make differentiation and
measurement of the separate effects extremely difficult, social scientists
are increasingly directing attention to the slighted role that social values
and ideals play in the determination of land use patterns in cities.

The sociologist usually views the city partly in the context of urban
ecology with its concern for the physical, spatial, and material aspects of
urban life, and partly in the context of social structure in the city with its
concern for human values, behavior, and interaction as reflected in such
social institutions as the family, the church, government, business, and so
on. Socially rooted factors of land use thus can be explained in terms of
"ecological processes" with their physical context and "organizational processes" with their social structural context. While in the classical traditions
of the field, sociologists have tended to view these aspects of city life in
separate compartments, in more recent approaches to the study of the

city, ecological processes are more closely associated with social behavior of people and groups and related considerations of human values and social action processes.

In recognition of the need for a fully rounded perspective, one that takes into account social as well as economic factors influencing land use patterns, this section attempts to summarize briefly what the sociologist identifies as the socially rooted processes exerting an influence on the location and arrangement of urban land uses. What the sociologist has termed "the basic ecological processes" are taken up first, followed by some very sketchy observations as to the ways in which the social behavior of people and groups influences land development.

Social Processes Affecting Land Use

Urban ecology is a term the sociologist has adapted from the biological sciences to describe the physical change processes in the city. In the natural science usage, ecology is concerned with the interrelations of living things and their environment. Plants and animals are classified into communities of living things with varying but distinct patterns of community development according to such interacting factors as the migration of species, climate and vegetation, topography and drainage, soils, and so on. Community patterns of development occur in a sequence of phases, what are referred to as processes of succession, converging in the most advanced sequence on a *climax condition.* This condition is reached when the community is stable and self-perpetuating, with all factors in appropriate equilibrium.

The application of this biological concept to human life and the human habitat is not difficult to follow. The urban community and its successive patterns and phases of community development, even the notions of populations in optimum adjustment to one another and their environment, have found their way into writings on urban ecology. In the natural science concept of ecology, there is a strong emphasis upon processes by which living things adapt to their environment, and so it is not surprising to find urban ecologists centering their attention on processes by which man adapts to his urban environment. As might be expected, economic forces figure prominently in explanations of these ecological processes. However, since our concern in this chapter is with man's social behavior, the discussion here will concern itself primarily with the socially rooted rather than the economic forces extant in these processes.

The primary and broadest basic process identified by urban ecologists —the one that describes the evolution and development of urban communities in time and space—is called *aggregation*. As typified in studies of dominance and subdominance of urban centers, it can be regional in its scope, but at the same time it has a localized frame of reference involving the sequences of change which occur within a particular locale. Ericksen has identified the most important localized subprocesses of aggregation as: (1) concentration and dispersion of services and populations, (2) centralization and decentralization, (3) segregation of populations into various distinctive areas, (4) dominance and the gradient of receding dominance in the successively more peripheral subareas of the community, and (5) invasion of areas by groups, giving rise to succession of one group by another.[17]

While all bear a relation to one another, subprocesses reviewed here will be grouped as follows: (1) dominance, gradient, and segregation, (2) centralization and decentralization, and (3) invasion and succession. Inasmuch as there appears to be implicit acceptance among urban ecologists that economic forces are controlling in the functioning of ecological processes in a regional framework, we will dispense with the intermetropolitan context and concentrate on subprocesses as they function internally within a single metropolitan center. Within this context, the subprocesses exist primarily through the mobility of residents and shifts of land uses in the course of the daily adjustment and change which is constantly occurring in the urban scene.

Dominance, Gradient, and Segregation

Viewed as a group, these three ecological processes offer a means of understanding the social aspects of the patterning of the city. Although most often used in a static context, these processes can also be used to describe change in the patterning. *Dominance* is used in the sense of one area in the city bearing a controlling social or economic position in relation to other areas. Usually dominance is considered in a vertical sense as applying to like use areas, although obviously there are patterns of dominance in a horizontal sense involving multiple use areas. *Gradient* is a term the sociologist has developed to indicate the receding degrees of dominance from some selected dominant center to the more distant locations relative to that center. *Segregation* is a related process of clustering. It is a selection process by which homogeneous units become grouped together to form clusters. Taken as a series, the ecologist employs these three processes to describe the way in which natural social areas develop.

These processes were first identified in a systematic fashion as part of the concentric zone conceptualization of the city (see the previous section).

---

[17] E. Gordon Ericksen, *Urban Behavior,* New York: The Macmillan Company, 1954, p. 155.

Thus the central business district is obviously one center of dominance, and the gradient of its influence over other business centers or even over other use areas can be described in each successive concentric zone. The clustering or segregative process, as manifest, for example, in the way used-car and automotive service centers, wholesale districts, or light-house-keeping apartment areas for single persons or working couples develop in one or more of these concentric zones, is also explained in this concept of the city. In the more conventional usage of the term "segregation," the various Puerto Rican areas, Negro districts, and so on are used as illustrations of the workings of the segregative process.

The sector theory explaining the distribution of high-value residential areas is also adaptable to describing these processes. For example, such processes are seen in the presumed controlling position of high-value areas, in the downward gradients noted in adjoining sectors, and in the clustering of uses of like character and intensity of development within certain segments of the pattern. The multiple nuclei concept is particularly graphic for describing dominance and subdominance within the urban center and is adaptable to explain each of the other related processes.

Taking up these processes separately, dominance is a term most frequently used to describe the economic positioning of cities in a whole constellation of communities, as discussed in Chapter 3. In a more localized and socially oriented context and with particular reference to land use, the process is most readily illustrated in studies of residential areas. Assuming some physical basis for delineating residential neighborhoods in a metropolitan area, they can be ordered into a system of dominant and subdominant neighborhoods, positioned according to prestige factors. Although these factors are closely related to land values or rental levels as employed by Hoyt in the development of his sector theory, prestige is a more socially rooted determinant of dominance. The actual measurements of prestige employed in identifying dominance and subdominance of course must recognize and allow for differentials in the values of people residing in the various neighborhoods. The foregoing application of the concept of dominance is but one of many that might be used. In place of studying the prestige status of various residential neighborhoods, one might examine these areas for patterns in the spatial distribution of poverty, disease, and so on, identifying dominant and subdominant areas of an entirely different order.

Gradient is directly related to the concept of dominance. The degree of increasing or decreasing intensity in prestige, poverty, disease, or whatever phenomenon is being observed, establishes the gradient or gradation from full dominance to total subdominance. The gradient extends from a point of greatest intensity or incidence to areas of low intensity or minor incidence. Thus, when instability is involved, as dominance recedes there is a gradual shift to a state of increasing stability the farther removed observations are made from the point of greatest dominance. Gradient is a concept frequently used to represent "decay" in population density, land values, or other phenomena exhibiting systematic gradations in spatial patterns.

Associated with the social processes by which use areas form a hierarchy or gradient is the segregating process that results in the identification of distinct prestige areas, islands of slums, areas of high incidence of disease, and so on. The extent and rapidity of the sorting that goes on day in and day out is a function of all attitudes, decisions, and actions at stake. They frequently involve such matters as deed restrictions, zoning, tightness of the housing market, family ties, location of place of work, school environment, and so on. These many and diverse factors produce both planned and unplanned results, and segregation occurs sometimes as a calculated result and sometimes as an unexpected result.

The implications of these processes for land use planning have never been fully explored. The urban ecologist has identified them in a descriptive "what is" or "what has been" context, but their research has yet to be directly oriented toward the operating needs of the city planner. To what extent can city planning recognize these social considerations and preserve desired natural areas? How are the social to be reconciled with economic considerations, and how are conflicts with broad social goals to be dealt with? Further empirical research is needed to establish what forms of the natural ordering of use areas described by the ecologist are important to recognize and provide for in land use planning and land development practices.

Centralization and Decentralization

Two pairs of reciprocal terms need to be distinguished at this juncture. One pair relate to the massing and spreading out of population in a regional setting. Sociologists have given these processes the terms *concentration* and *dispersion*. Since they generally apply to large territorial regions consisting of several scattered urban centers such as Bogue's 67 metropolitan regions (see Chapter 3) in which processes tend to be controlled by economic forces, these are not included in the present discussion. Centralization and decentralization, on the other hand, apply to a particular metropolitan area where socially rooted forces, though complexly related to the economic, are potentially distinguishable from them. *Centralization* usually refers to the congregation of people and urban functions in a particular urban center or its functional use areas in the pursuit of certain economic, cultural, or social satisfactions. *Decentralization* generally refers to the breaking down of the urban center with the accompanying ebb movements of people and urban functions to fringe areas or to new satellite centers.

Our concern here is not with the individualistic and philosophical concepts and proposals toward the creation of a wholeness of life as set forth in Ebenezer Howard's work on garden cities at the turn of the century or in the varying notions advanced in recent time by Wright, Saarinen, Gropius, Neutra, Le Corbusier, Sert, and other architects. Rather, we are presently concerned with the broad attracting and repelling processes as they stem from the basic values and ideals of people and groups.

Viewed in terms of the social institutions of the community, for example, business, industry, recreation, education, religion, etc., centralization involves the settlement of people and the related development of places of work, entertainment, education, and worship in a more or less compact relationship in a single center. Conversely, decentralization involves settlement patterns of a polynucleated order with the appearance of outlying centers of work, entertainment, education, and so on. One involves migration of people and economic activity into the central city, and one involves migration outward to fringe areas or nearby subcenters.

The establishment of social institutions in the course of centralization-decentralization processes occurs in response to both economically and socially rooted needs and wants. At one time, basic factors of convenience to raw materials, labor, and markets dictated central locations for economic institutions. Today modern technological developments in power, transportation, and communications permit the development of places of business and industry in outlying areas. While the location of workplaces tends to become a dominant influence affecting centralization and decentralization processes, social forces can function sympathetically with economic forces or they can run counter to them. Thus values concerning quality, convenience, and variety in the choice of stores, entertainment, and schools may be a deterring force in the decentralization process. On the other hand, fashion, ethnic conflict, the desire for an open-order pattern of living without the noise, confusion, hazards, and dirt of the densely developed areas of the central city may become motivational social forces working in unison with economic considerations to facilitate decentralization.

Invasion and Succession

Associated with both of the foregoing sets of processes is a third set which the sociologist calls invasion and succession. These two processes are usually linked in sequence. *Invasion* is the interpenetration of one population group or use area by another, the difference between the new and old being economic, social, or cultural. *Succession* occurs when the new population group or use types finally displace the former occupants or uses of the area. Of course, it is possible for an area to experience invasion but, through concerted action of local groups, never reach the succession stage.

Invasion of one population group by another is usually a spatial manifestation of the change processes at work in the social structure of the city. Spatial mobility is associated with social mobility, and, as the term implies, social mobility involves changes in social status or position. Thus vertical shifts from one social stratum to another usually involve spatial shifts, whereas horizontal social mobility within the same stratum has no special significance in the invasion-succession processes. Population group invasion is usually associated with residential areas, with one income, racial, or ethnic group penetrating an area occupied by another. The term is also used to describe shifts in land use as, for example, when business penetrates into residential areas or apartment districts take over areas of single-family homes. (In these examples, under the old "nuisance" approach to classification of land uses, residential areas are considered a "higher" order of use than business areas, and single-family areas a "higher" use than apartment areas.) Usually these displacements occur by an upper-status social group or a higher use giving way to a lower-status group or lower use, although the reverse may happen, as evinced in restoration projects (for example, the reclaiming by whites of the old aristocratic areas of Charleston, South Carolina, from former Negro occupants) or in the more formal procedures of urban redevelopment where local government assisted by federal funds can alter the whole complexion of an area and the functioning of ecological processes.

The principal consequence of invasion is a breakup of the existing population and land use makeup of an area. Succession is the culmination of this breakup, with the new achieving complete displacement of the old. Viewed in a land use context, business and industrial uses tend to follow transportation routes, creating ribbon developments along major thoroughfares or islands along railroads, sometimes jumping from one area to another. The process is less visible when changes occur within an area of the same land use, with upper-order shifts being less discernible than lower-order shifts. At the lower-order extreme where areas have gone through a series of general invasion-succession cycles, occupancy turnover, vacancy, slippage in the maintenance of structures, increasing intensity of use, and rising density of occupancy are some of the indicators of these processes.

The cycle is most graphically illustrated in residential areas. As invasion begins, families sensing the implications of these changes begin a quiet withdrawal in the interests of minimizing economic losses anticipated in lower-order succession of the area. As these withdrawals become evident, other families take the cue and the exodus of the old group accelerates until the new group for the most part is in possession of the area, thus completing the cycle. Ericksen describes this cycle of change in a sequence of six steps:

Step A. Equilibrium in the district, marked by lack of awareness on the part of the inhabitants of any invasion by an alien group.

Step B. Disequilibrium arising from the flight of several upper-strata members of the community. This flight is in response to rumors of invasion. . . .

Step C. The creation of new restrictive covenants or reinforcement of dormant covenants following from these rumors. . . .

Step D. The rush invasion by the in-migrants to exploit the outposts established earlier. . . .

Step E. Reintegration of the area as the alien group acquires cumulative power. Mass exodus of the old occupants takes place at this level. . . .

Step F. Change of community status. The new occupants organize and dominate the area. Thus orderly succession and a new equilibrium have taken place.[18]

In their broad gross effects, the processes of invasion and succession tie directly into the concentric zone theory of describing physical structure and change in the city. Indeed, these processes were first identified in a systematic way in terms of this conceptual scheme. In describing growth of the city in terms of expanding concentric rings, the theory anticipates the operation of these processes and the "filtering-down" process of residential occupancy, with the invasion-succession processes being most in evidence in the "zone of transition." It also gives recognition to the overall directional orientation of residential invasion processes. While short-run shifts can occur in any direction, the long-term orientation of invasion-succession shifts tends to be in the direction that the rings expand. However, assuming a positive and effective broad-gauge, long-range program of urban renewal is being vigorously pursued, it is probable that these ecological observations as to direction, and possibly the very nature of the invasion-succession processes, would be altered. The notion of control, of course, is inseparably bound up in city planning, and when applied in the pursuit of a program for a better physical living environment, all ecological processes may be influenced in the way they function.

As in the other ecological processes, the invasion-succession concept is a descriptive device which portrays mass tendencies resulting from individual and group decisions and actions in the community. The foregoing conceptual explanations imply that invasion and succession have the quality of a self-regulating law. They imply something of a universal rationale that guides people and groups into certain predictable courses of action. If

---

[18] *Ibid.*, pp. 215–216.

there are certain universals of human behavior involving certain predictable patterns of social action, these notions have great importance for land use planning. These considerations bring us to a discussion of the elements and dynamics of social behavior as a factor in land use planning.

Social Behavior as a Determinant of Land Use

It would be both presumptuous and beyond the scope of this discussion to attempt to review all the complex and great variety of factors involved in understanding the behavior of the urbanite. This is a task for the social psychologist and the sociologist. Yet it is essential to recognize the role of human values and ideals in the framework of group action if we are to develop an understanding of social behavior as it influences land use patterns in cities. In examining this aspect of land use determinants, it would also be well to recognize that there are a great many more questions in the minds of land planners than there are answers. Indeed, except for a few benchmarks such as Firey's work on land use in central Boston, this is largely an uncharted and undeveloped area.[19]

We shall first sketch out a conceptual framework to describe some of the major elements and the dynamics of human behavior as they relate to land use.[20] This will be followed by a discussion of social values and land use.

Human Behavior and Land Use

Expressed crudely, human behavior refers to the way in which people and groups conduct themselves, how they act in the context of the values and ideals they possess. These values and ideals, whether latent or manifest, are the product of human experience in a specific cultural, economic, and physical setting, and consist of a kind of superstructure built around the basic drives of human life (survival, procreation, etc.). Human behavior is two-directional. It conditions and is conditioned by this setting, and, in turn, actions in relation to the setting motivate and are motivated by values, both the unexpressed subconscious values and the expressed conscious ones.

Looking at urban land use patterns as the aggregate product of many individual and group actions in occupying and improving the land, we may view these actions as a form of human behavior activated by certain human needs and wants. In an oversimplified way, we may identify human

---

[19] *Op. cit.*

[20] The elements of this framework are drawn from a schema developed at the University of North Carolina. See F. Stuart Chapin, Jr., and Shirley F. Weiss (eds.), *Urban Growth Dynamics*, New York: John Wiley & Sons, Inc., 1962, pp. 2–5.

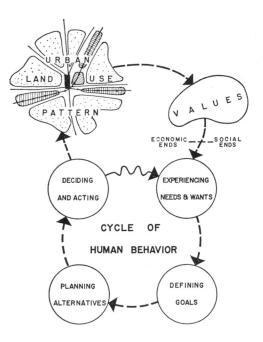

Figure 3. The Sequence of Action and the Influence of Values in Bringing About a Change in the Urban Land Use Pattern. Certain individual- or group-held values concerning the use of a particular parcel or area set in motion a four-phase cycle of behavior which culminates in the parcel or area being put to a particular use. This action sequence may bring into play new values or involve the values of other persons or groups, setting in motion new action sequences.

needs with values relating to the necessities of urban living, and we may identify *wants* with values concerning economic and social desires which supplement the necessities of urban living. The economic behavior of people and groups in seeking to satisfy needs and wants in the urban land market was taken up in the last section. Here we are concerned with their behavior and their antecedent values as they seek to influence land use in pursuit of their social desires.

As shown in Figure 3, certain individual or group values concerning, let us say, the renewal of a particular blighted area in an urban center produce a cycle of behavior. This cycle involves four phases: (1) experiencing of needs and wants, (2) defining goals, (3) planning alternative courses of action, and (4) deciding and acting. First, the values with economic and/or social ends in view result in the experiencing of a need or want for action to change this pattern of land use. Second, this need or want becomes crystallized into a resolution, for example, the philanthropist may simply conclude in his own mind that the slums must go and be replaced by safe and sanitary housing, the mortgage holders or an enterprising businessman may see a more profitable reuse, or the renewal agency may formally define and adopt a set of goals concerning the needed or wanted action. Third, in pursuit of these goals, the various alternatives for planning the area are established, for example, the possibility of undertaking rehabilitation measures combined with "spot" demolition of structures here and there *versus* complete area clearance and redevelopment of the area in new structures, streets, and uses. Finally, having examined the alternatives, the philanthropist, mortgage holders, entrepreneur, or renewal agency reaches a decision. A plan is selected and set in motion to achieve the goals. The final result is change in the urban land use pattern. This change may produce new values which set in motion a new series of actions that may further influence the pattern of land use in the area. The cycle thus follows a circular sequence, actually more nearly taking the form of a spiral rather than a circle, since no two cycles produce exactly duplicate results.

Now let us view urban land use patterns as influenced by the behavior of many individuals and groups. Figure 4 is a schematic representation of this complex, with the mass values held in common identified at the rim and the urban land use pattern appearing as the end product at the hub. The behavior of individuals or groups $(1, 2, 3, 4 \ldots n)$, the sum total of which forms the universe of all behavior with respect to a particular land use, is shown in a complex of action patterns similar to the prototype illustration (Figure 3). Obviously there are many combinations of action patterns not shown in the diagram. For example, two or more individuals or groups, each with their own value system and behavior pattern, might act or even plan and act cooperatively in the satisfaction of entirely different sets of values. Moreover, Figure 4 pictures actions relating only to a single change in the land use pattern. If all concurrent actions influencing the total pattern of uses were diagramed, the result would be a much more complex chart involving whole clusters of the Figure 4–type behavior patterns.

Viewing these series of individual and group actions occurring in a situation without guidance of an urban land development plan and its implementing regulatory and other planning controls, the resulting land use pattern develops or changes by a multitude of related and unrelated actions. These actions or behaviors have certain planned and unplanned consequences (in the diagram the planned consequences are indicated by a hatch at the core, and the unplanned consequences by white space). The *planned consequences* are planned in the sense that the group which conceived the land development or change anticipated and consciously brought about the intended end result. The *unplanned consequences* of human behavior are the resulting relationships, or more correctly the lack of relationships, between several independent actions such as to produce an unexpected end result. This may be an inconsistent or even an incompatible product in terms of the larger setting. Even assuming a guiding land use plan and conforming individual and group action, land development patterns can be expected to produce new responses and new and superseding values involving a changing alignment of people and groups in the subsequent cycles of behavior that develop. The dynamics of these changing values, alignments, and behaviors involve a dimension not presented in Figure 4.

The basic ecological processes discussed earlier in the chapter represent cross-sectional observations of the composite effects of mass behavior. Although there are many other effects of this behavior which are of interest in other fields, land use is the end product of particular interest here. The land use planner has an interest in observing these composite effects of behavior insofar as his proposals seek to modify them or are predicated on their continuance. In either case, it is important that he develop some understanding of the values which set behavior cycles into operation, for in the final analysis the success of his efforts is dependent upon how closely his land use planning proposals harmonize with group and mass values held in the community. This brings us to a discussion of the role of values in land use planning.

Social Values and Land Use

In the crude framework above, values are viewed as motivating behavior resulting in a certain organized form of action by people or groups. In this sense, values are logical constructs of the individual or the group with reference to desired ends. They can be latent or subconscious, and they can be articulated or conscious values. They may be classified as to content, for example, economic, social, political, religious, aesthetic, and so on, or they may be categorized by other means, for example, positive-negative, specificity, explicitness, and so on. The term *mass values* is used here to indicate a consensus of values shared by a majority of the people or groups in the community. Mass values have particular significance for urban-wide considerations of land use planning, but group values generally have significance for the more particularized and localized segments of land use planning. The most notable exception is the instance in which the influential people of the community composing the power structure function as a group. Such a group has very obvious importance to overall land use planning.

Firey's work in Boston involved an empirical investigation and the development of a theoretical framework to identify the role of values in the

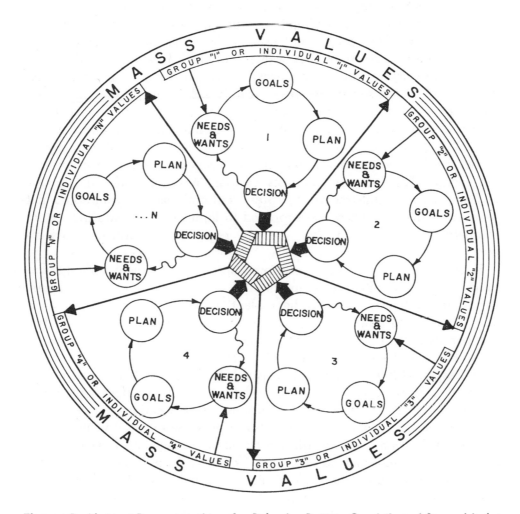

Figure 4. Abstract Representation of a Behavior Pattern Consisting of Several Independent Cycles of Human Behavior. This diagram shows that without conformance to a general land development plan, each of 1, 2, 3, 4 . . . *n* groups or individuals, motivated by mass values held in common and by distinct group or individual values, follows a sequence of distinct actions which in the aggregate tend to have rational and irrational consequences for urban land use. The rational consequences (shaded portions at the hub) are the intended changes in land use, and the irrational consequences (unshaded portion) are the unanticipated, often inconsistent relationships between two or more new or changed uses.

evolution of land use patterns. Disturbed by what he considered to be a general acceptance of a "rationalistic" approach to the explanation of land use with a strong explicit or implicit emphasis on self-regulating economic forces that distribute people and uses in the urban area, he studied sections of Boston to determine how values and ideals functioned with respect to past and existing land use patterns. In his own words, these rationalists (and he identifies several groups) "readily acknowledge the reality and effectiveness of social values in spatial adaptation; but they make no attempt to incorporate the empirical concession into their theoretical system. . . . All factual departures from the kind of spatial order called for by the theory are lumped together into a loose category of 'limiting' or 'complicating' factors. This category embraces 'custom,' 'moral attitudes and taboos,' 'political and administrative measures,' 'cultural biases,' 'traditional patterns,' and the like. These are supposed to limit or complicate the natural competitive process, but they are not regarded as ultimate causative factors." [21]

Firey set out to test two general propositions: (1) socially rooted values exert a causative influence on urban land use patterns, and (2) rationally functioning interests (what we have identified in the first part of the chapter as market-governed forces), in exerting a causative influence on land use patterns, stem indirectly from larger cultural systems and cannot be viewed as self-given ends in themselves. Studying locational trends in Boston's Beacon Hill, central area, and North End, he concludes with respect to the first proposition that space may be not only a productive agent, but also a symbol, and that people and groups choose locations not only in relation to market considerations but also in response to social values. In the Beacon Hill section, he identifies three kinds of influences which values exert on land use—what he terms the "retentive," the "recuperative," and the "resistive"—and on the basis of his tests concludes that "values are indeed self-sufficient ecological forces and that they have a very real causative influence upon land use." [22] In highlighting the origins and the preservation of historic sites in central Boston, he uses them as examples where symbolic attributes attached to an area become embedded in the social values of the people to the extent that "it appears that space has been divested of its role as a productive agent and . . . has been put to wholly uneconomic uses. . . ." [23]

With respect to the North End, the one distinctive Italian community in Boston, he points out that in this instance social values were not a result

---

[21] Firey, *Land Use in Central Boston,* pp. 20–21.
[22] *Ibid.,* p. 130.
[23] *Ibid.,* p. 168.

of fetishism where space is a conscious object of veneration as in the preceding two areas, but rather a result of processes of social organization where residence in the area to persons of Italian origin is a means of becoming identified with the Italian community and its distinctive values relating to occupation, family, choice of friends, group membership, and so on. On the basis of evidence presented on patterns of association and interaction, population movements and turnover, property ownership, and so on, he concludes that the North End is a symbol of "social solidarity" and that residence there is a token of identification with Italian groups and with Italian values. "Those persons who most fully identify themselves with Italian patterns tend to remain in the North End, in spite of the deteriorated, congested conditions which prevail there. Apparently the affect which attaches to 'one's own kind' outweighs awareness of the slum's undesirability as a place in which to live. Social values thus have an influence upon land use which is not at all limited to areas with congenial physical and architectural characteristics." [24]

The second purpose of his Boston study was to discover whether locational processes can be wholly separated from a cultural context. Here he concludes from his study of the retail center of Boston, the Back Bay, and the South End that "rational" determinants of land use are indeed themselves contingent upon a particular culture-bound value system and the cultural component is central to locational processes. The failure to recognize the cultural component in spatial adaptation he finds to be a major omission in existing formal theories which seek to explain land use. "All of them invest physical space with a 'non-cultural givenness,' and all of them consider social systems as passive, compliant and disparate adapters." [25]

Firey concludes his study with a theoretical construct suggesting the use of a "principle of proportionality" as a means of giving proper recognition to the role of values in the allocation of space to functional uses in the city. He discusses values in terms of a multiplicity of ends to be achieved in the location of land uses, with these ends requiring a certain balance, a degree of proportionality, in order that every component end of the community will in some measure be attained. He illustrates his theory of proportionality graphically in the form of a U-shaped curve (see Figure 5).

Let us imagine a city that is made up of certain ends defined for it by the value system of the society in which that city exists. We can postulate that there will be an hypothetical point [the lowest point in the U-shaped curve] at which the amount and "kind" [in terms of accessibility and applicability to the end in question] of space devoted to a particular end or function balances off with the spatial requirements of each other end or function comprising the city. At this point

[24] *Ibid.*, p. 220.
[25] *Ibid.*, p. 324.

the total deprivation of all the ends comprising the system is at a minimum. It is important to recognize that this "end-deprivation" is not synonymous with "cost" in the economic sense of the word, since it refers not only to the dearth of scarce goods but also to thwarting of intangible and non-empirical ends which are just as real functional requirements of a city. All of these ends and functional requirements must be attained, yet no one of them can be pursued to an unlimited degree lest others be unduly deprived. That point along the "deprivation continuum" of a particular end, at which point the degree of deprivation comports with a minimal deprivation of all other ends comprising the community, may be called point x. Now, by definition, any deviation away from x will entail increased deprivation to one or more of the other ends comprising the community as a system. Thus an allocation of too much space to park and recreational facilities will obstruct certain other requirements of the city as a functioning social system, such as commerce or manufacturing. Likewise the allocation of too little space to park and recreational facilities will obstruct the "best" functioning of the community as a system. Reasoning deductively, then, it may be suggested that departure from point x in either direction as to degree of deprivation of a particular end is accompanied by a *progressive* increase in deprivation to the system as a whole—more specifically, to one or more of the other ends comprising the system.[26]

In this statement of his theory, Firey appears to assume that there are limitations in the land area available for various uses—a built-in quantitative balance, as it were. If his principle of proportionality is applied to central city situations alone where the subject city is completely surrounded by independent and incorporated towns as in the case of Boston, the assumed limitation on space can be construed to apply. In most cities, particularly in the medium-size and small ones, the automobile has made larger land areas accessible to urban populations, suggesting that there are changing quantitative relationships rather than fixed limits on the availability of space. Of course, it might be argued that the time people are willing to spend in the journey to work may ultimately provide fixed limits to an urban area, but even here new developments in technology and changing attitudes as to the time people are willing to spend in commuting suggest that there is a changing quantitative balance.

Socially Rooted Values and Land Use Planning

The importance of viewing land use as having socially rooted explanations has been stressed throughout this section of the chapter. Social values and the behavior of people and groups activated by these values have significant implications for land use planning analyses of city planners. As a practical expediency at this stage of research development in the field, probably the points at which most attention should be focused are (1) the identifica-

---

[26] *Ibid.*, pp. 326–327.

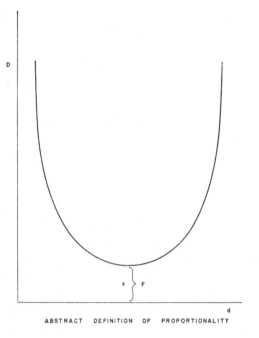

ABSTRACT   DEFINITION   OF   PROPORTIONALITY

Figure 5. Graphic Representation of Firey's Theory of Proportionality. "In the figure, *d* indicates deprivation of a particular spatially contingent end; *D* indicates
deprivation of all other ends comprising the system. At *x* along the *d* continuum the
overall functioning of the system is being least obstructed, or, to put the same thing
positively, the overall functioning is being most fully attained. Just enough space in
terms of area, and just the right distribution of space in terms of suitability (accessibility . . .) to the respective ends, has been allocated to the several ends comprising the system as to comport with the 'best'—i.e., least thwarted—functioning of
the system." (*Source:* Walter Firey, *Land Use in Central Boston*, Cambridge: Harvard
University Press, 1947, p. 327. Copyright, 1947, by the President and Fellows of
Harvard College.)

tion of mass and group values so that they may be taken into account in
planning proposals, (2) the determination of behavior patterns which are
important to the social well-being and mental health of urban residents,
and (3) the translation of these values and behavior patterns into physical
criteria so that the design of the land use plan can be made sensitive to
these aspects of urban life.

With respect to the first purpose, it is well to recognize that values are
difficult to identify and measure. This is particularly true of the hidden
unarticulated values. Social psychologists have developed indirect techniques for identifying and measuring some forms of these hidden values,
but comparatively little is known as to the validity of results. For example,
it has been suggested that the very attempt at identification may in itself

alter the values that are sought to be measured. In the case of the articulated values held by individuals and groups, techniques of attitude surveys are beginning to reach a high degree of refinement and development. The experimental work of the University of North Carolina studies in identifying satisfactions of urbanites with their social and physical environs provides some valuable methodological insights in the design of attitude studies for planning purposes.[27] On the other hand, the Detroit Area Study of the University of Michigan provides some important experience in longitudinal investigations of changes in attitudes.[28] More will be said of the utility of these surveys in later chapters.

Participant-observer studies of anthropologists and sociologists are helping to supply the planning field with a fuller appreciation of modes of human behavior of significance in land use planning.[29] They involve a specialized form of investigation which shows promise of adaptation to city planning needs and becoming a part of the continuing survey and study effort of planning agencies. Through lessons learned in family relocation in urban renewal and highway programs, local units of government have acquired a healthy respect for the social and mental health aspects of changes wrought by public works, and planning agencies can be expected to rely less on intuitive and more on investigative approaches in identifying the important patterns of human interaction. However, experimental work will be required in making these techniques more useful for planning, particularly in the use of sampling methods and in the development of more systematic ways of spatially defining the behavior patterns of different social groups and how these patterns relate to physical arrangements in the structure of the city.

To give recognition to values and behavior patterns in the design of the land use plan at present is a subjective procedure. This is true partly because of the impossibility of subjecting the synthesizing and aesthetic aspects of the design process to a rigid mechanical approach, and partly because of the limited operational knowledge and experience we have had in classifying values, in identifying dominant and critical ones, and in making the transition from values and behavior to desired patterns of land use. While there is thus much research needed to assist the planning practitioner in giving weight to socially rooted determinants of land use, un-

---

[27] Chapin and Weiss (eds.), *Urban Growth Dynamics.* See John Gulick, Charles E. Bowerman, and Kurt Back, Chapter 10, and Robert L. Wilson, Chapter 11, in *ibid.*

[28] See various bulletins in Detroit Area Study series, *A Social Profile of Detroit,* Ann Arbor: Survey Research Center, Institute for Social Research, University of Michigan.

[29] Examples of early studies of this kind are Robert S. and Helen M. Lynd, *Middletown* and *Middletown in Transition,* New York: Harcourt, Brace, 1929 and 1937, respectively. For a more recent example, with applications to planning, see Herbert J. Gans, *The Urban Villagers,* New York: The Free Press of Glencoe and The Macmillan Company, 1962.

doubtedly he in turn needs to give greater attention to emerging developments in the social sciences, even though at the outset it involves him in somewhat subjective interpretations covering this aspect of land use analysis.

The Public Interest as a Determinant of Land Use

This introductory orientation to land use planning has been one of singling out the more important considerations which set the emphases and condition the manner in which the land use planning task is approached. So far in this chapter, basic economic and social determinants of land use have been sketched out as they affect this task. The underlying significance to urban land use patterns of regional spheres of influence has been stressed, particularly in the way regional economic forces influence local economic growth. Through the eyeglasses of the economist, it was seen that the urban land use configuration is explainable in terms of the economic motivations of individuals and firms functioning in the urban land market. It was also seen that to the sociologist, urban land use has a direct relation to social processes and can be explained as the product of individual and group behavior in response to certain purely social as well as economic values. Though taken up separately, both ways of looking at land use have been presented as complementary, each complexly related to the other.

There is still another consideration to round out this introductory picture. While guided by these tenets of man's economic and social behavior in the community, the city planner must also view land use in the context of "the health, safety, and general welfare"—what is termed here "the public interest." The scope of the public interest is broad, the health, safety, and general welfare encompassing many things about the conduct of people in urban society. Our concern is with the public interest in land development, more particularly with public action that seeks to assure livability and sound development in the city as land is put to urban use. Not by any means dissociated from the other determinants of land use we have been considering, the public interest involves another dimension, another way of viewing land use. It involves the notion of control for public ends as they may be distinguished from private economic or social ends. These public ends are associated with "public interest values" which compose one segment of the larger system of mass values discussed above. These public interest values come into play in the legalistic actions of formal governmental organizations—what we refer to as "actions taken in the public interest." In place of focusing on economic and socially rooted actions discussed above, here we are primarily concerned with governmental actions to achieve livability in the urban setting and unity and efficiency in the overall land use pattern. The task of the city planner, then, is not only to develop a land use scheme fitted to the needs and sensitive to the wants of the urbanite, both economic and social, but also to harmonize these considerations with the public interest in a plan that maximizes livability in the city and insures sound development for the community as a whole.

Livability is used here to refer broadly to those qualities in the physical environment of the urban area which tend to induce in citizens a feeling of mental, physical, and social well-being according to the extent to which their fundamental day-to-day living needs and wants are satisfied. Thus defined, livability is both an individual matter and a community-wide concern—that is to say, actions of individuals or families in search of more satisfying living conditions have a random but cumulative effect of altering the land use pattern just as these same urbanites seeking satisfaction of their needs and wants through formal community action have an organized effect of altering the pattern of land development. In the first instance, actions are based on individual or family notions of livability; and in the second instance, they are based on shared notions of livability, these urbanites having discovered that they have a common public interest in livability. Thus livability in the city becomes a matter of public interest when there is consensus among city residents about the fundamental living needs and wants to be recognized as the urban area expands and develops.

In this section of the chapter we are concerned with the public interest rather than the individual interest as a determinant of land use. In such a context, the public interest connotes the notion of control. It involves control not only in the conventional action sense of imposing regulatory measures, passing on street and utility locations, renewing the outworn blighted areas of the city, and so on, but also in the preaction sense which is involved in the city planning process itself. Earlier we defined city planning as a means for systematically anticipating and achieving adjustment in the physical environment of an urban area consistent with social and economic forces and sound principles of land planning. Here we are concerned with livability derivatives of these principles that have come to be accepted as sound in the public interest. In addition and more generally associated with what is sound, we are concerned with livability-related considerations involved in achieving an efficient unity and harmony in the way in which the physical environment develops.

It is not necessary to establish that the public interest is, in fact, a determinant of land use. This is inherent in the notion of control as it is coupled with the public interest. Of more direct concern here are: What basic elements of the public interest prompt the use of controls, and what practical considerations affect the use of controls? Material presented below is organized in terms of these two questions.

Elements of the Public Interest Prompting the Use of Controls

The public interest is frequently used in law to refer to what the courts will sanction as a public purpose, whether under the police power, the power of eminent domain, or the power of taxation. For example, health, welfare, morals, and safety have become generally recognized tests of the public interest in American jurisprudence. Convenience, comfort, and prosperity are sometimes cited, but are less frequently allowed by the courts and usually only in combination with the other four tests. In a restricted sense, the courts thus provide a barometer of what are generally held to be the limits of the public interest. As indicated in the history of court actions, the public interest concept in a legal sense is an evolving one, tending to broaden in time as new elements become more generally sanctioned in a cultural context, but also tending to lag behind their social acceptance.

For planning purposes, a more advanced concept of the public interest is warranted, one which builds on the legal tests but which seeks forward-looking guideposts taken directly from the social currents of the times. In land use planning, the purposes usually identified with the public interest are five: health, safety, convenience, economy, and amenity. Morals come into play in some aspects of land use planning but play a relatively less important role. "Economy" may be identified with prosperity, and perhaps, by a stretch of the imagination, "amenity" may be associated with comfort in the legal definitions of the public interest. In all cases, it will become apparent that in the context of land use planning each of the five public purposes has broader meaning than that ascribed to it by the courts alone.

Health and Safety

Though they may be considered as separate public purposes, health and safety are frequently involved in combination and thus are customarily linked together. As might be expected, regulatory measures such as health, sanitation, housing, and building codes provide the principal operating definitions of the public interest. Such usages place a strong emphasis on constraints to prevent (or directives to ameliorate) conditions injurious or hazardous to the physical well-being of the people of the community.

In recent time there have been two notable developments toward a broader, more positive definition of health and safety in the public interest. First, in addition to a concern for physical health and safety, there is an emphasis on mental and emotional well-being. Second, there is not only the necessary emphasis on constraints in the interest of public health and safety, but stress is also being given to improved health and safety by planning and building it into the physical environment. In other words, contemporary thinking centers more on what is optimum or desirable than what is minimum or adequate in the interest of health and safety.

This trend was given impetus by the pioneering work of the Hygiene of Housing Committee of the American Public Health Association. As seen in the following list of criteria considered by the Committee to be a test of an *adequate* environment, many of the formerly optimal features of planning have advanced to the status of being regarded as minimal features:

1. Protection against accident hazards.
2. Protection against contagion and provisions for maintenance of cleanliness.
3. Provision of adequate daylight, sunshine, and ventilation.
4. Protection against excessive noise.
5. Protection against atmospheric pollution.
6. Protection from fatigue and provision of adequate privacy.
7. Provision of opportunities for normal family and community life, and protection against moral hazards.
8. Provision of possibilities for reasonable aesthetic satisfaction.[30]

Seen here are not only the "protection against" criteria invoked to safeguard the public from injurious and hazardous conditions, but also the more positive planning and design types of criteria proposing an environment developed for more optimal living conditions.

Many of the regulatory controls commonly associated with health and safety usually apply to individual structures or relate to specific practices or services carried on in the community. Illustrative of these are the requirement of a flush toilet and bath with hot and cold running water for each dwelling unit, the requirement of fire exits and fire escapes in hotels and places of public assembly, control over food handling, rodent and insect control, and so on.

Focusing attention more directly on land use planning, there are other forms of control exercised in the public interest. These are the controls which relate to the broad patterns of land use as opposed to the individual structure or a particular activity carried on inside the structure. The following are illustrative of public purposes to be served through proper planning of the location and internal arrangement of land uses:

[30] Committee on the Hygiene of Housing, American Public Health Association, *Planning the Neighborhood*, Chicago: Public Administration Service, 1960, p. vii.

1. Control of daytime and nighttime population densities.
2. Control over use and development of hazardous areas.
3. Control of exposure to accidents, noise, and atmospheric pollution.

Controls may take the form of *developmental measures* as involved in the programming and carrying out of public works or urban renewal proposals. They may involve the public acquisition of certain built-up or open areas in the community and the planning or replanning of these areas for specific uses. Such areas may be retained in public ownership and developed for such uses as recreation, low-rent housing, and so on, or they may be sold for private development in accordance with plans determined to be in the public interest. More generally recognized land use controls in the interest of health and safety take the form of *regulatory measures* involved in zoning, subdivision regulation, and the reservation of lands for public uses through official map procedures.

Density Controls

In a land use planning connotation and a control context, *density* is a measure of the designed population capacity of urban land. While density controls have been traditionally associated with residential areas, more recently the notion of controlled population densities has been extended to the work areas of the community—to the central business district and the industrial and commercial concentrations. In this extension of the concept, people present in an area during peak periods of congregation, rather than place of official residence, becomes the criterion of density. Obviously, the peak nighttime densities of residential areas tend to correspond with conventional measures of density as determined from U.S. Census enumerations. Thus, while tests of density in residential areas can be based on U.S. Census data, tests for work areas must be based on peak congregations of population, usually occurring during daylight hours. The extreme variations in density that can occur are indicated in Figure 6, which shows the variations in population density in Flint, Michigan, for various selected times of the day and night. Densities are shown in population per million square feet. In most planning studies densities are generally measured in families per acre in residential areas, and persons per acre in work areas.

The establishment of densities—what the designed population capacities for land development in various sections of the urban area should be—is a major concern of land use planning. The densities are generally based on what is considered desirable in the public interest from the standpoint of public health and safety. Regulation of residential densities has long been recognized as a means for controlling contagion, for insuring access to sunlight and air, and for a variety of other purposes identified in the

4AM   9AM   1 PM

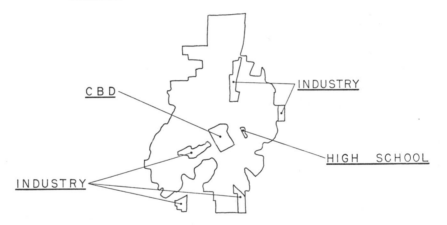

C B D   INDUSTRY

HIGH SCHOOL

INDUSTRY

3PM   6PM   11PM

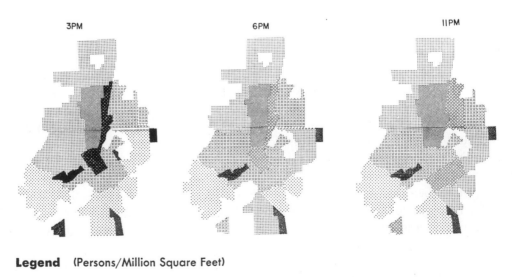

Legend (Persons/Million Square Feet)

0-99	200-299	400-499	600-699	800-899	1000-1249
100-199	300-399	500-599	700-799	900-999	1250-1499

Hygiene of Housing Committee listing above. Control of densities in both residential and work areas has received particular attention since World War II as a civil defense measure, but also in the interest of the peacetime health and safety of the people of urban areas. Indeed, even before the war, steps toward the control of the huge daytime densities in the heart of Manhattan and in the work centers of other metropolitan areas were being viewed as necessary in the interest of public health, safety, and convenience. Control in this instance would be concerned with the hazards of contagion and conflagration, mental well-being and physical fatigue from congestion, and the adverse effects of noise and fumes from traffic. Certainly it is well within the realm of possibility that density ceilings will be designed into work areas in the public interest in the same way that they are now established for residential areas.

As basic as the planning for certain designed population capacities is to the whole notion of control in the public interest, such measures must nevertheless be reinforced by regulatory devices controlling the intensity of land use and the occupancy of structures in order to insure that the designed capacity of the land is not exceeded. In this connection, zoning and subdivision control are fundamental effectuation devices. Moreover, in residential areas regulatory controls over the crowding of dwelling units and the doubling up of families are widely used (these are usually found in housing codes). By the same token, designed daytime densities in work areas will also require policing by suitable regulatory controls yet to be worked out. All of these applications of density control involve the public interest, and, as such, whether fully worked out and generally sanctioned by the courts or not, figure prominently in the land use planning task.

Controls Over Hazardous Areas

Depending upon physiographic conditions prevailing in a particular urban area, there are conditions and circumstances that warrant the use of control measures to protect man from himself, as it were. These are the situations in urban areas where land is subject to flood or difficult to drain.

Figure 6. Distribution of Population for Selected Times During the Day and Night, June, 1950, Flint, Michigan. The low point in the daily activities of this population occurs at 4 A.M. when most people are in their homes. During the daytime hours the population redistributes itself, until in Flint the largest concentrations occur at 3 P.M. at the time of shift changes at the five large industrial plants. (*Source:* Special tabulations prepared by the Institute for Research in Social Science, University of North Carolina, from the Flint Metropolitan Area Traffic Study, conducted by the Michigan State Highway Department in cooperation with the U.S. Bureau of Public Roads.)

The danger of flood would seem to represent a control in itself and serve to keep such land free of development, yet there are countless illustrations of families resettling in areas even after being flooded out of home and property on several occasions in their lifetime. Less dramatic, but nevertheless troublesome and a concern to the public health, is the situation where marshy places or areas difficult to drain are pressed into development. Where there is a polluted ground water supply, a condition that is common in most urban areas, the public health is especially affected where this water stands or tends to pond at the earth's surface. Typhoid fever can be a public concern anywhere, and malaria can become a major problem in the southern parts of our country.

The most effective means for controlling the use of these areas is by public acquisition, developing them as an integral part of the permanent public open space system of the community. However, the costs involved in public acquisition of all such areas or in carrying out corrective flood control or drainage projects may be prohibitive. Where this is the case and where there is no provision for federal or state participation in the costs, regulatory controls alone or in combination with the above alternatives may provide the only practicable solution. Although still in the process of experimental development, flood plain zoning is an example of a regulatory device employed in the public interest in these situations. The experience of Rhode Island with several hurricane disasters in recent years has become a matter of such great public concern in this state that the principle of flood plain zoning has been applied to regulate the settlement patterns of both summer and permanent residential areas. This regulatory measure has been used to supplement the more direct forms of control involved in state acquisition of certain shore lands and the construction of protective structures along the coast.

Thus, in much the same way that land use planning serves as a means for achieving a rational solution to the control of densities, it also provides a rational approach to the channeling of development into the good areas and discouraging development in areas unsafe or unhealthy for settlement. However, here also land use planning must be reinforced by the proper regulatory and public works measures to implement the planning solutions.

Control of Exposure to Adverse Environmental Influences

The third major public health and safety purpose to be served by land use planning relates to hazards developing out of (1) the heavy movements of automobile traffic and other forms of transportation and the adverse effect of their noise, fumes, or smoke on adjacent areas, and (2) the operations of industrial establishments with uncontrolled atmospheric or stream pollution or the noise they may create. While objectionableness has traditionally been measured in terms of the way that transportation routes and the lower-order uses (industrial and business) affect the higher-order uses (residential and public uses), there is a growing tendency to view these relationships not so much by functional use characteristics as by the standard of performance they achieve or the degree to which adverse influences are brought under control. Thus, in the same way that variations in density can be prescribed in the public interest in the different sections of the urban area, so can standards of performance be established for various areas in the community in the interest of public health and safety.

The effects of noise on fatigue are well known, and the adverse physiological effects on the respiratory system of smoke, dust, and gasoline fumes have recently received much attention in medical circles. These considerations and the hazards of heavy streams of traffic along major transportation routes and at employment centers are frequently cited as evils of the city. While the adverse effects can be abated, obviously these arteries and centers can never be eliminated, for they involve the very life and existence of urban areas.

These transportation and industrial hazards to public health and safety are perhaps most directly controlled by various technological abatement measures. However, land use planning offers a means of controlling *exposure* to adverse influences involved in these activities. Space, orientation, and internal design are all elements of land use planning which can be utilized to minimize exposure. Separation of inimical uses by space—by open space or by areas developed in uses that are mutually compatible—can be used as an alleviating factor. The selection of locations so that prevailing winds can serve to reduce rather than accentuate exposure to smokestack industries is another control mechanism of land use planning that can be used to advantage. The internal design of use areas can also assist in minimizing exposure—for example, a layout that discourages through traffic from moving through residential areas, the routing of transport along channels specifically designed for these facilities, the introduction of buffer or insulation strips of planted open space all serve to moderate the effects of adverse environmental influences.

Convenience

In the foregoing discussion of control, health and safety have been the prime elements of the public interest at stake. Though frequently viewed as a lower-order consideration of the public welfare, convenience is nevertheless closely associated with the public interest and constitutes a third major basis for the exercise of control. The courts have recognized public convenience to be an element of the public interest in upholding the construction of streets and highways as a public purpose, and viewed in combination with health and safety, convenience has been given judicial sanction as a basis for regulating the traffic using these streets and highways.

However, public convenience is not a function of the circulatory systems of the community alone. More basically it is a derivative of the locational arrangements of land use and the relationship that each functional use area bears to every other one. Thus convenience can be judged in terms of home-to-work, work-to-recreation, home-to-shopping, shopping-to-work, and a variety of other area relationships intrinsic to the urban land use pattern. It may also be judged in terms of relationships between wholesale and retail areas, retail and industrial areas, or other use combinations where the movement of goods rather than of people is the basis of judgment. According to the reasons for movement in the urban area, convenience is measured in miles or blocks of walking distance, or, more normally and in the modern-day sense, in minutes of transportation time. In transportation planning, convenience is viewed in terms of movement systems and the ease of moving large volumes of people or goods from one destination to another over these systems. Land use planning is concerned with the locations of these destinations which obviously play an important role in maximizing the ease of movement.

In addition to the location factor, convenience is affected by the intensity of land development, that is, the degree to which land is occupied and the density at which it is developed. Intensity of development in an urban area is influenced by such interrelated considerations as the character of the terrain and its drainage features, the pattern of land values, the whims of original landowners in the subdivision of property, the amenities of the area, the marketability of land titles, and so on. Now obviously, a spread-out pattern of development and the presence of low population densities (individually or in combination) tend to increase time-distance relationships between outlying sections of the built-up area and the center and between the various functional use areas. Further, the larger the metropolitan area, the more extreme these time-distance relationships tend to become. Thus intensity of development along with location is basic to the concept of public convenience.

It should be noted that while health and safety criteria dictate an emphasis toward low-order densities, convenience requirements favor an emphasis toward high-order densities. However, these seemingly disparate public purposes are in reality considerations of degree and do not need to be in conflict. In practice, a balance can be achieved in the land use planning process. For example, within the same development area it is possible to design for high *net* densities in the interests of convenience and for low *gross* densities in the interests of health, safety, and amenity.

In the light of the foregoing observations, convenience is obviously a public purpose that goes to the very heart of the land use planning task. Indeed, the land use plan may be viewed as a developmental control device aimed at achieving maximum convenience in the location and arrangement of land uses. Regulatory controls such as zoning and subdivision regulations then become the means for building convenience into the pattern of land development.

Economy

As the fourth major element of the public interest warranting control of land development, "economy" is a term associated with efficiency in the land use pattern and its public cost implications, whether in terms of municipal expenditures or cost to the urbanite in general. In a broader sense the public economy may be coupled with the general vitality of the urban economy as a whole and its implications for the revenue structure of an urban center. Since the urban economy is taken up later, we shall confine our discussion here to governmental and citizen costs of land development. In this usage, it has to do with land development from the viewpoint of the community as a whole as opposed to the viewpoint of the entrepreneur or the collective actions of many people functioning in the urban land market as discussed in the first chapter. What land use arrangement is most efficient and least costly to the municipality and to the citizen is the basic concern here in the exercise of control.

As an element of the public interest, economy is closely associated with convenience. Indeed, economy and convenience are frequently involved in tandem, just as health and safety are linked together. A land use scheme in which residential areas have easy access to schools and recreation areas also permits a more efficient and economical school plant or recreation program in terms of persons served and per capita costs. Convenient proximity of places of residence to places of work also makes for the most efficient and least expensive circulatory system in terms of public works expenditures or citizen outlay for gasoline or transit fares. In this sense, convenience has to do with expenditure of time and effort, whereas economy relates to the cost of this time and effort to the urbanite and to the city as an institution.

As in the case of public convenience, both the location of use areas and their intensity of development are key considerations of economy. The location of use areas affects public costs in a variety of ways. For example, it makes an obvious difference in public costs if industrial areas are located in relation to existing or proposed utility lines capable of supplying large amounts of water and handling heavy industrial waste requirements, than if these considerations are ignored. Similarly, it is a matter of public economy that the location of new commercial and industrial development occur where it can be efficiently served by existing fire protection facilities and by what would constitute an economical expansion of them. In still another example, it is important to give preference to areas where residential development can be located in relation to existing utility or school capacities or to areas where these facilities can be economically and efficiently extended. What is economical to provide in the form of streets, recreation areas, and other community facilities in relation to existing facilities also enter into the picture and also become, in effect, control factors in the planning of urban land uses.

In addition to location considerations, the intensity in the way land is put to use also affects the public cost aspects of land development. A spread-out pattern of development involves a greater mileage of streets and more lineal feet of water and sewer lines than more compact and densely developed settlement patterns. These considerations of the public interest of course must be balanced against the dictates of health and amenity where the emphasis is toward an open-order pattern of urban development. They must also be viewed in terms of community values, attitudes, and preferences and the taxes and other costs people are willing to assume in order to satisfy their wants. Again these considerations are intimately bound up in the land use planning process, and controls exercised in the public interest to achieve maximum economy are relative to other controls and the economic and social considerations at stake. Here too, land use planning may be viewed, then, as a kind of master control, but at the same time reinforced by effectuating regulatory controls such as zoning, subdivision regulations, and the establishment of major street locations and sometimes school and recreation sites through official map procedures.

Amenity

This is a term in more general usage in England than in the United States, and refers to the pleasantness of the urban environment as a place in which to live, work, and spend one's leisure time. It relates to the perceptual aspects of urban surroundings—their aesthetic appearances to the eye and the comfort and enjoyment offered to the other senses. Viewing all five elements of the public interest in the continuum of judicial acceptance,

amenity is situated at the lower end of the scale. It is not specifically excluded as an element of public interest in court decisions generally, but is
most frequently accepted in combination with one or more of the other
four elements. Yet in the array of public purposes to be served by land use
planning, from a social point of view it is of no less importance than the
other four as a basis for the exercise of control. While in judicial tenets it
may be viewed as an optimal rather than a minimal element of the public
interest, the increased importance being attached to amenity as a dimension of public health and mental well-being may well result in a more
positive recognition of aesthetics as a basis for the exercise of regulatory
controls in the future.[31]

Perhaps the major deterrent to a wider use of regulatory controls in the
interest of amenity is the range of variation inherent in public tastes. What
is attractive and pleasant in the living environment tends to vary with
every person. According to the values, whims, and beliefs of people, one
thing may be pleasing to some persons, and it may yield an entirely negative
response in others. It is this aspect of amenity that sets it off from other
elements of the public interest. Thus the difficulty of subjecting tastes to a
test of consensus may explain why amenity has not been accorded the
same recognition that health, safety, convenience, and economy have been
given in the courts. Nevertheless, there are extremes in the visual appearances of a city that evoke some degree of unanimity in response, either
of a positive or negative kind. For example, there tends to exist a general
consensus that highway entrances to one's city that are flanked by automobile graveyards are unsightly and should be regulated in the public interest. Other similar examples, perhaps of a more localized character, could
be cited in almost any community. But as we proceed upward on a scale
of from "bad" to "good," there may be less unanimity. Thus some people
would favor large open spaces in the townscape as a welcome relief to the
monotony of "urban sprawl." Some would place the emphasis on planted
green areas to relieve the drabness of concrete and steel. Some would feel
that the miles of structures and streets create variety and choice to match
every desire of the urbanite—from total anonymity to any amount of

---

[31] Indications of the changing judicial climate toward the use of the police power to regulate
aesthetics in the public interest appear in the U.S. Supreme Court decision of November 22,
1954, *Berman v. Parker* (23 LW 4012). "The concept of the public welfare is broad and inclusive. . . . The values it represents are spiritual as well as physical, aesthetic as well as monetary. It is within the power of the legislature to determine that the community should be
beautiful as well as healthy, spacious as well as clean, well-balanced as well as carefully
patrolled." This interpretation had a direct influence on the subsequent Wisconsin Supreme
Court decision upholding architectural control provisions in the zoning ordinance of Fox Point,
Wisconsin (*State ex rel. Saveland Park Holding Corporation v. Weeland*, 69 NW 2d 217). For
a more complete discussion of the problem, see J. J. Dukeminier, Jr., "Zoning for Aesthetic
Objectives: A Reappraisal," *Law and Contemporary Problems*, Spring, 1955.

neighboring that might be desired. As we proceed up the scale, we enter an area approaching unanimity again—this time of a positive form. Thus there are generally favorable reactions concerning tree-shaded streets that alleviate the heat of pavements and general approval of landscaped freeways that make driving pleasant and easy.

With recent advances in survey research methods and sampling techniques in the social sciences, the identification of these attitudes poses no major problems.[32] However, there are problems in interpreting responses obtained in such surveys. In the course of identifying negative and positive extremes of reaction, the displeasing or distasteful must somehow be connected with forms of physical development that elicit general approval. Where negative and positive responses are reciprocal with respect to particular features in the townscape, no problem exists. But where there is no positive counterpart to match up with an undesirable feature in the list of plus and minus aspects of amenity, difficulty is encountered. Corrective solutions which meet with general approval must be discovered by posing alternatives and singling out the solution which meets with the greatest approval.

Yet it can be expected that there will be a whole range of aesthetic considerations that are outside the experience of the people of a particular community. These may be advanced notions that heretofore have been given only experimental application in a few scattered localities. For example, this is true of the superblock principle in residential design.[33] The idea of residential areas with complete separation of pedestrian and trafficways may be totally foreign to the people of a community. In other situations, the city may not have advanced in its growth sufficiently to experience certain conditions that produce a marked reaction. This is true of a community facing a period of rapid growth for the first time. At the outset the local people have no particular convictions, but as urbanization accelerates, they form very articulate notions about developments they consider to be detrimental to the amenity of the community, the negative reactions tending to develop more rapidly than the positive ones.

The problem here is one of anticipating responses and matching up negative ones with solutions calculated to meet with favorable reaction.

---

[32] As noted earlier in the chapter, the underlying values that influence attitudes and beliefs are more complex to identify and measure.

[33] As pioneered by Henry Wright and Clarence Stein, town planners and architects of Radburn, New Jersey, the superblock, as the term implies, is an unusually large residential block which, in effect, is turned inside out, with pedestrian access provided by a system of internal walkways in a setting of landscaped open space, and with automobile access provided to individual houses from short dead-end streets or *cul-de-sacs* penetrating the block from the peripheral collector street. Superblocks are planned in clusters, with a system of interconnecting pedestrian ways that underpass or overpass the bounding collector streets. The superblock principle thus involves the element of safety as well as amenity.

At this point and at the present stage of development in this aspect of survey research, there is no alternative open to the city planner but the application of judgment backed up by experience and observation in other communities. Thus against a background of experience from communities of similar makeup where alternative approaches have been tried, a judgment is made as to the transfer value of each solution to a given locale of interest, with the one judged to be most suited to local circumstances being eventually selected. Here there is a fine line of distinction to be noted between what is experience and unbiased observation and what constitutes the values of the city planner himself. It is not within the scope of the public interest for the city planner to plan for Le Corbusier tower apartments or Frank Lloyd Wright Broadacres communities where the choice is made simply on the basis of his personal preference. This is quite different from the obverse situation where experience or knowledge of response in other similar situations is made the basis for his choice. The solution selected is made in the public interest, and this calls for an approach based on prevailing community concepts of amenity, not those of the planner.

In view of these problems of securing a consensus of tastes, control exercised to achieve attractive and pleasant civic growth and development is difficult to systematize into codes or laws. Present solutions rest with the land use plan reinforced by effectuation controls, both regulatory measures such as zoning, subdivision control, and the official map, and developmental measures that are involved in public works programs and urban renewal programs. At the same time amenity must be balanced against the other four elements of the public interest. Thus the introduction of open space into a city to give it greater variety in visual appearance and to introduce pleasant green areas for relaxation and leisure-time use also involves considerations of convenience and economy. The process of discovering this balance constitutes one of the basic tasks of land use planning.

Factors Conditioning the Use of Controls

Having reviewed the five major elements of the public interest which prompt the use of controls in land development, we can now proceed to examine some of the practicalities that condition the application of such controls and thus establish the way in which the public interest ultimately functions as a determinant of land use. Stated another way, it is now possible to highlight the factors involved in bringing the public interest considerations into equilibrium with the economic and social considerations covered in the first two sections of the chapter. How convergence of the public interest with the economic and social determinants of land use is accomplished, and how the synthesis is expressed in physical form in a land development plan constitute the very essence of the land use planning process.

As indicated earlier, controls employed in the public interest may reflect a range of community consciousness varying from optimal to minimal points of view. Thus in general terms, control over the physical setting of the city may be viewed at one extreme as an opportunity to realize the full potentialities of a safe, healthful, convenient, efficient, and pleasant place in which to live, with gradations to the other extreme in which control is viewed more in the sense of a necessary constraint to protect the public interest. What the point of acceptance or tolerance is will vary with the community and local circumstances. In one community, for example, there may be general acceptance of public ownership of riverfront lands as a means of control, with development secured through leasing arrangements or public works. In another community, there may be limited constraints over the private use of riverfront lands with little or no tolerance of the notion of public ownership as a means of control. In still other communities, there may be variations from both extremes. Within the same community, there may be unequal emphasis among the five elements of the public interest, with perhaps an acceptance approaching an optimal emphasis on one or two and a minimal approach to the other three or four.

Why a community accepts one element of the public interest, tolerates another, and perhaps even rejects another, or why one community exhibits a tolerant point of view in the degree of control exercised under one or more of the five elements and another shows a very low tolerance for control in the public interest are frequently matters of historical circumstance. The prevailing public temperament may have its origins in a public emergency caused by a San Francisco-type fire, a Pittsburgh-type flood, a Providence-type hurricane, or an economic collapse such as is involved in some New England communities with the wholesale withdrawal of textile plants. It may have its origins in a symbolic phenomenon—for example, a group sentiment concerning the community's historical heritage, a long tradition of nurtured community values concerning the past with accompanying pressures to protect the historical parts of the city. In other cases it may stem from a distinctive natural resource and a general desire to maximize its economic potential—our Miamis, Ashevilles, Tucsons, etc. In still other cases, it may have evolved over a period of time from a vigorous, forward-looking civic leadership with an accompanying growth in civic pride and awareness of the essentials of community livability— the outgrowth of nameless devoted individuals or groups: the work of the Daniel Burnhams in communities across the country.

Whatever the community or circumstance, obviously the temperament of the community—its mass community values and the extent that they are articulated in behavior that comports acceptance of control in the public interest—will dictate how far land use planning can go in providing for health, safety, convenience, economy, and amenity in the physical environment. So the task of land use planning becomes one of gauging the public temperament, discovering and recognizing levels of acceptance and tolerance, and balancing these considerations with local practicalities. This final aspect of bringing all public interest determinants of land use into focus in one perspective is concerned with local practicalities: (1) physical characteristics, (2) fiscal capabilities, (3) jurisdictional considerations, and (4) the political climate. All affect the extent to which control is necessary or feasible in the face of economic and social realities, and together they include the more practical considerations which condition the use of controls in the public interest.

Physical Characteristics

Perhaps the most tangible series of factors dictating the way in which controls are applied are the local physical characteristics. These include both the physiographic factors associated with the site of the urban area and the settlement characteristics that have been superimposed on the site. They involve then, on the one hand, the terrain, its drainage features, and the way in which the winds, the sun, and the climate warrant the use of controls. On the other hand, they involve the practicalities of the way in which the land has been developed, and more particularly the extent to which this settlement pattern can be altered through planning as a form of control.

Physiographic Factors

It was noted above that controls are invoked to minimize the ravages of the rivers and the sea where they impinge on the public health and safety. It was also observed that controls may be employed to take advantage of orientation with respect to prevailing winds to minimize exposure to smoke and fumes and maximize summertime and wintertime comfort and well-being. Controls may also be employed to insure that natural features of the landscape may be wisely and pleasingly utilized, providing the amenities of a pleasant living environment. All these considerations stem from physiographic features in the urban landscape.

While modern-day engineering is able and has wrought many changes on the earth's surface, it is rarely feasible to change the townscape in the sweeping way undertaken in many resource use and development programs in open country. Mountains and major drainage courses cannot be moved or appreciably altered without involving a multiplicity of property ownership rights and a whole complex of economic and social values running with the land and its relationship to prevailing patterns of land development. Yet at times the public interest may be so compelling and critical as to involve stringent control measures. Hibbing, Minnesota, moved to an entirely new site to permit open-pit iron ore mining on its original site, and there are a number of instances where whole towns were moved to new sites to make way for flood control works. However, these were small communities and represent the exception rather than the rule.

Nevertheless, the physiographic features of the city's site present some of the most obvious practicalities affecting acceptance of control in the public interest. In Pittsburgh, mountains and drainage courses represent very practical considerations, suggesting the probabilities of a higher tolerance toward certain developmental and regulatory forms of control than would be acceptable in Omaha in the plains area. To cope with local topographic problems, in Pittsburgh even the most minimal notions of public safety and economy can be expected to carry acceptance for costly public works programs (for example, highway projects, drainage control, etc.) and stringent subdivision and zoning controls. It happens too that the heavy coal consumption in this area (industrial added to the domestic) in combination with the local physiographic characteristics has made smoke abatement a health matter of considerable public interest, permitting high public tolerance limits to smoke control measures. Indeed, it is probable that physiographic features have been major factors in the development of an advanced public awareness of planning control measures here.

Land Use Factors

Closely related to the basic physiographic features of the urban locale, the character of existing land use is also a practical consideration that affects the extent to which controls are employed. In this connection, Abrams identifies five public purposes for which land use controls are employed in the public interest:

1. Guide the *use* of land to promote the advantageous development of the community (e.g., protection of factory, residential, commercial, park, parking, and other sites under a master plan).
2. Curb the *misuse* of land so that it will not injuriously affect the interests of the community (e.g., prevention of slum construction or unnecessarily intense development).
3. Prevent the *abuse* of land (e.g., prevention of abortive subdivisions, cut-over land).
4. Regulate the *nonuse* or *disuse* of land (e.g., taxation to enforce development,

clearing of unmarketable titles, keeping land from development, or restraining owners of occupied dwellings from discontinuing their use).

5. Guide the *reuse* of land for more appropriate purposes (e.g., urban redevelopment, slum clearance, and rehousing).[34]

In the context of this discussion, the first and fifth represent developmental forms of control, and the other three involve regulatory forms of control. All are concerned with needs or problems of land use and are generically referred to as planning controls.

The degree of acceptance of these public purposes and thus of the control measures themselves may be prompted by *reaction* to the misuse, abuse, or disuse of land, or it may be prompted by *action* to achieve certain goals in the use or reuse of land. In general, reaction to adverse conditions results in a stronger, more prompt exercise of control measures than action that is positively oriented toward certain new patterns of land use. In cities where there are large blighted areas with the accompanying human misery and deprivation, public acceptance of such control measures as slum clearance and redevelopment, rehabilitation, and conservation tends to be stronger and faster than the acceptance of controls used to promote orderly and attractive industrial districts, open space systems, shopping centers, or residential communities in new developments. It is human nature to be more immediately stirred by corrective needs than by the need for preventive measures.

The misuse, abuse, or disuse of land as seen in the slums is a very tangible basis for the use of controls. To be sure, vigorous campaigns by the leaders of the community must often dramatize the facts if public action is to develop in a concerted manner. Perhaps it is shock or horror—such as the rat that bit the child in a Chicago slum—which provides a symbol and the drama needed to arouse public indignation and create a demand for control measures. Thus when dramatized in terms of human misery, Chicago's 22 square miles of blighted and near-blighted areas and 50 square miles threatened by blight become a staggering fact in the public eye. The abstraction of a statistic then assumes a semblance of reality, and the prevailing slum conditions become the basis of a public issue, sometimes approaching the proportions involved in a fire, a hurricane, or other public emergency. Whether or not the newspaper campaign that ferreted out the rat incident in Chicago was a key element in the subsequent introduction of new control measures (for example, the community conservation law—a national "first" in Chicago) is difficult to establish. Undoubtedly a variety of considerations were involved. Nevertheless, the extended

[34] Charles Abrams *et al.*, *Urban Land Problems and Policies*, Housing and Town and Country Planning Bulletin 7, United Nations, 1953, p. 34.

scope of control measures employed for blight prevention and elimination was based on practicalities related to the character of land use. These conditions set in motion a chain of action patterns that served to alter tolerance limits toward controls used in the public interest.

Such other land use—related problems as the speculative subdivision of the land, traffic congestion, the shortage of parking space, fringe development overspilling the corporate limits of the central city, and so on, involve the use of other control devices. The exact kinds of control and the degree of acceptance of these control measures depend in each case on such factors as the acuteness of the problem, the public awareness of the needed corrective action, and other local practicalities.

Fiscal Capabilities

Fiscal considerations affecting the use of controls are so obvious as to require little amplification. Patently, the extent to which a community can acquire land in areas subject to flood, develop its public open space system, engage in urban renewal programs, or employ other forms of developmental control is directly related to its financial condition and its fiscal capabilities.[35] Even in the case of regulatory forms of control, the costs of administration may become a limiting factor. Few cities have a full complement of field investigators required for the enforcement of such regulatory measures as building, fire, housing, sanitation, and zoning ordinances. Accordingly budgetary appropriations affect the locality's ability to enforce regulatory measures and thus the extent of control exercised.

Granted that the fiscal capabilities of a municipality place limitations on the use of controls in the interest of public health, safety, convenience, efficiency, and amenity, it must also be recognized that these capabilities are a function of the taxes people are willing to pay balanced against their expectations for municipal facilities, services, and controls. All too often a control sanctioned by the majority of the people of the community is one thing and the capabilities for putting it into effect are another. Discounting the lag between the time that consensus is reached concerning the need for a new control and the time that may be involved in putting it into effect, we cannot overlook the fact that few people connect their demands for governmental action with the costs involved. In a formal sense an improvement, a service, or a control can easily be voted in, yet, even where

---

[35] While the fiscal capabilities for the exercise of controls would appear to be self-evident, it is startling to note how many master plans are developed without reference to the locality's financial ability for carrying them out. Master plans that are not carefully scaled to long-range estimates of local revenues, expenditures, and the debt structure of the community have limited utility, and their land development proposals tend to become ineffectual control mechanisms.

price tags are attached, for example in general obligation bond issues, few people associate the desired change with needed compensatory advances in the tax rate. What they demand as citizens is generally completely dissociated from their attitudes as taxpayers.

The foregoing observations indicate the inertia encountered in putting new controls into effect. However, there are variations among cities in the public sensitivity to the need for improving their fiscal capabilities. Attitudes in this respect involve economic and social values of civic leaders, influential civic groups, and the citizenry in general, and to assess these considerations requires not only a knowledge of patterns of citizen and group behavior as reflected in the history of past governmental reforms, but also an understanding of the present temperament of the community and its likely patterns of action in the face of present attitudes and their derivative values. Thus fiscal capabilities affect the extent to which controls are employed in a particular locality not only in terms of what is discernible on the surface in the existing municipal balance sheet, but also in terms of the underlying public temperament and what level of public support for progressive improvements in municipal government this temperament will sustain in the future.

Jurisdictional Considerations

Related to the physical and fiscal practicalities that affect the use of controls in the public interest, there are jurisdictional considerations which enter into the picture. These are the very real and practical problems associated with the multiplicity of political jurisdictions that have come into being in urban areas over the years. Most of these problems arise in connection with the financial plight faced by these separate jurisdictions, particularly the plight of central cities. As a consequence, control policies with respect to land development are being increasingly guided by considerations of the revenue-producing potentials of the various land uses.

Though artificial creations in the economic and social sense and inefficient and expensive to perpetuate in an administrative sense, jurisdictional factors continue to exert an influence on the way in which controls are applied. Indeed, they can be expected to remain a factor in the picture until effective metropolitan-wide governmental arrangements become a reality. Thus, no matter how logical it may appear for a central city to hew to certain metropolitan-wide land use objectives or how compelling these objectives may seem in terms of the public interest of the metropolitan community as a whole, so long as separate jurisdictions exist within one urban area, the central city will tend to exercise controls in the best interests of its own limited constituency. The same observation, of course, applies to all other political jurisdictions in the urban area.

Examples of these political realities are not difficult to find. The central city's policies concerning sewer and water extensions beyond its boundaries to adjoining incorporated or unincorporated areas tend to be a function of what is in the best interests of the central city. These jurisdictional considerations can thus exert an influence on the direction and rate of development in the urban area. Schools and other public facilities and services will usually be provided in each of the several jurisdictions, according to the public interest dictates of each particular jurisdiction rather than according to the public interest of the total metropolitan area.

Political boundaries affect other elements in the land use pattern. Apart from the way in which jurisdictional-based decisions on public facilities and services will tend to influence residential, commercial, and industrial land use patterns, the central city (or any of the adjoining political jurisdictions) may take more direct steps and embody in a zoning ordinance land use concepts that are conceived entirely in terms of its own set of interests. Clearly what is determined to be sound in the interest of one segment of the whole may be in conflict with what is sound in the public interest of the other segments of the whole, and further, what is established to be sound for each of these political jurisdictions may be quite another thing from what is best in the interest of the overall metropolitan area. And so, along with physical and fiscal considerations, the way the political boundaries are drawn represents a practicality affecting the use of controls.

The Political Climate

Implicit in the discussion so far is the notion that what is physically, fiscally, and jurisdictionally feasible in the exercise of developmental and regulatory forms of control is closely associated with what is politically expedient. As used here "the poitical climate" refers to what is acceptable to those elements in the community who wield influence and make decisions. In one sense, it relates to what is acceptable to the citizenry in general, in another, to what is acceptable to influential individuals and organized groups in the community, and in still another and in the conventional sense, to what is acceptable to the formal governmental structure—the mayor and city council. All three elements may be in harmony or completely at odds with one another. Where there is full harmony, it is tantamount to effective acceptance of a control measure, but where there is disagreement, the effective degree of acceptance is at the mercy of the dominant element in the community.

Using the term "control" in its broadest sense, the forms of control and degree of control which are acceptable depend upon attitudes that prevail and their more deeply rooted antecedent values. Thus the political climate in relation to any particular control measure involves an exceedingly complex web of value relationships which determine a certain alignment of attitudes, which in turn suggest the likely actions that these attitudes would elicit. To sort out these values, attitudes, and expected action patterns, to relate them to the power structure in the community, and to determine the dominant ones that would prevail under any particular set of local circumstances is an extremely complex proposition that would tax the most advanced research tools of the social scientist. This problem and all its technical ramifications, the substitution of judgment and empirical observation for scientifically based analyses of the political climate, and other similar methodological considerations are beyond the scope of this discussion.

It is sufficient for purposes here to recognize that the political climate, however complex in its origins and its functioning and in whatever way it is analyzed, is a basic practical consideration that affects the nature and extent of control exercised in the public interest. Physical practicalities may identify what is feasible from a technical or engineering viewpoint; fiscal capabilities and jurisdictional considerations may define these limits more narrowly; and political considerations may set still lower limits or entirely eliminate the use of particular control measures. Thus renewal of the blighted sections of a city may be clearly in the interests of public health and safety; a whole range of renewal measures may be technically and financially feasible; and an integrated series of redevelopment, rehabilitation, and conservation control measures may have wide support from civic groups and public agencies. Yet the kinds of measures and the degrees of control which are politically acceptable may be much more narrowly defined and limited in scope. According to the values and attitudes they hold, influential individuals or special-interest groups may exert pressure in the state legislature to block legislation supplying the necessary legal powers for certain renewal measures, or, if the legal authority already exists, they may seek to influence the forms of control sanctioned by the local governing body, and so on.

Though the political climate is a practical consideration which affects the control exercised over land development at a particular time, this is not to imply that land use planning is wholly governed by political expediency. The city planning agency aims toward what is consistent with economic and social forces and sound in the public interest. Its perspective includes the present, but its sights are set toward the future. Public objectives are patently concerned with things beyond the present, and plans for the fulfillment of these objectives are no more tied to what is presently politically feasible than to what the courts will allow today in the public interest. Thus in developing a land use plan, the planning agency is viewing land development against a backdrop of long-range considerations, among them the long-run political and legal eventualities. Yet at the same time the foundations are in the present, and progress in bringing plans into reality involves a day-to-day sorting and sifting process and the selection of the best move with reference to the prevailing political climate.

Our concern here has been related to the political climate as a factor affecting the use of controls rather than any detailed consideration of the dynamics of political action. More broadly, our concern has been to identify some of the more important practicalities which tend to condition the effectiveness of control measures utilized in the public interest. This concern in turn relates to a larger, more fundamental one of establishing how the public interest along with the economic and social factors affect the pattern of urban land uses. Let us now proceed to bring together these determinants of land use and examine their significance in relation to one another.

Relationships Among Land Use Determinants

Although urban land use determinants have so far been somewhat arbitrarily grouped into three classes, it is the purpose of this concluding section to show that these separate explanations of land use have little practical meaning unless viewed in one interrelated matrix. Basic to a full understanding of this matrix of factors shaping the pattern of land uses in an urban area, of course, is the need for an inclusive theoretical frame of reference mentioned at the outset. Until this kind of foundation theory is used to provide the guidelines for applied analyses of city planning, land use planning must somehow function as an open-ended process that seeks empirically the balance that is needed among the many factors summarized in the preceding pages.

Preparatory to the Chapter 2 discussion of theoretical work, it would seem to serve a useful purpose to bring together the concepts of the preceding chapters, array them side by side, and hypothesize some of the interrelationships involved. Such an organization of concepts at the very least should be helpful as a checkoff sheet to insure that all factors are considered in the technical studies undertaken in the land use planning process.

Interrelationships Among Determinants

Let us first draw upon the behavioral concept set forth earlier. According to this concept, land goes into use as a consequence of a myriad individual and group actions. Motivated by values, ideals, and resultant articulated attitudes held by the various organized and unorganized segments of the urban population, these actions follow a defined behavioral sequence that culminates in land use changes.

This concept appears to supply the common thread in all three ways of viewing the origins of land use patterns. In the first section of this chapter, there is a clear indication that land use is a consequence of the economic behavior of the urbanite in the urban land market. In the second section, land use is explicitly seen as being influenced by the urbanite's behavior in response to such culture-bound phenomena as customs, traditions, and beliefs. Finally in the last section, the health, safety, convenience, economy, and amenity controls employed in the common public interest can be viewed as the result of behavior consciously calculated to influence land use. In each of these approaches "forces" are sometimes spoken of as determinants. In the behavioral concept, various patterns of behavior are viewed as the ultimate determinants, with "forces" being used as intermediate abstractions to signify the interplay of factors in any particular phase of one or more behavioral cycles.[36]

Now by charting actions connected with each of the three major forms of urban behavior side by side (and there may well be more than three classes) and fitting them to a single sequence of the behavior cycle, interrelationships begin to suggest themselves (see Figure 7). Thus profit-making values concerning the use of the land result in a variety of behavior patterns in the urban land market which in the aggregate *tend* to produce purely economically motivated changes in the land use pattern. At the same time certain livability and culturally oriented values may have the effect of modifying these purely economic actions.[37] Such modifications may occur at the value-forming stage or they may occur in any phase of a behavioral sequence in one or more behavior patterns.

Each of the three forms of urban behavior *tends* to have pure consequences, but because of side effects the ultimate consequences to land use may be quite different from the originally anticipated results. In Figure 7

---

[36] The *behavior cycle* has been previously identified as a recurring sequence of phases in the action process: (1) experiencing needs and wants, (2) setting goals, (3) planning alternative courses of action, and (4) reaching a decision for action (see Figure 3). A series of related cycles are considered to be a *behavior pattern* (see Figure 4).

[37] *Livability* values refer here to public interest considerations of health, safety, convenience, public economy, and amenity. Obviously this segment of the whole has traditionally been of particular concern to the city planner.

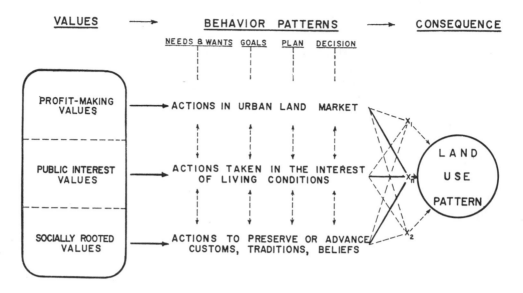

Figure 7. Interrelationships Among Land Use Determinants. Points x_1, x_2 . . . x_n represent points where all side effects of actions seeking changes in land use reach equilibrium, with a consequence of 1, 2 . . . n changes occurring in the land use pattern.

a crude generalization of this sequence of behavior is presented, with x being the point of equilibrium after all side effects have exerted their influence on a projected change in the land use. More particularly points x_1, x_2 . . . x_n represent the points where all behavioral relationships involving a series of n actions reach their equilibriums, resulting in 1, 2 . . . n changes in the land use pattern. Firey's theory of proportionality is a more formal statement of this general concept, and the point x on his U-curve representation of the theory (Figure 5) would correspond to point x in Figure 7.[38]

Broadly, many actions are evolving concurrently in the sequence suggested in Figure 7, with some in different stages of advancement in the behavior cycle than others. As suggested in the discussion of socially rooted determinants above, some have planned consequences in the sense that land use changes follow a conscious and rational course of evolution even though they may have undergone modification in the course of the behavior cycle in the manner described above. Some have unplanned consequences in the sense that there is a lack of relationship emerging from two or more planned actions, more particularly a lack of relationship among the one or more phases of each behavior cycle. The absence of such relationships

[38] Firey, *Land Use in Central Boston*, pp. 326–327. See the section on socially rooted determinants above for a summary of the theory.

results in unexpected, sometimes inconsistent, or possibly even incompatible uses of land.

Even with the consummation of one or more planned changes in land use and often with the emergence of unplanned consequences, new behavior cycles are set in motion with feedback effects upon human values in the community. Sometimes this feedback process starts before the consummation of the planned or unplanned changes in the land use patterns, and the final consequence is further modified by ensuing new behavior cycles.

A hypothetical illustration will make the dynamics of these behavioral concepts clearer. Let us say that a combine of builders motivated by profit values sets out to acquire at the outskirts of a city a sizable acreage of open land for development into a large-scale housing project including a regional shopping center. In one behavioral sequence they determine an income-producing need for this activity, define their objectives, consider the alternatives, and reach a decision to go ahead and acquire a site. The consequent purchase of a site involves a second sequence of behavior. They determine the extent of their profit needs, set their goals, consider alternatives, and again reach a decision. In this process they consider a variety of sites. With respect to Site No. 1, the developers' interpretation of public interest values indicates a possible stalemate that they can ill afford. First, they foresee difficulties in obtaining changes in zoning to permit the kind of development they have in mind, and second, they anticipate that prevailing public policies on extensions of sewer and water facilities will interfere with their plans.

In the case of Site No. 2, the public interest considerations are less important than the culture-bound values. Several members of the combine of developers are respected residents of the small-estate community surrounding Site No. 2, and have been accepted into the colony only after prolonged social maneuvering. Not only can strong opposition from this area be expected, but these resident partners of the enterprise face social ostracism if they permit their profit-making values to prevail. Because of social symbols held by the developers themselves, this highly promising site is eliminated from consideration. Thus in this behavior cycle, purely profit-making values do not lead to pure consequences, but rather the subsequent decision on Site No. 3 represents a modified decision in consideration of other values.

With the public announcement of intent to build on Site No. 3, a whole new pattern of behaviors occurs. One group of nearby residents, motivated by livability values, suddenly becomes organized, and in a series of behavioral sequences takes steps to thwart the new development. One element of the group opposes changes in zoning that would permit the development of a large shopping facility in the area, maintaining that the great traffic loads converging on the area would involve hazards to their children and noise and fumes to the general detriment of the area, that the flashing neon signs at night would have a disturbing effect, that the shopping center would deface the natural attractiveness of the area, and that all these considerations would have a cumulative effect of generally depressing property values for residential purposes in the entire surrounding area. Another element of the group, motivated by socially rooted values, opposes the proposed lower-order residential zoning on grounds of social disruptions. In effect, they maintain that the influx of lower-income groups alien to their symbols of social status will threaten the security of the group presently resident in surrounding areas. Both elements of the group organized initially as separate groups, but in the subsequent behavioral sequence, finding they had similar goals, they merged in the action phase of their missions.

Other groups may align themselves with the developer according to other values: the social need for more housing, the industry-attracting significance of an adequate supply of housing, the prosperity symbolism of outward signs of growth, and so on. As the behavior cycles move from value stimulus to action, these groups too may merge and function as one. Other new cycles may be introduced. For example, the consolidated opposition may seek support of political groups, or the developers and their sympathizers may seek support of influential persons in the community, bringing the community power structure into the controversy.

Obviously a whole new complex of values quite different from the original profit-making values have been introduced affecting the final outcome of this struggle. The whole scheme may be abandoned, a modified scheme may be adopted as a compromise, or the original proposal may be carried out. What happens and how it affects the configuration of land uses is a consequence of a variety of behavior patterns stemming from a variety of value systems. Thus the land use pattern evolves. Sometimes parts of it are based on actions stemming from a pure system of values unmodified by other systems; and sometimes, as the foregoing illustration suggests, these actions derive from interacting values, not purely profit-making, nor purely public interest or culture-oriented values, but a combination of several values.

Applications to Land Use Planning

What is the significance of this behavioral concept to the technical land use planning process? Now obviously the city planner cannot identify, much less keep tab on all the complex patterns of behavior that the average community sustains. Neither is it realistic to expect that his long-range land development plan will be shaped to accommodate all forms of land use–oriented behaviors. At the present level of research development in this aspect of social science, the immediate significance of such a concept is the purpose it serves in focusing attention on slighted or overlooked considerations in the technical procedures and in indicating the potentialities of fitting plan effectuation activities more successfully and less blindly to action processes.

Our concern here is primarily with technical rather than effectuation considerations. Accordingly, the foregoing discussion indicates a need for a *balanced* consideration of economic, socially rooted, and public interest factors throughout the land use planning process. This means that land use planning analyses must go beyond the customary emphasis on such public interest considerations as health, safety, convenience, economy, and amenity, and give more focused attention to the way in which the urban land market factors tend to site and arrange land uses and to the way in which culture-bound considerations such as customs, traditions, and beliefs influence the pattern of land uses. This kind of broadened emphasis leads the city planner into a number of uncharted areas much in need of researching. For example, how can he identify dominant patterns in land market behavior? Does the shifting pattern of land values provide an adequate index of market behavior? Or in the matter of customs, traditions, and beliefs, how are these identified and set forth in terms usable to the land use planning technician? More specifically, how does the typology and analysis of social areas such as Shevky and Bell have advanced assist in this task? [39] Future research must come to grips with these questions. Meanwhile more systematic and conscious attention must be directed to the use of available measures of economic and social factors that impinge on the distribution and arrangement of land use to insure that the needed balance is achieved.

Beyond these considerations is the need for recognizing the role that attitudes can play in technical studies in fitting the land development plan to the realities of urban behavior. While the identification of behavior patterns may seem to be a complicated appendage to the technical task of land use planning, sampling studies of attitudes may be expected to give perception into values held by strategic action groups and the community at large. Much has been written about "planning for people," but there is a strong possibility that some planning may reflect more of the values

---

[39] Eshref Shevky and Wendell Bell, *Social Area Analysis,* Stanford: Stanford University Press, 1955. See also Amos H. Hawley and Otis Dudley Duncan, "Social Area Analysis: A Critical Appraisal," *Land Economics,* November, 1957.

of the city planners themselves than those of the people of the community. A soundly conceived method of investigating attitudes in many respects provides information just as basic to the technical land use planning process as the land use survey. Not only would attitude data assist in establishing fundamental needs and wants of the urbanite, but it can be expected to provide insight into both immediate and long-range actions that follow from point x in Figure 7. The task is not "intelligent cooperation with the inevitable" in the live-and-let-live sense of the words, but rather one of seeking rational land use guidelines consonant with dominant attitude trends about the use of space in the city. Thus realistic land use planning must not only take into account the physical practicalities of the land and the existing uses it sustains, but it must also identify and interpolate from a changing base of the economic, cultural, and public interest values and project the kind of land development pattern that achieves a balance between all the relevant considerations.

Chapter 2

Toward a Theory of Urban Growth and Development

The strategic role that theory plays in man's quest for understanding and knowledge is so basic, so well documented, and so widely accepted that it seems unnecessary to stress its essential importance for the planning field. Yet until recently there has been very little effort within the profession going into theoretical research. A relatively young field such as planning normally faces a long period of "finding itself" before it begins to develop schools of thought and acquire theoretical traditions. Under the most favorable conditions theory building is a slow process, particularly so if it is to be systematic and rigorous by contemporary standards of scientific inquiry. The time involved from the first statement of theory, through the intermediate stages of empirical tests of its critical components, the successive reformulations and retests, to the stage when it becomes operational is painfully long. It is so long that components of theory often pass into operational use long before the full system can be made to work in practice.

The pressures on the profession to meet new emerging situations in creative and effective ways have been heavy in the post–World War II period, and the field has been pushed into maturing and assuming responsibility more rapidly than was generally anticipated. There is a growing sense of urgency that tactical efforts at solving urban growth problems require much stronger strategic support, and there is generally a new interest and sense of mission in advancing theoretical research. In the 'fifties there were several important efforts of this kind beginning to develop, and during the 'sixties some of this work can be expected to become operational. While there is this developing sense of need and expectancy from the profession, there is another reason for stressing the importance of theoretical research. Not only is it needed to advance knowledge and understanding in the field, but it supplies the guidelines, the rationale, and the *raison d'être* for planning studies undertaken in practice. Without these guidelines, the field remains in an *ad hoc* status. This is not to say that the field has been developing without theoretical foundations. Because of its close ties with such disciplines as economics, public administration, and sociology, and a conversancy with areas of theory in these fields relevant to planning, the profession has shown an alertness to and has put to use new developments from these related fields. Indeed, the results of research from these fields have often been received with more enthusiasm in planning than in the field from which they originated. But as the planning field expands further, it cannot remain dependent solely on the work of related fields, with "a little of this and a little of that" as a substitute for its own research and development effort. Indeed, the future growth of the profession is no less dependent on a basic research effort than is the case for the natural sciences, which have been emphasized so strongly in recent time.

At the present stage in the field's development, theoretical research is developing along two related lines. One major emphasis is on the *process of planning* and its relationship to decision-making theory, and the other focuses on the *subject matter of planning*: the urban complex, the larger region, and sometimes entire nations. In the sense that they constitute the means and ends of planning, they are related areas of theory specialization.[1] For purposes of land use planning we shall be concerned mainly with the second area of specialization, and particularly with urban spatial structure and urban growth. The first part of this chapter will be devoted to some general observations on the formulation of theory and on criteria of an adequate theory. This will be followed by a series of capsule summaries of various theoretical studies of urban spatial structure emerging from the planning field. Finally, some leads which even now in this early period of theory formulation stand out in the work reviewed are cited as guides for land use planning as outlined in subsequent chapters.

In passing it might be observed that perhaps at no point in this volume do the observations made in the Introduction about the swiftly changing status of work in the field apply more appropriately than to this chapter. It should be noted, too, that in a summary chapter of this kind, the nature of theory and the requirements of an adequate theory cannot be dealt with in detail. It would be well for the reader to build on this summary view from journal articles and monographs, and if his interests lean toward theory, he would be well advised to read broadly in the literature of social science theory.

---

[1] For a detailed discussion of this relationship see the author's "Foundations of Urban Planning," in Werner Z. Hirsch (ed.), *Urban Life and Form,* New York: Holt, Rinehart and Winston, Inc., 1963.

Criteria for an Adequate Theory

As used here, "theory" refers to a system of thought which through logical verbal or mathematical constructs supplies an explanation of urban areas —why they exist, how their growth and change occur, and what the basic structure and form components are in the urban scene. In addition to supplying an explanatory rationale, theory frequently provides a rationale for prediction.[2] By observation of the similarities or regularities in the behavior of phenomena in reality, it seeks to establish likely future states of these phenomena under differing assumptions of behavior. At still a third level of application, theory may supply guidelines for exercising choice among alternatives in the course of deciding on a plan. Thus, we see that there are different cut-off points in the development of theory which fall to the discretion of the researcher. It should be noted that utopian concepts of the city are not included here. While constituting an important area of study in the planning field, this kind of system of thought does not constitute theory in the usage of this chapter.

Normative and Explanatory Theory

At the outset it is useful to differentiate between theory which concerns itself with explanation (the what is and the why) and theory which is normative (the what ought to be). In emulating the dispassionate view of the physical sciences, social sciences have a predisposition to keep the normative element out of theory, making anything to do with the "what ought to be" a part of the application of theory and the choice among alternatives which comes into play when a theory is applied. This is the more detached approach. Occasionally the scientist will ask, "What will be the effect if this is assumed or that change introduced?" This takes him into a predictive type of theory and involves a more clinical approach. Of course, when these questions are asked, it is only one further step to pose questions in alternatives, and then to move into normative emphases. While the traditional social science disciplines lean toward the explanatory type of theory, it is the very nature of a profession which has a prescribing function in practice to favor theory with a normative emphasis. Actually, the kinds of theory which seem to be developing in the

---

[2] Prediction is used here in a time sense. Of course, in a formal hypothesis-testing usage, prediction concerns explanatory theory too. In this sense relationships are predicted, and tests are then made to establish the existence, direction, degree, and nature of these predicted relationships. In using prediction in a time sense, theory is dealing with probabilities, not absolute determinism nor the mysticism of prophecy.

field today follow both emphases. Some work focuses on the development of systems for explaining and predicting growth—the "what is," the "why," and the "what consequences" emphasis. This work seeks to understand more fully how the city grows and develops and how plans may alter these "normal" or "natural" processes. The normative theory may address itself to these same questions, but it also seeks to supply guidelines for discovering and analyzing various mixes of qualities, and how these might be put in optimal combinations to fulfill some predetermined requirements (goals). However, there is generally no intent to supply answers as to what the optimal pattern of development should actually be, only guides as to how to arrive at "what ought to be," once the community's development goals have been identified. To put it in operational terms, under normative theory on urban spatial structure, planners do not set goals; rather, they would employ this theory to determine the structure and form choices open to an urban area, given a certain combination of goals.

Formulation of Theory

Theory has been defined above as consisting of a system of thought used in explaining a phenomenon. In a formal sense, a system of thought is composed of subsystems made up of concepts, some of which are from known states of knowledge with known relationships, some of which consist of propositions of fact or relationships still to be proved. Since functional relationships are the connective links between components of theory and are at the root of explaining a phenomenon, the form of relationship becomes important. Ackoff has identified three forms of functional relationship which theory may put forward. One is the cause and effect relationship which involves *deterministic causality*—a relationship which has one and only one result. Another is what he calls a "producer-product" relationship which involves *probabilistic causality*—a relationship which due to chance factors yields variable results, but nevertheless results which tend to cluster around one theoretical end product. The third form of relationship may not involve causality at all; it is *correlation* and deals with the tendency for variables to behave in a similar manner together, that is, to change or not to change their values together. A finding of correlation does not establish causality, but it may be useful in inferring causality.[3]

As our state of knowledge in a field improves, many of the truths once taken to possess deterministic causality are found to involve probabilistic

[3] Russell L. Ackoff, *Scientific Method: Optimizing Applied Research Decisions,* New York: John Wiley & Sons, Inc., 1962, p. 16.

causality, sometimes only correlation. Even in the natural sciences, where we have long expected absolutes, there is now a sense of caution about deterministic relationships and a disposition to express relationships in terms of probabilities. In planning, where we are concerned with fixed improvements of long life, it would simplify our task immeasurably if we could construct all our theory in terms of deterministic causality. However, we know that land development and urban growth are so deeply involved with human behavior, and human behavior is so complexly affected by chance considerations, that we anticipate, at least at our present state of knowledge, that probabilistic causality is likely to be more prominent in our theoretical research when at length our directions of development in theory settle down and theories of land development and urban growth become widely accepted.

Causality has occupied logicians and scientists for a long time, and we cannot digress here to go into the long-standing controversy over the determinism and indeterminism of causality. For our purposes we shall note the sense of caution that goes with claiming cause and effect relations. But as Simon demonstrates in his series of essays on this subject, there are good and sufficient situations in empirical work where causation can be discussed with a clear conscience.[4] In any event, in a field which is just beginning to develop conceptual systems, we can anticipate that theory building will take advantage of the license of a "pick and shovel" approach and hypothesize deterministic causality until proved otherwise. When theory begins to reach more mature stages in the field and certainly when in more advanced work on theory interest becomes directly centered on the methodological aspects of theory testing, the differentiation between causation and association can then become quite important.

It will be helpful at this point to distinguish between levels of attainment in theory formulation. These levels fall into a descending order of scope from a "general theory" to a "middle-range theory" to a "small theory." Omitted from the list at the upper end is the notion of a "universal theory" and at the lower end of a "field theory." A universal theory is not included simply because it is doubtful that human behavior of so many diverse forms as that which is involved in the growth and development of urban areas can soon be reduced to one all-inclusive system. What is taken up in this chapter are the early stages of work of a middle-range character. Most of the conceptual systems aim toward becoming general theories, but to become full-blown theories of this level involves a rigorousness and systematicness that is not yet in sight. The middle-range theory is an intermediate level en route to a general theory. Usually limiting as-

[4] Herbert A. Simon, *Models of Man,* New York: John Wiley & Sons, Inc., 1957.

sumptions are necessary because of the state of the research arts. Small theories are generally associated with empirical studies of very specific dimensions and limited scope but where replication strongly supports hypotheses made in the theory. Perhaps the most primitive level of theory formulation is found in field theory, which is essentially a contrived rationale borne out in one particular situation but not replicated.

As suggested above, the statement of theory may consist of both proved and unproved concepts. Research concerned with urban spatial structure is likely to deal with such mixtures of concepts. An unproved concept consists of hypotheses, that is, statements of what is expected to be found when the hypotheses are eventually tested. In classical social science research, the test of hypotheses follows set rules in formulating the hypothesis, making assumptions, conducting statistical tests of the probability that a particular result is due to errors of different types, and reaching conclusions. When confirmed, a hypothesis may be stated as an empirical generalization and, under certain circumstances where theory reaches a formal stage of formulation, it may become a law. Formal statements of theory often involve preconditioning statements in the form of axioms or postulates. These are to be distinguished from assumptions which are preconditioning statements of a more technical character employed in the test of a theory or particular hypotheses composing parts of a theory.

In the formal traditions of theory building, scientific inquiry may explore statements of functional relationship by deductive or inductive means. It is beyond the scope of this discussion to go into the conventions involved in the formal formulation of deductive and inductive propositions. For our purposes, we will simply observe that a theory may be constructed so as to reason from a known general proposition to an unknown specific proposition, or it may be built around an approach which infers truth from empirical observation, with the validity of the theory being developed on the basis of consistency in findings from one case to another. The first is a deductive form of theory, and the second is an inductive form. While noting these conventions, we must hasten to point out that the state of theory formulation in the planning field has not yet reached a stage where these distinctions can be applied with any great meaning. They are briefly touched upon at this juncture to suggest the general kind of formal standards that the planning field must eventually seek to achieve.

Criteria of Adequacy

Where the objective of theory building is not simply a quest for truth for knowledge's own sake, but includes the eventuality of applying the theory in improving the lot of man (an objective which is characteristic of a profession), we are concerned not only with the conventions of formulating theory, but also with specifying performance criteria. We wish to insure that theory meets the requirements which we foresee will be important in its application in the field.

There are at least four criteria of adequacy which will be useful to bear in mind in reviewing the work summarized below.[5] One criterion holds that a theory must have a dynamic aspect if it is to have utility in representing the processes by which cities are structured and by which they grow. A second requirement is that the theory be susceptible of empirical verification, that it be capable of being tested. A third requirement is that the theory have an internal logic and consistency. The rigor of the logic and consistency may vary from a very general and somewhat summary form where concepts and relationships are very broadly stated to a very formalized form where all propositions and relationships are spelled out in detail. Finally, the theory must not be so abstract as to have no relation to reality. Indeed, it should seek to represent the phenomena under study as they actually occur or appear to function in reality.

As will become abundantly clear below, by these standards the present stage in theory building relating to urban spatial structure is spotty, and in general the field has a long way to go to measure up to requirements of this kind. The field appears to be still in a primitive stage of conceptualization of urban phenomena, still seeking to establish what the proper content of urban spatial structure theory should be. This simply underscores the observation made earlier about the urgency and the great need there is for fundamental research in planning.

Emerging Theoretical Orientations

It has been indicated that theoretical work in urban spatial structure is the type of theory which has special relevance for urban land use planning. In the usage here, urban spatial structure is concerned with the order and relationship among key physical elements of urban areas as they evolve and pass through transformations in time and space. But in all of the theoretical work so far undertaken, either implicit or as an integral part of the conceptual framework, is a second antecedent area of theoretical significance concerned with activities of people and their institutional entities and the interaction these activities create. Implied is a causal relationship between two pairs of concepts. One pair focuses on human be-

---

[5] Adapted from Rosalyn B. Post, *Criteria for Theories of Urban Spatial Structure: An Evaluation of Current Research,* unpublished manuscript, Chapel Hill: Department of City and Regional Planning, University of North Carolina, 1964.

havior: (1) place-related patterns of interaction (activities), and (2) patterns of interaction among different place activities (movements or, more broadly, communications). The other pair focuses on physical structure and form: (1) space adapted for activity use, and (2) channels developed for movements and other forms of communication. Depending on the scope intended, theoretical work may be concerned not only with spatial relationships between user activities and between space uses at a particular moment in time, but it may also extend to relationships in a dynamic framework, focusing on interaction patterns and on space use patterns and their interrelationships in an evolutionary sense over time.

As we have seen from various references in Chapter 1, an extensive amount of work of theoretical significance has been accumulating over the years, but it is widely dispersed through the social science fields and, for land use planning needs, is somewhat fragmentary and limited in its direct applicability. In a stricter usage, where emphasis is placed on linked systems of thought as we have been discussing them (for example, linkage between activity systems and land use patterns), the task of summarizing theoretical work is not so overwhelming. The problem is not so much one of identifying work from widely dispersed sources or of making selections from a great proliferation of work, but rather one of how far to go in summarizing conceptual systems that are so recent and, in some respects, still so tentative in the originator's thinking as to be still in a working stage of formulation. It is because of this tentativeness that we shall refer to them as conceptual frameworks or theoretical orientations rather than as theories per se.

It is premature to identify schools of thought in theory building, and there may be some question as to the meaningfulness of classifying tendencies in the work emerging today. At this stage only the most general observations about these tendencies can be made. We now turn to the conceptual systems which have been advanced in recent time.

A Communications Theory Approach to Urban Growth

Meier approaches the task of a theory of urban spatial structure by asking:[6] What, after all, is the quintessence of the city? Is there a common pattern that holds through time, one perspective in the behavioral sciences that provides a logical basis for building a theory of urban development? After examining human settlements as they emerged from the beginnings of civilization, following the changes as they might be seen by an archeologist, anthropologist, historian, and natural scientist, and after consider-

---

[6] Richard L. Meier, *A Communications Theory of Urban Growth,* Cambridge: The M.I.T. Press, 1962.

ing man's behavior in cities, looking at human activities as the economist, social psychologist, human ecologist, and political behaviorist might, Meier concludes that the one common element in all of these perspectives is *human communication*. Whether viewed in very concrete terms of marketplace transactions or in the more abstract notion of the transmission of culture, he is saying that the human communications process possesses all the requisite requirements of an organizing concept for a theory.

Meier conceptualizes the city in terms of systems of interaction prompted by man's urge to maintain communications (in the general sense) with his fellow man. At the present stage in man's state of development, transportation and communications technology supply the principal media of interaction. While noting that cities have always exerted a strong attraction for growth because of the opportunities for face-to-face transactions that they offer, Meier holds that technological developments are reducing the necessity for face-to-face interaction, and transportation overloads are imposing limiting conditions on opportunities for interaction through transportation systems. With the substitution of communications for transportation, communications becomes increasingly important as a focus for studying the city. In noting that overload crises in communications systems are in prospect, Meier anticipates control mechanisms being invoked to correct for these overload conditions. Thus, the communications system (in the narrow sense) offers what he considers to be the basis for understanding human communications (in the general sense) and the activity systems that arise out of the human relations involved.

Having satisfied himself on the validity of using a communications system as a basis for building a theory of urban growth, Meier develops a set of requirements for the communications process. Specifying that there must be (1) a sender, (2) a message, (3) a channel, (4) a receiver, (5) an attention span on the part of the receiver, (6) a common language, (7) time for the process to take place, and (8) one or more purposes to be served, he proposes to construct a representation of the city from the information content of communications flows. Information would be measured and recorded in a double-entry accounting system in much the same manner as origin and destination traffic studies record traffic flows today. The unit of measurement for information transmitted would be the "hubit," which Meier defines as "a bit of meaningful information received by a single human being"—a per capita concept of units of information received.[7] According to Meier, by obtaining a sample of communications flows in a metropolitan area, information theory can be used to construct a set of

---

[7] *Ibid.*, p. 131. A "bit" refers to the unit of information which can be handled in a binary system of digits, the system used in modern digital computers. By making use of the off-on combinations of an electrical circuit, the computer is able to carry coded messages in the binary system.

social accounts which can then become the basis for explaining activity systems.

Meier does not indicate fully the manner in which the framework would be used by a planner in a predictive application, say for the year 2000. However, he suggests that his concept of the "urban time budget," which estimates the proportions of a day's time a person would spend in various forms of public communication (as opposed to private or personal communications), would provide a means of making projections.[8] Given an estimate of the population for the year 2000 for a particular metropolitan area, one surmises he would construct a set of sender-receiver accounts of information flows or transactions broken down into "activity sectors," for example, leisure activity patterns of various forms, wholesale-to-producer or wholesale-to-retailer activity patterns of various types. On the basis of assumed states of technology, presumably he would trace out spatial loci of activities, and once location relationships are established, he would assign space to activities and modes of movement according to standards developed to correspond to the technology assumed. This aspect of his framework will undoubtedly be made clearer as he extends his work further.

In order to study some of the variables which he hypothesizes would affect the flows of information, he has undertaken two pilot-type, exploratory investigations of communications flows—one, of the January 1959 speculative activity that swamped the American Stock Exchange, and the other, of the functioning of a library system. In both studies he was able to investigate relationships among concepts of error, stress, and capacity in a communications system and demonstrate that these factors affect the dynamics of a communications system, indicating that the construction of activity patterns must ultimately take into account behavioral variables of the most complex order.

On the basis of this progress report on Meier's work, it is clear that it possesses a distinct behavioral emphasis on the study of the city, and tends more toward the explanatory than the normative emphasis. His work surely reflects a very strong feeling for the dynamic, not only in the usual time sense but also in his concern for constructing the evolutionary sequence in human behavior patterns. Clearly he is intent on empirical verification of this conceptual framework and builds it with this end in view. Surely there is a compelling logic in this system of thought concerning spatial organization and growth of cities. There is every indication that a formal and rigorous statement of theory will emerge. Perhaps because it is in a working stage of formulation, the internal continuity of the way in which the frame-

---

[8] *Ibid.*, pp. 48–54, 129–132. He excludes private communications as having no cultural significance and thus irrelevant in the study of the cultural processes of the city which shape growth.

work is eventually to be put to use is not entirely clear. How the analysis would proceed from sampling information flows, to identifying transactions, to constructing activity patterns, to defining space use patterns is not yet clearly established. As is perhaps true of any work which is still in progress, there are parts of the schema which are more developed and therefore more easily understood than other parts. Until the work nears a more formal stage of formulation, the exposition of concepts and analytical sequence is likely to remain uneven.

A Framework Emphasizing Human Interaction

Webber also utilizes interaction as the basic organizing concept of his theoretical system. He views urban communities in two related perspectives —one in which human interaction occurs in a particular metropolitan community, and one in which it extends to widely scattered places over the face of the earth.[9] He calls the first a "place community" and the second a "nonplace community." With modern transportation and communications developments having the effect of stretching distances, he notes that individuals, firms, organizations, and institutions more and more have contacts, conduct transactions, and maintain communications on a global basis. Thus their ties may extend to a variety of nonplace communities as well as exist within a particular urban place. To distinguish them from the urban place, he calls these nonplace communities "urban realms."

It is this total concept of the urban community which is the distinctive flavor of Webber's approach. He calls for an understanding of the interaction systems which extend into larger urban realms as well as those which fall within a particular metropolitan area. Thus he holds that the study of systems of interaction within the urban region is no longer a complete and sufficient scope for metropolitan planning. According to Webber's concept, what goes on within the spatial confines of an urban place must be interpreted in the framework of all of the ties that the community may have with the world at large. He notes that individuals may or may not engage in all of their activities in a place community and, according to whether they are scientists, manufacturers, or writers, their interest communities extend to differing realms. These same individuals may participate in several nonwork-related interest communities—in the arts, in recreation, in public service, and so on. In contrast, some persons such as the butcher, the factory worker, or the clerk may have interest communities which at present are completely contained within the place community. So today metropolitan planning requires a view which considers how the place

---

[9] Melvin M. Webber, "The Urban Place and the Nonplace Urban Realm," in Webber (ed.), *Explorations into Urban Structure*, Philadelphia: University of Pennsylvania Press, 1964.

population may also be a part of various realm populations, each with what Webber refers to as its own "space field" for interaction, some global, some national, and some in various regional contexts.

In both the place and nonplace view of the urban community, Webber emphasizes the importance of viewing the city as a "dynamic system in action." This dynamic feature is traced through "linkages," which he defines as "dependency ties" relating individuals, groups, firms, and other entities to one another. He terms these "the invisible relations that bring various interdependent business establishments, households, voluntary groups, and personal friends into working associations with each other—into operating systems." [10] His spatial counterpart of this aspatial view of linkages involves three related perspectives. First is a view of the city in terms of spatial patterns of *human interactions*—the flow of communications, people, goods, and so on; second is a view of the *physical form* of the city—the space adapted for various human activities and the pattern to networks of communications and channels of transportation; and third is a view of the city as a configuration of *activity locations*—the spatial distribution of various types of activities by economic functions, social roles, or other ways of classifying activities.

Using these three perspectives of the city, Webber develops a six-way cross-classification system for describing urban spatial structure. Under his schema, he would measure spatial linkages, that is, the flows of information, money, people, and goods; he would study the channels used and space forms adapted for human interaction; and he would examine locations of activities. These observations would be classified as follows:

Dimension	*Interaction Component*	*Physical Component*	*Activity Component*
Size of phenomenon	amplitude	capacity	volume
Degree to which phenomenon piles up in major concentric forms around a point	focality	nucleation	centralization
Propensity for phenomenon to pile up at points of lesser concentration	subfocality	subnucleation	subcentralization
Degree of pile-up per unit (e.g., pile-up per 100 contacts between people, per square mile of area, etc.)	intensity	density	concentration
Relative togetherness of like phenomena	affinity	clustering	localization
Relative degrees of mixture	insularity	separation	segregation

[10] *Ibid.*, p. 95.

With the elements of the metropolitan community thus identified, measured, and classified, Webber recognizes that there is still a step beyond, one of using this framework in the investigation of the directions that growth and development might take. While this step is still to be made, he indicates it would involve an analysis of interaction in terms of the locational behavior of various types of establishments.

In Webber's work we have a conceptual system which is extremely broad in scope but still in an early stage of development. Presently it consists of a framework for describing the city, one that is explanatory rather than normative. Webber emphasizes the importance of the dynamic aspect of a theory, but how the classification system above will be used and how he will use it in the behavioral approach he favors for the analysis of interaction systems is not yet entirely clear. We know that he places a high premium on making these systems continuous and dynamic, and so we anticipate that some kind of interaction model to represent these as operating systems will become a central concern in the next stages of his theory building. It is premature to examine the empirical content of his work in its present stage, but his concern for the problem of measurement in both the place and nonplace aspects of his schema indicates that empirical tests are very much in his thinking. Certainly Webber places heavy emphasis on achieving an internal logical consistency to his conceptual framework, and his concern for the study of locational behavior of the principal agents of interaction would indicate that as his work progresses he will be seeking a close representation of reality.

A Conceptual System Focusing on Urban Form

Lynch and Rodwin view the city as being made up of what they call "adapted space" for the accommodation of human activities and "flow systems" for handling flows of people and goods.[11] Although they differentiate between activities and flows on the one hand and adapted space and flow systems on the other, so far they have devoted their main effort to the latter level of analysis, which they equate with the study of "urban form." The distinctive feature of their conceptual system is the emphasis they place on the formulation of goals as an integral part of their framework. Their work begins with the study of urban form; it then focuses on the specification of goals; and finally it draws upon the goal-form analysis to indicate the nature of the planner's task in efforts aimed at shaping urban form in line with the goals that have been identified.

---

[11] Kevin Lynch and Lloyd Rodwin, "A Theory of Urban Form," *Journal of the American Institute of Planners,* November, 1958.

In their conceptual framework they are concerned first with a system for analyzing urban form. (Were they starting with activities and flows, they might well focus initially on a system for analyzing *interaction*.) Lynch and Rodwin propose evaluating urban form by six analytical categories: element types, quantity, density, grain, focal organization, and generalized spatial distribution. "Element types" is a category for differentiating qualitatively between basic types of spaces and flow systems; and, as might be expected, "quantity" has to do with amounts—a measure of the size of particular types of adapted spaces and flow systems. "Density," expressed either as a single measure or as a range of measures, has to do with compaction (of people, facilities, vehicles) per unit of space or capacity of channel. "Grain" is their term to indicate how various elements of urban form are differentiated and separated. Adapted spaces and flow systems may be fine-grained or coarse-grained according to the extent of compaction or separation in their internal components (houses, skyscrapers, streets) and how sharp or blurred these form elements are at the edges where transition occurs from one element to another. "Focal organization" is concerned with the spatial disposition and interrelations among key points in the city (density peaks, dominant building types, major breaks between forms of transportation). "Generalized spatial distribution" is the patterned organization of space as it might be seen from the air at a high altitude. This six-part classification system is the basic analytical tool they propose for classifying urban form.

The second major conceptual problem which the Lynch-Rodwin framework seeks to deal with is the formulation of goals utilizing this analytical tool. They point out that the problem is not alone one of identifying out of the multitude of possible goals those that have significance for urban form, but it is also one of specifying the goals in concrete terms which leave no doubt as to how they are to be realized. The identification of goals is one aspect of the problem, and the specification of content is a second aspect. With respect to the first, Lynch and Rodwin point out that goals must to some extent be determined in the normal democratic processes, with community-held goals being carefully differentiated from the planner's personal goals (which would tend to emphasize the goals of only one segment of society). But at the same time they would give careful attention in the choice of goals to the planner's goals as a professional and urban designer, where, they point out, he has a proper role to play in seeing that more advanced values take their place in the community value system beside the familiar ones of long standing. They suggest that the choice of goals have first a human and then an economic basis. Thus, goals relating to urban form are fundamentally concerned on the one hand with relationships between man and his environment and between man and man, and on the other hand with the efficiency of these relationships— maximizing the return and minimizing the cost in both a social and an economic sense. The specification of goal content derives from the analytical framework they devised in the first instance. Thus, the goals would be specified in terms of type of adapted space and flow system, quantity, density, grain, focal organization, and the spatial distribution pattern. Some would have quantitative emphases, some would deal more in qualitative concepts, and all would be subject to continuing checks as to relevance and reasonableness.

The final aspect of the Lynch-Rodwin framework is concerned with the application of the goal-form statements in the study of the city and in establishing what emphases will be needed in the plan that eventually is to emerge. Through the use of simple cross-classifications of the six components of their system of analysis applied to both adapted spaces and flow systems, they demonstrate how these two elements of urban form interact under different goal emphases. In sum, Lynch and Rodwin view the framework as a means for analyzing urban form in a systematic and logical manner. They think of it as a means of posing the problems for planning but they leave the solution to the planning task which follows from their framework.

This conceptual system has been developed to deal with a particular aspect of what we look for in a total system of theory. Although they acknowledge the important role which the interaction level of study has in theoretical formulations, so far Lynch and Rodwin have limited themselves to urban form, directing their attention to the physical implications of human interaction. Their work is concerned with the rationale of planning for the city rather than a framework for analyzing the structure of the city and explaining how growth occurs. In this sense they are providing a framework which has special significance for plan-making. In focusing on goal formulation, they have injected an essentially normative emphasis into their schema. However, they do not specify "what should be"; rather, they indicate how goal combinations can be analyzed in deriving "what should be" in a particular locality and how these in turn may be integrated systematically into the planning process. The importance of a theory being a dynamic one is recognized by Lynch and Rodwin, and, in the sense that the sequence from goal formulation to form analysis in their conceptual system has a continuous and dynamic interrelationship, it is dynamic in conception. But in the sense we have been using "dynamic" to signify the organizing aspect of theory which takes account of the evolutionary process of urban development, their framework is as yet incomplete. Their work reflects sensitivity to the importance of empirical verification. This has since become particularly evident in Lynch's studies of the perceptual form of the city.[12] They have given careful attention to the logical continuity of their conceptual system, and there is clearly a great sense of responsibility for tying their work closely to reality.

Accessibility Concepts and Urban Structure

Although all conceptual systems of the kind we have been discussing sooner or later become concerned with accessibility as an element inherent in the physical organization of space and movement systems, some work gives this concept a more central role in building theory. Much of the recent work on accessibility concepts has been primarily focused on transportation.[13] Although this work has had a very considerable impact on research in urban spatial structure, we do not attempt to include in this summary any report on work which is primarily transportation-oriented.

Guttenberg develops a theoretical approach to urban structure and city growth which utilizes accessibility as an organizing concept—what he calls "a community effort to overcome distance." [14] In the sense that human interaction is the underlying reason for minimizing distance, he is implicitly viewing interaction as the basic determinant of urban spatial structure. However, his work focuses primarily on the physical facility aspect of a total system of theory. In place of the simple two-part view (space use for activities and interconnecting systems of transport and communications), he identifies three components. He subdivides the first into "distributed facilities" and "undistributed facilities," with these being a function of the third component, "transportation." The rationale states that if transportation is poor, the workplaces, trade centers, and community services will tend to assume a pattern of distributed facilities; if it is good, these activities will assume more concentrated patterns in the form of

---

[12] Kevin Lynch, *The Image of the City*, Cambridge: Harvard University and Technology Presses, 1960.

[13] See work of J. Douglas Carroll and his associates in Detroit, Chicago, and Pittsburgh on metropolitan area transportation studies (for example, J. R. Hamburg, "Land Use Projection and Predicting Future Traffic," *Trip Characteristics and Traffic Assignment*, Highway Research Board Bulletin 224, National Academy of Sciences, 1959); see also the work of Alan M. Voorhees in the Baltimore, Hartford, and Los Angeles transportation studies (for example, C. F. Barnes, "Integrating Land Use and Traffic Forecasting," *Forecasting Highway Trips*, Highway Research Board Bulletin 297, National Academy of Sciences, 1961).

[14] Albert Z. Guttenberg, "Urban Structure and Urban Growth," *Journal of the American Institute of Planners*, May, 1960.

undistributed facilities. Thus, Guttenberg maintains that urban spatial structure is intimately tied up with the aggregate effort in the community to overcome distance.

In his framework, he sees the spatial gradation of density outward from distributed and undistributed facilities as a function of access. He points out that his distributed centers of activity acquire a value in accordance with the substitutability of that place for the chief place, with the physical density gradient outward from these centers corresponding closely with, but not necessarily directly coincident with, the economic density gradient. In the context of his framework, therefore, the slope of the economic density of gradient is closely related to transport efficiency as it enables outlying locations to substitute for more central locations.[15]

In examining the implications of growth for his concept of urban structure, he points out that the transportation system holds the key to the way in which growth proceeds. The transportation decisions made from one year to another will result in a constantly changing urban structure, with the emphasis shifting along the continuum between the situation with highly distributed centers to the situation with one major undistributed facility. He implies that there is some limit in the ability of the undistributed facility continuing indefinitely to function as the only major center as compared to the capacity that distributed centers have for absorbing growth. As growth occurs, structural adjustments to overcome distance can take the form of either new centers or improved transportation facilities. Commonly both occur. With the enlarged scale and resulting changed relationships between home, work, and various activity centers, population movements ensue. With these shifts the areas which do offer the accessibility that people seek develop, and those which do not, decline in a social and an economic sense. With growth, the enlarged scale alters the density gradient. If transport efficiency is improved favoring the substitution of outlying for central locations (as has been the case in Los Angeles), the slope of the density gradient is flattened, the region spreads out, and, depending upon the amount of population influx in relation to the area added, the density may go down.

How may such a view of urban structure and urban growth be used in

---

[15] Robert M. Haig made a similar point 35 years ago: "Since there is insufficient space at the center to accommodate all activities which would derive advantages from location there, the most central sites are assigned, for a rental, to those activities which can best utilize the advantages, and the others take the less accessible locations. Site rents and transportation costs are vitally connected through their relationship to the friction of space. Transportation is the means of reducing that friction, at the cost of time and money." See Robert M. Haig and Roswell C. McCrae, "Major Economic Factors in Metropolitan Growth and Arrangement," *Regional Survey of New York and Its Environs*, I, New York: Regional Plan of New York and Its Environs, 1927, p. 39.

anticipating urban form in the future? Guttenberg acknowledges that transport efficiency is not the sole variable. He notes that activities may choose a location in relation to a central place for reasons other than time-distance. For example, a change of economic composition in the region may produce new location patterns. However, assuming such other things are constant (similar economic conditions, terrain, tastes, and so on), he maintains that accessibility in terms of time-distance serves to sort activities spatially. If the additional assumption is introduced that the transportation system remains similar over time, he points out that there will be comparability in accessibility and therefore we may anticipate similar patterns in the distribution of activities in the region. He does not discuss the complexities of prediction involved when constraints are relaxed and one by one the elements held constant are allowed to vary, but it is clear that by introducing differing combinations of assumptions the interplay of these elements quickly becomes exceedingly complex.

In the present stage of its development, this conceptual framework centers mainly on the physical aspects of a theoretical system of urban structure and growth. Its distinctive feature is the emphasis it gives to the interplay between the location of urban activities and transport efficiency. In the sense that activity concentrations and transportation are continuously interacting and that accessibility provides an organizing rationale for urban structure and a regulating concept for urban growth, the framework is a dynamic one, supplying an evolutionary basis for explaining urban form. While it has a well-developed logical context and a direct relation to reality, Guttenberg's statement gives no indication as to how this framework is to be translated into an analytical system and given empirical form.

Other work which should be cited here includes Hansen's use of the accessibility concept in the analysis of the growth of residential areas and Voorhees' use of the concept in the analysis of other use activities.[16] However, both are primarily dealing with the pragmatic aspects of prediction rather than the formulation of a more general system of thought governing urban spatial structure. Hansen defines accessibility as "a measurement of the spatial distribution of activities about a point, adjusted for the ability and desire of people or firms to overcome spatial separation." [17] His concept of accessibility is very similar to Guttenberg's, and he has formulated a model which has useful immediate applications (see Chapter 12).

---

[16] Walter G. Hansen, "How Accessibility Shapes Land Use," *Journal of the American Institute of Planners,* May, 1959; Alan M. Voorhees, "Development Patterns in American Cities," *Urban Transportation Planning: Concepts and Application,* Highway Research Board Bulletin 293, National Academy of Sciences, 1961.

[17] Hansen, "How Accessibility Shapes Land Use," p. 73.

Economic Models of Spatial Structure

In some respects quite different from the approaches discussed so far, the economic models approach the conceptualization of urban spatial structure in the traditions of economic theory. The roots of this work go back to an agricultural land development concept advanced by von Thünen in the early 1800's; work in more recent time has been done by Alfred Weber, Lösch, Isard, and others.[18] The economic approaches discussed here make use of what is known in economics as equilibrium theory. Since forms of notation used in equilibrium theory are specialized and some of the technical aspects of the concepts involved in this theory are outside the scope of this discussion, this work is presented in somewhat abridged form. The student versed in economic theory will want to pursue this line of theoretical development in the original sources of work cited here.

Essentially the view taken in these approaches sees urban development processes as economic phenomena. The organizing concept is the market mechanism and the sorting process it provides in the allocation of space to activities. In the work on urban spatial structure this involves allocation of space in both quantitative and locational aspects to various users according to supply and demand relationships and a least-cost concept in an equilibrium system.

Wingo's work provides perhaps the most systematic and rigorous statement of urban spatial structure in the framework of equilibrium theory.[19] Traditionally economists have dealt with location as a constant, and there has been a disinterest or an unwillingness to examine location as a variable. In his work, Wingo lifts this constraint. He seeks to give explicit recognition to the way in which policy affects the market and how in turn these effects are reflected in urban spatial structure. In this sense, he is seeking to relate theory to real-world situations. However, in addition he seeks to bring developments in spatial models into closer harmony with general economic theory and to relate theoretical work on location to the broader concepts of the urban economy.

Directing his attention mainly to residential development, Wingo develops first a concept of transportation demand, considering the spatial

---

[18] J. H. von Thünen, *Der isolierte Staat in Beziehung auf Landwirtschaft und Nationalökonomie,* Hamburg, 1826; C. J. Friedrich, *Alfred Weber's Theory of Location of Industries,* Chicago: University of Chicago Press, 1928; August Lösch, *The Economics of Location,* New Haven: Yale University Press, 1954; Walter Isard, *Location and Space-Economy,* New York and Cambridge: John Wiley & Sons, Inc., and Technology Press, 1956.

[19] Lowdon Wingo, Jr., *Transportation and Urban Land,* Washington: Resources for the Future, Inc., 1961.

relationship between home and work. With the journey to work viewed as "the technological link between the labor force and the production process," he defines demand for movement as the total employment of an urban area multiplied by the frequency of work—in other words, the number of trips required to support the production process. As Meier has done, Wingo recognizes the propensity for urban society to substitute communications for transportation and stresses the necessity for taking into account technological developments in this respect. The supply aspect is expressed in terms of the capacity of a movement system—a measure of its ability to accommodate movements between home and work. Drawing on a somewhat similar concept of accessibility as that discussed above, he uses as a unit of measurement the cost of transportation based on the time spent in movement between points and the out-of-pocket costs for these movements expressed in money equivalents for distance and number of trips.

The central problem of this kind of economic model is to achieve an equilibrium distribution of households of particular rent-paying abilities to sites with a particular structure of rents. Wingo achieves this location equilibrium by substituting transportation costs for space costs. Thus, on the supply side, he utilizes transport costs to establish the distribution of household sites at varying position rents. He defines position rent as "the annual savings in transportation costs compared to the highest cost location in use." On the demand side, if prices for other goods competing for the household dollar are held constant, the rents households are willing to pay are based on the class utility concept, which holds that the greater the unit rent, the fewer the units of space consumed. Clearly this view of space use immediately involves density, and the smaller the quantity of space consumed in the more accessible locations, the higher the density. The spatial distribution of these densities in the urban area involves the density gradient concept noted earlier, with the slope falling off from the center of the city to the outskirts. To get at the characterisics of demand in the spatial context, Wingo constructs a demand schedule and utilizes appropriate position rents from this schedule to determine the point at which prices and densities are in equilibrium.

The economic model Wingo advances functions under the usual behavioral axiom that those who control residential space and households who seek space will each behave to maximize their returns. He specifies as givens: the locations of employment centers, a particular transportation technology, a set of urban households, the marginal value the worker places on leisure, and the marginal value households place on residential space. Wingo then uses his model to determine the spatial distribution of densities and rents, and the spatial distribution, value, and extent of land required for residential use. For the derivation of the elements to the model as well as the mathematical form, and for his discussion of the empirical advantages and limitations of the model, the reader is referred to the source.[20]

Although it is beyond the scope of this discussion to go further into this work as it relates to economic theory, we may note that as a theoretical system it is the most developed one considered so far. The market mechanism furnishes the dynamic aspect and organizing concept for the theoretical framework. The conceptual system is rigorously stated, and logical consistency is carefully observed throughout. Wingo has sought to maintain a close contact with the real world, and although empirical tests of this work are still to be made, we do have indications from experience cited below that this kind of economic model can be made operational.

Alonso uses the market mechanism in a somewhat different manner to distribute space users to urban land.[21] Instead of developing a demand function, he uses "bid price curves" which in interaction with the price structure of land are used as a basis for distributing agricultural, business, and residential users to sites (the space users he has selected for attention). Beginning at the center of the city, land is "put up for bid," and on the basis of these curves the bid for the most central site is compared to the next preferred alternative, with this preferred alternative being the marginal combination of price and location for that particular use. On the basis of the steepest bid price curve, the highest bidder takes the most central site; the next highest bidder corresponding to the second steepest curve takes the next most central site still available; and so on. For the first space user the price paid at the bid location is determined by the price at the marginal location, but for the next user what was a marginal location for the first user becomes the equilibrium location for him, with his bid price determined by the price at the marginal location for this site, and so on down the chain.

There are several models with more of an empirical content which should be noted. One is Herbert and Stevens' linear programming approach to distributing households by maximizing their rent-paying ability.[22] Harris integrates a refined version of this model into a system of growth models he has developed for the Penn-Jersey Transportation Study.[23] Another example comes from Artle's work on the Stockholm economy in which he

[20] *Ibid.* See p. 87 for the general form of the model.

[21] William Alonso, "A Theory of the Urban Land Market," *Papers and Proceedings of the Regional Science Association,* VI, Philadelphia: University of Pennsylvania, 1960. For a fuller statement, see Alonso, *Location and Land Use: Toward a General Theory of Land Rent,* Cambridge: Harvard University Press, 1964.

[22] John D. Herbert and Benjamin H. Stevens, "A Model for the Distribution of Residential Activity in Urban Areas," *Journal of Regional Science,* Fall, 1960.

[23] Britton Harris, "Experiments in Projection of Transportation and Land Use," *Traffic Quarterly,* April, 1962.

suggests the use of a simple regression model and an income-potential model for estimating the distribution characteristics of retail and personal service establishments in the metropolitan area and suggests a probability model to get at the clustering of establishments as they become distributed to retail sites.[24] Still another piece of work of particular promise for planning is found in Lowry's linked series of models to determine the distribution of various use activities in the Pittsburgh metropolitan area based on pre-established assumed locations of "basic" employment and on indices of trip distribution developed from an area-wide transportation study.[25] As another example, Garrison proposes a general simulation model of "urban systems" which would involve an analysis of urban structure and growth by means of a whole series of models.[26] Finally, the work of the RAND Corporation in the use of linked mathematical analyses should also be noted. [27] These are indicative of a whole series of developments in mathematical and economic models, but because they are presented primarily in methodological terms, those now in operational form are more appropriately taken up later (see Chapter 12).

Decision Analysis and the Structure of Cities

As still another approach to urban spatial structure, the author proposes that a conceptual system based on the *values-behavior patterns-consequences* framework referred to in Chapter 1 (in the discussion of human behavior and land use) offers an organizing concept for theory development. In its most basic form and viewing the components in reverse order, this framework seeks explanations for any particular man-induced phenomenon being studied (in this instance, urban growth and development) in terms of human behavior (interaction patterns), with such behavior patterns being a function in turn of people's values (or the attitudes held concerning interaction).[28]

In common with the view taken by several of the foregoing conceptual

---

[24] Roland Artle, *Studies in the Structure of the Stockholm Economy*, Stockholm: The Business Research Institute at the Stockholm School of Economics, 1959.

[25] Ira S. Lowry, *A Model of Metropolis*, Santa Monica: The RAND Corporation, August, 1964.

[26] William L. Garrison, "Toward a Simulation Model of Urban Growth and Development," Proceedings of the Symposium in Urban Geography, Lund, 1960, *Lund Studies in Geography*, Lund, Sweden: C. W. K. Gleerup, 1962.

[27] Issued from time to time since 1960, a series of memoranda contain reports of these investigations. (Processed material, Santa Monica: The RAND Corporation.)

[28] Based on the behavioral science schema developed by the Urban Studies Program, Institute for Research in Social Science, University of North Carolina. See Chapin, Introduction, in F. Stuart Chapin, Jr., and Shirley F. Weiss (eds.), *Urban Growth Dynamics*, New York: John Wiley & Sons, Inc., 1962.

systems, under this framework it is a behavioral axiom that human beings tend to concentrate at various places on the earth's surface in the satisfaction of needs and desires for interaction. Interaction is a form of behavior, then, growing out of complex interrelations among men and their various institutions—for example, the interrelations between individuals, or households, or firms, or the interrelations among individuals and households, households and firms, and so on. These interrelations may take rational or irrational forms. The term "behavior patterns" is used to refer to rational and overt forms of interaction, both the forms which cluster spatially into duplicating or near-duplicating patterns and remain relatively unchanged for extended periods of time, and the forms which take variable spatial patterns and appear in different locations from one day to the next. For example, common duplicating behavior patterns are involved in transactions between wholesale and retail firms or between customer households and a supermarket. A very well-known behavior which tends to appear in cluster-like patterns is visiting behavior. Nonclustering behavior patterns, those that are more scattered, less pronounced, and variable in spatial location from one day or week to the next, are illustrated in the circuits of salesmen visiting customer firms, or family drives on Sunday afternoons, or outings in the country. As brought out in more detail in Chapter 6, these patterns of interaction can be classified into *activities* ("within-place" interaction) and *communications* ("between-place" interaction), but for the present we shall think of the two as a related combination under the generic term "behavior pattern." Although as planners we are concerned with both clustering and nonclustering patterns of behavior, to get at the elements of urban spatial structure we are particularly interested in the way duplicating or clustered patterns build up in space. Further, we are concerned with clustered patterns in a time sense, that is, the repetitive aspects of these patterns in daily, weekly, or seasonal cycles.

Out of the universe of behavior patterns which are constantly evolving, then, certain ones have a spatial importance, show a tendency to duplicate in clusters, and occur in rhythmical and repetitive forms in the course of a day, a week, or a season. These behavior patterns are constantly undergoing adjustment and reformation in response to value orientations, but at the same time some of these behavior patterns have sufficient importance in their spatial, duplicating, repetitive characteristics as to produce outcomes in physical structure and form. As in most of the other conceptual systems reviewed here, these physical forms are composed of (1) *spaces* adapted to the various forms of place-related interaction, and (2) *interconnecting channels* for the various forms of movement-related or communications-related interaction—one growing out of the need for *activities* and the other for *communications* (in its narrower meaning). Yet to understand fully urban concentrations as outcomes of human actions requires an understanding of relevant antecedent behavior patterns and value orientations. Thus there is an evolutionary basis for the study of ordered arrangements of urban form we see on the ground, and our ability to predict how these arrangements may occur in the future is dependent upon our ability to anticipate the full evolutionary sequence. At the same time, it is necessary to recognize that this evolutionary sequence from values to interaction to outcomes is modified by a feedback aspect—by the effect that these outcomes may have on subsequent interaction and on value orientations, and all the secondary, tertiary, and other successive effects.

The means by which interaction patterns become translated into structure-form outcomes is found in the *location behavior* of households, firms, government, and institutional entities. Location behavior is viewed as a sequence of action in the same three-part framework, growing out of the needs and desires of day-to-day interaction. While occurring on a day-in-and-day-out basis, for any particular household or firm, location actions occur infrequently. The location action, then, constitutes a different type of behavior pattern from the daily activity patterns we have been discussing. But at the same time, the location action is the instrumentality by which the activity patterns of the first type are accommodated in physical form. For this strategic reason, under the present conceptual system location behavior is given special attention.

In our society, the marketplace and the council chambers of government (local and frequently nonlocal) provide the means by which location-specific activities and movements (or, more broadly, communications) are translated into place-fixed use areas and interconnecting circulation systems in the metropolitan area. These two mechanisms mediate location decisions. Neither can function without the other; each must be responsive to the other. In part because one involves many widely diffused and independent decisions while the other involves relatively few and concentrated decisions, and in part because government must represent the overriding public interest, in matters of space use and transportation it falls to government to assume leadership in seeking harmony between the two systems. Insofar as metropolitan planning is responsive to both systems, it becomes the means of securing this harmony.

Now clearly the manner in which the market and government interact in mediating location behavior is extremely complex. One way to follow this process is to focus on the *decision* as the critical point to the behavioral sequence in a location action. Under a decision analysis approach, of the many kinds of decisions by which space is adapted and put to use and movement systems established, two groups can be differentiated. One group involves what we may call "priming decisions" in the sense that they are seen to trigger the other group, what we may call "secondary decisions," with the two together accounting for development as a whole. Priming decisions are made in both the public sector (for example, those involved in major highway locations or utility locations) and in the private sector (for example, decisions on large-scale investment in land, on the location of industries with large employment or the location of major shopping centers or Levittown-type developments). They set the stage for secondary decisions, for example, park acquisition or street-widening decisions in the public sector, or small-scale subdivision, mortgage-financing, lot-purchasing, or home-building decisions in the private sector.

Priming actions tend to develop from single decisions or a mix of discrete decisions of some strategic importance in setting off a chain reaction of development, and secondary actions usually consist of clusters of decisions (for example, clusters of household decisions) stimulated by, but following from, the strategic actions. Because it would be impractical to unravel and deal with the separate effects of all kinds of decisions, the emphasis in this framework is on priming decisions—discovering what mix of these actions tends to trigger other actions and thus influence the course of events which accounts for the pattern of development that subsequently emerges. Therefore, under this conceptual system, land development is viewed as the consequence first of certain strategic decisions which structure the pattern of growth and development and then of the myriad household, business, and governmental decisions which follow from the first key decisions. This view of the land development process is a greatly oversimplified representation of what actually occurs. Initial investigations of the priming–secondary decision aspect of the rationale suggest that the "queuing order" or sequence of priming decisions bears an important relationship to the generating power which a mix of these decisions exerts on secondary decisions.[29] To take account of decision sequence and the differential lag times in the impact of different decisions may call for more detailed subclassifications of the present priming-secondary basis of classifying decisions. How much more elaborate the system can feasibly be made is a problem for future study.

Meanwhile an experimental model has been developed for testing this conceptual approach.[30] The initial emphasis of this work is on experimentation with household location. Although it will be discussed in Chapter 12

---

[29] F. Stuart Chapin, Jr., and Shirley F. Weiss, *Factors Influencing Land Development*, Chapel Hill: Institute for Research in Social Science, University of North Carolina, in cooperation with the U.S. Bureau of Public Roads, August, 1962.

[30] Thomas G. Donnelly, F. Stuart Chapin, Jr., and Shirley F. Weiss, *A Probabilistic Model for Residential Growth*, Chapel Hill: Institute for Research in Social Science, University of North Carolina, in cooperation with the U.S. Bureau of Public Roads, May, 1964.

more fully, briefly, the model is designed to test planning proposals which seek to shape growth and development into prescriptive forms that will fulfill interaction needs. As preconditions, it assumes the locations of major employment centers (the only "given" in the private sector), and it assumes certain location-specific government-prescribed public works decisions and policy positions. It then seeks to simulate market-mediated location decisions of households, firms, and institutions. It looks to the basic needs and desires of interaction and how these become translated into key decision factors such as space availability and the value man ascribes to land and its particular mix of access, amenity, and conveniences. In short, "given" certain postures of government plus an assumed pattern of basic employment, the model is addressed to the question: How can these location decisions shape those of the private sector to produce the pattern of development set forth in a plan? In the priming–secondary decision nomenclature, priming decisions are "givens," and the task of the model is to simulate secondary location decisions—a distribution of households to available and usable land pursuant to a predetermined evolutionary sequence of priming actions. The basic approach used in this model can be extended to other land use decisions, and it can be made to simulate the renewal of outworn areas.

Thus, if we consider priming decisions as structuring elements of urban growth and therefore of special concern in a metropolitan area plan, such a model then offers a tool for planning. Indeed, a distinctive aspect of this approach is its utility as an aid to decision-making by governing bodies, planning agencies, developers, and many other groups. If the influence on land development of a particular mix of priming decisions with a particular timing sequence can be simulated, this means that it is possible for governing bodies, for example, to take this knowledge into account in choosing among the decisions. A governing body might use the above model to study the effects of one particular decision, say a decision on the location of an expressway, and, holding all other factors constant, determine what the probable pattern of household settlement would be for each of several alternative routes and what each of these settlement patterns would mean in terms of other public costs. As suggested above, another application uses the model in an opposite way. Given several alternative schemes (for example, a compact single-centered emphasis in the pattern of growth, a diffused pattern of growth, and a cluster pattern of growth), each predicated on achieving one defined set of goals but following different policy emphases, the model might be used to establish what mix of priming decisions would tend to produce each form of development. With this kind of output from the model, relative long-range costs and benefits implied in each policy choice can be evaluated in reaching a decision on what plan and policy to pursue.

In effect, this model therefore is a simplified statement of the conceptual view of urban structure and growth set forth at the outset. The location decisions simulated by such a model are seen as satisfying interaction needs and desires of urban residents, firms, and other entities. Indeed, priming decisions are viewed as the result of pressures which arise from these daily interaction needs and desires. If this is the case, there is a premium on studying not only prevailing *activity patterns* but also *attitudes* of different population groups for insights they supply into the likely future stability of these patterns. It may be anticipated that future work on this conceptual system will emphasize two lines of research development: (1) the analysis of activity patterns from data obtained by home interviews, firm interviews, and so on, and (2) the analysis of attitudes from a paralleling line of inquiry in the course of these interviews.[31] These areas of inquiry are seen as supplying parameters for the location model. Chapter 6 indicates the direction in which studies of activity patterns and attitudes must move.

The conceptual system we have been reviewing is an explanatory one. It seeks an explanation of urban spatial structure through the study of location behavior and more particularly through the analysis of selected classes of location decisions and their sequence over time, and it seeks an explanation of location behavior in terms of daily activity patterns and related value systems. In this kind of approach norms may be introduced in the form of alternative choices in the decision process, but the normative aspect is not an integral part of the conceptual system. Particular stress is placed on the use models in making empirical tests of aspects of the system and in making the approach dynamic, with a direct relation to reality. In its present early stage of development, the framework is still loosely formulated. However, as experience in the use of models in testing the conceptual system accumulates, we can look toward a more rigorous statement of the conceptual system.

Comparative Aspects of Theoretical Approaches

There are some important similarities in these systems of thought we have been reviewing and some significant differences. Explicitly or implicitly each system is directly concerned with the development of a framework which identifies and describes regularities in patterns of human interaction

---

[31] For examples of attitude studies of urban residents, see John Gulick, Charles E. Bowerman, and Kurt Back, Chapter 10, and Robert L. Wilson, Chapter 11, in Chapin and Weiss (eds.), *Urban Growth Dynamics*.

in space and explains their origins and transformations in time wherever population aggregates in urban areas. Along with these rather fundamental relationships in space and time is a common concern for accessibility, a concept of great importance in spatial relationships. In describing interaction patterns, most of these conceptual systems make a distinction between patterns of intraplace and interplace interaction, the former having importance for the adaptation of space and the latter involving communications between spaces. "Space adaptation" and "communications," of course, are counterparts for "land use" and "circulation," which will be the pair of terms which will occupy us to an important extent in subsequent chapters.

While there is this fundamental common base, other similarities may be found when comparisons are narrowed to two or three approaches. Some similarities are based on acknowledged crossties, as in Meier's acceptance of Webber's urban realm concept, or in Webber's adoption of Meier's communications emphasis. Some appear to be simply parallelisms among the conceptual systems. Thus, while Wingo sees man's economic behavior in the marketplace as the medium which regulates location decisions, with adjustments introduced to take account of noneconomic factors influencing these decisions, the author's work in effect sees the urban social system setting the context for locations decisions, with government and the market serving as the medium which regulates location decisions.

Yet with these similarities and parallelisms, there are distinctive differences in approach. The differences are in part a function of the background, specialization, and research biases of the person advancing the approach. Beyond this, one senses differences in conception of what would constitute a proper set of criteria for theory building whether or not they are consciously considered in any particular approach. Meier's work reflects a unique perspective across the expanse of both physical and social sciences, and, drawing on this broad scope of interest, he directs attention to the opportunities for synthesizing elements from different fields in a theory of urban spatial structure. Deeply concerned with the implications of technological and social change for patterns of human interaction, Webber emphasizes the placelessness of many new forms of activities and the importance of the dynamic aspect of theory building to take these changes into account. Lynch and Rodwin have focused their attention on one part of the broad area we have been discussing, dealing with this part in some depth and laying particular stress on a normative approach. Wingo's work reflects a strong inclination toward a rigorously classical and systematic approach to theory building. Guttenberg has a sensitivity to the policy implications of theory and the alternatives open to metropolitan areas in making transportation choices. The author's work with his associates at

North Carolina places a strong emphasis on relating theory on urban structure and growth to theoretical work in public policy and decision-making.

It should be clear by this time that there is a significant effort going into theoretical research, a healthy variety to approaches being explored, and a developing emphasis on an experimental view. Some question the present-day emphasis in the social sciences on the use of experimental designs. This is in part a reaction against the heavy emphasis in these times on the natural sciences. The advent of symbolic logic and mathematical models is seen by some as a hocus-pocus and a dream world of faddism seeking to mystify with esoteric language and mathematical learning. There may be some excesses of this kind, but the real difficulties are more likely to come from the blind hope of formula-hunters who use models without looking into the qualifying conditions which apply in any particular situation. It should be noted, too, that the distrust and occasional eruption of impatience with the use of mathematics in theory building is not peculiar to the planning field. Old-line theorists in economics, political science, and sociology have frequently spoken out on this matter.[32] The planning field has come to this controversy more recently, but the arguments are not too different. Harris offers a cogent brief for the place of models in city planning, and the reader would do well to look up his comments on this subject if he has lingering doubts about the utility of mathematics in planning theory.[33]

Some Guides for Land Use Planning

What does this glimpse into examples of work in progress tell us about the scope and approach to be used in land use planning? Remembering the tentative nature of this work and the fact that it is still in the process of formulation, what can be said? What guides can be safely set down at the outset for the land use planning task? The answers to these questions are to be found in elements common to all the conceptual systems we have been examining. In this respect, this work provides at least two leads for the land use planning task we are about to take up—one concerned with a point of view about land use, and the other, with a process of study. These guides will be mentioned briefly here and will be reintroduced at different points in subsequent chapters.

---

[32] For arguments pro and con, see James C. Charlesworth (ed.), *Mathematics and the Social Sciences,* a Symposium, Philadelphia: American Academy of Political and Social Science, June, 1963.

[33] Britton Harris, "Plan or Projection: An Examination of the Use of Models in Planning," *Journal of the American Institute of Planners,* November, 1960.

What can be said about a land use point of view can be set down fairly simply in the form of two guiding considerations. The first is the notion that land use is concerned with human activity in a very broad sense. It is concerned with living patterns of households, productive patterns of industries, selling patterns of retail and personal service establishments, and the many other classes of activity patterns that exist and interact as elements in the urban social system. Thus, from this viewpoint, "land use" means a great deal more than existing or proposed improvements visible on the ground. Indeed, it may be said that space use has no intrinsic meaning separate and apart from human activity—the reasons for which the space was put to use in the first place. Land use maps of the conventional type are useful in answering the question "where" at a particular moment in time, but they tell us very little about "why," nor do they say very much about "where" *over time.*

This brings us to the second requisite of an adequately inclusive point of view toward land use. This is the view of land use as a constantly evolving and continuously changing phenomenon. An evolutionary view has great importance in one's outlook toward the land use plan. For example, if we take what is sometimes called the "unitary approach" in which emphasis is placed on the single, detailed scheme, we are essentially ignoring change, or we are taking the view that planning intercepts change, neutralizes it, and thus obviates the necessity of providing for it. More consistent with the trend of this discussion is the "adaptive approach"—an evolutionary scheme which through the medium of development policies is progressively adjusted in the flow of time to take account of unpredictable elements of technological and social change.[34]

Indeed, a proper recognition of this dynamic or evolutionary aspect of land development involves the very process of study followed in developing a land use plan. So finally, we may ask what guides grow out of the work we have been examining that offer assistance in organizing for the task of land use planning. Ultimately we may expect some very direct and tangible guides from theory itself. Indeed, when theory flows more directly into practice, and as we substitute more advanced systems of analysis for "hand" methods, the guidelines singled out here as leads may in fact be built into the analytical framework itself. Four emphases tend to crop up again and again in the work above:

The necessity of a system of analysis which is continuous rather than discontinuous.

---

[34] For a discussion of the "unitary" and "adaptive" views toward a plan, see Donald L. Foley, "An Approach to Metropolitan Spatial Structure," in Webber (ed.), *Explorations into Urban Structure,* pp. 63-75.

The importance of the system taking account of activity linkages where change in one element has the effect of altering the climate for change in another element. Recognition of the feedback influence which gives rise to the need for modifying change initially instituted.

Significance of the random aspect of human interaction and the importance of a probabilistic view toward development rather than a deterministic view.

The interrelation of policy, proposal, and action—phased to lead successively from one to the next.

These are complicated ideas, and we do not deal with them here. We simply note them in this summary form to come back to later.

Part II

Tooling Up for Land Use Planning

NARROWING OUR *focus from the general to the particular and shifting from a conceptual to an operational approach, we now enter upon a tooling-up phase in the discussion of urban land use planning. In making this shift, the emphasis will be increasingly directed toward methodological considerations. This is a phase concerned with data collection and data processing in preparation for land use planning analyses taken up in Part III. Involved here are studies of the urban economy, employment, population, attitudes and behavior, and the physical setting of the urban area. While the same kinds of studies are required in analyses for other components of the comprehensive plan, such as thoroughfares and transportation facilities, public utilities, and community facilities of all kinds, the emphasis here is primarily upon the special needs of land use planning.*

Of first importance in tooling up for land use planning are studies of the structure and vitality of the urban economy as key considerations in gauging the amount and rate of land development that is likely to occur in a city. Accordingly, considerable attention is given to methods of studying the makeup and general health of the urban economy. Analyses of employment and population prospects are extensions of these foundation studies, and supply the actual yardsticks needed for estimating amounts and rates of future land development. Then attention is focused on attitudes and behavior patterns to obtain insights into activity systems which must be accommodated in land use planning. But to apply data obtained from measurements of growth and studies of activity systems, it is necessary to have a basic description of the existing and past phsyical setting of the urban area. This is obtained from surveys and analyses of land use and vacant land in the urban area. Thus studies of the urban economy (Chapter 3), employment (Chapter 4), population (Chapter 5), activity systems (Chapter 6), and urban land (Chapter 7) are related prerequisites to the actual determination of land requirements and the subsequent development of a land use plan. However, along with these prerequisite studies, certain studies of a paralleling nature relate and contribute to the land use planning analyses. Transportation studies (Chapter 8) are of this category and particularly merit passing recognition, especially the relationship between traffic and land use.

The different methods presented in the following chapters have been selected for their general utility to land use planning analysis. Many of them have distinct shortcomings and may be open to question when used out of the accompanying context in forms of investigation or research where a higher level of accuracy may be required. Even within the present context some of the methods presented have limited utility, but these limitations are identified as the various methods are taken up below.

One common consideration in all types of studies taken up in the suc-

ceeding chapters is the early identification of a study area to represent what has heretofore been loosely termed "the urban area." As will be seen in Chapter 3 and will become evident again in Chapters 4 and 5, several systems of study areas are required and frequently used in background studies of planning. These are necessary and entirely proper so long as each system is internally consistent and serves a useful purpose within the framework for which it was intended. Nevertheless, ultimately cross comparisons at the urban level are useful and essential to land use planning, and it is in this connection that the question of the need for a common study area is introduced at this point. The urbanized area, *the reporting unit new to the U.S. Census in 1950, might prove ideal for planning purposes if data for previous census years were summarized on the same basis, thus permitting trend analyses.*[1] *Since its area of coverage in a self-regulating way adjusts according to changes in the urban settlement patterns observed in each census, the need for a fixed study area, constant for studies of the urban area—past, present, and future—becomes less crucial in the statistical reporting of population, economic, and other similar characteristics of the urban area.*

Since this more flexible approach is not at present feasible, it appears that the use of some suitable geographic area with constant boundaries is the next best solution. Ideally this area would correspond to what is later referred to as the planning area, *an area of special concern to land use planning but often quite different from the standard statistical areas employed in census summaries. But since the extent of this area and the specification of its boundaries generally remain fluid until the land use plan is firmed up, some other form of study area must be settled upon at this tooling-up stage of the land use planning process.*

The urban study area *has two major requirements. First, it should be an area officially used for reporting census information. Second, it should be larger than the census-defined urbanized area, but not so large as to be*

---

[1] An urbanized area is an area with at least one city of 50,000 population or more and the surrounding urban fringe which includes: (1) incorporated places of 2,500 or more; (2) incorporated places of less than 2,500 having a closely settled area of at least 100 dwelling units or more; (3) towns in New England states, townships in New Jersey and Pennsylvania, and counties elsewhere which are classified as urban; and (4) enumeration districts in unincorporated territory with a population density of 1,000 inhabitants or more per square mile, and other enumeration districts in unincorporated territory with lower population density provided they served to eliminate enclaves, close indentations in urbanized areas of one mile or less across the open end, or link outlying enumeration districts of qualifying density that were no more than 1½ miles from the main body of the urbanized area. This differs from the 1950 definition in the use of enumeration districts in place of blocks in constructing urbanized areas, a shift in density criterion from 500 dwelling units per square mile to 1,000 persons per square mile, and the inclusion of an entire town, township, or county under (3) as urban without the exclusion of portions. See Bureau of the Census, *1960 Census of Population,* Washington: U.S. Government Printing Office, 1961.

out of scale with and impractical to cover in land use and vacant land surveys. It should be an area that may reasonably be expected to contain the contiguous development functionally related to the urban center of interest that will be building up in the next 20 to 25 years. For the larger metropolitan centers, the Standard Metropolitan Statistical Area (SMSA) generally is a logical choice as the urban study area for employment and population analyses because of the availability of both standard census information and special census tabulations made for SMSA's.[2] The limits of these areas also usually extend beyond the contiguous built-up area of the central city. Where these areas involve impracticalities from a land use point of view, downward adjustments of the area and the data obtained

---

[2] As officially established by the Bureau of the Budget with the advice of the Federal Committee on Standard Metropolitan Statistical Areas (an interagency committee), SMSA's are selected on the basis of the following criteria (taken from Bureau of the Budget, *Standard Metropolitan Statistical Areas,* Washington: U.S. Government Printing Office, 1961):

POPULATION CRITERIA

1. Each SMSA must include at least:
   a. One city with 50,000 or more inhabitants, or
   b. Two cities having contiguous boundaries and constituting, for general economic and social purposes, a single community with a combined population of at least 50,000, the smaller of which must have a population of at least 15,000.
2. If two or more adjacent counties each have a city of 50,000 inhabitants or more (or twin cities under 1(b)) and the cities are within 20 miles of each other (city limits to limits), they will be included in the same area unless there is definite evidence that the two cities are not economically and socially integrated. [Areas may cross state lines.]

CRITERIA OF METROPOLITAN CHARACTER

3. At least 75% of the labor force of the county must be in the nonagricultural labor force.
4. In addition to Criterion 3, the county must meet at least one of the following conditions:
   a. It must have 50% or more of its population living in contiguous minor civil divisions with a density of at least 150 persons per square mile, in an unbroken chain of minor civil divisions with such density radiating from a central city in the area.
   b. The number of nonagricultural workers employed in the county must equal at least 10% of the number of nonagricultural workers employed in the county containing the largest city in the area, or be the place of employment of 10,000 nonagricultural workers.
   c. The nonagricultural labor force living in the county must equal at least 10% of the number of the nonagricultural labor force living in the county containing the largest city in the area, or be the place of residence of a nonagricultural labor force of 10,000.
5. In New England . . . towns and cities are used in defining SMSA's . . . [and] because smaller units are used and more restricted areas result, a population density criterion of at least 100 persons per square mile is used as the measure of metropolitan character.

CRITERIA OF INTEGRATION

6. A county is regarded as integrated with the county or counties containing the central cities of the area if either of the following criteria is met:
   a. If 15% of the workers living in the county work in the county or counties containing central cities of the area, or
   b. If 25% of those working in the county live in the county or counties containing central cities of the area.
   [Where data for Criteria 6(a) or (b) are not conclusive, other related types of information may be used based on such measures as telephone calls, newspaper circulation, charge accounts, delivery service practices, traffic counts, extent of public transportation, and extent to which local planning groups and other civic organizations operate jointly.]

106

from standard sources may be made to correspond to fewer counties or fractional parts of counties. Where parts of counties are employed, the limits are drawn around smaller civil division areas, such as townships, towns, or boroughs. For a smaller urban area not identified as an SMSA, a simple county or fractional parts of one or more counties may be used as the urban study area. Here, too, the limits are drawn around a suitable combination of recognized minor civil divisions.

One other general observation on the tooling-up phase merits attention at the outset. It relates to data collection. To avoid needless dissipation of time and effort, each of the studies covered in the succeeding chapters requires careful planning and disciplined execution. A "broadside approach" to data collection simply because "we may need the information sometime," rarely proves to be justified. Selectivity is essential, and this is possible only if the exact needs of the study are worked out in advance. This is such an elemental and self-evident aspect of survey operations that its mention would appear to be superfluous, yet the "broadside approach" continues to be used with consequent waste of time and effort spent in processing data not tabbed for a specific use, summarizing it, puzzling over possible uses for it, storing it, and eventually scrapping it.

Chapter 3

The Urban Economy

A knowledge of the structure and functioning of the urban economy is fundamental to all land use planning analyses. The destiny of an urban center is controlled by the extent and character of its productive or income-producing activity and by its general vitality. Studies of the economic basis for this activity hold the key to how the city has developed to where it is today and what its future prospects are. Stated another way, most metro-politan areas flourish because they serve as centers for the production and distribution of goods and services. Production and distribution functions create jobs, and employment opportunities attract people.

Viewed in these terms, the urban economy thus conditions the amount of land development that occurs. For example, an expanding economy with the implications it holds for new businesses and industries and population growth means more land going into use. Similarly, economic forces that are responsible for leveling off or declining trends in economic activity also exert influences on the pattern of urban land uses in the city. Apart from their significance in understanding the dynamics of land use changes, stud-ies of the urban economy have very fundamental implications for land use planning analyses. With a knowledge of the trends of growth, leveling off, or decline in economic activity, the city planner is better able to develop yardsticks (see Chapters 4 and 5) which assist him in estimating the extent and character of changing land requirements (see Part III) that form the basis for a land development plan. For example, studies of employment are a key element in population forecasts, and population estimates are used in scaling land development needs. Estimates of future land requirements for industrial uses are based on manufacturing employment trends, and future space needs for commercial uses draw upon employment trends in whole-sale trade, and so on. Plans for central, regional, community, and neigh-borhood shopping centers draw upon studies of population and purchasing power in and around the urban center.

The importance of economic studies and the fundamental role they play in land use planning will become apparent again and again in later chapters. This chapter considers first methods of analyzing the structure and functioning of the urban economy, and then takes up techniques for gauging its general vitality.

What is termed *the urban economy* is regarded here as a system of production, distribution, and consumption embracing the sum total productive activity within an urban center and that part of its hinterland which is dependent to a marked degree on facilities and services available in the city. Productive activity thus refers not only to manufacturing, agricultural, fishing, and extractive activity in which products are processed and/ or marketed, utilizing facilities and services of the city, but also to trade, finance, transport, government, and other services using the city as a base of operations. Thus defined, productive activity in a localized economic area possesses the characteristics and dynamics of a miniature national economy.

Because of the specialized and complex character of the work involved, a full-fledged analysis of the economy of an urban area in all its manifold aspects requires the skills of an economist. He is the specialist who probes into all the facets of production and distribution activities, employment trends, family income and expenditure patterns, and other elements which explain the economic structure and functioning of a city and give a picture of its general economic health. While the economist may be employed in the role of a specialist in these studies, the city planner as the generalist must not only know something of the scope of such studies, but he must also be prepared to execute limited types of investigations, particularly those that tie directly into land use planning analyses.

Two conceptual views are sometimes identified with the study of the urban economy, one regionally oriented, and the other urban-oriented. It is an underlying premise of the first approach that economic activity in any urban center of interest is affected by other centers of activity in its immediate region and is ultimately linked to the national economy as a whole. To put it another way, an urban center's *present* economic position in relation to other urban areas is dependent on what share of the regional and ultimately the national total of goods and services it produces in each line of local economic activity. Its *future* position is dependent on its capacity to develop new productive resources and expand existing ones in relation to other cities capable of engaging in the same activities within the same regional framework.

The urban-centered approach to the analysis of the urban economy begins at home (a given urban center of interest), but at the same time is externally focused, in that it seeks to explain the city's economic structure in terms of the goods and services it produces that are consumed outside the localized area of study. It identifies as the "base" of the urban economy the goods and services which are consumed externally. Thus any industry is classified as basic if it produces or distributes goods and services for "export" outside the localized area of study, and any industry whose goods and services are marketed at home is classed as service or nonbasic.

In the immediate succeeding sections of this chapter both concepts are considered in greater detail, premised on the necessity of viewing the urban economy from both a regional and localized vantage point. To obtain a fully rounded understanding of the urban economy, it is necessary to look first at national economic forces and trends and successively examine how they are influenced or altered in the larger regions of the United States, in the subregions, and so on down to the locale of interest. At the same time it is necessary to look at local productive activity, particularly local resources—the productive and distributive resources, labor resources, and the capital resources for financing new economic activity or for expanding established activities—and gauge the capacity for expanding the locality's productive activity *in harmony with regional factors*.

Regionally Oriented Approaches

A central consideration in the regionally oriented approach to the study of the urban economy is one of linkage—the interdependence of the locale with its region and a whole system of regions which make up the nation. In the American economy, differences in the distribution of natural resources and variations in the degree of economic organization, technological development, and labor specialization have the effect of increasing the interdependence of regions, and within them, their urban centers. If the economy of an urban area were self-sufficient, as is approached in the cultures of some parts of the world, there would be no need to relate the local economy to that of the region and the nation. However, in our mechanized and highly organized economy, where transportation and communication systems are developed to an advanced degree and where there is territorial division of labor, localized productive activity is conditioned by the interplay of forces in the region and nation.

The existence of spatial linkage is observed in a number of studies. Alfred Weber's work in the early 1900's on the theory of industrial location gives implicit recognition to the economic interdependence of regions in his "agglomeration analysis." [1] More recent studies of other economists working under different location theories, for example, Florence and his work on the

[1] Alfred Weber, *Uber den Standort der Industrien*, 1909. See also C. J. Friedrich, *Alfred Weber's Theory of Location of Industries*, Chicago: University of Chicago Press, 1929.

spatial dependence between industries [2] and Isard and his emphasis on space-economy analyses,[3] also lend credence to the fundamental importance of linkage factors in the study of a particular economy, whether national, regional, or local.

The foregoing references further recognize that there are marked variations in the linkage between cities and between regions as reflected in industrial location patterns. Duncan and his colleagues found this to be the case in their study of the gross flow of money between Federal Reserve Bank districts and within districts.[4] In pursuing his interregional space-economy analyses, Isard points to the volume of commodity flows from region to region as an indication of the extent of their economic interdependence. "If these flows are regarded as bonds which link components of the system to one another, it can be seen that the greater the magnitude of the flows in any area, the more highly interrelated are the components in that area." [5] Indeed, Isard hints at a system of economic dominance and subdominance among regions (very much along the lines of concepts of city hierarchy discussed later in the chapter), suggesting that through variations noted in interregional flows between aggregates of economic activity, hierarchical tendencies of varying order among regions may be identified.

From the foregoing, it should be evident that studies of the urban economy must recognize these elemental intra- and interregional relationships which profoundly affect the analysis and ultimate conclusions concerning the economic structure and functioning of any particular urban center. But having established the importance of a regional orientation to economic studies, how can regional influences be determined and made an integral part of studies of the urban economy, and how are regions identified for purposes of these analyses?

Three approaches to the study of regional spheres of influence are discussed below. The first, input-output analysis, is concerned with the dynamics of commodity flows between aggregates of industry. These aggregates or focal areas of economic activity can be single urban centers or a whole metropolitan complex of centers. Whatever study area is selected, the structure and functioning of its economy is viewed and analyzed in the

---

[2] P. Sargeant Florence, *Investment, Location and Size of Plant,* Cambridge: Cambridge University Press, 1948.

[3] Walter Isard, *Location and Space-Economy,* New York and Cambridge: John Wiley & Sons, Inc., and Technology Press, 1956.

[4] Otis Dudley Duncan, W. Richard Scott, Stanley Lieberson, Beverly Duncan, and Hal H. Winsborough, *Metropolis and Region,* Baltimore: The Johns Hopkins Press, 1960.

[5] Walter Isard, "Regional and National Product Projections and Their Interrelations," *Long-Range Economic Projection,* XVI, Studies in Income and Wealth by the National Bureau of Economic Research, Princeton: Princeton University Press, 1954, pp. 456-457.

context of the web of flows in a larger region and whole systems of regions. The second approach, a regional accounts system, in some respects is a more broadly focused version of the interindustry accounts system. While the input-output accounts are especially suited to analyze industrial linkage, the regional accounts approach (sometimes called a "social accounting system") is designed for analysis of all forms of income-producing activity. The third approach, an approximation analysis, uses conventional divisions of the nation into regions, subregions, and so on, and by crude step-down procedures from a larger parent area, develops gross measures of how the parts of the whole are estimated to share in total national productive activity.

Input-Output Analysis

Some recent empirically based theoretical work by Leontief [6] and some experimental extensions of it by Isard and others have resulted in the development of what is termed the "input-output technique" for measuring interindustry relationships in a given spatial setting—localized, regional, or national. The technique postulates that any given line of economic activity bears a measurable relationship to every other industry in the economy, and that these relationships can be set forth in a series of equations readily solved by computing machines. These interindustry relationships can be expressed in terms of what Leontief has referred to as a huge revenue expenditure accounting system.[7] The revenue side of the balance sheet shows how the output for every industry is distributed, and the expenditure side records for each industry the distribution of inputs per unit of output from all industries.

Table 1 indicates the basic structure of an input-output table of dollar transactions for a single region.[8] Read horizontally, the table shows output for each particular sector of the economy measured in terms of receipts from sales to every other sector, and read vertically, it shows input in terms of dollars spent in purchases in a particular sector from all other sectors. The final demand columns record purchases by households, governments,

---

[6] Wassily Leontief, *The Structure of the American Economy, 1919-1939,* Oxford: Oxford University Press, 1951.

[7] *Ibid.,* p. 11.

[8] To obtain some idea as to the detail possible in presenting the interindustry flow of goods and services both as to actual dollar transactions and as to input-output coefficients, the reader is referred to the published 200-sector tables (actually abridged from 500-sector tables) of the Interindustry Relations Study of 1947 for the United States as a whole, prepared by the Division of Interindustry Economics, U.S. Department of Labor. For a review of this project see W. D. Evans and M. Hoffenberg, "The Interindustry Relations Study for 1947," *The Review of Economics and Statistics,* May, 1952.

Table 1. Basic Format of Input-Output Table

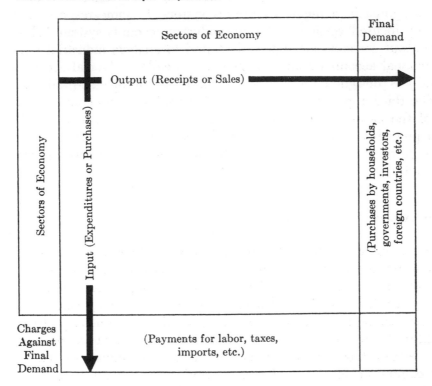

investors, and foreign countries—the dollar transactions after all intermediate processing and handling are completed. The charges against final
demand in the bottom rows are payments for labor, taxes, imports, and
others of a similar kind. Tables 2 and 3 illustrate how a table of coefficients
is constructed. Beginning with the dollar transactions (Table 2), the coefficient is derived by dividing each input in a given column by the total
of all inputs in the column. The resulting coefficients (Table 3) are read
by columns and indicate the cents of direct inputs per dollar of output.
Column 1 shows the input per dollar value of output from each of all the
other sectors supplying goods or services to Sector 1. The other columns
show similar relationships for other sectors.

Table 4, taken from Isard, presents a hypothetical matrix of coefficients
to illustrate how the input-output technique can be used in interregional
analyses.[9] For purposes of illustration, Isard drew this table to differentiate
between three kinds of regions according to the characteristic export indus-

[9] Walter Isard and Robert Kavesh, "Economic Structural Interrelations of Metropolitan Regions,"
The American Journal of Sociology, September, 1954.

Table 2. Interindustry Transactions in Hypothetical Region

	Sector 1	Sector 2	Sector 3	Households
Sector 1	$30	$20	$30	$25
Sector 2	60	20	80	30
Sector 3	10	40	60	50
Households	40	20	30	15
	(140)	(100)	(200)	(120)

Table 3. Interindustry Coefficients for Hypothetical Region (Cents of Direct Inputs per Dollar of Output)

	Sector 1	Sector 2	Sector 3	Households
Sector 1	.21	.20	.15	.21
Sector 2	.43	.20	.40	.25
Sector 3	.07	.40	.30	.42
Households	.29	.20	.15	.12

try of each, with Region I specializing in heavy manufacturing, Region II in light manufacturing, and Region III in agricultural and extractive activity. Reading by columns, any single column shows the cents' worth of input from each industrial class of activity in each region appearing in the stub of the table, per dollar's worth of output for the selected class of industry in a specified region at the head of the table.

The technique therefore establishes a basic relationship between the volume of output of any given industry in any given region and the volume of input required in the production process from all other industries in this and all other regions. Thus, for a factory engaged in producing aluminum cooking ware in a specified region, there are so many cents of input per dollar value of saucepan output attributable to one or more alumina reduction plants of the aluminum industry located in this and other regions in the matrix, and so many cents of input attributable to other industries contributing to the final product from this and other regions. Moreover, in addition to the first set of relationships, there are secondary ones, tertiary ones, and so on. Thus the input equivalent from the alumina reduction works for each dollar value of saucepan output involves second-round input equivalents from the electric power industry drawn upon in reducing alumina to aluminum, and this in turn involves third-round input equivalents in coal, machinery, and transmission lines used in the generation and distribution of power, and so on.

To explain the round-by-round analysis in terms of the Table 4 matrix,

Table 4. Hypothetical Intermetropolitan Transactions Table, 19xx[a] (Cents Worth of Inputs per Dollar of Output)

Industry Producing	Metropolitan Region I									Metropolitan Region II		
	Heavy Manufacturing (1)	Power and Communication (2)	Transportation (3)	Trade (4)	Insurance and Rental Serv. (5)	Business and Pers. Serv. (6)	Educational and Other Serv. (7)	Construction (8)	Households (9)	Light Manufacturing (10)	Power and Communication (11)	Transportation (12)
Metropolitan Region I:												
1. Heavy manufacturing	33	1	3	1	—	9	1	18	3	2	1	3
2. Power and communication	1	11	3	2	8	4	2	—	1	—	—	—
3. Transportation	2	2	5	1	1	1	2	4	3	—	—	—
4. Trade	1	—	2	—	2	3	5	9	12	—	—	—
5. Insurance and rental activities	1	1	3	5	7	5	4	2	12	—	—	—
6. Business and personal services	1	1	2	7	1	4	2	3	3	—	—	—
7. Educational and other basic services	—	—	—	—	—	—	1	—	10	—	—	—
8. Construction	—	4	6	—	10	—	1	—	—	—	—	—
9. Households	34	58	58	63	53	46	50	40	1	—	—	—
Metropolitan Region II:												
10. Light manufacturing	4	1	2	2	1	14	15	4	20	28	1	2
11. Power and communication	—	—	—	—	—	—	—	—	—	1	11	3
12. Transportation	—	—	—	—	—	—	—	—	—	2	2	5
13. Trade	—	—	—	—	—	—	—	—	—	2	—	2
14. Insurance and rental activities	—	—	—	—	—	—	—	—	—	1	1	3
15. Business and personal services	—	—	—	—	—	—	—	—	—	2	1	2
16. Educational and other basic services	—	—	—	—	—	—	—	—	—	—	—	—
17. Construction	—	—	—	—	—	—	—	—	—	—	4	6
18. Households	—	—	—	—	—	—	—	—	—	25	58	58
Region III:												
19. Agriculture and extraction	6	5	4	1	2	—	4	18	6	21	5	4
20. Power and communication	—	—	—	—	—	—	—	—	—	—	—	—
21. Transportation	—	—	—	—	—	—	—	—	—	—	—	—
22. Trade	—	—	—	—	—	—	—	—	—	—	—	—
23. Insurance and rental activities	—	—	—	—	—	—	—	—	—	—	—	—
24. Business and personal services	—	—	—	—	—	—	—	—	—	—	—	—
25. Educational and other basic services	—	—	—	—	—	—	—	—	—	—	—	—
26. Construction	—	—	—	—	—	—	—	—	—	—	—	—
27. Households	—	—	—	—	—	—	—	—	—	—	—	—

[a] Walter Isard and Robert Kavesh, "Economic Structural Interrelations of Metropolitan Regions," *The American Journal of Sociology*, The University of Chicago Press, September, 1954, p. 153. Copyright, 1954, by the University of Chicago.

| Industry Purchasing | | | | | | | | | | | | | | |
| Metropolitan Region II | | | | | | Region III | | | | | | | | |
Trade (13)	Insurance and Rental (14)	Business and Pers. Serv. (15)	Educational and Other Serv. (16)	Construction (17)	Households (18)	Agriculture and Extraction (19)	Power and Communication (20)	Transportation (21)	Trade (22)	Insurance and Rental (23)	Business and Pers. Serv. (24)	Educational and Other Serv. (25)	Construction (26)	Households (27)
1	—	9	1	18	3	1	1	3	1	—	9	1	18	3
—	—	—	—	—	—	—	—	—	—	—	—	—	—	—
—	—	—	—	—	—	—	—	—	—	—	—	—	—	—
—	—	—	—	—	—	—	—	—	—	—	—	—	—	—
—	—	—	—	—	—	—	—	—	—	—	—	—	—	—
—	—	—	—	—	—	—	—	—	—	—	—	—	—	—
—	—	—	—	—	—	—	—	—	—	—	—	—	—	—
—	—	—	—	—	—	—	—	—	—	—	—	—	—	—
2	1	14	15	4	20	6	1	2	2	1	14	15	4	20
2	8	4	2	—	1	—	—	—	—	—	—	—	—	—
1	1	1	2	4	3	—	—	—	—	—	—	—	—	—
—	2	3	5	9	12	—	—	—	—	—	—	—	—	—
5	7	5	4	2	12	—	—	—	—	—	—	—	—	—
7	1	4	2	3	3	—	—	—	—	—	—	—	—	—
—	—	—	1	—	10	—	—	—	—	—	—	—	—	—
—	10	—	1	—	—	—	—	—	—	—	—	—	—	—
63	53	46	50	40	1	—	—	—	—	—	—	—	—	—
1	2	—	4	18	6	28	5	4	1	2	—	4	18	6
—	—	—	—	—	—	1	11	3	2	8	4	2	—	1
—	—	—	—	—	—	3	2	5	1	1	1	2	4	3
—	—	—	—	—	—	2	—	2	—	2	3	5	9	12
—	—	—	—	—	—	4	1	3	5	7	5	4	2	12
—	—	—	—	—	—	1	1	2	7	1	4	2	3	3
—	—	—	—	—	—	—	—	—	—	—	—	1	—	10
—	—	—	—	—	—	—	4	6	—	10	—	1	—	—
—	—	—	—	—	—	40	58	58	63	53	46	50	40	1

Table 5 and the following explanation are taken from the work of Isard and Kavesh:

To illustrate the usefulness of input structure information, suppose a resource development program calls for an increase of one million dollars in the output of heavy manufacturing in Region I.[10] How will this affect the output of each activity in each region?

In column 1 of Table [4] are listed the coefficients which indicate the cents' worth of various inputs required per dollar output of heavy manufacturing. Multiplying these coefficients by one million gives us the direct inputs required to produce one million dollars' worth of heavy manufactures. These are called the first-round input requirements and are listed in column 1 of Table [5].

But to produce the first-round requirement of $330,000 of heavy manufacturing (item 1 in column 1, Table [5]) likewise requires a whole series of inputs. These can be obtained by multiplying column 1 of Table [4] by 330,000. And to produce the $20,000 of transportation (item 3, column 1, Table [5]) requires inputs which can be obtained by multiplying column 3 of Table [4] by 20,000. Similarly, the inputs required to produce each of the other items listed in column 1 of Table [5] can be derived.

It should be noted that the $340,000 which is listed in the ninth cell of column 1, Table [5], represents an increment of income received by the households in Metropolitan Region I. This increment results in increases in effective demand for a series of products. On the arbitrary assumption that two-thirds of this new income is spent, these increases in effective demand can be obtained by multiplying column 9, Table [4] . . . by 226,667.

Adding together all these inputs . . . necessary for the production of the first round of requirements yields the second round of requirements which is recorded in column 2 of Table [5]. In turn, the production of the second round of requirements necessitates a third round. . . . Furnishing a third round requires a fourth; a fourth round, a fifth; etc. Each of these rounds is recorded in Table [5]. It should be noted that the totals of the rounds converge. After a point it becomes feasible to stop the round-by-round computation and to extrapolate the remaining requirements.[11]

The input-output rationale thus involves (1) *an interindustry analysis* establishing in any given region the basic relationships existing between the volume of output for each industry and the volume of input required from all other industries in the production processes of each such industry, and (2) what Isard refers to as *a space-economy analysis* establishing relationships in the flow of commodities between regions which occur in fulfillment of input-output requirements in the interindustry analysis as given in Step 1 above. Step 1 derives a table of interindustry coefficients applicable to the region under study, and Step 2 derives a table of interregional-interindustry coefficients. Thus when these coefficients are applied to actual

---

[10] Isard has published with Robert E. Kuenne an actual case study of such a situation in "The Impact of Steel upon the Greater New York–Philadelphia Region: A Study in Agglomeration Projection," *The Review of Economics and Statistics*, November, 1953.

[11] Isard and Kavesh, "Economic Structural Interrelations of Metropolitan Regions," p. 155.

Table 5. Input Requirements (Hypothetical), by Round, for $1 Million Output of Heavy Manufacturing in Metropolitan Region I[a]

Industry Grouping	First-Round Input Requirements (1)	Second-Round Input Requirements (2)	Third-Round Input Requirements (3)	Fourth-Round Input Requirements (4)	Fifth-Round Input Requirements (5)	Sixth-Round Input Requirements (6)	Seventh-Round Input Requirements (7)	Sum of Rounds (8)
Metropolitan Region I:								
1. Heavy manufacturing	$330,000	$118,810	$ 47,793	$ 23,417	$ 13,407	$ 8,559	$ 5,884	$ 550,870
2. Power and communication	10,000	8,670	7,763	4,614	2,858	1,667	994	36,566
3. Transportation	20,000	14,910	7,417	4,508	2,516	1,475	871	51,697
4. Trade	10,000	31,440	15,687	11,021	6,042	3,573	2,060	79,823
5. Insurance and rental activities	10,000	32,940	18,965	12,612	7,135	4,155	2,430	88,237
6. Business and personal services	10,000	11,810	8,159	4,860	2,906	1,664	983	40,382
7. Educational and other basic services	—	22,700	10,077	7,463	3,945	2,359	1,344	47,888
8. Construction	—	2,600	4,759	2,731	1,789	1,031	622	13,532
9. Households	340,000	148,070	110,102	57,920	34,886	19,773	10,805	721,556
Metropolitan Region II:								
10. Light manufacturing	40,000	75,600	60,601	47,894	34,840	25,204	18,115	302,323
11. Power and communication	—	400	971	1,182	1,190	1,056	856	5,655
12. Transportation	—	800	1,781	1,821	1,601	1,309	1,016	8,328
13. Trade	—	800	2,364	3,044	2,858	2,470	1,963	13,499
14. Insurance and rental activities	—	400	1,696	2,689	2,706	2,490	1,972	11,953
15. Business and personal services	—	800	1,825	1,954	1,772	1,479	1,159	8,989
16. Educational and other basic services	—	—	670	1,387	1,394	1,275	1,033	5,759
17. Construction	—	—	104	325	446	455	391	1,721
18. Households	—	10,000	20,747	20,643	18,918	15,744	12,381	98,433
Region III:								
19. Agriculture and extraction	60,000	60,220	50,741	39,365	29,244	21,250	15,387	276,207
20. Power and communication	—	600	1,122	1,402	1,386	1,229	1,019	6,758
21. Transportation	—	1,800	2,430	2,360	2,085	1,673	1,310	11,658
22. Trade	—	1,200	3,226	3,541	3,481	2,922	2,385	16,755
23. Insurance and rental activities	—	2,400	4,646	4,962	4,701	3,917	3,156	23,782
24. Business and personal services	—	600	1,256	1,490	1,463	1,260	1,032	7,101
25. Educational and other basic services	—	—	1,600	1,876	1,969	1,680	1,397	8,522
26. Construction	—	—	372	664	719	682	581	3,018
27. Households	—	24,000	27,936	28,508	25,037	20,595	16,189	142,265
Total	$830,000	$571,570	$414,810	$284,253	$211,303	$151,006	$107,335	$2,583,277

[a] Walter Isard and Robert Kavesh, "Economic Structural Interrelations of Metropolitan Regions," *The American Journal of Sociology*, The University of Chicago Press, September, 1954, p. 153. Copyright, 1954, by the University of Chicago.

figures of output and results are summed up industry by industry, it is possible not only to have a measure of interindustry relationships but also to obtain a picture of the distribution of economic activity with respect to a given urban center of interest and with respect to the system of regions employed in the analysis.

The examples above illustrate in greatly simplified form the theoretical use of the input-output technique in analyzing existing productive activity within a localized, regional, or national economy. To estimate future productive levels, the technique assumes as "given" some reliable forecast of the effective demand for all the various economic lines for the system of regions involved in the study. Successively applying to the assumed future demand levels the input-output coefficients from the basic tables, the urban center's share of estimated future regional productive activity in all economic lines is determined.

This is not to imply that the set of values appearing in the basic tables of input-output coefficients will remain constant. These can change in time and will require adjustment. Over a period of time, changes in technology will necessitate adjustments in the basic tables, but these changes do not occur so rapidly that they cannot be anticipated and the appropriate adjustments made to the basic tables. Variations in price relationships also occur in time, but tests made by Leontief suggest that since there is sufficient degree of stability in the pattern of price relationships, here too adjustments can be estimated with a fair degree of accuracy.[12]

The basic principles of the input-output technique are not new to economic theory, but go back a great many years.[13] However, their applications to the analysis of the structural makeup of an economy are relatively recent and offer much promise to a wide variety of studies, among them city planning analyses of the urban economy. Methodologically the technique not only offers an important means of evaluating interindustry and interregional relationships in all their complexities, but by examining these relationships in the context of aggregates of industry in particular urban settings, it also permits analysis of the economic functioning of one urban center in relation to other urban centers in its region and other regions of the nation.

However, there are obstacles to immediate general use of input-output analyses for these purposes. There is the mechanical problem of data avail-

---

[12] Leontief, *The Structure of the American Economy, 1919–1939*, pp. 201–202.

[13] Evans and Hoffenberg cite a French work published some 200 years ago, *Tableau Economique*, by François Quesnay, Adam Smith's classic work, and the work of Leon Walras, a French economist, 100 years later, as containing some of the ideas which Leontief first applied in the modern economic environment. See Evans and Hoffenberg, "The Interindustry Relations Study for 1947," p. 97.

ability in the detail and form needed to trace interindustry-interregional flows of goods and services. This situation can be remedied in time, but the complex character of the procedural and mathematical operations involved is another deterrent to general usage of the technique. However, if the technique can be simplified to permit general understanding and use by the nonexpert and if it can be geared to utilize standard sources of data (or, alternatively, if the presently required data can become a part of the regularly reported statistics of a governmental agency), it offers much promise of becoming a widely used instrument for analyzing the structure and dynamics of the urban economy.[14]

Of course, where the technique is used in estimating future trends in the makeup of the economy, it faces a limitation common to all projective analyses, namely, the difficulties inherent in estimating future demand levels. Even in a context involving the use of highly qualified and carefully stated alternate assumptions, the input-output technique is no better off than other techniques. Here too, future demand levels must necessarily be presented by gross aggregate classes of industry and cannot extend to the same level of detail possible in analyses of current interindustry-interregional relationships.

One of the most promising uses of the technique in projective analyses is in experimental studies. These employ approaches closely paralleling those of the natural sciences. For example, using a hydraulic engineering prototype experiment, one can approach the study of an urban economy in this vein: If a certain series of flows are introduced into a given system of flows, what are the resultant rearrangements in this system of flows? Isard's interesting analysis of the impact of the new steel production and steel fabricating activity in the New York–Philadelphia industrial region triggered by U.S. Steel's Fairless Works furnishes a tangible illustration of the potentialities of such an approach.[15] The study found that chain reaction from the construction of plants with an estimated 3 million tons of new steel capacity would produce for this region in the period of a decade a minimum new employment in all forms of industry amounting to more than 180,000, with a resulting population equivalent estimated at 419,000 persons. Even though this study is concerned with expansion only in one sector of this region's economy, it illustrates the possibilities of this kind of projective analysis for city planning studies.

---

[14] Examples of the use of the input-output technique in metropolitan areas include Harold T. Smith, *The Kalamazoo County Economy*, Kalamazoo: The W. E. Upjohn Institute for Employment Research, April, 1960; Werner Z. Hirsch, "An Application of Area Input-Output Analysis," *Papers and Proceedings of the Regional Science Association*, V, Philadelphia: University of Pennsylvania, 1959.

[15] Isard and Kuenne, "The Impact of Steel upon the Greater New York–Philadelphia Region."

Income and Product Accounts

The social accounts system of analyzing the economy is not unlike the input-output technique. As its name implies, it is essentially a system of double-entry bookkeeping. In accounting for the dollar value of input and output exchanges among sectors in the economy, input-output analysis involves the use of a set of accounts. But it is also possible to set up accounts on the basis of asset changes without tracing interchanges in physical inventories. This is what is involved in income and product accounts. However, under this system we obtain a more inclusive view of all forms of income-producing activity.

Until recently an income and products accounts system has been viewed mainly as a tool for the study of the national economy and as an instrument of national policy. Over the past 25 years or so, Gross National Product (GNP) and other income statistics have become familiar indicators of national well-being.[16] On the basis of these statistics, analyses of national economic growth are made annually, and economic projections are becoming available at intervals.[17]

To apply these concepts to regions poses some different problems than those involved in a national system of accounts. For example, in national accounts when we achieve closure in the system by introducing the "Rest of the World" account, it is not difficult to visualize and make an analysis of the national economy as a system. It makes less sense to think of a region or a metropolitan area as a closed system because wherever we set the boundaries we know that we are arbitrarily cutting across important ties with other regions and metropolitan areas. In this age of specialization and interdependence among regions, the flow of income and products affecting a particular metropolitan area extends in complicated and constantly changing patterns to many other regions.

Hochwald points out that in setting up the national system as a closed one, we can see how past income generates present product flows. But on

---

[16] See footnote 4 in Chapter 4 for a listing and definition of various measures of national income.

[17] Regular reports are made by the National Council of Economic Advisers, Congress' Joint Committee on the Economic Report, and the U.S. Department of Commerce's Office of Business Economics. Recent projections include Hans H. Landsberg, Leonard L. Fischman, and Joseph L. Fisher, *Resources in America's Future,* Baltimore: The Johns Hopkins Press, 1963; Outdoor Recreation Resources Review .Commission Staff, National Planning Association, and Bureau of Labor Statistics, *Projections to the Years 1976 and 2000: Economic Growth, Population, Labor Force and Leisure, and Transportation,* ORRRC Study Report 23, Washington: U.S. Government Printing Office, 1962; and National Planning Association, *National Economic Projections,* published annually by the Association, Washington.

the regional level, there is some basis for taking the view that "strategic production decisions are made in response to expected 'foreign' market demand rather than local expenditures of past income. Regional accounts therefore are 'open' to trace the impact of external forces on local production flows; their design depends on the choice of exogenous and endogenous sectors used to trace relations between the region and the 'Rest of the World.'" [18] (Based on terms used in biology, "exogenous" refers to growth which originates from outside, and "endogenous" to growth which develops from inside.) This view underscores the importance of eventually having accounts of a common design on an "across-the-boards" basis for whole systems of regions.

Some have raised questions about the applicability of a social accounting system to the essentially different situation involved in setting up regional accounts. Others have questioned the use of this system of analysis on a regional basis because of the lack of the requisite data on a regularly reported basis and the cost of setting up and maintaining an adequate and complete set of accounts for regions. However, there are a growing number of economists who look with favor on the use of a properly designed system of regional accounts for selected kinds of regional analyses and who see the data problem as a temporary one. Until data are collected and summarized in terms of regions as an intermediate step in the compilation of national statistics, it is suggested that local surveys, including sampling studies, can be undertaken to supply data for a metropolitan area system of accounts which, with judicious interpretation concerning interregional economic relations, can be used in the study of local economic development and urban growth. Along with the perspective that this set of accounts gives of local economic activity, there seems to be little doubt that the estimates of income and product flows taken from these accounts are accurate enough to enable city planners to explore space needs for land use planning. Moreover, with "across-the-boards" analyses introduced as a comparative base and a "control," regional studies can be given the needed breadth of perspective in the interpretation of a local system of accounts.[19]

In a system of social accounts, the economy is seen as a mechanism for producing goods and services for final disposition as (1) household consumption, (2) private investment in industry and business, (3) govern-

---

[18] Werner Hochwald (ed.), *Design of Regional Accounts*, Baltimore: The Johns Hopkins Press, 1961, p. xvii.
[19] For a discussion of the importance of relating studies of the individual region with a national system of regions, see Harvey S. Perloff, "Relative Regional Economic Growth: An Approach to Regional Accounts," in *ibid.*

mental purchases, and (4) sales abroad.[20] With some adjustments in definitions, these same general sectors may be used in regional accounts. In this respect, of the four areas of final demand, we may think of the three exogenous elements (private domestic investment, governmental purchases, and foreign investment) as being independent of total income, and the fourth, the endogenous element (household consumption), as being dependent on total income. In its very simplest conceptualization, total income of course is the sum of exogenously determined income and endogenously determined income. But since, as we have noted, the exogenous element is independent of total income (as a mathematical function), this means that if we can establish a relation between the exogenous components and total income, we can estimate the level of personal consumption. Thus, if we know from an analysis of income data that total income tends to be 1.64 of the exogenous activity, we can use this relationship to estimate future endogenous activity. This is the multiplier effect obtained from a set of income and product accounts which can be used in introducing projections into the analysis.[21]

Leven sets forth in the most completely documented form so far available the techniques in the use of social accounts in the analysis of a metropolitan area economy.[22] The form of the accounts may be illustrated from his study for the Sioux City Planning Commission presented in Tables 6 and 7. Table 6 shows in summary form the total income for the three major sectors used in the analysis: production of goods for export, production of goods for investment, and production of goods for consumption.[23] Table 7 presents the summary of the various double-entry accounts which are used in constructing the consolidated income and product accounts statement in Table 6. Leven's Elgin-Dundee Area Study should be consulted for a detailed explanation of each item and the techniques used in assembling the data. Besides supplying data in a form needed in setting up accounts, local surveys of the kind Leven describes are important in the identification of imports of different categories.

---

[20] For a discussion of the theoretical aspects of social accounting applied to metropolitan areas, see Charles L. Leven, *Theory and Method of Income and Product Accounts for Metropolitan Areas, Including the Elgin-Dundee Area as a Case Study,* Pittsburgh: University of Pittsburgh Press, 1963.

[21] For a fuller discussion of the multiplier, see Charles M. Tiebout, "The Community Income Multiplier: A Case Study," in Ralph W. Pfouts (ed.), *The Techniques of Urban Economic Analysis,* West Trenton: Chandler-Davis Publishing Company, 1960; see also Tiebout's *The Community Economic Base Study,* New York: Committee for Economic Development, December, 1962.

[22] Leven, *Theory and Method of Income and Product Accounts for Metropolitan Areas.* See also Leven's "Regional Income and Product Accounts: Construction and Applications," in Hochwald (ed.), *Design of Regional Accounts.*

[23] In this analysis, governmental purchases which are prominent in national accounts have been absorbed into other accounts as indicated in the tables.

Table 6. Consolidated Income and Product Accounts, Sioux City Area, 1958 ($000) [a]

Value added in the production of goods for export	123,413	Sales of goods to the Rest of the World	734,437
Value added in the production of goods for investment	6,535	Purchase of goods by consumers	151,646
		Purchase of investment goods	21,690
Value added in the production of goods for consumption	72,852	Less: Imports of intermediate goods for production of goods for export	611,024
		Less: Imports of final and intermediate goods for investment	15,155
		Less: Imports of final and intermediate goods for consumption	78,794
CHARGES AGAINST GROSS AREA PRODUCT	202,800	GROSS AREA PRODUCT	202,800

[a] Charles L. Leven, "Regional Income and Product Accounts: Construction and Applications," in Werner Hochwald (ed.), *Design of Regional Accounts*, a Resources for the Future, Inc., publication, Baltimore: The Johns Hopkins Press, 1961. Leven notes that some slight revisions have been made since publication of the Sioux City Planning Commission report in 1959.

From accounts of the kind illustrated in Tables 6 and 7, Leven constructs the multiplier as follows:

$$k = \frac{1}{1 - \dfrac{Y_{end}}{T_t}}$$

where k is the multiplier, Y_{end} is the value added in the local market ($6,-535,000 plus $72,852,000—see Table 6), and T_t is total income (Gross Area Product of $202,800,000—see Table 6). This works out to be a multiplier of 1.64. This is interpreted to mean that, assuming the multiplier value remains constant, for every million dollars of additional value added for export, there will be approximately $640,000 of additional local economic activity. To put it another way, if a family moves into the area with an income level of $10,000, eventually total income would increase by $16,400.

In the use of such a multiplier in economic forecasts, previously prepared projections for a larger region would normally be required.[24] These projections presumably would be in balance with economic growth anticipated in all other regions of the nation. If local economic development programs are showing promise of seizing on competetive advantages in certain lines of new activity and there is therefore reason to develop alternative assumptions of growth in the local region, a modified set of estimates may be

[24] See National Planning Association, *National Economic Projections*.

introduced as a paralleling series of projections. Thus the multiplier, either held constant or modified or both, is used in conjunction with projections of exogenous activity in estimating total income. By reference to the more detailed "from-to" accounts (more detailed than Tables 6 and 7), the projected totals of final demand for consumption, for private investment, and for export can be distributed among subsector industrial categories.[25]

Table 7. The Parts of the Income and Product Accounts, Sioux City Area, 1958 ($000) [a]

Consumption Account			
Value added in the production of goods for consumption	72,852	Purchase of goods by consumers	151,646
		Less: Imports of final and intermediate goods for consumption	78,794
CHARGES AGAINST CONSUMPTION PRODUCT	72,852	CONSUMPTION PRODUCT	72,852
Investment Account			
Value added in the production of goods for investment	6,535	Purchase of investment goods	21,690
		Less: Imports of final and intermediate goods for investment	15,155
CHARGES AGAINST INVESTMENT PRODUCT	6,535	INVESTMENT PRODUCT	6,535
Rest of the World Account			
Value added in the production of goods for export	123,413	Net investment in the private sector of the Rest of the World	13,723
Excess of out-commuter wages over in-commuter wages	(−11,160)		
Net receipts of interest, rent, and dividends from abroad	475		
Excess of gifts received from over gifts given abroad	(−428)		
Excess of profits of outside branches of local firms over profits of local branches of outside firms	(−4,628)		
Less: Imports of final and intermediate goods for consumption	78,794		
Less: Imports of final and intermediate goods for investment	15,155		

[25] See Leven's "from-to" tables, "Regional Income and Product Accounts," pp. 194-195.

NET CURRENT PAYMENTS DUE TO THE AREA ON PRIVATE ACCOUNT	13,723	NET INVESTMENT IN THE PRIVATE SECTOR OF THE REST OF THE WORLD	13,723
Excess of direct and indirect nonlocal tax and nontax payments over transfer payments from nonlocal government	37,559	Net contribution to nonlocal government	37,559
NET CURRENT PAYMENTS DUE TO THE AREA	51,282	NET INVESTMENT IN THE REST OF THE WORLD	51,282

Saving and Investment Account

Purchases of investment goods	21,690	Undistributed profits of local corporations	3,416
		Personal saving	8,891
		Capital consumption allowances and statistical discrepancy	59,947
		Capital outlays of nonlocal government	718
		Less: Net investment in the Rest of the World	51,282
GROSS INVESTMENT	21,690	GROSS SAVING	21,690

ᵃ Adapted from Charles L. Leven, "Regional Income and Product Accounts: Construction and Applications," in Werner Hochwald (ed.), *Design of Regional Accounts*, a Resources for the Future, Inc., publication, Baltimore: The Johns Hopkins Press, 1961. Leven notes that some slight revisions have been made since publication of the Sioux City Planning Commission report in 1959.

Approximation Analyses

In identifying the linkage between the localized urban economy and its region and the nation, what is the alternative to the foregoing types of analyses which trace out the industry-to-industry and region-to-region flows of goods and services or income? As suggested earlier, another much less meaningful approach sometimes used is a comparative analysis as to how regions, subregions, and other more localized economic areas successively share in national productive activity, using such standard measures as value added by manufacture, wholesale sales, retail sales, and receipts from services. By taking cross-sectional readings of productive activity for all component geographical areas in a given system of study areas and expressing them as a percentage of the larger parent area, and by taking them for different periods of time, comparisons are drawn as to the relative position of each study area in each line of activity in relation to all other areas in that system and whether that position is improving, remaining constant, or deteriorating in time.

Such analyses thus employ ratio techniques involving the computation of a series of interlocking ratios of productive activity for the particular system of study areas considered to exert an influence on the localized areas being studied. Table 8 illustrates the form in which results can be summarized. It shows that successively smaller geographic areas examined from the nation as a whole down to the Charlotte SMSA are faring differently in the way they share in the economic growth of their respective parent areas. Whereas the South Atlantic states are showing steady increases in their combined share of U.S. growth in all three lines of economic activity, the trends are not so pronounced and indicate some slight reversals in a few of the subareas for some lines (even though in absolute terms there is growth across the boards). The table indicates in gross form the relative position of a metropolitan area in three major sectors of activity within the framework of a whole system of study areas. Such a table can be expanded to show subcategories of manufacturing, wholesale, and retail lines, depending on the detail reported by the census for the particular urban area being studied.

Where projective estimates are desired, this approach, as in the case of the input-output technique and the regional accounts approach, requires a "given" forecast of national productive activity. Such a forecast, of course, must be available broken down into the standard measures being employed, namely, value added by manufacture and wholesale and retail sales.

There are two variations on the ratio technique used in such projective analyses. The most common form expresses these standard measures of productive activity in terms of simple direct ratios of figures for a particular area to those of the larger parent area. Past values for these relationships are arranged in a time series and extrapolated by fitting a mathematical curve to the data. The projected region-to-nation ratio is then applied to the "given" absolute figures of the nation to obtain absolute values for the region; the projected subregion-to-region ratio is next applied to this resultant absolute regional estimate to obtain an estimate for the subregion in absolute terms; and so on. The other variation on the ratio technique employs the same procedure but introduces an element of control to the procedure by making tandem analyses of all subarea parts of the parent area and balancing the results with the total before proceeding to the next step-down. This is sometimes called the apportionment technique to distinguish it from the direct ratio step-down procedure first described.

Such an analysis reflects the combined effects of interindustry-interregional flows and indicates where gross changes are occurring in time, but it cannot trace flows between industries within and between regions. Thus it does not provide a direct measure of linkage, but only a crude cross-sectional view of the gross effects of commodity flows as they figure into the total transactions recorded for the selected system of study areas.

Table 8. Some Illustrative Indices Showing How Successively Smaller Geographical Areas Share in a Parent Area's Productive Activity

Geographic Areas Compared	Value Added by Manfacture				Wholesale Sales				Retail Sales			
	1929	1939	1947	1958	1929	1939	1948	1958	1929	1939	1948	1958
South Atlantic States as a per cent of U.S.[a]	8.0	9.0	9.3	10.1	6.7	8.3	8.6	10.0	8.0	10.4	11.3	12.8
North and South Carolina as a per cent of South Atlantic States	34.7	32.3	35.1	31.2	22.6	24.7	25.4	23.3	22.7	22.1	23.0	21.9
Piedmont Industrial Crescent as a per cent of North and South Carolina	59.1	72.9	50.0	48.8	53.0	48.1	56.1	55.2	33.5	35.4	35.9	35.8
Charlotte Standard Metropolitan Statistical Area as a per cent of Piedmont Industrial Cresent	5.7	4.9	6.6	8.6	33.2	38.5	42.8	47.7	16.2	14.9	15.1	17.2

[a] Forty-eight state basis.

A notable series of studies emphasizing interregional analysis has been made by Resources for the Future, Inc., a Ford Foundation–financed activity.[26] Such studies contain valuable benchmarks for metropolitan area analyses. Of special interest in this connection is the typology of SMSA's developed by Duncan and his associates and their analysis of 50 major cities in a regional framework.[27]

Delineating Regional Spheres of Economic Influence

As indicated above, regional concepts are introduced into economic analyses as a means of studying how small economic units—a particular industry or a grouping of economic activities that are represented by the urban center or complex of urban centers—are linked to one another, to the region, and to the national economy. However, there are certain practicalities that dictate the kinds of study areas employed in these analyses of linkage. At present the regionally oriented approaches to the study of the urban

[26] See Harvey S. Perloff, Edgar S. Dunn, Jr., Eric E. Lampard, and Richard F. Muth, *Regions, Resources and Economic Growth*, Baltimore: The Johns Hopkins Press, 1960; see also Landsberg, Fischman, and Fisher, *Resources in America's Future*.
[27] Duncan *et al.*, *Metropolis and Region*.

economy described above are dependent on the system of study areas for which U.S. Census data on productive activity are reported. As can be seen in Table 8, approximation analyses are undertaken entirely within the framework of conventional regional and political division delineations.

Input-output analyses also face limitations in the regions selected for study. In theory the term "region" is used in these studies in a fluid sense to denote a study area containing an observable series of commodity flows of specified internal consistency. If data requirements presented no problem, the system of regions thus employed would be derived in the course of the input-output analysis. But we know that there are restrictions involved in the form in which needed data are reported, and so, among those proficient in the use of the input-output technique, there is explicit recognition that regions employed in these studies also must be selected according to data availability. The same situation is involved in the regional accounts approach, particularly in relating a local region to a system of national regions.

Even though data availability places constraints on the selection of study areas, there is some latitude for choice. In the interests of providing more flexibility in the use of standard sources of data, there has been some recent effort directed toward recombining census areas into more functional study areas, with the result that there are now at least three systems of study areas from which to make a choice. There is first a subdivision of the country into regions on the basis of "regions of metropolitan dominance." [28] More recently, some work has been undertaken looking toward the use of assemblages of counties in a system of economically homogeneous study areas. Finally, there are the long-standing conventional series of census-reporting units consisting of regions, census divisions, and such political divisions as states and counties.

Metropolitan Regions

Metropolitan concepts of regionalism for the most part stem from urbanism studies of demographers and sociologists. In search of ways of describing metropolitan spheres of influence and the positioning of cities in a region according to their dependence on a single dominant metropolitan center, several such studies are suggestive of approaches which might be used in defining a region for economic analyses.

In the words of McKenzie, one of the first to emphasize the regional character of urban influences, "geographically the metropolitan region ex-

---

[28] Not to be confused with "metropolitan regions" in a more limited sense as used by the city planner in referring to a particular urban center and its immediate built-up area.

tends as far as the city exerts a dominant influence." [29] This region of influence is described in terms of "metropolitan dominance and subdominance." The concept likens a region to a system of magnetic fields, each surrounding a city and each, according to its relative economic strength, variable in its power to attract growth.

A city is defined as dominant when it occupies a controlling economic position in relation to all other communities in the surrounding region, particularly in such functions as services and wholesaling and in its capacity to attract industrial development. A dominant city exerts a strong influence over what types of economic activity develop in the immediate hinterland. A subdominant city, while being dependent on the larger center for one or more of its many specialized services and wholesale outlets, is a subservice and subwholesaling center for hinterland areas, with a more limited pulling power in the attraction of new industry. In order to survive, subdominant centers must specialize in the direction indicated by the dominant center, particularly in the trade and service functions but to a less extent in manufacturing activity.

Building on the earlier work of McKenzie, Bogue presents evidence that the cities of the nation group into regional patterns with definite and measurable ties with the major metropolitan centers of the country.[30] His study takes some 67 metropolitan centers with 1940 populations of 100,000 or more and divides the country into regions tributary to these 67 centers. Then, using as measures of dominance such census-reported indices as value added by manufacture, wholesale sales, retail sales, and receipts from services, it demonstrates how dominant and subdominant patterns in the economic positioning of cities can be identified within such regions, and clearly shows the interdependency and the interrelationships which exist among the cities of metropolitan regions.[31]

Figures 8 to 10 present three different metropolitan systems of regions in

---

[29] R. D. McKenzie, *The Metropolitan Community*, New York: McGraw-Hill Book Company, Inc., 1933, p. 70.

[30] Donald J. Bogue, *The Structure of the Metropolitan Community, a Study of Dominance and Subdominance*, Ann Arbor: University of Michigan, Horace H. Rackham School of Graduate Studies, 1949.

[31] In this study, metropolitan centers with 100,000 population or more were selected so as to exclude any such cities which were located next to, or very near, larger cities. The subdivision into regions was accomplished by connecting each center with adjoining centers by straight lines. These lines were bisected and the resulting midpoints were connected. The boundaries of each region were then defined by outlining the outer boundaries of all outlying counties the greater part of which fell within the geometric delineation. As might be expected, such a geometric approach to the subdivision of the country into metropolitan regions neglects such elements as physiographic features and transportation factors except insofar as these are reflected in the original siting of the urban center. While perhaps suitable for purposes of the original study, such an approach to defining regions would require adjustment if interregional comparisons are contemplated.

the nation. Figure 8 shows how the foregoing approach would break the country down into metropolitan regions. Figure 9 shows McKenzie's conception of metropolitan regions as defined by daily newspaper circulation. Figure 10 shows another early representation of the nation's regions of metropolitan influence as developed by the National Resources Committee.[32] In this study, regions were defined around 17 major metropolitan centers.

Duncan and his colleagues approached metropolitan dominance from a somewhat different view than that followed by McKenzie and Bogue.[33] Seeking to give recognition to intermetropolitan economic ties, they conceive of a particular metropolitan area as having a configuration of relationships with many centers located far beyond the surrounding hinterland area. After examining rank-size concepts, central place theory, and other approaches that might offer possibilities in the construction of spatial systems for the analysis of these intermetropolitan relationships, they conclude that the "spatial structure of the economy" is more appropriate as an emphasis than a "system of cities." Although they use SMSA delineations for city comparisons, they suggest the usefulness of an approach based on population potential as a convenient summarization view of intermetropolitan relationships.[34]

Homogeneous Economic Areas

As opposed to the essentially nodal concept of regionalism embodied in a metropolitan system of study areas, an approach based on economic homogeneity gives more direct recognition to the spatial distribution of economic activity. It takes into consideration the specialization of areas that occurs in selected economic activities, the interdependency among these areas, and the exchange which goes on between them, and it reflects the influence of resources and raw materials on the location of productive activity. Thus such an approach recognizes that the nation can be broken down into geographic areas of specialization that take into account contemporary trends in the territorial division of labor, differences in the distribution of resources, and the necessity for the flow of goods and services between sections of the country.

In recognition that these considerations led to a different order of regions,

---

[32] National Resources Committee, *Regional Factors in Planning*, Washington: U.S. Government Printing Office, December, 1935.

[33] Duncan *et al.*, *Metropolis and Region.*

[34] For the construction of isolines of population potential, see *ibid.*, pp. 551-553; see also Otis Dudley Duncan, Ray P. Cuzzort, and Beverly Duncan, *Statistical Geography*, New York: The Free Press of Glencoe and The Macmillan Company, 1961, pp. 52-56.

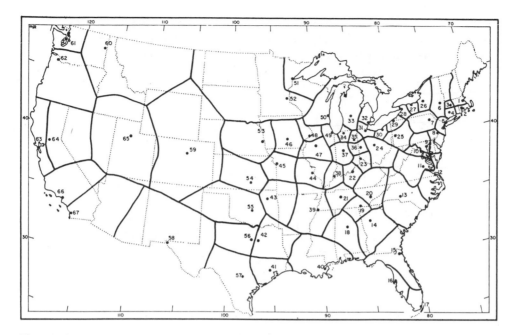

Figure 8. Regions of Metropolitan Dominance in 1940, after Donald J. Bogue. *Key to numbered regions:* 1—Boston; 2—Providence; 3—Springfield; 4—Hartford; 5 —New York City; 6—Albany; 7—Scranton; 8—Philadelphia; 9—Baltimore; 10— Washington, D.C.; 11—Richmond; 12—Norfolk; 13—Charlotte; 14—Atlanta; 15 —Jacksonville; 16—Tampa; 17—Miami; 18—Birmingham; 19—Chattanooga; 20— Knoxville; 21—Nashville; 22—Louisville; 23—Cincinnati; 24—Columbus; 25—Pitts- burgh; 26—Syracuse; 27—Rochester; 28—Buffalo; 29—Erie; 30—Cleveland; 31— Toledo; 32—Detroit; 33—Grand Rapids; 34—South Bend; 35—Fort Wayne; 36 —Dayton; 37—Indianapolis; 38—Evansville; 39—Memphis; 40—New Orleans; 41 —Houston; 42—Dallas; 43—Tulsa; 44—St. Louis; 45—Kansas City; 46—Des Moines; 47—Peoria; 48—Davenport–Moline–Rock Island; 49—Chicago; 50—Mil- waukee; 51—Duluth; 52—Minneapolis–St. Paul; 53—Omaha; 54—Wichita; 55— Oklahoma City; 56—Fort Worth; 57—San Antonio; 58—El Paso; 59—Denver; 60 —Spokane; 61—Seattle; 62—Portland, Ore.; 63—San Francisco; 64—Sacramento; 65—Salt Lake City; 66—Los Angeles; 67—San Diego.

Bogue and Beale turned their attention to developing a system of econom- ically homogeneous study areas.[35] Although the system of areas with which they emerged is defined mainly on the basis of homogeneity characteristics of concern to agricultural analyses, this system has utility for regional studies and many kinds of metropolitan planning analyses. Bogue and Beale

---

[35] See Donald J. Bogue and Calvin L. Beale, *Economic Areas of the United States,* New York: The Free Press of Glencoe and The Macmillan Company, 1961.

Figure 9. Metropolitan Regions as Defined by Daily Newspaper Circulation in 1929, after R. D. McKenzie. (*Source:* National Resources Committee, *Regional Factors in Planning*, Washington: U.S. Government Printing Office, December, 1935.)

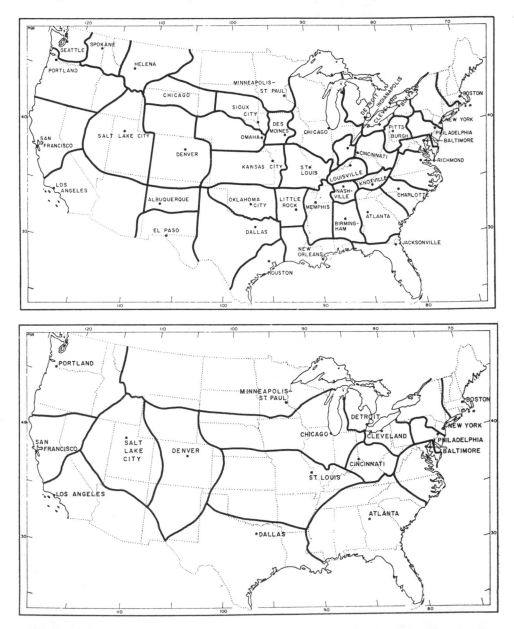

Figure 10. National Resources Committee's Delineation of Possible Planning Regions Based upon Composite Criteria of Metropolitan Influence, 1935. (*Source:* National Resources Committee, *Regional Factors in Planning*, Washington: U.S. Government Printing Office, December, 1935.)

have divided the 48 states into a system of 501 "State Economic Areas." [36] These consist of one or more counties with similar agricultural, economic, and social characteristics, including a special class of Metropolitan State Economic Areas which, with some exceptions, are equivalent to the SMSA's. Figure 11 shows the system of State Economic Areas. Selected economic and population data back to 1900 have been published for these areas. [37] For larger area analyses, Bogue and Beale have developed combinations of State Economic Areas consisting of some 119 "Economic Subregions," also shown in Figure 11. These are intermediate between the State Economic Areas and the next larger division consisting of 13 "Economic Regions," which in turn can be combined to form the largest geographical delineations, consisting of five "Economic Provinces" (see Figure 12). [38]

Conventional Census Areas

The systems of geographical areas employed in standard federal government summaries of population and economic statistics are obviously the most universally used sets of study areas for economic analyses. Not only do these sources provide data in the most convenient and directly usable form, but summaries are published at periodic intervals and thus permit the construction of time series for trend analyses. The sheer labor of tabulation involved in recombining small-area statistics to obtain summaries in terms of other areas becomes a deterrent to the use of new systems of study areas. Even more important, where new areas are created by aggregating small areas, there is the problem of missing detail in the publicly reported small-area summaries because of gaps in data where operations of individual firms would be revealed.

There are two systems of regions used in U.S. Department of Commerce summaries. One is the seven-region subdivision of the nation employed by the Office of Business Economics in their national income series and a few other Department of Commerce summaries (see Figure 13). [39] Information using this system of regions is generally not reported for areas smaller than states. The other system is the nine-region breakdown (called census divisions) used by the Bureau of the Census (see Figure 14). Because the Censuses of Population, Manufactures, and Business are all summarized by

---

[36] *Ibid.* See also Donald J. Bogue, *State Economic Areas,* Washington: U.S. Government Printing Office, 1951.

[37] *Ibid.*

[38] Donald J. Bogue, "An Outline of the Complete System of Economic Areas," *The American Journal of Sociology,* September, 1954.

[39] These delineations are based on the cultural-economic regions of the nation as defined by Howard W. Odum, *Southern Regions of the United States,* Chapel Hill: University of North Carolina Press, 1936. The only difference is the breakdown of Odum's Northeast Region into a Middle East and a New England Region.

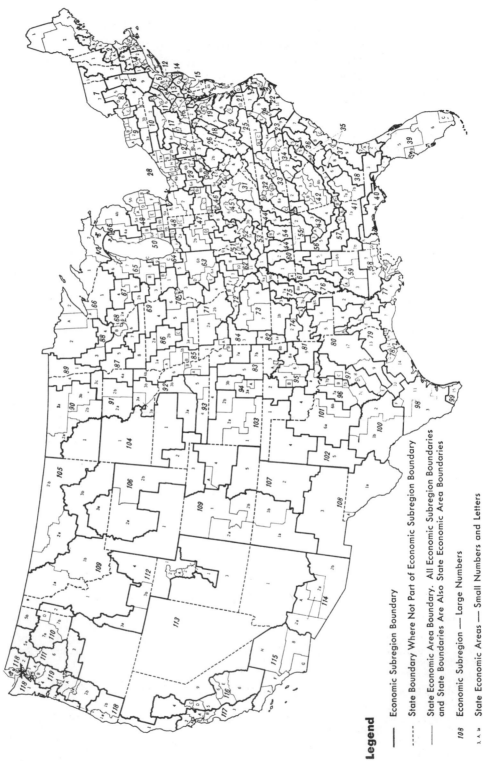

Figure 12. Economic Provinces and Economic Regions, 1950. (*Source:* Donald J. Bogue, "An Outline of the Complete System of Economic Areas," *The American Journal of Sociology*, The University of Chicago Press, September, 1954. Copyright, 1954, by the University of Chicago.)

states, counties, and cities as well as by census divisions, it is the most commonly used system of areas for economic studies.

Further empirical research in the identification of economic areas suitable for studies of economic linkage between the nation and its urban centers is clearly needed. While there are obviously obstacles to realizing completely the flexibility desired in input-output and social accounts analyses, certainly a more functional system of regions and subareas—perhaps on the order of the Bogue-Beale system of homogeneous economic areas—would assist in these analyses. It would appear that some new basis for reporting data on productive activity along the lines of the Bogue-Beale system of economic areas is needed to supplement the conventional system of areas presently used. Meanwhile experience dictates the use of the crude statistical regions and political divisions in general usage in census publications, namely, the nine-region breakdown in Figure 14, the states and the counties.

Figure 11. Economic Subregions and State Economic Areas, 1950. (*Source:* Donald J. Bogue and Calvin L. Beale, "Economic Subregions of the United States," *Farm Population*, Series Census BAE No. 19, Washington: U.S. Government Printing Office, June, 1953.)

Figure 13. Odum's Regions as Modified by the Office of Business Economics, U.S. Department of Commerce.

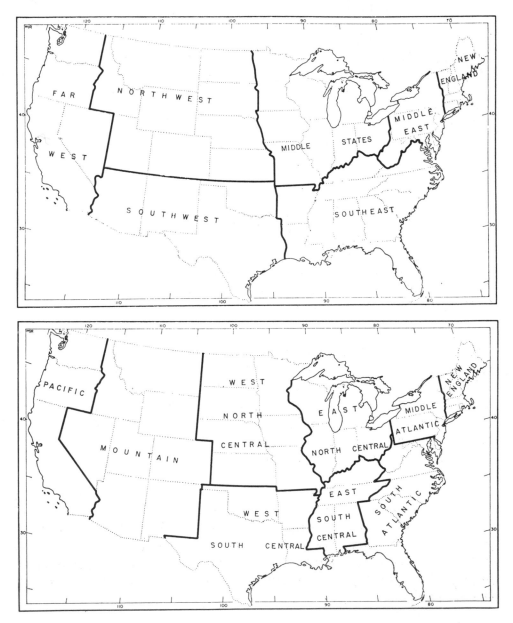

Figure 14. Census Divisions as Used by the Bureau of the Census.

The Economic Base: An Urban-Centered Approach

In contrast to the relatively few instances in which input-output and regional accounts systems of analyses have been used in studying the structure and functioning of the urban economy, the "economic base" approach has received rather extensive applications in city planning analyses. This is perhaps explained partly by the fact that the regional approaches in economic analysis have been adapted to urban studies only fairly recently, partly by the complexities of their analytical procedures, and partly by the mechanical obstacles involved in obtaining data in the form and detail required. In contrast, base analyses employ much simpler analytical procedures and are geared directly to standard sources of data which are regularly reported.

Base theory conceives the structure of the urban economy as made up of two broad classes of productive effort—the basic activities which produce and distribute goods and services for export to firms and individuals outside a defined localized economic area, and the service or nonbasic activities whose goods and services are consumed at home within the confines of this localized economic area. It thus seeks to make a distinction between productive activity which brings new money into the community (basic activity), and productive activity which simply recirculates money which is already there (service activity). The concept holds that basic industry is the key to a city's economic strength, and expansion in basic lines usually means growth in service activities and thus growth in the total economy. In other words, base theory maintains that new money can bring expansion capacity in basic lines and provide the base for growth in service lines. Moreover, it can create new jobs and improve levels of living among those employed on existing jobs, hence providing increments for still further growth.

Some base theorists see the concept as having parallels in international trade theory. Though viewing it in a much simpler context, they direct attention to "export balances" and how these balances become a measure of the strength of the urban economy in much the same manner that export balances have an important influence on the position of the national economy within the framework of international trade. They point out, also, that the balance-of-trade concept holds important implications for understanding changes in the urban economy. Thus, according to base theory, a rising export balance, or more particularly a rising balance of payments, has positive implications for the local economy, but where the export balance falls off and an excess of payments for imports over exports develops and continues over a period of time, this change has negative repercussions and the local economy faces a decline. It might be noted here that while the distinctions between export and local activity are similar in both the base approach and the income and product accounts system of analysis, there are very distinct differences that will become clearer when the systems are examined side by side. Some of these differences will become more evident presently.

Classification of Basic-Service Activity

Hoyt, whose experimentation and work in economic base analysis has provided the contemporary operational model of the base concept now in general use, repeatedly emphasizes that it is the extent to which a city can command income from beyond its borders which is the key element in its growth.[40] He observes that any one or a combination of the following activities are important basic sources for outside income: manufacturing, extractive industry, wholesale and retail trade, finance and banking, and special sources of income such as political, educational, institutional, resort, or amusement activities.

Under such a classification, the service or nonbasic activities are usually represented by local-serving stores, doctors, lawyers, banks, schools, city government, and so on. Base theory recognizes that all categories of economic activity cannot be sharply defined, and there will be some such lines producing for or serving the outside as well as local markets. Thus a portion of the goods of a department store or a portion of the services of a doctor, lawyer, or bank may be consumed beyond the metropolitan area and hence may be classified partly as basic and partly as service.

In dealing with this classification problem, Andrews, who has made perhaps the most exhaustive analysis of the base concept, has introduced some new distinctions into the classification of basic activities.[41] He has suggested that basic industries be analyzed separately as to whether they involve (1) the movement of goods, services, and capital to the consumer or purchaser, or (2) the movement of consumers or purchasers to the goods, services, and capital. In other words, he is proposing a classification

---

[40] See Arthur M. Weimer and Homer Hoyt, *Principles of Real Estate*, New York: The Ronald Press Company, 1960; Homer Hoyt, *The Economic Base of the Brockton, Massachusetts, Area*, Brockton, 1949; and other studies by Hoyt.

[41] Richard B. Andrews, "Mechanics of the Urban Economic Base," *Land Economics*, November, 1953, pp. 344–349. This is one of a series of articles on economic base theory and methods of analysis appearing over a two-year period in *Land Economics*, beginning with the May, 1953, issue. They have since been reprinted in Pfouts (ed.), *The Techniques of Urban Economic Analysis*.

which recognizes the peculiar nature of the export activity—whether an export transaction involves the purchaser coming into the area to receive his goods, services, or capital, or whether the nature of the transaction is such that he receives delivery out of the area. Along with this dual classification of basic activities, he identifies two classes of service activities as meriting separate analysis: (1) that which imports goods, services, and capital for local processing and/or distribution, and (2) that whose goods, services, and capital are entirely locally consumed.

While possibly there are urban areas where a basic-service system of classification can be applied with little or no qualification—particularly in the smaller communities engaged in activities that are mutually independent of one another—the larger the urban center and the more interdependent the lines of activity within this center, the greater the difficulty encountered in applying this system of classification. For example, in a particular metropolitan area, the entire output of, let us say, a number of parts manufacturers may be absorbed in a local exporting fabricating plant. Under the base concept, these parts manufacturers are service activities—their goods are consumed at home. The question arises as to whether it is meaningful to classify them as service activities when functionally they are actually a contributing element in an export activity. Even if it were possible to sort out activities, grouping together the interdependent lines for basic-service analyses, the complex interregional-interindustry relationships in the flow of commodities are not reported in a manner that would readily permit differentiation between "exports" and "imports" of each such functional grouping of "basic" industries so as to obtain a measure of the balance of payments of export over import activity. Moreover, further difficulty is encountered in identifying imports of competitors and taking these into account in classifying what proportion of the output is basic and what is service. Too, it might be observed that in many instances, the existence of these service or ancillary industries are frequently a crucial factor in attracting the basic industry to the urban center in the first place, suggesting that service lines may be more important in some cases in achieving urban growth than the pre-existence of basic activity there. These problems will be discussed further in the concluding section below.

Delimiting the Base Area

Base theory recognizes that the determination of what activities are basic and what ones are service can be markedly influenced by where the lines of the base area are drawn. If the city limits are selected as the perimeter of the base area, an entirely different description of economic structure is obtained than if the Standard Metropolitan Statistical Area or the grouping of several counties had been selected. Indeed, it is pointed out that an entirely misleading picture of the makeup of the economy is obtained if the base area is taken to be the incorporated area alone. How, then, is an area defined for the purposes of economic base analyses, or, for that matter, for any economic studies that the analyst desires to make?

As a point of departure, it is useful to examine the tests for defining a metropolitan area as advanced by Gras in 1922:

Where the systems of transportation begin to veer off toward other metropolitan centers.

The radius served by the metropolitan press and other advertising media.

The dependence of outlying financial institutions on the center for clearances and reserves.

Whether it is the center from which the retailers in a borderline town direct their supplies.

Whether the borderline town is independent or dependent upon the center for many of the following functions: (1) storage for the convenience of consumer, retailer, wholesaler, manufacturer, shipper; (2) whether the outlying producer markets directly to the local consumer or through the metropolitan machinery; (3) whether a borderline community communicates by rail, telephone, etc., through the center or independently of it; (4) where the borderline town sends its surplus products for disposal or storage; (5) whether a firm or industry which boasts its independence in some one respect, e.g., the marketing of its wares, is or is not dependent upon the center for its supplies and finances; and (6) whether the borderline town is too far away to avail itself of the central assemblage of museums, theaters, libraries, institutions of learning, and where it looks for guidance in fashions, tastes, and amusements.[42]

Obviously, even within the limits of these criteria, there is considerable latitude of choice for delineating the study area. In the absence of some systematic basis for indicating which of such criteria are most suitable to use as guides in defining a local economic area, the primary trade area is often selected as "the best fit."

Even accepting the expediency of using the primary or retail trade area as the local economic area, there is no universal agreement as to how the limits of this area are to be tied down finally. One approach identifies a "consensus area" of several available trade area delineations, using as the local economic area the grouping of counties which is most frequently included in these trade area delineations. The available trade area delinea-

[42] N. S. B. Gras in Thomas Adams, Harold M. Lewis, and Theodore T. McCrosky, "Population, Land Values and Government," *Regional Survey of New York and Environs,* II, Regional Plan of New York and Its Environs, 1929, p. 201.

tions may include ones identified in national studies,[43] those defined for the local newspapers by the Audit Bureau of Circulation, those defined by local credit, merchant, and similar groups, the area defined as containing the bulk of the charge accounts of local department stores, and so on.

An empirical approach to the problem was developed by Reilly on the basis of observations made in some 132 American urban areas in the late 'twenties and early 'thirties. His *law of retail gravitation* states that "two cities attract retail trade from any intermediate city or town in the vicinity of the breaking point approximately in direct proportion to the populations of the two cities and in inverse proportion to the square of the distances from these two cities to the intermediate town." [44] The breaking point is "a point up to which one city exercises the dominating retail trade influence, and beyond which the other city dominates." [45] The distance is measured along the most direct improved highway.

In addition to developing a formula to compute the location of breaking points, Reilly also supplies tables for those interested only in approximating these locations. He notes that in addition to population size and distance, there are other factors which may introduce variations in the definition of a retail trade area, for example, transportation facilities, lines of communication, business attractions such as delivery and credit services and banking facilities, social and amusement attractions, parking facilities, business leadership in the city, and so on. A comparison of Reilly's trade areas with those outlined by the Audit Bureau of Circulation for three North Carolina cities is shown in Figure 15.

Another technique for delineating the retail trade area is through a consumer survey. This may be done on a sampling basis by means of household interviews in which families indicate where they go for household goods and services. Because of the expense of conducting such a survey, it is not always practicable to consider the use of this technique in local economic studies. Sometimes, however, such surveys can be combined with consumer expenditure surveys or similar field studies made for other purposes, and sometimes it may be practicable to undertake a limited survey confined to the peripheral areas, where the survey is used to sharpen delineations established by methods described above. Another approach, the reverse of the consumer-type survey, namely, a sampling survey of retail

---

[43] For example, see delineations of the Commercial Research Division of the Curtis Publishing Company, *Market Areas in the United States,* Philadelphia: Curtis Publishing Company, 1956; Lewis F. Thomas and Robert M. Crisler, *A Manual of the Economic Geography of the United States Based on Trade Areas and Geographic Regions,* St. Louis: Educational Publishers, 1953.

[44] William J. Reilly, *The Law of Retail Gravitation,* New York: G. P. Putnam Sons, 1931, p. 9.

[45] *Ibid.,* p. 8.

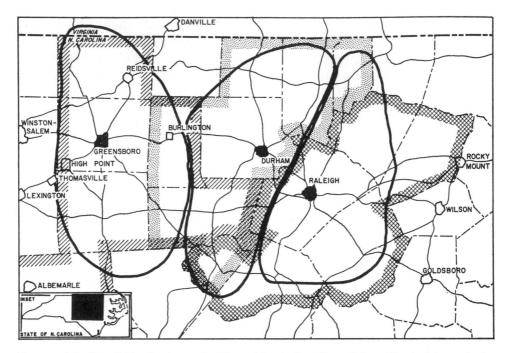

Figure 15. Retail Trade Areas in Three North Carolina Cities. Shaded boundaries identify trade areas as defined by the Audit Bureau of Circulation for local newspapers, and the solid heavy lines identify the theoretical trade areas determined by applying Reilly's law of retail gravitation.

and service establishments, is essentially the consensus approach described above. Still another approach, and usually combined with a parking survey, is the systematic recording of automobile license plate numbers of all cars parked in central or regional shopping centers. When these numbers are checked for home address on the license registration books, it is possible to estimate the extent of the retail trade area. Whatever approach or combination of approaches may be employed, usually the final result is translated into one or more counties, so that standard sources of data may be used in the economic analyses.

Measurement of Basic-Service Activity

Having briefly examined the rationale of the economic base concept, the generally accepted system for the classification of economic activity into basic and service components, and methods of delineating the local economic area, it is now possible to consider techniques of measurement. To apply the base theory to operational situations, some means of distinguishing and quantifying the basic and service components is necessary. According to the economic base concept, the measure employed must identify what lines of economic activity and how much of each line can be ascribed to one component or the other, and it must be capable of establishing the relative quantitative position of each basic line to every other one.

Andrews identifies six units of measure which are either in use or have been proposed for use at one time or another: employment, payrolls, value added, value of production, physical production, and dollar income and expenditure accounts for an entire urban area.[46] The last is the measure employed in social accounting analyses. It provides the most comprehensive and complete measure of economic activity, including a measure not only of goods and service transactions but also of capital. However, because of the complexity and difficulty of tracing monetary transactions, especially considering the form in which data are currently reported in standard sources, it is not yet widely used. The physical production, the value added, and the value of production approaches have advantages for analyses within particular sectors of the economy, but because they do not apply to some sectors of economic activity (even excluding capital transactions), the use of these measures is regarded as limited. Because of these difficulties, the two remaining measures are in most general usage, with employment commonly used as the primary measure and payroll data being used as a supplemental means of examining each basic line.

However, among those who have experimented with base techniques, it is generally recognized that, while offering certain obvious advantages in data availability, employment as a measuring unit for basic and service activity poses several problems. First of all, while providing a yardstick for production and distribution functions as basic activity, employment obviously has no meaning as a measure of capital export. Second, where historical studies or investigations of change are contemplated, raw employment data do not reflect important derivative considerations such as changing worker productivity (output per worker per unit of time). For example, if employment in a particular line is viewed as the quotient of the total annual output and the annual output per worker in that line, an increase in employment can be attributed to a variety of combinations of these two factors. Thus lower productivity at the same level of total output would yield an employment increase. Similarly, a constant value for worker productivity and an increase in output would have the same effect, or differential increases in both could result in rising employment. Moreover, if the analysis is extended to derivative considerations, let us say to

---

[46] Andrews, "Mechanics of the Urban Economic Base," *Land Economics*, February, 1954, pp. 52–60.

those of worker productivity, it can readily be seen that output per worker can increase because of rising wage rates, overtime work, more efficient management practices, improved machinery, and so on. Thus it is evident that the use of employment data alone as a measure may obscure a variety of underlying trends of change in the structure of the urban economy.

With or without qualifying assumptions concerning these factors, employment is the universally used unit of measurement in applications of base theory. In such applications, it is customary to express the basic-service relationship as a ratio of the number of workers in service or secondary lines to every worker in basic lines. (In some quarters this ratio has been expressed in terms of service workers per 100 basic workers.) Among those who have experimented with the technique, it is now generally recognized that the numerical value of this ratio varies from one urban area to another. For estimating or comparative purposes, a norm ratio of 1.5 to 2 service workers to every basic worker has been suggested.[47] While such fixed norms have been the object of some experimentation in making approximations of basic and service employment in studies of completely new towns or of towns facing a sudden very large expansion in economic activity, locally derived ratios are favored in the more usual situation in established urban centers.

Adherents of base theory point out that there can be a relatively sizable range of variation in the value of this ratio from urban center to urban center, even when allowances are made for differences in criteria used in setting the boundaries of the local economic area. Variations in ratio values of from 0.5 to 2.0 workers in service lines to every worker in basic lines are not uncommon. Students of the base approach also suggest that these values do not necessarily remain constant for long periods of time, pointing out that the detailed study of one center alone can show change in the ratio over a period of time depending upon changes in the economy of the urban area and national economic conditions. For example, using approximation methods discussed below, a test of one North Carolina city showed changes over a 20-year period from 1.46 to 1.11 to 1.48.

The preferred method of determining what proportion of current employment is engaged in activities which export, and what proportion is engaged in activities producing for local consumption, is through a local economic survey. Usually employing sampling techniques, such a survey establishes the percentage of sales during the preceding year which were local and nonlocal. Thus the survey determines the percentage of locally manufactured goods sold at home and in more distant places, the percentage

---

[47] See *Planning Community Facilities for Basic Employment Expansion*, Technical Bulletin No. 16, Washington: Urban Land Institute, September, 1951.

allocation of wholesale and retail sales, the percentage allocation of receipts in places of amusement, hotels, tourist establishments, garages, gas stations, and other service industries, the percentage distribution of bank depositors and loans, and so on down the list. Once these percentages are available, they are then applied to total employment figures (recorded in the survey) for each line of activity to obtain basic and service employment. This method is illustrated in the Albuquerque study.[48] These ratio estimators, of course, apply only in sectors of the economy in which employment is used as a measurement unit, which means that such sectors as private domestic investment are excluded from the analysis.

Even though such a survey yields primary data assembled especially for basic-service analyses, the method is not without its problems. For example, in some lines, particularly in manufacturing, results of such a survey obviously do not reflect figures for local consumption of goods from outside competitive manufacturers producing the same lines as the local establishments. To get at the net exports, then, would involve properly constructed sampling surveys of consumer firms and consumer households. But assuming these problems can be overcome, the survey itself can offer other difficulties. The survey method is just as accurate as the reliability of the responses received. Some interviewees may not want to reveal their markets. If the managements interviewed do not have their records ordered according to the delineation of the local economic area that has been selected to differentiate between local and outside markets, they are compelled to employ estimates. If it develops that estimates are required in a large number of cases, the possibilities of error are that much greater. Finally, there is the very compelling consideration of the time and expense involved in undertaking the sampling survey. Such surveys have been employed in several medium-size and small cities, but have never been undertaken in the large metropolitan centers. In these areas presumably the magnitude of the task and the cost have been deterring considerations.

An approximation technique, perfected by Hoyt and employed in his study for the New York Regional Plan Association, is frequently used when time and cost do not permit use of the approach discussed above. It makes use of data available from such standard sources as the Census of Manufactures, the Census of Population, Sales Management, Inc., publications, and other sources. This technique assumes that the population of a particular urban area consumes its proportionate share of the national production of goods and services and that all production in excess of this amount may be considered basic. For lines of activity where consumption tends to

---

[48] Federal Reserve Bank of Kansas City and Bureau of Business Research, University of New Mexico, *The Economy of Albuquerque, New Mexico*, Kansas City: Federal Reserve Bank of Kansas City, 1949, pp. 20–46.

vary with consumer income, the locality's share of the national purchasing power is used as a measure of local consumption, but in a few lines, such as the manufacture of food staples where consumption tends to be independent of income, the locality's population as a percentage of the national population is used as a measure of local consumption.

Thus basic employment in manufacturing is estimated by first determining, for each standard census classification of manufacturing activity, the percentage that the city's total number of workers in each line of activity is of the total number in each equivalent line in the country as a whole, and then comparing this figure with the city's share of the U.S. purchasing power or population.[49] For each line in which the city's showing in the employment ratio exceeds the city's showing in the purchasing power or population ratio, the increment in excess is attributed to basic activity. By converting these increments into employment figures and totaling them for all manufacturing lines, the technique arrives at a total basic employment in manufacturing.[50]

By similar analyses of wholesale and retail trade, finance, the professions, transportation government, and other classes of economic activity, the technique estimates basic employment in each of these lines. Totaled, these estimates are used as an approximation of all basic employment in the urban area.

This technique is sometimes used in estimating future changes in the structure of the local economy. Where projective estimates are attempted, this approach, as in the case of the other approaches discussed above, requires a "given" forecast of national levels of demand in each line. In generalized form, the procedure used involves: (1) analysis of past trends in each line of the local area's basic activity relative to national trends in these lines, (2) projection of these local trends forward in time, considering the estimated future national demand levels in each such line, and

---

[49] Estimates of a city's share of the total U.S. purchasing power for any year can be obtained from *Sales Management* magazine's "Survey of Buying Power" issue, published each year in the spring.

[50] A variation on this approach is used in the Cincinnati study which compares the total U.S. employment in each line of activity, expressed as a per cent of the U.S. population, to the equivalent local percentage. In using this approach, the Cincinnati study made various adjustments to correct for differences between national and local consumption characteristics. Another variation on this approach employs a "location quotient" and uses the ratio of national employment in an industry to total national employment to obtain a ratio to be applied to total local employment in estimating the local-serving or nonbasic component. Still another variation is the "minimum requirements" technique in which the location quotients for each sector of the economy for the entire universe of cities in the nation of the size group in which the study city falls are calculated and arrayed in rank order. The lowest ratio in each sector, no matter in what city it happens to occur, is used in estimating the proportion of local employment in that line which can be considered local-serving or nonbasic. (See Edward L. Ullman and Michael F. Dacey, "The Minimum Requirements Approach to the Urban Economic Base," *Papers and Proceedings of the Regional Science Association,* VI, Philadelphia: University of Pennsylvania, 1960.)

(3) expansion of basic employment estimates for the locality thus derived to total employment by applying an assumed future ratio of service to basic employment. The above procedure assumes the use of direct local to national ratios.

Criticisms of Base Theory

The seeming simplicity of the base concept as a means for analyzing economic activity in an urban area is probably responsible for much of its present-day appeal. Indeed, it may have obscured some of its limitations, for if it is interpreted in an unqualified manner, it can unwittingly lead to some fallacious and contradictory results. For example, Pfouts has suggested that an extension of base theory that adheres too closely to mercantilist doctrines and a favorable balance of trade is open to serious question, pointing out that the precursor system of thought, bent on supporting the homeland to the detriment of colonies and foreign nations, has largely been discredited.[51] Closely related to this question, Pfouts asks: Can all cities reasonably try to develop by promoting basic industry? Assuming basic industry is actually identifiable, can it be demonstrated that a large proportion of basic industry will always result in community growth and stability? Are there not other variables to consider such as the value of wage payments in basic industry? Similarly, even if it can be shown that an appreciable proportion of basic industry is necessary for urban growth and development, does it follow that this alone is sufficient for growth and development?

In some preliminary but exhaustive statistical tests, Pfouts has found evidence to suggest that there is no significant relationship between basic activity as measured by the above-described approximation approach and population growth.[52] Indeed, his tests suggest that if the crude dual classification of economic activity involved in the base system of analysis has validity, the service component may be more important as an indicator of growth potential than the basic component.[53] Having thus raised serious questions concerning this system of analysis, Pfouts then turns his attention

---

[51] From an outline of a study of *Economic Base Theory and Urban Development,* Chapel Hill: Institute for Research in Social Science, University of North Carolina, 1955.

[52] Ralph W. Pfouts, "An Empirical Testing of the Economic Base Theory," *Journal of the American Institute of Planners,* Spring, 1957. This and his article with Erle T. Curtis, "Limitations of the Economic Base Analysis," *Social Forces,* May, 1958, have been reprinted in Pfouts (ed.), *The Techniques of Urban Economic Analysis.*

[53] Relationships were examined in some 27 cities with an SMSA population between 100,000 and 300,000. In dividing them into diversified and manufacturing groups, Pfouts found that in the latter group a fairly strong relationship existed but that it was opposite of what would be expected from interpretations of the base theory.

to an alternative approach to the study of the urban economy. Drawing on general economic theory and supporting it with illustrative mathematical formulations, he poses the possibility of community income analysis as a substitute approach worthy of exploration. "Why should such great emphasis be placed on exports? . . . Are exports of such overwhelming importance that such variables as imports, savings, value-added, etc. can be safely neglected? . . . Surely it can be argued that imports, since they represent money leaving the community, should be given a place in considering the income stream within the community. Similarly, the amounts that individuals within the community save represent money withdrawn from the income stream within the community. These observations suggest that simple income models similar to national income models can be drawn up for the individual community." He is of course referring to the kind of approach discussed above as income and product accounts.

In a penetrating critique of the base concept as it has been used in recent years, Blumenfeld identifies what he considers to be a number of misconceptions and contradictory interpretations of base theory.[54] Acknowledging that the concept has some value in learning about market areas of local economic activity and about the competitive advantages and disadvantages of an urban center, he questions its meaningfulness in predictive studies, especially in metropolitan areas, and raises questions concerning the traditional distinction between basic and nonbasic activity. ". . . If an area produces its normal share of, say, electrical machinery, it would be completely erroneous to assume that this is 'nonbasic' industry working exclusively for the local market. It is entirely possible, and indeed quite probable, that most locally produced machinery is exported, while at the same time most locally consumed electrical machinery is imported." He points out that by carrying the quantification of import-export relationships to their logical conclusion, they get into the intraurban ramifications of purchases and sales between local economic activities in the production process. The distinction between basic and nonbasic then becomes "a function of the inner organization of the industry: the higher the degree of specialization and differentiation . . . the higher is the 'nonbasic' share." Blumenfeld then goes on to observe that if the economy of an urban area is thus viewed as an integrated whole of mutually interdependent activities, "the distinction between 'basic' and 'nonbasic' seems to dissolve in thin air." [55]

Blumenfeld notes that the applicability of the basic-nonbasic concept

[54] Hans Blumenfeld, "The Economic Base of the Metropolis," *Journal of the American Institute of Planners*, Fall, 1955. (The same article appears in Pfouts (ed.), *The Techniques of Urban Economic Analysis*.)

[55] *Ibid.*, pp. 120–121.

tends to decrease with increasing size of an urban center, suggesting that the numerical value of the ratio tends to be highest in small, relatively new cities and lowest in large, mature ones. He also notes that applicability tends to increase with increasing specialization and division of labor between centers and tends to decrease the greater the amount of nonwage income flowing into or out of a center. He maintains that the large metropolitan areas exist, survive, and grow because their highly developed business and consumer services enable them to substitute new export industries for those that decline, that these nonbasic activities are the permanent and constant element, indeed, the truly "basic" element of the metropolitan area economy, while the export activities are variable, subject to continual change and replacement, and thus more truly the "service" elements.

On the basis of these and other observations he makes in his critique, Blumenfeld urges an approach (especially in larger metropolitan area studies of the urban economy) which emphasizes in place of the basic-service dichotomy what he calls "criticality" and "balance of payments" studies. A criticality study would be concerned with the potential vulnerability of local economic activity from outside competition and the potential capacity of the local economic activity to expand into outside markets; and a balance of payments study would be concerned with actual sales—"all types of payments, and giving equal weight to both sides of the ledger [the import and the export sides]." [56]

If we disregard descriptive studies such as the "approximation analysis" noted above, we have been viewing the urban economy in terms of essentially three conceptual systems—input-output analysis, income and product accounts analysis, and economic base analysis. By now it must be apparent that there are similarities in all three systems, that by shifts in emphasis, by changes in measurement units, or by expanding or reducing the number of sectors included, one system becomes more like one of the other two. While general descriptive studies still seem to predominate in planning agency investigations of the economy, the next most common form of analysis is the economic base study. Both of these approaches serve a purpose in sketching out a general view of the urban economy. As the planning program advances to a more detailed stage, insights provided by the more detailed analyses of an input-output or regional accounts approach may be very important. In the final analysis the approach followed will be determined by the use to which the study is to be put and such considerations as budget for the study, the stage of the technical program, and so on.

---

[56] *Ibid.*, p. 122.

Vitality of the Economy

While the makeup of the urban economy, considered in terms of the extent of economic activity and population it supports, influences the amount of land which will go into use, the general health of the economy is an important determinant of the rate at which land will go into use. In short, the vitality of the local economy is a key consideration in whether land development is active or sluggish in the urban area and whether whole areas stagnate and become vulnerable to urban blight.

The general vitality of the economy is customarily described in terms of such factors as stability, balance, worker productivity, and quality of economic leadership. Stability refers to capacity of the economy both to weather the business cycle over the years and to absorb the seasonal business changes in any single year. Balance is usually expressed in terms of diversification in productive activity, and productivity refers to output per worker at prevailing wage levels for the prevailing standard work week.

In assessing the susceptibility of an urban center to fluctuations in national economic activity, Ernest and Robert Fisher have suggested that the character of local industry, the scope of its markets, and its relative diversification and concentration will be particularly important considerations.[57] With respect to the character of local economic activity, they note that industries least susceptible to fluctuations tend to be: (1) those whose products and services cater to a broad consuming base as measured by personal and corporate income, for example, industries dealing in low- and medium-price lines as opposed to high-price lines; (2) those producing goods and services the purchase of which is least postponable by the consumer, for example, nondurable as opposed to durable; (3) those that have the most favorable prospects for long-term growth of demand; (4) those in the extractive category that have substantial resource reserves on which to draw; and (5) those dealing in consumer goods and services as opposed to those dealing in producer goods and services (except where producer goods industries are producing for stable types of consumer goods industries).

With scope of the market measured in terms of population served and its purchasing power, the Fishers observe that the greater the scope, the more stable the urban economy tends to be. In the matter of diversification and concentration, they mention that a wide spread in the type of economic activity as between manufacturing, trade, construction, and so on, in addition to variety within the manufacturing category alone, is more con-

---

[57] Ernest M. and Robert M. Fisher, *Urban Real Estate*, New York: Henry Holt and Company, 1954, pp. 280–294.

ducive to a stable urban economy. Where these conditions exist and where there is spread of employment and payrolls among a variety of firms and no marked interdependence among these firms, more stable conditions are apt to exist. "Probably the most favorable combination is represented by an economic base composed of numerous strong, independent firms (preferably dominated by industries, such as government, with relatively small income volatilities) with complementary labor requirements and high average wages and salaries, turning out a large variety of low-priced, nondurable consumers' goods and services distributed widely over separate markets, from a community whose operating statement and rate of savings are both positive and whose balance sheet reveals a great number of comparative advantages held by it over rival areas." [58]

Although not without their limitations, there have been some attempts to develop objective measures of the cyclical stability of various kinds of economic activity. One such measure has been suggested by Denison.[59] It employs a technique of classifying private nonagricultural industries in the nation as a whole with respect to their sensitivity to cyclical changes in the level of national income. The Denison study first computed the percentage that the income of each private nonagricultural industry in the nation was of total private nonagricultural income for the years from 1929 to 1947, inclusive. Taking the span from 1929 to 1937 as containing the downward movement of the business cycle in the last great depression, for each industry, the study next used a straight-line interpolation between these years to obtain percentages for 1932 and 1933 which might have been expected had 1932 and 1933 been prosperous years and had the trend (assumed to be linear) been the only factor which affected the industrial distribution of income from 1929 to 1937. Next, for all industries the ratio of the actual percentage to the hypothetical percentage was computed separately for the two depression years 1932 and 1933 and then averaged to give a single ratio. The final ratio, termed the "stability ratio," was used as a measure of cyclical stability during the depression.

Those industries whose income trend was exactly like that of the aggregate of private nonagricultural industries had a stability ratio of 1.00. A higher ratio indicated that income originating in the industry fluctuated less during the depression than the income of the aggregate of industries. Those industries which had no cyclical variation maintained a ratio of 2.11. A ratio below 1.00 indicated that the particular industry's income was more affected by the depression cycle than the income for the private nonagri-

---

[58] *Ibid.*, p. 301.
[59] Edward F. Denison, "Industrial Composition of National Income," *Survey of Current Business,* December, 1948, pp. 11–27.

cultural industries as a whole. The practical minimum ratio was zero, though theoretically it could be negative. Table 9 shows Denison's grouping of private nonagricultural industries by degree of sensitivity, with the range of the stability ratio shown beside each group.

This measure of the relative cyclical stability of various lines of private nonagricultural economic activity was developed primarily with the purpose in view of examining fluctuations in the national economy. It has certain limitations when applied to the economy of a particular urban center. The characteristics observed in the national scene should not be attributed to local industries without a careful analysis of the pattern of relationships among industries, within the local area and within the larger region. For example, while a durable goods industry, such as one producing furniture, may generally be regarded as sensitive to national fluctuations, it may have a long record of highly stable sales made largely to stable nondurable goods industries. In the final analysis, investigations into factors of this kind provide the surest means of assessing the susceptibility of the local economy to fluctuations.

In a study of the effects of diversification of manufacturing industry on local economic development, Rodgers developed a gross measure of diversification and applied it to 93 SMSA's with manufacturing employment exceeding 20,000.[60] Using 22 industrial groups appearing in the U.S. Census of Population, he developed indices of diversification for the 93 SMSA's. Table 10 is Rodgers' illustration of the procedure for deriving his "refined index" as applied to Indianapolis. After ranking employment percentages from highest to lowest, he sums the cumulative percentage totals to obtain his "crude index of diversification." Where industries are absent, he uses totals of 100 per cent. Thus in the extreme situation where a single industry contains all the recorded manufacturing employment, the crude index would be 2200, or the situation of least diversification. By applying this procedure to the totals for all 93 SMSA's, he found that the crude index for all urban centers was 1553. The derivation of the refined index is indicated in Table 10.

These computations were made for all 93 SMSA's and the refined indices divided into five broad groups: highly diversified (Group I), moderately diversified (Group II), average diversification (Group III), moderately specialized (Group IV), and highly specialized (Group V). Figure 16 shows the geographical distribution of the 93 SMSA's and the regional

[60] Allan Rodgers, "Some Aspects of Industrial Diversification in the United States," *Papers and Proceedings of the Regional Science Association,* I, Philadelphia: University of Pennsylvania, 1955.

Table 9. Classification of Private Nonagricultural Industries by Stability Groups[a]

GROUP I (highly insensitive)—2.06 to 1.38

Tobacco manufactures
Air Transportation (common carriers)
Religious organizations
Educational services, not elsewhere classified
Nonprofit membership organization, not elsewhere classified
Legal services
Utilities: electric and gas

Insurance agents and combination offices
Local railways and bus lines
Miscellaneous repair services and hand trades
Telephone, telegraph, and related services
Medical and other health services
Highway freight transportation and warehousing
Anthracite mining

GROUP II (markedly insensitive)—1.32 to 1.14

Insurance carriers
Personal services
Local utilities and public services, not elsewhere classified
Pipeline transportations
Real estate

Food and kindred products
Highway passenger transportation, not elsewhere classified
Printing, publishing, and allied industries
Business services, not elsewhere classified
Engineering and other professional services, not elsewhere classified

GROUP III (average cyclical sensitivity)—1.13 to 0.88

Chemicals and allied products
Leather and leather products
Water transportation
Railroads
Private households
Paper and allied products
Amusement and recreation, except motion pictures
Wholesale trade

Retail trade and automobile services
Motion pictures
Apparel and other finished fabric products
Services allied to transportation
Hotels and other lodging places
Radio broadcasting and television
Security and commodity brokers, dealers, and exchanges
Banking

GROUP IV (markedly sensitive)—0.87 to 0.64

Textile mill products
Crude petroleum and natural gas production
Bituminous and other soft coal mining
Commercial and trade schools and employment agencies

Rubber products
Furniture and finished lumber products
Miscellaneous manufacturing industries
Contract construction

GROUP V (highly sensitive)—0.56 to —0.35

Electrical machinery
Nonmetallic mining and quarrying
Transportation equipment except automobiles
Nonferrous metals and their products
Stone, clay, and glass products
Automobiles and automobile equipment

Machinery (except electrical)
Iron and steel and their products, including ordnance
Lumber and timber basic products
Products of petroleum and coal
Metal mining
Finance, not elsewhere classified

[a] Adapted from Edward F. Denison, "Industrial Composition of National Income," *Survey of Current Business,* December, 1948, p. 15.

Table 10. Illustration of Method for Determining Index of Diversification as Applied to Indianapolis Industrial Area, 1950[a]

	Employment by Industrial Group	Per Cent	Ranked Percentage [b]	Cumulative Addition [b]
1. Lumber and wood	831	1.08	13.33	13.33
2. Furniture	1,085	1.41	12.47	25.80
3. Stone, clay, and glass	1,200	1.56	11.32	37.12
4. Primary metals	4,092	5.32	9.73	46.85
5. Fabricated metals	6,256	8.13	8.19	55.04
6. Machinery except electrical	9,596	12.47	8.13	63.17
7. Electrical machinery	10,256	13.33	6.63	69.80
8. Transportation equipment	4,444	5.78	5.78	75.58
9. Motor vehicles	7,488	9.73	5.32	80.90
10. Professional equipment	636	0.83	2.94	83.84
11. Miscellaneous durable	1,571	2.04	2.87	86.71
12. Food and kindred	8,712	11.32	2.59	89.30
13. Tobacco	43	0.06	2.04	91.34
14. Textiles	1,996	2.59	1.98	93.22
15. Apparel	1,524	1.98	1.56	94.88
16. Paper and allied	2,262	2.94	1.41	96.29
17. Printing and publishing	5,101	6.63	1.08	97.37
18. Chemical and allied	6,300	8.19	0.97	98.34
19. Petroleum and coal	424	0.55	0.83	99.17
20. Rubber	2,210	2.87	0.55	99.72
21. Leather	173	0.22	0.22	99.94
22. Not specified	745	0.97	0.06	100.00
Total	76,945	100.00	Crude Diversification Index	1,697.71

$$\text{Refined index} = \frac{\text{Actual crude index} - \text{Crude index for all industrial areas}}{\text{Crude index for least diversity} - \text{Crude index for all industrial areas}}$$

Example: Indianapolis

$$\text{Refined index} = \frac{1698 - 1553}{2200 - 1553} = \frac{145}{647}$$

Refined index = 0.224

[a] Allan Rodgers, "Some Aspects of Industrial Diversification in the United States," *Papers and Proceedings of the Regional Science Association*, I, Philadelphia: University of Pennsylvania, 1955.

[b] Figures in these columns are rearrangements of percentage figures in the second column, and thus do not correspond with industrial categories in the stub of the table.

variations in diversification based on 1950 census data with the legend showing the range of index values used for each of the five groups. The Flint SMSA was the most specialized (index value of 934) and the Philadelphia SMSA the most diversified (index value of 36). The reader is referred to Rodgers' paper for interpretations of the regional distribution patterns and to his supplemental studies of changes in diversification patterns in time. He observes that "any index of this nature tends to mask elements in the pattern of individual areas. Thus high indices can result from concentration on one or more industries. In addition, the index gives no indication of the composition of industry in an area, such as employment in the production of durable versus nondurable goods, which may be highly significant in an analysis of diversification."

In a very useful research monograph, Rapkin and his colleagues have developed an index by which it is possible to measure some of the factors of diversification and concentration cited above from the work of the Fishers.[61] It utilizes two elements of economic diversification: the relative number of industries operating in a local area, and the distribution of employment among these industries. Applied to a particular locality, the index involves the statistical computation of the extent to which the number of workers in each industry deviates from the average number of workers per industry to indicate the degree of diffusion or concentration of employment. While evaluation of all factors affecting diversification involves a more extensive analysis of the economy, such an index is useful in quantifying two important factors of diversification.

Most efforts toward evaluating the whole range of factors affecting the vitality of the economy are somewhat subjective extensions of the economic base type of analysis. For the most part, these approaches examine the national and local record of employment for the urban area's existing basic industries in relation to the business cycle and note which ones are subject to marked seasonal variations in employment. Then, considering local labor, capital, and natural resources, a tentative list of industries is prescribed as offering good prospects for diversifying the economy, matching local skills and other resources, and having high levels of productivity.

The work of Denison and that of Rodgers contribute some useful techniques for identifying weaknesses in the makeup of the economy, but clearly the range of techniques for evaluating the vitality of economic activity in a metropolitan area needs to be extended. Some attempts have been made to develop composite measures of vitality based on wage categories,

---

[61] Chester Rapkin, Louis Winnick, and David M. Blank, *Housing Market Analysis, a Study of Theory and Methods,* a Housing and Home Finance Agency research monograph, Washington: U.S. Government Printing Office, December, 1953, pp. 88–90.

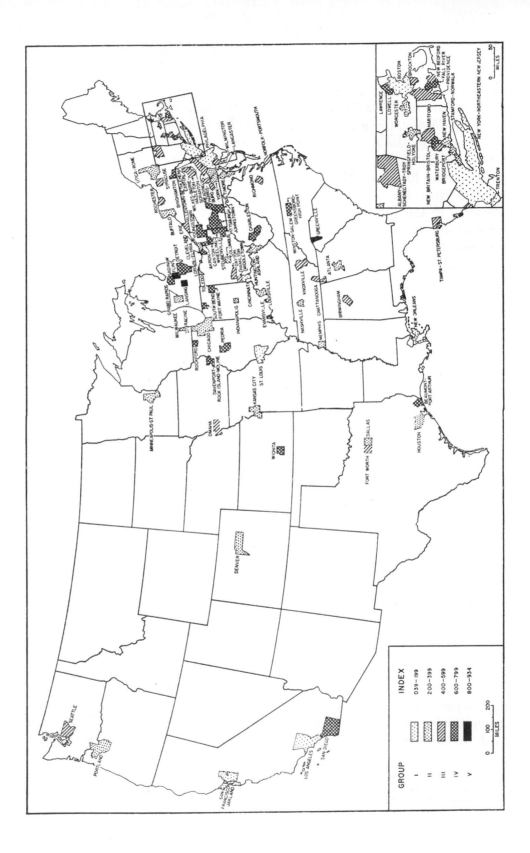

productivity, skill levels, and stability, but eventually such efforts must be tied more directly into one or more of the three basic approaches to the analysis of the structure of the economy.

Figure 16. Industrial Diversification in 93 Standard Metropolitan Statistical Areas, 1950. This map shows the distribution of cities by the degree of diversification as determined by Rodgers' refined index. The range varies from highly diversified (Group I) to highly specialized (Group V). (*Source:* Allan Rodgers, "Some Aspects of Industrial Diversification in the United States," *Papers and Proceedings of the Regional Science Association*, I, Philadelphia: University of Pennsylvania, 1955.)

Chapter 4

Employment Studies

In the foregoing discussion of the structure and vitality of the urban economy, it was seen that employment is one of the most common units for measuring economic activity. Although imperfect as a measure of many qualitative aspects of economic growth, if allowances are made for these imperfections, it represents an extremely useful unit of measurement for scaling land development requirements. It is this kind of application of employment data that is of ultimate concern here. A review of the more broadly focused analyses in all their complex aspects that the economist might undertake for his needs is beyond the scope of this discussion. Moreover, to be consistent with our own admonishments above, the studies described in this chapter are morally bound to those which have specific application to land use planning analyses. In particular, these have to do with techniques of forecasting employment in the urban study area.

In the land use planning process, the employment forecast serves two specific purposes: (1) it provides information of concern to population studies which in turn are used in estimating space needs for residential areas and community facilities, and (2) it supplies a direct yardstick for use in scaling land requirements for industrial and commercial areas. As brought out in some detail in Chapter 5, perhaps the most important variable affecting the population growth of an urban area is the migration component. Since migration tends to be regulated by economic opportunity, that is, employment prospects, the employment forecast provides the means for estimating the effect that migration will have on population trends in the urban study area. The second purpose has a more obvious application to land use planning. In industrial areas, space requirements are estimated on the basis of adopted industrial density standards, that is, manufacturing workers per acre of industrially used land, or standards of a more detailed nature based on floor area, shift size, and structural density. In wholesale areas, space requirements are derived from various floor area standards of employees per square foot of building space in wholesaling, truck terminal, and related warehousing uses, and in business areas, office space requirements are developed on the basis of floor area standards relating employment in professional services, finance, insurance, and real estate to space taken up in this category of use. In such applications, employment forecasts thus play a vital role.

General Considerations of Forecasting

At the outset, some comment is perhaps in order concerning the skepticism sometimes encountered outside the field in the use of employment forecasts in city planning studies. Some of this reaction is warranted, especially where it is premised on the loose use of forecast data or techniques without regard to the elemental qualifications and assumptions which go with the forecast. However, where there is real understanding and prudent recognition of these limitations in city planning analyses, there are mitigating circumstances which may not be generally recognized by people outside the field.

In most applications of forecast data in land use planning—for example, in estimating industrial land requirements—there is some latitude for inaccuracy. The use of industrial employee density standards in conjunction with a forecast of manufacturing employment yields a tentative estimate of the new acreage required to accommodate normal industrial expansion. But then in the same way that civil engineers introduce safety factors which make the designed capacity of a bridge considerably in excess of maximum loads anticipated, the city planner usually provides for an "industrial reserve" or a safety factor in his estimates of space requirements which introduces into the result an increment well over the amount of land estimated to be needed to take care of normal growth and expansion.

Even if we concede the possibility of forecast inaccuracies being large enough to be critical in these calculations, the effect of such inaccuracies tends to be relatively insignificant compared with the variability in results which are possible with only slight differences in the choice of the standard used for the future employee density. Thus there may be reason for greater concern over the choice of standard to which forecast data are applied. But apart from these considerations, there are other moderating elements in the picture. Implicit in the planning process itself as we have been viewing it is the necessity for periodically reviewing and restudying plans in the light of new and unforeseen developments. There is thus the continuing opportunity to adjust for forecast inaccuracies. Not to be overlooked, too, is the element of control which zoning and other similar plan-implementing measures exert and the effect that these may have in influencing the accuracy of the forecast.

The foregoing discussion is not to minimize the hazards inherent in developing employment forecasts, but rather to point out that city planning applications of forecast data are not so exacting in their requirements as perhaps those of labor market analysts and other consumers of forecast data. Certainly these moderating circumstances do not absolve the city planner from careful examination of the sources of data he employs and for recognizing the limitations of the forecast techniques he may be using.

It should be noted that the techniques taken up in this chapter are not concerned with prediction, but rather with methods for estimating levels of future employment, provided the assumptions which go with the techniques are found to apply during the forecast period. Some of the more obvious types of assumptions are: "continued high levels of employment with a constant rate of unemployment at roughly x per cent of the civilian labor force," "no major recession," "no outbreak of war," and so on. These types of assumptions would generally be associated with the "high" estimate. Variations downward from these and other assumptions that may be involved would be set to a "low" forecast estimate. This way of looking at forecasting techniques does not preclude for planning purposes the selection of a "single best estimate;" it simply underscores the fact that forecasts are based on certain fundamental assumptions and not on intuition, divine guidance, or some special superhuman knowledge of things to come.

In some quarters, reservations of another kind are sometimes voiced, and anything to do with economic projections is viewed with suspicion. In this respect, we will simply repeat what the congressional Joint Committee on the Economic Report has observed, namely, that economic forecasting "is here to stay as long as individuals, private business, and democratic governments are free to make their own decisions. Only in an authoritarian state can we be relieved of this necessity; there, projections become commands." [1]

There are various available series of data generically included under "employment statistics." In order to be assured of internal consistency and the general accuracy of analyses undertaken, not only should distinctions between the various series be clearly understood, but also it should be ascertained that the series selected are available and the same for the whole range of study areas employed, from the nation down to the urban study area. In the more recent decades, the U.S. Bureau of the Census decennial reports carry statistics which permit direct transcription or the isolation of such series as the total labor force, the civilian labor force, total employment, nonagricultural employment, manufacturing employment, and

[1] Joint Committee on the Economic Report, 83rd Congress, 2nd Session, *Potential Economic Growth of the United States During the Next Decade,* Washington: U.S. Government Printing Office, 1954, p. 2.

so on. The Bureau's Census of Manufactures and Census of Business carry other series for different years, the former, for example, carrying a series on manufacturing wage earners as well as manufacturing employment, and the Bureau's *U.S. Statistical Abstract* carries average annual employment. The monthly estimates used in computing the latter series along with a series on production workers broken down by Standard Industrial Classification (SIC) categories are issued by the Bureau of Labor Statistics in their monthly bulletin, *Employment and Earnings*.[2] There are obvious differences in some of these series, and there are frequently variations in series which on the face of it would appear to be similar, the differences occurring because of different data collection methods used in the original instance. Since there is no substitute for the investigator digging in and learning his data sources and their limitations for himself, the reader is simply alerted to these problems, and except for a few distinctions necessary to explain techniques, it is expected that he will find these things out for himself in the course of developing his own forecasts.

In the following sections of the chapter, two general groups of forecasting methods are discussed: the analytical methods and the short-cut methods. The former develop employment estimates from an analysis of the major antecedent variables which determine employment. In their most elemental form, they utilize the relationship:

$$\frac{\text{Total output}}{\text{Output per worker}} = \text{Employment}$$

and develop estimates of future employment from forecasts of production and worker output data, with a forecast being developed for each component according to an analysis of its principal antecedent variables.[3] The more commonly used short-cut methods utilize one or more series of employment statistics direct. Manifestly, they are simpler to apply and are less time-consuming to complete.

Both groups of methods require as a point of beginning certain estimates for the future (derived or "given") appropriate to the series being used. Thus the analytical methods require initial estimates of future total output and output per worker for the nation or the region within which the urban study area is situated from which to begin the analysis. Similarly, the short-cut methods must have an estimate of the civilian labor force, total employment, or other similar unit of measurement for some geographic area larger than the urban study area. Once a point of beginning

---

[2] The SIC classification system is now used as the basis for detailed breakdowns by type of industry in all published federal agency sources. See Bureau of the Budget, *Standard Industrial Classification Manual*, Washington: U.S. Government Printing Office, 1957.

[3] Future production or output is used here in a loose sense referring more precisely and correctly to *future demand*.

is established, most analytical and short-cut methods utilize ratio or correlation procedures, either direct or by apportionment, as a means of connecting the initially derived or "given" data to the urban study area.

The forecaster will want to use several methods as a means of gauging
the reasonableness of estimates derived. Although the methods discussed
below have never been subjected to systematic statistical tests of validity, obviously the forecaster will attach greater weight to some results
than to others. Until mass statistical tests can be made of these methods on
a comparative basis, the importance attached to results from various methods will depend upon such factors as the liberties taken by the forecaster
as necessitated by gaps in trend data, his "common sense" observations
as to variations in the accuracy of procedures employed in the various
methods, and so on.

The particiular kinds of applications that are to be made of results from
the various forecasting methods are a factor to be taken into consideration
in the selection of methods. As mentioned above, population studies require estimates of total employment. Land use planning analyses require
breakdown estimates for at least the manufacturing and frequently the
wholesaling and warehousing-trucking components of the total, and the
professional services, finance, insurance, and real estate categories. All
methods presented below will yield estimates of total employment, but for
purposes of developing breakdowns for special components, some methods
may prove to be better than others, according to the peculiarities of the
data series used in the forecast and the detail available in that series for
the urban study area of interest.

Analytical Forecasting Methods

The analytical methods are closely tied up with the regionally oriented
approaches to the study of the urban economy, and thus involve much the
same order of complexity and the same limitations that were identified
with these approaches in Chapter 3. Discussed below are extensions of
these approaches. The first section indicates how input-output analysis can
be used in developing employment forecasts. This is followed by a discussion of the use of income statistics within the context of a system of regional
accounts and within the framework of the approximation approaches to
the study of regional spheres of economic influence.

The principal advantage of an analytical method is the greater accuracy
theoretically obtainable by separate analysis of each individual component
(total output and output per worker) that affects the final employment

estimate derived. In the short-cut methods these separate effects are obscured, but in the analytical methods, the behavior of each variable in the past can be observed separately and used as a guide in estimating its likely behavior in the future. In practice, this seeming advantage may become the principal disadvantage, for with more variables to account for, there are more chances of error entering into the forecasting procedure. Whether it proves to be an advantage or disadvantage depends on the experience of the forecaster, the care with which each variable is examined for hidden influences, and the availability of suitable and reliable basic data for periods sufficiently far back in time to permit observation of trends.

Forecasts by Input-Output Analysis

In the earlier discussion of the input-output technique, our attention was centered around the derivation of the basic table of interregional-interindustry coefficients which contained the matrix of relationships in the flow of commodities between all industries within and external to a given spatial setting. In terms of our present concern, this spatial setting would be the urban study area, that is, the Standard Metropolitan Statistical Area or whatever other delineation of this area has been settled upon for the tooling-up studies. Further, the table of coefficients, let us say, is Table 4, with Metropolitan Region I being our SMSA and Regions II and III being all other areas within the sphere of economic influence of our SMSA.

Now according to the analytical approach requirements, we must have as a point of beginning certain given estimates. In input-output analysis one such set of "givens" would consist of estimates of the effective demand for all the various economic lines listed in Region I or our SMSA for, let us say, the year 1975. Assuming adjustments have been made in the values contained in the table for anticipated changes in the local economy by 1975 as discussed in the last chapter, these future demand levels can be applied industry by industry to the adjusted coefficients to obtain the 1975 output in, let us say, constant 1965 dollars. By summing up the results for all industries in our SMSA, we obtain an estimate of the total output for the forecast year. Obviously, by using a more detailed industrial classification than the one employed in our illustrative model (Table 4), it would be possible to obtain subtotals of output for manufacturing and for other desired detailed categories.

To complete the analysis, the other set of "givens" required would consist of estimates of 1975 labor productivity for all industries and for the subcategories, manufacturing, wholesaling, warehousing-trucking, and the professional, finance, insurance, and real estate services. To maintain internal consistency to the analysis, these estimates would be expressed in dollar output per worker in constant 1965 dollars for all industry and for each of the desired subcategories. If reliable estimates of this order are not available as "givens," then estimates would have to be developed on the basis of assumed levels of labor productivity based on subassumptions relative to technology, management efficiency, and so on.

With these data available, the actual employment estimates are obtained by dividing values for estimated future output by the appropriate values for output per worker. While the procedure thus described is conceptually a simple one, obviously to put it into operation involves several problems. First and foremost, except for some possible few situations where data may have been especially assembled for an input-output matrix, there are no presently available sources of data in the form needed to construct the matrix. These and other problems related to the input-output technique itself have already been covered. But assuming the necessary matrix were available, there is the further problem of the "givens" and their availability by industrial categories used in the matrix, or for that matter by broad combinations of these categories. If they are not given, it is outside the competence of the field of city planning to deal with the many variables involved in deriving estimates. These factors and the problem of technical know-how in the execution of input-output analyses thus represent deterrents in the use of this method at the present time.

Forecasts Using Income Statistics

The alternative to the use of dollar measures of transactions between industries (which concentrate particularly on intermediate transactions before goods reach a final demand form for consumption) and worker productivity in these transactions as the components of the ratio for deriving employment is to go to a broader, more inclusive accounting system involved in income and product statistics. Here we are concerned with all forms of income-producing activity, investment and trade as well as industrial production.

The forecast of employment levels from regional accounts data follows procedures generally paralleling those noted above. For the numerator of the ratio, income and product figures are taken directly from projections of accounts developed from the social accounting analysis described in Chapter 3. "From-to" tables would supply the income estimates for the sectors desired in the forecast. As in input-output analysis, we require estimates of future income per worker in each category employed in the analysis. These would be based on special local studies of productivity trends in various sectors, or in the absence of data for these studies they rely on analyses of national trends adjusted for local variations and on assumptions as to future changes in various lines.

Income statistics can also be used in approximation analyses to estimate future employment by the analytical approach. Here national forecasts are allocated to local areas by apportionment procedures. As the term "apportionment" implies, this is a system of analysis which determines how smaller geographical areas share in estimates (of whatever kind) previously prepared for a parent area: the nation, a region, or perhaps a State Economic Area. It is a technique which has had some use in short-cut employment forecasts but which has had more general use in population forecasts. Customarily it utilizes "step-downs" through intermediate areas until the share of the given locale of interest is determined. In each step-down operation apportionment to all parts of the whole (for example, all regions of the nation, all subregions of the region of interest, etc.) is made and results are balanced out against the total before the procedure is carried to the next smaller set of geographical areas. In this way an interlocking relationship is worked out from the largest to the smallest area. The number of such step-downs is dependent upon how large the local area's share of the original parent area's total is likely to be (in terms of employment, population, etc.), and the larger the share, the fewer the number of intermediate step-downs required. Step-downs are usually accomplished either by ratio or by correlation procedures.

In the context of the present discussion, the apportionment technique determines first, on the basis of past trends, how each region can be expected to share in estimated future national annual production or output, and then determines, on the basis of estimated future annual levels of output per worker for each region, the number of future workers this productive activity will support. Of course, the point of beginning is some reliable national forecast of both production and output per worker. Once regional apportionments have been made, the whole process is repeated on a subregional level within the region of particular interest, and apportionment of the region's share of national totals is made to subregions. The process is repeated further until the urban study area is reached. The basic requirements of this method, then, are (1) two series of data for trend analyses, one indicating past production trends and another showing past worker output trends, both being required for the whole system of geographical areas being employed in the analysis, and (2) suitable national forecasts of both production and output per worker.

Considering the total output component first and the problem of selecting a series of data, it may be noted that there are various measures of national production in common usage. Those for which statistics are reported annually are Gross National Product, Net National Product, National Income, Personal Income, and Disposable Income.[4] One or more of these income concepts are frequently used as measures of the nation's total production, with Gross National Product (GNP) usually favored, being considered the most stable measure of productive activity. While estimates for all five income series are summarized for individual years on a national basis, unfortunately no systematic summaries are yet available showing breakdowns as to how all states and counties share in these totals.

Some studies have attempted to bridge this gap.[5] In the analysis of the changing economic structure of regions and smaller geographic areas relative to national trends, the Personal Income series may be used as a measure of total productive activity. It is closely correlated to GNP and is available broken down by states, with new summaries appearing annually in the August issue of *Survey of Current Business,* published monthly by the U.S. Department of Commerce. At the county level the "effective buying income" series of data, which are similar to Personal Income and published

---

[4] See U.S. Department of Commerce, *National Income,* a supplement to the *Survey of Current Business,* 1954; *U.S. Income and Output,* Washington: U.S. Government Printing Office, 1958; and the July issue each year of the *Survey of Current Business* for data on these national income series from 1929 to the current date. For the period 1909 to 1928, see J. Frederic Dewhurst and associates, *America's Needs and Resources,* New York: The Twentieth Century Fund, 1955. These income concepts have been defined by the U.S. Department of Commerce as follows:

"*Gross National Product* is the market value of the net output of goods and services produced by the nation's economy, before deduction of depreciation charges and other allowances for capital consumption. . . . [It] comprises the purchases of goods and services by consumers and government, gross private domestic investment and net foreign investment.

"*Net National Product* is the market value of the net output of goods and services produced by the nation's economy. . . . [It] comprises the purchase of goods and services by consumers and government, net private domestic investment and net foreign investment.

"*National Income* is the aggregate earnings of labor and property which arise from the current production of goods and services by the nation's economy. . . . [These] earnings consist of the compensation of employees, the profits of corporate and unincorporated enterprises, net interest and the rental income flowing to persons.

"*Personal Income* is the current income received by persons from all sources, inclusive of transfers from government and business but exclusive of transfers among persons. . . . Personal income is measured as the sum of wage and salary receipts, other labor income, proprietors' and rental income, interest and dividends, and transfer payments.

"*Disposable Income* is the income remaining to persons after deduction of personal tax and other payments to general government.

"*Gross National Product* (GNP) is considered to be the most stable measure of productive activity and to be more precise statistically than Net National Product. Net National Product is less than GNP by the amount of depreciation charges, and certain other capital consumption allowances. Theoretically Net National Product and National Income should be equal, but the latter is actually smaller due principally to certain indirect taxes received by the government which are included in the former. Personal Income is less than National Income principally by profits retained by corporations and by corporate profits taxes, after allowance has been made for net interest paid by the government and transfer payments, which are not included in National Income. Disposable Income is the smallest of the five indices and is the same as Personal Income, except it excludes income taxes."

[5] One such study by Michael Cabot on which the techniques discussed here are based is described by the author in "Employment Forecasts for City Planning," *Journal of the American Institute of Planners,* Spring, 1954.

annually in the May issue of *Sales Management* magazine, may be used for estimating purposes. Since this magazine carries state as well as county statistics, for estimating purposes it is possible to relate this series to the Personal Income series. By adjusting the buying income data to represent Personal Income equivalents in constant dollars for some base year, say 1965, the state's Personal Income can be allocated to counties or combinations of counties by apportionment procedures. The approach is somewhat circuitous, but until such time as Personal Income data or some similar series tied into national projections are reported by counties, this will serve as a reasonably satisfactory procedure for approximation purposes.[6]

A suitable forecast compatible with national projections of productive activity has been identified as a needed "given." For this aspect of the analysis, projections made in connection with major economic studies which become available from time to time may be used.[7] The projections prepared by the National Planning Association are especially useful in this respect. In addition to the annual estimates for the nation as a whole which can be apportioned by the above-described procedures to a metropolitan study area of interest, NPA's periodic projections for regions and states provide a direct ready source for estimating how smaller areas in the region or state are likely to share in the projected growth.[8] In using such estimates, the analyst will want to examine the assumptions which go with the projections with respect to national defense expenditures, the general economic outlook, price levels, and so on.

Let us now consider the problem of the other component of this estimating procedure, that of selecting a suitable series on annual output per worker which would satisfactorily reflect labor productivity trends. To obtain the worker productivity data required in the analyses, it is necessary

---

[6] Income data on a county basis are frequently available from university sources. For example, see Scott Keyes, Felix C. Rodgers, and Wallace E. Reed, *Personal Income in Illinois Counties, 1950, 1954, 1956, 1958, 1959*, Urbana: University of Illinois Bureau of Community Planning, 1962.

[7] For example, see Hans H. Landsberg, Leonard L. Fischman, and Joseph L. Fisher, *Resources in America's Future*, Baltimore: The Johns Hopkins Press, 1963; the President's Materials Policy Commission (Paley Commission), "Foundations for Growth and Security," *Resources for Freedom*, I, Washington: U.S. Government Printing Office, 1952.

[8] National Planning Association, *National Economic Projections* (dated), issued annually since 1960. See also NPA's technical supplements for regional and state projections, issued irregularly. For illustrative state projections, see Outdoor Recreation Resources Review Commission Staff, National Planning Association, and Bureau of Labor Statistics, *Projections to the Years 1976 and 2000: Economic Growth, Population, Labor Force and Leisure, and Transportation*, ORRRC Study Report 23, Washington: U.S. Government Printing Office, 1962, p. 420.

It will be of interest to note that NPA's approach to economic projections begins with an employment analysis and from this derives GNP and Personal Income projections rather than following the procedure discussed here. NPA indicates this was done partly because employment series are more readily available and partly in the belief that firm and household migration decisions and thus economic growth can be traced through state industry employment trends (*ibid.*, p. 294).

to consider the number of working units per year (hours, days, etc.) at selected time intervals into the future, and the output per worker per unit of time for these same selected time intervals. Here, too, obstacles are encountered in finding a suitable series. Small-area breakdowns on the daily output per worker and the number of days worked per year are not available. To bridge this gap and to make the analysis consistent with the previously described Personal Income measure of output, a productivity index combining these two elements in the form of a series of curves on *Personal Income per worker* can be developed. Following correlation procedures similar to those described for step-downs of total output, Personal Income per worker estimates can be prepared for counties or groups of counties, using the state series on Personal Income and county equivalents in conjunction with an appropriate state and county employment series to obtain an estimate of worker productivity on a county basis.

Utilizing national production and worker output data, this technique thus develops estimates as to how local areas share in or relate to state estimates by developing and applying step-down relationships. As the step-down is accomplished, estimates of future employment are computed. By using "high" and "low" assumptions throughout, results could be presented in terms of a range within which the future employment might be expected to fall.

As noted above, ratios instead of correlation procedures could be used as another variation on the apportionment technique. In place of correlating size of subarea Personal Income or subarea productivity against size of parent area Personal Income or productivity, a time series is constructed expressing the smaller area increments as percentages of the parent area totals. Utilizing the same model described above, projections are made of the percentage series, and future percentage values obtained are applied to "given" absolute-figure estimates of the parent area for the forecast date to obtain absolute figures in future time for the subareas. A major advantage of the correlation procedure is the greater accuracy possible in the projection operation. Since data are plotted by size of Personal Income and magnitude of productivity, they follow a more regular pattern. It is thus possible to fit a curve to the data with greater ease and less hazard than is involved in fitting a curve to a time series which is susceptible to greater fluctuations.

This particular application of the analytical approach to employment forecasts yields only estimates of *total employment* as derived from output and output per worker data. The series of data used in these analyses do not carry breakdowns by industry groups, and at present it is necessary to use short-cut methods for breaking out subtotals on the manufacturing, wholesaling, warehousing-trucking, and other desired categories.

Short-Cut Forecasting Methods

The short-cut forecasting methods are much more simply applied than the foregoing analytical methods. Since they use employment statistics direct without becoming involved in projections of total output and output per worker, the procedures generally require much less time and effort in the actual work of carrying them out. Moreover, because there are several employment series reported on a small-area basis the forecaster is permitted more latitude in the choice of data sources, and the mechanical task of forecasting is generally facilitated.

There are two classes of methods in this group. While both utilize step-down procedures in determining the urban study area's share of the "given" estimate for a larger geographical area, one class accomplishes the step-

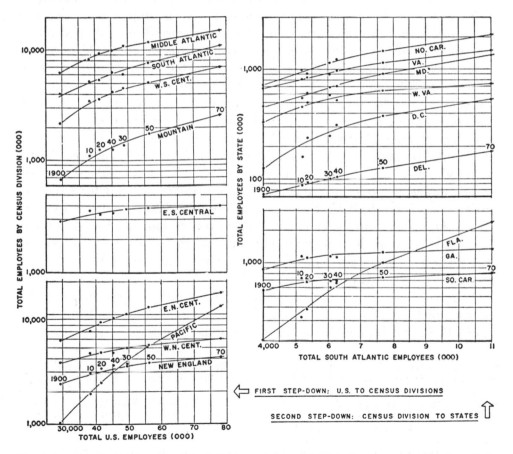

Figure 17. Illustrative Charts of First and Second Step-Downs Apportioning Estimates of Future National Employment to Smaller Geographic Areas.

downs by an apportionment technique and the other employs direct step-downs, omitting the proration analyses of all parts of the whole. The chief weakness of the latter technique is that it ignores the manner in which the economic structure of the region, the subregion, and the smaller subareas selected for the step-down operation may be changing relative to the structure of all other regions, subregions, etc., that are included in each parent area. Here too, correlation or ratio procedures can be used to accomplish step-downs, the latter being the most commonly used.

Apportionment of National Employment Estimates

Following the same general apportionment procedures described above under analytical methods, two series of employment data may be used in this short-cut method of forecasting: the Bureau of the Census employment series reported decennially (corresponds to April employment) or the Bureau of Labor Statistics employment series reported monthly and on an average annual basis. The latter series is not directly available in small-area summaries, but breakdowns may be estimated from data of the local or state employment security office.[9] Appearing with total employment statistics is a series on production worker employment, compiled on the basis of sampling surveys of industrial firms and summarized in a historical form by categories in the Standard Industrial Classification. The total employment data are compiled on the basis of sampling surveys of households. Although available at less frequent intervals, the decennial census has an advantage of possessing the internal consistency needed for planning analyses, and for SMSA's there is considerable detail reported by SIC classes in manufacturing categories. However, it too has its limitations. Breakdowns for small areas were not undertaken before the 1930 census, and manufacturing employment is not listed as an integral part of the decennial census before that time.

Figures 17 and 18 illustrate apportionment step-down procedures in the forecast of total employment using the decennial census employment series.[10] The same sources for a "given" national, regional, or state forecast

---

[9] For national summaries in a historical series, see Bureau of Labor Statistics, *Employment and Earnings Statistics,* Washington: U.S. Government Printing Office, 1961. For current data in this series, see *Employment and Earnings,* a monthly bulletin of the Bureau of Labor Statistics. Caution should be used in relating "covered employment," which refers to employment covered by the Old-Age and Survivors Insurance Program, to national summaries in the foregoing BLS series. State and local employment security offices report on "covered employment."

[10] This illustration of the use of apportionment procedures taken from A. C. Hall, Jr., *A Forecast of Employment for the Raleigh Metropolitan Area, with a Study of Basic-Nonbasic Composition,* unpublished manuscript, Chapel Hill: Department of City and Regional Planning, University of North Carolina, 1955.

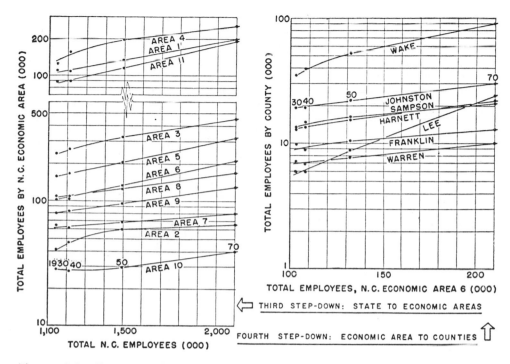

Figure 18. Illustrative Charts of Third and Fourth Step-Downs Apportioning Estimates of Future National Employment to Smaller Geographic Areas.

which would be used in an analytical approach may be consulted in this procedure.[11] Figures 17 and 18 are suggestive of the system of geographical areas which might be employed in step-downs. The previously mentioned problem of fitting regression curves to data available only since 1930 is evident in the third and fourth step-downs (Figure 18).[12] Although this illustration of the method correlates size of subarea employment to parent area employment to effect the actual step-downs from one series of geographical areas to the next smaller series, data could have been ordered in time series, and ratio procedures used to accomplish the step-downs. As in the previous examples of the use of apportionment procedures, in each

---

[11] See National Planning Association, *National Economic Projections*; Outdoor Recreation Resources Review Commission Staff *et al.*, *Projections to the Years 1976 and 2000.* Other sources for projections include the Bureau of the Census, *Current Population Reports,* issued irregularly, and the Bureau of Labor Statistics releases (for example, see *Interim Revised Projections of U.S. Labor Force, 1965–75,* Special Labor Force Report No. 24, Washington: U.S. Government Printing Office, 1962).

[12] To alleviate difficulties encountered here, studies of employment trends by state or university agencies are sometimes available and can be used to guide the forecaster in fitting curves to his data.

Table 11. Illustrative Estimates of Employment for Various Geographical Areas as Derived by Apportionment Procedures, 1970[a]

Area	1970 Adjusted Employment (000)
Census Divisions	
New England	4,200
Middle Atlantic	15,000
East North Central	16,000
West North Central	6,200
South Atlantic	11,000
East South Central	4,000
West South Central	7,000
Mountain	2,600
Pacific	12,000
U.S.	78,000
South Atlantic States	
Delaware	150
Maryland	1,350
District of Columbia	540
Virginia	1,500
West Virginia	740
North Carolina	2,100
South Carolina	820
Georgia	1,400
Florida	2,400
South Atlantic	11,000
North Carolina	
State Economic Area 1	200
State Economic Area 2	65
State Economic Area 3	450
State Economic Area 4	250
State Economic Area 5	315
State Economic Area 6	210
State Economic Area 7	80
State Economic Area 8	170
State Economic Area 9	130
State Economic Area 10	40
State Economic Area 11	190
North Carolina	2,100
N.C. State Economic Area 6	
Franklin County	13
Harnett County	22
Johnston County	30
Lee County	24
Sampson County	21
Warren County	10
Wake County	90
N.C. State Economic Area 6	210

[a] See bottom of following page.

level of the step-down operation, figures for all parts of the parent area are balanced out against the parent area figure before the analysis is repeated at the next lower level. Table 11 gives a summary of results obtained following these procedures. Estimates are purely illustrative.[13]

To extend this analysis to include estimates of manufacturing employment, two alternative procedures could be followed.[14] One involves duplication of the foregoing apportionment procedures, using given national estimates of future manufacturing employment in place of total employment. The other requires a study of local trends in manufacturing employment, and by use of ratio or correlation procedures, involves the construction and projection of a curve showing the relationship between the manufacturing subcategory and total employment. Both approaches face the same limitations in not having decennial census data on manufacturing employment available prior to 1930. For large cities of the country, it is possible to get around this problem by using the Census of Manufactures series to approximate local trends in manufacturing employment for decennial years prior to 1930.[15] This adjustment procedure can be used in either of the two alternative approaches.[16] For smaller cities, the second alternative is perhaps the most satisfactory approach. Figure 19 illustrates how the total employment estimate derived in Figures 17 and 18 can be broken out into major census subcategories by correlation procedures. However, until trends can be established over a longer period of time than is presently possible from decennial census data, results from the application of these procedures in small cities must be regarded with some reservation.

---

[13] The curves in Figures 17 and 18 were smoothed by means of moving averages and fitted to the data by eye. Mathematical curves would normally be computed, thus yielding more valid estimates than those appearing in Table 11.

[14] Because decennial census series do not carry breakdowns in the detailed form needed to break out wholesaling and warehousing-trucking as separate subcategories, it is not feasible to develop estimates for these groupings of activities in the same way as described for the manufacturing subcategory. For estimating procedures suitable to these subcategories, see the discussion of ratio methods below. Estimates for professional services, finance, insurance, and real estate categories would be obtained in the same manner as described for the manufacturing subcategory.

[15] In the period prior to 1930 of particular interest here, the Census of Manufactures reports for "principal cities" rather than for counties or for Standard Metropolitan Statistical Areas that contain these cities. Thus, in order to maintain consistency to the analysis, it is necessary to adjust figures given in the Census of Manufactures for both area and year reported in estimating decennial census equivalents.

[16] In using the first approach (the apportionment procedure), step-downs of manufacturing employment below the state level must be accomplished on the rather crude basis of using "the urban study area" and "rest of state" in lieu of the system of geographic areas utilized in the third and fourth step-downs shown in Figure 18.

---

[a] Adapted from A. C. Hall, Jr., *A Forecast of Employment for the Raleigh Metropolitan Area, with a Study of Basic-Nonbasic Composition*, unpublished manuscript, Chapel Hill: Department of City and Regional Planning, University of North Carolina, 1955.

Note: This table is introduced to illustrate the "balancing-out" procedure. The figures used are illustrative only and based on 1955 information.

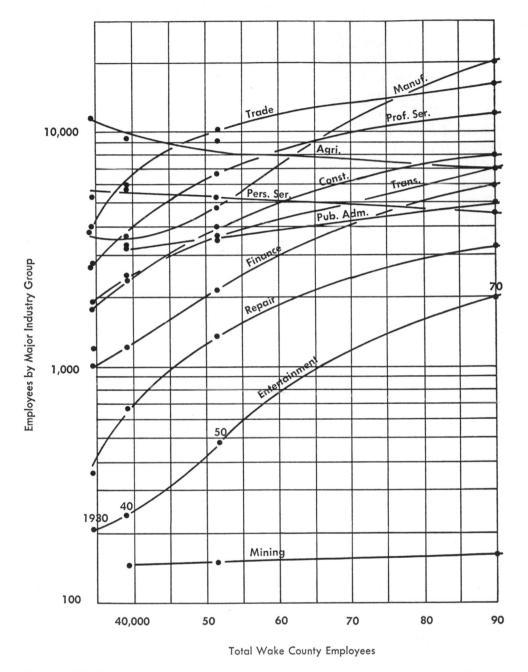

Figure 19. Illustrative Chart of County Employment by Major Subcategories Plotted in Relation to Total County Employment.

The foregoing discussion indicates how ratios of gross employment can be used in the apportionment of "given" national, regional, or state estimates to systems of smaller subareas. However, for the detailed stages of a city planning program, this approach may not be accurate enough. Even when total employment is "broken out" into major sectors as indicated in Figure 19 as an integral part of the step-down analysis, important trend changes within subsectors of the economy may not be adequately reflected nor important shifts in competetive advantages between regions or states fully reflected. Intuitively we know that as different subsectors and subregions develop or decline in their positions relative to other subsectors and subregions, the totals we have been dealing with on a gross basis in the analysis shown in Figures 17 and 18 would be modified in the more detailed investigation. (It would be rare that differential gains and losses would exactly cancel one another.)

The National Planning Association's work on regional and state projections suggest corrective procedures which could be introduced to advantage. Indeed, where NPA state projections are used as the "given" forecast for estimating future employment of counties or combinations of counties in a particular state, procedures comparable to those employed by NPA in developing their regional and state projections may be followed in developing substate projections. The NPA methodology differentiates between commodity and noncommodity employment.[17] It makes the assumption that the latter will locate in relation to the former and further that the former will locate in relation to where the new capacity in that commodity line has tended to concentrate in recent time.

In accordance with these assumptions, attention focuses first on commodity employment projections. For this component the NPA technique calls for three successive approximations of employment levels in the major commodity sectors using what they call "a trend-supply-demand approach." In the first approximation, they apportion their forecast national *increases* in employment (or decreases) by commodity sector among the regions and the states in accordance with the way increases (or decreases) were distributed in the immediate past decade. These increases were added to the threshold year for the forecast to give the first approximation of the estimated total commodity employment on the forecast dates.

In the second approximation, they examine national trends of various supply and demand factors in the various commodity sectors for anticipated location shifts and how these might alter the first approximation. For each

[17] Outdoor Recreation Resources Review Commission Staff *et al.*, *Projections to the Years 1976 and 2000*, pp. 295–297.

line this stage of analysis focuses on a region's and a state's supply of skilled labor; its access to raw materials and materials from intermediate processing, to low-cost transportation, and to linked complexes of industries important in the processing of the commodity; and the prospects of each industry improving its competitive position in gaining access to large-scale external economies. Trends thus observed are used in modifying the first approximation.

In the final approximation, they take into account market factors. After adjusting for projected changes in each commodity line's relative position (decline or gain) as determined in studies of the relative position of the sector in the United States as a whole, regional and state projections for all commodity lines are expanded to a trial total employment figure on the basis of projections of the ratio of commodity to noncommodity employment. Using this trial total employment estimate, ratio procedures are used to expand employment projections to population estimates. Then on the basis of these estimated gains in market size, commodity employment approximations previously obtained in market-oriented sectors are re-examined and adjusted as necessary to reflect the growth in market. The final total employment figures are thus based on this third approximation of commodity employment expanded to reflect the noncommodity employment.

Estimation by Direct and Indirect Ratio Procedures

By far the most commonly used approaches to estimating future employment in a locale of interest utilize simple ratio procedures. These procedures estimate how a particular urban study area will share in the projected employment of some larger geographic area (usually the nation). They may be used in a series of indirect step-down analyses involving successively smaller areas, until estimates for the urban study area are finally determined, or they may be used in direct local-national analyses.

As in the apportionment approach, the rationale of these procedures is based on the premise that local employment trends are a function of national trends, and given a reasonably reliable national forecast, local estimates can be derived which possess a sufficient degree of accuracy for planning purposes. Such a premise usually carries with it a corollary that the larger the employment of the local study area the greater the degree of accuracy in the final result. As in the other methods, forecasts can be developed with a series of alternate assumptions, with the end results being expressed in terms of high and low estimates bracketing a range of possibilities.

The Basic Procedures

In the direct local-national ratio approach, percentages of local to national employment are computed for past decades from census reports and ordered in a time series. A curve is fitted to the data and projected to the desired forecast date. The value of the projected ratio thus obtained is then applied to the given estimate of future national employment to obtain the estimate of future employment in the urban study area. The step-down variant of the ratio approach follows essentially the same procedure in each successive step-down analysis. Thus curves of the employment ratios are developed and projected—the region-to-nation ratio, the state-to-region ratio, and so on. Beginning then with given employment estimates for the nation, absolute estimates of employment for each of the intermediate geographic areas are determined in turn by applying the appropriate projected ratios to absolute figures derived in the last preceding step. This step-down operation is repeated until an estimate for the urban study area is finally derived. The mechanics of this operation are identical with those of the ratio procedures used in short-cut population forecasting taken up in the next chapter. These two ratio methods are the simplest to apply and are in most common usage.

Special Problems Resulting from Military Bases

Some urban areas contain military establishments which pose a special problem in employment forecasting, particularly where the military forces represent a substantial proportion of the total labor force. Under any circumstances forecasts in these situations are difficult, but the problem is especially troublesome when the military activity does not have official permanent status. While military employment (officer and enlisted personnel) is not included in employment totals utilized in land use planning analyses of civilian land requirements in the urban study area, obviously the military strength of the installation has a bearing on the local civilian economy. Accordingly, employment forecasting procedures must include studies of military strength as a basis for estimating future civilian employment in the area.

In general, the most feasible short-cut approach involves a segmental forecasting procedure which deals separately with the following three components of total civilian employment: (1) direct military-related civilian employment (persons employed by the military), (2) indirect military-related civilian employment (an increment composed of persons employed in retail establishments, domestic employees, etc., attributable to the presence of military personnel), and (3) all other forms of civilian employment (nonmilitary-related). Future estimates of the first two segments are predicated on future military strength. Past trends in employment in the first component are obtained by analysis of civilian payroll records of the military establishment. The indirect military-related civilian employment trends are more difficult to establish. This segment can be crudely approximated for various census years by comparative analysis with other cities of similar size not affected by military activity, but the economic structure and employment levels of which are similar to those of the nonmilitary segment of the economy of the city under study. In much the same way that service-basic ratios are developed in conventional economic base analyses, ratios are computed here for past periods of time of both direct and indirect military-related civilian employment as per cents of military strength. The trend in the values of each series of ratios are then used as bases for estimating future values to be used as "multipliers" applied to the estimated future military strength of the local base. Depending upon the international situation and security policies prevailing, these estimates of future military strength can sometimes be obtained through military channels. If such estimates are not available, it is necessary (and it is desirable in any case in order to check the reasonableness of estimates secured) to estimate local military strength from national data using conventional ratio step-down procedures.[18] In thus developing these estimates, alternate "high" and "low" assumptions set to such alternatives as "war" and "normal peace-time" conditions are usually identified. Once local estimates of future military strength are available, estimates for the two military-related segments are computed in absolute terms.

The third segment of the forecast concerned with nonmilitary-related employment is developed, using the ratio procedures described above for communities where no military installation is involved. With absolute values for this last segment of local civilian employment thus prepared, the final step is simply one of summing up the three separately derived segments to obtain the estimated total future civilian employment. At best, these procedures yield very crude estimates, and consequently it is particularly important in using this kind of short-cut approach to review continu-

[18] The aggregate military strength of all installations of any particular county can be approximated in each decennial census by taking the difference between total labor force and the civilian labor force. To step down a national forecast would involve the use of state 1950 and 1960 estimates obtained in the same manner, perhaps supplemented by 1955 estimates by states appearing in Table C, *Current Population Reports*, Series P-25, No. 132. In estimating past trends at the state level, it may be helpful to compare military strength with military-connected population (military personnel and families) by consulting the annual July 1 estimates which appear in a November or December release of the P-25 Series of *Current Population Reports* (see Series P-25, No. 229, for a recapitulation for 1950 to 1960). Estimates of military-connected population are obtained by taking the difference between resident population and civilian population.

ally and revise estimates in the light of changing international, national, and local conditions.

Estimating Manufacturing and Other Subcategories

As noted earlier in the chapter, planning analyses usually require a forecast of total employment broken down into subcategories. The breakdown into industrial subcategories selected, of course, is dependent on the detail desired in planning analyses. For example, in comprehensive planning studies, the two-, three-, and sometimes four-digit SIC classes of manufacturing activity may be important. In preliminary planning studies, perhaps an estimate of only three or four subcategories is all that may be needed. However, it should be noted that the choice of subcategories used in breakdowns will also be influenced by the detail available in the "given" forecast.

Either apportionment or simple ratio procedures may be used in determining a particular study area's share of a larger area's projected employment by subcategories. For the detailed breakdowns, it is customary to carry subtotals in the detail desired through all step-downs used in deriving local projections of total employment. If the point of departure for step-downs used in the projection is a "given" state set of projections, the procedure is more abridged than it would be if national projections were the source used. For preliminary planning studies, the minimal breakdown into subcategories will usually include at least a manufacturing subcategory, a wholesaling category, and some measure of office-related employment, often the finance, insurance, and real estate subcategory. Of these three classes, the wholesale classification presents some complications since if "trucking and related warehousing" is to be included in the same subcategory as "wholesale with stocks," both the Census of Business and the Census of Population will need to be consulted.[19]

In summary, the freedom of choice in forecasting methods will depend on the uses to be made of results, the series of data available for the locale of interest, the general accuracy desired, and the time the analyst is willing

---

[19] The following procedure may be used in developing estimates of the two components. From a graphic plot of national data on wholesaling employment (Census of Business series) arranged in a time series, equivalents for decennial census years are approximated. These national estimates are then expressed as percentages of total national employment (decennial census series), with the resulting ratios plotted in a time series and extrapolated. The ratio thus obtained for the forecast date may then be applied to the "given" estimate of future national employment to establish in absolute terms a national estimate of future employment in wholesaling. Following the usual step-down procedures (by apportionment or by simple ratios), an estimate of the wholesale component is obtained for the local county or combination of counties. Since "trucking and related warehousing" is a subcategory in the Census of Population, no conversion to decennial census equivalents is necessary. Step-downs are made as above, and the two components are combined. See the discussion of space needs of wholesale and related uses in Chapter 11 for classes of wholesaling included in the wholesale component.

to spend in deriving estimates. Because total output and output per worker are analyzed separately as antecedent factors affecting levels of employment, the analytical methods theoretically yield more accurate results than the short-cut methods. At the present time, however, the problem of data availability handicaps the use of these approaches. Furthermore, they are more complex and time-consuming than other methods. Due to these considerations, city planning agencies have favored short-cut approaches. Although these methods have never been subjected to systematic statistical tests for accuracy of results, conceptually the apportionment approach appears to be superior to the simple ratio procedure because of the manner in which it takes into account employment trends in other related areas that share in overall trends. However, within the limitations noted above, several methods should be used as a means of checking the reasonableness of estimates to be used in population and land use planning studies.

Chapter 5

Population Studies

In the last two chapters it was seen that analyses of the structure and vitality of the urban economy and the employment opportunities which the economy can support provide the means of gauging the growth potential of an urban area. These studies were identified as basic to land use planning—indeed, the starting point for all city planning. But to be entirely useful in planning analyses, this growth potential must be expressed in terms of the population it can be expected to sustain—the size of population, its composition and characteristics, and its spatial distribution. Population *size* gives an indication of the overall dimensions of the physical environment and supplies a basic yardstick for the estimation of space needs for various categories of land use. When the time element is introduced and future trends in population size are estimated, these trends become the basis for estimating future dimensions and future space needs. Investigations of population *composition* extend these analyses to such qualitative considerations as age groups, household sizes, and income composition of the population. Thus studies of population composition assist in estimating residential space requirements for various dwelling types consistent with existing and anticipated family sizes, income levels, and the needs of each segment of the life cycle. They assist in determining the amount of space needed for recreation areas, schools, and other community facilities for all segments of the population—small children, teen-agers, families, and old people. Finally, investigations of population *distribution* provide clues as to how these various land uses and facilities should be located in the urban area. Thus, population studies not only provide a means of scaling total space needs for selected land use categories at different periods of time in the future, but also give an indication as to how these total space needs should be allocated to different parts of the urban area at any particular time. We shall see in later chapters that, while demographic analyses of population distribution assist in identifying trends, forecasts of the future distribution involve the kinds of investigations discussed in the next chapter which seek to secure insights into why people locate their homes in the cities where they do.

In much the same way that fully rounded economic studies and employment analyses require the assistance of the economist, a full-fledged study of population in the urban area requires the know-how of the demographer. He is the specialist equipped with the training and background to undertake the more complex investigations, and it is important to recognize when his skills are needed. While the city planner normally lacks the training to carry out a complete range of demographic studies, he must be prepared to execute several types of analyses. Chief among those required in tooling up for land use planning are studies concerned with (1) estimating the current population, (2) population forecasts, and (3) analyses of the composition and distribution of population. Methods involved in making these studies are taken up in the three sections of the chapter that follow below.

Sound demographic analysis is predicated on accurate and systematically recorded population data for the area under study. There are two sources commonly recognized as meeting these requirements—the complete periodic census enumeration, and a system of continuous population registration. In the United States, we employ the first approach to provide our basic source of information, whereas in some parts of the world—for example, in the Scandinavian countries—continuous registration of births, deaths, moves, separations, and so on provides an up-to-date record at all times of general population statistics and is used in lieu of the regular census. To supplement these, a third major means of obtaining population data is by estimation. Common methods of estimation include sampling procedures, statistical or mathematical projection procedures, or the use of data series collected for purposes other than demographic analysis. Many of these methods are taken up in the first two sections of this chapter.

At the outset some general observations on census sources are perhaps in order. Although the following general sources are cited to give an indication of the range of publications available, the population analyst can best learn his sources by perusing these publications for himself and locating the various data series he needs. He can thus discover the form in which each is summarized and become familiar with the limitations and changes which have been introduced from census to census. Most information employed in population analyses comes from Bureau of the Census publications, either from decennial census reports or from selected special series issued annually or on a periodic basis. The decennial reports of particular interest are those containing data by small geographic areas. In the censuses since 1940, paperback bulletins on the number of inhabitants and the characteristics of population are issued for each state in the first and second years following the census.[1] These Census of Population bulletins, along

---

[1] Beginning in 1950, the paperback Census of Population bulletins have been assembled and

with a similar paperback series for the Census of Housing issued by states, carry small-area data for the county and various minor civil divisions. Two other series of paperback bulletins of special interest to city planners are the Census Tract bulletins by SMSA,[2] and the Block Statistics bulletins by city.[3] Vital Statistics reports are a special annual series compiled from state health department records and are used in several population estimation techniques taken up below.[4] The Bureau of the Census periodic releases in *Current Population Reports* (see especially Series P-25 and occasional reports in Series P-20 and P-23) provide projections as well as estimates of current national and state population. In addition to published data, certain unpublished data are also available from the Bureau of the Census on a special request basis for the cost of photocopying the tabulations, and during periods that decennial census summaries are being processed for publication, arrangements may be made to obtain at cost photostatic copies of machine tabulations in advance of actual publication dates.

The investigator can best determine these sources and understand their limitations in the framework of the specific tooling-up studies in which they are to be used. We can now proceed to review these studies—first, those concerned with estimating current population for postcensal periods; next, those employed in estimating future population prospects; and finally, those devoted to analyses of the characteristics and distribution of population in the urban study area.

Estimating the Current Population

Since land use planning analyses begin with the present, one of the first concerns is the current population size of the urban study area. Even if

republished by states in hardback editions. These are generally more handy to use than the conventional summary volumes which appear three or four years following the census. For compiling data from censuses before 1950, the standard summary volumes will normally need to be consulted, however.

[2] Census tracts are defined locally in consultation with the Bureau of the Census and consist of permanently established small-area divisions of counties or SMSA combinations of counties containing roughly 2,500 to 8,000 persons. They are laid out with a view to permit comparisons from census to census (for more information, see Bureau of the Census, *Census Tract Manual*, latest edition, and other processed materials of the Bureau). In 1960, 180 local areas were tracted, all being SMSA's except for two counties in New Jersey.

[3] Selected Census of Housing data have been published for cities of 50,000 or more on a block basis since 1940. By 1960 the number of cities and localities in the United States and Puerto Rico included in these bulletins was 467 (published in 421 bulletins).

[4] See National Vital Statistics Division, U.S. Department of Health, Education, and Welfare, *Vital Statistics of the United States,* Washington: U.S. Government Printing Office, published by individual years (roughly a two-year lag in publication).

the technical work involved in developing the urban land use plan is scheduled around a decennial census period in order to have ready access to accurate and detailed population data, we know that public and private development is not scheduled according to census periods, and if the planning agency is to carry forward the detailed planning studies in implementation of the various features of the plan, it soon becomes involved in developing postcensal population estimates. Indeed, up-to-date population estimates are so crucial to all forms of city planning work that many planning agencies have made it a regular and continuing staff function to develop new estimates annually.

A local census, either a complete enumeration or a survey using a carefully structured sample, obviously provides the most satisfactory result. From their surveys of state and city agencies engaged in making local population estimates annually, the Bureau of the Census has identified the following methods in common usage: the migration and natural increase method, the proration method, the censal ratio method, the vital rates method, the ratio-correlation method, the dwelling unit method, and various composite methods.[5] We shall treat the more common forms of these methods under three categories: (1) the migration and natural increase method, (2) the censal ratio methods, and (3) methods based on symptomatic data. The first approach is used more extensively by state agencies; the second group of methods are used to some extent by both state and city agencies; and the third group have been more widely used by city planning agencies, especially the dwelling unit method. In general, the selection of method will depend upon the uses to be made of the estimate, the level of accuracy required, and the time and staff experience available. As indicated below, the experimental tests which have been made indicate that some methods are decidedly superior to others, but much more rigorous tests of the relative accuracy of all methods are needed before it will be possible to type them in order of preference for specific planning or other uses.

Migration and Natural Increase Method

Of several variants of this method, two developed by the Bureau of the Census are discussed here. The Bureau's Method I was first described in

---

[5] Commonly used mathematical methods, such as arithmetic and geometric projections, and estimation by use of natural increase data alone, are not considered sufficiently reliable to be included in this résumé of methods. For reports on the use of these methods, see Bureau of the Census, "Local Population Estimates Prepared by State and City Agencies: Mail Survey of 1960," *Current Population Reports,* Series P-25, No. 244, March 8, 1962. See also earlier surveys cited in this report.

1947,[6] and its Method II was first spelled out in some detail in 1949,[7] with a later improvement of it brought out in 1956.[8] Both approaches utilize the same elemental procedure, essentially one of adjusting the last census figures of the locale of interest to reflect changes that have occurred to date, considering separately the effects of two major determinants of these changes, migration and natural increase. More particularly, both approaches are based on the following formula: "The civilian population of an area at the close of a period is equal to its population at the start of the period plus natural increase (the excess of births over deaths) during the period, plus the net migration during the period, minus the net loss of population to the armed forces. The total population is equal to the civilian population plus the number of persons in the armed forces stationed in the area." [9]

Translated into procedural steps, both approaches derive the current estimate of total population as follows:[10]

1. Civilian population at the time of last census.
2. Natural increase from last census to current date.
3. Estimated net civilian migration for the same period.
4. Net loss to the armed forces during the same period.
5. Estimated current civilian population (sum of Items 1, 2, and 3 minus Item 4).
6. Military personnel stationed in the area.
7. Estimated current total population (sum of Items 5 and 6).

The difference in Methods I and II is the technique of estimating the net migration component, with tests by the Bureau of the Census indicating that Method II, though more time-consuming and complex, results in more accurate estimates on the average.

Computing the Natural Increase

The first ingredient of both methods of estimating the current population is the natural increase which has occurred between the date of the last census and the current date. The amount to be added for this component

---

[6] See Bureau of the Census, "Suggested Procedures for Estimating the Current Population of Counties," *Population—Special Reports*, Series P-47, No. 4, April 30, 1947.

[7] For a comparison of the two approaches, see Bureau of the Census, "Illustrative Examples of Two Methods of Estimating the Current Population of Small Areas," *Current Population Reports*, Series P-25, No. 20, May 6, 1949.

[8] See Bureau of the Census, "Illustrative Example of a Method of Estimating the Current Population of Subdivisions of the United States," *Current Population Reports*, Series P-25, No. 133, March 16, 1956. See also modifications discussed in Series P-25, No. 165, November 4, 1957.

[9] Bureau of the Census, *Current Population Reports*, Series P-25, No. 20, p. 1.

[10] Adapted from Bureau of the Census outline of Method II. See *Current Population Reports*, Series P-25, No. 133, p. 2.

(in rare instances, it may be a subtraction) is simply computed from vital statistics data reported on an annual basis, and consists of differences between births and deaths as reported by place of residence, summed up for all years since the last census. Since the official date of the decennial census is April 1, care must be exercised to adjust data as reported on a calendar year basis so that only the appropriate fractional parts of the census year and the terminal year are included in this estimate. In this connection the necessary adjustments can be made by linear interpolation.[11] In addition, certain adjustments will usually be necessary to correct for underregistration of births and sometimes deaths.[12] Since there is a lag in the publication of *Vital Statistics of the United States,* local figures for the last two or three years must be obtained from the state health department or vital statistics office or from local health agencies.

Adjustment for net migration, the other major determinant of population change, is approximated in both Bureau of the Census Methods I and II by reference to school enrollment changes from the last census date to the current date. Implicit in both approaches is an assumption that the rate of net migration for the population as a whole during this period is similar to the estimated net migration rate of school children.

Net Migration by Census Bureau Method I

This approach uses the total change in the elementary school enrollment from the last census date to the current date, taken as a per cent of the census date enrollment as a rough indicator of net migration occurring during this period. The elementary school grades normally used are the second through the eighth grade, and, in order to use this approach, data must be available for all schools of this level in the urban area on the census date and the date of the current estimate. The approach calls for a careful examination of enrollment recording techniques to insure that there is consistency in the method of counting pupils in both years (for example, checking to see that counts for all local schools are given on a common date, checking on the consistency in the inclusion or exclusion of parochial schools, etc.). It may also require conversion of data from months used in school reports to the months involved in the population estimating procedure for both initial and terminal dates. This adjustment of enrollment data may be made by determining the monthly average change and then adding or subtracting to correct the data for the census month (April) and

---

[11] See procedures suggested by the Bureau of the Census, *ibid.,* p. 3.

[12] See suggested procedures, *ibid.,* pp. 3–4; for information on completeness of birth registrations, see National Vital Statistics Division, *Vital Statistics of the United States,* I, explanatory material, last annual report.

the month selected as the current date, or it may be estimated by linear interpolation.[13]

With the data thus checked and adjusted as necessary, the percentage change in enrollment from the last census date to the current date is computed as follows:

$$\frac{\text{Total change in enrollment to current year}}{\text{Base year enrollment}}$$

To eliminate the influence of what might be considered normal change in enrollment, the percentage change in national enrollment during this period is subtracted from the local percentage thus derived.[14] After careful examination of the result for reasonableness, this figure is then used as the estimated crude net migration rate. This rate is applied to the civilian population of the study area at the last census plus one-half of the births occurring between the last census and the current date (as corrected for underregistration).[15]

Net Migration by Census Bureau Method II

As compared with the foregoing approach where the percentage change in school enrollment is used as a determinant of net migration, this method develops an estimate of the hypothetical enrollment based on natural increase alone, with the difference between the hypothetical and actual enrollment being used as the key determinant of net migration. More specifically, the procedure calls for the following series of steps. First, the population age groups which would be in elementary grades 2 through 8 on the current date are identified in the last census reports according to their then age-group equivalents.[16] These groups are broken out into individual years, with the current elementary school–age population tabulated as it would appear in the last census, thus showing children of preschool age, lower–grade level school ages, and if the current date of the estimate is in the second half of the decade, including some children of minus 1 and other unborn categories. These children are "survived" year by year to the

[13] See procedures suggested by the Bureau of the Census, *Current Population Reports,* Series P-25, No. 20, p. 11.

[14] For national summaries of school enrollment, see *Current Population Reports,* Series P-20. October enrollment data appear generally in a July release in the year following.

[15] The inclusion of half the births in this total for purposes of computing the net migration assumes that newly born persons between the time of the census and the current date were alive for only half the period and would therefore be present for net migration at only half the computed rate (or to simplify computations, the full net migration rate is applied to half the births).

[16] Probably the Bureau of the Census reasons for selecting grades 2 through 8 are, first, to include a span of years where enrollment tends to be most stable, and, second, to facilitate the identification of appropriate age-group equivalents in published census categories.

current date by applying the appropriate age-specific survival rates (determined by reference to standard life tables). The unborn children will of course appear in the analysis beginning at the date corresponding to their birth year, with the actual data on births determined from vital statistics reports. As in the other analyses above, the number of live births for the appropriate years must be corrected for underregistration. The result from following the above procedure produces an estimate of the number of elementary school–age children based on natural increase alone.

However, not all children of school age are in school, and it is therefore necessary to convert the elementary school–age children into an enrollment equivalent. The conversion is usually made by a ratio procedure, that is, by noting what the number of children in school in grades 2 through 8 is as a per cent of children in the elementary school–age bracket at the time of the last census, and under the assumption that the same relationship continues to the current date, this ratio (called the "enrollment factor") is used to convert the "survived" elementary school–age figure to its enrollment equivalent. The difference between the enrollment thus derived and the actual enrollment is attributed to migration. This result, expressed as a per cent of enrollment at the time of the last census, is used as the net migration rate for the entire population. As in the other approach, this rate is applied to the civilian population of the study area at the last census plus one-half of the births occurring between the last census and the current date (corrected for underregistration). The analyst should consult *Current Population Reports*, Series P-25, No. 133, for detailed procedures of computing net migration under Method II.[17]

Estimating Persons Away in Armed Forces

Since World War II persons away in the armed forces have become a particularly important factor in population studies. While the military element in the nation's population in prewar years remained more or less fixed at about half a million, since 1950 this element has fluctuated from six to eight times this number, with as many as a million and a half entering and leaving the service in a single year. It is thus understandable that this segment of the population must now be given special consideration.

Estimates of the net loss of persons to the armed forces between the last census and the current date are made by ratio procedures. First, the most recent estimates of the losses of persons to the armed forces on a state basis are consulted in *Current Population Reports*, Series P-25. The appropriate

---

[17] For improvements on estimating net migration under Method II, see Bureau of the Census, *Current Population Reports*, Series P-25, No. 165.

state estimate is selected and adjusted forward to the current date by procedures suggested in *Current Population Reports*, Series P-25, No. 133. Then, assuming that losses to the armed forces in the county of interest will be in the same proportion that the county's male population 18 to 24 years old is to the state's at the time of the last census, this county-state ratio is applied to the adjusted amount of the net state losses to the armed forces between the last census and the current date to obtain an estimate of the net county losses to the armed forces during this period.

The remaining Steps 5, 6, and 7 of Methods I and II are reasonably straightforward. The problem of estimating military personnel in local military installations was discussed in the last chapter.

Censal Ratio Methods

"Censal ratio method" is often used to refer to any method utilizing ratio procedures. For our purposes, we shall include under this group of methods the simple apportionment and direct ratio techniques, and cover methods using ratio procedures with symptomatic data in the next section.

As described in the last chapter, the apportionment principle determines how systems of successively smaller geographical areas share in a previously prepared estimate for a larger geographical area, balancing subarea shares with the parent area total at each level to which the apportionment procedure is carried before proceeding to the next smaller system of geographical areas. If the previously prepared estimate is for the state containing the urban study area (obtained from *Current Population Reports*, Series P-25), the apportionment may be made to all counties of the state or it may be made to combinations of counties as involved in the use of State Economic Areas (see Figure 11). If the previously prepared estimate is for the nation, apportionment would first be made to major census divisions (see Figure 14), then to the several states in the census division of interest, and so on down to the local level. However, most applications of this method use the "provisional estimates" of state population prepared annually by the Bureau of the Census.

The simplest form of the ratio procedure makes a direct step-down from Bureau of the Census state population estimates to one particular county or SMSA without examining trends in other counties or combinations of counties. Except for the very large SMSA's or metropolitan combinations of counties, the direct step-down should be used with caution. Both the apportionment and the direct step-down forms of the censal ratio method usually assume that a particular county's (SMSA's) estimated yearly increase (or decrease) in the share of new population in the state added since the last decennial census will follow trends in the way that the county (SMSA) has shared in state increases in the decade prior to the last census. The projection of the trend in censal ratios is commonly accomplished by fitting a least squares line to the data.

Methods Based on Symptomatic Data

This group of methods derive estimates of the current population by reference to observed trends in data series which are found to bear a close relationship to population change and for which current data are available. Using ratio procedures to adjust the last census figures forward to the current date, they employ such series as vital statistics, school enrollment, listings in city directories, electric meter, water meter, or telephone installations, dwelling unit counts from land use surveys, registered voters, and so on. The suitability of the series is judged in terms of the consistency and accuracy of the way in which data are assembled and reported, the frequency with which the series are published (monthly, semiannually, or annually), and the degree of significance in the relationship it possesses to population trends. Obviously the series must be reported at least on the census year and the year of the current estimate in order to establish the necessary relationships.

Vital Statistics Rate Technique

Observing that the number of births and deaths occurring each year in a given area is roughly proportional to the size of the area's population, Bogue has set forth a technique designed to use vital statistics data as a symptomatic measure of population change.[18] He describes the sequence of steps as follows:

1. Compute crude birth and death rates (average of a two-year base around the last census year) for the subarea and the parent area.
2. Express the crude death rate of the subarea as a ratio of the crude death rate of the parent area. Make the same computation for the birth rate.
3. Make an independent investigation of how the crude birth rates and crude death rates of the various subareas have behaved in the recent past in relation to the trend of vital rates in the parent area. If a definite change-of-ratio with the passing of time is indicated for any class of subareas, devise a set of correction factors to be applied to the ratios for the base year in order to obtain "corrected" ratios for the year of estimate.
4. Compute a crude birth and crude death rate for the parent area for the year

[18] Donald J. Bogue, "A Technique for Making Extensive Population Estimates," *Journal of the American Statistical Association,* June, 1950.

for which a population estimate is desired. (Choose as a parent area a state or other unit for which the Bureau of the Census makes a regular postcensal estimate. The Bureau of the Census estimate can be used as a base to compute the vital rates for the parent area.)

5. Multiply the crude death rates for the parent area obtained in Step 4 by the corrected death ratio of the subarea obtained in Step 3 to obtain an estimated crude death rate for the subarea. Repeat for births.
6. Divide the estimated crude death rate of each subarea into the number of deaths registered for the year and allocated to residents of the subarea. Repeat for births. This yields *two estimates* of the subarea population, one based upon death and one based upon birth data.
7. Average the two estimates to obtain a single population estimate.
8. Adjust the population of all subareas to equal the total population of the parent area. This yields an estimate for the population as of July 1 of the year for which the rates have been computed.

Bogue made rough tests, applying the technique to assorted geographical areas: states and census divisions, cities in three states where state censuses were available, and cities in California where special censuses were available at the time he was experimenting with the technique. Where comparisons were possible, results indicated that the technique compared favorably with the migration and natural increase method.[19] Generally, it showed a greater consistency of accuracy in areas not subject to major population upheavals and in the larger geographical areas analyzed. When applied to cities (as opposed to counties containing the built-up area of these cities), it indicated a strong tendency to overestimate the population.

Composite Methods

Some approaches break down the estimation process into various age segments of the population, with the postcensal estimate derived by totaling up the estimates of the individual segments. These have come to be called "composite methods." Generally these approaches utilize various symptomatic data series for different age groups in the population. For example, Bogue and Duncan have used death statistics to estimate the "45 and over" group, birth statistics for the "18 to 44" and "under 5" segments, and Method II techniques of the migration and natural increase approach for estimating the "5 to 17" age category.[20] Results of Bureau of the Census

---

[19] An average difference of 3.6 per cent per state and 1.8 per cent per census division as compared with an average difference of 4.2 per cent for state estimates of the 1930 population, using school enrollment data as reported by Henry S. Shryock, Jr., *The Postcensal Estimation of Population in the United States,* University of Wisconsin, Ph.D. thesis, 1937.

[20] Donald J. Bogue and Beverly Duncan, "A Composite Method for Estimating Postcensal Population of Small Areas, by Age, Sex, and Color," in National Office of Vital Statistics, *Vital Statistics—Special Reports,* Vol. 47, No. 6, August 24, 1959.

tests on a state basis of the above illustration of the composite method indicate that it compares favorably with Method II.[21]

Regression Method

This method utilizes a multiple regression equation to project population, with the independent variables consisting of ratios of a county's (or SMSA's) share of births, deaths, elementary school enrollment, and/or other symptomatic data at the time of the last census to its share at the next preceding census.[22] This type of approach assumes that the mix of factors used as independent variables have behaved in the same way relative to one another during the period since the last census as they did between the last two censuses. Some preliminary tests made of this method on a state basis show that it is only slightly less accurate than Method II, the composite method, and the vital rates method.[23]

Other Symptomatic Series

Other approaches based on the use of symptomatic series include the proration method and variants on the previously discussed censal ratio method, including the dwelling unit method. Essentially a form of the apportionment technique, the proration method allocates new population to counties using the proportion of population to the selected symptomatic series as it existed in each county at the last census (for example, using a series on voter registration). Proportions for each county are applied to the increase in state population obtained from *Current Population Reports,* and by the familiar balancing-out step the new population is prorated to all the counties. Thus such an approach assumes that the proportional distribution of the state's population among the counties has not changed since the last census. The censal ratio method applied to a symptomatic series simply relates population to some basic indicator such as school enrollment, voter registration, city directory listings, or connections to electricity at the time of the last census. The ratios thus derived are then applied to the current data in the selected symptomatic series to establish population estimates for the current date. More refined forms of this method of estimation use

---

[21] Meyer Zitter and Henry S. Shryock, Jr., "Accuracy of Methods of Preparing Postcensal Population Estimates for States and Local Areas," a paper presented at the annual meetings of the Population Association of America, Philadelphia, April 26, 1963.

[22] For an example of the use of this method, see David Goldberg, Allan Feldt, and J. William Smit, *Estimates of Population Change in Michigan: 1950–1960,* Michigan Population Studies No. 1, Ann Arbor: Department of Sociology, University of Michigan, 1960.

[23] Zitter and Shryock, "Accuracy of Methods of Preparing Postcensal Population Estimates for States and Local Areas."

two or more indicators. Such an approach can be extended to all counties of the state and results adjusted to balance with the Bureau of the Census' current estimate for the state. Since Bureau releases are for July 1, ratios should be developed for the same dates where such an extension of method is contemplated.

In a study of 39 counties in Washington, Schmitt tested the following six series of symptomatic data using the proration and censal ratio techniques: live births, deaths, school enrollment, automobile registrations, voter registrations, and welfare recipients.[24] In ex post facto analyses, he estimated the 1950 populations and then checked results against the actual 1950 returns. Under the proration method, he found the voter registration series yielded the best results (an average error of 8.7 per cent), and, as might be expected, he found the welfare recipient series the least accurate (an average error of 25.2 per cent). Under the censal ratio method, the enrollment-based and voter registration series yielded better results than other series (both with average error of 7.0 per cent), with the "straw man" series on welfare recipients again being least accurate (average error 33.2 per cent). According to several statistical tests (standard deviation and critical ratio tests as well as the arithmetic mean), Schmitt improved his results by using various combinations of weighting in these series, but points out that these results cannot be considered conclusive, indicating the possibility of differing results in other areas with differing economic conditions and differing systems of recording these series of data.

The dwelling unit technique is a form of the censal ratio method used extensively by city planning agencies. Its popularity is probably due in large part to the fact that planning agencies, in the normal course of their work, maintain statistics on building permits for new and converted DU's as information required in housing and residential area analyses. In this method, the ratio of the number of dwelling units to population at the time of the last census is applied to a current dwelling unit count to derive a crude approximation of the current population. Most applications of the method assume the same average household size that prevailed at the time of the last census. For greater accuracy, trends of change in household size would be investigated and adjustments introduced where the size appears to be changing since the last census. This method has shortcomings where systematic reporting of building permits is not maintained for an entire metropolitan area. Differential standards of reporting from one jurisdiction to another and the reliance on field surveys to cover fringe areas where no building permit system exists undermine the accuracy of this method.

---

[24] Robert C. Schmitt, "Short-Cut Methods of Estimating County Population," *Journal of the American Statistical Association*, June, 1952.

Comparative Results from Various Methods

Following the completion of both the 1950 and 1960 census returns, the Bureau of the Census undertook comprehensive reviews of postcensal estimation methods. In the 1950 review, attention was devoted to the two variants of the migration and natural increase method, Bogue's technique of using vital rates as a symptomatic series for gauging population change, and two commonly used mathematical projection methods.[25] Although the study was primarily oriented toward a reassessment of Bureau of the Census methods of estimating postcensal state population, it presents important information on the use of these methods in cities. In this particular part of the study, it tested 1950 postcensal estimates developed from 1940 census counts on 92 cities having a 1940 population of more than 100,000. On the supposition that an average of the results of two methods involving rather different assumptions would tend to eliminate extreme errors, two additional tests were made following this averaging procedure.

In recognition of the probability of differences in accuracy according to city size and the rate of population change occurring, the study also tested the results of estimates by grouping the 46 larger and the 46 smaller cities on the basis of the 1950 census, and by grouping the 46 cities with higher and the 46 cities with lower rates of change in the 1940–50 intercensal period. Table 12 shows the average percentage deviation from 1950 counts of results from these methods and according to these groupings.[26] Of the methods tested, the migration and natural increase method employing Census Method II for estimating the net migration showed the lowest percentage deviation from actual counts, with the two averaged results showing even lower deviations. As might be expected, the larger the city and the slower the rate of change, the more accurate the result. In a later extension of these tests applied to a series of metropolitan counties (as opposed to cities used in the first tests), results were very similar to those shown in the first column of Table 12, except that the vital rates technique made a somewhat better showing.[27]

Two sets of tests against 1960 census returns provide some additional experience. One set undertaken by the Bureau of the Census, although

[25] Jacob S. Siegel, Henry S. Shryock, Jr., and Benjamin Greenberg, "Accuracy of Postcensal Estimates of Population for States and Cities," *American Sociological Review*, August, 1954.
[26] Average percentage deviation was one of five statistical tests used. For results of other measures of accuracy, see original source, *ibid.*
[27] Bureau of the Census, *Current Population Reports*, Series P-25, No. 178, p. 6. Following the same order as that used in the stub of Table 12, the results obtained in applying these seven methods to metropolitan counties showed average deviations as follows: (1) 9.21 per cent, (2) 6.57 per cent, (3) 6.29 per cent, (4) 18.25 per cent, (5) 16.42 per cent, and (7) 6.86 per cent.

Table 12. Accuracy of 1940-Based Postcensal Estimates by Various Methods Measured by Average Percentage Deviation from 1950 Population Counts[a]

| | | Average Percentage Deviation | | | |
| | | Population Size | | Rate of Change | |
Postcensal Estimating Method	All [b] 92 Cities	46 Larger Cities	46 Smaller Cities	46 H-R [c] Cities	46 L-R [c] Cities
1. Migration—natural increase (Method I)	8.34	8.05	8.63	7.94	8.74
2. Migration—natural increase (Method II)	6.53	6.32	6.73	7.44	5.61
3. Vital statistics rates (Bogue technique)	9.33	9.06	9.60	10.48	8.18
4. Arithmetic extrapolation	9.60	10.27	8.92	14.79	4.40
5. Geometric extrapolation	9.33	9.97	8.69	14.24	4.42
6. Average of methods 2 and 3	4.93	4.22	5.63	5.77	4.08
7. Average of methods 1 and 2	5.96	6.04	5.88	5.98	5.94

[a] Adapted from data summarized by Jacob S. Siegel, Henry S. Shryock, Jr., and Benjamin Greenberg, "Accuracy of Postcensal Estimates of Population for States and Cities," *American Sociological Review,* August, 1954.

[b] Cities with more than 100,000 population in 1940.

[c] H-R means "high-rate," L-R means "low-rate."

concentrating mainly on the accuracy of various methods in developing state estimates, examines Method II and the vital rates technique applied to 25 of the nation's larger SMSA's (involving 65 counties).[28] In these tests Method II showed an average error of 6.7 per cent for the SMSA's (7.5 per cent for counties), while the average error for SMSA's by the vital rates technique was 4.0 per cent. The other set of tests, undertaken by the Study Group on Postcensal Population, attempts to get a clearer picture of the relative accuracy of several of the methods applied to counties.[29] As noted from Table 13, in these tests the vital rates technique made a better showing than Method II, and in the one series of tests including the composite method, the latter approach made a better showing than either the vital rates or Method II. It may be noted too that the techniques appear to yield more accurate results in metropolitan counties than in rural counties.

The results from tests of 1950 and 1960 postcensal estimates suggest that with further testing some conclusions may eventually be forthcoming that

[28] Zitter and Shryock, "Accuracy of Methods of Preparing Postcensal Population Estimates for States and Local Areas."

[29] Public Health Conference on Records and Statistics, "Preliminary Report of the Study Group on Postcensal Population Estimates," Washington: National Vital Statistics Division, U.S. Department of Health, Education, and Welfare, June 11, 1962.

Table 13. Tests of Postcensal Estimating Techniques Applied to Counties in Three States—Average Percentage Deviation of 1950-Based Estimates for 1960 from 1960 Census Counts[a]

	Average Percentage Deviation								
Postcensal Estimating Method	Ohio (88 counties)			Montana (56 counties)			Oregon (36 counties)		
	Metro-politan	Other Urban	Rural	Metro-politan	Other Urban	Rural	Metro-politan	Other Urban	Rural
Migration—natural increase (Method II)	4.5	4.2	8.6	14.3	18.4	13.3	4.5	5.7	4.0
Vital statistics rates	3.3	3.3	5.6	5.7	9.2	15.3	2.7	5.4	6.2
Composite (Bogue-Duncan form of method)	2.4	2.9	3.9	N.A.	N.A.	N.A.	N.A.	N.A.	N.A.
Average of Method II and vital rates technique	2.6	2.3	5.5	4.3	9.3	9.3	2.9	4.3	4.0

[a] Adapted from Public Health Conference on Records and Statistics, "Preliminary Report of the Study Group on Postcensal Population Estimates," Washington: National Vital Statistics Division, U.S. Department of Health, Education, and Welfare, June 11, 1962.

would indicate which of these methods are better suited for metropolitan as opposed to smaller urban counties and for fast-growing as opposed to slow-growing situations. However, it is evident that still more rigorous testing of all methods as applied to urban areas is needed before they can be satisfactorily grouped for levels of accuracy and typed as to preference for particular kinds of planning analyses. In this connection much more attention needs to be directed to uses of postcensal estimates in planning studies, for within this one field that makes use of current population data there is some latitude for variation in accuracy. Where the current estimate is required as the beginning point for the population forecast, the most accurate possible estimate is needed. On the other hand, where estimates are used in broad-gauge analyses of existing community facilities such as the general adequacy of park space or playground area, approximation approaches may be warranted, particularly when it is considered that the standard of space per unit of population selected will tend to introduce more variation in results of the analyses than the population figure selected.

Population Forecasts

Perhaps the single most important population study for planning purposes is the population forecast. Certainly current population estimates and studies of the present composition and distribution of population are essential as a point of beginning in planning analyses, and in the continuing task of revising and detailing features of the resulting plans. They also serve an important function in day-to-day decisions relating to all kinds of public works and land development activities. Yet frequently the original and initial comprehensive plan studies undertaken in an urban area and their subsequent major revisions can be scheduled around a decennial census period to take advantage of the detailed and accurate data available only at these particular times. But no amount of scheduling obviates the necessity for studying future population prospects, for no planning activity is fulfilling its proper function unless plans are developed within a context of a continuum of needs extending from the present into the foreseeable future.

What is foreseeable and what period into the future should be selected for population forecasts depends a great deal upon the past growth characteristics of the urban study area, how large it is, and the specific uses to be made of the forecast. Obviously the conditions that are likely to prevail within the next ten years can be estimated with greater assurance than those that develop over a longer-range period. Too, the period that is foreseeable in one community may be quite different than what would be reasonable in another. As suggested earlier, areas in the throes of a spectacular and particularly a sudden growth cycle present more difficult problems than those experiencing growth at a slower pace. At the same time this very rapidity of change makes the necessity of a population forecast more pressing. It was also noted that population estimates for small urban areas were more subject to error than estimates for metropolitan areas. The same difficulties hold for forecasting procedures, but the hazards are more accentuated.

In the face of these problems, the forecaster is confronted with differing needs as to a forecast date. Different urban land uses have different life spans for amortization, and depending upon their space-using characteristics and the relative urgency there is to reserve land for each particular use, planning analyses often require varying forecast periods. Thus the difference in the magnitude of investment between a water supply system and a park system and the difference in the gross space needs involve differing demands in the length of the period into the future that must be taken into account. In providing for water requirements, an urban center must make a heavy initial investment in large property acquisitions, reservoir area preparations, impounding dams, and so on, and this entails looking further into the future than is necessary in acquiring and preparing land for recreation needs. One kind of decision involves eventualities 50 to 60 or perhaps even 100 years into the future, and another may involve considerations only five or ten years ahead at a time. Yet estimates suited to each decision are essential to the process of planning, and each with its varying assumptions and limitations as to accuracy must be taken into account and accorded its place in population studies.

While there is no reason why the land use plan, or for that matter the comprehensive plan, cannot be developed with variable ultimate terminal dates for varying land use categories, it is customary to present these plans with development proposals brought into synchronization in time. As brought out in Part III, a metropolitan area's plans may be set forth in at least three time scales: (1) the scale of time involved in a goal scheme (often called the "horizon-year plan," sometimes a "policies plan"), (2) the scale of time commonly recognized in the comprehensive plan (variously called the "master plan, "general plan," or "guide plan" covering a 20- to 25-year period); and (3) the scale associated with the capital improvements plan (usually the five- or six-year period embraced in the capital budget). Clearly, different time scales call for different concepts of accuracy. In dealing with generalized space use and circulation requirements in the goal scheme, an approximate population size is all that is needed, that is, whether the metropolitan area is likely to reach 5 million rather than 2 million or 500,000 rather than 100,000. At the comprehensive plan time scale, an estimate within 10 per cent is considered desirable, and at the capital budget planning level, where exactitude in population forecasts may become even more crucial (for example, as in the case of planning for schools), greater accuracy is desired, usually within 5 per cent.[30]

While the planning profession needs to give further study to standards of accuracy and establish tolerance limits for error in different types of planning analyses, this kind of research will not of itself result in improved forecasts. Given some specification of the accuracy levels required, demographic research is still needed in perfecting techniques best suited to each kind of need. In this connection, it is noteworthy that many demographers will not involve themselves in forecasts for small areas. Traditionally they have worked with large areas—the nation, regions, and states—but they have been reluctant to engage in work on small areas because of the problem of meeting their own standards of accuracy. They acknowledge the needs of city planners and recognize the dilemma, holding out hope that demographic research will in time remedy this situation.

It is understandable that the population specialist leans toward this position, yet there are moderating circumstances in planning applications

[30] The tolerance limits for error are relatively ill-defined in planning practice, and the problem warrants some careful research. Obviously, the minimization of error, especially at the 25- and 5-year time scales, will be more critical for some elements of the plan than for others. Until standards of accuracy are more clearly defined by the profession for different elements of the plan and for different time scales, decisions on methods to be employed in forecasting population will necessarily remain indecisive.

of forecasts that demographers are not always aware of which tend to offset the hazards of inaccuracy. In the first place, some applications are less demanding of the high levels of accuracy that demographers strive for in their own uses of population data. Planning standards are sometimes variable in actual practice, and often the final decisions made will depend less on the population forecast than on the selection of the standard. But more directly related to the mechanics of the land use planning process, the use of safety factors in translating forecast data into land requirements permits greater tolerance limits for error than might be required in other applications. As pointed out in the discussion of employment forecasts, this is as much of a standard practice in planning as it is in civil engineering, where, for example, safety factors are introduced to make the designed capacity of a bridge much greater than the estimated maximum load that it will bear. But more fundamental than those considerations, the very nature of the planning process itself calls for a continuing activity of review and restudy, thus affording the opportunity to adjust continually for error.

The need for both city planning and demographic research on population forecasting and the need for improved communications between the fields are thus evident. Yet these considerations are not justification for overlooking the hazards involved, the fundamental limitations of small-area forecasts, and the need for caution in statements concerning the results. Too, many of the limitations are of a more fundamental order than those of technique and procedure. As Dorn implies in painting the broad picture in this respect, there are pitfalls in population estimation of a broad nature that apply to all forecasting work, for the nation as well as regions and on down to small-area forecasting.[31] The influence of economic conditions on the rate at which families are formed and on the voluntary control of fertility, the impact of technology and scientific developments on family life, the effect of advances in medicine on birth and death rates, and so on —these are fundamental considerations that profoundly affect the accuracy of any population forecast regardless of the size of the area being studied.

General Considerations

Before taking up the various methods of forecasting population, it would be well to sketch in some of the factors which affect results. If the effect of annexation, consolidation, and other forms of change in the territorial limits of the urban study area are disregarded, population change occurs by deaths, births, and migration. Any forecast, whether or not the method

[31] Harold F. Dorn, "Pitfalls in Population Forecasts and Projections," *Journal of the American Statistical Association,* September, 1950.

actually makes direct analysis of these three variables, either explicitly or implicitly involves assumptions with respect to each. Deaths have been traditionally the most stable of the three variables and therefore the least troublesome to forecast. Birth rates involve more complex antecedent factors, and the effect, for example, of peace or war, prosperity or depression on marriage rates and the rate at which families are formed are more difficult to assess. These factors, of course, are related to the values and attitudes held, the elusive natures of which were brought out in Chapter 1. In this connection, it has even been intimated that the power of suggestion from advertisements of automobile manufacturers and the housing and appliance industries in "fortuitously" dropping their old two-child stereotype of the American family in favor of families with three and sometimes four and five children may have an influence on attitudes toward family size.[32] These factors obviously make the task of forecasting births difficult.

Migration is also difficult to estimate with any degree of certainty. In his valuable bulletin on forecasting techniques, Stanbery succinctly summarizes the principal causes of migration as:

1. The desire for better economic opportunities. Interstate migration is largely a movement from areas with relatively low planes of living to areas with higher income levels.
2. The attraction of milder or more suitable climates in other areas.
3. Desire for better living or housing conditions. This applies particularly to short distance migration within the same general locality.
4. Movement for reasons of health, education, or retirement.[33]

Of these causes, the first is the most important, and in the average community generally is responsible for the major percentage of migration. As pointed out in the previous chapter, one major reason for undertaking employment studies is to determine the probable extent to which in- or out-migration in response to economic opportunity may affect the future population prospects of the urban study area. Here again, such basic considerations as prosperity or depression, peace or war, and so on, can have a very marked influence on the volume of net migration.

This brings us to a consideration of the desirability of developing the forecast in terms of high and low estimates and the importance of identifying the assumptions coupled with these estimates. It is customary to express a forecast in terms of a range of possibilities bracketing what ap-

---

[32] From commentary on "Baby Boom" appearing in "The Reporter's Notes," *The Reporter*, August 11, 1955.

[33] Van Beuren Stanbery, *Better Population Forecasting for Areas and Communities*, prepared for the U.S. Department of Commerce, Washington: U.S. Government Printing Office, September, 1952, p. 5.

pears to represent the most probable range of conditions prevailing during the forecast period. This does not necessarily mean that the range is developed to cover all eventualities, that is, from total peace to all-out war, but rather to represent the likely direction of things at the time of the forecast, with a full realization that periodically review studies must be made to re-examine these assumptions in the light of more recent developments.

Stanbery identifies the following as *basic assumptions,* either explicitly stated or implied in most forecasts:

The form of government and the political, economic, and social organization and institutions of the United States will remain substantially unchanged.

No all-out war, internal revolution, nation-wide devastation, epidemic, or other disaster will occur.

No large-scale epidemic, destruction by military action, fire, earthquake, or other disaster will occur in the area or within the geographical or economic region to which the area is closely related.[34]

In making these the characteristic basic assumptions, he implies that economic conditions are the basis for supplemental or *special assumptions.* Such conditions as "no major recession and continued full employment" might thus be identified as a "high" assumption, and "a downswing in the business cycle, with unemployment leveling off at x per cent of the civilian labor force" as a "low" assumption. To such a general range of conditions assumed by the forecaster are added various others which may pertain to purely local circumstances. Thus if there is a military base in the locale, certain supplemental assumptions are introduced concerning international conditions and the general size of the armed forces. In an area dependent on extractive resources, the conditions selected will pertain to the degree of exploitation public policy permits and the extent to which conservation measures such as sustained-yield timber farming are practiced, and so on. In the more common situations, assumptions may relate to the structure and vitality of the economy, with "high" and "low" conditions, for example, being attached to "improvement" and "no change" alternatives.

As in the case of employment forecasting, the development of high and low projections bracketing the most probable size of the future population does not preclude the selection of a "single best estimate" for planning analyses. This estimate may vary according to the use that is to be made of it. Thus, "in planning the future water supply for a community, the high population projection would probably be used to assure an adequate supply for the largest expected population. But for estimating probable

---

[34] *Ibid.,* p. 3.

minimum revenues from the project, the low projection might be used in order to be on the safe side." [35]

The foregoing comments relate to the selection of a "single best estimate" from a forecast by one method with high and low alternatives. There is also the problem of selecting the "single best estimate" from forecasts using several methods. This involves the matter of accuracy of the various methods, particularly as they apply to small-area forecasting. What experience is available in testing the accuracy of the different methods will be taken up later. For the present, it can be observed that in the absence of the needed systematic testing of results from the various commonly used forecasting methods, most population analysts make their choice of methods on the basis of a priori judgments from their experience in the use of a few of these methods. The problem then becomes one of selecting on these grounds the particular estimate that will be used for planning purposes. As noted above, there may be two estimates instead of one, depending upon the use to be made of the forecast. For land use planning purposes, a single estimate is generally used, with the choice being made with a bias more to the high than the low side. This is based on the reasoning that it is better to err on the high than on the low side in the estimation of space needs for housing, industry, and other land uses. The decision is not so immediately crucial as it would appear, however, for, as noted above, the choice of standard and the extent of the safety factor introduced into analyses of space requirements are means for compensating for possible extreme errors in choice of the forecast estimate. In effect, the decision as to the bias to be used, if any, is postponed until the land use planning analyses are undertaken, when, by means of these adjustment devices, *an effective best estimate is selected for each use,* the nature of the adjustment being dependent upon how crucial it is to provide a margin of safety for that particular use.

With these general observations as a background, we turn to a review of some of the most common forecast methods used in small-area studies. Five methods or groups of methods will be summarized: (1) the cohort-survival method, (2) the migration and natural increase method, a variation on the first, (3) forecast methods based on estimates for larger geographical areas, (4) forecasts based on estimates of future employment, and (5) the mathematical and graphical extrapolation methods. The first two may be classed as analytical approaches in that they base future population estimates on an analysis of the major components of population change; the other methods are sometimes considered short-cut approaches in that they deal only with the combined effects of these components.

[35] *Ibid.,* p. 11.

The only one of the five approaches which yields data on age composition and sex composition directly is the cohort-survival method, although, as noted later in the chapter, crude ratio procedures are sometimes used with other methods in approximating age-sex breakdowns of the estimated future population.

Cohort-Survival Method

This method is modeled generally after the analytical approach used in developing estimates for the nation as a whole. It is the most complex of the methods taken up here, and because of the special and often very technical problems encountered in the course of the estimation procedure, it requires an experienced population analyst to execute the forecast. Briefly, it is a method that adjusts figures from the last census forward by age groups and sex groups year by year to the date of the forecast, with separate adjustments made for each of the three major components of population change: deaths, births, and net migration. A variation on this approach records the change in population by five-year intervals, using a fertility ratio to fill in data for new persons appearing in each new 0–4 age group. (The fertility ratio is the number of children aged 0–4, inclusive, per 1,000 females of child-bearing age at the end of this five-year time span.)

Each variable is estimated separately and adjustments are made to establish what the next year's population (or that of the next five-year interval) is expected to be. Separate tables are developed for males and females, and additional separate tables can be developed for whites and nonwhites where large proportions of nonwhite population make it advisable to make these breakdowns. Also, a separate series of these tables is developed for low and for high estimates. Death rates (age-specific or by five-year intervals) are determined from standard life tables. Age-specific birth rates or, alternatively, fertility ratios for five-year intervals are estimated by reference to special studies of long-range trends in local birth rates. Net migration rates (age-specific or by five-year intervals) are estimated by reference to studies of past trends in migration and future employment prospects. Unless wartime conditions are anticipated as one contingency of the forecast, death rates would be the same for both low and high estimates. Birth rates or fertility ratios and net migration rates would vary according to low and high assumptions that are established for the locality. As noted above, they are the most difficult to estimate. In some locales there will be available for reference use previously prepared state tables on one or more of these last variables, some possibly with an urban classification for the state as a whole. If there are such materials available, they can rarely be used without adaptation to a particular locale and a particular set of local assumptions.

Table 14 illustrates in generalized form the mechanics of the procedure for carrying estimates forward to the date of the forecast. It illustrates the variation on this method that makes the analysis by five-year intervals and employs fertility ratios. The arrows indicate how each cohort is carried forward from the base date (in this instance the 1960 census) to the forecast date, with illustrative detail shown for tracing changes in the 1960 age group, 0–4 years. The first succession of steps derives from abridged life tables for the appropriate age groups, death rates which are used in computing the number of survivors from each age group to be carried forward to the next age bracket at the beginning of the next five-year period.[36] In the next succession of steps, the net in- or out-migration is estimated by age groups for the same intervals of time and entered as the second adjustment shown in Table 14.[37] The sum of the survivors and the in- or out-migrants from the original age group furnish the estimate for the next higher age group at the beginning of the next five-year period. The circled figure, the new 0–4 age group, is obtained by applying the approximate fertility ratio to the number of females of child-bearing age (usually 15-44) at the beginning of the last period.[38] Although these steps illustrate the procedure in a general way, obviously there are certain

---

[36] For references on life tables, methods of developing abridged life tables, and methods for computing survival rates from these tables, see A. J. Jaffe's Bureau of the Census publication, *Handbook of Statistical Methods for Demographers,* preliminary edition, second printing, Washington: U.S. Government Printing Office, 1951, Chapter 2.

[37] Values for net migration are developed in special studies of past trends of net migration rates for various age groups and the way in which future rates will reflect low and high assumptions of the forecasts as determined from studies of the urban economy. Past net migration rates for each ten-year age group can be established by surviving the population of one age group to the next higher age group from one census to the next census, using actual birth and death data (corrected for underregistration), with the difference at the terminal census date between the expected and the actual population in each age bracket being used to compute the net migration rate for each age group in the particular intercensal period. Five-year age-group rates are developed from the ten-year age-group rates by customary demographic procedures. See Jaffe, *ibid.*

[38] Fertility ratio values are obtained from special studies that must be made of local trends in the past and how these trends may be expected to function in the future under low and high assumptions. In turn, these assumptions must be based on alternate estimates of the marriage rate and the number of children per marriage, or, in other words, on trends in the size of completed families.

The estimation of future fertility rates has received renewed attention by demographers in the past several years. For general tables, see Pascal K. Whelpton and Arthur A. Campbell, "Fertility Tables for Birth Cohorts of American Women," in National Office of Vital Statistics, *Vital Statistics—Special Reports,* Vol. 51, No. 1, January 29, 1960. For discussions of problems and techniques, see Ronald Freedman, Pascal K. Whelpton, and Arthur A. Campbell, *Family Planning, Sterility, and Population Growth,* New York: McGraw-Hill Book Company, Inc., 1959. For a report on a continuing annual survey of fertility, see Morris Axelrod, Ronald Freedman, David Goldberg, and Doris Slesinger, "Fertility Expectation of the United States Population: A Time Series," *Population Index,* January, 1963.

Table 14. Sample Work Table Illustrating Forecast Procedure by Cohort-Survival Method Using Five-Year Intervals—Female Table (One of Two Tables for "Low" Estimate)

Year	0-4	5-9	10-14	15-19	20-24	25-29	30-34	35-39	40-44	45-49	50-54	55-59	60-64	65-69 etc.	Total Females
						Age Groups (Females)									
1960	256	231	283	315	395	373	287	275	228	183	144	133	100	66	3340
1965															
1970															
1975															
1980															

(For years 1965, 1970, 1975, 1980 the diagonal cohort projections are shown:)

XXX Survivors
±XX Net migrants
XXX

special adjustments required along the way to account for underenumeration in particular age groups, underregistration of births and deaths, and the deaths and births of migrants.

Migration and Natural Increase Method

This method is a simpler form of the analytical approach and is similar in many respects to the migration and natural increase method used in estimating current population. Forecasts derived from this method involve separate analyses of two components in place of three as in the cohort-survival method, and provide estimates only for the total population, without breaking out age-sex components. It starts with a current estimate of the population, and by introducing adjustments first for migration and then for natural increase on a year-by-year basis, it develops annual estimates into the future until the forecast date is reached.

Table 15 is a sample work table used in the method, illustrating the accrual aspects of the procedure. Taking up first the migration component, low and high net migration rates may be estimated by reference to past trends and assumptions as to future economic conditions (determined from study of urban economy) and other relevant factors (for example, enrollment prospects in areas where there are educational centers). The past net migration rates may be computed by procedures similar to those cited under the cohort-survival method, except that the population is "survived"

Table 15. Sample Work Table Illustrating Forecast Procedure by Migration and Natural Increase Method —"Low" Estimate Table

Year	Population (1)	Net Migration		Pop. After Adjustment for Net Migration (±) (4)	Natural Increase		Pop. After Adjustment for Natural Increase —Next Year's Pop. (7)
		Rate (±) (2)	Amount (±) (3)		Rate [a] (5)	Amount (6)	
1965							
1966							
1967							
1968							
1969							
1970							
.							
.							
.							
1985							

[a] Some forecasters introduce a crude correction step here to recognize that part of the natural increase among migrating families during the year shown in the stub of the table is already accounted for before they arrive or after they leave the community. Accordingly, they apply the natural increase rate to the full amount in Column 1 and to half the amount in Column 3 on the assumption that half of the births and deaths in migrating families occur after in- or out-migration.

from each past census period to the next as a total rather than by age-sex groups.[39] Using mathematical or graphical procedures, a general future trend line is first established from a graphic plot of both past net migration rates.

Then adjustments from this trend line in the form of supplemental curves are subjectively developed based on the low and high assumptions as to economic conditions and other factors. Among his suggestions for supplemental investgations, Stanbery lists the following considerations as aids in making these subjective determinations.[40]

1. Past relationships between the direction and volume of net migration in the area and the levels of national economic activity and rise, or decline, in per capita real incomes.
2. The relative rates of increase of employment and population nationally and in the area during decades of rapid national economic expansion (1920–30 and 1940–50), and during periods of slower expansion (1930–40).
3. Outlook for economic development and expansion of employment in the area during the period of the forecast.

On the basis of these considerations, Stanbery suggests that the forecaster

[39] A rough check of the ten-year net migration for the period 1950 to 1960 can be obtained on a county, SMSA, or State Economic Area basis by consulting Bureau of the Census, "Components of Population Change, 1950 to 1960, for Counties, SMSA's, State Economic Areas, and Economic Subregions," *Current Population Reports,* Series P-23, No. 7, November, 1962.

[40] Stanbery, *Better Population Forecasting for Areas and Communities,* p. 68.

then proceed to decide whether minimum and maximum net migration during the forecast period appears likely to vary upward or downward from the smallest and largest volumes of net migration observed during past decades, finally establishing low and high levels to be introduced into the analysis.

As an alternative to estimating net migration by these procedures, an approach based more directly on results of employment forecasts may be used. Local net migration as derived above for past decades is expressed as a percentage of employment in past periods of time, with the trend extended by mathematical or graphical extrapolation procedures to the forecast date. The resulting ratio is then applied to low and high estimates from the employment forecast to provide estimates of future net migration. Since this approach is based on the assumption that migration is a function of employment opportunity, obviously it is not fully applicable to such urban areas as retirement, educational, or health centers.

Estimates of future natural increase rates may be made on the basis of subjective extensions of past minimum and maximum rates somewhat parallel to the first approach above to estimating net migration, or they may be developed by reference to previously prepared vital statistics projections for larger geographical areas. Local natural increase rates for past years in time are computed from recorded resident birth and death data. Intercensal estimates of population for rate computations (here and for net migration rates) are usually based on a linear interpolation of the population for the census figures at the beginning and ending of the decade. Under the first approach, these past rates are examined for minima and maxima and for trend indications, and after deciding on likely low and high assumptions for the future, alternative curves of the future trend in the natural increase rate are developed. It should be noted that because of the relatively short period for which the local vital statistics contained in national summaries are available by place of residence (since 1936), and in view of the extreme depression and wartime fluctuations in births experienced in most communities for which these data are available, conventional extrapolation procedures are likely to be difficult if not unfeasible. Thus these curves will usually be based largely on a subjectively reasoned approach rather than on the extrapolation of past trends. The alternative approach uses as a guide estimated future crude birth and death rate trends previously prepared for a larger area, and by observing relationships between rates of the local and larger area in the past, develops trends for future local rates under low and high assumptions.[41]

With separate analyses of net migration and natural increase rates com-

---

[41] For use of this approach in a short-cut version of the migration and natural increase method, see *ibid.*, pp. 71–73.

pleted, data are transcribed to Columns 2 and 5 of the appropriate "low" and "high" tables as illustrated in the sample work table (Table 15). Using the current population estimate as the point of beginning (the figure at the head of Column 1), it then becomes a simple matter of arithmetic to develop the entries in Columns 4 and 7 and arrive at a population estimate for the forecast date.

Estimates Based on Forecasts for Larger Areas

This method employs a previously prepared forecast for some larger geographical area—usually the nation, the region, or the state—and by ratio procedures establishes how the local area may be expected to share in the forecast population of the larger area. Population ratios may be established direct between the larger area and the urban study area, or they may be developed as several interlocking series of ratios, stepping-down estimates for the larger area to the urban study area through a system of intermediate areas. The latter approach has two variations. One employs *apportionment procedures in a multiphased analysis* of all parts of each parent area (the nation, the region, or the state), balancing estimates for all subareas with the parent area total before proceeding to the next step-down. The other makes *direct step-downs in a single-phased analysis,* without reference to the way other subareas of the system may be sharing in the parent area total. The procedural principles of both were discussed in some detail in the last chapter.

As brought out in the use of these techniques for employment forecasts, the population of the smaller area is expressed as a percentage of that of the larger area for past decades. These ratio values are plotted in a time series, and a curve is fitted to the data and projected to the forecast date. The projected ratio is then applied to the given future population estimate of the larger area to obtain the absolute population figures for the smaller area. Such a procedure is followed for both low and high estimates selected from the given series of estimates for the larger area (for example, low and high estimates of the future population of the nation or the state of interest as released periodically in the Bureau of the Census, *Current Population Reports,* Series P-25). If a system of intermediate areas is used, the above-described procedure is repeated until an estimate for the urban study area is finally derived. If the apportionment technique is employed, estimates for all subareas in the selected system of geographical areas are balanced with the larger-area estimate before this procedure is carried to the next smaller system of study areas.

Table 16 is a sample work table illustrating the sequence to the step-

Table 16. Sample Work Table Illustrating Forecast Procedure Using Previously Prepared Estimates of Larger Geographic Areas—"Low" Estimate Table

Year	U.S. Population	Census Division Population	C.D./U.S.	State Population	S./C.D.	SMSA Population	SMSA/S.
Census							
1900							
1910							
1920							
1930							
1940							
1950							
1960							
Estimates							
1970							
1980							
1990							
2000							

down procedure in a single-phased analysis, using the census division and the state as the intermediate types of areas between the nation and an SMSA of interest. If the local study area is a city, the step-down procedure usually employs *urban* population ratios in place of ratios based on *total* population figures (giving due consideration to changes in the census definition of "urban").

A special application of this approach is usually used in areas with large military installations. Because of extreme fluctuations in troop strength that frequently occur even at the more permanent bases and in view of the semitransient character of this segment of the local population, the analysis of the separate effects of migration, births, and deaths involved in the first two methods above becomes extremely complex—so complex and with such a variety of qualifications that population analysts generally consider the use of ratio techniques better suited to these situations.

For small urban centers where the military installation tends to maintain a dominant position in the local economy, generally the most satisfactory procedure to follow is to break down the forecast analysis into three parts —one concerned with the military personnel and their dependents present in the area, one dealing with the military base-related civilian population, and the other treating the nonbase-related civilian population. Separate low and high estimates are developed for each component and results are summed up for the forecast date to obtain the total population or the civilian and military population as may be desired. Analysis of the military component first deals with military strength, employing ratio techniques to establish the share that local installations may be expected to have in state or national military strength under alternative assumptions as to the future size of the armed forces, and then, by reference to past minimum and maximum levels of dependent population present, establishes assumed low and high estimates for the full component of military personnel and dependents.[42] Next, the military-related civilian component is estimated, either by reference to previously prepared employment forecasts and the expansion of these estimates to full population equivalents (using techniques discussed in the next section below), or, on the basis of analyses of the past relationship between military-related civilian population and the military strength of local installations, by development of assumed future ratios to be applied to the low and high estimates of future military strength. Finally, the nonmilitary-related civilian component is estimated for the forecast date using conventional ratio procedures described above.

In larger metropolitan areas where military-related civilian employment needs are reasonably well contained by the local labor market, the foregoing approach can be simpified, using only military strength and civilian population as the components of the ratio analyses. Stanbery's population forecast for the county and city of San Diego is a well-documented illustration of this last approach.[43]

Estimates Based on Employment Forecasts

Where employment forecasts have been previously prepared for the urban study area, this method is often used as a basis for making population projections. Using the same basic ratio principle involved in the last-described method, the method expands future employment figures to labor force estimates which in turn are expanded to population equivalents. The method thus assumes fairly stable relationships between these series. Obviously the method is not suited to the study of retirement centers, university communities, resort cities, and in areas with similar kinds of special circumstances affecting these relationships.

The employment forecast, the point of beginning for analyses by this

[42] For analyses of past trends of military-connected population at the state level as of July 1, see the November or December release on provisional estimates of the population by states in the P-25 Series of *Current Population Reports*. By taking the difference between resident and civilian population, it is possible to estimate the size of military population (with dependents). See Series P-25, No. 229, for a recapitulation of these data for 1950 to 1960.

[43] Van Beuren Stanbery, "Population Analysis and Projections, County and City of San Diego," San Francisco: Industrial Survey Associates, May, 1953, processed.

method, has been discussed at some length in Chapter 4. Two sets of ratios are computed for past periods of time—one expressing employment as a percentage of total labor force, and the other expressing labor force as a percentage of population. Each set of ratios is ordered in a time series, and curves are fitted to the data and projected. Future values of these ratios are then successively applied to expand employment estimates to population estimates. The process is repeated for low and high estimates of future employment. In this connection, Stanbery points out that forecasts by these procedures commonly assume that there will be unemployment no greater than 10 per cent of the labor force in the area.[44]

Mathematical and Graphical Methods

Of the great variety of methods falling within this category and from time to time propounded for local population analyses, those encountered most frequently include arithmetic and geometric projections, trend extrapolation by the method of least squares, and estimates based on the logistic curve. The previously described forecasting methods employing ratio techniques commonly make use of the first three of these projection methods as a means for extrapolating ratio curves forward in time. However, when applied directly to population data, especially in long-range forecasts, these methods have limited utility, it being generally conceded that no mathematical law yet discovered can wholly or consistently contain the forces governing population growth.

The arithmetic and geometric projections assume that the same forces affecting population change in the past will continue to apply in the future. Applied to data plotted on plain coordinate graph paper, the arithmetic approach results in a straight-line projection and assumes the same *numerical change* for similar periods of time. The geometric projection is represented by a straight line on semilogarithmic graph paper, signifying similar *rates of change* for similar periods of time. Under the method of least squares, a best-fitting straight-line equation is developed to fit a time series plot, and the mathematical extension of this curve provides estimates of population at selected dates in the future. In effect an extension of the method of least squares, the use of multiple regression as a technique for making projections is sometimes used. In using this technique, usually some symptomatic series of data, for example, time series on births, deaths, and net migration, are introduced as independent variables, with the total population being the dependent variable. When used in a linear form, this approach, like the least squares method, is most useful for short-term fore-

---

[44] Stanbery, *Better Population Forecasting for Areas and Communities,* p. 33.

casts. The logistic curve is an S-shaped curve developed by Raymond Pearl and Lowell J. Reed based on their work with the growth phenomena of fruit flies. Their Logistic I and their subsequent modification of it in Logistic II are mathematical representations of an S-shaped curve developed from studies of the growth of national population, and the use of the curve in a local situation assumes that the population growth pattern is behaving similarly to national growth phenomena. To apply this curve, the slope of the population growth curve in the local area must have passed through a decceleration period from an initially rising rate of increase. Under these circumstances a logistic curve fitted to the data is then used to establish future population estimates.

Accuracy of Methods

Earlier it was noted that there was a need for more rigorous tests of the accuracy of postcensal methods of estimation. The need for similar, more systematic tests of forecast methods is even greater. On the basis of what tests have been made, there appears to be some agreement that the longer the forecast period, the smaller the area for which projections are made, and the more rapid the growth that occurs during the forecast period, the less accurate the results tend to be. But reports on these tests have been quite inconclusive on the relative accuracy of the commonly used forecasting methods, and very little attention seems to have been given to what methods appear to be best suited for varying forecast periods, growth characteristics, and size ranges of urban areas.

Schmitt and Crosetti present some valuable information on two of the five groups of methods reviewed above.[45] In ex post facto analyses of 20 cities in which they "forecast" population for 1940 and/or 1950 and compared results with actual census counts, they tested the short and long forms of the ratio technique (identified above as forecasts based on previously prepared estimates of larger areas, using direct and intermediate area step-downs), three mathematical methods (arithmetic, geometric, and logistic curve projections), and the analogy method (not included in the series of methods reviewed).[46] The five most populous urban areas in the

---

[45] For a report of tests on ratio techniques, see Robert C. Schmitt and Albert H. Crosetti, "Accuracy of the Ratio Method for Forecasting City Population," *Land Economics*, November, 1951; for a report on the extension of tests to other methods, see Schmitt and Crosetti, "Short-Cut Methods of Forecasting City Population," *The Journal of Marketing*, April, 1953.
[46] Considered one of the less reliable methods, this approach matches up the recent growth characteristics of the given city with those experienced by one or more other cities in the past, and then, using as a guide the recent growth trends of the prototype cities, projects the population growth of the city of interest forward in time.

four census regions were selected, with tests being made for both the central cities and their Standard Metropolitan Statistical Areas, and for 10- and 20-year periods. On the basis of their tests they arrive at the following conclusions:

1. The logistic curve, arithmetic projection, and two forms of the ratio method produced almost equally accurate results, on the average, in population forecasts for cities and metropolitan areas. These four methods were much more accurate than either the geometric projections or the analogy methods.
2. Twenty-year forecasts were less accurate—but not excessively so—than projections covering only a 10-year period.
3. Metropolitan forecasts differed little from forecasts for central cities in degree of accuracy.[47]

In generalizing on these results, they state that "the high degree of forecasting error characteristic of the ratio method indicates it to be of limited value to city planners," concluding after their later more extended series of tests that there is no foolproof short-cut approach to small-area forecasting.

Although tests of these methods used in large-area forecasts do not necessarily indicate what would be best in small-area work, it may be noted that studies by the Bureau of the Census of a broader range of forecasting methods as applied to states did not produce conclusive evidence of the superiority of any one method over all others tested.[48] These tests included the cohort-survival method, ratio and apportionment approaches, and arithmetic and geometric projections. While it was concluded that no method was clearly superior to the others, the cohort-survival method, the apportionment approach, and one form of the ratio technique were found to produce consistently the best showings.

Siegel's comparison of results from some 99 forecasts for small areas with 1940 and 1950 census returns brings out some interesting tendencies in the direction that errors appear to take. In these forecasts, involving all groups of methods reviewed above, he found that nearly two-thirds underestimated the population. "This type of bias appears to be characteristic of work done in the thirties and forties in the measurement of population growth to 1950. The opposite type of bias, however, may be characteristic of these same forecasts so far as population changes during future decades are concerned. . . ."[49]

---

[47] Schmitt and Crosetti, "Short-Cut Methods of Forecasting City Population," p. 424.

[48] Helen R. White, "Empirical Study of the Accuracy of Selected Methods of Projecting State Populations," *Population Index*, July, 1952.

[49] Jacob S. Siegel, "Forecasting the Population of Small Areas," *Land Economics*, February, 1953, p. 80.

Population Characteristics and Distribution

To round out the population series of tooling-up studies, it is important to include some brief consideration of the types of analyses of population characteristics and distribution that are useful to land use planning. While most investigations of this kind are best carried out as part of the specific land use planning analyses in which they are to be used, sometimes they may be scheduled in advance in conjunction with general demographic studies. Certainly they should be outlined at the time the above-discussed studies of current and future population are planned so that the original basic studies are conducted with these needs in view. Then, as and when population composition and distribution data are needed, it becomes a simple procedure of extending the original basic population studies to obtain the breakdowns in the form desired.

Population Characteristics

Of the variety of ways of breaking down the total population, urban-wide land use planning analyses generally utilize breakdowns of three kinds: age, income, and household size. Other ways of breaking down the total population—by sex, by race, by nationality, by educational background, or by other categories—may provide useful background insights into the general makeup of a city's population, but with the possible exception of racial composition, these have more limited utility in land use planning studies. While the U.S. Supreme Court has removed any vestigial legal reasons for separate attention to different racial elements of the population, city planning will continue to find special studies of racial composition to be of importance. These may be important in forecasts where there appear to be distinct differences in birth, death, or net migration trends among whites and nonwhites. Where this is a factor (and it is likely to become less and less important as economic opportunities for Negroes improve), it may be that forecasts of each racial component of the total would yield a more reliable forecast of total population than if race were ignored.

Age composition data are important primarily for school and recreation planning analyses, with forecasts of age composition being of special concern in determining long-range facility needs and land requirements for school and recreation sites. As noted previously, the only type of population forecast in which age data are developed as an integral part of the projection procedure is the cohort-survival method. Where this method is not employed, a ratio technique is often used to approximate how the estimated total future population will be distributed among the various age categories. This application of the ratio technique involves the same elemental procedures followed in other applications of the technique described in this and the preceding chapter. For past census periods each selected age group is expressed as a per cent of total population, and resulting ratio values for each age group are then plotted in a time series. Curves are fitted to the data for each age group, and the projected ratios for each such age group are read off these curves for the forecast year and are applied to the total population estimate for that year to obtain an approximation of the number in each age group in absolute figures. Although curves can be subjectively adjusted to reflect known trends affecting age composition (for example, in retirement centers, an anticipated increase in immigrant elderly couples, or changes in the rate that families are being formed, changes in the number of children per family, etc.), this technique must be regarded as a crude substitute for the cohort-survival technique which gives these factors more systematic consideration.

A more refined approach has been detailed by Hamilton and Perry in which, using decennial census data, they estimate the age composition for the decade ahead, say 1970, by examining the proportional distribution of each 1960 age group as it was in 1960 and as it was ten years earlier in 1950.[50] They express the relationship in the following form:

$$P_x^7 = (P_{x-10}^6 \cdot P_x^6) / P_{x-10}^5$$

where P_x^7 is the population of age group x in 1970; P_x^6 is the population of age group x in 1960; P_{x-10}^6 is the population of age group $x-10$ in 1960; and P_{x-10}^5 is the population of age group $x-10$ in 1950. The projections for the under-10 age group in 1960 may be estimated assuming that age-specific fertility rates prevailing in 1960 (or in some other recent period) will remain constant until 1970.

Family income characteristics for small areas became available for the first time in the 1950 census, the data being obtained on a sampling basis from every fifth family covered in the population enumeration. While it will take another two or three decades before this information can begin to be used satisfactorily in trend analyses (assuming valid adjustment factors for the changing value of the dollar), it has considerable immediate value in housing market analyses, particularly when such studies are scheduled and executed at the time of the decennial census. For example, with respect to the rental market alone, in establishing how the supply of housing

---

[50] C. Horace Hamilton and Josef Perry, "A Short Method for Projecting Population by Age from One Decennial Census to Another," *Social Forces*, December, 1962.

at various rental levels actually matches up with the number of renting families at the income levels that correspond to these rental levels, it is possible to obtain a crude picture of the under- or oversupply of rental housing which may exist for renting families of different income brackets. As will be seen in a later chapter, this kind of information has application in land use planning analyses in providing a guide for establishing the proportion of undeveloped and redeveloped land to be allocated to different residential density classes. In the future, as trend information on income characteristics can be established and applied in forecasts of the housing market, we can expect improvements in this land allocation procedure.

Household-size information also has application in residential land use planning studies. Households are defined by the Bureau of the Census as being made up of all persons occupying a housing unit (dwelling unit in 1950 census), including the related family members and also the unrelated persons who may be residing in the housing/dwelling unit, such as roomers, foster children, wards, or employees. A household may consist of one person living alone in the housing/dwelling unit or a group of unrelated individuals sharing the housing/dwelling unit.[51] To be distinguished from family-size data used in the 1930 census, household-size characteristics became a standard item of information beginning with the 1940 census. Household-size data have important applications in housing market analyses, with the percentage distribution of households by size providing guides in estimating overall space requirements for the various classes of residential structures applicable to the city under study. Studies of trends in the total number of households and the differential trends among the several typical size categories, along with studies of the rate of family formation, provide bases for estimating future household sizes. The same kinds of ratio procedures used in estimating future age composition can be used in estimating future household sizes, with investigations of economic trends, the rate of family formation, and birth rates providing the basis for the formulation of the high and low assumptions used in projections.

Spatial Distribution of Population

Not only do land use planning analyses require estimates of the future population composition for the urban area as a whole, but they also require an indication as to how the total population and how selected composition

---

[51] The difference in definition between a housing unit and a dwelling unit is so slight that for the purposes of analyses discussed in this book, we shall consider them the same and use the term *dwelling unit* (DU).

groups will be spatially distributed in the urban area. Thus estimates of the distribution of the future total population among the various neighborhoods have obvious implications for the study of residential areas and their community facilities. Moreover, while urban-wide age composition analyses are used in estimating the total land requirements for schools, estimates of the residential distribution of school-age children will provide guides as to how the estimated total land requirements should be allocated to the different parts of the city. Similarly, studies of the spatial distribution of various income groups and household-size categories among the different neighborhoods provide clues for the geographic patterning of residential densities. The application of these population studies and the other considerations involved in establishing future density patterns are taken up in a later chapter.

For purposes of the present discussion, we will allude to two approaches to the study of population distribution. One relates to daytime population distribution, or, more correctly, how people distribute themselves at different hours of the day or night; and the other is concerned with the residential distribution of population, or the place of residence where people are enumerated by the U.S. Census. The so-called daytime population study has received attention in demography only recently, and this is largely because data are not generally available in the form necessary for detailed studies of this kind. What work that has been done in daytime population analysis has been concerned with current population rather than future estimates. Besides the uses that daytime population data have in civil defense studies, they have important applications in transportation and parking studies, and as noted in Chapter 1, have potential utility in studies concerned with the establishment of "density ceilings" in the central business district and industrial areas.

Developed around sources of information presently available, two techniques have been employed in estimating the accumulation of population in various functional use areas for different hours of the day or night. At the University of North Carolina, a technique was devised to order data for this purpose from origin and destination surveys used in the series of metropolitan area traffic studies undertaken cooperatively by state highway commissions and the U.S. Bureau of Public Roads.[52] The data available from these studies were obtained principally from home interviews on a sampling basis, supplemented by information obtained from persons traveling by car into the urban area from beyond the home interview area.

---

[52] Industrial Areas Study, *Population Distribution—Spatial and Temporal,* Chapel Hill: Institute for Research in Social Science, University of North Carolina, September, 1952. This study examines daytime-nighttime population distribution patterns in Flint, Grand Rapids, Erie, Minneapolis–St. Paul, and in the Philadelphia-Camden area.

Using punch cards containing these data and beginning with the "low point" in the daily activity patterns of the normal household (usually 4 A.M.), machine tabulations of trip cards were made of the differences between the arrivals and departures of persons from each use area (composed of smaller-unit zones used in the traffic surveys as reference areas for trips) for each hour of the day and night. The result was a tabulation of the approximate number of people present in each use area for all hours of a 24-hour period—a general picture of the ebb and flow of people in a metropolitan area during a particular span of time.[53] Figure 6 shows how results may be summarized for a city in terms of density patterns for selected hours of the day.

The second technique is one devised by the Bureau of the Census for use by civil defense agencies in studying potential disaster areas resulting from air attack.[54] It provides a rough estimate of the total daytime population during the normal working and school hours of the day, broken down by census tracts or enumeration districts. The technique begins with the residential distribution of population recorded in the last census, and then adjusts these data, first, by subtracting out, tract by tract, workers, school population, and others assumed to be away from home during the major portion of the day. It then calls for the addition of the labor force (adjusted to include commuting workers from outside the urban study area), the school population, and estimates of people away from home for other reasons into those census tracts or enumeration districts where the Census of Manufactures, local school attendance summaries, and other sources of information indicate tracts or districts of concentration. Detailed notes on these procedures are furnished in *Civil Defense Urban Analysis*.

Turning now to the second approach to the study of population distribution, namely, one concerned with the residential distribution of the population, two somewhat similar techniques are taken up briefly. The first is a general-purpose form of small-area analysis, and the second is a zonal form. Both are used in estimating how the forecast total population of the urban area as a whole can be spatially distributed to small areas, and both

---

[53] Although providing perhaps the most detailed and accurate estimates that can presently be obtained (short of a census especially designed to obtain daytime population distribution data), results from this technique are nevertheless approximate. This is true for several reasons. For example, origin and destination traffic survey records do not yield the actual count of people present in each use area at the beginning point of the 24-hour analysis. To obtain an estimate of the 4 A.M. distribution of population requires adjustments of residential distribution figures (customarily used as the beginning point) to account for "graveyard shifts" present in work areas at 4 A.M. Other problems relate to "walking trips" and train commuter trips which are not recorded in some of these surveys. In effect, then, results obtained by this technique tend to understate the daytime population in work areas.

[54] Federal Civil Defense Administration, *Civil Defense Urban Analysis*, Washington: U.S. Government Printing Office, July, 1953, pp. 78–81.

can be used to determine how these small-area estimates of future population break down into age groups and other subtotals of population characteristics.

In general, both techniques employ apportionment procedures, and within the limits of the holding capacity of each small area derive estimates as to how neighborhoods, census tracts, or other small areas share in urban area population growth.[55] These estimates are based on trends in the way each small area in a selected system of areas has fared relative to the urban area as a whole. Under the general-purpose technique, ratios of the population of the central city and of each of the suburban areas to the urban study area population are computed for past census periods and plotted graphically. Then, considering holding capacities and residential building trends in each component small area, these curves are extrapolated into the future. This same procedure can be repeated to determine how smaller areas such as census tracts or neighborhoods share in the above derived subtotals.

The zonal technique utilizes groupings of census tracts in the form of a series of concentric zones around the central business district as the basic system of delineations for small-area analysis. The gross density and the percentage of total metropolitan area population are computed for each zone for past census periods and extrapolated. The extrapolated densities for all zones are then adjusted to take into account holding capacities and housing vacancy rates, and these results are used to adjust percentages of total metropolitan population expected to be found in each ring. The estimate of future population for the urban area as a whole is then apportioned to the various rings using the adjusted percentages as guides. Once population estimates are obtained for each concentric zone, these totals can be apportioned to smaller areas, that is, neighborhoods or census tracts, following similar procedures.[56]

The purpose of this chapter has been to summarize the available methods and techniques for population analyses required in land use planning studies. It is perhaps unnecessary to draw attention again to the varying degrees of accuracy that may be expected from the use of these methods

---

[55] The holding capacity may be considered here to mean the maximum possible population the land can accommodate at residential densities permissible under the combined application of the zoning ordinance and housing code. As discussed in greater detail in a later chapter, technically the holding capacity is the saturation point in the number of dwelling units an area can absorb under assumed densities of residential development. Thus in order to convert the holding capacity as expressed in terms of dwelling units to population-holding capacity, it is necessary to estimate future household sizes, multiplying the number of dwelling units an area is expected to contain by the average future household size in that area.

[56] The foregoing "hand" techniques for estimating the future residential distribution of the forecast total population of a metropolitan area are now being supplanted by mathematical techniques of the kind briefly described in the last part of Chapter 12.

and techniques in estimating the current population, the future population, and the composition and distribution of population in urban areas. Nor is it necessary to stress that as these types of studies are undertaken one after another, each successive task, built as it is upon the preceding study, becomes vulnerable to cumulative errors. Yet as hazardous as these studies appear to be, the risks involved do not obviate the necessity for these studies. They are "musts" for urban land use planning analyses. But even with the moderating circumstances involved in city planning applications of data derived in these studies cited throughout the chapter, the population analyst is obligated to seek the maximum possible accuracy consistent with the uses to be made of the data. Meanwhile, it is hoped that as demographers can be persuaded to give greater attention to small-area population analyses in their research efforts, some of the cruder techniques discussed above can be replaced with more reliable ones that can be put to use in city planning studies.

Chapter 6

The Study of Urban Activity Systems

So far we have been concerned with tooling-up studies which provide a perspective of the metropolitan area as it relates to a larger region, and to studies which supply a basis for scaling economic and population growth. We now turn our attention to the activities which go on within the metropolitan complex. In Chapter 2 the importance of viewing the city as a center for interaction and the need for identifying patterns of human and institutional interchange were emphasized. Picking up the interaction theme, this chapter is primarily concerned with various kinds of urban activity systems which take spatial form in the metropolitan area, particularly systems which assume importance in the structure and organization of the area. To some extent we will see how analyses discussed in Chapters 3, 4, and 5 can be extended and given spatial meaning, but to an important degree we will be concerned with an additional and distinct kind of tooling-up study.

At the outset it should be noted that much of what is taken up in this chapter is still to be made a part of standard operating procedures of planning agencies. Traditionally planning agencies have jumped directly into land use studies, essentially looking at the effects of activity systems rather than seeking to define and understand activities themselves as producers of land use patterns. At the same time it should be recognized that there are no fully tested techniques of analysis or, for that matter, methods for surveying and identifying activity systems. It takes time and a considerable amount of testing to develop survey and analytical techniques suited to this task, and so, in this chapter, little more than an approach can be outlined and a review undertaken of what experimentation has been carried on to date. The perfection of techniques proposed here thus remains to be achieved, but there is little doubt that these techniques will soon be in general use.

An Approach to the Study of Activity Systems

There is a fair degree of consensus today in the work on urban spatial structure that, whatever future pattern of land development is proposed, this pattern must be designed to fit as closely to the activity systems of the people who will be living in the metropolitan area as our knowledge and methods of analysis will permit. In this respect, the problem the city planner faces is twofold: (1) he must examine and interpret systems as they have evolved to date, and (2) he must use these observations and knowledge about basic changes in urban society to anticipate the space-related kinds of activities of persons and institutions which are likely to be dominant in the metropolitan area in the future. In this chapter we will be primarily concerned with the first of these problems, but in order to insure that investigations of activities will lead directly into the forecast aspect of the problem, some attention will need to be given to the eventual uses of information in land use planning. To assist the reader in this respect, tie-ins to later chapters will be cited along the way.

Clarification of Terms

Before developing the outlines of an approach to the study of activity systems, it will be useful to define more clearly the meaning imputed here to "activity systems" and in the process indicate more precisely the requirements of an approach consonant with the operational pattern of planning agencies as they are constituted today. Let us begin first with the extraterritorial aspects of interaction. There are two aspects of human interaction which must be taken into account: (1) the systems which have no specific boundaries but which may be region-wide, nation-wide, or world-wide at any particular moment in time, and (2) the systems which tend to have a locus in a particular metropolitan area at a particular time. To give some differentiation in the spatial meaning of these two kinds of activity systems, Webber has suggested the term "urban realm" for the first kind of interaction to distinguish it from the more conventional term "urban or metropolitan area" for the second.[1] While our concern here is with the *place* kind of "metropolitan community" rather than the *nonplace* kind, it will be important to obtain some perspective of both if we are to deal realistically with the one. Thus, if, as Webber predicts, interaction in the urban realm increases in importance and urban area interaction becomes

---

[1] Melvin M. Webber, "The Urban Place and the Nonplace Urban Realm," in Webber (ed.), *Explorations into Urban Structure,* Philadelphia: University of Pennsylvania Press, 1964.

relatively less important, it is strategic to recognize these changes in the study of any particular metropolitan area.[2]

A second kind of distinction to be noted is in the view we take of interaction within the metropolitan area itself. As we shall use the term, "interaction" will refer to two interrelated components—the *activities component* and, broadly, the *communications component* (and usually with particular reference to the *movements subcomponent*). As we shall see later when interaction systems are translated into physical elements in the metropolitan area, it is helpful to think of the activities component as "within interaction" in the sense of its occurring within particular adapted spaces, and viewing the communications component as "between interaction" in the sense of its involving person movements, goods movements, and message flows between particular adapted spaces. In land use planning we give special attention to the activities component. But of course bringing land use and transportation proposals into balance in the form of a comprehensive plan involves both "within" and "between" interaction. So clearly these two interrelated components cannot be disassociated in land use or in transportation planning, if a sound and unified general plan is to be achieved.

A third consideration to be noted is the dynamic aspect of interaction. Whether we are analyzing its place-nonplace aspects or investigating its activity-movement relationship, interaction is a continuously evolving phenomenon, with the nature of interaction at any particular moment being reshaped by the feedback effects from interaction immediately preceding. This aspect of interaction is intrinsic to the very nature of human behavior and needs no laboring. The classification system we use must be sensitive to the way this dynamic aspect affects spatial patterns of activities. It is particularly important in classifying activity systems to distinguish between activities which involve relatively slow changes in spatial distribution and those which may be more volatile, for obviously planning solutions will be different for each class of activity system. But even more important is the need for a continuing inventory system which serves as an "advance warning system" for anticipating important changes in the locus of activity patterns. As we shall see presently, the attitude study plays an important role in scouting out these changes.

In setting out to examine and interpret interaction systems, we will be primarily concerned with systems that tend to be recurrent. So a fourth

[2] Webber raises some challenging questions concerning present-day planning emphases and how well suited prevailing concepts of planning are for giving adequate consideration to the far-reaching changes in interaction systems that are now in progress, particularly in view of the steady rise in importance of interaction in the urban realm and the relative decline in importance of interaction within urban areas.

consideration will be one of identifying recurring activities but differentiating between those systems which tend to recur in identifiable spatial patterns and those which recur in more random patterns in space. The first type has significance in translating activity systems into proposed land use configurations or in making the connection from identified movement systems to particular proposals for transportation routes. The second type places a premium on ingenuity in urban design in integrating into the conception of space arrangements opportunities for random interaction even though these activity systems may not be directly reflected in urban spatial structure.

A final distinction to be noted is that interaction can be of a private and a public nature. Our concern here is more directly with interaction which involves the public interest and has a relationship to the physical layout of the community rather than to private relationships between individuals or single transactions between particular firms which normally do not involve these community considerations. We may sum up by noting that in any particular urban area the approach followed will be concerned primarily with (1) metropolitan area interaction (but in the framework of the ties which extend to the larger urban realm); (2) the activities component of interaction (but in close relationship to the communications component); (3) some form of continuing inventory (though recognizing that periodic "cross-section" readings may be the only immediately practical expedient); (4) interaction systems of a recurrent nature and with tendencies to cluster into spatial patterns (yet taking note of the types of recurring random activities and movements); and (5) patterns of interaction of community-wide significance (but giving consideration to privacy in individual relations and firm transactions where the public interest is not directly involved).

The Nature of Activity Systems

"Activity systems" is defined here as behavior patterns of individuals, families, institutions, and firms which occur in spatial patterns that have meaning in planning for land use. Just as the analysis of movement systems—the related component of interaction—has become the basis for transportation planning, the study of activity systems serves a corresponding purpose in land use planning.

It may assist in clarifying our task of outlining an approach if we consider briefly the movement component of interaction. There exist distinct techniques for the analysis of goods movements and person movements in a metropolitan area. In the analysis of person movements there have been some remarkable advances in the use of survey research methods for the identification of "desire lines" of movement and in the assembly of these strands into flow systems of significance for transportation planning. As remarkable as this progress has been, there are many aspects of movement systems that pose difficult and complex problems for the transportation planner—many of them in the realm of human behavior. For example, to date in the area of forecasting traffic movements, the emphasis has been on studying *what* people do, with relatively little attention devoted to *why* they choose to do what they do. A traffic projection based on how people have behaved in the past implicitly assumes people will behave on the average the same way in the future. Unfortunately the problem is not that simple. The assumption of a constant mode of behavior is not a tenable one for rapidly expanding communities and for long-range plans. Intuitively we know that man's behavior is continually changing in response to his social system. So in order to anticipate trip behavior of persons more accurately, transportation planners are beginning to turn to attitude studies and the social psychology of trip behavior.

The task of developing an approach to the analysis of activity systems faces similar considerations. Indeed, since the two are so interdependent, *trip behavior between places* cannot proceed far before the "why'" problem becomes inextricably involved in *activity behavior within places*. While the interrelatedness of these aspects of urban behavior will be constantly before us, the basic concern of this chapter is to explore techniques for studying activity systems, particularly the definition of spatial patterns these systems take and the identification of attitudinal factors that produce variation in these patterns.

Essentially we are seeking to define a survey instrument which will assist us in studying the metropolitan area from the vantage point of the first two components in the *values – behavior patterns – outcomes* framework introduced in Part I. These two components are at the heart of a first-stage analysis; land use surveys focus on the last component and represent a second stage in land use investigation. Survey techniques for this "outcomes" component are taken up in the next chapter. As brought out in Chapter 2, we do not view space use as a direct outcome of daily activities. We view it as the outcome of a special kind of behavior—what was identified as location behavior. It may be helpful to think of daily activities as a *basic form of behavior* in the urban social system, and location actions as an *instrumental form of behavior* prompted by the basic form. The way in which urban planning recognizes and accommodates this instrumental form of behavior is taken up in Part III. From studies of the kind outlined in the last part of this chapter, we wish to lay the groundwork for Part III by discovering what the basic daily activity patterns are in the urban social system and what insights can be gained as to changes in these patterns through the investigation of attitudes as they condition activities.

A Typology of Activity Systems

Before taking up survey techniques appropriate for the study of activity systems it is necessary to identify a general typology of activity systems which will be used throughout this and later chapters. As a center of inter-action, the metropolitan area accommodates a number of major activity patterns each of which involves classes of subsystems. The major classes and the principal agents of the larger system may be set down as follows:

Activity Agents	*Activity Types*	*Activity Systems*
Firms	Productive activities	Goods-producing activities (extraction, processing, communications, distribution) Service activities (to firms, institutions, households, and individuals)
Institutions	General welfare activities	Human development activities (education, religious, and recreation) Basic community service activities (police, fire, water, waste disposal, etc.) Activities for welfare of special groups (labor, social, etc.)
Households and individuals	Residential activities	Income-producing activities Child-raising and family activities Education and intellectual development activities Spiritual development activities Social activities Recreation and relaxation Club activities Community service, political activities Activities associated with food, shopping, health, etc.

Obviously this is not a complete statement of a classification system, for the indicated activity systems can be extended and each of these subdivided into subsystems. Also as activity systems are broken down into subsystems, it is clear that they become interconnected at various points, depending on whether a user or supplier perspective is assumed. In this respect, as a general rule, the activity classification followed here will be determined from the vantage point of the agent. Thus, one class of activities of interest is associated primarily with *individuals and families* as entities, and in the analysis of space use taken up later, the location-specific base of the home or place of residence will be important. Another class of activities is centered around *firms* involved in supplying goods and services (even though firms provide the places of work for members of households). Similarly, we will be concerned with the spatial locus of the activity patterns of *institutions* as they carry on their human development and public service functions in the urban setting (even though they fulfill needs or supply services to households or firms). While interaction is thus not confined to discrete firm, organization, or household systems but involves firm-organization, firm-household, and organization-household interrelations, it is useful to this analysis to group systems and subsystems according to agents of interaction.

The study of localized spatial patterns of firm activities is a logical extention of the investigations of the urban economy in both its internal and external aspects. Thus, for activities involved in supplying goods, we may need to extend the work discussed in Chapter 3. To identify linkages, we can no longer use aggregations of economic activity, but must turn to a micro-economic approach involving measures of transactions between firms or clusters of firms.[3] We are concerned here with space-related aspects of these linkages, and we are concerned with the trends and likelihood of future shifts in linkages, as they are modified by basic economic and technological changes. Thus, we wish to examine extraction, processing, and assembly activities each as they may be operations in themselves and each as they may be linked to one another. This kind of analysis is important eventually in identifying transportation and other channels of communication required for "between interaction" and in defining the space needs and site development requirements for "within interaction" among linked parts of each major industrial complex.

Similarly, we are concerned with spatial patterns in communications and distribution activities. For example, in wholesale distribution we are concerned with goods transfers between wholesaler and producer, between producer and wholesaler, and between wholesaler and retailer. While in the past wholesale activity in any particular locality has involved considerable "between interaction," it is quite possible that when the dominant recurring interestablishment patterns of transaction are clearly identified, location adjustments may be effected through land use planning to reduce the amount of "between interaction." Within the industrial establishment,

---

[3] "Linkage" has been defined as "a relationship between establishments characterized by continuing or frequently occurring interaction." See Robert B. Mitchell and Chester Rapkin, *Urban Traffic, a Function of Land Use*, New York: Columbia University Press, 1954, p. 111. For a fuller discussion of the linkages between establishments, see John Rannells, *The Core of the City*, New York: Columbia University Press, 1956.

with new emphases on economies of scale, large manufacturing firms are increasingly handling their own wholesale distribution. This will mean a changing balance in linkages, with the "within interaction" supplanting the "between interaction" in some cases. Here, too, changing technology and its likely future impact on interaction patterns is exceedingly important and must be investigated thoroughly.

It is evident from the nature of activities of retail firms dealing in goods and services that they are in daily contact with other firms and with households. Thus, we may anticipate that spatial patterns of retail activities will tend to bear a close relationship to interaction patterns of all other agents in the metropolitan area. Moreover, with less fixed capital investment to cope with, retail firms are able and do adapt more readily to changes in these patterns of interaction in the metropolitan area. Perhaps because of the volatile aspect of retail activity, city planners have given these activity patterns more attention than others. In retail lines catering to households, establishments dealing in *convenience goods and services* in the past traditionally sought to maximize "within interaction" opportunities. Except for specialized or fancy goods establishments, this type of activity originally located within walking distance of their residential market areas. But with the widespread use of the automobile and the development of new merchandising methods and large drive-in shopping centers, "between interaction" has become ascendent in this line of retailing. Trade areas for *consumer goods and specialized services* have similarly undergone adjustments —some involving suburbanization to superhighway interchange points and some regrouping in the new regional shopping centers. Even as these changes are in progress, automation and developments in merchandising are producing still other changes in retail activity patterns. In the retail sphere too, then, the analysis of activity patterns is essential to the study of land use.

We tend to think of institutional activities of churches, welfare groups, fraternal orders, and various society headquarters as entities which need no particular attention, being self-sufficient activities well able to fend for themselves. Indeed, unless they happen to cluster together into centers for their own convenience, planners have not often given much thought to their needs. Yet if land use planning is to achieve development patterns that match up efficiently with activity systems, these too merit investigation. Some will strongly emphasize "between interaction" because it is in the very nature of these particular functions to maintain contact with widely distributed entities in the metropolitan area. Thus, intuitively we recognize that a museum, the city hall, or special church denominations seek locations that will take advantage of "between interaction" and be strategically close to major systems of movement. On the other hand, with branch library systems, suburban churches, or subcivic centers, the emphasis may be on "within interaction," and their functions considered as part of a bundle of several activities. Here, too, investigations of past activity patterns will not offer a fully adequate or valid approach for activity patterns in the future. The planner will not only need to give much more positive attention to these activity systems, but he will also need to stretch his efforts to discover indicators of long-range shifts in these systems.

Finally, in this system of activity classification there is the household or family and the manifold activity systems associated with the individual members of the family. The daily activity systems of households are particularly complex to identify and organize in spatial patterns, and perhaps this accounts for the fact that planning agencies have tended to rely heavily on an intuitive view of family activity systems. However, with modern survey research methods and sampling techniques now developed so that they are operationally feasible tools, planning agencies can be expected to undertake this kind of survey as one of its primary investigative techniques.

While our concern in this chapter is with the "within interaction" (activities spatially localized within defined activity zones), very clearly survey research focusing on individuals and families must be concerned with both *between* and *within* interaction systems. Only by having a complete picture of individual and family interaction patterns can the spatial distribution and the changing locus of such patterns be defined. With scientific advance and the substitution of communications for some kinds of movements systems, we can expect some significant changes in these activity systems. It is therefore important to view the within and between forms of interaction in concurrent studies. This would seem to support the notion of combining the home interview studies that transportation agencies undertake with the kind of survey research study that planning agencies undertake.

Household behavior is infinitely more complex than firm behavior or other forms enumerated above. To anticipate behavior with greater understanding and accuracy, it becomes necessary to investigate why people are motivated to engage in the activities they do. This involves investigations of attitudes and their implications for future behavior—particularly attitudes that may lead to activity patterns with spatial significance for planning.

To sum up, urban land use planning requires insights into the fundamental characteristics of activity systems. The concept of "activity systems" as used here is concerned not only with the identification of spatial patterns of these systems as they exist but also why they take the form they do and how activity patterns are likely to change in the future. The concept recognizes that different agents—firms, institutions, and families and individuals

—call for differing types of activity investigations. The concept further views behavior patterns of these entities as they may be manifest in particular spatial forms as having important value-based areas of investigation. This is particularly important in the household sector and involves the study of attitudes and motivations as they relate to activity patterns of spatial significance.

Survey and Analysis of Activities

The foregoing discussion has sketched in the general requirements for defining and classifying activity systems. In this final section, illustrative material on the content of activity surveys and some forms of data summarization are discussed. The aim is to indicate the general directions this kind of investigation must take in the future as it becomes a part of the normal operations of a planning agency.

In general, activity systems of firms and institutions involve a survey approach of a somewhat different kind than what is involved in surveys concerned with activities of individuals and families. In surveying firms and institutions not only are we dealing with smaller numbers of entities, but we are also dealing with activity types that are more institutionalized in form. Their activities are defined and instituted to an important degree by formal policies, procedures, and corporate or legalistic actions. To define spatial patterns of activity and to understand why and how they change, not only do we need to investigate the volume of "to-from" interactions, but we also need to examine the corporate system, the political system, or the organizational system, as the case may be, and determine how activity patterns are regulated by the system which generates the activity. For families and individuals, the study of activity patterns is somewhat more complex. While the social system with its cultural sanctions of various kinds functions to provide some measure of regulation to these patterns, surveys in this instance are dealing with less regimented forms of behavior which may therefore be prone to whim and nonconforming patterns. The classification system used must be sensitive to the way this dynamic aspect affects spatial patterns of activities.

To indicate the desirable scope of activity surveys, illustrative material from the three basic activity groups is presented below for a few selected activity systems (see Tables 17-20). The outlines are suggestive of the content—not inclusive. It will be noted that each illustrative outline not only covers a series of question areas which seek to establish the present spatial patterning of activities and the intensity of interaction involved in these patterns, but also contains an area of questioning focusing on factors which may serve to alter these patterns in the future. The latter aspect of the survey (covered in Content Area 4 in Tables 17-19 and 6 in Table 20) clearly involves the most complex kind of investigation and requires special attention in research and experimentation in the future.

Of course, the design of the study and the organization and conduct of the surveys are very important areas which, until the planning field develops its own expertise, standards, and procedures, require the assistance of survey research specialists. Particularly important in the basic design of the survey are decisions on sampling methods and the selection of confidence limits as these affect the problem of generalizing results from the sampling survey to the full universe. With respect to survey operations, such considerations as the design of the interview questionnaire, the pretesting of schedules, the conduct of the survey including field checks on the coverage and conduct of interviews, the coding of data, and eventually the machine processing of results in punch card form are also technical areas of considerable importance. Since standard works on social science research methods can be consulted for general guidance, these aspects of the activities study are omitted in the discussion below.

Firm Activities

The first basic activity group we wish to consider focuses on productive activities—man's activities in supplying his fellow men with goods or services. Activities in the goods category can be thought of as consisting of extraction, processing, and distribution; and activities in the services category can be subdivided into various industrial, business, professional, and personal services. Extraction has to do with the procurement of raw materials; and processing involves the refining of raw material, the fabrication of components from these materials or other components, and eventually the assembly of components into products for final consumption. Distribution activities at the wholesale level involve the transport, breaking down, redistribution, and storage of goods, and, at the retail level, the assembly, display, and eventually delivery of goods to the final consumer. In the services category, for industry and business, there are a variety of repair and maintenance services. Serving firms, institutions, and households are a wide range of professional services covering such classifications as law, medicine, finance, engineering, architecture, accounting, and so on. Finally, catering to individual and household consumers, there are various personal services—hairdressers, barbers, photographers, laundries and cleaners, funeral services, and so on. Breakdowns into the first elemental sub-classes may be summarized as follows:

Goods	Extraction	Agriculture Forestry Fishing Mining Construction
	Processing	Manufacturing (refining, fabricating, and assembly)
	Communications	Transportation Communication Utilities
	Distribution	Wholesale Retail
Services	Business	Finance, insurance, and real estate Etc.
	Consumer	Personal Amusement Etc.
	Professional	Medical Legal Etc.

This tree system of classification can obviously be extended and carried to great detail. However, in developing classifications of this kind, it is important to bear in mind that interaction is not confined within the systems thus defined, and many of the services exist in combination with goods-producing activities.

The object of the firm survey is to obtain a general picture of the spatial patterns of interaction among activities and to obtain a measure of the intensity of this interaction. We wish to have the activity information in sufficient detail to enable us to classify space use for purposes of land planning. The study of the urban economy built around a social accounts approach can easily be adapted to supply the basic information required in making an activities analysis.[4] Indeed, the economic studies outlined in Chapter 3, the activities investigations taken up in this chapter, and surveys of manufacturing, wholesale, and retail space use taken up in Chapter 11 should all be planned and carried out as one combined planning survey.

[4] For example, this could be accomplished by additions to firm interview forms used by Charles L. Leven, *Theory and Method of Income and Product Accounts for Metropolitan Areas, Including the Elgin-Dundee Area as a Case Study,* Pittsburgh: University of Pittsburgh Press, 1963.

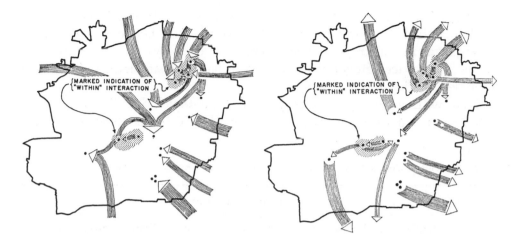

Figure 20. Interaction in Processing Activities. The figure to the left presents linkages from the vantage point of input relations, and the figure to the right pictures linkages in terms of output relations. Clearly the input of one plant may be the output of another plant in the metropolitan area. As shown here, the to-from representation of "within" interaction involves approximately the same areas. The dotted pattern suggests that these areas may be treated as one class of land use in land use planning.

The content areas of the interview schedule will vary somewhat with the subclass of activity system. Consider processing activities, that is, activities engaged in the manufacture of goods for final consumption. Table 17 illustrates the kinds of content areas which would be covered in interviews with the management of firms engaged in these activities. As suggested by this table, it may be that in some surveys both industrial services and the processing of goods can be appropriately incorporated into the same schedule. The stub titles indicate the basic uses of the data in the activity analysis. Question Areas 1 and 2 enable us to classify the activity. Question Area 3 is comparable to the group of questions commonly included in household interviews to get at "background variables" which become the basis of tabulating data into subcategories so that investigators can determine whether responses vary to any significant degree among these various subclasses. The content of this part of the questionnaire would also be dictated by needs in space analyses taken up in Chapter 11. Question Area 4 is aimed at determining the technological and other factors which might modify spatial patterns of this activity in the future. In this area both factual and open-ended questions would seek to get at these factors. Question Areas 5 and 6 identify nodes of linked activities, and Question Area 7 is concerned with assembling information on the intensity of interaction between nodes. Figure 20 is a simplified representation suggestive of the way in which tabular summaries of "from-to" data can be used to define recurring patterns of "within" and "between" interaction among firms in a metropolitan area. This kind of analysis provides the basis for defining space categories to be used in land use summaries of the kind discussed in the next chapter.

Even with a survey of this general type developed into an operational form and with the proper determination of the confidence we may

Table 17. Question Content Areas for Survey of Firms Engaged in Processing or Industrial Services

Purpose	Question Content Areas
Classifying Activity	1. *Name by which this plant is known* and its address. Name, address, and city of this firm's main offices.
	2. *The principal products and/or services of this plant.* Indicate on a value-added basis the relative importance of each product or service as a per cent of total. Indicate last year's output. Show SIC classifications used in reporting to census.
	3. *The principal characteristics of plant and site.* For example, obtain information on the average annual and the seasonal range of total employment and size of largest shift; total floor area and first floor area; total site area and used site area; use of site (facilities on site, e.g., ground area taken up in different processing or service activities under different roofs, parking and loading areas, open and roofed storage areas, landscaping, etc.); types of utilities, their ownership, and characteristics of their operation (average daily figures on water use, waste disposal, power consumption, etc.); and so on.
	4. *The principal variables likely to affect the future activity patterns.* Obtain information on automation, changes in processing operations, management policy, and other factors likely to alter activity patterns.

Identifying Nodes of Activity	5. *Sources of major goods and/or service inputs*
	
	   a. List *this firm's* processing plants or outdoor operations or its service facilities or sites at other local or nonlocal locations which are linked to this activity.
	
	   b. List *this firm's* storage or stockpiling facilities at other local or nonlocal locations which are linked to this activity.
	
	   c. List local and nonlocal locations of *other major suppliers* of parts or other materials (principal ones in terms of value or bulk) or of services (principal ones in terms of value or criticalness to operations).

	6. *Destination of major goods and/or service outputs* (obtain data similar to that listed under Question Area 5). For each separate location listed under Question Areas 5 and 6, give name by which facility is known and address. (For nonlocal locations, identify only city and state; and for local facilities, use grid coordinates of location as determined from metropolitan area map.)

Determining Intensity of Activity, or Interaction

7. *Magnitude and frequency of interaction.* (List the "from" entry [input source] and "to" entry [output destination] with respect to this firm as separate entries.)

a. *Intrametropolitan area interaction*

(1) GOODS TRANSFERS

From (Coded to grid coordinate location)	To	Amount (last yr.)* (% all inputs by total value, or % all outputs in terms of value added)	Means of Tfr. (Indicate if by truck, RR, pipeline, etc.)	Frequencies (For example, no. truck pickups last year, etc.)
This plant 381–392		5% output	truck	10 deliveries
420–630	This plant	22% input	truck	100 pickups

(2) SERVICE CALLS

From (Coded to grid coordinate location)	To	Amount (last yr.)* (% all man hours of services received ... or provided)	Frequencies (Total no. service visits last year)
This facility 326–520		2% provided	50 visits
238–518	This facility	10% received	100 visits

b. *Interaction with outside world* (goods* or services)

From (Indicate city and state of location)	To	Amount (last yr.) (% in measures corresponding to above definitions)	
This plant New York, NY		500 vehicles	10% output
Venezuela	This plant	1,000,000 tons	55% input

*Intrametropolitan and "outside world" amounts should total to 100% for goods and/or services.

place in the results, the picture of activity patterns is essentially a static mosaic for the particular moment in time that the survey is made. Content Area 4 should be designed to supply some of the leads for developing a more dynamic view of activity systems and simulating the activity patterns under various assumptions concerning the future. Two lines of effort are needed here—one focused on changes in processing methods as a variable, and one focused on management policies and practices as the other variable. With respect to the first, we not only seek information from management in the metropolitan area under study, but we also consult sources which can provide a picture of the more basic trends. Thus, through one series of questions in Content Area 4, we are in effect attempting to extend our view into the future through the collective insights of present-day management concerning changes that can be anticipated in the future in the form of technological improvements in processing operations. We know, of course, that this is not enough, and frequently even the most forward-thinking person in the management level in a particular metropolitan area will not be able to anticipate changes of a more fundamental nature—for example, the social implications of automation and all the complex feedback effects that begin to regulate what previously appeared to be entirely technical matters. How the planner is to get at the factors which escape the notice of firm management cannot be set down in any "how to do it" procedure. In this respect a continuing research activity at universities and in government which brings the latest thinking and knowledge to the planning analysis is certainly a necessary element in the picture.

The other aspect of the study of firm activities is concerned with determining the "play" that the corporate system permits in activity patterns and the kinds of information required in order to comprehend fully the extent of variation in activity patterns that may be instituted by short-term changes in corporate policies and practices. Content Area 4 would therefore also include questions designed to get at these sources of change in activity patterns.

So far we have been directing our attention to processing activities. At the present state of development in the study of activity systems, we do not attempt to do more than suggest directions in which planning agencies will need to move in surveying firms in a metropolitan area. Different activity types will require variations in what has been suggested above for processing activities. Thus extractive activities will involve a modification of the outline presented in Table 17. Wholesale distribution will involve other modifications. To indicate how variations in approach will need to be devised, let us consider retail trade and services.

Table 18 is suggestive of the content areas that a questionnaire designed to identify activity patterns of firms engaged in retail trade or services might cover. As in the study of processing and related service activities, we are interested in coordinating investigations and generally economizing on staff effort going into tooling-up studies. So, besides supplying information on activity patterns, this schedule would also be designed to serve needs in both the analysis of the urban economy (Chapters 3 and 4) and the study of space needs (Chapter 11). Since in retail trade we are dealing here with an activity which is concerned with the marketing of goods to the consumer, as might be expected, patterns of "between" and "within"

Table 18. Question Content Areas for Survey of Firms Engaged in Retail Trade and Services

Purpose	Question Content Areas
Classifying Activity	1. *Name and address of this establishment.* If part of chain or branch, indicate other outlets or branches in metropolitan area. Indicate also if there is specialization of goods and services provided by any such branches or outlets. If this is not firm's headquarters, give name and address of main offices (if in a different city, give city and state). Indicate whether this is owned or leased space.
	2. *The principal products and/or services of this establishment* based on sales volume. Indicate SIC classification used in reporting to census.
	3. *The principal characteristics of structural facility and/or site.* For example, obtain information on average annual employment, seasonal range of total employment, and size of largest shift; total floor area, total first floor area, and total sales area; total site area, total used site area, and area devoted to various site uses (ground area taken up in main and accessory activities under separate roofs, in parking and loading areas, landscaping, etc.); and so on.
	4. *The principal variables likely to affect the future volume of business* and the suitability of this site for doing business. Explore implications of new merchandising practices (discount houses, contractual arrangements for customer service, etc.), changing patterns of customer buying, changing patronage habits, and so on.

Identifying Nodes of Activity	5. *Origin of goods or services received*
	
	  a. List *this firm's* off-site warehouse and storage facilities linked to this establishment at local and nonlocal locations.
	
	  b. List *other major suppliers* linked to this establishment, local and nonlocal.
	
	6. *Destination of goods or services delivered*
	
	  a. List branch or service centers not at this location which are used by this establishment for repair or other specialized services or for intermediate handling of goods before delivery to consumer.
	
	  b. From a census tract map of metropolitan area outline individual tracts or combinations of tracts receiving major proportion of local deliveries or services (clustered delivery areas).
	
	For each separate location or zone listed under Question Areas 5 and 6, give name by which facility is known and address (for nonlocal locations, identify only city and state); assign code numbers to these addresses; for local facilities, use code numbers to mark locations on metropolitan area map. These code numbers should be used in Question Area 7.

Interaction	7. *Magnitude and frequency of interaction* (use format similar to that shown in Table 17).

interaction are concerned mainly with assembly of goods from wholesalers or other distributors, the display of goods, or the delivery of goods to consumers. Service firms tend to be more involved in dispensing than receiving services, although there will be instances in which a service activity subcontracts to obtain specialized services needed in order for them to supply general services. While drawn up to fit the activity characteristics of retail trade and services, as can be seen in Table 18 the question content areas follow a line of inquiry parallel to that of Table 17. Thus, the first block of questions would seek to classify the activity, describe the physical plant and the site at the focal point of the activity, and determine the conditions affecting the spatial configuration of interaction of the retailer with the supplier and consumer. The second block of questions is concerned with pinning down the spatial locus of activity. This involves identifying nodes of activity. The "from" aspect of retail trade and services, that is, the relations with wholesalers, can be analyzed in a manner similar to the approach suggested above from processing firms. The "to" aspect, however, involves a somewhat different approach and, as suggested under Content Area 6, deliveries or service calls are more practicable to analyze by grouping them into clusters and viewing the centroid of the cluster as the destination of that group of deliveries. It should be noted that many retail trade and service lines no longer provide deliveries (in effect passing these costs on to the consumer), and the customer drive-in pickup system has developed as a substitute (not without higher public costs, however). A significant portion of this form of interaction is investigated as "shopping activities" of households.

Because of the more volatile aspect of retail trade and services pointed out earlier, questions in Content Area 4 assume particular importance. Not only is capital investment a less inhibiting factor, with the result that firms can change locations more readily, but the market at the retail level is more temperamental and subject to the vagaries of whim, style, and prestige, particularly in lines that are not classified as necessities of everyday living. So we see merchants themselves employing survey techniques to study the market potential. However, their needs are of a somewhat different order than what a planning agency needs to know. From the vantage point of an activities study, the line of questioning would seek to identify the "play" in activity patterns arising from polar extremes in merchandising practices, customer buying patterns, and store patronage habits. Questions are designed to provide the means for estimating the extent of change in retail activity patterns under differing assumptions concerning merchandising trends, consumer goods consumption, and store patronage. Of course a continuing sampling survey operation will permit surveillance of trends and assist the planning agency in anticipating short-run changes in activity patterns.

In the foregoing illustrations of activity studies, the outlined content areas assume that the investigation of service firms can be combined with surveys of goods-handling firms. It may be that some services are better studied in a survey especially designed for that service. Thus, activity patterns of some professional or personal services may need to be examined in individual studies. However, before attempting to outline and undertake separate surveys, it is well to determine to what extent the needed information can be obtained through other surveys—from surveys of households, nonservice firms, and institutions that must be undertaken in any event.

Institutional Activities

The activities of institutional entities are very similar in general character to the class of firm activities referred to as "services" and, not unlike firms, the patterns are determined in many respects by policies and procedures of a relatively formal kind. Because of the similarities between institutional and firm activities, we will not dwell at length on this type of activity. Breakdowns into general activity classes are as follows:

Human development
- Educational activities—organized (offered in schools, etc.) and unorganized forms (available through libraries, museums, etc.)
- Religious activities (provided through churches, bible schools, etc.)
- Health activities (offered through hospitals, clinics, fund-raising groups, etc.)
- Recreation activities of organized nonprofit form (available through public recreation programs, YMCA activities, etc.)

Community development
- Protective services and related activities (e.g., police, fire, courts, etc.)
- Public safety and inspection services
- Public works and maintenance activities (streets, water, wastes, parks, etc.)

Group welfare
- Labor, professional welfare activities
- Economic development activities
- Political action activities
- Social action activities

Here, too, the classification system is open-ended. Obviously, as suggested in the second column, the system can be extended to subclasses of much greater detail.

Table 19. Question Content Areas for Surveys of Nonprofit Organizations

Purpose	Question Content Areas
Classifying Activity	1. *Name and address of this organization.* If not headquarters, give address of main offices. (If main offices not local, give only city and state.) 2. *Type of organization and purposes.* Indicate whether this is religious, civic improvement, government, health, welfare, or other type of agency, and further clarify the nature of organization by listing its principal purposes. 3. *Principal characteristics of facility and site.* Indicate annual average employment level and describe facilities. If facility and/or site shared with other organization(s), give total space allocated to this organization and all other sharing organizations (include floor area and site analyses as below). If this facility is exclusively for use of this organization, give total floor area and first floor area, total site area and used site area, use of site (space in facilities under separate roofs on this site, parking and service areas, special outdoor use areas, utility requirements, etc.) 4. *Factors likely to affect future activities of this organization.* For example, do long-term changes in leisure time, medical requirements, welfare loads, governmental services, and so on, indicate changes in activity patterns.

Identifying Nodes of Activity	5. *Origins of goods and/or services regularly received by this facility*
	
	    a. List locations of own branch facilities which supply this facility with goods and/or services regularly.
	
	    b. List goods and/or services this firm requires regularly from other entities.
	
	6. *Destinations of goods and/or services this facility regularly supplies.* From a census tract map of metropolitan area, outline individual tracts or combinations of tracts receiving major proportion of goods or services provided by this facility. Identify the individual large users.
	
	For each separate location or zone outlined under Question Areas 5 and 6, give name by which branch or supplier is known and address (for nonlocal locations, identify only city and state); assign code numbers to these addresses; for local facilities, use code numbers to mark locations on metropolitan area map. These code numbers should be used in Question Area 7.

Interaction	7. *Magnitude and frequency of interaction* (use format similar to that shown in Table 17).

As can be noted from headings in the illustrative outline of content areas in Table 19, surveys suited to these classes of activity will tend to follow a line of questioning quite similar to that involved in investigations of retail trade and services. Of course, Content Area 4 relating to factors that are likely to affect activity patterns in the future will be handled somewhat differently. There will be parallels—for example, the investigation of the organizational system: how the institution is constituted and how it functions to regulate activity patterns. However, the forces of technological and other basic changes external to the organizational system have different implications for each institution. Some organizations' activities may be appreciably affected by increases in leisure time, others by the general economic outlook, and still others by broad changes in the trends in literacy and educational levels being achieved. Questions in Content Area 4 will therefore need to be developed around the particular features that are distinctive to each institutional entity surveyed.

As in the case of firms providing retail services, an accent of surveys of institutional activities is on the provision of services. But here, in place of providing them in the marketplace, they are supplied as a public or non-profit service. For some activities we can anticipate emphasis of "within interaction"—for example, educational activities within a defined residential area through the medium of a school. For others, there will be an emphasis on "between interaction," as in supplying medical services from a general hospital to an entire metropolitan area or in the case of a union local serving members throughout a city. Specific questions in the several content areas will therefore need to be prepared to recognize whether an activity is urban-wide in scope of operation or more localized in its service area. The content of the survey schedule will also need to recognize that the pile-up of activities into recurrent spatial patterns will tend to be more pronounced when services are provided at the base of operations of an activity. Where the nature of the activity involves performing services at widely distributed points, it is possible that clusters of recipients of services can be identified by census tracts in much the same way that was suggested for deliveries of retail firms. However, it may be that services are provided in a random pattern and therefore are not susceptible to grouping for space analyses.

Individual and Household Activities

As noted above, the activity systems of individuals and households are perhaps the most difficult to analyze of the three general classes considered in this chapter. Without the leavening effect of highly institutionalized norms of behavior of the two other classes of activity and with a much larger number of agents involved, we expect and do find a much greater degree of variability in activity patterns. This is not to imply that the social system does not influence and regulate to some degree the activities of residents of a metropolitan area. Clearly much of the behavior of individuals and households in their manifold and complex activities conforms to norms imposed by the social system. There is a whole field—sociology—which devotes its efforts to studying human behavior in these multifarious forms. The planner cannot go deeply into the many considerations behind the behavior patterns that interest him. However, he does have a direct concern with the spatial distribution of human activities and the identification of attitudinal variables that will assist him in understanding more fully how and why these spatial patterns of behavior change.

An analysis of activity patterns in this third basic group needs to differentiate between a wide range of activities involved in the typical day of each member of the household. A general classification of the principal classes of activities might consist of the following:

Income-producing	On-the-job activity, moonlighting Professional activity (union, professional societies, etc.) Activity to improve income-producing potential (evening school, inventing, writing, etc.)
Child-raising and family activities	Overseeing and participating in play Overseeing children's study, practicing, etc. Expeditions with children Family outings, picnics, etc.
Education and intellectual development	Attending school, college, adult classes, etc. Attending meetings for improvement of education, arts (PTA, Art Guild, Music for Children) Participating in drama, orchestra, Great Books, and similar group activities Attending plays, exhibitions, etc.
Spiritual development	Attending and participating in church activities Taking part in organizations concerned with human welfare
Social activities	Attending and participating in organized social activities (country club, city club, athletic club, etc.) Engaging in informal forms of socializing (visiting friends, dating, attending parties, etc.)

Recreation and relaxation	Attending spectator events (ball games, races, fights, etc.) Participating in recreation activities with others (golf, tennis, bowling, softball, swimming, fishing, etc.) Individual forms of physical and mental relaxation (taking naps, gardening, walking, reading, viewing TV, working on hobby, crafts, etc.)
Club activities	Taking part in special-interest clubs (Garden Club, Stamp Club, etc.) Attending luncheon or dinner clubs (Rotary, Altrusa, etc.) Attending meetings of patriotic groups (Legion, DAR, etc.) Attending fraternal groups (Masons, Elks, Eastern Star, etc.)
Community service and political activities	Attending and/or participating in civic improvement activities (LWV, Civic Assn., etc.) Serving on City Council, Planning Board, etc. Political action activities Fund-raising activities and similar volunteer efforts
Activities associated with food, shopping, health, and similar needs	Meals at home, restaurants Shopping (convenience, specialty, and consumer goods) Visits to doctor, hospital Home and yard maintenance

Two aspects of this classification of individual and household activities should be noted. First, the breakdown to the right for most categories in the left-hand column reflects two fundamental ways of classifying activities —activities which are highly institutionalized and activities which are more individualized in nature. Thus, on the one hand individuals or households may be drawn to activities which are formally organized; on the other hand they may prefer to use informal means of fulfilling their individual and household needs and desires; or (and more typically) they may choose both. The second conclusion to be drawn from such a classification is the reciprocal nature of some of the activities in relation to the other activity types discussed above. This is particularly true of the institutional category of activities. Thus firms or institutions are suppliers of activities but at the same time the individuals or households are the users. Of course, here we are viewing activities from the vantage point of the individual or household taking part in the activity rather than from the viewpoint of the institution or firm patterns of activity involved in supplying the service.

From inspection of the individual and household activities in the above list, it is clear that a number of activities are home-based and therefore of limited significance for spatial analyses. Particularly noteworthy are the large number of activities which we suspect will involve "between" forms of interaction, that is, movement from home to other places. Yet we can recognize in this list a number of activities which either normally take place in the residential community or which through positive planning could take the "within" form of interaction. Therefore, a survey of this general class of activities must look at the entire range of activities of individuals and households if all options of choice are to be taken into account.

In this general class of activity we are concerned with the definition of specific recurrent behavior patterns, both clustered and random ones, and we are interested in attitudes—their range of variation and the extent of consensus. Intuitively we know that activity systems of individuals and families tend to fall into certain recurring patterns. From observation and experience, we know that income-producing activities of the household involve the journey to work as a type of activity. Similarly, we see that child-raising involves outdoor play activities, family outings, and various school-centered child and adult programs. We know that socializing—whether in the form of gossiping over the back fence or visiting friends or relatives, or whether in the form of outings or supper parties—involves other activity patterns of differing spatial significance. And we know that participation in civic affairs, church activities, and meetings of fraternal groups involve still others. Survey research enables us to sharpen our understanding of the spatial characteristics of these activities, to determine which ones cluster and which ones are random, and to ascertain how clustered activities build up in intensity at particular locations.

The value basis of household activity patterns is a more elusive area of investigation. In defining attitude areas of study, it may be helpful to go back to the distinction made in Chapter 1 between needs and wants. There we equated needs with necessities of living, and we linked up wants with desires which supplement these necessities. Activity patterns tied to needs can be reasonably well analyzed on the basis of direct questions on individual and household activities interpreted in terms of technical norms. For the *need* aspect of an activity study, the main value of attitude questions is for sounding out residents on how the upgrading of minimum standards may affect activities and how economic conditions would serve to expand or constrict activities at this "need" level.

For activity patterns tied to *wants*, attitude questions are more crucial. Some attitudes in this area must be related to an individual's or household's economic status. If responses are to be useful in making meaningful and practical inferences, stratification of the sample of households by economic group will be important. At the "want" level, attitudes will be more ephemeral, and as planners our concern is to discover the range of choice desired and to provide a variety of opportunities by which households in the different socio-economic groups may fulfill their special and variable wants. Attitude investigations dealing with wanted or desired activities will frequently get into matters of taste and considerations of prestige and livability. In the next chapter we will examine these factors as considerations in location behavior. Here livability enters into consideration in terms of how daily activities may be modified when people have the means or time beyond what is required for the necessities of life. What choices or what substitutions will they make in leisure-time activities, in buying habits and shop patronage patterns, in mode of transportation, and so on? The game technique suggested below is especially suited for studying "wants" as opposed to "needs" in daily patterns of activity. However, many activities fall into both the "need" and the "desire" area and are not readily classified as one or the other by available norms. These are the networks of social patterns in the immediate residential environment and the larger urban area. Some are "needs" from a mental health point of view (for example, visiting patterns), and yet are not normally associated with the necessities of daily life.

Table 20 is suggestive of the content areas to be included in a sampling survey of households. Such a survey is logically integrated with the standard origin and destination (O-D) survey undertaken in transportation studies. Thus the respondent is asked to identify major activities of various members of the household during the preceding 24-hour period, regardless of whether or not they involved movement between places. The objective is to be able to identify specific recurrent behavior patterns which will enable the planner to make analyses of space use and travel and develop an integrated set of proposals for land use and transportation set forth in the comprehensive plan.

Content Area 6 provides the means for determining the basis of variability in activity patterns. The social psychologist can be of great assistance in designing this part of the questionnaire, in developing sharply focused questions, and in analyzing and interpreting results. However, this form of technical assistance is no substitute for the task the planner must assume in clearly defining what it is he is trying to obtain from the survey. Fuzzy thinking here can lead to expensive and unusable results. Certainly experimentation should occur only in pretests or preferably in special research studies—not in a full-scale survey. In this connection, experimentation in this type of survey has been going on for several years at the Center for Urban and Regional Studies at the University of North

Carolina. Wilson's work on livability taken up in the next chapter is an example of research undertaken to experiment with the use of attitude studies in planning analyses. In this chapter our concern is with studies of attitudes which may give important insights into variables affecting activity patterns rather than attitudes toward the city and the neighborhood as factors affecting location behavior that concerned Wilson.

Content Area 4 in Table 20 is designed to record current patterns of activity of various members of the household. Figure 21 shows the spatial configuration of two kinds of leisure-time activities as plotted from results

Table 20. Question Content Areas for Household Survey

Purpose	Question Content Areas
Classifying Activity	1. *Address of this dwelling unit* (DU). Mark location on metropolitan area map.

2. *Household characteristics.* List persons in household in some such manner as follows:

Person Code	Relationship to Head of Household	Age Code	Sex	Years of Education	Occupation (use SIC code)
Ⓐ	*Head	g	m	16	3571
B	*Housewife	g	f	14	none
C	*Daughter	b	f	3	in school
D	*Son	d	m	11	in school
E	Mother-in-law	i	f	12	none
F	Roomer	h	m	8	2782

Age Code	
0– 5	a
6–10	b
11–13	c
14–16	d
17–20	e
21–30	f
31–45	g
46–65	h
Over 65	i

Include roomers but not visitors

Referring to list, circle respondent and mark with asterisks respondent's basic family. Give aggregate income last year for all working members of this basic family, including income from rents, securities, alimony, and other sources. Indicate whether this basic family rents this DU or owns structure containing DU. Give number of years this family has lived in this DU, and give number of moves made since living in this metropolitan area. List other cities by name and number of years this family has lived in them.

3. *Characteristics of this structure and this DU.* Indicate type of structure (one-family, multifamily, rooming house, trailer, motel, hotel, institution). For structures designed for more than one family, give number of DU's, number of stories taken up in DU's, and location of this DU (floor and location on floor). Indicate nonresidential use of space and amount of floor area for each separate use. Give lot size, ground floor area of principal structure and other structures (indicate use of such other structures), space reserved for deliveries, space reserved for parking (indicate number of parking places), etc. [If this survey is combined with housing and environmental quality investigation, questions on these aspects of structure and surroundings should be included here.]

Identifying Activity Patterns and Their Intensity

4. *Activities of individual members of household.* Diagram, in some such manner as the following, all major activities of all members of household for previous 24-hour period:

Person Code	a.m. 6 . .	noon . .	p.m. 6 . .	midnight . .	a.m. 5
A	→'←————————1————→'←——2——→'←————sleep————
B	→'←3→'←4——→'←5→'←6→'←——2——→'←————sleep ————
C	→'←———7a———→'←8——→'←9→'←———sleep————
D	→'←———7b—→'←10——→'←——11——→'←———sleep————
E	——→'←12———→'←13→'←14→'←13→'←———sleep————
F*	——→'←———15———→'←16→'←17→'←——sleep————

*Obtain if possible from respondent, otherwise leave postcard.

a. *Activities recurring daily* during typical weekday (list in general order given in diagram and note location on gridded metropolitan area map):

Activity	Coded Location	Usual Means of Reaching	Activity	Coded Location	Usual Means of Reaching
1 Work	653–237	his car	7a School	325–475	walk
3 Housework	home	N.A.	7b School	456–378	bus
6 Children & housework	home	N.A.	etc.		

b. *Occasional activities* from previous 24-hour period (list all other activities in general order given in diagram and note location on gridded metropolitan area map):

Activity	Av.No. Times per Mo.	Coded Location	Usual Means of Reaching	Activity	Av.No. Times per Mo.	Coded Location	Usual Means of Reaching
2 Dinner party	5	213–654	his car	11 Movies	10	563–335	m's car
4 Conv. shopping	15	325–470	her car	etc.			

Other occasional activities which did not happen to occur during previous 24-hour period:

a Lodge meeting	2	478–321	his car	c Consum. shopping	2	561–333	bus
b Baby-sitting	4	neighbor-hood	walk	etc.			

5. *Trip-making behavior of individual members of households.* (Using standard O-D home interview reporting forms, indicate all trips for various purposes to various locations for previous 24-hour period.)

Change Factors

6. *Attitudes and preferences on activities and environment*

a. *Attitudes about activities identified in Content Areas 4 and 5.* Use questions on satisfactions with present typical daily pattern of activities, both as to necessities of daily life (work, school, shopping, and similar activities) and as to leisure-time activities. Also use questions which determine the degree of pleasure or irritation with existing facilities and spatial relationships as these contribute to or intrude on ease of interaction. [If this survey is combined with a study of attitudes on living qualities of city as these attitudes affect location behavior, this content area would be greatly expanded.]

b. *Use of supplemental techniques* (in addition to direct questions under a). For example, use of a game technique to investigate choices of leisure-time activities:

1. *First stage*—ask respondent to indicate preferences as suggested in Figure 22. Then at conclusion of game ask how satisfied he is with his choice.

2. *Second stage*—referring to Figure 22, indicate to respondent that it is now several years later and that the work week has been reduced and he now has two afternoons (total of eight daylight hours) or eight new white stamps (marked "D" to indicate dividend) he can now insert on the game sheet. When he has made his new choices, ask respondent to indicate satisfaction.

of Content Area 4 questions used in an experimental survey based on Table 20. Content Area 6 is designed to identify factors which produce variation in activity patterns over time. Figure 22 is a prototype form of a technique which is being tested by the author in experimental attitude surveys relating to household activities. It employs the game technique which social psychologists have used in other kinds of surveys with considerable success and which proved to be effective in Wilson's surveys. The trade stamp game is based on the general concept of a time budget. The respondent is given a game sheet, identifying various choices open to him for spending his leisure time and a limited number of stamps to paste onto the sheet. There is an element of forced choice in this technique in the sense that the respondent must accept as rules of the game certain preconditions. For example, there are only a certain number of daylight and evening hours available to the respondent to be allocated in the game; furthermore, the amount of time spent for a particular activity must conform to specified rules. After making his budget for leisure time under his present-day income and family situation, the respondent is asked to make choices for additional leisure time made available under conditions of an assumed shorter work week. This kind of approach permits the investigator to identify choices of marginal nature. Where a substantial proportion of

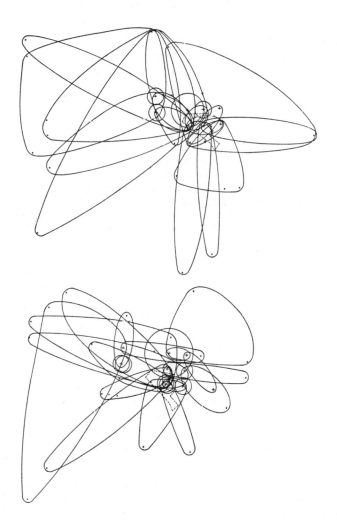

Figure 21. Illustrative Household Activity Patterns from Pilot Study. These diagrams show spatial patterns of two types of activities as determined from interviews with a simple random sample of households in a census tract flanking downtown Durham, North Carolina. Data comparable to that shown in Content Area 4 of Table 20 provided the basis for these plots. The top figure shows recreation patterns, and the lower figure shows visiting patterns. The activity places are indicated by black dots, and places of residence are designated by plus signs. Locations are plotted to the centroid of the grid cell. The dotted line delimits the CBD.

respondents make similar choices, the technique offers a useful means for estimating changes in activity patterns under assumed changes in automation and a shorter work week. The game also provides insights into whether current activity patterns match up with preferences. Divergence between actual and preferred activities may assist in defining missing facilities or missing areas of institutionalized activity.

Figure 22. Choice of Leisure-Time Activities—Trade Stamp Game.

Instructions: In this game we are borrowing the trade stamp idea — the green stamps that merchants give you when you are buying something. However, we will use black and white stamps. You will paste in your supply of stamps in the boxes below according to the way you would like to spend your free time. Assume that during the next 7-day week, after subtracting out the time taken up in sleep, work, meals, grocery shopping, doctors' visits, and similar necessities, you have a total of 28 evening hours (black) and 16 daylight hours (white) distributed as follows to use as you see fit for any of the activities you wish to choose below:

Your stamp supply corresponding to hours and days of the week is diagrammed as follows:

M   T   W   Th   F

Sat.   Sun.   morning

afternoon

evening

One hour of free time spent during daylight hours takes a white stamp, and one hour of free time spent in the evening takes a black stamp. You have to spend the full amount of time budgeted for any choice below, and you have to use black or white stamps specified unless there is a choice. Black squares take black stamps; white squares take white stamps; and hatched squares take either black or white stamps. Lay your stamps on the boxes in appropriate numbers and color, and after you are satisfied with your choices, paste them in.

1. INCREASING YOUR INCOME

A second, night job (choice of one, two, three, four, or five blocks of working time—one to five full evenings a week)

Making hobby pay

Baby-sitting

Overseeing rental prop., investments, etc.

_____
(specify other)

2. IMPROVING YOURSELF BY FURTHER EDUCATION OR IN OTHER WAYS DEVELOPING YOURSELF

Night classes

(Choose 1 or 2 blocks)

Museum visits

Art gallery

Concert

Theater (stage)

Great Books group

Research and writing

_____
(specify other)

3. RECREATION AND RELAXATION

Activity Shared with Others

Golf   ☐☐☐☐

Tennis   ☐☐☐

Dancing (folk or social)   ▨▨▨

Bowling   ▨▨

_____ ☐▭
(specify other)   (mark off)

Shared or Individual Activity

Fishing   ☐☐☐☐ ☐☐☐☐
(must take both)

Boating   ☐☐☐☐

Movies   ▨▨▨▨

Window shopping   ▨▨▨▨

Individual Activity

(Choose as many hours as you wish)

Taking a nap   ▧▧▧▧

Reading   ▧▧▧▧

Gardening   ☐☐☐☐

Crafts, other hobbies   ▧▧▧▧

_____ ☐ ▭ ▭ ▭
(specify other)   (mark off)

(Choose as many hours as you wish)

Television   ▧▧▧▧

Walking   ▧▧▧▧

Playing musical instrument   ▧▧▧▧

_____ ☐▭
(specify other)   (mark off)

4. DOING THINGS WITH FAMILY

Campout (must take all weekend)   ☐☐☐☐ ☐☐☐☐

Outing   ☐☐☐☐ ☐☐☐☐
(must take both)

Picnic   ☐☐☐

Going to zoo   ☐☐☐

Taking drive   ☐☐

Activities or play with children or grandchildren   ▧▧▧▧ (Choose as many as you wish)

_____ ☐▭
(specify other)   (mark off)

5. SOCIAL ACTIVITIES

Evening at friends' house or entertaining in your home   ▨▨▨

Playing cards   ▨▨▨▨

Group picnics, socials   ▨▨▨▨

Dating   ▨▨▨▨

Visiting in neighborhood   ▧▧▧▧ (Choose as many as you wish)

Telephoning or writing letters   ▧▧▧▧

_____ ☐▭
(specify other)   (mark off)

6. CHURCH ACTIVITIES

    Regular Sunday   ☐☐
      services

    Evening meeting   ▦

    Choir practice   ▧

   ———————————   ☐
    (specify other)   (mark off)

7. PARTICIPATING IN COMMUNITY SERVICE AND POLITICAL ACTIVITIES

    Volunteer service   ▧ ▧ ▧
      (United Fund, Boy   (Choose as many
      Scouts, etc.)   units as you wish)

    Special interest groups   ▧
      (PTA, LWV)

    Official activities   ▦
      (School Bd., Planning
      Bd., Recr. Commission)

    Political work (precinct   ▧
      activities, campaign-
      ing, etc.)

   ———————————   ☐
    (specify other)   (mark off)

8. PARTICIPATING IN CLUB AND ORGANIZATIONAL ACTIVITIES

    Club activities   ▧
      (crafts, Garden
      Club, French
      Club, etc.)

    Fraternal groups   ▦
      (Masons, Elks,
      etc.)

    Supper or luncheon   ▧
      group—time
      added to meal
      (Rotary, Kiwanis,
      etc.)

   ———————————   ☐
    (specify other)   (mark off)

From preliminary tests of the technique, it appears to get at activity preferences more successfully than direct questions. As might be expected, the pattern of choices shows variation with socio-economic group, working-nonworking adults, and adults in different stages of the life cycle. In a simple random sample of households interviewed in a test area, leisure-time activity choices of those in the upper socio-economic group clustered more strongly around continuing education and cultural functions than those in the lower group, whereas the lower group preferred to devote a larger proportion of their leisure time to recreation and relaxation than their opposites. Within the recreation category, the lower group showed a higher intensity of preference for TV, gardening, and bowling, the higher group a higher intensity for reading, golf, and attending collegiate sports events than their opposites. While the results are not particularly important in themselves, they indicate the possibilities of making interpolations in activity patterns for anticipated changes in age composition of the population or marked escalation of income levels over a time interval represented in the planning period.

In summary, the activities study sketched out in this chapter is a necessary part of the typical planning agency series of tooling-up studies. It is essential to the study of land use. Three basic activity classes—productive activities, general welfare activities, and living activities—each require investigation with instruments especially designed for that class of activity. There are many subclassifications, but essentially the firm, the institution, and the household are the basic agents used in defining general classes of activity. The content areas of an activities study should be blocked out and integrated with a movements study and other basic planning surveys. The typical survey seeks to obtain sufficient information to classify the activity, to define nodes of activity, to determine the intensity of activity between nodes, and to identify the factors that modify activity patterns. The last task is normally the most complex and involves investigations of attitudes as the "regulators" of behavior and thus crucial determinants of activity systems, present and future.

Chapter 7

Urban Land Studies

The fifth series of tooling-up investigations required in land use planning seek to describe the salient features and facts about land in the urban area and its surroundings. These studies provide information on the physical setting that accommodates the economic activity, and the population and their activities, which are analyzed by methods and techniques taken up in the preceding four chapters. The present chapter goes into nine types of background studies which furnish information related to the use, nonuse, and misuse of urban land—information which contributes to the analyses and decisions reached in the land use planning process taken up in Part III:

1. Compilation of data on physiographic features, mapping the urban setting.
2. The land use survey.
3. The vacant land survey.
4. Hydrological and flood potential study.
5. Structural and environmental quality survey.
6. Cost-revenue studies of land use.
7. Land value studies.
8. Studies of aesthetic features of the urban area.
9. Studies of public attitudes and preferences regarding land use.

As these types of studies are successively described in the sections below, it will become apparent that there is considerable variability in the precision and detail to which survey and analytical techniques are carried. To an important degree, this is a reflection of the unequal attention which has been accorded these various types of urban land studies in research to date in the field of urban planning and contributing disciplines.

In general, the mapping of the urban area, as discussed in the first section below, provides the medium for recording and presenting information on the natural features of the urban setting and the manner in which these have been altered and put to use in streets, blocks, and lots for urban living. Not included in the discussion of mapping below are certain other obvious investigations such as the geology and climatology of the urban area and its larger region, which round out the picture of the physiographic character of the urban setting.

Land use surveys are concerned with classifying and recording space in use. As suggested in Chapters 2 and 6, the land use classification used must be conceived in terms of the classification of urban activity systems. The second section below discusses survey techniques for gathering data to be applied in subsequent chapters in land use analyses. There are a variety of forms for summarizing data thus assembled. A common one consists of a graphic presentation of dominant land uses by activity groups —work areas, living areas, leisure-time areas, and so on, each with its assemblage of specific land uses. Although there are other forms of presentation, the *land use map* and its statistical summary are the traditional means of summarizing the use of ground area. Space use maps involve summaries of use by floor area. In coastal areas the use of water areas is still another class of use to be included in surveys. However, in this chapter we shall be concerned mainly with ground area use and floor space use.

The vacant land survey classifies and records the use capabilities of the lacework residual pattern of inlying vacant parcels and the open land at the periphery not yet in urban use. This survey results in what is usually referred to as a *land capabilities map* and a statistical summary of the general characteristics of vacant and open land, considering topographic and drainage factors and the kinds of public utilities and other improvements presently serving these areas. The land use and vacant land maps thus account for all land in the urban study area.

The hydrological study provides information about water areas important in determining uses to be made of adjoining land areas. It examines the natural drainage system and brings to bear information on flood potential which is needed in later land use planning studies.

The structural and environmental quality survey classifies and records the physical condition of structures in the city, the quality of their environment, and other factors associated with urban blight and obsolescence. This survey involves investigations of social, health, and economic as well as physical indicators of blight. It results in what is usually referred to as a *blighted areas map* and supplemental statistical summaries of the incidence of physical deterioration and obsolescence. This study indicates where there may be flexibility for replanning. The blighted areas map along with the land capabilities map furnish a picture of the areas where the major growth of the future must be accommodated—one through *urban renewal* and the other through *urban extension,* the two basic processes of urban growth.

Cost-revenue studies of land use examine prevailing public policies and practices in supplying services and facilities for various classes of land use in differing areas of governmental jurisdiction, and develop cost-revenue estimates indicating the implications for municipal finance of land development at various intensities and densities under existing or assumed changes in prevailing policies and practices. These studies are concerned with the economy of land development as a public interest consideration as opposed to the economics of development arising through the operations of builders and developers functioning within the framework of the urban land market.

As indicated in Chapter 1, studies of land values, both spatial and temporal aspects, provide clues as to the way land has been priced in the urban land market and thus what the most economic use of land might be. These studies have a direct relationship to land use and vacant land analysis and provide a basis for taking into account the implications that land use proposals hold for the structure of prevailing land values.

Studies of aesthetic features of the urban area identify distinctive locations and vistas, or foci and axes, natural features with special development potentialities, special building groupings with symbolic significance, and so on. Finally, studies of public attitudes and preferences in the use of land supply important information to be taken into account in fitting the land development plan to livability concepts of the people of the urban area. All of the foregoing list of studies contribute material which is relevant to analyses and decisions faced in the land use planning process. Existing and developing techniques used in each type of study are taken up in greater detail in the following sections of this chapter.

Mapping the Urban Setting

Since maps provide the medium for recording and summarizing data descriptive of the urban setting, it would be well at the outset to review briefly mapping needs and techniques requisite to the study of land and its uses. The need for base maps will vary with every city. Cities with an established city planning activity will generally have a selection of base maps available for mapping the urban setting and for making planning studies. Depending upon the financial resources of the planning agency, and to some extent the professional pride of the city planner and thus his office policy in keeping his basic "tools" up to date, mapping offers no problem in most such cities. It is in the smaller community where resources are limited or in the community where planning is a newly established function that the following discussion is particularly applicable. It also applies in cities where planning has never been established as a permanent and continuing service of local government, where there are periodic flurries of planning activity and then lapses of time with little or no activity.

Land use planning analyses call for a variety of maps which not only provide a basic description of the physical layout of the urban area and its physiographic features but also provide a base for plotting and analyzing information assembled in surveys discussed later in the chapter. The typical types of reference maps used in developing the base maps, the kinds of base maps, and the major steps involved in preparing planning base maps are taken up briefly in the subsections that follow.

Types of Reference Maps

Depending somewhat on the resources of the city but more frequently on the active interest on the part of the engineering department, the tax assessor, or some high-ranking city or county official in maintaining accurate mapped information on the city and its environs, any one or more of the following types of maps may be available: engineering maps, topographic maps, property or tax maps, miscellaneous reference maps. The original base for these maps may be drawn from a controlled aerial photographic mosaic, from engineering surveys, or by compilation from miscellaneous sources.

Few cities will go to the expense of mapping beyond the corporate limits, and so, for planning purposes, where studies must be made on an urban-wide basis, the maps listed above must usually be considered reference maps. However, where the corporate limits include the planning area, or where reasonably accurate maps in one or more counties inclusive of the planning area are available at uniform and satisfactory scales, such maps may be used directly as base maps for city planning.

If available, engineering maps are usually maintained in the public works or engineering department of the city. They are generally drawn in ink on tracing linen and maintained in the form of an atlas of from two or three to a large number of sheets, depending upon the scale used and the size of the city. They are usually laid out with reference to a local, state, or U.S. Geological Survey plane coordinate system and indicate major reference and control points of triangulation, traverse, and level systems. They show street right-of-way lines and sometimes curb lines; railroad rights-of-way and sometimes track locations; streams, rivers, and lakes; culverts, bridges, and grade separations; corporate limits lines; and so on. Scales are generally 50 or 100 feet to the inch. These maps are used by the engineering force as a central set of records for all engineering work and as a point of departure for local surveys in connection with street improvements, subdivisions, and other engineering studies where accuracy is important. Such maps provide a useful reference to the planning agency in subdivision review work, site planning studies, and for all kinds of detailed investigations, including work on setback lines or street lines, the preparation of official maps, redevelopment studies, and so on.[1]

The situation with respect to topographic maps has been improving rapidly since World War II. Where previously many cities either relied upon small-scale U.S. Geological Survey maps or went to great expense to obtain engineering surveys for large-scale detailed topographic maps, the improvement and more extensive use of multiplex photogrametry equipment used in conjunction with limited ground control surveys now permit the preparation of extremely accurate large-scale topographic maps. Keyed to a grid layout of the urban area, these maps are usually prepared in the form of an atlas consisting of several sheets, the number being dependent upon the horizontal scale of the map and the extent of the built-up area. These maps are the principal reference work for the natural features of the area, indicating land forms by contour lines and showing natural drainage lines, rivers, streams, ponds, and marshy areas, some even showing wooded areas, rock outcroppings, and sink holes. Such maps generally show the used width of streets, railroad tracks, principal structures, and political boundaries. They sometimes indicate benchmarks and other triangulation and traverse monuments, depending upon the contract specifications when the mapping is undertaken. Large-scale maps prepared from engineering or aerial surveys in atlas form usually are made at 200 feet to the inch on a horizontal scale, with contour intervals at two, five, or ten feet vertical scale, depending upon the desired detail and local terrain conditions. USGS quadrangle sheets have an R.F. (representative fraction) of from 10,000 to 65,000 depending upon the date of the survey, the practices of the original surveying agency, and the prevailing accepted scale at that time.[2] Contour intervals of these maps are generally 10 or 20 feet, depending on the topographic characteristics of the particular area involved.

Property maps (sometimes called tax maps) are usually developed from aerial photographs because of the ease in identifying fence lines, structures, and other physical features in the townscape which can be tied to property lines. Occasionally where comprehensive engineering surveys have

---

[1] The term "official map" is sometimes erroneously considered to be simply a base map prepared by the city. The term has a much more specialized meaning. An official map is a document in map form, usually recorded, which together with supplementing notations identifies existing and proposed streets, and frequently such other public facilities as existing and proposed school sites, playground, parks, and so on, depending upon the scope of the official map legislation of a particular state. It is a plan implementation instrument by which the local legislative body places on record its official intentions as to locations and dimensions of such facilities, particularly as to widenings, expansions, extensions, and new facilities.

[2] The R.F. system of scaling maps is commonly used by geographers where large land areas are being mapped, and is found on Army Engineer maps as well as Geological Survey and Coast and Geodetic Survey maps. On a map with an R.F. of 10,000, an inch measured on the map is equivalent to 10,000 inches on the ground, or a graphic scale of 833 feet to the inch.

been made, a city will use a set of reproduced tracings of the engineering maps and insert property line data on the basis of field surveys and a search of property records maintained by the city or county. In some cases, usually in small communities, a property map may be compiled entirely on the basis of recorded subdivision plats and deeds, relying on simple traverse surveys to provide controls and fill in critical gaps. These maps usually show street rights-of-way (opened and unopened streets), property lines, railroad and utility easements and rights-of-way, watercourses and lakes, and political boundaries. Maps developed on the basis of aerial photographs may show dimensions of property lines, whereas those based on engineering surveys often contain bearings as well as lengths of property lines. Scales range from 50 to 600 feet to the inch, with 50 feet being used in central areas, 100 to 200 feet in the remaining built-up areas, and 400 to 600 feet in outlying areas where acreage tracts predominate. These maps are usually developed for the tax assessor's office, but are exceedingly important reference maps for the planning agency, particularly for detailed land use surveys, subdivision review work, zoning administration, and site planning studies of all kinds.

There are a great variety of miscellaneous reference maps useful to the work of the planning agency, among them insurance maps, county and state highway maps, census maps, historical maps, and the various types of commercial maps frequently prepared for sale in larger cities. Prepared primarily for fire insurance underwriters, the insurance atlas provides useful material for planning purposes on structures, showing the outline shape, the number of stories to buildings or sections of buildings, the type of construction, and the street number of each structure or the separate address in each such structure. The planning office will frequently find county maps prepared by the county or the state highway commission useful in studies of peripheral areas where city maps leave off. Although most census maps are based on maps supplied from local sources, frequently they will provide the only readily available source on minor civil division lines such as town, township, or borough lines.

Planning Base Maps

In urban areas where no satisfactory planning base maps are available or where for one reason or another none of the foregoing types of reference maps is completely satisfactory for city planning purposes, it is probable that sooner or later the planning office will find it necessary to prepare a series of base maps suitable for planning studies. Most planning offices will require at least two series of base maps in addition to the available reference maps described above: (1) what we shall call general-purpose maps, and (2) the detailed planning base map.

The general-purpose map is the type which cities frequently have published in quantity. It shows streets and street names, perhaps an index of street names, corporate limits lines, railroads, perhaps the major public buildings, lakes, rivers, and so on. Where this map covers the entire metropolitan area of interest, this conventional city map can be used for generalized studies, records, and displays or for rough work maps. Where the coverage does not include the entire urban area of interest, the planning agency must develop a new general-purpose base for its own special needs. Generally, this type of map should be available in three sheet sizes, ranging from the wall-display size down to a table size and letter size. These maps vary in scale for each sheet size according to the extent of built-up area and the general shape of the area covered. For example, the wall map may range from 200 feet to the inch, for the small communities of 10,000 or under, to 2,500 scale, and, in a few cases, as much as a mile to the inch for the large metropolitan area. Table maps may vary from 500 feet to two miles to the inch, and letter-size maps on 8½ by 11–inch sheets may be upward of several miles to the inch. The latter series of general-purpose maps may need to be greatly simplified by the elimination of street names, and for the larger metropolitan areas, the elimination of all but the major streets.

The other type of base, what we refer to as the detailed planning base map, merits more detailed consideration. This is a base which is prepared in atlas form, usually to the same scale as the topographic maps so that they may be used as overlay maps in conjunction with contour maps. The atlas may be keyed to the same grid system employed in the atlas of topographic sheets or it may be composed in terms of planning districts or natural planning areas as taken up in Part III. It is usually prepared in two or three series. One shows street right-of-way lines, railroads, watercourses, lakes, and civil division lines. This map is frequently combined with the second, which shows, in addition, property and easement lines. The third series have structures added. The first and second series are used for neighborhood studies and detailed studies of all kinds, and the third series are used for maintaining office records of all kinds, including land and structure uses, plots of building permits issued, a map of house numbers, zoning analyses, plots of new subdivisions, and so on.

Preparing the Detailed Base Map

Procedures for preparing the planning base map will vary from urban center to urban center according to available reference maps and the budget available for the mapping activity. Accordingly, the suggested procedures outlined briefly below must be adapted to each particular situation.

In general, the first step is the assembly of all available reference maps and the selection of one consistent series of maps as a control for the development of the new base. Scale, accuracy, inclusiveness of coverage, and street and property line data available at the selected scale are all factors which enter into the selection of the control map. The smallest suitable scale for the subsequent plot of structures on this base is 200 feet to the inch, and perhaps the largest suitable scale without involving sheets of unwieldy size or sheets too limited in the area covered to obtain relationships from block to block is 100 feet to the inch. With the possible exception of the central business district area, where considerable detail must frequently be plotted and therefore the larger scale may be preferred, for most purposes 200 feet to the inch is perhaps the best multipurpose scale. It permits inclusion of the average low-density neighborhood on a single sheet and conforms to a commonly used scale for aerial and topographic maps which, if not used as control maps for the preparation of this planning base, often must be used in conjunction with the planning base map in many types of city planning analyses.

The second step is the determination of the area to be mapped, which will generally be the *planning area*. For plan presentations at the horizon-year time scale where detail is not important, general-purpose maps will generally be adequate for planning analyses and presentations. The identification of the planning area is more important at the intermediate time scale, generally involving a period from 20 to 25 years in the future and commonly called the *planning period*.[3] The planning area will usually show all the present built-up area with an ample allowance for expansion beyond, especially along major highway approaches. In metropolitan areas the planning area obviously extends beyond the corporate limits of the central city to include all suburban areas considered to be functionally related to the urban center. In a few cases where the corporate limits extend considerably beyond the built-up area, the planning area may be defined to coincide with the corporate limits. Since population data are reported only by minor civil divisions, these lines may be a factor in establishing the limits of the planning area. Although somewhat arbitrary so far as growth and expansion of the urban center is concerned, county or township lines may be sufficiently close to the functional delineation to be usable as the planning area. Other factors to be considered in drawing the planning area limits are locations of school attendance areas, watershed areas affecting the city water supply, limits of major drainage areas related to sanitation and

[3] For considerations involved in selecting the planning period, see the discussion under population forecasts in Chapter 5.

storm drainage systems, outlying municipally owned property, and so on. Procedures for delimiting the planning area are taken up in greater detail in Chapter 9.

A third step is to select the coverage of individual sheets of the atlas. Where a uniform grid system is employed, this step becomes a mechanical one of laying out a grid pattern over the selected planning area. Where an attempt is made to recognize natural planning areas such as residential neighborhoods or industrial districts (see Chapter 9), each individual sheet must be composed with special care. Since no two planning districts are likely to be of the same shape or size, particular attention must be given to sheet orientation with respect to the direction of the north point and the selection of a sheet size which will contain the largest planning district to be included in the atlas. In some cases where there are odd-shaped or unusually large planning districts, it may be necessary to develop the sectional base sheet in two parts if the size of the atlas is not to become too unwieldy for convenient use on an ordinary desk or table.

Once these preliminary preparations have been completed, the successive steps which follow become somewhat mechanical operations. The result of the next steps is the preparation of what we call Base A, Base B, and Base C. Base A is simply a street map; Base B is Base A with property and easement lines added; and Base C is Base B with structures added. Some planning agencies may be interested in having base maps of all variations on the initial Base A. Others may be interested only in Base B and Base C, and some in Base C only. The appropriate modification to procedures summarized below can be made to fit the needs of the planning agency.

Assuming all three bases are desired, the fourth step is the preparation of a preliminary pencil drawing on tracing linen of Base A, showing the street network. If the reference base being used is sufficiently accurate for planning purposes, street right-of-way lines can be traced directly on the linen. If other reference sheets are to be used in establishing right-of-way lines, it may be necessary to trace off the center lines of the street network from the reference base, with rights-of-way dimensioned in by reference to other sources of information. Streets which are open are usually shown in solid lines, and streets which are dedicated to public use but not open are usually shown in broken lines. Base A also includes railroad rights-of-way, watercourses, political boundary lines. Political boundaries are usually shown in heavy dash and dot lines of appropriate weight to distinguish them from other lines.

From the preliminary drawing of Base A, a print is made; and to this print are added data which will be required later for Bases B and C. Property lines and easements to be used on Base B are obtained from tax maps or, in the case of acreage tracts, identified on aerial photographs by reference to fence lines and use lines (after being checked against other data sources), or they are obtained from various engineering drawings, subdivision plats, deed records, and other reference maps described above. Structure data to be used on Base C are obtained from aerial photographs and insurance atlases. In general, property and easement lines are shown in broken lines of a lighter weight than those used for right-of-way lines. Property lines may be broken or unbroken lines, and easement lines are shown in dashes and dots to differentiate them from property lines. Structures are shown in bold heavy solid lines with the shapes of commercial, industrial, and public buildings following the approximate true shapes observed in photographs or the insurance atlas and with residential structures represented by symbols of uniform size, usually in the shape of an open square. All such representations of structures are located as closely as possible to actual location with reference to property lines. In residential areas, only the principal structures are shown, with sheds, garages, and other outbuildings accessory to the residential use omitted.

The result of the foregoing step completes the preliminary compilation work done in the office. The sixth step is a field check of the preliminary work sheet compiled on the Base A print. This step is usually combined with the detailed land use survey discussed later in the chapter. In this stage of the mapping activity, street and lot discrepancies are discovered on the ground. Theoretically no corrections of this order should be necessary, but in practice some changes here and there will usually be necessary. By public usage, a street right-of-way differing from the platted right-of-way may need to be recognized. In certain sections of a city, there may be considerable deviation in the lot layout discovered on the ground from that compiled from office records and subdivision maps. Recent aerial photography will usually obviate most of these difficulties in the original compilation work, but in sections not covered by photographs or where the photography is not of recent date, this field checking activity will often reveal that a superseding plat has been followed in the actual land subdivision as carried out on the ground. The field work also includes verification as to whether streets are opened or closed, visual checks of building setbacks in relation to property and street right-of-way lines, the insertion of new structures, and so on.

In the intensively developed sections of the city, field checking must generally be done on foot, but in most outlying residential areas it can be done by a "windshield survey." In peripheral sections of the planning area, distances between structures, building relationships to property lines, streams, and natural features may be estimated closely enough for planning purposes by use of the automobile speedometer, rangefinders, and similar makeshift means. In these rural sections, it is frequently simpler to make the necessary field notations in colored pencil directly on aerial photographs.

Upon completion of field work and after conducting any further investigation into official records in follow-up on any discrepancies uncovered in the field, Base A can be finally drawn in ink. From the completed Base A maps, reproduced tracings can be made and Base B data on property and easement lines added; and from the completed Base B maps a second set of reproduced tracings can be made and Base C data on structures inserted. When completed, the necessary prints can be made from these base maps, the desired data inserted with colored pencils or inks, and bound in atlas form as a set of records for analysis and general office reference use.[4]

Because of the time and expense involved in preparing these base maps, it is most important to establish systematic procedures for keeping them up to date. Within the area of subdivision jurisdiction, it is possible to keep abreast of these changes and make additions as they occur. These additions or changes can be plotted on special "correction prints" as they are formally approved. In the case of new structures or converted buildings, in cities or counties where building codes or zoning ordinances are in effect, it is possible to keep an up-to-date plot of these changes through the building inspector. This can be done by providing him with a set of prints of Base C and arranging with him for the systematic addition of structures as building or, preferably, occupancy permits are issued. Where the planning area extends beyond the limits of the subdivision jurisdiction or in peripheral areas where building inspection procedures are not applicable, it becomes necessary to make periodic field checks to insure a complete record of changes in the physical setting. By consolidating these correction sheets and maintaining them on an annual basis, it is possible to develop comparative data from year to year on rates of change, directions of growth, and locations of conversion activity.

Land Use Classification and Surveys

In a sense the foregoing mapping activity serves as an inventory of natural features of the urban setting. As noted at the outset, there are other features

---

[4] These procedures for mapping and for relating the mapping to the land use survey, of course, apply to a map system of recording and storing land use data. They are applicable primarily to cities under 100,000. Mapping requirements of large urban areas are increasingly being met by automatic map plotters utilizing aerial photographs. Where punch card systems of data storage are used, data plotting by machine methods is replacing the hand methods discussed above. The technology of mapping and printing out data by machine methods is developing rapidly and revolutionizing mapping work in large city planning offices.

about the landscape of a man-made character that must be investigated in preparation for the land use planning task. Among these, the classification and survey of land use are basic.

It should be noted at this point that, although "land use" is used throughout this book in a generic sense, in a narrower meaning and particularly in recent time planners have become more and more concerned with "space use" within buildings. The land use survey has traditionally been concerned with the use of ground space. It has classified and recorded uses of developed land according to "functional activities" carried on in the urban center. While the term "activities" has always been closely associated with land use, it has generally been linked to various classes in an intuitive and generalized manner. Thus, there are one or more industrial use classifications to represent goods-producing and goods-handling activities; one or more commercial use classifications to represent wholesale and retail distribution and the related storage and service functions; one or more "public" and "quasi-public" categories to identify various services of a general welfare nature; and one or more categories to represent residential uses of land. For initial generalized studies, a classification system based on the use of ground space still serves a purpose.

As suggested in Chapters 2 and 6, more and more the planner is seeking classification systems compatible with a whole range of new tools he is beginning to acquire. He is now interested in the classification and assembly of data about the use of space inside buildings (floor space) as well as on the land (ground space). He is still concerned with the use of land as a descriptive tool, but more fundamentally he is interested in land and space uses as they reflect specific clusters of human activities. Thus he must classify and inventory uses of space and land in a manner which is meaningful in terms of activity systems discussed in the last chapter. As noted there, more and more human interaction has ties far beyond the physical confines of the metropolitan area of concern. In land use surveys the planner is therefore seeking to classify and record uses as they tie into both local and nonlocal activity and communication systems. In sum, he requires a classification scheme which is compatible with these systems of interaction and which at the same time will serve as an all-purpose approach to inventorying land use whether it involves a survey of ground space use of the most generalized character or an investigation of floor space use of the most exacting type.

Before turning to the problem of classification of space, it will be useful to consider briefly the various forms in which land use data can be presented. As might be expected, forms of presentation have been changing as new developments in classification and data processing have occurred. For general descriptive studies, one of the oldest and simplest forms for

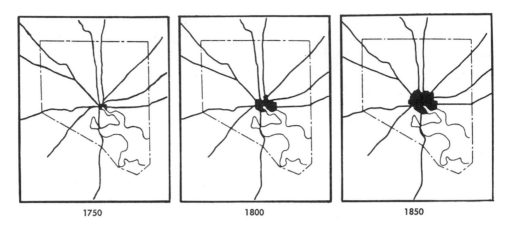

Figure 23. Use of Land Development Diagrams to Show Historical Growth Patterns in the Development of the Urban Area. (*Source:* Baltimore Department of Planning.)

presenting data on the use of ground area is the *land development diagram* showing the distribution of land in urban use without distinguishing between classes of uses (see Figure 23). By reference to land development records for selected intervals of time, supplemented by historical maps of the urban area, these diagrams can be used to show the historical changes in the extent of built-up pattern of the urban area as it has expanded over the years. However, with advances in the use of automatic data-processing systems in the analysis of land development patterns, it is now practicable to prepare such diagrams in forms more useful for analysis. In place of the gross visual basis for studying the intensity of development shown in Figure 23, it is now possible to depict land development patterns in a standardized and measured form of use intensity usable in machine methods of analysis, either in terms of overall patterns or on a small-area basis pinpointed to specific locations. Figure 24 divides up land area into cells of uniform size and, on the basis of subdivisions of each cell into nine subcells, records the proportion of each cell taken up in urban land use in terms of ninths.

More commonly, land use data are summarized both statistically and in map form according to specific ground use categories such as residential uses, business uses, industrial uses, and so on. For general studies, particularly in the small and medium-size urban centers, these studies are usually done "by hand." Figure 29 shows the conventional land use map for the same urban center shown in Figure 24. This is the most common form for presentation of land use patterns. It is the type of presentation a city planner finds useful in analyses of relationships among land uses in generalized patterns. Sometimes, however, the data are summarized by plotting uses on separate maps as shown in Figure 30. For large metropolitan areas where

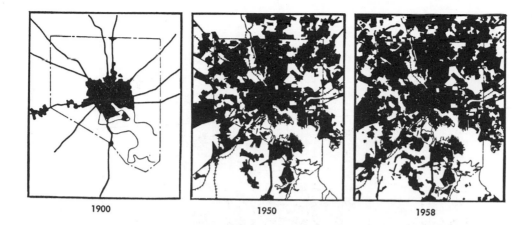

1900   1950   1958

machine methods of data handling are used, individual uses, for example, residential uses, can also be presented in the manner indicated in Figure 25. This shows in standardized form not only the distribution of land in residential use but also the pattern of residential densities (in this case, the number of dwelling units per residential ninth).

For analyses involving indoor and outdoor space use, still another type of presentation may be used. This involves the mapping of space use (usually for particular areas, such as the central business district) by a series of overlays or individual maps, each presenting the use of space for one of the various stories at, above, or below ground level. Murphy and Vance have carried this type of presentation a step further and introduced the concept of a "height index" and an "intensity index." [5] The height index simply shows the ratio of space on all floors devoted to a particular class of use being studied (for example, central business space as studied by Murphy and Vance) to the *total ground floor space;* the intensity index is the ratio of space on all floors devoted to a particular class of use being studied to the *total floor space on all floors.* Conceivably these concepts could also be expressed in terms of area in indoor *and* outdoor space. Summary gradations in these measures can be mapped for each class of use with standard crosshatch patterns either by blocks, as done for central business districts by Murphy and Vance, or by standardized grid cells. The latter system of summarizing data on maps would of course be used where ADP methods of data handling have been instituted and would offer opportunities for machine print-outs of maps.

The applications of land use studies are many. One of the applications of immediate and direct concern to the chapters that follow is in the prep-

[5] Raymond E. Murphy and J. E. Vance, Jr., "Delimiting the CBD," *Economic Geography,* July, 1954, pp. 208–209.

Figure 24. Intensity of Land Development. The gradation from a white to a black pattern indicates the compactness of urban development in the sense of the degree to which land is taken up in urban uses. Black indicates that all land in the grid cell is taken up in urban use, with gradations in tone through successively lighter grays signifying less and less of the area of the grid cell being in urban use.

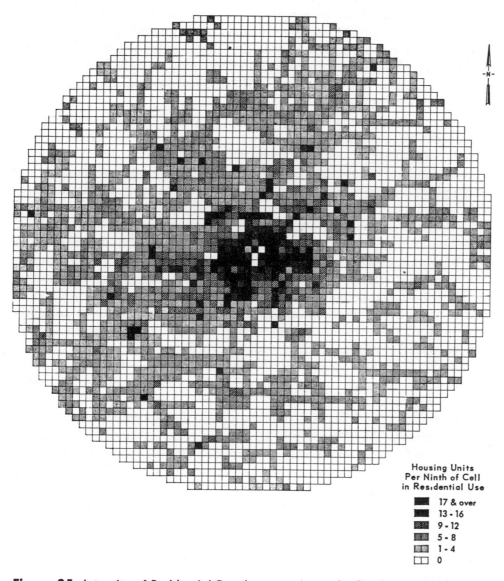

Figure 25. Intensity of Residential Development. A standardized form for recording the degree to which land area in a city is pre-empted for any particular use—in this case residential use. The darker the crosshatch pattern the more dense the residential development.

aration of a *preliminary land use plan*—a generalized scheme of proposed
land development which provides an initial guide and working basis for
developing the land use plan part of the *comprehensive plan*. In the preliminary studies we are concerned mainly with ground space use. In the
more exacting comprehensive plan studies that eventually follow from these
preliminary plan studies, space use analyses may include both floor area
and ground space use. These form the basis for the land use proposals in
the comprehensive plan.

Land use surveys have equally tangible applications in the whole array
of transportation studies and utility service area analyses involved in these
elements of the comprehensive plan for the urban area. In thoroughfare
studies, land use data are basic to the analysis of traffic generation and
assignment. Land use information is important in parking studies. Similarly
it is an essential element in mass transportation studies. The pattern of
ground space use as derived from generalized land use maps is a basic
reference in locating major thoroughfares, parking areas, and transit routes
and terminals, and the detailed Base C type of land use presentation is
fundamental in the first preliminary design of thoroughfares and parking
facilities. Both the generalized and the detailed land use maps are invaluable in transit, trucking, railroad, and airport studies. Moreover, in utility
studies of all kinds—in estimating existing and future needs for the expansion of water, sewerage, power, and other utility systems—land use data
provide an important source of information with respect to service areas
and how the demands on utilities are concentrated or dispersed within
these service areas.

The applications of land use information are not restricted to urban-wide
planning studies. The Base C type of detailed presentation showing ground
space use is fundamental to studies of residential neighborhoods; and used
in conjunction with floor space use, they are essential to analyses of central
and outlying business areas, and organized or planned industrial districts.
It is a basic reference for redevelopment and rehabilitation plans under
federally aided urban renewal programs. In addition to area studies of these
types, such land use maps are a primary source of information for site
planning work: for example, on recreation areas, school sites, housing
developments, and shopping centers.

Land use maps, in terms of both ground and floor use, have a great
variety of operational as well as planning uses. For day-to-day problems and
operation, they are the city planner's "encyclopedia" for many routine and
urgent matters. They provide a basis for responding to citizen petitions
and council, mayor, or city manager referrals of all kinds, and they furnish
a ready reference for discussion of complaints, problems, and ideas offered
by daily visitors to the planning office. The usefulness of these maps for

record purposes, for subdivision review, and for zoning studies and petitions has already been pointed out. Too, the uses of these maps on day-to-day matters are not confined to the city planning office alone. Copies with acetate overlays attached for plotting purposes are frequently to be found in city council chambers and in the mayor's or city manager's office.

Land Use Classification and Coding Systems

Because of the great variations which exist among uses, it is necessary to classify and record land and space uses on some systematic basis. This gives rise to a classification system, and if modern data-processing methods are to be used, it gives rise to a coding system. Classification is a systematic means of *grouping* like categories of land use in the pursuit of some predetermined purposes, and coding is a systematic means for *recording* land uses in line with these purposes. Classification permits planners to deal with "families" of land use in various kinds of analyses, and coding permits quick access to land use data and the rearrangement of data into family combinations. In this connection the Urban Renewal Administration and the Bureau of Public Roads in their coding manual stress the importance of differentiating between *parcel* characteristics (as in location, area, ownership, etc.), *structure* characteristics (for example, type of building, total floor area, ground floor area, etc.), and *land use* characteristics (whether residential, manufacturing, etc.).[6] The coding system used in recording land use should be distinct from coding systems used in recording characteristics of the parcel or structure.

From these observations and the partial listing of the ways in which land use data are used in planning analyses given above, it is evident that before a system of classification is finally adopted, much thought and study must go into the detail and form in which data are needed in both immediate and ultimate applications. A system too narrowly conceived, too bound to one kind of application, can severely handicap a planning agency's general program, and once a classification system has been adopted, later corrective changes can create problems. Just as studies of population trends can be seriously disrupted by changes in census categories from one census to another, similarly every time basic changes in the land use classification system are introduced, the opportunities for trend studies are curtailed. More important, in the task of periodically adjusting long-range plans to significant new changes in trends, every revision in the classification

---

[6] Urban Renewal Administration and U.S. Bureau of Public Roads, *Standard Land Use Coding Manual—a Standard System for Identifying and Coding Land Use Activities,* Washington: U.S. Government Printing Office, June, 1964.

system will present a whole series of problems in reorganizing the analytical framework employed. These problems and the sheer expense of corrective land use surveys (as distinct from the necessary periodic resurvey of land use under one classification system as discussed in a later subsection below) place a premium on care and forethought in the initial selection of a classification system.

Because of early zoning practices of grouping uses by nuisance characteristics and because of similarities in analytical approaches to land use planning followed in more recent years, there is considerable uniformity in classification systems to be found from one city to another. There has been a continuing interest in the United States in developing a standard classification system such as those existing in England and many countries abroad, and it may be that agreement on at least some of the purposes of such a classification system will come to be sufficiently widespread to enable the profession to adopt a standard classification system. Perhaps the power of persuasion will come through adoption of some uniform coding system.[7] Several are beginning to emerge and will be discussed below. Most of them have been influenced by the Standard Industrial Classification (SIC) system developed under the auspices of the U.S. Bureau of the Budget to standardize data collection systems within the federal establishment. As its title implies, its primary purpose is the classification of industries, and so from the point of view of planning its purpose is somewhat overspecialized.

There are some distinct advantages in a standard classification system. For example, standardization simplifies problems of communication among members of the profession and with the general public; and in a profession where there is the degree of job mobility found in the junior positions in the city planning field, there is less waste motion in integrating new personnel into staff operations. Also a standard classification assists in determining the transfer value of analytical methods successfully employed in one city for use in the solution of problems in other cities; and it offers opportunities for comparative studies and more systematic research into urbanization trends.[8] On the other hand, blind adherence to a standard classification system can result in an entirely inadequate appraisal of land use characteristics peculiarly local in nature or of special local interest. Moreover, standardization can involve cumbersome and time-consuming formalities in the initial adoption and subsequent amendment of a system, with attendant dangers of inflexibility and delays in the mechanics of keeping the system up to date.

---

[7] It should be noted that since groupings are employed in coding systems, there is a built-in classification system of sorts associated with each such coding system.

[8] For a fuller discussion of the need for a standard classification system, see Robert M. Sparks, "The Case for a Uniform Land Use Classification System," *Journal of the American Institute of Planners,* August, 1958.

Apart from the purely local requirement which may be dictated by climate, topography, local policy, and many other local factors, there are some considerations of general application worth noting at this juncture. In the first place, there are the primary uses of a classification which must be borne in mind, and there are secondary applications of land use data. The needs of a primary order may be thought of as the technical requirements of the planning agency's own on-going program, and the secondary applications are more of a service category, a service provided to public and private agencies or groups in the urban area either on a special report basis or in the form of current and continuing reports on land use changes. While the discussion here is concerned with the technical planning needs, the importance of secondary uses of data should not be underestimated, for attention to these needs may play a useful role in strengthening the planning agency's position and general prestige in the metropolitan area.

Within the primary category, there are a variety of applications not by any means restricted to the land use planning needs under discussion here. The range of these applications roughly corresponds to the scope of the planning agency's program:

1. Applications relating to the comprehensive plan and its various component elements.
    a. The land development plan (private and public use, including all major land-using community facilities such as school, recreation, and other similar uses).
    b. The transportation plan (thoroughfares, rapid transit, and rail, air, and water systems of moving people and goods, and their terminal facilities).
    c. The public utilities plan (the underground, surface, and overhead distribution and collection systems, including supply, disposal, and generation facilities).
2. Applications relating to the principal plan effectuation measures.
    a. Regulatory measures (zoning, subdivision control, etc.)
    b. Public developmental measures (public works programming and capital budgeting, urban renewal programs, etc.).
    c. Civic education and public support measures (graphic presentation requirements in exhibitions, films, television shows, publications, etc.).

The above listing is based on the usual definitions of the planning functions of a planning agency. If other functions are assigned to the agency, this list would be expanded.

Each of the above types of studies or programs has its own specifications as to the applications to be made of land use data. So, to achieve its optimum usefulness, the land use classification system must anticipate so far as possible the exact needs of each application. To avoid a wasteful land use survey operation, this means that the system adopted must reflect *known specific applications*, eliminating from consideration uncertain or unexplored possible applications, as promising as they may seem, until such time as they have a demonstrated worth.

Turning now to land use planning applications of land use data, we may note two general and controlling specifications: *specifications of a mechanical character* that are involved in data-processing requirements and the graphic presentation of the land use pattern, and *specifications of an analytical character* that are involved in the study of activity systems and the procedures of land use planning. We cannot go into the mechanics of automatic data-processing (ADP) techniques here. There is a whole body of literature and a variety of training manuals and machine programs which may be consulted.[9] We will simply note that for ADP purposes the coding of land use must usually be by categories consisting of multiples of ten, which is the number of punch positions normally used in the basic column of the standard punch card for storing coded data. Thus, for the basic column, digits 0, 1, 2, 3, 4 . . . 9 may be used; and if these prove to be too limiting, then a pair of columns can be used—00 to 99—or three columns, and so on. The SIC system utilizes ten major categories:[10]

0 – agriculture, forestry, and fisheries
1 – mining, construction, and ordnance manufacture
2
3 } manufacturing
4 – transportation, warehousing, communication, and utilities
5 – wholesale and retail trade
6 – finance, insurance, and real estate
7
8 } services to individuals and businesses, including education, the arts, nonprofit
     organizations, and households
9 – government

Each of these major categories is subdivided into two-, three-, and four-digit subcategories, with each successive digit furnishing further detail within the major category. Thus, under SIC Category 4 are:

40 – railroad transportation
41 – local and suburban transit and interurban passenger transportation
42 – motor freight transportation and warehousing
43 – (unassigned presently)

---

[9] For example, see Harold Borko (ed.), *Computer Applications in the Behavioral Sciences,* Englewood Cliffs, N.J.: Prentice-Hall, Inc., 1962. See also Roger L. Creighton, J. Douglas Carroll, Jr., and Graham S. Finney, "Data Processing for City Planning," *Journal of the American Institute of Planners,* May, 1959. For the simpler data-processing operations such as key punching and card sorting, see manuals prepared by manufacturers of data-processing equipment.
[10] Bureau of the Budget, *Standard Industrial Classification Manual,* Washington: U.S. Government Printing Office, 1957.

44 – water transportation
45 – air transportation
46 – pipeline transportation
47 – transportation services
48 – communication
49 – electric, gas, and sanitary services

The third- and fourth-digit breakdowns carry these subcategories to further detail as to type of facility or establishment.

The same nesting approach is now used in most land use coding systems which have been developed for urban planning. These coding systems also accept many of the SIC classifications, especially in the manufacturing categories, since these are now so widely used for the reporting of statistics important in planning analyses.[11]

The other mechanical consideration in establishing a classification system has to do with graphic presentation and the number of categories that can be clearly recognized in map form. In this connection in the selection of land use categories, practice varies according to the scale and use of the presentation and the size and character of the urban area. In general, small-scale color presentations of land use and most black and white renditions contain relatively few land use categories in order not to detract from the readability of the map. Generally, ground space use maps show areas of residential, business, industrial, and public-institutional uses, with vacant or nonurban areas left blank. Large-scale detailed land use maps of the Base C type can show a breakdown of these major land use classes in as much detail as desired. Generalized or detailed ground and floor space use maps prepared for office reference use may show more classes than those used for public displays or in popular publications. Fewer classes are generally needed in small communities than are required in large urban centers, and within cities of similar size there may be some variation in land use categories necessary to bring out special classes of uses peculiar to one city. For example, in Washington, D.C., federal office building areas might be distinguished from other public use areas, or in cities such as Butte, Montana, where mining operations are carried on within the urban area, these uses would be given special identification. Table 21 presents a system of major land use categories typical of the kind used for presentation purposes, with one variant for maps showing uses by land areas and another for maps showing detail by floor area and open ground areas. It also indicates colors most commonly used for these categories.

---

[11] For example, see Land Classification Advisory Committee of the Detroit Metropolitan Area, *Land Use Classification Manual,* Chicago: Public Administration Service, 1962; Albert Z. Guttenberg, "A Multiple Land Use Classification System," *Journal of the American Institute of Planners,* August, 1959; and Urban Renewal Administration and U.S. Bureau of Public Roads, *Standard Land Use Coding Manual.*

Table 21. Illustrative Major Urban Land Use Categories for Generalized and Detailed Land Use Map Presentations

---

Generalized Presentations by Ground Area

Residence	Industry and related uses—indigo blue
Low density—yellow	Wholesale and related uses—purple
Medium density—orange	Public buildings and open spaces—green
High density—brown	Institutional buildings and areas—gray
Retail business—red	Vacant or nonurban use—uncolored
Transportation, utilities,	
communications—ultramarine	

Detailed Presentations by Building Space Use and Open Air Use [a]

Residence [b]	Industry and related uses [c]—indigo blue
Low density—yellow	Extensive
Medium density—orange	Intermediate
High density—brown	Intensive
Retail business [c]—red	Wholesale and related uses [c]—purple
Local business uses	Public buildings and open spaces [c]—green
Central business uses	Institutional buildings and areas [c]—gray
Regional shopping centers	Vacant or nonurban use—uncolored
Highway service uses	
Transportation, utilities,	
communications—ultramarine	

---

[a] Overlays or separate maps are required to show uses by floor area.

[b] A figure for the number of dwelling units in each structure and a symbol for dwelling types (single-family, duplex, row housing, garden apartments, multistory apartments, etc.) are sometimes inserted on maps to supply supplementary information.

[c] Symbol may be used to differentiate between various subcategories.

A classification system based on the foregoing ADP and presentation requirements does not reflect the detail and the organization of uses employed in the analytical procedures of land use planning. So fundamentally the major categories included in the classification system must reflect basic activity systems of the kind outlined in Chapter 6. At the same time, the system must be divisible into subclasses that are capable of recombination into groups of spatially related uses important in land use planning procedures outlined in Part III. The coding system given in Table 22 is based on the activity systems of Chapter 6, and permits recombinations of uses required in the procedures for preparing the land use plan.[12] The table also indicates equivalent codes used in the Detroit, SIC, and HHFA-BPR systems.[13] Obviously, it can be extended into three- and four-digit or as many

---

[12] A somewhat different view of "activities" is taken by Albert Z. Guttenberg in his proposals for resolving the problems which have grown up around the ambiguity in the meaning of "land use." See Guttenberg, "A Multiple Land Use Classification System."

[13] Land Classification Advisory Committee of the Detroit Metropolitan Area, *Land Use Classification Manual;* Bureau of the Budget, *Standard Industrial Classification Manual;* and Urban Renewal Administration and U.S. Bureau of Public Roads, *Standard Land Use Coding Manual.*

subgroups as may be required in the more refined types of analyses involved in preparing the comprehensive plan. Table 23 illustrates one kind of recombination of uses from Table 22. This particular regrouping of land uses was developed for general analyses undertaken in preparing a preliminary land use plan. For more refined analyses required in the later studies for the comprehensive plan, other more detailed forms of recombinations are usually undertaken.

The Land Use Survey

Once a land use classification system has been established—one which recognizes mechanical as well as analytical requirements—the task of planning and carrying out the land use survey can proceed. Considerations in the selection of the type of survey, the advance preparations, and the actual conduct of the survey are taken up in the pages immediately following.

Types of Surveys

In general, two kinds of surveys have been in usage for a number of years: what we shall call the "inspection" type and the "combined inspection-interview" type. In turn, the inspection survey may be of two kinds—one using a field notation system of recording land uses directly on maps and the other using a system of coding uses on field schedules which are keyed to reference maps. The permanent form in which land use data are to be stored has a bearing on the choice between these two survey techniques. In general, the former is best suited to a map type of data storage system, and the latter for a punch card storage system. The inspection-interview type of survey (sometimes called the "real property survey") has not been used appreciably in recent years, but because of opportunities it affords for obtaining accurate data on space use by floor area, it may come into more common use in the future. In effect, this is a more elaborate form of the inspection type of survey using a card system of data storage.

The mapping form of inspection survey is the simplest type of land use survey and is best suited to the needs of small cities and towns where it is generally more practicable to make planning analyses "by hand." It is usually organized and executed by the planning agency primarily for its own needs. This type of survey commonly uses aerial photographs as the field source material, although the survey may be combined with the field checking of planning base maps as noted earlier in the chapter. When these two operations are combined, data are recorded directly on the preliminary prints of the various sectional sheets as previously compiled in the office.

Table 22. A General Activity and Land Use Coding System Related to Systems in Current Use

General Activity System and Two-Digit Land Use Coding System [a]	Equivalent Codes Under Detroit, SIC, or HHFA-BPR Systems [b]
1. *Extraction Activities* (including stockpiling and assembly of material incidental to these activities)	HHFA-BPR 8 (Resource production and extraction, including related services and processing)
10 Agriculture	DS 10 (SIC 01, 02; and HHFA-BPR 81 similar)
11 Agricultural services, including hunting and trapping	DS 11 (SIC 07; and HHFA-BPR 82 similar)
12 Forestry	DS 12 (SIC 08; and HHFA-BPR 83 similar)
13 Fisheries	DS 13 (SIC 09; and HHFA-BPR 84 similar)
14 Mining, including on-site ore preparation	DS 14 (SIC 10, 11, 12, 13, 14; and HHFA-BPR 85 similar)
19 Other not elsewhere classified	HHFA-BPR 89
2–3. *Processing Activities* (including refining, fabricating, assembly, storage, parking, and other space usues incidental to these activities)	DS 2–3 or SIC 2–3 or HHFA-BPR 2–3 (Manufacturing)
20 Food and kindred products	(HHFA-BPR 21)
21 Tobacco manufacturers	(HHFA-BPR 396)
22 Textile mill products	
23 Apparel and other finished products made from fabrics and similar materials	(HHFA-BPR 23 except 236)
24 Lumber and wood products, except furniture	
25 Furniture and fixtures	
26 Paper and allied products	
27 Printing, publishing, and allied industries	
28 Chemicals and allied products	
29 Petroleum refining and related industries	
30 Rubber and miscellaneous plastics products	(HHFA-BPR 31)
31 Leather and leather products	(HHFA-BPR 236)
32 Stone, clay, and glass products	
33 Primary metals industries	
34 Fabricated metal products, except ordnance, machinery, and transportation equipment	
35 Machinery, except electrical	(HHFA-BPR 342)
36 Electrical machinery, equipment, and supplies	(HHFA-BPR 343)
37 Transportation equipment	(HHFA-BPR 344)
38 Professional, scientific, and controlling instruments; photographic and optical goods; watches and clocks	(HHFA-BPR 35)
39 Miscellaneous manufacturing industries, including ordnance, construction, and related activities	DS 17, 39 modif. of SIC 15–17, 19, 39, HHFA-BPR 39, 341, 66

4. *Communications Activities* (including related rights-of-way, storage, service, parking, and other areas incidental to these activities)

HHFA-BPR 4 (Transportation, communications, and utilities)

    40 Railroad transportation and related transfer and maintenance facilities

DS 40 modif. of SIC 40 (HHFA-BPR 411, 419 in part)

    41 Local passenger systems and related maintenance, including terminals for cross-country stage lines but not including commuter lines operated over railroad rights-of-way and not including highway rights-of-way

DS 41 modif. of SIC 41 (HHFA-PBR 412, 419 in part, 421, 429)

    42 Motor freight transportation and related transfer and maintenance facilities

DS 42 modif. of SIC 42 (HHFA-BPR 422 similar)

    43 Highways and related maintenance facilities

DS 432 or HHFA-BPR 45

    44 Water transportation and related transfer and maintenance facilities

SIC 44 (DS 44 except 447; or HHFA-BPR 44 similar)

    45 Air transportation and related terminal transfer and maintenance facilities including landing areas and incidental space reservation (excluding military)

DS 45 modif. of SIC 45 (HHFA-BPR 43 similar)

    46 Pipeline transportation and related transfer, tank farm, and maintenance facilities

SIC 46 and 5092 (DS 447 and HHFA-BPR 491 similar)

    48 Other communications and related transfer and maintenance facilities including telephone, telegraph, radio, television, and post office

SIC 48 plus postal services (DS 471, 481, 70; and HHFA-BPR 47, 673)

    49 Electric, gas, water, and waste disposal services, including processing and storage, rights-of-way, and related facilities

SIC 49 (DS 47 except 471, 48 except 481; and HHFA-BPR 48 similar)

5. *Distribution Activities* (including customer or employee parking, loading, service, and other related areas)

HHFA-BPR 5 (Trade)

    50 Wholesale trade—*with storage on premises* (includes merchant wholesalers, wholesale and industrial distributors, manufacturers' sales branches and wholesale assemblers, and other warehousing functions involving storage on premises, except stockpiling under Activity Systems 1, 2, 3, 4 above)

DS 15, 18, 46, 50 or SIC 50 not included under 51 below (HHFA-BPR 51 with auxiliary code of 0 similar [c])

    51 Wholesale trade—*without storage on premises* (includes wholesale agents and brokers, and manufacturers' sales offices and representatives, freight forwarders)

DS 50 or SIC 50 not included under 50 above (HHFA-BPR 51 with auxiliary code of 1 or 2 similar [c])

52 Retail trade—building materials, hardware, and farm equipment	DS 52 or SIC 52 or HHFA-BPR 52
53 Retail trade—general merchandise	DS 53 or SIC 53 or HHFA-BPR 53
54 Retail trade—food	DS 54 or SIC 54 or HHFA-BPR 54
55 Retail trade—automotive dealers, auto accessories, and gasoline service stations	DS 55 or SIC 55 or HHFA-PBR 55
56 Retail trade—apparel and accessories	DS 56 or SIC 56 or HHFA-BPR 56
57 Retail trade—furniture, home furnishings, and equipment	DS 57 or SIC 57 or HHFA-BPR 57
58 Retail trade—eating and drinking places	DS 58 or SIC 58 or HHFA-BPR 58
59 Retail trade—miscellaneous retail stores	DS 59 or SIC 59 or HHFA-BPR 59
6. *Service Activities* (including customer or employee parking, loading, service, and other related areas)	HHFA-BPR 6 (Services in part)
60 Firm headquarters not located in conjunction with Activity Systems 1, 2, 3, 4, and 5 above	HHFA-BPR auxiliary code 1^c (parts of SIC 1–5 and DS 1–5)
61 Finance, insurance, and real estate	DS 60 (SIC 6; and HHFA-BPR 61 similar)
62 Personal services	DS 61, 767 or SIC 72 or HHFA-BPR 62
63 Miscellaneous business services	DS 62 or SIC 73 or HHFA-BPR 63
64 Automobile repair and services, metered or fee parking lots and garages	DS 63 or SIC 75 (HHFA-BPR 641, 46 in part similar)
65 Miscellaneous repair services	DS 64 or SIC 76 (HHFA-BPR 649 in part similar)
66 Commercial amusement services	DS 65 (SIC 78, 791–793; and HHFA-BPR 721, 7312, 739 in part similar)
67 Hotels, motels, trailer parks	SIC 701, 7031, 7042 (HHFA-BPR 15; DS 06–08 similar)
68 Medical and health services except hospitals, sanatoria, convalescent and rest homes	SIC 801–804, 807, or DS 67 except 675 (HHFA-BPR 651 except 6513, 6516)
69 Other professional services including professional associations, labor unions, etc.	SIC 81, 861–863, 89 (DS 675, 68, 781–783; and HHFA-BPR 652, 659, 683, 699 in part similar)
7. *General Welfare, Community Service, and Non-commercial Leisure-Time Activities* (including parking, service, and other related areas)	HHFA-BPR 6, 7 (Services; cultural, entertainment, and recreation in part)
70 Education, including parochial schools	DS 74, 75 (SIC 821, 822, 824, 829, part of 866; and HHFA-BPR 681, 682)
71 Libraries, museums, art galleries, historical sites, arboreta, botanical gardens, etc.	SIC 84, 823 (DS 761–763; and HHFA-BPR 71 similar)

72 Recreation not elsewhere classified, including playgrounds, parks, and related open space; golf courses, country clubs, riding academies, winter sports areas; auditoriums, stadiums, race tracks, fairgrounds; outdoor water recreation; hunting and fishing preserves, and summer camps

DS 8 (HHFA-BPR 722, 723, 729, 7311, 74, 75, 76; and SIC 7032, 794, parts of 91–93 similar)

73 Churches and other religious services

SIC 866 not included under 70 and 74 and 6551 (DS 764, 765; and HHFA-BPR 691 similar)

74 Hospitals, sanatoria, convalescent and rest homes

DS 77 or SIC 806, 809, part of 866; or HHFA-BPR 6513, 6516

75 Protective services—military and civilian, including police, fire, correctional, institutions, etc.

HHFA-BPR 672, 674, 675 (parts of SIC 91–94; and DS 71, parts of 73 similar)

76 Governmental services not elsewhere classified—city, county, state, federal and other domestic or foreign headquarters or offices

HHFA-BPR 671 (parts of SIC 91–94 not included under 48, 70–72, 74, 75; parts of DS 72, 73 similar)

77 Service and welfare organizations and their headquarters—Council of Social Agencies, Red Cross, Salvation Army, Boy Scouts, etc.

HHFA-BPR 692 (SIC 867 and DS 786 similar)

78 Nonprofit membership groups such as patriotic, veterans, fraternal, civic, political organizations

SIC 864, 865, or DS 784, 785, or HHFA-BPR 699

79 Other institutionalized services not elsewhere classified

(parts of HHFA-BPR 699 similar)

8. *Residential Activities*—nontransient space for housing

HHFA-BPR 1 (DS 01–05, SIC 702, 704, 88 similar)

9. *No Activity*—unused space (improved and unimproved land, water areas, etc.)

DS 9; HHFA-BPR 9 (Undeveloped land, water area)

---

[a] The italicized headings correspond to the general activity systems identified in Chapter 6; items listed in Roman type correspond to commonly used land use categories, grouped here the way they are for coding purposes. Obviously certain compromises are made in order for the system to conform to SIC categories important to planning analyses for the access they insure the analyst to standard sources of census statistics. This general coding system can be extended into three- and four-digit categories by reference to other systems indicated in the right-hand column.

[b] For Detroit System, see Land Classification Advisory Committee of the Detroit Metropolitan Area, *Land Use Classification Manual*, Chicago: Public Administration Service, 1962. For SIC codes, see Bureau of the Budget, *Standard Industrial Classification Manual*, Washington: U.S. Government Printing Office, 1957 and subsequent supplements. For HHFA-BPR System, see Urban Renewal Administration and U.S. Bureau of Public Roads, *Standard Land Use Coding Manual—a Standard System for Identifying and Coding Land Use Activities*, Washington: U.S. Government Printing Office, June, 1964.

[c] The HHFA-BPR System has introduced a one-digit "auxiliary" series of categories to show a link between certain auxiliary functions and their parent functions: 0—not an auxiliary; 1—central or administrative offices; 2—sales office; 3—research and development laboratory; 4—warehousing and storage; 5—automobile parking; 6—steam and power plant; 7—vehicle garage (maintenance and storage of vehicles); 8-9—(open codes).

When aerial photographs are used, photo interpretation techniques can be used to advantage prior to the field survey. Either sectional base maps or blown-up photographs can be used as field sheets. As a variation on these procedures, some surveys have effectively reduced time spent in the field by the use of dictaphone equipment in survey automobiles. Here some form of property- and block-numbering scheme inscribed on field reference maps is required in dictating field observations on land use. Where time and resources do not permit the detailed type of study as involved in surveys using Base C–type maps for field sheets, or where only the generalized type of land use information by land area is required, a copy of the general-purpose wall map cut up into convenient-size sheets is sometimes used for field survey purposes.

The machine-adapted type of inspection survey is best suited for the large metropolitan areas, certainly in areas of a quarter of a million population and upwards and frequently in urban areas down to a 100,000 size, where property assessment and land use studies are integrated into one record system. This type of survey was first used on a large-scale basis when the modern transportation studies were introduced in the 'fifties. As planning agencies have experimented with this type of survey, innovations have been introduced which now permit the use of data from these surveys in both land development and transportation analyses of the most advanced forms. While field reference maps are still required for orientation, coding, and space use measurements, the basic forms used for field notations are generally designed to double as data collection *and* coding sheets. These sheets are used in key-punching operations in transferring recorded field observations to punch cards. The cards can be used in simple sorting equipment, or when the data are transferred to magnetic tape by card-to-tape converter more advanced equipment may be used for computations or for advanced forms of machine operations where tests are made of land development and transportation proposals.

Either type of inspection survey can be expanded to include other investigations for planning purposes. The field survey of vacant land characteristics is often included in the land use survey. Details of this type of survey are taken up in the next section of this chapter. For the preliminary land use plan, a general visual appraisal of the condition of structures is frequently combined with the land use survey. Appraisal techniques are covered in a later section of this chapter. Other data sometimes assembled at the time of the land use survey include facts relating to setbacks and sideyards and notations on incidental uses in residential areas for use in zoning analyses. Also sometimes combined with the land use survey are investigations relating to street conditions. Whether streets are open or not must be checked for purposes of completing the planning base map. With reference to paved

Table 23. A Land Use Classification Recombining Functional Classes of Uses into Spatially Related Clusters of Uses for Land Use Planning Analyses

---

Industrial and Related Uses [a]

Intensive class [b]	At this extreme are establishments manufacturing jewelry, optical instruments, etc.
Intermediate class [b]	
Extensive class [b]	At this extreme are oil refineries, ship-building yards, railroad marshaling yards, quarries, etc.

Wholesale and Related Uses [a]

Close-in class [b]	At this extreme are merchant wholesalers serving retailers, etc.
Outlying class [b]	At this extreme are wholesale assemblers, truck terminals and distribution centers, warehousing, etc.

Region-Serving Retail and Related Uses [a]

Central business district	Retail group, office group (including wholesale agents and brokers), amusements, civic center, transportation passenger terminals, etc.
CBD satellite centers	Auto sales and service centers, farm machinery centers, farmers' markets, outlying office centers, appliance sales centers, etc.
Regional shopping centers	(Planned)
Highway service centers	Motels and related services, drive-in roadside services such as restaurants, outdoor theaters, carnivals, golf-driving ranges, etc.

Region-Serving Recreation, Education, and Cultural Uses

Close-in class [b]	Spectator sports, museums, auditoriums, lodges, large churches, etc.
Intermediate class [b]	Medical centers, colleges, large institutions, etc.
Outlying class [b]	Golf courses, fairgrounds, park reservations, etc.

Residential Communities

Residential uses	Various residential density classes
Local business uses	Neighborhood and community shopping centers, corner groceries, and other retail outlets serving day-to-day household needs [a]
Schools	Elementary, junior, and senior high schools [c]
Recreation areas	Playgrounds, community recreation centers, local parks, etc.
Institutional uses	Neighborhood-serving churches, etc.

Streets, Railroad Tracks, and Transit Lines [d]

Vacant and Nonurban Uses

---

[a] Floor area as well as land area data are summarized for these categories. Land space taken up in railroad spur lines, parking areas, loading space, outdoor storage areas, or similar functions associated with these uses are summarized as separate subtotals of land area.

[b] Activities falling within each of these classes are defined locally.

[c] In cities where there is but one consolidated high school, such a use would be classed as a region-serving recreation, education, and cultural use.

[d] Consisting mainly of rights-of-way, this residual category is used to make acreage tabulations sum up to an urban area total.

streets, notations are sometimes made as to whether or not the street has curb and gutter, what the pavement width is, and for unpaved streets, what the used or effective graded width is. Along with data on right-of-way widths, this kind of information is used as reference material for subdivision review and for capacity analyses in thoroughfare planning studies.

The inspection-interview type of survey is generally carried out on a cooperative basis with other public agencies. The old WPA real property survey technique was the forerunner of this type of survey. Contemporary versions of this kind of survey may be jointly sponsored by planning, housing, and redevelopment agencies, and they vary in detail and content according to the interests of the sponsoring agencies. In some cities, a combination tax record and space use form has been used in inspection-interview surveys, and in others, a combination local population or school census and land use survey form has been used. Whatever the form, some basic reference map is needed in order to key questionnaire and inspection forms to a systematic property- and block-numbering scheme. Both key maps and data sheets or cards are used in the field.

Advance Preparations

The key importance of determining just how the results of the survey are to be used in advance of the actual field survey, as mentioned earlier in the chapter, cannot be overemphasized. A careful examination of existing sources of data should be made as part of the step in planning the content of the survey so as to avoid unnecessary duplication of effort, and there must be a very specific predetermined use for every item finally included in the survey. Time spent in collecting data of the "we may need" variety rarely proves justified. Unless the specific use is known in advance, the exact kind of observation to be made in the field may be ill-defined, and even though the hunch was correct, the form is likely to be incorrect.

Once the type and scope of the survey has been determined, all field procedures can be set down in memorandum form or in a "Manual of Standard Field Procedures." This aspect of advance planning is most important in large urban areas where several field workers are involved, and particularly important in inspection-interview surveys. Standard practices in surveys of this kind call for one or more pretests of field schedules in order to clear up any problems of ambiguity and to eliminate or modify items which present practical difficulties of one kind or another in the field. Test surveys are also helpful in improving on standard definitions and general field instructions. After the manual is issued in final form, a formal briefing session for all field workers is held, short test surveys are made where results are discussed, and each worker is "checked out" in all aspects of his assignment. Such briefing sessions may also be held in the course of the survey where unforeseen problems develop. The purpose of these preparations and precautions is one of minimizing error due to interpretation of instructions and to secure maximum possible uniformity on all items of subjective observation or judgment.

Conducting the Land Use Survey

Field survey procedures will differ according to whether data storage is to be in punch card or map form. Procedures for each will be considered briefly below.

Surveys predicated on the use of punch card methods of storing data presuppose that most information obtained in the field will be processed by machine. The punch card is presently preferred as a basic storage medium for machine work because of the ease with which updating of data can be done where continuous land use inventory systems are contemplated. However, with film optical sensing devices for input to computers (FOSDIC) of the kind pioneered by the Bureau of the Census coming into use, it may be that magnetic tape or other storage media will supplant the punch card. It is beyond the scope of this volume to go into these developments, and those who wish to go more deeply into data storage and retrieval systems and the machine-programming aspects applicable to the land use study will want to consult some of the machine manuals and other sources developing from this field of specialization.

To indicate the general nature of the land use survey which is designed to lead into machine methods of analysis, we shall run through some of the more elemental aspects of the survey.[14] For this purpose, punch cards are assumed as the storage medium, and we will direct our attention primarily to the relatively simple type of inspection survey, uncomplicated by inclusion of data forms which are involved where land use surveys are combined with tax assessment, structural quality, or other surveys.

This type of land use survey is usually organized into two parts—a space use survey for central areas to be covered on foot, and a land use survey for fringe areas to be covered by automobile. The discussion here applies mainly to the first more complex part of the survey. This survey is based on a field listing procedure in which investigators equipped with reference maps and especially designed forms for use in clipboards traverse the survey area and list space uses in a predetermined systematic manner in much the same way that the census taker makes his head count. The listing

---

[14] The approach covered in the next few pages illustrates the general principles of field listing. For other techniques of field listing, see Urban Renewal Administration and U.S. Bureau of Public Roads, *Standard Land Use Coding Manual.*

Investigator _____ **Sheet No.** _____

Field Check	Office Check	OK to Punch
date	date	date	initials

Card No. ☐ Tax Map No. ☐☐ Pl. Dist. No. ☐☐ Cen. Tract No. ☐☐☐ Block No. ☐ Grid Coordinates ☐☐☐ x ☐☐ y

For this portion entries made in field in course of survey →

← Entries made in office after field survey →

Line Number	Parcel No. in Block	Street Face Code	Parcel — No. Parking Spaces This Parcel: Inside Parking	Outside Parking	Parking on Facing Sts.	Struct. No. on This Parcel	Structure — Floor Area This Structure in 100 ft.² (x-resid.)ᵃ: All Floors	Grnd. Floor	Floor No. This Use (x-resid.)ᵃ	Floor — Unit No. This Floor: Estabs. (x-resid.)ᵃ	DU'S (x-nonres.)ᵃ	Type of Activity This Space (Describe)	Space Use — Amt. Fl. Area This Space Use on This Fl. in 100 ft.² (x-resid.)ᵃ	Outdoor Sp. Use This Parcel in 100 ft.² excl. pking, loading (x-resid.)ᵃ	Space Use Code (for 2-digit code)	Resid. Density Code (x-nonres.)ᵃ	Grnd. Area in 1,000 ft.²: Parcel Total	Off-Street Parking	Off-Street Loading	Zoning Code This Parcel

ᵃ The notation "x-resid." or "x-nonres." signifies that an x would be entered in this column (meaning not applicable) where this space is residential or nonresidential, respectively. This distinction is made because, in this form, floor area measurements would be listed only for structures of a nonresidential character. Special rules apply where ground space on a parcel is in use but contains no structures, or where both outdoor and indoor uses are involved.

form is usually designed to serve not only as the field form but also as the coding sheet. This is done in order to make the space use classification decisions in the field and avoid sources of inaccuracy that frequently develop when uncoded notations made in the field are coded in the office after completion of field work. The field form therefore reflects the coding system to be used in the one or more 80-column standard punch cards. Figure 26 illustrates a general-purpose form for field listing in central areas. In this particular form floor area detail is obtained only for nonresidential structures. Where resources permit, the survey could provide for floor area measurements in residential structures as well. Special forms may be designed for special studies, for example for CBD (central business district) studies where more elaborate field listing may be undertaken. For outlying areas where structures are more scattered and where data are listed from an automobile, a more simplified form is used.

In the particular form illustrated in Figure 26 a separate punch card is used for each line. For each new space use listed in the field, a new line number is required. Thus in this type of form the space use is the basic observational unit. The field lister receives his assignment by blocks. At the start of the field survey, he receives a sketch of the block prepared from tax maps or large-scale aerial photographs on which are shown parcel or property lines and known structures. For Line One, he numbers the first parcel visited *1*; the first structure stopped at, *1*; the first floor investigated, *1*; and the first space use recorded, *1*. If the block he is covering is a single-family type of residential area, Line Two will generally involve an entry *2* for both the next parcel and the structure visited, with *x* inserted in the columns set aside for floor data. (In this form floor numbers and floor area data are recorded only for nonresidential structures.) However, if he is covering a business area, Line Two might well contain a *1* entry for the parcel, structure, and floor level since there will frequently be several space uses on the first floor of such a commercial structure. The appropriate column under "unit number this floor" differentiates between listings on the same floor.

Space use is described in a longhand entry (for example, "barber shop" or "heating contractor's supply yard") and then coded according to the space use coding system established at the outset (for example, a system such as that outlined in Table 22). It should be noted that the use of both written and coded entries here permits an office check on the classification

Figure 26. Illustrative General-Purpose Field Listing Sheet for Space Use Survey Conducted in Developed Areas of a City for Studies Where Data Are to be Stored on Punch Cards.

decisions being made by the field lister. For nonresidential space uses at the first or ground floor level where there are both outdoor and indoor uses of space, one line can be used to record both. Where a parcel is taken up entirely in a nonresidential outdoor use, x is entered in columns where structure data, floor level, and indoor space use measurements are normally entered. Obviously a variety of special coding rules are necessary in a general-purpose form of this kind.

The investigator proceeds systematically around the block and enumerates parcels, structures, floors, and space uses in a well-defined and orderly sequence. When he checks in at the office with field listing forms completed for a full block, he turns in his sketch map on which he has numbered parcels and structures corresponding with the numbering sequence shown on the field listing form. After the field work is checked, areas are measured by nomograph, residential densities determined, and zoning code entered. When office entries have been checked, the block listing is approved by a supervisor for key punching. Once cards are punched, machine contingency checks are made to screen out errors in coding, transcription, and key punching. After punch cards clear this check, various summary machine runs of the cards are made and summary punch cards prepared for the basic geographic unit to be used in ground space analysis. Thus, in order to make land use analyses by land area, summary cards may be punched by parcel, by block, or by grid cell. Here special rules are required in determining the "principal land use" for the particular geographic unit used in summarizing ground area use. Other summary cards prepared might include nonresidential floor area space use, residential densities, and zoning classification.

Now let us turn to land use surveys where maps are the basic means of storing data. This type of approach also divides the survey area into sections to be covered by automobile and by foot. For the outlying sections covered by automobile, at least two and sometimes three field workers are needed in each car. A driver and one or two plotters equipped with plotting boards, colored pencils, and copies of the land use classification system for occasional reference use are needed. For the more intensively developed sections where field work must be done on foot, field personnel can work individually on a block-by-block assignment basis.

Although there is some uniformity in the basic essentials of field plotting procedures, each planning office generally develops its own system of field notations to fit the circumstances, time schedule, and final product desired. For inspection surveys where detailed building and land use are desired, Figure 27 is suggestive of a system of field notation. The upper drawing indicates what the field worker has to start with, showing the kind of

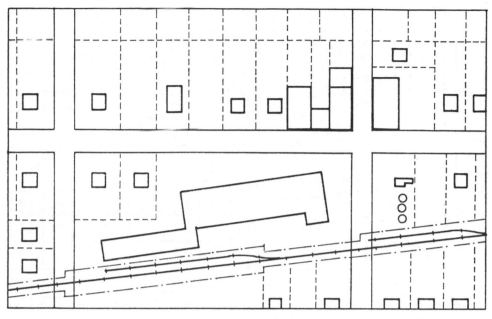

Section of a Typical Base C Print for Field Survey.

Figure 27. Detailed Building and Land Use Mapping in Inspection-Type Surveys.

The Same Print After Entry of Field Notations.

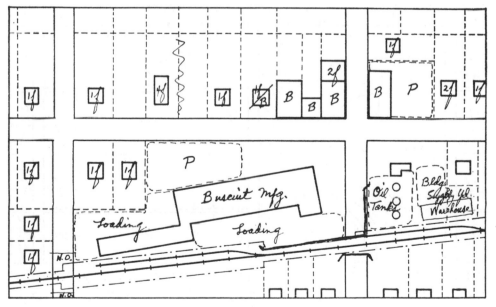

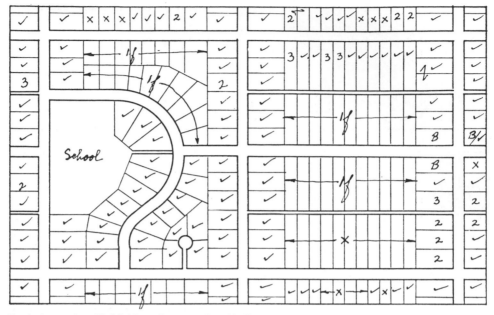

Technique A—Field Notations with DU Count.

Figure 28. Generalized Land Use Mapping by Area in Inspection-Type Surveys.

Technique B—Field Notations by Area Only.

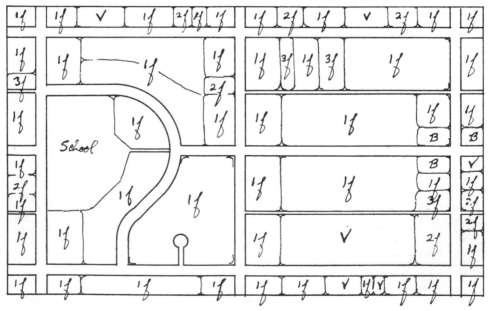

material plotted on field sheets in the office from relevant existing sources of information and maps. The lower plate shows the same drawing after the entry of field notations. It should be noted that to begin with, the Base C print contains street, railroad easement, and property lines and all principal structures. As shown in the lower plate, a notation concerning the number of families in each residential structure is made; business structures are identified along with their accessory parking (indicated by letter *P* in this drawing); and for industrial structures, the nature of industrial activity is identified. Storage yards, loading and parking areas, and other open areas in use are outlined and type of use identified. New structures are added; use lines are related to property lines, and where discrepancies occur, these are noted for later checking against property maps and other records back in the office; and miscellaneous notations as to whether or not a street is open (in the drawing, *N.O.* is used for "not open"), a residence over a business (a diagonal line drawn through the structure with an *LB* for local business noted in the front part of the building and *1f* for one-family dwelling unit inserted over the rear portion of the structure) and other similar special notations are inserted. The memorandum or manual of instructions prepared in advance of the survey will contain standard symbols and other types of notations to be used in the field.

For inspection-type surveys where results are to be presented only in terms of generalized land use by area (on Base B or general-purpose maps), there are two basic techniques. These are identified in Figure 28 as Technique A, where a count of dwelling units is required, and Technique B, where there is no need for assembling information on the number of dwelling units. Where the development of a land use plan is an immediate objective, either the detailed land use mapping procedure (Figure 27) or Technique A of the generalized land use mapping procedure (Figure 28) is required. The field notation symbols used usually vary from city to city, and those shown in Figure 28 can be modified in many ways to suit the purposes of any particular office. In the upper plate, a dwelling structure is indicated either by a check for a one-family house or by a figure appropriate to the number of dwelling units in the structure. Vacant lots are indicated by a symbol *X*, and nonresidential uses are indicated by the appropriate initial or by writing in the name of the use. Although the illustration shows a field base with property lines, Technique A can be used on an ordinary street map, either on a general-purpose map or on a Base A type of map. In the lower plate of Figure 28, only aggregate use areas are noted in the field, using some such identification system as that indicated. Obviously land use mapping can be done much more rapidly using Technique B, and field work is most time-consuming in the detailed land use survey shown in Figure 27.

Presentation of Land Use Data

The results of the land use survey may be summarized both in map form
and statistically. Figure 29 shows a generalized presentation of land use by
land area—the conventional land use map. Figure 30 utilizes the land
development diagram technique of graphic presentation to show land use
by general category of use. Color versions of Figure 29 which are prepared
for general office reference use often carry as many as ten or more categories of uses, and by use of supplementary symbols on structures or lot
areas in the Base C type of presentation, an even greater number of categories can be shown. Figure 25 illustrates a standardized form of presentation where ground space data are transcribed from machine print-outs of

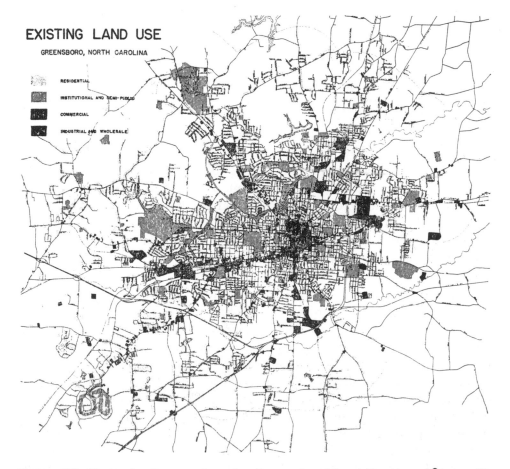

Figure 29. Illustrative Presentation of a Conventional Land Use Map. (*Source:* Department of Planning, Greensboro, North Carolina.)

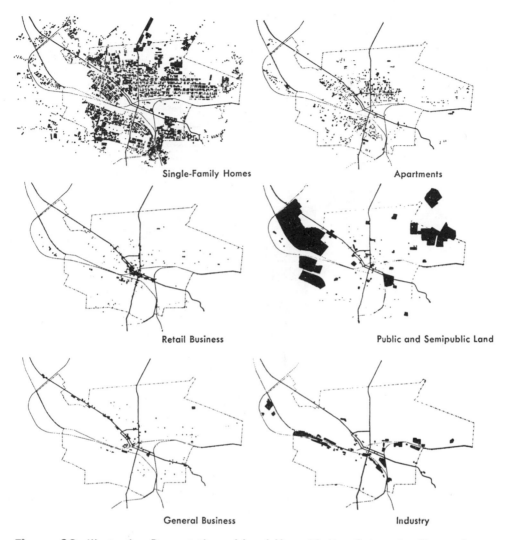

Figure 30. Illustrative Presentation of Land Use with Use Categories Shown Separately. (*Source:* Tennessee State Planning Commission.)

land use data processed on a grid cell basis by a computer. Figure 31 is a machine-produced land use map which eliminates the land transcription work in Figure 24.[15] The latter has to be produced by a draftsman as an overlay over the machine print-out of data (printed to the same scale as

[15] For a detailed discussion of computer methods of graphing, data positioning, and symbolic mapping developed by Edgar M. Horwood, see Urban Renewal Administration, *Using Computer Graphics in Community Renewal,* Washington: U.S. Government Printing Office, January, 1963.

Figure 31. Illustrative Machine Print-out of Land in Development. This print-out shows used land as a per cent of total land per quarter square mile in Erie and Niagara counties, New York. Each dot is equivalent to 5 per cent of a quarter square mile, that is, there can be a maximum of 20 dots to a quarter square mile. The machine program for this print-out was developed by the Upstate New York Transportation Studies, an agency of the New York State Department of Public Works established for the purpose of preparing comprehensive transportation plans for metropolitan areas in upstate New York. These studies are carried out in cooperation with the U.S. Bureau of Public Roads, local city and county governments, and other state departments. (*Source:* Upstate New York Transportation Studies.)

the desired map scale). Map presentations of floor space use are normally prepared only in connection with detailed analyses of particular areas of a city such as the central business district. A separate map is required for each floor level. For office analyses, these maps are prepared as multiple overlays, and for published reports separate plates for each floor level in either black and white or color are commonly used.

The statistical summary of land use is typically prepared in terms of acreage devoted to each category of use employed in the survey, with an added category to summarize the acreage of land that is vacant or in non-urban use. Acreages are frequently summarized in terms of percentages, usually in terms of the developed portion of the city proper, the fringe areas, and the planning area as a whole as covered in the survey. Percentages based on *developed areas* as opposed to *total area* provide a more meaningful form of summary for intercity comparisons or for comparisons between existing land use and proposed land use as set forth in a land development plan. Table 24 is a typical tabular summary of the land use based on the conventional classification systems which have been in use in recent years. It tabulates acreages and the per cent of the total area as well as the developed area found in each particular use category. Table 25 indicates how land use can be summarized using activity systems as a basis for tabulating use categories as suggested in an earlier section of the chapter. Tabular summaries of space use by floor area are usually developed in terms of square feet of floor area at ground level and the total floor area. Such space use summaries are designed to fit the needs of special studies, for example, the study of the central business district.

Acreage and percentage summaries of the order shown in Table 24 are prepared primarily as a quantitative description of land use, and are employed in land use planning analyses and in zoning studies in implementation of the land use plan. As indicated above, occasionally these percentage summaries are used to compare the urban center of interest with other centers of similar functional type and size, but since there are variations from one part of the country to another and even from one urban area to another in the same region, these comparisons have limited utility in technical studies.[16] Large variations in the way the limits of the study area are drawn, be it city limits lines, planning area, or some other defined study area, differences in topography, regional variations in residential living patterns, the differential impact of long-established planning controls which may be in effect, and many other factors introduce variations of varying magnitude. Even averaged percentage summaries for cities of varying sizes have limited use, and certainly should not be considered as valid

[16] For statistics on some 53 central cities, 33 satellite cities, and 11 urban areas, see Harland Bartholomew, *Land Uses in American Cities,* Cambridge: Harvard University Press, 1955.

Table 24. Illustrative Summary of Land Uses, Augusta, Georgia, Planning Area, 1952

Class of Use	Total Planning Area			Inside City Limits			Outside City Limits		
	Acres	Per Cent of Total Land	Per Cent of Developed Land	Acres	Per Cent of Total Land	Per Cent of Developed Land	Acres	Per Cent of Total Land	Per Cent of Developed Land
All residential	4,268.5	9.4	37.6	2,144.5	35.1	38.8	2,024.0	5.5	36.6
One-family	3,823.0	8.4	33.7	1,868.4	30.6	33.9	1,954.6	5.0	33.6
Two-family	251.3	0.6	2.2	183.3	3.0	3.3	67.5	0.2	1.2
Multifamily	194.2	0.4	1.7	92.3	1.5	1.6	101.9	0.3	1.8
Retail business	299.6	0.7	2.6	162.7	2.7	2.9	136.9	0.3	2.3
Wholesale and other [a]	441.8	1.0	3.9	185.0	3.0	3.4	256.8	0.7	4.4
Industrial [b]	814.8	1.8	7.2	257.1	4.2	4.8	557.7	1.4	9.6
Transportation and utilities	189.4	0.4	1.7	138.4	2.3	2.5	51.0	0.1	0.9
Streets and railroad rights-of-way	3,150.3	7.0	27.8	1,477.0	24.2	26.8	1,673.3	4.3	28.7
All public	1,568.6	3.5	13.9	846.3	13.9	15.3	722.3	1.8	12.4
Public	1,299.7	2.9	11.6	577.4	9.5	10.4	722.3	1.8	12.4
Military [c]	268.9	0.6	2.3	268.9	4.4	4.9	—	—	—
Institutional	597.7	1.3	5.3	300.8	4.9	5.5	296.9	0.8	5.1
Water areas	367.0	0.8	—	129.8	2.1	—	237.2	0.6	—
Vacant and nonurban	33,473.6	74.1	—	465.4	7.6	—	33,008.2	84.5	—
Total	45,171.3	100.0	100.0	6,107.0	100.0	100.0	39,064.3	100.0	100.0

[a] "Other" refers to "general business," a classification used in the original study to denote uses falling between the retail and the industrial categories (includes, for example, building, plumbing, and heating suppliers, trucking terminals, amusement parks, race tracks, and other large space-using businesses).
[b] Includes extraction activities, for example, clay extraction pits.
[c] Includes an arsenal and a military reservation (but not Camp Gordon).

standards or yardsticks for land use planning, for average observed conditions in a selected number of cities will rarely measure up to positive land planning standards fitted to the needs of one particular urban center.

Practice in the measurement of land use areas differs with the method of data storage. For surveys involving punch card data storage, where each space use, floor, or parcel is measured separately, nomograph templates may be used in place of a planimeter. However, these techniques are now giving way to machine methods in which the operator, using a "joy stick," guides a stylus over a large-scale aerial photograph, and in the process automatically computes areas and punches cards. For surveys where maps are to be used as the basis for storage of land use data, the more painstaking method of planimetering areas is commonly used. In small urban areas

Table 25. Illustrative Summary of Land Use in Selected Activities and Subcategories for Metropolitan Region, 19xx

Activity and Subcategory	Region as a Whole Acres	Per Cent of Developed Land	Central City Acres	Per Cent of Developed Land	Suburban City A Acres	Per Cent of Developed Land	Etc.	Sector A Acres	Per Cent of Developed Land	Sector B Acres	Per Cent of Developed Land	Etc.
					Suburban Areas			Rest of Region				
Extraction	xxxxx	xx	xxxxx	xx	xxxxx	xx		xxxxx	xx	xxxxx	xx	
Processing												
Industry Group A	xxxxx	xx	xxxxx	xx	xxxxx	xx		xxxxx	xx	xxxxx	xx	
Industry Group B	xxxxx	xx	xxxxx	xx	xxxxx	xx		xxxxx	xx	xxxxx	xx	
Etc.	xxxxx	xx	xxxxx	xx	xxxxx	xx		xxxxx	xx	xxxxx	xx	
Communications												
Railroads	xxxxx	xx	xxxxx	xx	xxxxx	xx		xxxxx	xx	xxxxx	xx	
Highways & streets	xxxxx	xx	xxxxx	xx	xxxxx	xx		xxxxx	xx	xxxxx	xx	
Electric, gas, sanit.	xxxxx	xx	xxxxx	xx	xxxxx	xx		xxxxx	xx	xxxxx	xx	
Etc.	xxxxx	xx	xxxxx	xx	xxxxx	xx		xxxxx	xx	xxxxx	xx	
Distribution												
Wholesale	xxxxx	xx	xxxxx	xx	xxxxx	xx		xxxxx	xx	xxxxx	xx	
Retail	xxxxx	xx	xxxxx	xx	xxxxx	xx		xxxxx	xx	xxxxx	xx	
Services												
Firm headquarters	xxxxx	xx	xxxxx	xx	xxxxx	xx		xxxxx	xx	xxxxx	xx	
Finance, ins., real estate	xxxxx	xx	xxxxx	xx	xxxxx	xx		xxxxx	xx	xxxxx	xx	
Amusements, hotels, etc.	xxxxx	xx	xxxxx	xx	xxxxx	xx		xxxxx	xx	xxxxx	xx	
Personal	xxxxx	xx	xxxxx	xx	xxxxx	xx		xxxxx	xx	xxxxx	xx	
Etc.	xxxxx	xx	xxxxx	xx	xxxxx	xx		xxxxx	xx	xxxxx	xx	
General welfare												
Education	xxxxx	xx	xxxxx	xx	xxxxx	xx		xxxxx	xx	xxxxx	xx	
Cultural facilities	xxxxx	xx	xxxxx	xx	xxxxx	xx		xxxxx	xx	xxxxx	xx	
Recreation	xxxxx	xx	xxxxx	xx	xxxxx	xx		xxxxx	xx	xxxxx	xx	
Protective & misc. governmental services	xxxxx	xx	xxxxx	xx	xxxxx	xx		xxxxx	xx	xxxxx	xx	
Welfare organizations	xxxxx	xx	xxxxx	xx	xxxxx	xx		xxxxx	xx	xxxxx	xx	
Etc.	xxxxx	xx	xxxxx	xx	xxxxx	xx		xxxxx	xx	xxxxx	xx	
Residential												
Density Group A	xxxxx	xx	xxxxx	xx	xxxxx	xx		xxxxx	xx	xxxxx	xx	
Density Group B	xxxxx	xx	xxxxx	xx	xxxxx	xx		xxxxx	xx	xxxxx	xx	
Etc.	xxxxx	xx	xxxxx	xx	xxxxx	xx		xxxxx	xx	xxxxx	xx	
No activity (unused space)	xxxxx	–	xxxxx	–	xxxxx	–		xxxxx	–	xxxxx	–	
Total	xxxxxxx	100	xxxxxxx	100	xxxxxxx	100		xxxxxxx	100	xxxxxxx	100	

under 100,000, the generalized presentation prepared on a wall map can be used to measure land areas in various uses, but Base C land use maps will yield greater accuracy and are generally the most satisfactory source for most planning studies. However, where a planning program is just getting under way and where plans are at a preliminary broad-stroke stage of development, statistical summaries drawn from a generalized land use presentation can serve a legitimate and useful interim purpose. In the more mature stages of the planning program, when preliminary planning studies are progressively refined and carried to greater detail, the more accurate measurements of land use will be required.

In the course of measuring land use acreages from maps, it is desirable to tally measurements by the system of planning areas or districts developed for land use planning analyses (see Chapter 9). Thus planning district summaries are developed as subtotals to the summary for the urban area as a whole. The actual measurement procedures employ a simple mechanical technique. Two or more transparent overlays are used with each sheet of the land use presentation. One has all planning district and corporate limits lines drawn on it and is used as a master check sheet. Other transparencies are used to "collect" land uses in terms of land area, that is, for each use category, lots and tracts are traced off and fitted together into a single puzzle-like pattern. As each lot or tract is traced, it is checked off on the master check sheet. When all areas have been taken off for each use, each planning district, and each incorporated area, the areas of the resulting saw-toothed polygons are measured with a planimeter. Averages of three measurements thus made are entered in the appropriate places in a tally work table. When all planimetering is completed and all use categories, including streets and vacant land or areas in nonurban use as separate categories, and all planning districts and separate incorporated areas are totaled, the result is checked with the area obtained by planimetering the urban area as a whole.

Keeping Land Use Data Up to Date

The work of assembling and summarizing land use data as described above represents a considerable expenditure of time and funds. It would therefore appear that every effort would be made to maintain this basic tool in up-to-date form so as to avoid a repetition of this operation in the immediate future. Yet because no systematic procedure has been developed for keeping account of changes, many planning agencies must repeat this whole operation more often than necessary.

Steps for keeping land use "data files" up to date are relatively simple if the necessary arrangements are made. Within the jurisdiction of the building codes and/or zoning ordinances in effect, updating can be worked out in conjunction with building inspection or the issuance of occupancy permits. For punch card systems of data storage, as inspections are completed or occupancy permits issued, a coding form is filled out for a new or correction card for the appropriate deck of cards. For map systems of data storage, the correction becomes a simple extension of procedures previously described for updating base maps. As inspections are made or occupancy permits issued, changed uses can be noted at the time the structure is plotted in the atlas of "correction prints," a new set of which is supplied annually to the building inspector's office. Of course, in cities not requiring occupancy permits or where this permit requirement is not enforced, some changes in use will go undetected. For example, this would be the case when changes occur from one permitted use category to another within a particular zoning district where no alterations in the structure are made. However, this type of change will normally not affect land use summaries because of the broad categories employed.

One difficulty arises where undetected violations occur, particularly in residential areas where alterations are made inside a structure to accommodate additional families—alterations which are not easily detected. Another problem relates to peripheral areas beyond the jurisdiction of building codes and zoning ordinances. As in the case of keeping base maps up to date, these outlying areas must usually be covered by special land use surveys at periodic intervals, usually once a year in portions of the urban area where there is indication of considerable building activity.

No matter what precautions are taken to keep a survey up to date, it is doubtful that a land use survey, however carefully carried out, can be depended upon for more than ten years. Not only do changes occur which go undetected by procedures described above, but in this span of time the emergence of new analytical procedures can be expected to modify data requirements. For example, in recent time we have seen the beginnings of changes in the classification as to "light" and "heavy" industry, which was developed according to the nuisance characteristics of the use, to a new classification system based on locational and space requirements of each type of industrial use. With the development of performance standards for industrial uses, more flexibility is permitted in the grouping of manufacturing activities and a much more positive approach is replacing the old negative emphasis in the classification of these uses. Moreover, as automation proceeds, there will be a continuing need for periodic resurveys. Automation is also having an impact on office-type activities. In addition, we may soon see a system of classes developing in business areas based on daytime population densities, where standards of maximum permitted densities or "congestion limits" become the basis for land use groupings. These and other developments in the technical requirements of this relatively new and changing field undoubtedly will make it necessary to make resurveys from time to time. Moreover, since long-range plans will be requiring major review and some revision from time to time, the timing of these resurveys will tend to fall into schedule with these periods of reassessment and restudy.

Vacant Land Study

Were only a simple picture of the use and nonuse of land desired, the vacant land category in the land use survey would provide an adequate description and summary of vacant land. But since we are concerned with a basic description of the capabilities of vacant land for urban use and development, we must look at vacant and open land as something more than a residual category in the land use survey, something that is amenable to classification in some detail and the subject of special attention in land use planning.

The purpose of classifying vacant land is to determine its suitability for various forms of urban development: for industrial, residential, recreational, and other classes of land use. The vacant land study identifies the potentialities of vacant and open land for development, taking into account the physiographic features and the presence or absence of such man-made improvements to the land as streets and drainage facilities, accessibility to railroad and other transportation facilities, and the existence on or near the site of public water mains, a sewerage system, and other utilities. Whereas the vacant land study identifies the potentialities of open land for various uses, land use planning studies as described in Part III finally determine the proposed future use of vacant areas.

As noted in the preceding section of the chapter, the total amount of vacant and open land is customarily obtained in the conventional land use survey. To obtain a more detailed classification of vacant land requires either an extension of the land use survey or a separate study. Either alternative has its problems. If vacant land is classified as part of the land use survey, such an approach cannot be entirely effective in taking into account the full range of land requirements necessary in land use planning studies, since the result of the land use survey itself is a necessary prerequisite to the formulation of these requirements. On the other hand, duplicating surveys of the urban area involved in a separate land use and a separate vacant land survey rarely can be justified.

To circumvent this dilemma, a simplified system of vacant land classification can be developed and integrated into the land use survey. This system appraises vacant land as to its general suitability for development. In the course of the vacant land analysis, it is subdivided into additional categories, and still later in the execution of land use planning analyses, it is generally extended and appropriate subdivisions made to apply to each particular use category.

Vacant Land Classification

The simplified vacant land classification system is based on two kinds of determinations: first, use capabilities from the standpoint of topography and drainage characteristics, and second, use capabilities from the standpoint of improvements available to the parcel or tract. As suggested above, later in the actual land use planning process other factors are taken into account, such as the availability of the property for development, the land value structure, cost-revenue considerations, and so on.

Topographic Characteristics

Terrain and drainage characteristics are usually determined partly from sources of information in the planning office and partly from field observations. Office sources consist of topographic maps and aerial photographs, and where these are available, they provide a suitable basis for estimating the terrain characteristics of the large open areas and rural fringe sections of the planning area. The field survey is generally confined to the classification of the scattered vacant lots and parcels interspersed in the built-up portions of the urban area. Although field surveys can be employed in the classification of all parts of the planning area (and this will be necessary where no topographic maps are available), usually they are used only to get at the characteristics of the relatively small parcels where topographic maps cannot be expected to give an entirely satisfactory or accurate assessment of prevailing conditions.

The typing of vacant land according to topographic characteristics proceeds from an initial tentative classification to successively more refined categories. In its initial and simplest version, this system of classifying vacant land contains two basic categories: prime and marginal land. Lots, tracts, or areas judged suitable for building use are classed as *prime* for urban development. Lots, tracts, or areas judged unsuitable for building without extensive preparation or modification of the terrain are defined as *marginal* land. Generally marginal land is too low (that is, it is marshy or subject to flooding), or it is derelict land (for example, abandoned quarries) or it is too steep to be suitable for building. Prime land is all other land. "Suitability for building" is generally a matter for local determination, since standards as to slopes that are considered economical to put into use will vary in different communities and in different parts of the country. For example, in San Francisco greater slopes are acceptable for building purposes than in midwestern cities. Here the demand for land is sufficiently great and the supply sufficiently short so that greater slopes are considered economic to develop. In the Piedmont area of the South, where generally there is an ample supply of vacant or open land on level or rolling terrain located where reasonable time-distance standards are attainable once development occurs, slopes up to 15 per cent are considered economical to develop.

The mechanics of making this initial and preliminary evaluation of the topographic capabilities of vacant land are relatively simple. In the course of the land use survey, the scattered lots and small parcels within the built-up portion of the planning area are tentatively classified as to whether they are prime or marginal according to predetermined standards appropriate to the urban area under study. Where punch card data systems are used, the land use classification system employed will need to have subdivisions under the "no activity" or "unused space" category (for example, under Category 9 of Table 22) to provide for the desired subcategories in classifying the drainage and topographic characteristics of vacant land. For a mapping type of land use survey, a similar advance determination will be required so that classifications of vacant land can be made on a first tentative basis. The actual notation used in plotting the land classification on field sheets will vary with the preferences of the city planner. The simplest procedure is to enter the tentative class designator on the outlined area so classified. To avoid confusion with other symbols used in the land use survey, this class designator can be circled. Thus when vacant land classification is undertaken in conjunction with the land use survey, Figure 27 and Technique A of Figure 28 would carry a circled vacant land designator in place of the X.

At the conclusion of the field survey and after ground space use has been set down on the land use map, this preliminary classification of vacant land can be extended to the large underdeveloped tracts and open land in fringe areas of the city. This first presentation of land classification is made on an overlay tracing over the land use map. First, all vacant lots and parcels classified in the field are outlined and their appropriate classification noted from the field sheets, and then, by reference to topographic maps, the larger vacant tracts and the open land are classified. Of course, if topographic maps are not available, classification of these areas must be made in the field. Some special investigations may be necessary to establish the outlines of areas subject to periodic flooding as discussed in the next section below. These facts can sometimes be obtained from local, state, or federal sources where some agency maintains official stream gauge stations. Where no such records are available, old newspaper files may carry some account useful in establishing high-water marks. It may even be necessary to spot check the residents or management of businesses in certain areas to obtain firsthand accounts as to water levels during high-water periods. The end product of this initial land classification operation is a graphic representation of "buildable" and "unbuildable" areas, that is, prime and marginal land.

For land use planning purposes, further refinement in the classification of topographic characteristics is needed. In the modern-day era of spread-out, single-story industrial plants, it is useful to introduce subclasses under the prime land category in order to identify areas with special terrain potentialities for industrial, wholesale, and related uses. Slope standards will vary to some extent from one locale to another, but within a relatively small range. For example, in the Piedmont area of the South, prime in-dustrial land is usually limited to areas where the slope does not exceed 5 per cent. In making refinements to the vacant land classification system to recognize these special topographic considerations, it is useful to introduce a tract-size criterion in conjunction with the slope differentiations that are made. Thus if the "prime" class of vacant land is to contain a special slope category for industrial and related uses, rather than opening this subcate-gory to every small parcel in the entire urban area, it is desirable to refine this subclass further by setting some lower limit to the size of vacant areas to be included. As brought out in Chapter 10, a tract of five acres or larger is a criterion sometimes used for cities, with one acre or larger being more appropriate for towns.

Once standards as to slope and tract size have been established, a refined classification system can be developed. In place of the simple two-class system, three classes can be substituted, let us say *Class 1 Prime, Class 2 Prime,* and *Marginal.* Thus in the Piedmont cities of the South, "Class 1 Prime" might be defined as all vacant areas five acres or more which have slopes of 5 per cent or less, and "Class 2 Prime" might be defined as all other land from 0 to 15 per cent slope. On the basis of the refined classification, a second overlay is developed to show the distribution of vacant land ac-cording to the new subclasses.

Improvement Characteristics

The final refinement of the classification system introduces further sub-classes according to improvement characteristics. Thus Class 1 Prime land is subdivided into categories to denote whether railroad and major thoroughfare systems are in close proximity to the area and whether all the necessary utilities are available at the edge of the area. Varying degrees of combination are possible as suggested in the following list:

Subclass Designator	Improvements
1A	All improvements available
1B	All improvements but water
1C	All improvements but water and sewer
1D	All improvements but water, sewer, and power
1E	Only railroad and highway
1F	Highway only
1R	Raw land

Obviously the list could be extended to include other combinations, for example, railroad and water only, water and sewer only, and so on.

In the same way that the Class 1 type of vacant land can be subclassified, Class 2 Prime can be detailed into subcategories of varying combination:

Subclass Designator	Improvements
2a	Platted and all improvements installed
2b	Platted, all improvements except sewer
2c	Platted, all improvements except sewer and water
2d	Platted but no improvements
2r	Raw land

Here, too, combinations other than those listed are possible.

Obviously, a classification system which accommodates every possible combination can become unwieldy. To simplify the system and reduce the number of categories, combinations can be developed and graded to fit local needs. The footnotes of Table 26 present a simplified set of subcategories fitted to the particular needs of one small city, and generally typify the nature of the simplified vacant land classification system which evolves in the course of following the steps described above. A third and final overlay is prepared to show how vacant land is classified under this refined version of the classification system.

The above-described vacant land analyses aim to classify the urban use capabilities of both vacant parcels scattered through the urbanized area and the open farm land and wooded areas beyond which fall within the planning area. Open land can also be classified for its agricultural, forestry, or sometimes its mining use capabilities. In some parts of the country where land has special capabilities for these nonurban uses, it is important to carry out land capability analyses which get at these considerations in land use planning. For these studies, soil surveys and geologic maps are basic sources of reference, and soils specialists, foresters, and geologists need to be consulted in setting up appropriate use capability categories. Studies of these kinds have applications in classifying open land for urban as well as nonurban use capabilities. For example, soil surveys are used in identifying areas where load-bearing characteristics of the soil would not support industrial structures or where septic tank systems of waste disposal are impractical. Another use is in the analysis of the potentialities of an area to support tree farms at a commercially profitable level of production, a use which has potentialities in some parts of the country in a comprehensive program for the conservation of open spaces in urbanizing areas.

Presentation of Vacant Land Data

Somewhat like the land use presentation, vacant land data are generally presented in map form and in a tabular summary. The map is called a

Table 26. Illustrative Summary and Classification of Vacant Land, Aiken, South Carolina, Planning Area, 1956

Planning District	Class 1 Prime a (acres)				Class 2 Prime b (acres)				Marginal c (acres)	Total (acres)	Per Cent of Total
	A	B	C	Total	A	B	C	Total			
1	0.0	13.2	70.7	83.9	42.2	526.5	652.9	1,221.6	73.2	1,378.7	13.8
2	43.8	93.0	165.4	302.2	43.4	256.2	2,165.2	2,464.8	157.6	2,924.6	29.3
3	145.0	132.0	275.8	552.8	84.9	273.8	1,291.3	1,650.0	8.7	2,211.5	22.2
4A	3.1	7.2	90.5	100.8	63.2	66.2	253.4	382.8	0.0	483.6	4.9
4B	0.0	0.0	0.0	0.0	34.5	56.7	22.1	113.3	0.0	113.3	1.1
4C	0.0	294.9	49.5	344.4	0.0	484.5	2,025.9	2,510.4	0.0	2,854.8	28.6
CBD	0.0	0.0	0.0	0.0	8.5	1.0	0.0	9.5	0.0	9.5	0.1
Planning area total	191.9	540.3	651.9	1,384.1	276.7	1,664.9	6,410.8	8,352.4	239.5	9,976.0	100.0
Per Cent total	1.9	5.4	6.5	13.8	2.8	16.7	64.3	83.8	2.4	—	100.0

a *Class 1 Prime* is here defined as vacant land suitable for industrial or wholesale use, situated within 500 feet of a railroad or major thoroughfare, and in parcels not less than one acre, with a slope of 5 per cent or under and well drained. *Subcategory A:* sewer and water line within 500 feet; *Subcategory B:* water line within 500 feet; *Subcategory C:* no sewer or water line within 500 feet.

b *Class 2 Prime* is here defined as vacant land suitable for residential or other nonindustrial or nonwholesale uses, with a slope of 15 per cent or less and well drained. *Subcategory A:* sewer and water line within 200 feet; *Subcategory B:* water line within 200 feet; *Subcategory C:* no sewer or water line within 200 feet.

c *Marginal* is here defined as vacant land with slopes in excess of 15 per cent, areas subject to flooding or marshy, and derelict land unsuitable or uneconomic to develop.

land capabilities map, and the patterns appearing on this map look somewhat like a photographic negative of the configuration of patterns appearing
on the land use map. In effect, all areas in urban use are "punched out,"
and the resulting lacework pattern is the portion of the planning area of
central interest in this presentation. A suitable color or black and white
legend is developed to correspond to the various vacant land categories
and subcategories and a vacant land map is prepared to show the distribution patterns of land with varying developmental capabilities.

The resulting presentation, while providing a reasonably complete picture of vacant areas, does not show, of course, areas which are *available*
for urban use. Whether the property owners are willing to release their
property for urban development, whether there is a clear title to the land,
and whether property held in trust or restricted as to its future use by
covenants running with the property, offer complications as to its use
potentialities—these factors must be determined by supplementary investigations. While it would be possible to refine a "gross" vacant land
presentation to a "net" presentation taking these factors into account, in
practice these determinations are best left to the land use planning stage
of analysis. By the time such analyses are completed and the vacant
areas actually needed for urban expansion during the adopted planning
period ahead are determined, there may be no immediate need to look
into these matters for all portions of the area surveyed. Moreover, it is only
when the whole range of considerations relating to urban expansion needs
are before the city planner that he is able to reach a decision as to whether
such availability factors are overriding or not. In some instances it is per-
fectly conceivable that "unavailable" property is of such vital importance
to the sound growth and expansion of the urban center that the power of
eminent domain would be invoked to obtain a piece of property and clear
the title for the use indicated in the comprehensive plan. Obviously these
determinations are made in the planning rather than the survey stages of
a planning program.

In addition to the map presentation of vacant areas, a tabular summary
is prepared as a means of facilitating later land use planning studies of
vacant land usable and vacant land required for each land use category in
the foreseeable future. Table 26 typifies the tabular summary used in
vacant land studies. In the same way that land use summaries are prepared in terms of planning districts and the one or more incorporated
communities in the urban area, the vacant land tabulation is prepared
with subtotals in order to recognize these functional and political units
separately. The larger the urban area the more important is this type of
summary.

Flood Damage Prevention Studies

In some respects related to the vacant and open land analysis above, the fourth type of investigation under the heading of urban land studies is the hydrological study and other kinds of analyses in planning for flood damage prevention. This type of investigation has been brought to the forefront by the work of the Tennessee Valley Authority [17] and its efforts to bring into the thinking of local governmental officials an appreciation of the two complementing ways for the prevention of flood damage: (1) flood control works which aim to keep water away from man, and (2) control of flood plain development through planning and regulatory efforts which aim to keep man away from water. It is this latter aspect of flood damage prevention which is of primary concern here.

Studies of the hydrology of the watershed area require the expertise of engineering specialists. In many states, the Corps of Engineers have made flood control studies, and state water resource agencies have made exhaustive studies for water conservation. These studies provide basic source materials, especially the former, but frequently they need to be carried a step further and brought into relationship with local planning efforts. The local flood damage prevention study draws on these sources to define areas involved in the "highest flood of record," the "standard project flood," and the "maximum probable flood." The first is the area along a river or stream which has actually been inundated by the highest known flood for which records are available. Since this is not necessarily the most severe flood possible, engineers have sought a more meaningful delineation of potential flood areas based on a coincidence of the most critical conditions noted in meteorological and flood data from a wide surrounding area. They have termed this the "standard project flood." In TVA's studies of flood damage prevention, the "regional flood" is comparable to the Corps of Engineers' "standard project flood." The regional flood area is the area affected should a storm of this composite intensity strike the area under study. The maximum probable flood is the maximum flood of reasonable regional expectancy taking into account present knowledge, and the affected area is the most extensive of the three. The intermediate concept (standard project flood) is generally used in planning. The cost of absolute protection for the third eventuality is so great that engineering works built rarely

---

[17] TVA's work is reflected in the Goddard Task Force Report for the ASCE Committee on Flood Control, "A Guide for the Development of Flood Plain Regulations," New York: American Society of Civil Engineers, January, 1962. See also Tennessee Valley Authority, *A Program for Reducing the National Flood Damage Potential,* Washington: U.S. Government Printing Office, 1959.

achieve this level of protection. Present-day thinking favors the design of dams, dikes, and other protective works at the standard project flood level, drawing on planning and the implementing regulatory controls to keep man from using unprotected areas in ways which would endanger life and property to a serious degree.

The basic hydrological studies go into a number of factors. Among these is the investigation of flood profiles showing the slope of the stream at low flow and the elevations reached by the flood of record. Maps and cross-sections are developed to show the stream bed and the top of the stream bank in relation to the low flow and crest level of the highest flood of record, the standard project flood, and the maximum probable flood. Investigations also go into the period of inundation, the rate of rise, the velocity of flood waters, the frequency of flooding, obstructions that affect crest levels, and the land use encroachments on the flood plain. These studies are used in the design of the permanent flood control structures and in identifying floodways which must be kept free of certain kinds of encroachments. In many areas there may be a delay of some years before needed permanent flood control works can be scheduled and built. In these situations, for land use planning purposes, a "stage one" set of floodway lines would be identified on higher ground assuming no flood control works and a "stage two" set of lines on lower ground assuming construction of protective works.

Once floodway lines are determined, the planner is able to introduce refinements into his land capability classification system as discussed in the immediate preceding section.[18] Thus, depending on the hazards involved, various parts of the flood plain carry special classifications in the land capability analysis. In addition to a "prime" and a "marginal" classification, a "limited use" category is required to take account of flood hazards in urban areas situated on rivers and streams. In land use planning analyses taken up in Part III, areas classified in the most restricted categories would become earmarked for open space uses such as outdoor recreation spaces and parking; land in intermediate classes would be considered for storage functions and structures where minimum floor levels and certain standards of construction are prescribed; and so on. Beyond the land use planning stage, of course, is the plan-implementing stage in which zoning, building code, and other regulatory measures are amended to effectuate these as well as other features of the land use plan.

While the foregoing discussion has been largely concerned with vacant and open areas, flood damage prevention studies obviously have important applications in developed areas wherever growth has encroached upon

---

[18] See suggestions of Jerrold A. Moore, *Planning for Flood Damage Prevention,* Atlanta: Engineering Experiment Station, Georgia Institute of Technology, 1958.

the flood plain. In these areas, urban renewal offers opportunities for corrective action, and the land use plan would utilize flood plain analyses to pin down areas for immediate and long-range remedial action.

Structural and Environmental Quality Survey

As noted earlier in the chapter, urban growth is accommodated by physical renewal and expansion of the city. While expansion occurs primarily by the filling in of vacant land and by urban extension into open land, renewal is usually associated with the built-up sections of urban areas. In its broadest meaning, *urban renewal* is a form of recuperative change in the physical city by which the outworn or outmoded structures and facilities and, in time, whole areas are altered or replaced in response to pressures of economic and social change. In this sense, urban renewal is a process that has been going on as long as cities have existed and flourished. However, in the years since World War II, the term has assumed a more specialized meaning and has come to be associated with the prevention and elimination of blight. Thus "urban renewal" is now being used to refer to the planned regeneration of built-up areas through an integrated program of redevelopment, rehabilitation, and conservation.[19] We now speak

---

[19] Although the term "urban renewal" in some circles includes the replanning of predominantly open areas where improper land subdivision in the original instance has had a blighting effect, in the city planning field it is generally used to refer to replanning in predominantly built-up areas, with the term "reclamation" being used to refer to replanning in predominantly vacant areas. Adapting from the American Institute of Planners' definitions, all the terms we have been using can be summarized as follows:

Redevelopment is the revision or replacement of an existing land use and population distribution pattern through the acquisition of a predominantly built-up area, and the clearance and rebuilding of this area according to a comprehensive metropolitan-wide plan—a plan which reflects positive long-range land use and population policies.

Rehabilitation is the improvement or restoration of a predominantly built-up area which, though consistent with a comprehensive plan in terms of intensity of development and land use patterns, is in a stage of incipient blight. It may involve the reduction of population densities, the acquisition and clearance of scattered deteriorated buildings, the repair, modernization, and provision of sanitary facilities, the provision of street, park, or other public improvements, or cleanup and maintenance work on the part of property owners.

Conservation is the preservation of predominantly built-up areas that are in "good" condition. These are the areas which are substantially in keeping with land use and population density requirements of a comprehensive plan but which require continuing systematic code enforcement, and may require public improvements to insure continued private investment therein.

Reclamation is (a) the reassembly and replanning of prematurely subdivided and relatively unsettled land which in many cases can never be put to proper use with proper population densities because of tax delinquency, clouded titles, or substandard subdivision design, and (b) the acquisition of land for public or institutional uses in areas so located or of such topographic characteristics as to be impractical, unsafe, or unhealthful for standard private development.

Urban extension is the acquisition and development (or the restriction of the use) of open unsubdivided land to provide for sound expansion of existing small urban centers or for the creation of completely new towns in the hinterland of existing metropolitan centers.

of "urban renewal programs," and in this sense urban renewal is a means of effectuating those portions of the land use plan that deal with blight prevention and elimination in built-up areas of the city.

The fifth kind of urban land study, the survey of structural and environmental quality, provides the necessary information for identifying renewal areas, indicating the portions of the built-up area where there is freedom to modify the existing land use pattern. Its purpose is to identify various degrees of blight in the urban area, culminating in a generalized designation of *treatment areas*—areas for clearance and redevelopment, areas for rehabilitation, and areas for conservation.

Urban Blight and Treatment Areas

To pin down the origins of urban blight soon involves the investigator in the study of very complex cause and effect relations, and he quickly discovers that there is a long way to go before definitive techniques for identifying root causes become available. Yet if efforts at treatment deal with effects rather than causes, clearly little is achieved in the long run in the elimination and prevention of blight. Until knowledge of these cause and effect relations is more perfect, the planner must be careful in his analyses of blight to view his work in a perspective of what is already known in an economic and social sense in this respect.

In its most elemental form urban blight is usually defined as an economic dislocation. It is frequently argued that an antiquated system of property taxation constitutes one very basic source of economic dislocation, and its disrupting effects are reflected in certain cycles of change in the character and intensity of land use: the premature obsolescence and the physical deterioration of large areas. No one yet has successfully demonstrated the interplay between these complex and subtle aspects of urban blight, and clearly we need much more rigorous research into the nature and the progression of cause and effect relations. For our purposes here, we are concerned with the immediate practical problem of measuring structural and environmental quality. When we use the term "treatment areas," we must recognize that we are using it in the sense of providing a basis for an attack on part of the problem of urban blight. A full-scale attack would go into considerations of a very fundamental character. For example, the education level of the people, their employment opportunities, their attitudes, and their dreams and hopes all impinge on the problem of urban blight and the effectiveness of urban renewal in purely physical terms.

In the usage here, urban blight refers to the physical aspect only. We use it to imply deterioration or the existence of deficiencies in the quality of structures and their immediate environment. Implied also are a range of conditions which are measurable and can be defined downward or upward from a set series of "standards" which in turn are based on generally recognized criteria of health, safety, and other elements of the public interest. The standards employed and thus the range of conditions to be identified with each type of treatment area are matters of local determination. Locally adopted standards relating to buildings, their design, occupancy, and sanitary facilities are generally specified in building, housing, fire, and sanitation codes; and environmental standards relating to the design of lots, blocks, and streets, population densities, and the type and intensity of development are included in subdivision regulations and the zoning ordinance. Where inadequate or no standards have been adopted, upgrading or setting of trial standards for survey purposes must be accomplished by reference to general standards (for example, minimum standards of health and safety for residential areas of the Hygiene of Housing Committee of the American Public Health Association [20]) or by reference to standards in force in communities of similar size and character which appear to be most consistent with local objectives.

Three types of treatment areas have been mentioned above. Clearance or redevelopment areas, the first type, are areas in which urban blight has advanced to such a degree that by local standards nothing short of clearance is practicable. Present are what may be termed simple and complex forms of blight. *Simple forms of blight* include such physical characteristics as structural deterioration, missing sanitation facilities, structures in disrepair or lacking in elemental maintenance, presence of trash and rubbish accumulations in yards, adverse environmental influences such as noise, odors, dust, and so on, and missing community facilities such as schools, playgrounds, public water and sewerage systems, and adequate street and drainage facilities. Usually associated with simple forms of physical blight are certain social and economic indicators of blight. Social indicators of blight include presence of abnormally high rates of juvenile delinquency, venereal disease, and similar results from other health and welfare indices; and economic indicators include concentrations of tax delinquent and tax title properties, declining property values, and presence of an abnormally large number of building vacancies. *Complex forms of blight* are said to exist when an area contains a mixture of incompatible land uses (the classic illustration being the glue factory located in the residential area), obsolete or impractical layout of lots, blocks, and streets, unsafe and unhealthful

---

[20] Committee on the Hygiene of Housing, American Public Health Association, *Planning the Home for Occupancy* and *Planning the Neighborhood,* Chicago: Public Administration Service, 1960; see also their pamphlet on *A Proposed Housing Ordinance,* New York: American Public Health Association, 1952.

conditions existing or possible when marginal land is in use, particularly land subject to floods, marshiness, or tidal flows. In terms of local standards, simple forms of blight may be present to such a degree that these factors alone constitute a basis for designating an area for clearance and redevelopment. Even if simple forms of blight have not advanced to the degree where local standards would call for clearance, if complex forms of blight are present, clearance and redevelopment obviously offer the only ultimate rational type of treatment for the area.

The second type of treatment area is the rehabilitation area. This is an area where usually only simple forms of blight are present, and where the overall degree of blight, according to local standards, has not progressed to the stage where so-called "rehabilitation measures" will not restore the area to standard condition. Rehabilitation measures include such activities as spot condemnation of structures, enforced building repairs, or provision of missing sanitary facilities through code enforcement, a public improvements program for the provision of missing community facilities, and a campaign for voluntary cleanup, painting, and improved building maintenance standards.

Conservation areas, the third type of treatment area, make up the balance of the built-up portions of the city. They are areas in what might be termed "standard condition"—the areas to be protected from urban blight and to be maintained at least at their present standard of development. Strict and continuing enforcement of zoning and a minimum housing standards ordinance and vigilance as to the maintenance of community facilities and private property are key conservation measures.

While the foregoing distinctions are generally recognized in professional planning circles, other groups such as real estate and home-building organizations use these terms in other connotations. For example, it is not uncommon to find rehabilitation and conservation being used interchangeably, nor to find a whole array of differing meanings in use from city to city or even in one locality. It is thus most important that these terms be carefully defined to avoid any unnecessary confusion and misunderstanding.

Survey Techniques

With this introduction to the characteristics of blight and how various gradations in quality are linked with various forms of treatment, it is appropriate now to consider briefly the types of surveys and their potentialities for land use planning analyses. It must be noted at the outset that for land use planning purposes, as desirable as it may be, it is not often feasible to undertake on a metropolitan-wide basis the more elaborate types of surveys of structural and environmental quality that have been developed in recent years. Nevertheless, it is important to be familiar with the alternatives so that should opportunity permit a more elaborate survey, this may be used in lieu of the less exacting alternatives. Not to be overlooked in this connection are the increasingly promising opportunities for undertaking more detailed types of structural and environmental quality surveys jointly with urban renewal and public health agencies. Taken up first are survey techniques for residential areas followed by a brief summary view of techniques for the investigation of commercial areas.

APHA Appraisal Technique

Perhaps the most precise and comprehensive type of survey for use in residential areas is the American Public Health Association's appraisal technique.[21] Including provisions for the appraisal of environmental as well as dwelling conditions, it employs a penalty scoring system applied item by item for various features in the structure and its surroundings that have been found to be diagnostic of urban blight. It can be used to measure both the extent of deviation from minimum standards and the detailed nature of housing conditions which adversely affect the health, safety, or the essential livability of dwelling units and their residential environment. The technique was developed, tested, and refined to its present form over a period of years by a group of public health specialists, city planners, sociologists, and others composing the membership of the Association's Committee on the Hygiene of Housing.

Under this technique, two separate appraisals are made: one of dwelling conditions, and one of the quality of the environment. Dwelling appraisals are made on an individual dwelling unit basis and include items on deterioration, maintenance and state of repair, safety and sanitation factors, adequacy of heating and lighting, degree of room crowding, and so on. The environmental quality schedule covers such items as land crowding (defined in terms of coverage and adequacy of yard space), lineal feet frontage of inimical land uses on the block, adequacy of water and sewerage facilities in the block, adequacy of schools, recreation areas, and other community facilities in the area, and the extent of hazards and nuisances in the area from traffic, railroads, and industry. The scores obtained from these two schedules can be combined to give a "housing score" as shown

---

[21] Committee on the Hygiene of Housing, *An Appraisal Method for Measuring the Quality of Housing: A Yardstick for Health Officers, Housing Officials and Planners*, Part I, "Nature and Uses of the Method," 1945, Part II, "Appraisal of Dwelling Conditions," 1946, Part III, "Appraisal of Neighborhood Environment," 1950, New York: American Public Health Association.

Table 27. Summary of Gradations in Housing Quality Under APHA Appraisal Technique[a]

Graduation of Quality	Environmental Score	Dwelling Score	Total Housing Score
A—Excellent to good	0–19	0– 29	0– 49
B—Acceptable	20–39	30– 59	50– 99
C—Questionable	40–59	60– 89	100–149
D—Substandard	60–79	90–119	150–199
E—Unfit for habitation	80 and over	120 and over	200 and over

[a] Committee on the Hygiene of Housing, *An Appraisal Method for Measuring the Quality of Housing: A Yardstick for Health Officers, Housing Officials and Planners*, New York: American Public Health Association, 1945–50.

in the illustrative results from the use of this technique in Figure 32. Table 27 indicates the range of quality possible in the use of the technique, showing the corresponding range of penalty scores for each of the environmental and dwelling schedules and for the combined total of both. Blocks with Grade E scores generally fall into areas classed as clearance areas, and those with Grade C tend to be classed as rehabilitation areas, with blocks carrying a Grade D score being assigned to clearance or rehabilitation areas according to the nature of the items which have the highest penalty ratings and the scores prevailing in the surrounding blocks. Blocks with Grades A and B scores will usually be classed as conservation areas. For details on the individual items in the schedules and the scoring system, the reader is referred to the APHA manuals cited above.

The APHA technique can be used for both a complete house-to-house coverage of an urban area or a sampling survey of the area. Under federally assisted urban renewal programs of slum clearance and area rehabilitation, low-ratio sampling surveys have been used for screening purposes, that is, for identifying in generalized form the treatment areas. Such a survey is then followed by a house-to-house or high-ratio sampling resurvey in the areas tentatively identified in the screening survey as most in need of attention. For land use planning purposes, the first screening survey is usually the only coverage necessary. This survey may involve either the use of an abbreviated schedule or the conduct of a low-ratio sampling study employing the full schedule.

Continuous Real Property Inventory

In cities where a positive code enforcement program has become accepted practice and is adequately financed, there is an opportunity to develop

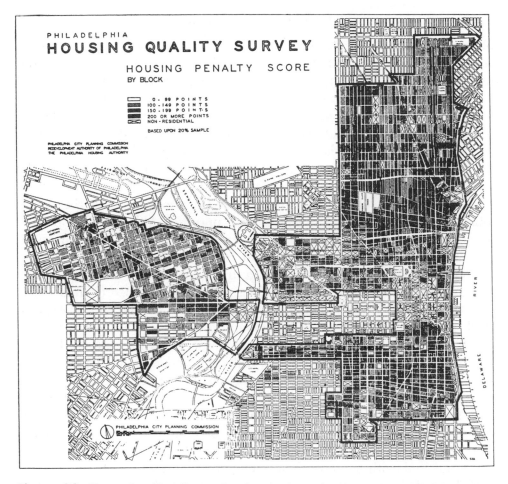

Figure 32. Illustrative Map Presenting Results from the Use of the APHA Technique for Appraising the Quality of Housing. (*Source:* Philadelphia City Planning Commission, *Philadelphia Housing Quality Survey,* 1951.)

and maintain records of structural and environmental quality on an up-to-date basis. Under a well-organized program of this type, a record is maintained on every structure and its environmental character. At periodic intervals each structure and its premises are reinspected. While such inspections cannot go into great detail since they are made primarily to ascertain the conformance of structures to code provisions, the very act of reinspection at regular intervals permits the keeping of records in the form of a continuous inventory. Obviously, such a source of information, especially if data are summarized on punch cards, can readily be used in the identification of treatment areas for land use planning purposes.

Census of Housing and Land Use Survey Sources

Short of a continuous real property inventory, an APHA type of special survey, or a study combined with some other inventory such as the land use survey, a property appraisal study for tax purposes, or one conducted in conjunction with a housing market analysis, the only remaining alternative for the evaluation of structural and environmental quality is the use of standard sources of data such as are available in the decennial Census of Housing and in the planning agency's own map and land use records. Such sources are crude substitutes for surveys especially designed for the measurement of structural and environmental quality, but they are by no means unsuitable for the identification of treatment areas in the generalized form required for land use planning purposes. Although they present a variety of mechanical problems as noted below, many and perhaps most planning agencies find it necessary to resort to these sources.

For those portions of the urban area in residential use, the conventional sources of information are the U.S. Census bulletins entitled *Census Tracts* and *City Blocks* for the condition of structures, and the Base C type of land use maps for data on environmental conditions. The census sources on structural condition and housing unit sanitary facilities are used in defining areas containing simple forms of blight, and land use maps supplemented by local sources of information on community facilities can be used in identifying such complex forms of blight as inimical mixtures of uses and obsolete lot and block layouts. For the areas covered by block statistics (usually incorporated areas of 50,000 population or more), maps can be prepared showing by block the proportion of housing units with structural and with sanitary deficiencies. In SMSA's where census tracts have been defined, the picture thus obtained by blocks can be extended on a tract basis to the limits of the SMSA. Similarly, by reference to various local sources of data, blocks deficient in essential community facilities can be mapped, and the proportion of lineal feet frontage of inimical uses, substandard lot sizes, and other environmental deficiencies can be plotted on a block-by-block basis.

By relating the mapped data to standards in housing, building, zoning, and subdivision codes, hatch patterns can be used on this series of maps to represent degrees of substandardness. After both structural and environmental criteria have been thus applied, a crude composite scoring system is sometimes devised to assist in the final delineation of treatment areas. To make for greater consistency in this task, weights are sometimes assigned each of the selected criteria to assist in making the final allocation of blocks into one of the three treatment categories. Unless statistical tests of the accuracy of such an index have been made, the analyst should avoid imputing any precision to such a "scoring system," if, indeed, it can be dignified by such a term in the first place. Though it is far too subjective and crude to be construed as a valid scoring system, it can assist in systemizing the application of judgment in the course of designating areas for possible clearance, rehabilitation, and conservation.

It may be helpful to note briefly the criteria the Bureau of the Census used in the 1960 census in classifying housing units by condition and plumbing facilities. There is some difference in the summary categories on sanitary facilities used in the bulletins on *City Blocks* and *Census Tracts*:

City Blocks	*Census Tracts*

Sound Housing Units	
With all plumbing facilities	With all plumbing facilities
Lacking some or all facilities	Lacking only hot water
	Lacking other plumbing facilities

Deteriorating Housing Units	
With all plumbing facilities	With all plumbing facilities
Lacking some or all facilities —inside flush toilet	Lacking only hot water
Lacking some or all facilities —no inside flush toilet	Lacking other plumbing facilities

Dilapidated Housing Units

A housing unit was classified as "sound" if it had no defects or only slight defects. It was classified as "deteriorating" if it needed more repair than would be corrected in the normal course of maintenance and possessed defects of an "intermediate" nature which if left untended to would lead to serious structural damage. It was classified as dilapidated if it was determined to be unsafe or inadequate shelter owing to one or more critical defects, to a combination of intermediate defects which occur in sufficient number to require extensive repair or rebuilding, or to inadequate original construction (structures built of makeshift materials and inadequately converted cellars, sheds, or garages not originally intended as living quarters).[22]

Examples of slight, intermediate, and critical defects are given on the following page.

---

[22] Paraphrased from standard introduction to *City Blocks* bulletins of *U.S. Census of Housing: 1960*, Series HC(3), Washington: U.S. Government Printing Office, 1961, p. x.

Slight Defects	Intermediate Defects	Critical Defects
Slight damage to porch or steps	Shaky or unsafe porch steps	Sagging walls, floor, or roof
Small cracks in walls, plaster, or chimney	Holes, open cracks, or missing material over small area of floors, walls, or roof	Holes, open cracks, or missing material over large area of floors, walls, roof, or other parts of structure
Slight wear on floors or doorsills	Deep wear on stairs, floors, or doorsills	Damage by storm or fire
Broken gutters or downspouts	Rotted window sills or frames	
Lack of paint	Broken or loose stair treads or missing balusters	

It is to be noted that summary tabulations make it possible to derive separate summaries for condition and plumbing facilities. This is a distinct advance over the definitions used in the 1950 census which did not permit separate counts of housing units with structural deficiencies and plumbing deficiencies.

Appraisal of Commercial Areas

Techniques for identifying blight in commercial areas have received attention only relatively recently, and there is therefore less experience to draw on in outlining procedures for appraising the quality of these areas. As yet no calibrated techniques for analyzing the quality of retail areas have come into general use, although various economic indicators (vacancy rates, declining rental rates per square foot of floor area, and so on), measures of the structural condition of retail buildings, and the adequacy of parking and loading facilities, capacities of fronting streets, and mass transportation facilities have been used in various ways in CBD studies to support renewal proposals.

For appraising the quality of industrial and wholesale areas, two efforts are particularly noteworthy. One of these, the Detroit study of industrial corridors, provides an example of a windshield survey technique especially suited to land use planning analyses of a preliminary or generalized nature.[23] Like the APHA technique for appraising residential areas, this approach differentiates between structural and environmental factors of blight. Criteria used in estimating the degree of structural obsolescence and deterioration were walls broken, cracked, or out of plumb; foundation rotting, broken, or cracked; chimney, stairs, and other building appendages

---

[23] Detroit City Plan Commission, *Industrial Renewal,* 1956.

rotting, broken, or parts missing; buildings of wood frame construction; vacant structures; and major buildings more than one story in height except for specified situations. A three-point rating scale was devised based on the proportion of structures in a block with one or more of these factors present. Criteria used in appraising the industrial environment were conflicting land uses, overcrowding of land, inadequate streets, parking, and off-street loading, and nuisance elements. When one or more of these conditions was found in an extreme degree, a block's numerical rating of structural condition had an x added; when these conditions were present to a considerable degree but not to a sufficient degree to injure the area seriously, a slant line (/) was added; and where the block had a generally sound environmental setting, it received no symbol. In the summary ratings, Class 4 blocks (3x, 3/, or 3) were considered to exhibit an extreme tendency toward obsolescence and deterioration. Class 3 blocks (2x) were held to be showing considerable tendency in this direction. Class 2 blocks (1x or 2/) were listed as showing a moderate tendency, and Class 1 blocks (2, 1/, or 1), a slight tendency toward obsolescence and deterioration. Class 4 areas generally called for clearance and redevelopment as the form of treatment, Class 3 a combination of redevelopment and conservation, and Classes 2 and 1 conservation of variable urgency.

The St. Louis approach follows the APHA pattern as to scope, field procedures, and rating system.[24] It is best suited for detailed studies following the preliminary land use planning stages of a local planning program and is especially useful in defining project areas for renewal. The technique has not had extensive testing, and there is presently no mechanism for organized supervision in the use of the instrument and in the analysis and interpretation of results as has been achieved by the American Public Health Association in the use of their housing appraisal technique. The APHA has a requirement that personnel using the technique must attend APHA-sponsored training institutes as a condition for permission to use the technique. Control is exercised through the copyright the APHA holds.

The technique is an inspection-interview type and involves the use of a structure schedule and an occupancy schedule covering a wide variety of items relative to individual establishments. Illustrative of the detail are items covering such *building features* as access and egress, type of construction, age, story and ceiling heights, floor characteristics, and column spacing; such *building appurtenance* items as fire escapes, fire protection systems, heating systems, characteristics, and utilities; such *building condition* items as structural condition, plumbing, wiring, heating, and infes-

---

[24] St. Louis City Plan Commission, *Measuring Deterioration in Commercial and Industrial Areas,* a Housing and Home Finance Agency demonstration project, St. Louis: City Plan Commission, 1957.

tation; such *building occupancy* features as design use, nuisances, and convertibility; such *site features* as shape, topography, rail facilities, and loading and parking facilities; and the presence of *code violations* of various kinds. In the field a one- to nine-point scale is used to rate these features, and in the office these results are converted to a penalty score for each structure.

The environmental schedule is designed for analysis on a block basis and covers such items as the block's location with respect to traffic arteries, mass transportation, and utilities. It also rates adjoining street conditions such as the character of traffic, the grades, right-of-way and pavement widths, number of traffic lanes, condition of pavement, curb, and gutters, on-street parking conditions, street lighting, and sidewalk conditions; and it evaluates block size, mixtures of land use, expansion opportunities, desirability of location, and vacancy history. The environmental score is added to each individual structure score. A median score is then computed for each block, and then the block is given a classification A to E according to its median combined score. The range of scores permissible in each class are graded in much the same way as the APHA summary in Table 27. The study should be consulted for details.

Summary of Survey Results

When all use areas in the built-up portion of the urban center have been classified into treatment areas according to locally adopted standards of structural and environmental quality, a map showing the generalized patterns of these treatment areas is prepared. This is the *map of urban renewal areas*. In those portions of the urban area identified for clearance and redevelopment, there is a full measure of freedom for modifying the land use pattern. While in areas earmarked for rehabilitation only minor changes in land use are generally possible, there is some flexibility for modifying the intensity of development through the spot elimination of substandard structures.

The presentation of urban renewal areas by the foregoing procedures is based on the extent that urban blight is present in the respective treatment areas. Subsequent analyses in Part III of location and space requirements may indicate additional areas where land use patterns need revision. Although for practical reasons it is highly unlikely that large areas of this kind could be altered in use and intensity of development, it is possible that certain clearance and redevelopment areas may be enlarged because of considerations other than urban blight.

For land use planning purposes, the foregoing kind of analysis yields a summary of acreages expected to become available for reuse through clearance operations during the planning period. By following procedures similar to those employed in establishing the use potentialities of vacant land, it is possible to apply to renewal land a classification system such as that presented in Table 26. The final result of following this procedure is a summary of the supply of renewal land by planning districts tabulated according to topographic characteristics and the level of improvements available at the site. Obviously the designation of certain areas for clearance and redevelopment will involve in later analyses acreage deductions for various land use categories in the tabular summary of existing land uses such as that shown in Table 24. Similarly in subsequent land use planning analyses, it will involve deductions in the inventory of dwelling units available during the planning period.

Cost-Revenue Studies

The kinds of urban land studies covered so far have been largely concerned with the development of a basic description of the physical characteristics of land in the urban area as a step in tooling up for land use planning. But along with these characteristics of urban land, the decisions finally reached in the land use planning process must take into account the public costs of supplying community facilities and service to land as these compare with tax revenues received. While it is beyond the scope of this summary treatment of the subject to go into basic and very complex questions of tax structure and public finance, available techniques for determining cost-revenue relationships for different uses of land under prevailing policies and levels of service will be briefly reviewed.

Related, but in many respects distinct from land value studies (which are concerned with the economic worth of land and its improvements on the open land market), cost-revenue studies aim to provide information on the governmental costs of supplying public improvements and services to urban land as these costs relate to the revenue available to finance such improvements and services. For purposes of land use planning, these studies are concerned most directly with cost-revenue comparisons for various uses of land at varying locations and at varying densities and intensities of development. Thus a primary element that must be taken into consideration in reaching land use planning decisions is how much it will cost to provide public improvements and services at particular locations in relation to revenues that can be anticipated at these locations. But density and intensity of development are related to location. Thus for residential development, it is important to investigate differentials in cost-revenue relationships in fringe areas where scattered settlement patterns tend to occur as opposed to those of the more concentrated development found in closer-in locations. It is also important to know what the differential effects on these cost-revenue relationships will be when development occurs in these locations at low, medium, and high densities. By the same token, in industrial, commercial, and retail business areas, it is important to know how these relationships will differ in developments ranging from an intensive to an extensive use of land.

However inadequate methods of analysis have been in the past, cost-revenue studies have long been employed in various special-purpose investigations. For example, they have been undertaken to estimate the magnitude of the financial drain that blighted areas and slums represent to a city, to evalute the financial implications to the central city of "the flight to the suburbs," and to set forth the fiscal considerations of annexation for the annexing city and for the area being annexed. Only in the years since World War II have the applications of these studies to land use planning begun to receive serious recognition, and since 1950 an increasing number of cost-revenue studies have been initiated.[25]

The earliest studies have had a strong influence on methods in use in the past 30 years.[26] But in the years since World War II, deficiencies in the methods of computing costs and revenues have been noted.[27] While a great deal more research is needed in perfecting methods of conducting cost-revenue surveys, some valuable guidelines for these surveys are beginning to emerge. Lichfield has focused attention on the use of cost-benefit analysis techniques as a means for evaluating plan proposals, and the work of Wheaton and Schussheim and that of Isard and Coughlin provided prototype studies in cost-revenue analysis.[28] The material on the following pages is taken from the work of Esser at the University of North Carolina.[29]

Methods of Analysis

The methodological problems in estimating the allocation of costs of public improvements and services to specific use areas are more complex than those

---

[25] See Ruth L. Mace, *Municipal Cost-Revenue Research in the United States,* Chapel Hill: Institute of Government, University of North Carolina, 1961.

[26] These include such studies as R. B. Navin, *An Analysis of a Slum Area in Cleveland,* Cleveland: Metropolitan Housing Authority, 1934; and *The Income and Cost Survey,* Boston: City Planning Board, 1935.

[27] Mace, *Municipal Cost-Revenue Research in the United States.*

[28] Nathaniel Lichfield, "Cost-Benefit Analysis in City Planning," *Journal of the American Institute of Planners,* November, 1960; William L. C. Wheaton and Morton J. Schussheim, *The Cost of Municipal Services in Residential Areas,* a Housing and Home Finance Agency and U.S. Department of Commerce monograph, Washington: U.S. Government Printing Office, 1955; and Walter Isard and Robert E. Coughlin, *Municipal Cost and Revenues Resulting from Community Growth,* West Trenton: Chandler-Davis Publishing Company, 1957.

[29] George H. Esser, Jr., *Urban Growth and Municipal Services: Uses and Methods of Cost-Revenue Analysis,* Chapel Hill: Institute of Government, University of North Carolina, 1957.

involved in estimating revenues. Indeed, much more research is needed before available methods will be entirely satisfactory for direct application in land use planning studies. For example, most work in this field has been concerned with cost allocation for residential areas. Although some proto-type studies have dealt with industrial and retail uses,[30] more research and experience in the application of cost-revenue techniques to nonresidential uses are needed. The approaches discussed here deal primarily with residential uses.

Early work and most of the more recent studies which attempt to allocate costs for public improvements and services to residential uses have relied heavily on approximation techniques in making measurements of the cost incidence, without checking what it actually costs to provide improvements and services to a given area. Moreover, they have made allocations generally on the basis of assessed valuations, with some variations (for example, costs of road construction and maintenance have been assigned to residential uses in terms of the lineal feet of improvements or services involved). The faulty assumption implied here is that assessed valuation is a reliable measure of services consumed. While frankly recognized in most studies as a means of getting around the complexities of making actual measurements of cost, the very use of such approximation approaches has obscured two factors which are considered crucial to obtaining reliable results.

The first such factor relates to the base which is to be used in cost allocations: the need for an approach which recognizes that some costs are more properly chargeable to the *community as a whole* while other costs can be traced more directly to *properties* alone. A concrete illustration based on a widely accepted public policy in street improvement work will serve to point up the reasoning behind the differentiation being made here. When a street is under consideration for paving, its financing is usually accomplished in one of two ways. If the street is a major traffic artery which is used by all the people of the community, the cost of paving is generally made chargeable to the entire community, that is, out of general funds. On the other hand, the cost of paving a local street which is used primarily by the residents of a particular area is usually financed by property assessments charged against abutting property owners who directly benefit by the improvement. One is a cost that is chargeable to people of the community as a whole, and the other is a cost chargeable to property. Following the same general reasoning, cost-revenue analysis should differentiate between (1) costs which are essentially property-related and (2) costs which involve improvements and services for the people of the community as a

---

[30] Examples are found in the work of Robert J. T. Longabaugh, "Cost-Revenue Implications of Various Industrial Land Use Patterns," unpublished manuscript, Chapel Hill: Department of City and Regional Planning, University of North Carolina, 1960; and Raymond J. Green, *The Impact of the Central Business District on the Municipal Budget*, Washington: Urban Land Institute, 1962.

Table 28. Cost Measurement of Residential Area Activities, Greensboro, North Carolina, 1956[a]

Basic Operational Activity	Self-Supporting	Activity Performed by	Unit of Activity	Unit of Cost[b]	Method of Finance	Unit of Time	Unit of Incidence	Residential Portion	Unit of Residential Cost
Police patrolling[c]	—	City	Patrol car beat	$51,264	Operating	Annual	15,000 people	50%	$25,632
Detective	—	City	Per patrol car beat	8,635	Operating	Annual	15,000 people	50	4,318
Fire fighting									
Station	—	Purchase	Pumper company	72,182	Bond	30 years	10,000 people	75	54,137
Engine	—	Purchase	Pumper company	20,623	Capital	10 years	10,000 people	75	15,467
Equipment	—	Purchase	Pumper company	34,339	Capital	10 years	10,000 people	75	25,754
Company	—	City	Pumper company	48,802	Operating	Annual	10,000 people	75	36,602
Fire alarm									
Boxes	—	City	Box	155	Capital	30 years	—	100	155
Circuit	—	City	Wire-mile	150	Capital	30 years	—	100	150
Fire prevention	—	Company personnel	—	—	—	—	—	—	—-
Traffic signing									
Initial	—	City	Sign	12	Capital	4 years	—	100	12
Replacement	—	City	Sign	5	Operating	4 years	—	100	5
Street paving	Assessment (partial)	Contract	Street-mile	22,295	Revolving	15 years	—	100	22,295
Paved street maintenance									
Resurfacing	—	Contract	Street-mile	10,388	Revolving	15 years	—	100	10,388
Other	—	City	Street-mile	398	Operating	Annual	—	100	398
Sidewalk construction	Assessment	—	—	—	—	—	—	—	—
Street signing	—	City	Sign	18	Capital	10 years	—	100	18
Garbage collection	—	City	Collection route	11,139	Operating	Annual	750 houses	100	11,139
Street cleaning	—	City	Street-mile	61	Operating	Annual	—	100	61
Building inspection	Fee	—	—	—	—	—	—	—	—
Street lighting	—	Contract	Lamp	22	Operating	Annual	—	100	22
Water and sewer construction	Assessment and rates	—	—	—	—	—	—	—	—
Water	Rates	—	—	—	—	—	—	—	—
Sewer	Rates	—	—	—	—	—	—	—	—

[a] David L. McCallum, *A Case Study of the Cost of Governmental Activities in Single-Family Residential Areas of Different Density*, unpublished manuscript, Chapel Hill: Department of City and Regional Planning, University of North Carolina, 1956.

[b] Includes apportioned cost of supplementary activities.

[c] Local records not maintained on a basis to permit use of more precise measurement units.

whole.[31] Examples of costs considered to be chargeable to people in the urban area as a whole are schools, libraries, recreation, health and welfare services, traffic regulation, major streets, and so on. Examples of costs considered to be incident to particular parcels of land are residential street, water, and sewerage systems, some aspects of police protection, fire protection, and so on.

It is recognized, of course, that the classification of these improvement and service costs into one or the other category is not always a clear-cut choice and that there is a gray area between the black and the white where choices will tend to be somewhat arbitrary. Yet if no attempt is made to differentiate between these two classes of cost, the effect is to conceal actual costs incurred by the municipality in the development of new property. Thus in place of residential areas being "a net liability" in cost-revenue comparisons as is commonly concluded when a single base for cost allocation is used, under the more realistic two-class system of cost allocation, all but unsoundly developed property, particularly slums, will generally show up as paying their fair share of property-related costs. However, as will be seen in the illustrative material below, there can be a wide variation in the extent to which land development at various densities is contributing to the costs of improvements and services for the community as a whole.

The second conceptual consideration is the necessity of recognizing that different parts of the urban area will require different levels of service. For example, the central, intensively developed sections of the city usually require higher levels of fire protection than the suburban fringe areas. Within the central area, business uses may require more frequent garbage collection than residential areas. Thus levels of service may vary with the density of population, the use of the land, the powers and functions of the governmental unit having jurisdiction in the area and their policies, and so on. Moreover, since these conditions and policies vary with urban area, cost experience in one area may have little transfer value in another.

Turning now to cost allocation procedures, we refer to a pilot study made by Esser and McCallum in Greensboro, North Carolina.[32] This study aimed to develop and apply a methodology of measuring the incidence of improvement and service costs to residential property. It made detailed in-

---

[31] It is interesting to note that the division of functions among the metropolitan government of Toronto and its several constituent municipalities roughly corresponds to the distinction being made here for purposes of cost-revenue analysis. In general, the metropolitan government assumes responsibility for functions that serve the people of the urban area as a whole, and the several municipalities assume responsibility for property-related functions.

[32] David L. McCallum, *A Case Study of the Cost of Governmental Activities in Single-Family Residential Areas of Different Density,* unpublished manuscript, Chapel Hill: Department of City and Regional Planning, University of North Carolina, 1956.

Table 29. Annual and Amortized Capital Costs for an Illustrative Fringe Area Residential Development Designed to Varying Densities, Greensboro, North Carolina, 1956[a]

Annual and Amortized Periodic Costs	Minimum Lot Size (in square feet)							
	6,000		9,000		18,000		36,000	
	Sub-division Total	Average per House [b]	Sub-division Total	Average per House [b]	Sub-division Total	Average per House [b]	Sub-division Total	Average per House [b]
Annual Costs								
Police patrolling	$ 5,991	$ 6.41	$ 4,544	$ 6.41	$ 2,288	$ 6.41	$ 1,314	$ 6.41
Detective	1,009	1.08	765	1.08	385	1.08	221	1.08
Pumper company	12,833	13.73	9,732	13.73	4,901	13.73	2,815	13.73
Other paved street mainte-nance	2,974	3.18	2,872	4.05	2,114	5.92	1,691	8.25
Garbage collection	13,887	14.85	10,530	14.85	5,302	14.85	3,045	14.85
Street cleaning	456	.49	440	.62	324	.91	259	1.26
Street lighting	1,607	1.72	1,430	2.02	902	2.53	660	3.22
Total	38,757	41.45	30,313	42.75	16,216	45.42	10,005	48.80
General activities [c]	3,004	3.21	2,349	3.31	1,257	3.52	775	3.78
Total annual costs	41,761	44.66	32,662	46.06	17,473	48.94	10,780	52.59
Amortized Capital Costs, Years 1–4								
Fire station	$ 633	$ 0.68	$ 480	$ 0.68	$ 242	$ 0.68	$ 139	$ 0.68
Fire engine	542	.58	411	.58	207	.58	119	.58
Fire equipment	903	.97	685	.97	345	.97	198	.97
Fire alarm boxes	62	.07	52	.07	41	.11	47	.23
Fire alarm circuit	15	.02	15	.02	14	.04	11	.05
Street signing—initial	117	.13	96	.14	66	.18	30	.15
Street paving	11,105	11.88	10,727	15.13	7,895	22.11	6,316	30.81
Street signing	97	.10	88	.12	49	.14	36	.18
Total	13,474	14.41	12,554	17.70	8,859	24.81	6,896	33.63
General activities [c]	1,044	1.12	973	1.37	686	1.92	534	2.60
Interest on bonds	184	.20	140	.20	70	.20	40	.20
Total, years 1–4	14,702	15.72	13,667	19.27	9,615	26.93	7,470	36.43
Total, annual and amortized capital costs, years 1–4	$56,463	$60.39	$46,329	$65.34	$27,089	$75.88	$18,251	$89.02
Amortized Capital Costs, Years 5–15								
Less traffic signing—initial	$ −117	$−0.13	$ − 96	$−0.14	$ − 66	$−0.18	$ − 30	$−0.15
Less general activities [c]	− 9	− .01	− 7	− .01	− 5	− .01	− 2	− .01
Plus traffic signing—replacement	+ 49	+ .05	+ 40	+ .06	+ 28	+ .08	+ 13	+ .06
Plus general activities [c]	+ 4	+ .00	+ 3	+ .00	+ 2	+ .01	+ 1	+ .00
Net change, years 5–15	− 73	− .08	− 60	− .08	− 41	− .11	− 18	− .09
Total, years 5–15	14,629	15.64	13,607	19.19	9,575	26.82	7,453	36.35
Total, annual and amortized capital costs, years 5–15	$56,390	$60.31	$46,269	$65.26	$27,048	$75.76	$18,233	$88.93

(Table 29 continued.)

Annual and Amortized Periodic Costs	Minimum Lot Size (in square feet)							
	6,000		9,000		18,000		36,000	
	Sub-division Total	Average per House [b]	Sub-division Total	Average per House [b]	Sub-division Total	Average per House [b]	Sub-division Total	Average per House [b]
Amortized Capital Costs, Years 16—								
Less street paving	$ −11,105	$ −11.88	$ −10,727	$ −15.13	$ − 7,895	$ −22.11	$ − 6,316	$ −30.81
Less general activities [c]	− 861	− .92	− 831	− 1.17	− 612	− 1.71	− 489	− 2.39
Plus resurfacing	+ 5,174	+ 5.53	+ 4,998	+ 7.05	+ 3,679	+10.31	+ 2,943	+14.36
Plus general activities [c]	+ 401	+ .43	+ 387	+ .55	+ 285	+ .80	+ 228	+ 1.11
Net change, years 16—	− 6,391	− 6.83	− 6,173	− 8.71	− 4,543	−12.73	− 3,634	−17.73
Total, years 16—	8,238	8.81	7,434	10.48	5,032	14.09	3,819	18.62
Total, annual and amortized capital costs, years 16—	$49,999	$53.47	$40,096	$56.55	$22,505	$63.03	$14,599	$71.20

[a] David L. McCallum, *A Case Study of the Cost of Governmental Activities in Single-Family Residential Areas of Different Density,* unpublished manuscript, Chapel Hill: Department of City and Regional Planning, University of North Carolina, 1956.

[b] Discrepancies in adding columns caused by rounding numbers.

[c] A 7.75 per cent factor used as a measure for apportioning costs of general activities.

vestigations of the operations and service areas of various municipal agencies under the prevailing quality and intensity of service permitted under existing financial policies of the city. Table 28 presents a summary of these cost measurements.[33] Next, these cost data were applied to a land area at the fringe of the city considered prime for residential development. Designs were developed for this area at alternative residential densities, with development into lots of 6, 9, 18, and 36,000 square feet. Table 29 is a summary of annual and amortized capital costs and public facilities and services for future periods of time, and indicates how costs vary according to density.

Revenue estimates from these residential developments include property taxes (developed on the basis of building trends and actual tax assessments derived from a representative sample of residential properties in the ranges indicated) and the probable income from gasoline, beer and wine, intangible, and franchise taxes. The final cost-revenue comparisons derived from this analysis are presented in Table 30. From this table it is seen that under prevailing local service levels and financial policies for the provision of improvements and services in this city, residential areas

[33] For a detailed discussion of the derivation of cost data, see *ibid.*

Table 30. Cost-Revenue Comparisons for an Illustrative Fringe Area Residential Development Designed to Varying Densities, Greensboro, North Carolina, 1956[a] (Costs Expressed in Dollars per Dwelling Unit per Year)

	Lot Size and Price Range						
	6,000 sq. ft.	9,000 sq. ft.		18,000 sq. ft.		36,000 sq. ft.	
	$7,000– 9,000	$7,000– 7,500	$11,000– 12,000	$12,500– 13,500	$20,000– 21,000	$19,000– 20,000	$40,000– 41,000
1956–61							
Revenue [b]	$69.01	$67.19	$ 93.10	$104.51	$164.75	$155.67	$278.69
Annual operating costs	45.08	46.47	46.47	49.48	49.48	53.12	53.12
Amortized capital costs	15.46	19.01	19.01	26.67	26.67	36.17	36.17
Total costs	60.54	65.48	65.48	76.15	76.15	89.29	89.29
Difference	8.47	1.71	27.62	28.36	88.60	65.38	189.40
1961–71							
Revenue [b]	79.03	77.20	103.11	114.52	174.75	165.68	288.71
Annual operating costs	45.08	46.47	46.47	49.48	49.48	53.12	53.12
Amortized capital costs	15.39	18.92	18.92	26.55	26.55	36.08	36.08
Total costs	60.47	65.39	65.39	76.03	76.03	89.20	89.20
Difference	18.56	11.81	37.72	38.49	98.72	76.48	199.51
1971—							
Revenue [b]	79.03	77.20	103.11	114.52	174.75	165.68	288:71
Annual operating costs	45.08	46.47	46.47	49.48	49.48	53.12	53.12
Amortized capital costs	8.55	10.22	10.22	13.83	13.83	18.35	18.35
Total costs	53.63	56.69	56.69	63.31	63.31	71.47	71.47
Difference	25.40	20.51	46.42	51.21	111.44	94.21	217.24

[a] David L. McCallum, *A Case Study of the Cost of Governmental Activities in Single-Family Residential Areas of Different Density*, unpublished manuscript, Chapel Hill: Department of City and Regional Planning, University of North Carolina, 1956.
[b] From 1956 to 1959, it is estimated that revenue from property taxes would range from 89 per cent of the total revenue for the 6,000-square-foot property to 93 per cent for the higher-valued 36,000-square-foot property. From 1960 on, it is estimated that revenue from property taxes would range from 76 per cent, respectively, of the total revenue.

developed to sound standards at any one of the listed densities would return their fair share of property-related costs. The figures appearing opposite the "difference" item in the stub of Table 30 indicate how much a house and lot at the quoted price ranges at different densities will be contributing toward the costs of community-wide improvement and services. Particularly noteworthy is the relatively small difference in this figure in similarly priced developments with 6,000- and 9,000-square-foot lots, suggesting that from a cost-revenue standpoint, this city might adopt 9,000 square feet as a minimum lot size without making an appreciable difference in net cost.

Applications to Land Use Planning

The above-described pilot study is indicative of the kinds of tests it is possible to make in developing a land use plan. By applying sample tests to areas proposed for residential development and redevelopment, it is possible to estimate the impact of future development on a municipality's fiscal structure. When similar detailed cost measurement methods are used in cost-revenue comparisons for business, wholesale, and industrial areas, it is possible to assess the net cost implications of providing improvements and services as set forth in the entire land development plan.

At the same time, it is well to recognize that the "break-even" point in municipal finance involves considerations which are outside the scope of land use planning and the tests we have been discussing. While land use planning can and should give proper consideration to optimum cost-revenue relationships in the land use patterns proposed in a land development plan, more fundamental readjustments may be called for in the basic tax structure of the urban area and in the governmental arrangements for tax administration. Thus there is a need for caution to avoid distorting land development standards, where remedial action is more properly obtained in the tax field. Studies which seek to establish a break-even point, concluding that homes costing less than a certain amount will upset this break-even point, should be used cautiously unless keyed in with a basic re-examination of the tax structure.

Where remedial action gets into questions of tax structure, these lead to problems of tax relationships among the various governmental jurisdictions to be found in metropolitan areas. While solutions to these problems are not within the scope of land use planning, they have implications for the way in which cost-revenue studies are approached. Obviously cost-revenue tests will encounter variations in service policies among these various jurisdictions. Suburban municipalities can be expected to pursue policies of quite a different order than those being followed by the central city, and among suburban communities, there may be some range of variation. These policies may be in conflict with one another, and they may well continue thus until metropolitan government becomes a reality. The task of testing land use planning proposals for cost-revenue relationships under these circumstances is difficult enough for the central city planner, but the task for suburban city planners is even more difficult. In the face of these problems, the soundest approach would seem to be the pooling of effort on the part of the various planning agencies in the metropolitan area in the development of one urban-wide land use plan that is sound in every other respect, and then jointly testing such a plan for its cost-revenue implications under alternative combinations of service policies. The very act of focusing attention on different combinations of consistent and inconsistent cost-revenue relationships may hasten the time when financial policies are developed on a metropolitan-wide basis. An illustration of an effort in this direction is the Hartford Capitol Region Planning Agency's study of the municipal tax implications of five alternative patterns of regional growth.[34]

Land Value Studies

As brought out in Chapter 1, the structure of land values in the urban area has a very considerable influence on the way in which individuals seek to use land for various purposes, in various locations, and at various densities. While traditionally the city planner has been preoccupied with social objectives—what we have referred to as public interest considerations—he cannot proceed far in his land use planning studies without taking into account value-use relationships of urban land. He encounters too many forcible illustrations of these relationships in his day-to-day work not to be aware of their implications. The repeated approaches to planning commissions for the rezoning of corner lots for filling stations and the continual requests of all kinds for rezoning properties from one category to a "lower" category are manifestations of urban land market forces.

Land use planning proposals and the subsequent implementing decisions reached in the system of use districts and permitted densities and intensities of development adopted in a zoning ordinance seek a balance between the economic and "social" use of land. Of necessity, then, a very vital part of the tooling-up process for land use planning is an investigation of the structure of land values. It indicates whether various proposed locations of particular uses or groups of uses are feasible in terms of land costs, whether individuals, firms, or developers are likely to take up the land in the use and intensity of development that may be proposed from a public interest point of view.

Since it is the very nature of the real estate market that land and building values are constantly changing, it is never possible to obtain a precise picture of the pattern of values. The task of appraising the value of property is an extremely complex and time-consuming kind of study. By the time a study is completed, in the course of the survey itself, some of the details have undergone change. Fortunately the needs of land use planning are such that changes in detail have little direct consequence. It is the

[34] Capitol Region Planning Agency, *Municipal Taxation and Regional Development*, Hartford: Capitol Region Planning Agency, March, 1963. See also the Agency's *Regional Plan Alternatives*, issued in November, 1961.

broad pattern of values, their general gradations upward or downward, and their trends of change which have most direct application to the work of the city planner for the generalized level of detail with which he is working in his land use planning analyses.

Land values are normally computed in urban areas on a front-foot basis and on an acreage or area basis in fringe areas and in open country. In calculating the value of a particular urban lot or tract, applied to the front-foot unit values are adjustment factors to take into account varying lot or tract depths and corner influences. Valuations of structures and other improvements are estimated separately by reference to rates of depreciation applied to original costs, to depreciated replacement costs, or by other means.

Valuation data are presented in map form to show the geographic patterns of values. Land and building values may be presented separately or in the form of a combined property value map. For the study of vacant and open land, the pattern of land values alone are needed; for the study of renewal areas and other built-up areas where the public acquisition of land and buildings may be involved, the combined form of property value map is generally needed.

In general, market value appraisals, even on a sampling basis, provide the most accurate source of information for constructing land value maps. Where no recent comprehensive study of property values has been undertaken or where no funds are available to finance such a study, assessed values as prepared by the city and county tax offices are frequently used as a substitute source of information. These values usually bear only very approximate relationships to true market values, and such relationships may vary from one part of the city to another. According to local assessment practices, assessed values are usually pegged under the estimated "true" value by some established percentage relationship. Figure 33 illustrates a land value map based on assessed valuations. Various critical areas on such maps can be crudely spot checked by reference to known sales prices in land or property transactions at dates corresponding to those of the tax information. These investigations serve to evaluate in a rough way the extent to which assessed valuations deviate from market values for land and properties in different locations. Rough indications of trends in land values in different parts of the urban area may be noted by reference to a historical series of land value maps, that is, graphic presentations of the patterns of values such as that shown in Figure 33 for past intervals of time. However, to insure comparability, adjustments must often be made to correct for changes in relationships between assessed and market values, and in the change in the value of the dollar during the periods under observation.

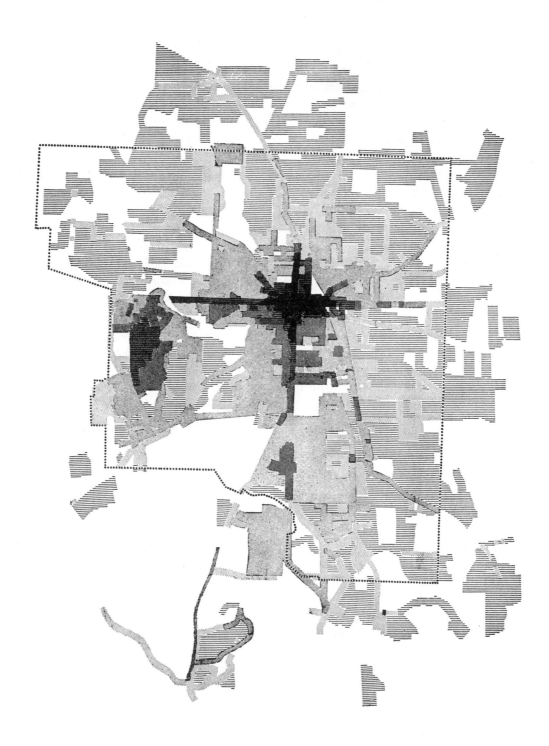

Studies of Aesthetic Features of the Urban Area

Along with the more utilitarian features of urban land, land use planning is also concerned with the perceptual aspects of the urban environment, its aesthetic qualities, and the preservation and development of natural features in a manner calculated to enhance these qualities for the enjoyment of city residents. Seemingly this aspect of land use and development would require no special emphasis, for aesthetics has long been linked with the basic objectives of city planning—indeed, as we have seen, the very origins of city planning and its early development possessed a strong aesthetic orientation. Yet as the field has developed and matured and as the kinds of tasks city planners are called upon to undertake have multiplied, taking them into engineering, economic, and social science investigations of all kinds, the aesthetic aspects of land development have sometimes been slighted as "old shoe" or "frilly." Fortunately, this point of view appears to be only a transient phase in the maturing of the profession, and since World War II, urban aesthetics has assumed a far more important role in the total approach to urban development.

Perhaps more responsible for the lull in this aspect of land use planning is the inherently fugitive character of norms as they apply to aesthetics and the difficulties of defining and ordering aesthetic factors into anything approaching an analytical framework. However, some recent research into the perceptual qualities of cities is beginning to point the way toward a more systematic approach to the creative use of aesthetic features in land use planning, one that is developing more on a reasoned and less on an intuitive basis. Lynch has observed that urban areas possess distinct and recordable qualities that affect an individual's perceptual satisfactions with the urban environment.[35] In addition to the generally recognized factor of size, he suggests that density, grain, the outline or shape, and the

Figure 33. Illustrative Map of Assessed Land Values. The highest front-foot values are shown in black, with the wide vertical hatch being the lowest and the blank areas being either tax-free or assessed on an acreage basis. The expected decrease of values outward from the CBD is graphically illustrated by the finger-like extensions of high-value land following the main radials. The large pocket of high-value land north of the CBD is the country club residential district, and the scattered small pockets are shopping centers or industrial tracts. (*Source:* Greensboro Department of Planning, "Land Use Plan, Greensboro Metropolitan Area," 1948.)

---

[35] Kevin Lynch, "The Form of Cities," *Scientific American*, April, 1954.

internal pattern of cities are all dimensions of the urban area that can be
observed. These affect the pleasantness of city living, the subconscious or
conscious awareness, the positive and negative response that people experience in following the daily path to and from work, in making shopping
trips, or in taking an occasional outing. The placement of key functional
areas and buildings, the location of circulation routes, and the siting of
residential and other areas in relation to each and every other feature,
and how they relate to the sun, prevailing winds, and existing vistas—all
of these considerations are elements of aesthetics which enter into the land
use planning task.

Williams' approach to studying the aesthetic characteristics of cities is
especially well suited to recording features for the preliminary land use plan
for which a general reconnaissance is sufficient.[36] What he terms the "visual
survey" consists of two parts: one which identifies three-dimensional characteristics of the city's site and the man-made features which have been
added to the site, and a second which records significant paths and vantage
points from which the city can be visually perceived. For purposes of the
first part of the survey, he has developed a classification of city sites into six
basic ground forms:

1. Level or gently sloping or rolling sites.
2. Sloping sites, backed by hills or steeper slopes.
3. Valley or gorge sites.
4. Amphitheatrical or fan-shaped sites.
5. Bowl-shaped sites.
6. Ridged or hilltop sites.

Williams then classifies man-made features into the following five forms:

1. Urban textures.
2. Green areas.
3. Circulation facilities.
4. Paved open spaces.
5. Individually significant architectural masses, including vertical slab-like, mas-
   sive, and horizontal forms.

For purposes of the second part of the survey, he has developed five ways
in which the city may be perceived: the panorama, the skyline, the vista,
the urban open space, and through the experience of the individual in
motion.

On the basis of this system for studying the perceptual aspects of the
city, the observer may actually conduct a "visual survey" in the field and
record the features about the city that are important to take into account
in both land use planning and more detailed later stages of site planning.

[36] Sydney H. Williams, "Urban Aesthetics," *The Town Planning Review,* July, 1954.

Important ground forms can be sketched or noted directly on a map by reference to topographic maps and aerial photographs and by field observation. Man-made features particularly important to preserve and visually accentuate in subsequent planning studies can be outlined or spotted, and significant skyline views, vistas, and open space systems to be utilized and enhanced in future development can be similarly noted and supplemented by sketches. A sketchbook and photo album record of the important features observed in the field would provide a valuable additional means for summarizing data collected in the field.

Lynch's approach to the perceptual form of the city in a sense is an extension of some of the more basic observations made in the foregoing type of survey and is more suited to the advanced and detailed work necessary in the development of the comprehensive plan.[37] He has developed two complementing parts to his investigative technique. In one the planner systematically records key perceptual features in a field survey, and in the other a sample of the population is interviewed to obtain insights into the extent that the people of the community are sensitive to the features noted in the first survey. Lynch focuses on what he calls the "imageability" of the city—the features about the city that persist as an image in a person's memory.

In the first aspect of the investigation, two or three trained observers make independent reconnaissance trips on foot, by automobile, and by other common means of movement. These trips are made during the daylight and nighttime periods of the day, along both preselected paths and paths of their own selection. When these investigators have completed their surveys, they prepare field analysis maps and report on both strengths and weaknesses recalled about the pattern of the city, particularly with respect to paths, edges, nodes, districts, and landmarks. In the second paralleling investigation involving interviews with a representative sample of the city's population, Lynch has respondents draw sketches—one showing the person's conception of the important and interesting features of the city, a diagram that a visitor to the city might use to find his way about, and the other showing for one or two imaginary trips the routes and observations a person would be able to make along the way. In addition each respondent lists what he considers to be the most distinctive parts of the community and answers a few standardized questions directed to all respondents. From these investigations the "public image" is compared with the visual forms recorded by the trained observers. Lynch recommends a second somewhat similar survey of a smaller sample of residents to pursue in greater detail the dominant images discovered in the first set of interviews. This is fol-

---

[37] Kevin Lynch, *The Image of the City,* Cambridge: Harvard University and Technology Presses, 1960.

lowed by an intensive field investigation of these elements by the crew of trained observers. He sees this type of investigation as a continuing one which supplies what is needed in treating the visual form of the urban region in plans for its future development.

Jacobs and Jones propose another kind of survey approach.[38] Concerned with the study of significant historical values as well as aesthetic features, they have directed their attention to devising a survey technique which can be used in defining these kinds of features so that a positive effort can be made to conserve them in plans for renewal and growth areas. Under their visual classification system, attention is directed to (1) "sensory material," that is, color, texture, pattern, shape, and rhythm, (2) noteworthy "forms," both of an isolated kind and as an interrelated series of forms, and (3) "expressions" of historical or symbolic significance. Results of investigations are evaluated in terms of indifference curves of the kind that economists use in the analysis of supply and demand functions, and conventional perspective sketches are used to portray findings of particular relevance in the conservation of historical or cultural features of aesthetic significance.

Livability Studies and Land Use

One final form of investigation warrants consideration in this list of tooling-up studies. This is the livability investigation whch seeks to get at expectations and preferences of people in a particular urban area as to the makeup and qualities a city should possess as development proceeds. Restating the meaning attributed to "livability" in Chapter 1, it may be defined as the sum total of the qualities in the urban setting which induce in the residents a feeling of satisfaction and a sense of well-being.

To define livability qualities in the city which evoke feelings of satisfaction among urban residents involves two related kinds of investigative effort—one concerned with the behavior of residents and the other with their attitudes. The first gets at their choices or preferences as observed or inferred from their modes of behavior, and the other gets at them directly or indirectly from statements of attitude or feeling. Here we are not directly concerned with activity systems as discussed in Chapter 6, nor are we concerned with a public opinion poll as a device for seeking approval or disapproval from among a set of stated alternatives. Rather, the concern here is with location behavior and related attitudes which stem from livability considerations.

An investigation of livability must cover at least two mutually related

---

[38] Stephen W. Jacobs and Barclay G. Jones, "City Design Through Conservation," a processed monograph available from the authors, Ithaca: Cornell University, 1960.

areas—the urban resident's sensitivity to socio-economic dimensions of livability and his response to livability as a physical concept. As brought out in Chapter 1, the socio-economic dimension involves what we can call a "need" and a "desire" level of livability. For example, a person's feelings about livability tend to be colored by his sense of job security and the opportunities he has for mixing with friends, seeing relatives, or in other ways engaging in social interaction. These socio-economic considerations may be equated with "needs." But frequently also figuring in the urban resident's feelings about livability is a concern for prestige. Actions and attitudes of this dimension may be classed under the heading of "desires." Prestige is a mercurial aspect of livability. It is variable from one social group to another and changes from time to time. It exists by virtue of some consensus of tastes and is generally exclusive to one stratum of society. Scarcity is a factor affecting the intensity of desire for a prestige quality, and when it becomes widely available it begins to lose its importance as a livability factor. While these considerations may not be a particularly valid basis for developing plans, they are factors which have a pronounced effect on location behavior of urban residents, which is a matter of direct concern in developing plans. Consequently attention needs to be directed to the social dimensions of location behavior—to underlying social desires as well as fundamental social needs. But until rigorously tested survey instruments and standardized scales for interpretation of results are available, the investigation of this aspect of livability will remain relatively general and of limited usefulness.

Physical dimensions of livability are less elusive, and survey research techniques are beginning to be used in determining how the physical livability of the city affects the sense of well-being of urban families. However, studies of this kind must be developed in the context of livability in the larger sense, and survey techniques must be developed to get at the relative weight of physical as opposed to socio-economic considerations.

Wilson's work at North Carolina's Center for Urban and Regional Studies constitutes a pioneering effort of this kind.[39] Drawing on earlier exploratory work in widely divergent situations—in Radburn, Harlem, Fresh Meadows, Greenbelt, and various North Carolina communities—and with consultation from a social psychologist, he designed and tested a survey instrument aimed at identifying key livability factors. Applied to carefully constructed samples of families in two North Carolina cities, the survey instrument identified sources of satisfaction and irritation through three lines of investigation. One focused on factors affecting the respondent family's past

[39] Robert L. Wilson, "Livability of the City: Attitudes and Urban Development," in F. Stuart Chapin, Jr., and Shirley F. Weiss (eds.), *Urban Growth Dynamics*, New York: John Wiley & Sons, Inc., 1962.

behavior in picking a home location; another dealt with the family's sensitivity to various features and qualities about their city and their own particular residential community through a series of attitude questions; and a third utilized photographs and a game device to secure insights into a respondent's livability concepts on a more ideal plane.

The technique deals with very concrete and abstract considerations of livability. For example, each respondent is asked about past moves and reasons for these moves; he is asked to indicate his general satisfaction with his city as a place to live and with his neighborhood; and then attitudes are elicited on particular characteristics in his city and his neighborhood. In this aspect of the survey, livability is pursued on a broad basis. Socio-economic as well as physical dimensions are introduced in order to get some measure of the relative importance of physical factors. At the more abstract level, a person is shown some photographs of strange cities and is asked to indicate which of a series of characteristics (cleanliness, friendliness, crowdedness, dirtiness, etc.) most nearly characterizes his feeling about the pictures. Having done this, the respondent is asked to apply the same list of characteristics to his own neighborhood. In addition to the "warm-up" aspect which tended to sharpen the respondent's basis of evaluating his own neighborhood, this particular feature provides insights into desired qualities.

Two games are used in the interview, both revolving around the respondent's winning his dream house in a TV give-away program. In both games the respondent is told that in addition to winning a house he is receiving from the sponsors of the program a budget of so many markers. On one side of the game board, in effect, he is choosing his neighborhood, and within his budget he "shops" for a lot at the residential density he is willing to live without making too heavy sacrifices in the character and convenience of facilities and services he wants, each of which is also priced at so many markers for varying time-distances away and for varying levels of service. On the other side of the board, choices are similarly made on improvements and public services available to the lot. These games provide valuable insights into factors which affect the urban resident's location behavior, and the analysis of results by income group offers a means of estimating differences in attitudes among various socio-economic groups.

This type of study represents a new kind of investigation in the list of tooling-up studies. It is aimed at replacing the intuitive approach to defining living qualities which are so important to the design phase of land use planning. Beyond these applications, it can be expected to provide data important in setting the parameters for some of the land development models which planning agencies will increasingly be using in testing out plan alternatives.

Chapter 8

Transportation and Land Use

In Chapter 6 an approach to the study of *activity systems* (place-related patterns of interaction) was introduced. It was emphasized there that what people do at particular places—in residential communities, work areas, various places of leisure-time activity, and so on—cannot be separated in our thinking from the other form of interaction which we have classed as *movement systems* or in a broader sense communications systems. Chapter 7 dealt with techniques of studying land use or land available for use to accommodate activity systems. Although it is beyond the scope of this book to go into a paralleling coverage of transportation planning, we would be remiss not to indicate how the interrelationships between transportation and land use planning noted earlier continue in the tooling-up phase. Of course, as noted again in Chapter 12, this theme continues in both the design and test stages in arriving at a land use plan. Accordingly, in this chapter we sketch in some of the fundamentals of studying movements and circulation systems to the extent necessary to clarify relationships between transportation and land use.

Transportation and Land Use Relationships

Transportation is essentially a service which enables people, firms, and various other entities to carry on activities at sites selected for these purposes in separated locations. Just as sanitation systems with their water supply and waste disposal facilities represent another necessary service, thoroughfares and transit systems and their terminal facilities exist to make it possible for concentrations of people, firms, and other human institutions to carry on their activities in different locations in space. From studies of location behavior of these entities, in conjunction with land use studies of the kind described in the last chapter, we know that a major consideration in selecting a location is the accessibility that any particular activity has to certain other activities. The very heart of transportation planning is concerned with the design of circulation systems which maximize accessibility for essential movements between linked activities, giving due consideration to safety, comfort, and amenity as well as cost.

These interrelationships between transportation and land use have been known for some time. In the 'twenties in the regional plan survey of New York, Haig emphasized them in taking the view that transportation is the means for reducing the "friction of space" between activity sites.[1] Mitchell and Rapkin have noted that "specialization of urban activities makes it necessary for establishments and their members to communicate with each other, and consequently there is a pervasive tendency for establishments to make accessibility a major locational consideration. The pattern of land uses is thus a large dependent system in which choice of location of an establishment is made in terms of spatial distribution of others with which it interacts. For some this means access to the largest number of persons, firms, or households—a central location; for others it means convenience in regard to an inexpensive channel of goods-movement; and in still other cases it means actual proximity."[2] More recently, as discussed in Chapter 2, Wingo has investigated the accessibility function as an economic phenomenon in the framework of equilibruim theory, and Guttenberg has utilized accessibility as an organizing feature in his conceptual view of urban spatial structure.[3]

The fundamental nature of these relationships is becoming more and more recognized in practice. In terms of technique, there has been a steady progression of advances made in putting into practice the interrelationships which have long been stressed at the theoretical level. Backed by a strong research and development emphasis on the part of the Bureau of Public Roads, the large metropolitan transportation studies have had a major influence in this respect. The improvements introduced in transportation analysis in the Detroit, Chicago, and Pittsburgh sequence of studies, the important exerimentation at Penn-Jersey, and the subsequent studies following these early leads have brought about successive advances in the analysis of these relationships. The latest studies have been in the direction of making land use and transportation analyses an integrally related process, and in the Minneapolis–St. Paul study we see the administrative arrangements catching up with the logic of analytical techniques. For the first time the transportation planning sponsor (Bureau of Public Roads)

---

[1] Robert M. Haig and Roswell C. McCrae, "Major Economic Factors in Metropolitan Growth and Arrangement," *Regional Survey of New York and Its Environs*, I, New York: Regional Plan of New York and Its Environs, 1927, p. 39.

[2] Robert B. Mitchell and Chester Rapkin, *Urban Traffic, a Function of Land Use*, New York: Columbia University Press, 1954, p. 132.

[3] Lowdon Wingo, Jr., *Transportation and Urban Land*, Washington: Resources for the Future, Inc., 1961; and Albert Z. Guttenberg, "Urban Structure and Urban Growth," *Journal of the American Institute of Planners*, May, 1960.

had a counterpart sponsor in land development planning (Housing and Home Finance Agency), and also for the first time the land use and transportation plans were treated as complementing systems of proposals in the transportation planning process.

Even as these advances were developing, there were indications that other more fundamental changes in approach were in prospect. The Penn-Jersey Transportation Study's exploratory work in the study of the location behavior of households undertaken as a means of estimating the future patterning of residential areas foreshadowed the introduction of more systematic approaches and more rigorous analytical techniques coming into use in land use planning. Voorhees' use of attitude studies in getting at the range of variability in trip-making behavior to be anticipated under differing conditions of home environment and the Twin Cities Metropolitan Planning Commission's use of survey research to get at attitudinal bases of activities as well as movements represent important new developments in the improvement of transportation and land use analyses.[4] Yet even with these steps forward, there still remains a missing element which we may anticipate will be in the picture more and more in the future. This has to do with the need for more systematic consideration of activities as we have discussed them in Chapter 6 as a prior level of analysis to the study of land use. As noted there, we may expect that activities and movements as forms of human behavior will become increasingly the focus of an analysis which precedes the investigation of land use and transportation facility relationships.

Essentially what this means is an effort at forecasting future patterns of human activity—work patterns, shopping patterns, leisure-time patterns, firm linkage patterns, and so on. Such forecasts will require, first, the know-how for constructing existing activity patterns from results of sampling surveys of the kind outlined in Chapter 6, and, second, the development of models which will enable us to simulate spatial configurations of activity patterns under various possible changes in technology, economic levels, social structure, and the underlying attitude and habit systems of urban residents. Once techniques for estimating future activity patterns have been developed, it will then be possible to use these results as parameters for land development models of the kind discussed in Chapter 12. With these improvements in activity and land use analysis, we can anticipate the handling of the dynamic aspect of land use and transporation systems with greater sophistication than has been possible to date. We can expect that the interplay between these two systems can be simulated more meaning-

---

[4] Alan M. Voorhees, "Community Planning Survey, Albany, New York," unpublished study, 1962; and various unpublished work papers concerned with basic research for the Joint Inter-agency Land Use–Transportation Planning Program outlined in *Meeting the Challenge of Metropolitan Growth*, St. Paul: Twin Cities Metropolitan Planning Commission, January, 1963.

fully, with the feedback of one upon the other taken into account on more nearly parallel levels of accuracy. Whatever emerges, we can be sure that transportation and land use models will be useful mainly in studying the implications of proposals, not as an automated substitute for the planning that must go into any particular system of proposals. Of course, we can anticipate that more and more, supplemental models will be introduced as subsystems to the basic activity and trip generation models. These will enable the land use and transportation planners to take into account a wider range of factors (in place of treating them as constants) and to assess more accurately how various alternatives under consideration will affect other parts of the total system. However, land use and transportation plans must still be designed and choices must still be made. The plan which finally emerges as the recommended one will be just as imaginative as the planning that goes into it in the course of this process.

The Transportation Planning Study

To analyze the sufficiency of existing transportation networks and to estimate future requirements in this respect involves two basic investigations paralleling and coordinated with the land use–related studies discussed in the last chapter. One is concerned with the investigation of persons and goods movements and the other with transporation facilities—the location, capacity, condition, and level of service of thoroughfare and mass transportation facilities.

For studies of movements, the transportation engineer has developed a variety of survey techniques. The overall direction and magnitude of vehicular movements are established by a *traffic volume survey*. Comparable surveys of mass transportation provide measures of the volume and direction of movement of people by transit facilities for different hours of the day and night. The purposes of movement and the places between which the movements occur are obtained through an *origin and destination survey*. Volume measurements are obtained by traffic counts, procured by persons or by mechanical devices recording traffic at selected stations throughout the thoroughfare network. The O-D survey obtains information on intra- and intercity movements, and the most reliable data are obtained by home interviews (usually organized on a sampling basis), supplemented by information procured by stopping a sample of the vehicles passing through the "cordon line," a line drawn around the urban interview area. Special information on commercial movements is obtained from truck and taxicab operators. Results of the traffic volume survey provide a measure of the total movement over the system of streets surveyed, showing the actual *travel lines* of all traffic in the aggregate. Although surveys permit summaries of movements by 15-minute intervals, results are usually mapped for the peak hour or a 24-hour period. The O-D survey results can be used to establish for various trip purposes, for similar time intervals, *desire lines,* that is, what the travel lines would be if straight-line routes were provided between various origins and destinations.[5] The results also show the mode of transportation and the relative importance of these desire lines at different times of the day for each mode.

While these surveys provide a description of the extent and nature of person and goods movements, they do not explain directly the factors that produce these movements. These explanations are bound up in the land use arrangements of the city and the nature of activities carried on in various functional use areas that we have been discussing. Apart from viewing activity systems as a variable in trip-making behavior, the transportation planner deals with other variables. Thus, besides considering differences in trip generation rates of, say, household activities as opposed to firm activities, he must also consider the intensity at which activities are carried on in places accommodating these activities. High density of residential development or high density of employment obviously creates high demands for movement. At the same time the rate of demand for households is a function of income, car ownership, transit usage habits, and time-distance considerations; and the rate of demand for firms is a function of sales volumes, time-distance to markets, perishability of product, and other goods movement factors. To analyze movements, it is therefore necessary to include in the basic transportation survey an investigation of a wide range of variables.

The other major survey involved in a transportation study is concerned with routes and facilities available to accommodate these movements. For thoroughfares, this aspect of the transportation study goes into such considerations as right-of-way widths, roadway capacity, the type and condition of surfacing, location and capacity of terminal parking facilities, and so on. For mass transportation, it assembles data on such things as type of system, its routes, and their capacities; the amount and condition of rolling stock; the location and character of terminal locations; the service levels; and so on.[6]

---

[5] For a more complete discussion, see National Committee on Urban Transportation, *Origin-Destination and Land Use,* Procedure Manual 2A, and *Conducting a Home Interview Origin-Destination Survey,* Procedure Manual 2B, Chicago: Public Administration Service, 1958.

[6] Techniques in general usage for the conduct and analysis of the major types of transportation surveys are summarized in the work of the National Committee on Urban Transportation. For a general overview of the transportation planning process, see the Committee's *Better Transportation for Your City,* Chicago: Public Administration Service, 1958.

From information obtained in these surveys of movements and facilities, routing systems are classified. For example, in the case of thoroughfares, both functional and design systems of classification are employed. In regard to the first type, most classification systems identify two major *functional classes* of trafficways—the *radial* and the *circumferential* (sometimes called a crosstown or loop). A third functional class of thoroughfare sometimes distinguished from these two primary classes is the *connector,* which, as its name implies, serves as a connection between two or more major radial or circumferential systems of movement or between major focal points of traffic.

Another system of classification in general usage specifies the *design classes* of streets. According to the size of the urban area and local preferences, it may consist of upwards of three classes. The National Committee on Urban Transportation has suggested four classes: the expressway system, the major arterial system, the secondary arterial system, and the local street system.[7] The expressway system generally includes freeways, all parkways with full control of access, and those expressways where there is at least partial control, for example, where there are limitations of intersections at grade, prohibition of private driveway connections, and so on. The major arterial system consists of all major streets and those expressways and parkways with lower-order controls over access. The secondary street system consists of the connectors between the local street system and the higher-order systems and feeder streets which pick up and distribute traffic within residential neighborhoods and communities. Not generally included in the thoroughfare network is the residual class, the local street system which is designed primarily to provide access to adjacent land uses.

On the basis of these surveys, the transportation system as it exists today is summarized and evaluated. At this juncture it is necessary to spell out in explicit form the goals to be achieved in the transportation system and the principles and standards to be followed in achieving these objectives. Commonly, goals are set forth in terms of such criteria as (1) reducing time spent in movement and generally promoting the convenience of the users of different systems, (2) maintaining an adequate measure of safety and taking into account tension and other considerations of health, (3) minimizing capital and operating costs from a public point of view and a user point of view, and (4) promoting sound land development. Principles generally define location and design guides to be followed in the planning of the transportation systems, and standards give minimum specifications in the location and design of facilities and define acceptable levels of service.

Once these ground rules of the transportation study are established, an

---

[7] *Ibid.*

analysis of future travel patterns in the metropolitan area is undertaken. These aspects of the study involve inputs from land use planning analyses in estimating the magnitude of future movements. The results of these studies in turn are used in traffic assignment models which take into account mode of transportation and choice of routes in each system. While it is beyond the scope of this book to get into the complexities of these models and the transportation planning procedures followed in translating trip projections thus obtained into networks and facilities, we may note that this process must be integrated into the land use planning process as taken up in Chapter 12. The plan that emerges from this process represents a choice made from a range of alternatives, each tested for its sufficiency against the goals established at the outset. This plan, together with the land use plan, are the principal components of the general plan.

Part III

Land Use Planning

WE COME NOW to the land use planning process itself. It is a process which looks to the basic theoretical orientations set forth in Part I for its conceptual guidelines. Drawing on the information developed from the kinds of studies set forth in Part II, it seeks to fashion a balanced and integrated set of proposals for the future use of land in the urban area which are generally consistent with theoretical precepts and yet workable in every practical sense of the meaning.

It is useful at the outset to consider broadly the relationship of urban planning to public policies, particularly developmental policies. As suggested in the Introduction and as is evident throughout Parts I and II, city planning is viewed as a process—a series of evolutionary and rationally organized steps which lead to proposals for guided urban growth and development. Various meanings have been ascribed to "developmental policies" or, more specifically, "urban land use policies." Some view these policies as something akin to a statement of general principles for planning, and they are thus formulated before plans are developed. Others consider them to be embodied in the plans themselves, and when a plan is officially adopted, the proposals contained in the plan become official urban land use policies. Still a third usage considers them to be statements of the directions in which the urban area should move in order to achieve the objectives of, and implement the proposals contained in, a plan. For example, in this sense policies might take the form of general specifications for zoning, urban renewal, and so on. In the usage of the term here there are present elements of all these meanings.

Urban land use policies are considered here to be a series of guides to consistent and rational public and private decisions in the use and development of urban land. They are maxims to guide land development decisions in principle. They give direction to the urban planning process, but they also become conditioned by the findings and proposals developed from the planning process. We may conceive of the formulation of policies as proceeding from the general to the particular, with each level of policy-making supplying the foundation for subsequent more detailed policy determinations. But within the planning process the preparation of a specific plan proposal for the coordinated development of urban land is in many respects contingent upon a variety of prior policy decisions. Thus in a very fundamental sense the planning process must play an important role in supplying policy alternatives and pressing for decisions from the earliest and broadest level of policy formulation on down to the more detailed levels of policy determination. This aspect of the planning function can therefore be considered one of supplying alternatives at progressively more detailed levels of decision-making, with each successive stage in policy formulation building on previously made choices of a more general character.

To illustrate, the hierarchy of policy decisions might follow roughly in this order. Perhaps the highest order of policy decision could be viewed as a choice between urban development stabilized at a certain level (measured in terms of economic development, employment, population, land area in development, and so on) and urban development proceeding on an indeterminant and noncontainment basis. Conceivably there could be gradation of several choices here rather than these two extremes. In any case, involved in this illustrative choice are a variety of social, economic, and public interest considerations relating to public finance, health, safety, convenience, and the general amenities of urban living. A decision on the first alternative—containment of urban development at a particular level—would involve in the planning implementation of the decision an emphasis on balance within the limits of a known size of ultimate growth. A decision on the noncontainment alternative would involve an incremental approach to the development of land, transportation, and community facilities, one which accommodates the needs of growth as and when they occur, but still according to a plan.

A second level of policy decision might relate to the basic orientations in the way land development and transportation systems are to be accommodated. Although there are gradations here too, this decision might be posed as a choice between concentrated expansion concentric to existing patterns of development and dispersed expansion to a polynucleated array of outlying centers. In its purest form the first land development alternative involves the presumption of a single major center with functionally related suburban outlets of business and radial developments of industry and commerce generally concentrated along existing or proposed railroads and highways. The indicated transportation system is essentially the conventional web pattern consisting of major radial arteries and transit routes fed by auxiliary crosstown, feeder, and local service systems. In the purest form of the second alternative, though the downtown area of the central city would continue as the dominant center for certain metropolitan-wide functions, it is supplemented by functionally differentiated or somewhat independent centers of business and industry, each providing a substantial proportion of the employment and services for its own surrounding localized area. Here we are dealing with high-order freeway and rapid transit systems providing interconnections between centers, with a series of lower-order web systems of circulation emanating from each major terminus of the higher-order systems.

Following from the above succession of decisions are many other related policy considerations. For example, a third-order series of policy decisions might relate to homogeneity versus heterogeneity of development among functional use types and among various activities within each use type.

They might involve questions of intensity of development, what might be referred to as "open-order versus *closed-ranks" development patterns. Along with intensity would be questions of density of use: high, medium, or low residential densities and high, medium, or low daytime population densities, and so on. These decisions again bring into play social, economic, and public interest considerations, the decision seeking to strike a balance in such factors as cost-revenue implications for local finance, health, safety, convenience, and the desired level of amenities to urban living.*

The above illustration is indicative of the kind of hierarchy of considerations involved in policy formulation, with policies at each level feeding into the planning process and the findings of the planning process subsequently feeding back into policy decisions. Now obviously many public policy decisions affecting urban development emerge without following such an idealized sequence. Indeed, probably in very few American communities have urban development policy and planning developed in any way approaching such a sequence. But while the full sequence may not be achieved, it is important to note that policy decisions generally do tend to evolve from the general to the particular. In this connection it should also be noted that where decisions are made out of sequence, the point of entry into the hierarchy automatically tends to force decisions of a higher order without the opportunity for deliberate consideration of the broader or more elemental choices involved in these higher-order decisions. It might be noted, too, that there is a dynamic aspect to the foregoing more or less static rendition of the relationships between policy and planning. Just as we think of planning as a continuing process, we must also view policy formulation as a continuous activity. That is, policies may be reconsidered and modified from time to time under changing circumstances. Entire new ones, some being the obverse of policies previously in effect, may be adopted, setting in motion a whole new cycle of policy and planning.

With some modification, the so-called progressive planning approach *can be phased into this kind of policy-making sequence.*[1] *This particular system of planning analysis called for a six-point sequence:*

1. Develop a first estimate of existing conditions and significant trends in the urban area. *In scope this estimate encompasses the full range of planning studies; as to detail, it is abbreviated and general, to be progressively rounded out as the program proceeds.*
2. Determine the principal and most pressing problems and needs, briefly evaluate them, and develop an interim program. *This stage involves the development of a generalized sketch plan intended to serve as a starting point for*

---

[1] First perfected in test demonstration studies by the National Resources Planning Board at the beginning of World War II, the "progressive planning approach" was later set down in *Action for Cities,* Chicago: Public Administration Service, 1945.

352

later phases of the program. As current problems and needs come more fully into perspective and longer-range aspects of the program get under way, the interim sketch plan is progressively refined.

3. Formulate a detailed program indicating priorities for undertaking component studies of comprehensive plan. *This is the step which determines the end product and the time schedule to be followed.*

4. Carry out detailed plan studies according to program and priority. *This phase is essentially one of progressive refinement of studies initiated earlier on an abbreviated basis and presented in generalized form.*

5. Integrate various plan studies into comprehensive plan. *This is the stage in which the individual plan proposals are synthesized and inconsistencies and conflicts are eliminated.*

6. Revise plans as conditions alter their applicability. *This will be a continuing activity of observing trends, revising studies, and adjusting plans.*

Following what might be regarded as a circular *rather than a* straight-line *sequence, this approach can be made to gear directly into the cycle-like sequence described above by which policies become formulated and adopted. As policy decisions are reached of a broad and general nature, planning solutions can be developed in generalized form. As these solutions are reviewed and decisions are reached of a more detailed order, the planning process picks up from there to carry the solution to a more detailed stage. Thus both policies and plans are progressively refined to the point where an acceptable plan proposal emerges. But as conditions alter the applicability of earlier findings and proposals, policies and plans are reviewed and often modified. This explains the emphasis in the field on* planning *rather than on* plans.

The above procedural framework can be modified in several ways, not only to give more direct recognition to the relationship between the technical program and policy-making, but also to introduce into the system provision for reviewing various policy alternatives. While the same basic procedures can be followed in plan-by-plan studies of various community facility elements included in the comprehensive plan, it is more useful for our purposes here to set the procedure in terms of the land use and transportation plans. The staging of the technical program can be summarized as follows:

1. *Preliminary Planning*
   a. *Make reconnaissance surveys and develop a first estimate of existing conditions and significant trends in the urban area.*
   b. *Determine the principal and most pressing problems and needs, briefly evaluate them, and develop an interim program.*
   c. *Identify land development goals for the growth of the metropolitan area and develop generalized horizon-year schemes to define alternative growth patterns, spelling out the basic policy assumptions of each.*
   d. *Consult decision-making groups for policy guidance.*

    e. *On the basis of indicated policy preferences, carry the planning analysis from the generalized scheme to the preliminary plan stage. This will generally mean taking one basic horizon-year policy orientation and developing perhaps two or three preliminary land use plans geared to a 20- to 25-year planning period. These comparative plans focus on policy considerations of a more specific order than those involved in the horizon-year proposals and usually provide for differing policy assumptions for transportation and/or land development.*

    f. *Develop comparative data on plan alternatives (cost-benefit estimates, time-distance estimates, relative living qualities featured, and so on).*

    g. *Consult again with decision-making groups for further policy guidance.*

2. *General Land Use and Transportation Plan*

    a. *Carry out basic surveys and tooling-up studies, review results, and develop coordinated work program for land use and transportation planning.*

    b. *Carry forward activity studies and land use analyses, and develop provisional land use plan.*

    c. *On the basis of the provisional land use plan and studies of trip-making behavior, estimate future travel patterns, make trip distribution and assignments to transit and thoroughfare networks, and finalize the provisional transportation plan.*

    d. *From tests and subsequent adjustments of provisional land use and transportation proposals, firm up general land use and transportation plan.*

    e. *Prepare capital improvements program showing time schedule, capital and operating costs, and methods of financing.*

3. *Comprehensive Plan*

    a. *Carry out other detailed plan studies, for example, studies of school site requirements, recreation and open space needs, water and waste disposal needs, and so on; obtain policy guidance and develop plans.*

    b. *Integrate various plan studies into comprehensive plan and introduce adjustments in overall public improvements program and capital budget.*

    c. *On the basis of a continuing inventory system and periodic restudy, revise plans as conditions alter their applicability.*

The importance of gearing the technical aspect of the program to policy-making is clearly suggested in the steps listed for the preliminary planning stage. Although not listed as specific steps, consultation with policy-makers will be important in the second stage when provisional plans emerge and again in the third stage when the comprehensive plan emerges.

This approach supplies a sequential framework for the analytical procedures of land use planning taken up below. It is thus clear that the city planner utilizes techniques of analysis that are variable in their detail, the level of detail being fitted to the stage that has been reached by the city council and planning commission in the formulation of public policy. While the city planner is not barred from proceeding immediately to the most detailed level of land use planning, by moving too far ahead of policy decisions he runs the risk of assuming policy choices which never materi-

354

alize, thus removing his proposals from the realities of political action and eventual fulfillment.

The procedures and general approach discussed in the following pages apply primarily to the preliminary planning level of analysis in the sequence outlined above, and more particularly to the 20- to 25-year planning period. Each kind of analysis can be carried into the more exacting studies, and in the larger metropolitan areas machine methods of data analysis can be substituted to advantage for "hand" methods. Chapter 9 presents an overview of the entire land use planning framework; Chapter 10 takes up location requirements for various uses of land; Chapter 11 sets forth approaches for estimating space requirements for each of these uses; and finally, Chapter 12 discusses the applications of these analyses in the design of the urban land use plan and indicates how land development models used in conjunction with transportation models can be employed to check out the implications of various policy alternatives.

Chapter 9

The Plan and Its
Analytical Framework

In no aspect of the planning process is the city planner dealing with more fundamental, more important determinants of guided physical expansion and renewal than he is in the development of the land use plan. Land use data assembled and plotted as described in Chapter 7 record these patterns as they have occurred in the past, whether in haphazard or in guided form. The land use plan reflects an analysis of urban activity systems and a carefully studied estimate of future land requirements for expansion and renewal, showing how development in the urban area should proceed in the future to insure the best possible physical environment for urban living, the most economic use of land, and the proper balance in use from a cost-revenue point of view. Fundamentally, then, the land use plan embodies a proposal as to how expansion and renewal should proceed in the future, recognizing local objectives and generally accepted principles of health, safety, convenience, economy, and the general amenities of urban living.

Definitions and Applications

While there appears to be general agreement on these fundamentals of land use planning, there are in usage a variety of connotations to the term "land use plan." As might be expected, "land use map" is sometimes loosely and interchangeably used with "land use plan," especially among lay groups such as planning commission members and citizen groups in general. Even among professional planners, this confusion is not entirely unheard of. More prevalent and similarly a source of confusion is the interchangeable use of "zoning plan" and "land use plan." Finally, considerable vagueness persists as to the functional relationship of the land use plan to the comprehensive or master plan.

Although distinctions between these terms are made below for purposes of clarifying the land use plan concept employed herein, it should be remembered that in American city planning practice there is as yet no full agreement on these meanings. Nevertheless, there is considerable agreement on some terms in professional circles. The land use map is generally recognized for what it is, simply a map showing how the land and structures on the land are used for urban purposes at a particular time, past or present. The land use plan is generally recognized as a proposal for the future use of land and the structures built upon the land. As a proposal, it is more than a map; it embodies a whole array of principles and the assumptions and reasoning followed in arriving at this proposal. Thus, while the land use map is a factual description of the urban setting, usually as it exists today, the land use plan is a generalized but scaled presentation of a scheme for the future development of the urban area.

The so-called "zoning plan," as an adjunct to a zoning ordinance, is generally conceived as a scheme of districting an urban area for purposes of regulating use, density of population, coverage of lots, bulk of structures, and so on. Zoning is one of several legal devices for implementing the proposals for land development as set forth in the land use plan. As a legal instrument, it is exacting in detail. The land use plan is concerned with use and intensity of development but is generalized in form. The usage of "zoning plan" in place of "zoning map" in some cases may be intended to convey the notion of a proposal as opposed to an officially adopted map of zoning districts, but even as a proposal the zoning plan is, or should be, aimed at *achieving* the objectives of the land use plan. Thus the latter is a prerequisite of the former. Indeed, no zoning ordinance and its accompanying districting scheme are likely to be comprehensive in scope and sound in content unless based on a previously prepared land use plan.

Apart from these rather elemental distinctions, there are variations in the connotation attached to "land use plan" when it is properly used to refer to a generalized proposal for the future development of an urban area. In many parts of the country, by legislative definition or by common usage, the "land use plan" is used to refer to that portion of the master plan which is devoted to proposals for industrial, commercial, business, and residential uses—the so-called *private uses* of land, the public uses being covered by the term "community facilities." In other cases, while being construed as a part of the master plan, proposals for both *public and private uses* of land are considered to be a part of the land use plan. For example, San Francisco is guided by the following statement from its city-county charter: "The master plan . . . shall include a land use plan showing the proposed general distribution and the general location and extent of housing, business, industry, recreation, education, and other categories of public and private uses of land, and recommended standards of population density and building intensity." [1]

This is the essential meaning of the term as it is used here. But within the framework of the "progressive planning approach," there is some latitude for variation in the extent of detail that may appear in such a plan at any particular time. In the earliest stage, it is current practice to develop two or more preliminary land use plans, each to explore and present a different policy emphasis. In the usage of this book, *the preliminary land use plan* is a study plan which emerges from this initial planning stage. It presents a first general but comprehensive estimate of land use requirements relative to location and amount of land to be reserved for each public and private use. As pointed out earlier, the analytical framework presented here is developed to correspond to this general level of detail. The preliminary land use plan is usually developed concurrently with the preliminary thoroughfare plan, and these two generalized studies in combination provide a point of departure for the development of *the general land use and transportation plan*. This plan is sometimes viewed as an intermediate step toward the comprehensive plan, and it is sometimes regarded and may be adopted as the first element of the comprehenhive plan. Under the first view, studies of community facilities are completed and adjustments in the general land use and transportation plan introduced before adoption; in the second, as each of these community facility elements are completed, it is adopted, with the necessary amendments to the general land use and transportation element of the plan accomplished at the same time. Thus in the framework of this concept, *the comprehensive plan* is a synthesis of these component, more detailed plans, including not only systems of use areas, but all forms of circulation and their terminal facilities and all kinds of utility requirements, the rudiments of which were first outlined in overall form in the preliminary land use plan and the preliminary thoroughfare plan.

In short, the preliminary planning stage first examines land development alternatives presented for a horizon year in generalized form. Then on the basis of a chosen land development policy emphasis, this stage proceeds to the development of 20- to 25-year schemes (presented to scale) as study plans of the way in which differing transportation and other policies would affect land development. The selected scheme or study plan emerging

---

[1] San Francisco Department of City Planning, *Land Use Section of the Master Plan of the City and County of San Francisco*, January, 1953, mimeo., p. 1.

from this preliminary planning stage becomes the *parti* for the second stage in which the general land use and transportation plan is developed.

Inherent in the progressive planning approach is a recognition of the need for an overall general plan to guide day-to-day operational decisions of the planning office and to provide a basis for rational solutions for zoning and subdivision control problems, urban renewal programs, and similar pressing needs until such time as the comprehensive plan is developed. The preliminary land use plan selected at the conclusion of the first round of studies (hereafter referred to sometimes as the "land use plan") may serve as an interim guide. Where decisions on public facilities must be made prior to the adoption of a general land use and transportation plan or a comprehensive plan, the land use plan chosen in the preliminary planning stage provides a useful guide to land acquisition for such public facilities as schools, playgrounds, firehalls, and so on. It becomes a useful guide to private developers, particularly promoters of large-scale developments such as residential communities, shopping centers, organized industrial districts, and so on. As previously mentioned, it is a guide for zoning, subdivision control, and urban renewal studies. And finally, it is of invaluable assistance to public and private agencies concerned with utilities and transportation. It indicates areas where water, sewerage, and private utility systems are likely to encounter new or increased demands in the future, and insofar as the future land use pattern is a factor, it provides the necessary kind of information for making rational decisions concerning major airports, military air bases, transit extensions, railroad routing, and so on.

One further observation should be made here concerning the material covered in this and subsequent chapters. We are in a stage of development in the field in which improvements in methods of analysis are almost a daily occurrence. Mathematical models and systems analysis techniques are being tested as aids in developing plans. While recognizing the great importance of these developments, even if these systems had had time for shakedown tests, it is perhaps more useful in a text of this kind to keep the focus on the underlying rationale of the analytical process in its most elemental form. In directing the emphasis in this direction, the discussion here serves not only as a learning tool but also as an aid to understanding and evaluating the more complex and exacting approaches which must eventually be used. So the reader is cautioned that the "hand methods" presented in the following pages are useful mainly as estimating techniques for preliminary planning and as a general reference system for the more advanced forms of analysis involved in the later stages of the progressive planning approach.

With this general introduction to the land use plan, we may now turn to the analytical procedures. At the outset it is helpful to obtain an overview of these procedures first in terms of what the table of contents of a land use plan report would show, and then in terms of the sequence which would be followed in the technical studies.

Elements of the Land Use Plan Study

Although there can be many variations in the way they are grouped and presented, in general the basic elements of the study will include the following: a statement of local objectives; a discussion of existing trends in the use, nonuse, and misuse of land; a presentation of future land use requirements including a statement of the principles to be followed and the assumptions made; a description of each sketch land use plan among the alternatives presented; and the identification of proposals involved and policies implied in each. In a later stage in the progression of planning studies in which a general land use and transportation plan emerges, the content of this type of report includes recommendations for the implementation of the plan.

Statement of Objectives

Broadly, land use objectives are guides to the way in which land development should proceed in fulfillment of basic needs and wants of residents, firms, and institutions of the metropolitan area concerning interaction opportunities, living qualities, costs, and minimum levels of health and safety. The presumption is that in the course of the tooling-up studies, the residents, the management of firms, the local governments, the various organizations, and other institutions in the metropolitan area would have been consulted on their development requirements and that out of this reconnaissance the range of expectations and the extent of consensus can be evaluated and a statement of goals derived. Referring to the cycle identified in Figure 3 of Chapter 1, by this time tooling-up studies have probed into values and provided insights into needs and wants of these entities or their agents, and the task is to define goals as a basis for presenting planning alternatives and subsequently reaching a decision on a general land use plan.

More specifically, the statement of objectives broadly identifies the kind of urban environment it is expected that proposals of the plan will achieve when development subsequently occurs in the metropolitan area. The identification of goals grows out of the staff work of the planning agency, but the goal-setting function is generally that of the policy-making groups of the metropolitan area.

While there may be similarities in objectives, the priority and emphasis will tend to vary from one city to another. The following statement of the Hartford region objectives taken from a study of regional growth alternatives is illustrative of broadly stated land use planning objectives:[2]

1. Provide for the orderly growth and development of the region while preserving a measure of diversity among its parts.
2. Allocate land in the region, recognizing that it may become a scarce resource, to be conserved rather than wasted.
3. Satisfy the multiple needs of a society with increasing amounts of leisure time in general, and preserve the amenities associated with the region's "open character" in particular.
4. Maximize the opportunity for a wide range of choice in residential living arrangements in general, and serve the varying housing needs of the region's population in particular.
5. Help promote sound economic development and assure employment stability of both the region and the state.
6. Minimize conflicts with residential areas and facilitate the provision of required public services, particularly transportation and utilities.

The alternative approaches developed on the basis of these objectives in this particular region assumed basic acceptance of the notion of channeling growth into areas around defined regional and subregional centers (as opposed to indiscriminate dispersion throughout the region); a ceiling on development in terms of population size; a reservation of permanent open space of a certain proportion of total development; and a certain proportion of new dwelling units devoted to multifamily housing. Obviously, other regions would emphasize other aspects of development in their set of conditioning assumptions. However, the important thing to note here is that these assumptions in effect represent that planning agency's interpretation of the values that residents of this region hold, constituting in their view a valid basis for setting goals.

It should be noted that while one and only one set of goals is involved, there are different approaches that can be followed in achieving goals. This, of course, is why alternatives are introduced in the preliminary planning stage. As indicated earlier, these alternatives frequently feature contrasting transportation policies. While the general land use and transportation plan

---

[2] Capitol Region Planning Agency, *Regional Plan Alternatives*, Hartford: Capitol Region Planning Agency, November, 1961.

which emerges in the next stage in the progressive planning approach may be predicated on the same goals, it is possible that in the course of reviews of the preliminary sketches, where problems and issues are brought more clearly into view, refinements and modifications will be introduced. Also, it should be noted that the underlying rationale of the progressive planning approach takes cognizance of the likelihood that goals may need to be re-examined over time.

Existing Conditions and Future Needs

With the objectives set forth, the next section in the land use plan report is generally a description of the urban setting as it is today. This usually consists of a presentation of the results of the urban land studies, including maps and tabular summaries as discussed in Chapter 7. This would be the section in which activity systems would be featured (Chapter 6).

Following the summaries of existing land use characteristics, the use capabilities of vacant, open, and renewal land, and so on, there is a major section concerned with the summary of future land use requirements. This describes requirements of both a qualitative and quantitative character. In the former category is a statement of principles setting forth relationships to be observed in setting aside areas for various land uses. This statement deals with the *relationships in the broad patterns of use areas and the location criteria for each specific class of use* employed in the design phase of the plan. In the second category is a statement of *space requirements for each class of use*.

Plan Alternatives and Policy Implications

Once the land use planning requirements have been presented, the section of the report devoted to the plan alternatives follows naturally. Here, in accord with objectives, the limitations of the existing pattern of uses, and the principles and requirements previously established, the basic features of alternative sketch plans and the qualities of each are set forth and the policy implications identified.

To obtain policy guidance on higher-order choices in metropolitan growth and development in a hierarchical array of policies of the kind noted in the Introduction to this part of this book, as noted earlier many planning agencies are beginning to break the preliminary planning stage down into at least two phases. In one phase, plans may be presented for a horizon date in the metropolitan area's development, say 40 or 50 years ahead.

Generalized representations of growth patterns are commonly presented in comparative form: the nucleated, lineal, compact, lattice, and so on. In the Hartford study, five different patterns are presented and their qualities and policy implications identified.[3] In Washington's *A Plan for the Year 2000,* not only are a range of alternatives presented, but the planning agencies preparing the report recommended a pattern.[4] In the Bridgeport region, one of three alternatives for the year 2000 was recommended.[5]

In the second phase, alternatives are set forth in the 20- to 25-year conventional time span of the general or comprehensive plan. These plans are fitted to land forms, and space allocations to uses of various intensities are presented approximately to scale. It is possible that other intermediate phases would be introduced where policies need further clarification. In some metropolitan areas the policy choices may be presented and decisions reached without formal publication of alternative schemes. In these instances formal publication may not be undertaken until the second stage of the process identified earlier, with the general land use and transportation plan being featured. The chapters that follow are concerned with techniques that would be used mainly in the scaled phase of preliminary planning.

In the later stages of the progressive planning sequence, a single concept of metropolitan growth and development thus becomes the guide for developing the comprehensive plan. At the general land use and transportation plan stage, the report includes sections on priorities and the programming of costs. Usually a last section of the report at this stage formulates a tentative program for the implementation of the plan. If the plan is adopted by the planning commission, the program assumes some official significance and provides the basis for interim action on developmental matters until such time as the comprehensive plan is adopted and its implementing program supersedes the interim one. Broadly, this program is customarily concerned with zoning, subdivision control, a housing code, and similar *regulatory measures*; a public works expenditure program, an urban renewal program, and similar *developmental measures* for public and private action; *public policies* for re-enforcing plan proposals with respect to such matters as supplying or extending services, tax reform, and so on;

---

[3] *Ibid.* A follow-up study, *Municipal Taxation and Regional Development,* Hartford: Capitol Region Planning Agency, March, 1963, examines the implications of various alternative growth patterns for taxation to the local taxing jurisdictions.

[4] National Capital Planning Commission and National Capital Regional Planning Council, *A Plan for the Year 2000: The National Capital,* Washington: U.S. Government Printing Office, 1961.

[5] Greater Bridgeport Regional Planning Agency, *Recommended Development Policies, Preliminary Regional Plan,* Trumbull, Conn.: Greater Bridgeport Regional Planning Agency, June, 1963.

and a *program for the continuing involvement of the community* in the planning process.[6]

General Sequence to Technical Studies

With this organization of the general elements of the land use plan *report* in mind, we can now proceed to outline the major phases in the work of carrying out the land use planning study—*the procedures*. Planning the technical work procedures is a crucial part of the whole operation.[7] Once the nature of the end product has been identified as set forth above, it is important to chart the sequence to the land use planning analyses as a basis for overall guidance and economy of staff effort. This sequence can be organized into three phases.

Initial Spadework

Delineation of Study Areas

The first phase is best labeled as "initial spadework." It is essentially concerned with completing and bringing together the results of tooling-up studies needed in the land use planning analysis. But as pointed out in Part II, in summarizing the data needed from these studies, it is necessary to identify a system of study areas to be used in these analyses. As a practical matter, these delineations must be made in advance of land use planning studies. They include the "planning area" and the subdivision of this larger area into subplanning areas, what we have termed "planning districts."

In general, the *planning area* includes the dominant urban center of special planning interest, the adjoining incorporated or unincorporated areas built up in urban uses, and the vacant land or open country beyond which is expected to go into urban development by the end of the planning

---

[6] For a discussion of the implementation aspects of a planning program, see the author's "Taking Stock of Techniques for Shaping Urban Growth," *Journal of the American Institute of Planners,* May, 1963.

[7] In the later stages of the progressive planning sequence, work programming has become so important that planning agencies are beginning to adopt techniques for controlling data preparation and analysis along lines similar to the "critical path" concept now widely used as a control over the timing and delivery of components in logistics, production, and construction operations. This kind of control becomes particularly important in computer operations in which tests of alternative policies are made in developing the general land use and transportation plan. For a discussion of these control techniques applied to a transportation study, see Roger L. Creighton, "Perting a Transportation Study," a paper presented at the annual meeting of the Highway Research Board, Albany: Upstate New York Transportation Studies, January, 1963.

period, generally a 20- to 25-year span of time. In some metropolitan centers, where there are one or more separate planning agencies functioning in segments of the total metropolitan planning area, local expediency may dictate the usage of the term "planning area" in each locality to refer to its area of planning jurisdiction as defined by state act, the municipal charter, or local ordinance. In the context of the usage here and for comprehensive land use planning studies, it is a larger area. It is larger than the urbanized area, but generally smaller than the Standard Metropolitan Statistical Area as defined by the Bureau of the Budget.

While the immediate concern here is with this localized metropolitan planning area, in the populous urbanizing parts of the country, *urban regions* constitute a study area of still larger scope. Using density and interaction criteria, Pickard defined 21 urban regions in the 48-state area of the United States following the 1960 census.[8] The developing importance of the interregional and intercontinental dimensions to human interaction and its increasing significance for planning in specific metropolitan areas was brought out in Chapter 2. In the future we may anticipate that in some way these extraterritorial considerations of the planning area will be introduced into planning analyses, possibly in the framework of a still larger system of study areas or possibly in the context of interaction studies somewhat dissociated from geographic concepts of space organization.

Defining the Planning Area

The actual procedures employed in delineating the planning area are based on the following considerations. Once the built-up area is roughly defined, the resulting outline is extended outward into open country, considering the general growth prospects and the likely directions of expansion as affected by natural and man-made features. These features include the broad pattern of natural drainage areas, especially the sections of the area which are economic to sewer, and such special features of the area as lakes and hills which are likely to attract growth, the pattern of highways, transportation facilities, and so on.

The extent of area likely to go into development is approximated in terms of square miles by using a rough average density of persons per square mile existing in the presently built-up area and applying this figure to crude estimates of the increase in population of the county or counties, the towns or townships, or the incorporated areas, whichever appears most appropriate to local circumstances for approximation purposes. The resulting rough estimate of the total amount of land likely to go into development

[8] Jerome P. Pickard, "Urban Regions of the United States," *Urban Land,* Washington: Urban Land Institute, April, 1962.

is then distributed around the perimeter of the built-up area according to anticipated directions of expansion activity and other factors cited above. Finally, the resulting outline is generalized to follow lines readily identified on the ground, such as watercourse lines, ridge lines, highways, civil division lines, and so on. As noted earlier, these lines may be drawn to follow civil division lines entirely for convenience in statistical analyses of census data. Whatever basis is used, such delineations of the planning area are tentative and may be subject to revision for land use planning purposes according to suggestions made in Chapter 11. For later detailed studies in the progressive planning sequence where machine methods of data handling are used, the planning area and its system of planning analysis subareas may take a more geometric form consisting of a complex of grid cells in quarter, half, or square mile units, with saw-toothed delineations still closely corresponding to natural features.

Defining Planning Districts

The delineation of planning districts within the planning area involves other factors. Planning districts may be either natural areas or somewhat arbitrary areas useful primarily for analytical purposes. In urban areas where there has been a long-established planning program and residential neighborhoods, or other forms of natural planning areas have been previously identified and are established for planning purposes, the planning districts employed for land use planning may be identical with these. Appropriate extensions of this system of districts to allow for new neighborhoods may be necessary. Planning districts of this type usually aim to recognize the service area of an elementary school, but often must be modified according to the number of people or families present and the density of population in relation to the existing school plant, and the physical barriers present such as railroads, thoroughfares, watercourses, and large areas of nonresidential use.

In situations where no such delineations have been previously made, a somewhat arbitrary system of planning districts may be used or developed for analysis purposes. These may follow census tract boundaries or some other previously developed breakdown of the urban area into small statistical areas. There are certain very obvious advantages to using census tract breakdowns, namely, those of having census data available for the system of subareas to be employed in land use planning analyses. In urban centers which have not been tracted or in situations where it is considered more expedient to depart from census tract lines, a rather simple procedure can be employed. This is based on a rather crude but nevertheless useful division of land use categories into those which for land use planning purposes are studied on an urban-wide basis, and those which are tied to local subareas (see the breakdown in Table 23). In the former category are industrial areas, wholesale areas, the central business district, institutional areas, upper-level schools, and recreation areas serving the city as a whole. In the latter category are residential areas and their service facilities such as elementary schools, local shopping centers, playgrounds, and local parks.

Once the industrial, wholesale, institutional, and other land areas not tied to residential community analysis have been identified and blocked out on a map, only the balance of the urban area—the living areas—needs to be broken down into planning districts. The simplest procedure to follow is first to trace off on an overlay placed over the land use map the pattern of existing residential areas. In order to include in the system of planning districts new undeveloped areas as well as the existing built-up areas, the resulting pattern is then extended out to the limits of the planning area by blocking in all vacant and open land areas identified in the vacant land analysis as potentially suitable for residential use (for example, all of Class 2 Prime type of land as defined at the foot of Table 26). Then on the basis of readily recognized barriers, such as railroads, thoroughfares, watercourses, or large nonresidential areas, a perimeter outline is drawn in generalized form. Planning district dividing lines are then drawn, similarly generalized and following major barrier lines, so that planning districts are not much in excess of one mile in the longest dimension and contain or can accommodate roughly from 1,000 to 5,000 persons each, according to prevailing densities. The general concept employed here is a series of planning districts which represent multiples of the elementary school service area.

The planning districts as previously delineated or as identified by the above procedures are numbered or named for convenience of reference in the subsequent land use planning analyses.

Completion of Tooling-Up Studies

Once a system of study areas is defined, the results of various prerequisite studies can be summarized in terms of these areas. It is recognized that these studies may have been completed earlier and published for general planning purposes, but if data have not been summarized by these study areas in a form usable for land use planning analyses, "completion" may mean re-examination of earlier studies. The prerequisite studies include an analysis of the urban economy, employment and population studies, the activities study, the land use and vacant land surveys, and other studies discussed in Chapters 3, 4, 5, 6, and 7. Scheduled concurrently with this work are the paralleling preliminary thoroughfare plan studies.

Local priorities may dictate the initiation of work on the land use plan alternatives before the formal completion of work on prerequisite studies. If this should be the situation, tooling-up studies should be sufficiently advanced to have produced the following minimum required information:

Current and forecast urban area *population*—total and by school-age groups.

Current and forecast urban area manufacturing, wholesale and office-related *employment*.

Map and tabular summary of *existing land use* by planning district.

Map and tabular summary of *vacant and renewal land* characteristics by planning district.

Summary of current *stock of dwelling units* by structure type and by planning district.

Summary of currently *substandard dwelling units* by structure type and by planning district.

Data on cost-revenue relationships for developments in varying locations, at varying densities and intensities of use, and information on the general pattern of land values and their trends in the urban area should be available early in the analytical sequence.

Estimation of Future Land Requirements

The second major phase in the sequence is the development of what might be termed *qualitative* and *quantitative* land use requirements. This phase goes to the very heart of the analytical procedure. In the first part of this phase—the one relating to qualitative aspects of the analysis—principles and standards governing the location of individual uses and the relationships between uses are formulated, and a schematic land use diagram is prepared for each of the several alternatives being studied. If studies of urban activity systems have been undertaken, these would identify prevailing patterns of interaction, and investigations of household preferences and firm and organization policies with reference to trends in leisure time, automation, and technological change would supply guidelines to changes that may be indicated for future patterns. These diagrams are the first sketch studies for the future patterns of uses, showing in principle "desirable" use relationships and locations matching up with expected patterns of interaction. These serve as references for the study of space requirements and a guide and beginning point in the development of each preliminary plan among the alternatives being presented.

The estimation of space requirements, the quantitative aspect of the analysis, is the most complex and time-consuming part of the analytical procedure. Essentially it is concerned with the estimation of the acreage required to accommodate the expansion anticipated during the planning period for each activity. Built into the procedure is a means for adjusting estimates of land requirements that are derived so as to reflect anticipated future public or private renewal activity and any displacement of existing uses occasioned by these processes of change. Although the final product of these studies is expressed in terms of acreage, the intermediate analyses made in arriving at space requirements utilize different measurement units, for example, employees, dollar sales, dwelling units, population, and so on. Since differing policy assumptions are involved in the different alternative schemes being developed and since the process of developing space requirements proceeds from activity to activity following a particular *parti* for each alternative scheme, the application of space estimates to each scheme must be made in separate analyses.

While the "dimensioning-in" of new space needs fitted to the old pattern of the metropolitan area produces a different structure and form for each plan alternative, the basic analytical procedure is the same for all. As intimated above and in the earlier discussion of land use classification, space needs for region-serving uses are dealt with first. These are uses studied on a planning area basis—uses not directly tied to residential communities such as industry, wholesale and region-serving retail business, recreation, education, and cultural uses. Following these analyses, space requirements for uses associated with residential areas, namely, housing, schools, recreation, local business, and neighborhood-type church uses, are analyzed as an interrelated group of uses. In place of the planning area, here the planning district becomes the primary unit area of analysis.

The tabular and mapped summary of the supply of vacant and renewal land previously classified according to various topographic and improvement characteristics should be available for reference use in these analyses. According to the preferences of the analyst, estimates of space needs for all uses may be completed before trial geographic distributions of uses are attempted (by reference to the previously developed schematic location diagram), *or*, as the acreage requirements for each use are developed, trial distributions may be made to areas defined as vacant and renewal land. In the latter approach a cumulative record is maintained in both tabular and map form of trial land use proposals for each plan alternative. In some respects, the "dimensioning-in" of space requirements on a trial basis as the space needs for each use are derived is the more convenient approach since the derivation of space requirements for some uses is contingent on the manner in which space needs of other uses are distributed. On the other hand, if the first approach is followed, proper adjustment for this contingency may be made later. In either approach, it must be emphasized that at this phase of the study, location and space requirements are developed and tested irrespective of potential conflict (thus the continual reference to *trial* distributions above).

Design of Land Use Plan

The third and final phase to the procedure is a design stage. For each basic policy emphasis being studied, this stage consists of collating preliminary proposals as to location and distribution of various types of land uses as developed in the preceding phase of the work and preparing a sketch plan which best fits activity patterns, livability concepts, and cost considerations. Along with activity, livability, and cost-revenue considerations, the derivation of each scheme takes into account land value, physiographic, and visual factors. Some plan alternatives may have quite different implications for transportation than others. So, in addition to an explicit statement of the basic land development policies around which each scheme is developed, the policy assumptions with respect to transportation are also made explicit. With all this information at hand, then begins a "cut and fill" process, a process of ironing out conflicts in location. These are of two orders: conflicts between the land use pattern and the transportation scheme, and conflicts between the different land uses. Each land use category is reviewed for the economic feasibility of development in the locations indicated, considering the fiscal abilities and legal authorities of the one or more municipalities and counties which may be involved for realizing the plan in the planning period.

Once location conflicts are brought into harmony, space requirements are re-examined as necessary and the space needed for each use is brought into overall balance. For each plan alternative, the final result is the best practical, most economical, and most attractive design for all uses, fitted to the topography and the existing land use pattern and articulated with the circulation system.

Chapter 10

Location Requirements

Location requirements take the form of guiding principles and standards for the placement of uses on the land. Involving a whole range of physical, economic, and social considerations, these requirements derive from the basic interaction needs of residents, firms, and institutions within the metropolitan area and far beyond. As noted in Chapter 2, through market-mediated and government-set location decisions, the activity and movement components of interaction are given physical form as space uses and transportation systems. In the advanced stages of planning, land development models may be used to study location requirements. For example, in the conceptual system centered around decision analysis set forth in Chapter 2, priming decisions may be studied in *parti* form as alternative skeletal plans following principles and standards set down in this chapter, and the secondary decisions can be generated by a model, that is, the filling in of residential use patterns, local shopping areas, recreation spaces, and so on. However, in the preliminary planning phase all location decisions are studied by "hand methods" of analysis. So location requirements as discussed here are concerned with principles and standards in a simplified form suited to an estimation level of accuracy.

In their most elemental form, location requirements relate to health, safety, convenience, economy, and the general amenities of urban living. They involve consideration of danger from floods and other health and safety hazards, the nearness or remoteness of one use from another in time and distance, their compatibility and the social implications of these uses to the people of the community, the economic feasibility of developing particular uses in particular locations considering the pattern of land values and site development costs, the practicalities from a cost-revenue point of view, and livability and general attractiveness as factors of location.

How these considerations are expressed in terms of principles and how principles are subsequently translated into standards of location are fundamentally matters of local determination. Different urban areas will have different natural advantages, different fiscal capabilities, different concepts of convenience, amenity, and livability in general. Theoretically these differences should result in different emphases from city to city in statements of principles and standards. However, in practice most such statements are very similar. They are similar partly because in their fundamentals all such statements stem from a common core of widely recognized general principles of design, and partly because few cities have yet attempted detailed investigations of public attitudes concerning such factors as amenity and convenience, which are less conducive to standardization than such other elements of the public interest as health and safety.[1]

General Principles

General principles relating to the location of land uses customarily identify three major functional areas in the urban complex: the work areas, the living areas, and the leisure-time areas. The major work areas consist of those parts of the city devoted to manufacturing, trade, and the services. The living areas are viewed as the residential communities and their accessory community facilities such as neighborhood stores, playgrounds and local parks, and elementary schools. The leisure-time areas are generally considered to include the major educational, cultural, and recreational facilities of the urban center consisting of colleges, museums, concert halls, libraries, colosseums, golf courses, large public parks and wildlife reserves for hiking, picnics and outings of all kinds, and similar facilities.

In the broadest possible context, principles relating to these three areas generally read somewhat as follows:

Work areas should be located in convenient proximity to living areas where there are nearby interconnecting transit and thoroughfare routes to insure easy access back and forth, and should be in convenient proximity to other work areas where uses accessory to one another have access to interconnecting truck routes. Some work areas should be in locations accessible to heavy transportation facilities and large-capacity utility lines. Work area locations should provide sites adequate in size, economic to develop, and attractively situated for the particular uses intended.

Living areas should be located in convenient proximity to the work and leisure-time areas where there are nearby transit and thoroughfare routes to insure easy access back and forth. They should be in convenient proximity to large open spaces and should include smaller open spaces to insure an open-order character of development, with residential areas in easy walking distance of accessory community facilities. They should be located in areas protected from traffic and

---

[1] See previous references to the potentialities of attitude studies for city planning in Chapters 1, 6, and 7.

incompatible uses, in areas economic and attractive to develop, and in areas where desirable residential densities with a range of choice can be insured.

Leisure-time areas should be located in convenient proximity, by thoroughfare and transit, to living areas. Cultural activities and spectator sports should be central and on sites adequate for their purposes, and major parks and large open spaces should be located so as to take advantage of natural or unusual features of the landscape and provide for a variety of outdoor recreational and other activities.

In such a statement, such terms as "convenient proximity," "easy access," "adequate in size," "easy walking distance," "economic to develop," and "desirable densities" immediately pose problems of definition. These are points in the statement of principles where definitions will vary somewhat according to the size of the urban area. Here, too, value and policy questions are involved which vary from city to city, even within the same general size range. Definitions of these terms appear in the standards as adopted to fit a particular local situation.

The factors involved in a more detailed formulation of principles relating to the location of land uses are suggested below according to the category of land use. It should be noted that, with some exceptions, this listing recognizes the same location groupings developed in the land use classification scheme shown in Table 23.[2] It should also be noted that even this listing is very general in form. While it is in keeping with the generalized character and level of detail required for the preliminary land use plan, location factors are considered in greater detail in the course of developing the general land use and transportation plan.

Manufacturing Areas

1. Reasonably level land, preferably with not more than 5 per cent slope, capable of being graded without undue expense.
2. Range of choice in close-in, fringe, and dispersed locations.

   Extensive manufacturing: large open sites for modern one-story buildings and accessory storage, loading and parking areas in fringe and dispersed locations, usually 5 acres as a minimum, with some sites 10, 25, 50, or 100 or more acres depending on size of urban area and economic outlook for industrial development of extensive lines of activity.

   Intensive manufacturing: variety of site sizes for modern one-story or multiple-story buildings and accessory storage, loading, and parking areas in close-in and fringe locations, usually under 5 acres.
3. Direct access to commercial transportation facilities; in fringe and dispersed locations, access to railroad, major trucking routes, cargo airports, and, in

---

[2] A number of uses which involve certain special location factors or are popularly regarded as possessing certain nuisance characteristics have been grouped together as a miscellany under the heading "public service facilities." Such uses will be found distributed among other headings of the land use classification system in Table 23.

some urban areas, deep water channels; and in close-in locations, for a major proportion of sites, access to both railroad and trucking routes, with the balance adjoining trucking thoroughfares or, if appropriate, port areas.

4. Within easy commuting time of residential areas of labor force and accessible to transit and major thoroughfare routes directly connected with housing areas.
5. Availability of utilities at or near the site such as power, water, and waste disposal facilities.
6. Compatibility with surrounding uses, considering prevailing winds, possibilities of protective belts of open space, development of "industrial parks," and other factors of amenity both within the manufacturing area and in relation to adjoining land uses.

Wholesale and Related Use Areas

1. Reasonably level land, preferably with not more than 5 per cent slope, capable of being graded without undue expense.
2. Range of choice in close-in and fringe locations, site sizes usually under 5 acres.
3. Direct access to trucking routes and major street system for incoming goods and outgoing deliveries; frontage on a commercial street or in well-served wholesale centers essential; railroad access for minor proportion of sites or centers.
4. Suitability for development of integrated centers, with consideration for amenity within the development and adjoining areas.

Region-Serving Business Areas

1. Adjoining heavy traffic flows, central to their tributary trade area.

    Central business district: location close to peak flow of traffic and pedestrians where retail, professional, financial, and related services can be conveniently accommodated and made easily accessible to adequate parking, transit, and regional transportation services for clientele and employee groups patronizing or working in CBD.

    Regional business centers: (a) regional shopping centers: location close to two major arterials tributary to trade area (50-100,000 families); site adequate to accommodate peak parking needs and a complete line of shop and store types, eating and entertainment facilities, and branch business and financial services sufficient to fill several hours of a shopper's time (30 to 150 acres); and (b) satellite CBD centers (office centers, automobile sales and service centers, appliance centers, farmers' market and service centers, etc.): locations on intersection of radial and circumferential arteries and on one or more major transit routes, with adequate parking and service areas.

    Highway service centers: locations in outlying areas on major highway approaches to urban area where sites are adequate for integrated design of drive-in services and motel accommodations and proper consideration is given to highway safety, roadside beauty, and general amenity of adjoining uses.

2. Suitability for development as one center internally arranged or, where appro-

priate, in an integrated series of subcenters, with consideration for parks and other open spaces, approaches, and general amenity within the area and in adjoining use areas.

Public Service Facilities

1. Suitable locations, adequate in size for following uses, as determined by special studies: civic center, subcenters, and general civic services; cemeteries; water works, sewage disposal facilities, and garbage and refuse disposal facilities; gas works, power plants, and substations, and communications facilities; transit yards and service facilities; railroad terminals, marshaling yards, and service facilities; port facilities; overland bus and union truck terminals and servicing facilities; helioports, landing strips, and major airports; military installations; and so on.

Region-Serving Recreation, Education, and Cultural Facilities

1. Reasonably level land for facilities involving structures, accessory parking, and active recreation areas, with perhaps not more than 5 per cent slope, capable of being graded without undue expense; for large open spaces and public reservations, land with a variety of natural features and no limitations as to slope and drainage characteristics (often includes land not practical for other urban uses).

    Major parks, public reservations, and golf courses: acreage sites in fringe and outlying areas, ranging from gently rolling terrain for golf courses to topography with variable features for parks and reservations.

    Colleges, medical centers, and institutions: fringe locations on level to rolling terrain in areas protected from traffic and incompatible uses; site adequate to accommodate buildings, accessory parking, outdoor uses, and grounds, with due consideration to approaches and amenity of surroundings.

    Cultural facilities, large churches, and spectator sports: level sites in central locations (out of high-value areas) adequate to accommodate building, accessory parking, and landscaping, with due consideration to approaches and general amenity of surroundings.
2. Suitability of unusual land forms and natural drainage creeks for incorporation into an integrated open space system in urban area, serving as natural breaks between functional use areas and providing connective links between recreation areas and large public and institutional open areas.
3. Direct access to major thoroughfare and transit or stage routes with direct and easy connections to the residential communities of the urban area.

Residential Communities

1. Terrain with variety, offering fairly level, rolling, and hillside sites depending on topographic characteristics in the urban area, but avoiding steep or irregular sites and low or poorly drained areas; slope usually under 15 per cent.
2. In close proximity to major thoroughfares and transit system with direct connections to work and leisure-time areas; bounded but not penetrated by major

streets; and internally served by a system of collector and service streets fitted to the terrain with due consideration to drainage, sunlight, and views.

3. Suitability for integrated design of residential areas and their related shopping, school, church, and recreation facilities, including the community-serving and the neighborhood-serving facilities.

  Local shopping facilities: sites adequate for shops, accessory off-street parking and loading, and landscaping; convenient to specific local tributary trade areas and accessible for receiving goods: (a) neighborhood-serving store group within convenient walking distance of families served (within convenient driving range, in low-density areas), with due consideration for pedestrian access and amenity of surrounding areas; and (b) community-serving shopping center on major radial thoroughfare, usually at the intersection of a major crosstown street, situated toward in-town edge of tributary trade area, and located with due consideration for integrated design of center and amenity of adjoining areas.

  Schools: reasonably level sites, with upper-level schools within convenient commuting range and lower-level schools within easy walking distance of age groups served (except in low-density areas, where convenient driving range rather than walking distance becomes crucial consideration); sites adequate for buildings, recreation facilities, and landscaping, and located with due consideration for safety of children and amenity of surroundings.

  Churches: reasonably level sites, adequate for parking and landscaping, and convenient to potential membership; for neighborhood-serving churches, walking convenience important, and for community-serving churches, accessibility to major street system important.

  Playground areas and parks: (a) reasonably level playground and recreation center sites, usually in conjunction with schools, within easy walking distance of age groups served (within convenient driving range, in low-density areas), and adequate for appropriate active recreation facilities and circumscribing planted strips; and (b) quiet parks on steep, level, or low sites and fingers of open space along watercourses and in low areas, integrated with active and passive recreation areas and the larger open space system of the urban area according to the opportunities offered by land forms in locale.

4. Range of choice in residential densities, with high densities in close proximity to permanent open spaces and nearest to the thoroughfare and transit systems and community-serving shopping centers; with lowest densities in the interstices between thoroughfare and transit systems.

These are illustrative of the kinds of factors which would be covered in a detailed statement of guiding principles for the location of various functional use areas within the framework of the land use plan. Again it should be noted that there will be variations from one urban area to another. Cities in mountainous areas will have emphases differing from those in the Great Plains; climate will produce differing emphases; resort, government, transportation, and other specialized centers will have their special considerations; and even the size of the urban area will be a factor in playing up certain features and de-emphasizing others.

Location Standards

Standards are a set of yardsticks established for measuring the excellence of quality in elements of the community's makeup, in this case use locations. Standards established in laws generally take the form of *minimum standards* which have come to be recognized as necessary in the public interest. For planning analyses, we use *"desirable" standards,* an excellence of quality somewhere between the minimum and optimum situation —something practicable to achieve in the great majority of applications. In this sense, standards are not absolute, but more in the nature of guides or criteria to be followed under average circumstances. Where there is a marked range of variation in circumstances, variable standards of location may be warranted.

Convenience Standards

As suggested above, standards supply measurement units for terms appearing in the statement of principles. In dealing with standards for the location of uses, time and distance criteria are primary units for the measurement of convenience. Thus "close proximity," "convenient driving range," "easy walking distance," and "accessible to railroad, transit, or utilities" are defined in time or distance standards, usually in terms of minutes or miles of travel.

For purposes of the preliminary land use plan, these convenience standards are usually locally established adaptations from general standards developed by nationally recognized authorities from long experience and intimate familiarity with the testing and use of varying standards. Access standards adopted by the Committee on the Hygiene of Housing for time and distance relationships between the dwelling and various community facilities are widely used as general standards.[3] However, adaptations must be made in each locale on the basis of judgment and general observation of prevailing community habits. Compiled from the land use plan studies for an urban area of about 100,000 population, Table 31 serves to illustrate the form in which such standards are expressed for generalized land use planning analyses. Obviously these standards are based on a certain set of local conditions with respect to terrain, prevailing residential densities, local transportation systems, school and recreation policies, and other considerations which would not necessarily be duplicated in another community of the same size or even in the same region.

---

[3] Committee on the Hygiene of Housing, American Public Health Association, *Planning the Neighborhood,* Chicago: Public Administration Service, 1960, p. 9.

Table 31. Illustrative Time-Distance Standards for Selected Uses in Urban Area of 100,000 Population

Use of Facility	Controlling Standards
Employment centers	20 to 30 min.
Central business district	30 to 45 min.
Local shopping center	½ mile or 10 min.
Elementary school	½ mile
Junior high school	1 mile or 20 min.
Senior high school	20 to 30 min.
Playgrounds and local parks	½ mile
Playfields and recreation centers	1 mile or 20 min.
Public park or reservation	30 to 60 min.

For later studies in refinement of the preliminary land use plan, convenience standards should be developed on the basis of much more detailed study. For example, in the case of time-distance between residential areas and places of employment, the controlling standard used for illustrative purposes in Table 31 in all probability would be replaced by a series of several standards. Sampling attitude surveys can be expected to identify a variety of variables, such as cost and pleasantness of travel, which would provide a basis for the development of more exacting specifications, probably taking the form of variable standards. The location of the employment center itself may be found to be a factor to be recognized in location standards. Thus, where employment centers are planned for peripheral locations, lower time-distance standards may be indicated than those used in more centrally located employment centers. "The value which a worker places on time, and the degree to which he is willing to make a specified journey to work will depend upon many variables. Age, sex, race, occupation, economic class, cultural group, reason for working, will all be important determinants of the evaluation of the journey to work by individuals. No gross generalizations can be made as to the 'optimum' journey to work, nor can generalizations be made as to how far employees as a whole are willing to journey to their jobs."[4] However, for particular segments of the population situated in particular sections of the urban area, standards may be developed which on the average match up with dominant preferences as to travel times or distances to various functional use areas, considering convenience, cost, and other factors.

Similarly, in more detailed studies of school needs, variable standards

[4] Planning Advisory Service, *The Journey to Work: Relation Between Employment and Residence,* Information Report No. 26, Chicago: American Society of Planning Officials, May, 1951, p. 5.

may be substituted for the single crude standard used in the preliminary land use planning analyses. A map of school sites with half-mile circles described around each site provides only the very crudest measure of location adequacy. Even when time zones are substituted for distance circles, variations in concepts of convenience in different parts of the urban area suggest that variable standards may be more realistic than one uniform standard. These concepts will vary with different residential densities, different income groups, and so on. Similar observations may be made concerning shopping facilities and recreation areas. Indeed, convenience standards for all uses should be carefully re-examined and refined as work proceeds from the preliminary land use plan toward the comprehensive plan.

Performance Standards

Another form of location standard is the so-called "performance standard." Deriving from health, safety, and, to some extent, the amenity elements of the public interest (as opposed to convenience as taken up above), in present usage performance standards provide criteria for testing the degree of hazard or nuisance from land use activities creating smoke, dust, noise, glare, odor, or fumes, or from activities generating traffic or producing wastes. To date they have been largely applied to industrial and related activities, although they have applications for other uses, for example, tests of glare, noise, and traffic association with spectator sports, recreation uses, carnivals, revival meetings, and so on.

Since O'Harrow's study in 1951, much attention has been given to the use of performance standards as a basis for the location of industrial activity.[5] Borrowed from earlier applications in building codes, the principle of the performance standard is based on the use of tests to determine whether a particular industry (or, originally, a particular building material) conforms with established basic criteria or standards of acceptability. Largely associated with industrial zoning, performance standards are increasingly being used as the basis for determining the location qualifications of various industries for admission to particular classes of zones. The degree to which hazards and nuisances are brought under control through technological and planning measures becomes the test. The performance approach renders obsolete the old basis of zoning under which industries were arbitrarily grouped into "light," "heavy," and "unrestricted" manufacturing districts.

---

[5] Dennis O'Harrow, "Performance Standards in Industrial Zoning," in *Planning 1951*, Chicago: American Society of Planning Officials, 1952.

It should be noted that performance standards are as yet imperfectly developed, some being more highly developed than others. Thus research on standards of smoke pollution, dust, glare, and noise is more advanced than what has been accomplished with fumes and odors. The measurement of most of these nuisances presently requires special equipment, and for interpretation of findings, some technical knowledge is necessary. Moreover, being a tool of zoning, performance standards presently focus on minimum rather than "desirable" standards. However, recognizing that the land use plan provides the basic rationale for a system of zoning districts, we may anticipate that with the advancement of research, upgraded forms of performance standards will be used in the future as general location criteria in land use planning analyses.

Security Factors of Location

Security factors pose still another order of location criteria—criteria that are based in some measure on public safety but perhaps more fundamentally on national well-being. With the atmosphere of unsettled global conditions following World War II and the prospect of international tensions continuing for an indefinite period into the future, increasing attention has been centered on security factors of planning. Historically a factor in the layout and development of individual cities, security now encompasses nations, indeed continents. While protection of the populace is of fundamental concern, the protection of industrial areas, the means for prosecuting war, is an objective of particular concern.

The great concentration of the nation's industrial resources in a relatively few metropolitan areas has grave implications for national well-being in event of an enemy attack. The vulnerability of these resources and the cities in which they are located prompted the establishment in 1951 of a national program for industrial dispersion. In effect until 1959, the program was based on voluntary action of localities and industrialists and called for future plants to be built outside highly industrialized or densely populated areas and away from military installations. As incentives to conform with the policy, new plants which located according to dispersal criteria could avail themselves of accelerated tax amortization and loan privileges. While the Office of the Assistant Secretary of Defense for Civil Defense continues to provide advice and guidance on the relative vulnerability of various locations under consideration, the fallout implications of later developments in thermonuclear weapons have become the center of attention and in some respects have deflated continuing efforts to minimize vulnerability from industrial concentrations.

If the importance of a dispersal program is accepted, it becomes apparent that the urban land use plan offers an important means for effectuating workable dispersal objectives within any particular metropolitan area. The extent to which national dispersion criteria can be integrated into local industrial development principles and standards should be the subject of a special study. While certain general principles of dispersal may be applied in the preliminary land use plan, the application of dispersal criteria in detail are probably best undertaken in the refinement and extension of the preliminary land use plan.

Trial Application of Principles and Standards

With location requirements for each major class of land use established as set forth above, it is possible to develop generalized growth patterns roughly scaled to a horizon year, say 50 years hence, and carry through the first-level review of policy directions that might be followed in accommodating growth in the preliminary planning phase. As indicated under the discussion of development objectives and plan alternatives in Chapter 9, this stage initially is one of determining policy preferences of decision-making groups from among the most elemental choices open to the metropolitan area in absorbing the economic and population growth anticipated. In many parts of the country, growth of dramatic proportions is in prospect, and it is at this stage that the potentialities of a long-term and consistent policy orientation can be first demonstrated to policy-makers. This is also the stage at which goals are identified from attitude and activity investigations made in the course of tooling-up studies. On the basis of a recommended set of developmental goals, the alternative ways in which growth can be accommodated are presented. For contrast purposes, usually a growth pattern is developed signifying how development would occur under a "no-policy orientation." Then under various preconditioning assumptions and certain explicitly stated and set policies, alternative growth patterns are offered such as the concentration of growth around a constellation of satellite centers and subcenters; the channeling of growth into selected drainage corridors; growth by controlled diffusion into selected drainage basins; compacted expansion around existing dispersed centers; radial or stellate pattern of growth along main communications lines; and so on. Next, differentials in living qualities are identified and the relative cost implications approximated by comparing lineal miles of transportation facilities, sewer interceptors, and water mains required to accommodate each of the development patterns.

Each growth pattern involves a different combination of policies. For example, for the nucleated pattern, a policy mix might specify: (a) establishment of defined utility service areas in selected drainage basins where "utility cores" of fixed capacities suited to each have been developed; (b) development of a coordinated express transit and expressway system, with stations and access points set at predetermined locations central to these service areas; and (c) regulation of residential densities, permitting urban densities only in the service areas of public utility systems and related to transportation stations and access points. Other policy mixes can be identified to favor other growth patterns. With the alternatives thus presented (including the "no action" alternative), costs and benefits can be evaluated in general terms. While it is unlikely that such policies would be formally adopted, this kind of review can be expected to produce a fairly clear indication of preference from decision-making groups.

On the basis of this kind of guidance, the preliminary planning stage next comes to focus on a series of plan alternatives based on second-order policy emphases. It is now possible to develop in *parti* form for the 20- to 25-year period ahead an initial schematic representation of each of several variations on the prototype pattern selected from the horizon-year schemes. At this point, a number of the tooling-up studies mentioned in Chapter 7 come into play. Among them are: the land capability study, blighted areas study, cost-revenue study, land value study, visual survey, and attitude studies. Although detailed applications of these studies are not warranted at this stage of the study, each one serves a reference purpose in blocking out locations in schematic form. The land capabilities analysis brings to bear studied consideration of the terrain and drainage conditions and the utility and transportation services available in different areas. The blighted areas study shows what sections of the city are expected to be available for redevelopment during the planning period and indicates land capabilities in areas slated for renewal. Cost-revenue and land value studies serve as guides to the feasibility for the use of land contemplated at these locations. The visual survey identifies locations where there are distinctive views and other similar features which are important developmental assets to be considered in the placement of various uses. Finally, attitude studies will provide a picture of dominant public preferences and expectations in the future development of the urban area.

At this second level of refinement, variations on the basic transportation policy selected in the first-level review are sketched in and land use patterns diagrammatically fitted to land forms and related to drainage patterns. In this process the locations for each use are first roughed out on overlays fitted to the land forms in vacant and renewal areas. Eventually, according to location principles and standards of this chapter, a trial scheme of the distribution of uses for each *parti* emerges. While analyses of space requirements in the next phase of the study may modify this tentative selection of locations and final determinations must thus be made in the synthesizing process of the design phase, nevertheless, for these later phases of land use planning it becomes a guide and a beginning basis for the development of alternative land use plans for the scaling in of space needs taken up in the following chapter.

Chapter 11

Space Requirements

In shifting the focus of the land use planning study from the derivation of location requirements to the estimation of space needs, fundamentally we are seeking a basis for scaling the land area needed to accommodate growth in the urban area expected in the next 20 to 25 years. More particularly, having established in principle *where* each category of use should be located in the future, we are now interested in estimating *how much* land will be needed for each such use. Once these estimates are available, it is then possible to firm up the alternatives for the preliminary land use plan, initially "testing out the various locations for size" and eventually arriving at plans reflecting the best possible balance in land utilization that is commensurate with the generalized level of study employed in analytical procedures throughout the whole sequence of study. This final balancing task is taken up in the last chapter.

Again it is emphasized that the objective of this chapter is to outline estimation techniques for the preliminary planning phase in the progression of analyses leading to a general land use and transportation plan. While land development models now utilize much more exacting methods of analysis than presented here, the analytical framework outlined in successive sections of this chapter supplies in an elemental form a description of many of the operations involved in the more advanced stages of planning. In this sense, it therefore also serves as an introduction to the underlying analytical sequence followed in these later stages.

In this chapter the whole range of tooling-up studies of Part II are brought into play. Studies of the urban economy, employment, and population provide measures of the growth potential, and the several kinds of urban land studies indicate the general character of existing development and provide the basis for determining the space-using characteristics of various land use categories developed to their present intensity of use.

While techniques for estimating space requirements vary according to the class of land use, there is a common methodological pattern to the analysis of all classes. Integrating into the procedure the kind of trial tests alluded to earlier for checking the space needs of each land use against the supply of land as the various use categories are successively analyzed, the operation can be summarized as consisting of three major steps. The first involves a recapitulation of the existing characteristics of development for the particular land use category being studied. Thus the present distribution of the use between inlying and outlying locations is examined, and variations in the intensity of use in each of these parts of the urban area are determined.

The second step is directly concerned with space requirements. It involves first the derivation of space standards appropriate to each class of use and then the application of these standards to the appropriate growth index previously developed. Density standards are employed for industrial and residential uses, with employees per net or gross acre of land used for manufacturing purposes being the measure for the former, and families or dwelling units per net or gross acre of land used for residential purposes being the measure for the latter. For schools and certain types of recreation areas, local adaptations of general empirical standards of minimum site sizes for designated multiples of school or total population are customarily used as standards. For retail business uses, standards are based on trade area population or the volume of retail sales per unit of retail floor area, and wholesale standards are based on wholesale employment per unit of wholesale area. Thus in such analyses the measure of growth is generally taken from the employment, population, or some other forecast, and the estimate of space requirements is obtained by applying the standard to this growth increment.

The third and final step in this analysis is the balancing of space requirements as derived in the preceding step against the supply of land. The supply of land is all vacant land, summarized in a form somewhat like Table 26, plus all land slated for clearance during the planning period under an urban renewal program, summarized in a similar form. The balancing of need against supply is done separately for each class, with the acreage needed for each use being compared with the supply listed under the classification appropriate to that use in the table of vacant and renewal land. Cumulative tallies of deductions from the vacant and renewal land summary are maintained as the analysis of space requirements for each use is successively completed. Overlays are prepared showing the distribution of the vacant land taken up by each use and the distribution of residual vacant land after each deduction is made. The deduction tallies are usually maintained in subcategories according to the basic characteristics of the vacant land originally employed in the vacant land classification system (see illustrative Table 26). Thus if deficiencies should be encountered in the supply of land classified for one use, vacant land with alternative use potentialities can be considered for reclassification to the use class where the shortage develops. If such a reclassification is impractical or does not fully accommodate these deficiencies, then it will be necessary to extend the limits of the planning area, classify the additional vacant land thus brought into the planning area, and revise the summary of the supply of land upward accordingly.

Generally, however, the limits of the planning area tend to be drawn rather generously in the first instance, and so this balancing operation will usually show a surplus rather than a shortage in the supply of vacant and renewal land. The surplus can run so high that the delineation of the planning area may appear unrealistic. However, so long as the total excess of land is not unreasonable, that is, is not over what is considered locally to be an adequate allowance for flexibility (usually roughly 25 per cent of the total amount of land estimated to go into use during the planning period), there is no particular need to contract the boundaries of the planning area. In this connection it should be noted that such a flexibility factor is over and above the safety factors introduced in the course of detailed calculations made in the analyses of space requirements as discussed in the various sections of this chapter below. Such a flexibility factor allows for deviant choices of individuals and firms who may acquire land in excess of the estimated need, and it allows for land which may be held out of use because of personal preferences or whims of a few property owners or because of legal complications which make the land unavailable for immediate development.

If the surplus of vacant land is considerably in excess of estimated needs plus the flexibility allowance, it is usually desirable to tighten up the planning area delineation initially assumed, to bring it more in line with what space requirement analyses show to be a planning area of practical size. This, of course, involves acreage deductions from the appropriate classes in the land use and vacant land summaries. In the actual sequence of procedures employed in determining space requirements, the contraction of planning area boundaries, if it is found to be necessary, is made after running through the analyses for all classes of land use.

The whole trial distribution procedure in which space needs are balanced against supply of vacant and renewal land must be viewed of course as tentative until the final design phase of the land use planning is reached, for it is only at this phase of developing the different land use plan schemes that location decisions can finally be reached. However, the trial distribution of total space requirements is an essential step in reaching these final decisions.

The balance of the chapter describes the techniques in common usage for estimating space requirements of each class of land use. Uses not tied to small-area analysis are taken up first, followed by uses customarily analyzed by planning districts, namely, the residential communities and their accessory community facilities. It should be noted that for ease of analysis we estimate space needs for assemblages of uses according to the way activity patterns tend to group together in space, and we are in effect extracting uses of different activity systems listed in Table 22 and recombining them in mixes of the kind outlined in general form in Table 23.

Manufacturing Space Requirements

For purposes of a generalized result such as is required in the preliminary land use plan, estimates of space requirements for manufacturing areas are usually obtained in four steps as follows:

1. Determine the salient characteristics of existing manufacturing uses in the urban area, existing industrial densities, and the prospects for future manufacturing activity as determined in previous studies of the urban economy.
2. On the basis of these studies and considering modern-day industrial plant requirements, develop local standards for future industrial densities.
3. Apply industrial densities to future manufacturing employment estimates to obtain estimated land requirements.
4. Determine from summary of vacant and renewal land how supply matches up with estimated need, and, referring to location requirements, make a trial distribution into areas considered prime for industrial use, carrying over the surplus for reallocation in the vacant land tally.

The first step above is the equivalent of the industrial survey carried out in later comprehensive planning studies. For an abbreviated type of study involved in preliminary planning, it consists of organizing data assembled in the land use survey and the study of the economy, and determining existing industrial densities.

Existing Industrial Densities

Two types of breakdowns are prepared to describe these characteristics of existing manufacturing uses: first, a summary of the acreage and employment of manufacturing establishments for the *urban area as a whole* broken down by density classes of manufacturing activity; and then a breakdown of the totals in this summary *by central city and by outlying incorporated and unincorporated fringe areas* making up the balance of the planning area. Converted to industrial densities, the first breakdown provides a measure of the intensity of development in the urban area as a whole for the selected density classes of manufacturing activity, and the second provides a crude indication as to how the intensity varies by density class from the central city to outlying areas.

Industrial density is defined as the number of manufacturing employees per gross industrially used acre.[1] As applied to particular density classes, it refers to the gross industrially used acres in that class. The term "gross" refers to all land within the property lines of the plant site, including building areas, landscaped grounds, parking and loading areas, outdoor storage and waste disposal areas, and to half of the area of all drives, streets, highways, or railroad spur lines bordering the property.

The number and the definitions of density classes of manufacturing activity in common usage vary from one city to another. Depending somewhat on the size of the urban area and the nature of manufacturing activity present, a breakdown by density classes may or may not be necessary. For example, in urban areas under 100,000 with a fairly diversified character of manufacturing activity, a breakdown by density classes may unnecessarily complicate the analysis and thus prove to be impractical. For larger urban centers, two or more classes may be required. Probably for most preliminary land use planning studies, not more than two or three density classes will be required. A study of the Detroit Metropolitan Area Regional Planning Commission illustrates the use of two broad density classes, extensive and intensive manufacturing areas, with a range of subcategories for special uses.[2] The "intensive" category was defined as including all manufacturing activities with 40 or more workers per net industrial acre, with "extensive" applying to those activities with fewer than 40. An early study of the Philadelphia City Planning Commission employed three density classes, intensive, intermediate, and extensive, with differing definitions to suit the needs of its area.[3]

Density Standards for the Future

Having examined the density characteristics of existing manufacturing activity in the urban area and the range of variation from central to out-

[1] Some planning agencies use the "net" measurement, which includes the industrial building site plus outdoor storage, parking, and loading areas, presumably eliminating undeveloped portions of the industrial site, bounding or internal streets, and railroad spurs included in a "gross" measurement. However, this usage is generally connected with analyses of existing manufacturing areas, rather than in the context of land use planning studies for future industrial areas. For estimating future land requirements, gross measures which include streets, railroad spurs, and similar service facilities are simpler to apply to vacant and open land in dimensioning the land use plan.

[2] Detroit Metropolitan Area Regional Planning Commission, *Industrial Land Use in the Detroit Region,* February, 1952, mimeo., p. 7.

[3] Philadelphia City Planning Commission, *Industrial Land Use Plan,* December, 1950, pp. 8–9.

lying areas, the next and second step is the development of density standards to be used in estimating space needs for industrial expansion in the
future. These are generally developed as adaptations of the existing densities, considering modern-day trends in site sizes among various industrial
uses. Densities for activities which the study of the urban economy suggests are likely to develop in the area in the future and would be entirely
new to the area are generally estimated on the basis of studies made in
other cities where these activities presently exist.

As might be expected, density standards tend to vary from one metropolitan area to another, depending to some extent on its size and the
industrial makeup of the economy. For example, in the Roanoke metropolitan area (about 150,000 population in 1960) a single density standard
of 19 workers per net acre was used in estimating future requirements.[4]
The standards originally adopted in Philadelphia were:[5]

Density Class	Workers per Acre	
	Net	Gross
Intensive	147	50
Intermediate	40	18
Extensive	18	6

As an average gross density for all manufacturing, Cincinnati has used
30,[6] Copenhagen, 20,[7] and the British new towns, 30.[8]

In the early Philadelphia study, different density standards were introduced to differentiate between different intensity groupings of industry.
Looking toward further refinement and revision of earlier studies, the
Philadelphia City Planning Commission commissioned two additional studies which illustrate ways in which the accuracy of standards can be improved upon. In the first, the effect of industry moves within the metropolitan area was studied.[9] This study noted that in the period from 1943
to 1954 space needs tended to be variable according to the move patterns
of industries to sites where expansion needs are accommodated in existing
buildings as opposed to sites where expansion is accommodated by the

---

[4] The Roanoke Valley Regional Planning Commission, *A Land Use Plan for the Roanoke
Valley Region,* Roanoke: Department of City Planning, June, 1963.

[5] Philadelphia City Planning Commission, *Industrial Land Use Plan,* pp. 8–9.

[6] Cincinnati City Planning Commission, *Industrial Areas,* June, 1946, p. 46.

[7] *Storkobenhavn,* udarbejdet 1947, Egnsplankontoret.

[8] Patrick Abercrombie, *Greater London Plan 1944,* London: His Majesty's Stationery Office,
1945, p. 52; and T. A. Jeffreys, "New Towns Technique," *Journal of the Town Planning
Institute,* November-December, 1946, p. 12.

[9] Institute for Urban Studies, University of Pennsylvania, *Industrial Land and Facilities for
Philadelphia,* Philadelphia: City Planning Commission, 1956.

building of new structures. Two new standards were introduced for each major density category. The standard for the old intensive category was replaced by two new ones; and the intermediate category was broken down into two subcategories, with two standards assigned to each. The study proposed no change in the extensive category since too few cases were available for an analysis of moves in this industrial category. Applying one standard to the turnover in employment anticipated in moves from old quarters to larger old quarters, and applying the other to the employment expected on new sites with new structures, the resulting separate segments by density category were then combined to arrive at aggregate space requirements. The new standards proposed were:

| | Workers per Net Acre [a] | |
Density Class	Space Added by Turnover of Old Sites	Space Added by New Sites
Group I—Intensive	256.4	79.3
Group II—Intermediate-Intensive	241.8	59.5
Group III—Intermediate-Extensive	29.8	49.5

[a] Estimated from Table 23 in Institute for Urban Studies, University of Pennsylvania, *Industrial Land and Facilities for Philadelphia*, Philadelphia: City Planning Commission, 1956.

In a later study which became the basis for the standards subsequently used in the Philadelphia comprehensive plan published in 1960, the Philadelphia City Planning Commission went into a floor area basis of analysis of the kind discussed briefly below.[10] For preliminary planning purposes the use of acreage standards is common practice. For large metropolitan areas the order of detail noted in the table above may be important in the preliminary planning phase; for the smaller metropolitan area, a simpler approach is warranted.

Estimating Space Needs

The foregoing type of standard when applied to the appropriate estimates of *increases in manufacturing employment* may be used as one basis for determining the amount of land required for new industry. To make allowances for replacements of existing industrial plants in character with move patterns and contemporary trends toward the spread-out one-story

[10] Arthur D. Little, Inc., *The Usefulness of Philadelphia's Industrial Plant: An Approach to Industrial Renewal*, Cambridge: Arthur D. Little, Inc., January, 1960.

type of development, the approach used in Philadelphia is especially appropriate for the large metropolitan area. In smaller centers, it may make more sense to use a second approach. Where there are relatively few moves, the impact of these shifts can be approximated by applying locally derived density standards to appropriate estimates of *total forecast manufacturing employment*. The difference between this result and the acreage presently in manufacturing use is then taken to be the estimated additional land needed for industrial use. Since all plants cannot be expected to rebuild to these standards during the planning period, the latter approach in effect introduces a "built-in" safety factor to allow for a greater industrial growth than is foreseen under normal circumstances.

Even with the introduction of such a safety factor, the resulting estimate of space requirements is generally regarded, especially in small urban areas, as insufficient to cover the contingency of very large installations desiring to locate in the area. To cover such an eventuality and at the same time to give some recognition to the importance of protecting prime industrial sites in anticipation of needs even beyond the immediate planning period, frequently a planning agency will earmark additional areas as "industrial reserves." There is no standard practice in estimating space requirements in this category. It is largely a subjective matter, tempered somewhat by the supply of land in fringe and dispersed locations appropriate for industrial use. In urban areas situated in level country where there is virtually an unlimited supply of open land adjacent to highway and railroad transportation facilities and within reasonable range of existing utility lines, it is less important to provide an industrial reserve. In hilly and mountainous areas, the protection of prime industrial land is a matter of considerable importance, and planning agencies are much more likely to provide for an industrial reserve.

The foregoing procedures apply in arriving at *overall estimates* of industrial space requirements for an urban area. In the large metropolitan area it may be desirable to differentiate between inlying and outlying areas in the density standards adopted. Higher land values and the additional taxes usually involved in incorporated portions of the urban area may dictate as a practical consideration a dual system of density standards, with a higher range of densities for density classes located in the inlying areas than those being used for corresponding classes in the outlying areas. In many urban areas, by "natural selection," the intensive, intermediate, and extensive density classes distribute themselves in inlying, fringe, and outlying locations more or less automatically in recognition of these practical considerations, and it is thus unnecessary to employ a dual-standard system.

Table 32. New Space Requirements for Industrial Areas, 19xx

Density Class	Acreage Requirements			
	Central Areas [a]	Fringe Areas [a]	Outlying Areas [a]	Total
Intensive	xx	xx	xx	xxx
Intermediate	xx	xx	xx	xxx
Extensive	xx	xx	xx	xxx
Planning area total	xx	xx	xx	xxx

[a] As a practical necessity, these areas are usually differentiated by designation of the central city as constituting "central areas," suburban incorporated cities as "fringe areas," and unincorporated areas at the outskirts of the planning area as "outlying areas." This table obviously applies to large metropolitan areas and would be simplified when used for smaller urban centers.

Trial Distribution Scheme

Having arrived at an estimate of the total amount of land needed for future industrial growth broken down by density classes, the final step is one of matching up the supply of vacant and renewal land having industrial use potentialities with the estimated need for industrial land. In this step the acreage requirements for future industrial expansion are tentatively dimensioned into areas considered to be prime land for industrial use as established by the previous analysis of location requirements. (This would be Class 1 Prime land in the illustrative classification system of Table 26.) Whether or not a system of variable density standards is being employed, gross allocations are first made on the basis of proportions of total industrial expansion expected to occur in the central city of the urban area and in the outlying portions.[11] This procedure provides a crude control in the dimensioning process. This proportion is estimated on the basis of observed past trends in the rates of industrial growth in these two portions of the urban area, but considered in the light of the supply of vacant and renewal land in the central city available for the absorption of industrial development. Once tentative allocations have been made on this basis, allocations are made to each of the two portions of the urban area by density classes. The pro rata share of expansion in each portion of the urban area is tentatively dimensioned into vacant and renewal areas according to estimated proportions of subtotals each density class will

[11] In large metropolitan areas, it may make more sense to group certain suburban communities with the central city for purposes of these breakdowns, and in some it may be possible to establish an intermediate ring of incorporated communities between the central city and the outlying fringe area as in Table 32.

absorb in the future. The final result may be summarized as indicated in Table 32.

After a trial distribution has been made, the surplus land not required in the foregoing allocation process is earmarked for possible absorption by other land use classes according to analyses to follow. Appropriate overlays are prepared identifying land allocated for industrial use and the residual areas available for other uses. It should be emphasized that the above allocations of land for future industrial use are tentative at this stage of the analysis. As noted earlier, these remain tentative until the final design phase of the land use planning procedure is reached.

Detailed Industrial Planning Studies

The above crude procedures for the estimation of space requirements are reasonably satisfactory for purposes of the generalized or preliminary land use plan. However, as attention is directed toward revision and refinement of these first investigations, looking toward the development of a comprehensive plan, studies of a much more detailed nature covering a wider range of considerations are required. The general character of these later, more detailed studies is indicated below.

Detailing the Space Needs

The above-described approach to estimating space requirements is geared to analyses of general aggregates of manufacturing activity. In effect, the broad groupings of manufacturing activity for which employment data are reported in the Census of Population have imposed limits on the level of detail that is possible. Furthermore, to the extent that the land use survey is planned and conducted to furnish data of a general-purpose character, this basic source of information imposes similar limitations. Consequently, when the comprehensive plan studies come to focus on industrial space requirements, it is generally necessary to undertake an industrial survey, often a combined survey of industrial and wholesale activities.

Essentially this survey is an establishment-by-establishment study involving interviews with the management, and as noted in Chapter 6, it would be combined with the activities study. Although the survey may serve several needs, for industrial land use planning purposes, the planning agency will want to obtain such detailed information as: past and present employment by shift; total land area within the property lines of each establishment and how this area is taken up by the plant and auxiliary buildings, by outdoor storage and waste areas, and by parking and loading facilities; floor area data; water use, waste disposal, and other operating characteristics of the activity; transportation and utility services available to the plant site; and so on. Such surveys must be carefully structured to the data requirements of space analyses undertaken later in the study.

Muncy's research into space requirements for industry provided considerable insight into the kind of detail required for more advanced analyses.[12] Her work indicated ways of classifying industries in much greater detail than is customarily used in preliminary land use planning studies, and among other things suggested the advisability of using floor area standards and of computing industrial densities on the basis of shift employment as opposed to total employment. Her studies of floor space per employee, structural density (ratio of the ground area of the factory and its accessory structures to the total land area of the plant site), and other site relationships provided important clues for the derivation of more precise industrial density standards for various classes of manufacturing activity. Although relating floor space to acreage on a somewhat different basis, Table 33 gives an illustration of the way in which standards can be developed using SIC categories of manufacturing. All these considerations should be taken into account in detailed land use planning studies of industrial space requirements.

Planned Industrial Districts

In connection with more detailed studies of industrial land use, investigations should include consideration of organized or planned industrial districts. Just as entire residential communities or shopping centers are now planned and built as integrated developments, modern-day industrial areas are increasingly being developed as planned industrial districts. Usually an enterprise under one management for marketing industrial sites on a sale or long-term lease arrangement, these developments are laid out in acreage lots of varying size especially designed for modern industrial operations. Employee parking and loading areas are required; water, waste, power, and fire protection facilities adequate for contemporary types of industrial operations are provided; and special attention is given to railroad and trucking facilities and, in some cases, to water and air transportation. Some of the more enterprising developments are conceived as "industrial parks," reserving areas for special common facilities such as lunchrooms, exhibition space, and recreation and park areas, and providing

---

[12] Dorothy A. Muncy, *Space for Industry, an Analysis of Site and Location Requirements,* Technical Bulletin No. 23, Washington: Urban Land Institute, July, 1954.

Table 33. Illustrative Floor Space and Acreage Standards Used to Determine Industrial Space Requirements by Zone, Philadelphia, 1960[a]

	II Inner Zone		III Outer Zone		V Far Northeast	
Floor area ratio [b]						
Present (1959)	2.50		1.00		.30	
Future (1980)	1.50		.60		.30	
Class of Industry	Floor Space per Worker (sq. ft.)	Workers per Acre	Floor Space per Worker (sq. ft.)	Workers per Acre	Floor Space per Worker (sq. ft.)	Workers per Acre
Food	600	109	700	37	1,200	11
Tobacco	250	261	250	105	—	—
Textiles	500	131	500	52	500	26
Apparel	175	373	225	116	—	—
Lumber and furniture	700	93	700	37	700	19
Paper	500	131	500	52	500	26
Printing	400	163	400	65	400	33
Chemicals	600	109	600	44	600	22
Petroleum and coal	—	—	—	10	—	5
Rubber	350	187	350	75	350	37
Leather	375	174	375	70	—	—
Stone, clay, and glass	600	109	600	44	600	22
Primary metals	—	—	1,200	22	1,200	11
Fabricated metals	400	163	600	44	650	20
Nonelectrical machinery	450	145	450	58	450	29
Electrical machinery	220	297	300	87	350	37
Transportation equipment	—	—	400	65	400	33
Precision instruments	350	187	500	52	600	22
Miscellaneous	400	163	400	65	400	33

[a] Excerpted from Table 7, "The Plan for Industry," in Philadelphia City Planning Commission, *Comprehensive Plan for the City of Philadelphia*, 1960.
[b] Ratio of total floor area of building to its site area.

for control over landscaping and the architectural design of structures.

Based on the experience of some of the pioneering organized industrial districts, manuals are available describing methods of planning, organizing, financing, and developing these industrial districts.[13] Although oriented mainly toward detailed site planning and development work, they provide useful insights into general land use planning requirements. Of particular interest is the general magnitude of these developments. One analysis of

---

[13] See Theodore K. Pasma, *Organized Industrial Districts*, a U.S. Department of Commerce publication, Washington: U.S. Government Printing Office, June, 1954; and Urban Land Institute, *Industrial Districts: Principles in Practice*, Technical Bulletin No. 44, *Industrial Districts Restudied*, Technical Bulletin No. 41, and *Planned Industrial Districts*, Technical Bulletin No. 19, Washington: Urban Land Institute, December, 1962, April, 1961, and October, 1952, respectively.

tract sizes of established industrial districts indicates that 80 per cent of the districts have tracts of less than 500 acres. The average tract is about 454 acres. Of the older, established districts, the average acreage comes to 1,182.[14] In identifying acreages of this magnitude for possible development as planned industrial districts, the land use plan must not only take into consideration topographic, transportation, utility, and other requirements normally associated with studies of industrial needs, but it must also give special attention to land ownership patterns and the actual availability of tracts for the industrial use contemplated. Obviously, the availability of unsubdivided land in as few ownerships as possible with clear land titles is an important consideration affecting the feasibility of developing such districts.

Space Needs of Wholesale and Related Uses

Of all the major use categories customarily included in the land use plan, the class referred to as "wholesale and related uses" is generally treated with the least specificity. Indeed, it has often been combined with manufacturing or given only vague recognition in a "general business" category. This is, of course, a reflection of the lack of attention accorded the wholesaling function in planning research and the need for studies which define the space-using characteristics of wholesale uses and provide techniques especially suited to the measurement of space requirements.

It has been common practice to relegate to this category all commercial uses of a nonindustrial and nonretail nature. Yet an investigation of the range of uses that thus fall within such a category clearly suggests the need for some form of subgrouping within this category, possibly some reallocation of uses to industrial or CBD office categories in recognition of variations in function, location, and space-using characteristics. While a great deal of further research is needed in this general area, for purposes of the preliminary land use plan, three general subgroups warrant recognition: wholesaling and warehousing proper, trucking and related warehousing, and the subcategory "other." This categorization is dictated primarily by standard employment data available in the Census of Business and the Census of Population which are used in conjunction with land use information for the estimation of space requirements. Of these three subcategories, the first two submit to a crude form of systematic analysis, with space requirements for the "other" subcategory being developed on a case-by-case consideration of the uses which fall within this miscellaneous group locally.

---

[14] Pasma, *Organized Industrial Districts*, p. 7.

Of the Census of Business' five-category classification of wholesalers, four categories could be included under our classification *wholesaling and warehousing proper:* merchant wholesalers, manufacturers' sales branches and offices, wholesale agents and brokers, and wholesale assemblers.[15] The fifth category, petroleum bulk stations, is more appropriately included in the final miscellaneous classification called "other," since it possesses distinctly special space-using characteristics. Merchant wholesalers generally predominate in this first class. They employ warehouses for assembly, storage, and distribution of goods and are the establishments traditionally associated with wholesale uses. They include retail distributors, who deal in commodities for retail outlets, and industrial distributors, who deal in goods bought for further processing or for business consumption. Manufacturers' sales branches and offices, a mixed group, function in effect to bypass merchant wholesalers. As the name implies, they are the manufacturers' own outlets. Sales branches require warehousing as well as display space, while sales offices require only display and office space for taking orders, which are then handled directly from the manufacturing plant. Wholesale agents and brokers are middlemen who require only display and office space.[16] They do not handle or acquire title to goods but only arrange sales between producers and retailers or wholesale merchants. Wholesale assemblers, who collect farm output for distribution to other wholesalers or to retailers, include farm-produce packers, shippers, cooperative marketing associations, and storage stations (for example, grain elevators, tobacco warehouses, cotton gins, milk depots, etc.).

The *trucking and related warehousing* category as used here refers to common carrier trucking facilities. These are the trucking firms which require terminals for assembly and breakdown of truck-load lots in connection with over-the-road hauls, and include accessory warehousing, repair and service facilities, and employee dormitories and similar services. They serve largely manufacturers and wholesalers, deriving only about 10 per cent of their business from CBD activities.[17]

---

[15] The Bureau of the Census defines wholesale establishments as "those productive units which are engaged in selling merchandise to retailers, to industrial, commercial, institutional, or professional users or to other wholesalers, or acting as agents in buying merchandise for or selling merchandise to such persons or businesses." The wholesale part of a business is counted as a separate establishment if it is operated functionally on a separate basis, and where businesses deal in both retail and wholesale trade, the business is classified in the category with the majority of sales. (*Source:* Bureau of the Census, *U.S. Census of Business: 1958,* Washington: U.S. Government Printing Office, 1960.)

[16] In line with the comments above, manufacturers' sales offices and wholesale agents and brokers would be more properly classified with CBD office uses for detailed land use planning analyses. This is reflected in the division of this activity in Table 22 into the "with storage on premises" and "without storage on premises."

[17] See Planning Advisory Service, *Motor Truck Terminals,* Information Report No. 21, Chicago: American Society of Planning Officials, December, 1950.

With this brief introduction to wholesale and related uses, we may now examine techniques for estimating space requirements. This analysis includes a sequence of four steps:

1. Analyze the characteristics of existing wholesale and related activities in the urban area.
2. On the basis of anticipated growth in wholesale activity as determined in studies of the urban economy and expected changes in the intensity of use, estimate future ratios of land area per employee for inlying and outlying locations.
3. Apply these ratios to future wholesale employment estimates to obtain estimated land requirements.
4. Determine from summary of vacant and renewal land how supply matches up with estimated need, and, referring to location requirements, make a trial distribution into areas identified as having potentialities for this use, earmarking the surplus for use in subsequent analyses of other uses.

A more detailed explanation of these steps to the analysis follows.

Existing Wholesale Areas

For the generalized results required in the preliminary land use plan, the first step is simply one of organizing data assembled in the land use survey and studies of the urban economy and employment in a form suitable for evaluating the general character and intensity of development in areas presently used for wholesale purposes. The acreages of wholesale use for the urban area as a whole are abstracted from the land use summary, including breakdowns by subcategories for wholesaling proper, trucking, and other related uses. If these wholesale breakdowns were not compiled from map or punch card analyses of the land use survey, new summaries of land areas in wholesale use of course would have to be made. In addition, summaries by major subdivisions of the urban area are required, and in order to permit comparative analyses with employment data, usually the central city and the balance of the planning area are the selected subareas. Summarized in percentages, these breakdowns by area give a crude indication of the relative concentration of wholesale uses in the inlying and outlying portions of the urban area.

By recapitulating wholesale employment data by the same functional and areal categories,[18] and applying these to acreage figures, it is possible to compute existing ratios of employees per wholesale acre for each of these categories and for the urban area as a whole. Measures of the exist-

---

[18] Census of Business employment figures are available separately for major cities and Standard Metropolitan Statistical Areas. Crude adjustment of SMSA figures to a planning area basis is made by reference to local sources of employment data for establishments beyond the planning area but inside the SMSA.

ing intensity in the use of wholesale land (the percentage coverage of land areas by wholesale structures) may be computed from Base C land use maps or by reference to insurance atlases.

Future Land Area Ratios

With a knowledge of the characteristics of existing development in wholesale use, it is possible to proceed to the development of standards of wholesale acres per employee. For purposes of the preliminary land use plan, the most expedient procedure in developing such standards at present is one of examining existing ratios for their sufficiency and subjectively upgrading those which appear to possess inadequacies for the character and intensity of development judged reasonable for the future. Thus if existing development as a whole in any one of the three functional subcategories of wholesaling, in either the inlying or outlying areas, appears to be crowding the land by comparison with some selected local "model" development or modern developments elsewhere, appropriate adjustments upward may be made. Such elements as the percentage of the land covered by structures and the observed adequacy of parking, loading, and service areas would provide the basis for making these adjustments.

It should be noted that the floor space per employee is a more valid basis for developing standards than land area per employee. In later detailed studies in revision of the first crude estimates developed by the above procedures in preliminary studies, a special establishment-by-establishment survey (probably combined with the industrial survey suggested earlier) would be designed and conducted to obtain, among other things, floor area data. Floor area ratios would then be used as base standards, with land area ratios developed from these base standards by applying appropriate parking standards and expansion factors to take into account loading and other on-site space requirements. Illustrative of standards for one metropolitan area obtained by such an approach are the following:[19]

Activity	Employees per Net Acre
Wholesaling proper [a]	32.0
Trucking-warehousing	10.0
Petroleum bulk stations	3.0

[a] Merchant wholesalers, manufacturers sales branches, and assemblers only.

These results were based on an analysis of floor area data obtained in a

[19] George M. Beaton, *Planning for Wholesale and Related Functions,* unpublished study, Chapel Hill: Department of City and Regional Planning, University of North Carolina, 1955.

survey made by the Advance Planning Division of the Nashville City and Davidson County Planning Commission.

For general approximation purposes, crude employee density standards for "wholesale and related uses" are commonly used. Illustrative of this kind of standard are those used in a Baltimore study where for estimating purposes, 25 employees per net acre was the standard used in the central city area as compared to 10 employees per net acre in the larger four-county area.[20] In the Roanoke area, a density of 10 employees per net acre was used as one general area-wide standard.[21]

Future Space Requirements

Once space standards for future wholesale development have been derived, space requirements can be estimated by applying these standards to estimates of future employment developed as described in Chapter 4. It is customary to increase the estimates thus derived by a percentage (commonly 25 to 50 per cent) to provide for flexibility in choice. Land requirements would be broken down to show the space needed by the end of the planning period for each subcategory of wholesale activity used and for the central city and the remainder of the planning area. Table 34 indicates the kind of summary of space requirements which should finally emerge from these analyses. The "extensive" and "intensive" subcategories at the head of the table are shown to indicate the possibility of using dual standards. Thus in the central city there may be intensive wholesale developments near the CBD and more extensive types in outlying locations. By the same token fringe areas may require dual standards.

Trial Distribution Scheme

The final step in the procedure compares the supply of vacant and renewal land judged to have wholesale use potentialities with the estimated need as established by procedures described above, and makes a tentative distribution of these acreage requirements according to location criteria established by studies discussed in Chapter 10. Using the same procedure employed in the analysis of manufacturing areas, allocations are first made to central city and outlying portions of the urban area on a proportional basis to serve as a control in the dimensioning process. Here too, pro-

---

[20] Baltimore Regional Planning Council, *Industrial Land Requirements,* Baltimore: Maryland State Planning Commission, May, 1959.

[21] The Roanoke Valley Regional Planning Commission, *A Land Use Plan for the Roanoke Valley Region.*

Table 34. New Space Requirements for Wholesale and Related Uses, 19xx

Wholesale Categories	Central City Ext.[a]	Central City Int.[a]	Outlying Area Ext.	Outlying Area Int.	Total Ext.	Total Int.
	Acreage Requirements					
Wholesaling and warehousing proper	xx	xx	xx	xx	xxx	xxx
Trucking and related warehousing	xx	xx	xx	xx	xxx	xxx
Other (petroleum bulk stations, etc.)	xx	xx	xx	xx	xxx	xxx
All wholesale and related uses	xx	xx	xx	xx	xxx	xxx

[a] "Ext." is an abbreviation for "Extensive," "Int." for "Intensive."

portions are estimated on the basis of observed past trends of growth in these two segments of the urban area relative to one another, and on the supply of vacant and renewal land in these areas available for wholesale development, particularly considering any ceilings on growth imposed by space limitations of in-town locations. Of course, this procedure must recognize any assumptions previously made concerning decentralization of wholesale uses. Then, in the framework of these controls, total acreage requirements are tentatively dimensioned into vacant and renewal areas previously identified as having potentialities for wholesale use or into areas carried over in the surplus tally as not needed for manufacturing uses. The map of vacant and renewal areas and the overlay of surplus industrial lands provide ready references for this dimensioning process. Finally, all land not needed to fill out space requirements for wholesale and related uses is carried over in the surplus land tally for absorption in other use categories in analyses that follow, and the accompanying overlay map is modified to show the locations of the surplus vacant land available at the conclusion of this analysis.

Space Requirements for Region-Serving Business Areas

Perhaps the most complex and difficult problems the average metropolitan area faces today are found in the business areas, particularly in the central business district. Foremost among these are traffic congestion and the lack of adequate parking. Although the immediate concern of investigations described below is with land use, proposals for the movement of people and goods to and from and within the central area and certainly the storage of vehicles during business hours of the day profoundly affect land use planning proposals. Indeed, these transportation elements are large space-using activities themselves. Obviously, if optimum parking conditions prevailed, vast areas would be taken up in storage of cars, even if the space were provided in multideck mechanized parking lofts. And if it were feasible to finance the drastic surgery that would be required in central areas so that all people with destinations in the CBD could drive there and find terminal parking space, great swaths would have to be cut through built-up areas in all directions simply to accommodate the traffic. These costs would be staggering. Even if the auto millennium were here and every person entering the CBD daily had an automobile enabling him to make the trip by car, the overall costs for completely "automobilizing" the CBD would be astronomical. Thus transit becomes an important leveling factor in striking some kind of practical balance—transit planned in effective balance with automotive transportation and its parking requirements.

The integrated solution to these problems is the subject of special CBD improvement studies. While the kind of generalized approach to these problems involved in developing the preliminary land use plan falls far short of providing solutions in the detail that ultimately will be required, it does assist in identifying the broad relationships involved and the general outlines of solutions that must be worked out in later refined types of studies.

For purposes of a preliminary plan and the generalized result desired, a very broad-gauge type of approach to the estimation of business space requirements is generally used. For the fully detailed analysis of space needs undertaken in comprehensive plan studies, a whole array of specialized investigations of retail, service, office, and other commercial functions is required. Although detailed floor area analyses, purchasing power studies, and other specialized types of investigations are alluded to at the end of the discussion below, our main concern here is with a type of analysis commensurate in detail with those undertaken in space analyses of other uses. It should be noted that, as a beginning point in preliminary studies, analyses of space needs usually assume continuation of the present balance in the use of automotive and transit modes of transportation. In the final design stages of the generalized plan, when a preliminary transportation plan becomes available, adjustments may be necessary in order to bring these initial assumptions into harmony with those of transportation studies.

As noted in Chapter 10, three types of region-serving business areas are involved in this general use category. These are the central business district, various satellite business centers, and highway service centers. The satellite centers include certain decentralized CBD-type business activities seeking larger and lower-value sites and escape from the downtown congestion (for example, auto sales and service centers, office building centers, etc.), and the so-called "regional shopping center," the type of facility planned and engineered for the automobile age. Since fully satisfactory estimates of space requirements for regional shopping centers and highway service centers involve specialized investigations not normally feasible for inclusion in preliminary land use planning analyses, these types of business areas will be taken up briefly at the outset before attention is centered on the CBD and its satellite business centers.

Regional and Highway Service Centers

Decisions relative to developing regional shopping centers require particularly exacting studies because of heavy initial investments involved in this type of center. These include purchasing power analyses, investigations of buying habits, surveys of family expenditure patterns, and a variety of other studies. Having removed these studies from the scope of the present approach, and with the relatively limited experience with this new type of business area generally available to serve as a guide, for purposes of the preliminary land use plan the only feasible procedure for the present is simply to insure that, if such a center seems warranted, a generous reservation of land is made for it in the most strategic location. General guides in this respect were presented in Chapter 10.

Space requirements for highway service types of business areas are dependent upon studies of both inter- and intraregional traffic movements and the makeup of these movements. According to the characteristics of this traffic, one or more types of business centers may be warranted. Thus, along major tourist routes these studies may indicate the need for tourist service centers. For these centers site sizes will be conditioned by space requirements for one or more modern motel accommodations on sites easily seen from the highway yet set back from the noise of passing traffic, plus their accessory restaurant and automobile service facilities. Along major trucking routes, a few sites for facilities to serve the 24-hour schedules of the trucking industry should be anticipated. Special sites for these needs will be less important where truck terminal centers are planned in peripheral locations.

In addition to these transient forms of business, highway service centers may be warranted to cater to the needs of the local metropolitan area, providing for outdoor theaters, drive-in refreshment and produce stands, auction centers, automobile service areas, and so on. In the average small and medium-size metropolitan area, say 250,000 or under, where site planning review requirements are anticipated in the implementing zoning provisions, a single type of highway service center may suffice. In the larger metropolitan areas, two or three types of highway service centers may be desirable to meet the needs of specialized service facilities. The number and spacing of these centers will normally be determined on the basis of estimates of purchasing power to be tapped from either transient or localized sources or both. The space requirements for any particular center will depend upon the number and character of facilities estimated to be needed in each such center and how they can be provided within the framework of an integrated site plan. For preliminary land use planning purposes, these analyses are necessarily very general, and since aggregate space requirements are somewhat nominal as compared to those of other land uses, the generalized land use plan frequently carries only symbols as to strategic locations and the spacing of such centers in outlying rural sections of the planning area, specifying in the text of the plan the criteria to be employed in the future establishment of these highway service centers.

Study of CBD Characteristics

Turning now to the central business district and satellite business centers, the analysis of space needs entails a sequence of three steps:

1. Delineate the CBD study area and satellite business centers and analyze existing space usage by floor area and ground area.
2. On the basis of this analysis and studies of retail business trends in the primary trade area, develop estimates of probable changes in intensity of use, parking needs, and so on, and determine future space needs.
3. Determine from vacant and renewal land summary the amount of land available for CBD expansion and determine what additional space is expected to become available due to decentralization moves of wholesale and manufacturing uses presently in CBD. Establish space deficit, if any. As necessary, earmark for CBD expansion strategically located areas, and summarize data on areas presently in other uses needed for CBD expansion. Repeat these space investigations for satellite centers.

The first step involves the definition of the CBD study area and any satellite business centers which exist at present or are anticipated to develop, and the compilation of floor area and acreage data relative to uses located in these areas from Base C–type land use maps or punch card sources. Since what may reasonably be expected to be the limits of the future CBD cannot be firmly established until the full sequence of this analysis is complete, the CBD study area as defined in this first step is tentative. In general, it is drawn so that it is overly generous in extent. The delineation recognizes the directions in which the CBD is currently expanding, and is traced out to include immediately adjoining areas in wholesale and manufacturing use previously identified as being likely to relocate in outlying areas during the planning period. It also recognizes locations of any adjoining renewal areas, and is drawn to include the major portions, if not all of the "inner loop," the major belt street ringing the CBD as defined in the preliminary thoroughfare scheme.

It should be noted that the CBD study area is therefore larger than the CBD as seen today or as defined by various empirical methods for research analyses of CBD structure. Nevertheless, such empirical methods are useful in defining the CBD core which can then be used as a basis for delineating the larger study area. Particularly useful in this respect is Murphy and Vance's "central business index method." [22] Defining the central business district in terms of whole blocks, this method utilizes two general tests, supplemented by special rules to take care of civic center uses and special situations. A block in which the ratio of the total area in central business uses on all floors to the total ground floor area has a numerical value of one or more would be included in the CBD. In the terminology of the authors, this block would have a "central business height index" of one or more. Any additional blocks where the percentage of the floor area on all floors in central business uses is 50 or more would also be included. The terminology used here is "central business intensity index." Central business uses are defined as those involved in "the retailing of goods and services for a profit and the performing of various office functions."

Once a CBD study area is tentatively defined, major subfunctional areas are defined, recognizing principal concentrations of retail shopping, entertainment, finance, offices, and such other functional groupings as represented by the civic center or the wholesale district and manufacturing areas which may be present. In this connection, unless special attention was given in the land use survey to the detail required in the analysis of the CBD study area and satellite business centers, a special resurvey may be required.[23] Assuming the necessary detailed information is available, in each subfunctional area, acreages occupied by structures in each dominant class of use, acreages devoted to off-street parking lots, and the residual acreage (alleys, landscaping, outdoor sales space, etc.) are tabulated. In addition to these subarea summaries, an overall summary for the entire study area is developed in two parts, one to show ground acreages by major class of use, and the other to show floor area for retail uses and

[22] Raymond E. Murphy and J. E. Vance, Jr., "Delimiting the CBD," *Economic Geography*, July, 1954, pp. 209–219.
[23] In this connection, the reader should be familiar with the detailed kind of CBD survey developed by Murphy and Vance, *ibid.*, pp. 204–209.

office uses broken down into subtotals as to area on the first floor and area above the first floor.

In addition to the CBD analysis, it is necessary to investigate the characteristics of any distinct satellite region-serving business centers that exist in the metropolitan area. Generally, similar procedures are followed in delineating and analyzing these centers. For scattered region-serving business establishments, a miscellaneous "all other" category is used in area tabulations.

Future Space Requirements

Having established the existing physical characteristics of the CBD study area and satellite centers, the second step draws on this information and, by using crude proportions relating space to the appropriate "multiplier," develops estimates of future space requirements. A crude estimate of the needed increase in aggregate floor space to be devoted to retail uses in the CBD and all satellite centers may be computed in proportion to the increase in population expected during the planning period in the primary trade area.[24] Sometimes a retail sales index is used as a "multiplier" in lieu of retail trade area population growth. A rough measure of the needed increase in aggregate floor space to be devoted to office use may be computed proportional to the increase in employment expected during the planning period in the professions, finance, insurance, real estate, and similar office-related categories of the employment forecast. Once the aggregate increments of increase have been determined, they are allocated to the CBD and satellite business centers in proportion to the assumed extent that each will share in the overall increases. These percentages are based on existing proportions adjusted subjectively to reflect observed trends or any planned modifications in these areas which might alter these trends.

Next, according to assumptions as to an average height of building in which this aggregate floor space will be accommodated in the CBD and each center, estimates of the amount of additional ground floor area which will be needed in all business areas during the planning period are devel-

---

[24] Murphy and Vance report that there appeared to be no significant relationship between floor space and primary trade area population in the nine small-city CBD's they studied, but their studies do not take into account all region-serving retail areas—retail floor space situated in satellite business centers and in scattered locations as well as in the CBD proper. Certainly further study is needed covering more cases and experimenting with different definitions of floor area identified with the retail function and different delineations of the tributary trade area before the use of a population "multiplier" is rejected or unconditionally accepted as a method of estimating space requirements.

oped. Next, according to locally adopted standards relating parking space to floor area, the amount of additional ground area in off-street parking required (1) to accommodate the new retail and office uses, and (2) to make up deficiencies in off-street parking for existing retail and office uses is estimated and added to this acreage in all business centers. Then, on the basis of observations of existing relationships between the loading and yard areas to retail floor area of the present retail shopping areas, standards considered reasonable and adequate for the new retail development in the CBD and for outlying centers are adopted and applied, and the amount of space needed for these purposes is added into these cumulative totals. Finally, these totals are adjusted upward by an amount judged to be adequate to allow for drives, landscaping, and waste area and to provide a safety factor for unforeseen needs not covered in the foregoing analysis. Table 35 indicates the estimation procedure in greater detail.

The foregoing procedures apply in estimating space requirements for retail and office functions. For other functions, such as civic center needs and its accessory parking areas, rail, bus, and possibly helicopter terminal facilities and their accessory parking areas, central park areas and other uses to be accommodated in the CBD, special estimates of space requirements are necessary. (Techniques for estimating space needs for these functions are taken up under other sections of this chapter.) The sum total of these needs, when added to the acreage presently in use for retail shopping and office purposes, yields a grand total of the net area required for the future development of the CBD.

Dimensioning the Future CBD

Finally, these total net space requirements are fitted into the block pattern of the CBD study area and other centers that exist or as this pattern may be modified by street adjustments or by renewal measures. The process of "dimensioning in" space needs in the CBD takes into account criteria previously established and such tempering elements as the prevailing directions of expansion, land values in the central area, the preliminary thoroughfare scheme, the pattern of railroads in or near the CBD and other relatively fixed features, natural or man-made. Close-in vacant and renewal areas are first examined for their suitability as expansion areas for the CBD. Then the manufacturing, wholesale, and general commercial areas in the downtown section expected to become available by the natural processes of decentralization and succession are investigated for their adaptability to CBD uses. Finally, any additional area needed may involve the earmarking of acreage for CBD purposes from residential areas, usually areas where old residences have been converted into rooming houses or light-

Table 35. Estimating Net Increase in Space for Retail and Office Functions in CBD by Component Analysis, 19xx

Type of Space Use	Space in Thousands of Square Feet		
	Retail	Office	Combined Total
Total floor area	xxxx [a]	xxxx [b]	xxxxxx
Ground floor area	xxx [c]	xxx [d]	xxxx
Ground area for new parking [e]	xxx	xxx	xxxx
Ground area for new loading [f]	xxx	xxx	xxxx
Other ground area [g]	xxx	xxx	xxxx
First subtotal of ground area			xxxxxx
Allowance for flexibility [h]			xxxx
Second subtotal of ground area			xxxxxx
Deficiencies in parking and loading for existing uses [i]			xxxx
Total ground area required			xxxxxx

[a] Before this entry can be inserted, assumptions as to the distribution of new region-serving retail space must be made. To illustrate, it might be assumed that 50 per cent of new floor area is to be accommodated in the CBD, 30 per cent in satellite centers, and 20 per cent in all other locations. Under such assumptions, the entry would be 50 per cent of the aggregate new floor space expected to be added in the metropolitan area during the planning period.

[b] As in the case of the retail item, assumptions concerning the distribution of office space are introduced here. If, for example, 90 per cent of new office floor area is expected to develop in the CBD, then the entry here would be 90 per cent of the aggregate of all new floor area in office uses expected in the metropolitan area during the planning period.

[c] For estimating purposes, an average story height for retail uses is assumed here. If, for example, upon examining the prevailing average height to which retail uses build, it seems reasonable to expect new uses to build to an average of 1.9 stories, then to derive this entry, the total floor area in the entry immediately above would be divided by 1.9.

[d] Two assumptions are involved here. First, the per cent of floor area in offices in the CBD which can be expected to be added to floors above retail activities already provided for in the entry immediately to the left is assumed, let us say 40 per cent. Second, as in the case of retail structures, an average story height of CBD office buildings is assumed, say 5 stories. Then, under this example, the entry here would be 60 per cent of the total new office floor area expected to be added in the CBD (60 per cent of the item immediately above), divided by 5.

[e] Assumed parking ratio standards are introduced and applied to *total* new floor area figures. Differential standards may be used, or a crude general standard may be applied to the entry for combined floor area in the right-hand column. If a portion of the parking area is to go into multideck structures, a procedure similar to that followed in Note d would be followed in order to "factor out" the space in upper-deck areas and obtain a ground area total.

[f] On the basis of design standards, an estimate of space required for new loading areas is made in this entry. Crude standards for both retail and office structures are sometimes developed on the basis of a survey of areas presently judged to be well served in this or other cities. Some studies have used rough estimators such as one square foot of loading area for every 20 square feet of *total* floor space.

[g] This is to take care of waste area and private open spaces not included in estimates above. According to anticipated changes in the intensity to which ground area is to be used, an entry for these space needs is made here. On the basis of recent construction in the CBD, some studies simply follow the trend observed, adjusted or unadjusted, and increase the ground floor area by, say, 10, 20, or 25 per cent to provide for "relief space" and planted areas.

[h] The flexibility factor is an allowance for unforeseen expansion in the CBD, including at the same time latitude for choice of location among leasing users of CBD floor area. This factor is estimated locally on the basis of vacancy rates assumed reasonable for the period ahead and an adequate allowance for flexibility. It usually takes the form of a simple per cent increase of the aggregate ground area represented in the first subtotal, say a 20 per cent increase.

[i] This entry involves an analysis of the adequacy of present off-street parking provisions. It reflects the aggregate deficiency in parking and loading areas that must be treated as new space requirements under assumptions concerning the elimination of on-street parking and loading and any significant changes in driving habits anticipated.

housekeeping apartments (sometimes referred to as the "area of transition") bordering on the present central business area. While clearance of limited portions of these occupied areas may be achieved by blanketing them into clearance areas under the local public renewal program, for the most part stimulation for clearance and redevelopment into new CBD uses during the planning period must come from indirect means such as zoning changes, stiffening of fire regulations, promotional programs, and so on.

The problems of guiding expansion of the central area along sound and orderly lines and controlling the speculative forces commonly present in areas of transition are particularly acute and difficult. Planning proposals are dealing here with an area which is largely built up and where properties (usually composing an area much larger than can be absorbed in the foreseeable future) are valued by their owners for a use that may not develop for a great many years, if at all. These problems of plan implementation are beyond the scope of this discussion. However, it is clear that much more positive implementation measures are required in central areas, perhaps along the lines of a central business improvement district authority, backed with new forms of redevelopment powers.

Following the dimensioning process, any increments of vacant and renewal land not taken up in these analyses are entered in the surplus land tally, and any necessary modifications in the overlay maps keyed to the

Table 36. Total Space Requirements for CBD and Satellite Region-Serving Business Centers, 19xx

| | | Net Acreage of Ground Area | | | | |
| | | Deductions from Other Uses | | | | |
Type of Center and Use [a]	Total Needs	Residence	Wholesale	Mfg.	Other	Total
Central business district	xx	x	x	x	x	xx
Retail uses	xx	x	x	x	x	xx
Office uses	xx	x	x	x	x	xx
Civic uses and parks	xx	x	x	x	x	xx
Transportation uses	xx	x	x	x	x	xx
Other uses	xx	x	x	x	x	xx
Satellite business centers	xx	x	x	x	x	xx
Center A	xx	x	x	x	x	xx
Center B	xx	x	x	x	x	xx
Etc.	xx	x	x	x	x	xx
Other scattered	xx	x	x	x	x	xx
Total	xx	x	x	x	x	xx

[a] Acreage figures for each center and type of use include parking, loading, and other miscellaneous areas associated with these uses.

tally are made. In the central areas of the city this step may involve very few if any changes in the tally and key maps. Finally, data are summarized relatively to areas tentatively identified for use invasion. Table 36 illustrates the way in which these analyses may be summarized. Since most if not all new acreage requirements involve invasions into built-up areas, therefore making the summary of vacant and renewal land of relatively limited utility, it is usually simpler to prepare this table in terms of *total space needs* rather than in terms of new space needs as done in other use analyses. While space requirements for the central park areas, the civic center, and public service uses requiring central locations are taken up later in the chapter, these needs are recapitulated in the table as part of the CBD space summary. This table also records the deductions in acreages presently in other uses so that these may be taken into account in space analyses of other affected use categories. Not shown in the table but necessary for later analyses of the housing inventory is a tabulation of the number of dwelling units affected, by type of structure.

Later Detailed Investigations

As noted at the outset of this discussion of region-serving business areas, a variety of more exacting investigations are necessary in the refinement of this first generalized approach as the planning agency moves toward the development of a comprehensive plan. This is not to imply that there are highly developed techniques available for all phases of these investigations. On the contrary, the tools available for these purposes are variable in their precision and adequacy, and when these investigations are initiated, it soon becomes evident that there are a great many aspects of business area analysis which are urgently in need of research attention. However, there are several kinds of investigations particularly noteworthy for later more detailed stages of planning.

Some of the more detailed studies involve extensions of techniques noted above. In the analysis of CBD space requirements, detailed studies generally break out subcategories within such major sectors as manufacturing, wholesale trade, retail trade, and finance–insurance–real estate which are commonly found in the central area at present. Within the framework of metropolitan-wide analyses of each major sector, future CBD functions are defined and growth prospects of each investigated. For retail activity, aggregate retail space estimates for the entire metropolitan area are usually based on population growth in the retail trade area (usually larger than the metropolitan area). In place of using square feet of floor area per 1,000 population as in preliminary planning analyses, population growth is usually translated into retail sales potential, either in terms of sales per capita or of sales per family of different median income levels. Separate measures may be used for general classes of retail activity, for example, for consumer goods, shopper goods, or convenience goods. Aggregate estimates of retail sales are then distributed to subsidiary market areas—consumer and shopper goods to regional and intermediate shopping centers and convenience goods to intermediate and local shopping centers—according to estimates of the distribution of population or families as determined from the residential areas analysis taken up in a later section of this chapter and studies of the rest of the trade area. The Philadelphia comprehensive plan utilizes an approach of this general type.[25]

At least two additional refinements may be introduced. The first is a relatively recent development, and the second is a refinement of the technique above. Relatively new on the scene is the use of models to distribute retail activity to particular sites. For example, Artle uses a producer-type model to distribute establishments and simulate clustering tendencies.[26] Conceivably the locations selected could be tested by a consumer-type model of the kind proposed by Huff, which utilizes the properties of the conventional gravity-type model (see Reilly's use of the gravity concept discussed in Chapter 3) in a probability form to simulate customer behavior in patronizing shopping centers.[27] The other kind of submetropolitan type of detailed investigation focuses on market survey techniques of the kind used by Huff but is directed to the analysis of a particular shopping center's competitive position with respect to others in the surrounding area. These investigations give particular attention to analyses of purchasing power, family expenditure patterns, and consumer buying habits. Such analyses are used mainly for the study of retail functions or business areas, having only limited application to office functions.

This approach to estimating retail requirements calls for estimates of the effective buying income in the retail trade area and how it is distributed among various income groups. This information is obtained in conjunction with a survey of family expenditures. Typical family expenditure patterns of these various income groups are spelled out for purposes of identifying the major kinds of retail facilities that are associated with goods and services

---

[25] Philadelphia City Planning Commission, *Comprehensive Plan for the City of Philadelphia,* 1960.

[26] Roland Artle, *Studies in the Structure of the Stockholm Economy,* Stockholm: The Business Research Institute at the Stockholm School of Economics, 1959.

[27] David L. Huff, *Determination of Intra-Urban Retail Trade Areas,* Los Angeles: Real Estate Research Program, Graduate School of Business Administration, University of California, 1962.

purchased. In this connection, it has been found that the volume of goods and services purchased bears a relationship to the floor space required to handle the indicated volume of business. Once a measure of the volume of business by income group for various retail categories has been determined, a study of patronizing habits is made to establish what places the different income groups in various sectors of both the immediate urban area and outlying portions of the trade area select for what kinds of purchases. Besides providing insight into the many and complex variables affecting consumer purchase habits, this study provides a means of linking the spatial distribution of total space in retail use with the spatial distribution of the various income group families patronizing these business areas.

While the Census of Business provides data on retail sales for various categories of establishments, the only means presently feasible for connecting these sales with the income and geographic distribution of families making the purchases reflected in these sales is through the above kinds of studies. Since forecasting techniques are most satisfactory if developed in terms of population units in these analyses—in this case the family—we therefore need family expenditure information for various income levels represented in the trade area, and according to the way these income groups are distributed spatially.

The procedures for these analyses can go into great detail, and their most detailed applications are found in shopping center analyses. In one of the earliest and most fully documented studies, Lillibridge, in applying market analysis techniques to a Chicago redevelopment area, shows how the Bureau of Labor Statistics' family expenditure studies may be used for estimation purposes in lieu of a sampling survey of families.[28] The Real Estate Research Corporation's analysis of Englewood Plaza in Chicago, an illustration of a study using a sampling survey, introduces an interesting geometric zonal and sector scheme for the analysis of families potentially served by this facility.[29] Smith provides other insights into the use of these techniques in the analysis of shopping centers.[30]

Whether the study is centered on a particular shopping facility or its scope is the entire range of business areas in the city, there are obviously variations in the technique that can be employed in pursuing the basic procedures—variations in short cuts that may be taken and variations in the

---

[28] Robert M. Lillibridge, "Shopping Centers in Urban Redevelopment," *Land Economics,* May, 1948.

[29] Real Estate Research Corporation, *Economic and Legal Analysis, Perimeter Plan for Englewood Plaza,* published by the author, 1953.

[30] Larry Smith, "Economic Potential of Proposed Shopping Center," *The Appraisal Journal,* January, 1959.

methods of assembling data required at various stages of the analyses. But most techniques begin with the family or household as a unit, and by analysis of expenditure patterns of various income groups, build up estimates of gross retail sales for various retail locations. These estimates broken down by store type are translated into floor space, which in turn can be expanded into acreage requirements by using appropriate parking ratios, loading area factors, and so on.

Forecasts involve a variety of intangibles and uncertainties about the future which are difficult to assess. Buying habits are affected by changes in technology, fashion, and whim, which in certain lines are difficult if not impossible to anticipate with any reliability. (For example, in the entertainment field the widespread purchase of television sets has had an effect upon family expenditures for the movies.) Moreover, changes in patronage habits are difficult to anticipate. The place of patronage is affected not only by such elements as parking, traffic congestion, and the physical convenience and attractiveness of the business center, but also by customer loyalties, which depend upon management policies on such things as sales, opening and closing hours, merchandising practices, and other similar factors. Changing income levels and inflationary-deflationary forces also offer formidable problems in forecasting. While these difficulties would seemingly raise serious questions as to the utility of these detailed analyses, it should be remembered that these sources of possible inaccuracy would have a relatively limited effect on the acreage space requirements, since parking and off-street loading areas constitute such a large proportion of the total space needs.

Space Needs of Public Service Facilities

As used here and in the preceding chapter, the "public service" land uses correspond with activity systems identified in Chapter 6 as communications and general services. They are a group of uses composed mainly of activities which, though assembled here as a group, are often widely distributed in a spatial sense. They appear together here simply because the derivation of total space requirements needs first a metropolitan-wide perspective. When distributed and eventually dimensioned into the plan, many of them can be summarized as parts of other assemblages—the CBD, industrial parks, residential communities, and so on. Thus, if existing land uses have been grouped and summarized following the pattern proposed in Table 23, the space needs for uses examined in this section would be summarized as subcategories of the major categories under which they fall in this table.

Accordingly, the civic center, the central post office, the state and federal functions, the various passenger stations, and headquarters for the various public utilities requiring access to the general public would be included in the CBD, possibly with branch offices or facilities in satellite business areas or community shopping centers. Similarly, such facilities as freight terminals, railroad marshaling yards and service facilities, port installations, power plants, gas works, and garbage and refuse disposal plants might be studied in conjunction with manufacturing uses, thus forming the category referred to in Table 23 as "industrial and related uses." Some uses with special location considerations—uses which do not properly fall within any of the broad functional use categories, such uses as cemeteries, water works, sewage disposal plants, power substations, refuse land fills, and airports— would continue to be handled as special uses. All these miscellaneous public service uses are grouped together for purposes of this discussion simply to emphasize their special nature and the necessity of seeing them in an urban-wide perspective and reserving space for them in addition to that which may be provided for under the general use category in which they fall.

For the most part, space requirements for these facilities are determined on the basis of special studies of the individual needs of each facility and the site size dictated by these needs. Obviously, the variety of special investigations involved in arriving at accurate space requirements for each type of facility are more appropriately covered in the comprehensive plan studies.[31] For the level of detail required in the preliminary land use plan, the need for new or expanded public service facilities, especially for the large space users, is established on the basis of interviews with the appropriate public or company officials. Crude estimates of space needs are made facility by facility based on the judgment of these officials, any pertinent special investigations they or their consultants may have made in the recent past, and the general experience with the particular facility that may be gained from other cities. Some of the general considerations involved in

[31] For the reader's convenience, some of the references for these more detailed studies are listed as follows: Planning Advisory Service, *Cemeteries in the City Plan*, Information Report No. 16, July, 1950, *Municipal Waterfronts: Planning for Commercial and Industrial Uses*, Information Report No. 45, December, 1952, and *Rail Lines and Terminals in Urban Planning*, Information Report No. 82, January, 1956, all issued by the American Society of Planning Officials, Chicago; S. J. Schulman, "Public Utilities and Related Service Facilities," in Mary McLean (ed.), *Local Planning Administration*, third edition, Chicago: International City Managers Association, 1959; American Public Works Association, *Municipal Refuse Disposal*, Chicago: Public Administration Service, 1961; Robert Horonjeff, *The Planning and Design of Airports*, New York: McGraw-Hill Book Company, Inc., 1962; Federal Aviation Agency, *Small Airports*, January, 1959, and *Heliport Design Guide*, December, 1959, Washington: U.S. Government Printing Office; and for highly technical installations such as power plants, electric substations, railroad marshaling yards, and railroad service facilities, few of which are treated in city planning sources, standard engineering texts in these fields should be consulted.

estimating space requirements for civic center and subcivic center facilities are taken up briefly below.

The Civic Center

Except in a few of the very large metropolitan areas, the civic center is usually situated on the edge of the retail shopping section of the central business district. The site selected and the intensity with which the site is developed are often markedly influenced by the pattern of land values, although other important considerations such as the accessibility to the major street network and transit system are also involved. Generally, the site should be near but not in the high-value area and out of the path of retail expansion; it should be in an area where there are good approaches and adequate space for a pleasing grouping of buildings, for open green areas, and for parking space—in general, sufficient space for the proper setting and symbolic treatment normally associated with the civic center. Some facilities such as fire or police stations or an auditorium located in the group may impose special requirements as to location. For example, these facilities require a location which permits easy and quick access to the thoroughfare system. All these factors are considered in principle in connection with the establishment of location requirements as taken up in Chapter 10.

The estimation of space requirements for the civic center must first take into account the functions to be housed in the center: the city hall, the county courthouse, state and federal buildings, if any, the public library, museums, the civic auditorium, and any other types of functions that may be contemplated. Once decisions have been reached on the activities ultimately to be accommodated, it is then necessary to determine how intensively the site is to be developed: whether buildings are to be low, one- or two-story, or multistory buildings. This decision is dependent to some extent on land values and the size of the chosen site and to some extent on design objectives in the massing and grouping of buildings on the site in relation to approaches and vistas. However, once decisions have been reached on the character of buildings to be provided, space needs then become a matter of summing up the ground area required for these buildings and the areas determined to be needed for accessory parking, public grounds, and related park areas. Of course, floor space requirements of each function to be housed in the center, present and future, are essential to the study. Initially, for purposes of site selection, these may be rough estimates assembled on the basis of preliminary scaled diagrams of alternative space arrangements for each function. The architect should be available for consultation at the earliest possible stage of these studies, and certainly in the execution of site development sketches and studies.

Subcivic Centers

There are certain public service functions which must be organized on a district basis. Thus, except in the case of very small communities, fire stations are provided in selected locations to serve certain subareas of the city. In the large metropolitan areas, it eventually becomes necessary to decentralize a number of the functions. However, it is not always feasible to consolidate in the same subcenters all decentralized civic functions. While there is need for branch offices at outlying focal points where the public can pay utility and tax bills, secure permits and licenses, and, in some sections of the community, have access to public health personnel for routine clinical examinations, at the same time efficient police and fire districting may call for substations at entirely different locations.

In this connection, it will be helpful to outline some of the location criteria and other factors which affect the derivation of space requirements of branch facilities for public service functions. In general, branch municipal offices should be located near the focal point of several residential neighborhoods, preferably near or adjoining community shopping centers. According to the overall districting system and other specialized needs of each facility, there may be consolidated with the branch municipal office a fire station, a precinct police station, a health clinic or station, and a branch library.

The extent of fire districts and local service areas which govern the location of fire stations is strongly influenced by the recommendations of the National Board of Fire Underwriters who set standards for the administrative organization, equipment, and location of fire stations for fire insurance rating purposes.[32] Intensively developed high-value areas (usually contained in special "fire districts" defined in the city's fire code) require higher-order standards than other sections of the urban area. For example, for pumper companies, a direct street-travel distance to business and industrial areas of no greater than three-quarters of a mile is recommended, and for compactly developed residential areas, a distance no greater than a mile and a half; for ladder companies, standards of maximum direct travel distance are one and two miles, respectively. The actual space requirements

---

[32] See the Board's *Standard Schedule for Grading Cities and Towns of the United States with Reference to Their Fire Defense and Physical Condition*, New York: National Board of Fire Underwriters, 1956; and see also *Planning the Location*, Bulletin 176, March, 1959, and *Planning the Building*, Bulletin 175, March, 1959, New York: National Board of Fire Underwriters.

for firehalls are dependent upon the type of fire company and therefore the size of ground floor area in the firehall, any outdoor facilities required for practice drills, the visual clearance needs for the particular site, landscaping, and so on.

District or precinct police stations are located on the basis of other criteria. Since contact with the public is not of primary importance, the location of these stations is determined by the district lines and by the speed and efficiency of moving personnel and equipment into these established service areas. Police districts in commercial areas and close-in densely populated areas are usually small and patrolled on a beat system, while outlying districts are larger and are covered by patrol cruisers. On the other hand, public health centers, clinics, or stations are generally needed only in certain areas of the city. Generally, the out-patient department of the city hospital contains the specialized facilities for the city as a whole, with clinics and stations for routine examinations being provided in the densely populated areas where the disease incidence rates tend to be high. Obviously, there would be only a few instances in which the application of the individual location criteria for fire, police, and health stations would result in the same location.

The provision of branch libraries depends not only on the population size of the library system's service area, but also on local policy matters such as separate school and public library systems *versus* a combined system, the use of bookmobiles, and so on. American Library Association standards call for all residential areas being within the service area of a public library, and where a branch library system is the adopted local policy, a local service-area radius of not more than one mile is recommended.[33] In making adaptations of these standards to local needs, San Francisco favored, in principle, large branches serving 25,000 to 50,000 population, but recognizing that in areas of low population density or in situations where barriers exist, a service-area population of 10,000 to 15,000 may be warranted. The facility should be located in or adjoining a community shopping center or some similar center which is a point of congregation for the residents of the service area. The space requirements are determined by the ground floor area of the ultimate-size building required, parking areas for automobiles and bicycles, and landscaping.

Post offices generally seek business center locations. In addition to the independent or central post office in the downtown area, outlying post office "stations" are provided in cities of medium size and upward. Stations outside the corporate limits of the area served by an independent post office

---

[33] San Francisco Department of City Planning, *Report on a Plan for the Location of Public Libraries in San Francisco*, April, 1953.

are called "branches." Stations and branches are located at the focal points of shopping, usually in large community shopping centers. They may be in government-owned buildings, but post office policy calls for leased quarters as a general rule. Since all mail deliveries originate from the independent post office, space requirements for stations and branches are minimal.

Space for Regional Recreation, Education, and Cultural Uses

This section is concerned with land uses developed to accommodate the activity subsystem identified in Chapter 6 as human development activities —space used for recreation, education, health, and other similar activities. Here we are concerned with region-serving forms of these land uses. As in other use categories discussed so far, for the generalized result required in preliminary planning, this class of use also employs only broad-gauged estimating techniques. For most of this category of region-serving uses, the same general procedural sequence followed in other land use classes applies equally well here. Thus the first step is an analysis of the existing facility in terms of its adequacy for the population groups served and the sufficiency of the site size for the particular facility developed there. In the light of these findings and available general standards adapted to the local situation, the second step first derives total acreage requirements for the correction of existing deficiencies and the accommodation of future growth, and then distributes the total acreage thus derived to appropriate vacant, renewal, or sometimes occupied sites in the urban area according to location criteria previously developed as discussed in Chapter 10. The final step involves deductions from the supply of vacant and renewal land for the indicated tentative uses, with appropriate notations sketched in on overlays indicating locations of areas absorbed for region-serving recreational, educational, and cultural uses, and those areas still unearmarked for specific use at the conclusion of this series of analyses.

Open Space Systems

In this general group of space uses is included what has come to be known as open space. While open space is frequently associated with outdoor recreation, it has also come to have significance as a land reserve to introduce relief from what might otherwise become uninterrupted development. In recent years a great deal of interest has become centered on the problem of the disappearance of open space in metropolitan areas. For a time, city planning agencies seemed to be carrying on a monologue on the need for reserving open space. Then Whyte's magazine article crusade to bring the problem before the public and his proposal for the establishment of open space easements touched off a general push for public action.[34] Fortuitously, the great interest of the press in the growth of cities following the 1960 census and their speculations on the megalopotanean spread of urban regions lent momentum to public interest in open space conservation. On the crest of this interest Congress established a public open space grant program under the Housing and Home Finance Agency, and with this means of implementing open space proposals, what had once been an academic exercise has become a reality.

Conservation is not the only basis of interest in open space. The continuing trend in western society toward a more advanced technology and a wider use of automation has served to focus more attention on leisure-time needs. While it is beyond the scope of this discussion to go into these trends, there is no doubt that one result of changes in leisure-time patterns will be a greater demand for open spaces to accommodate recreation needs. This is made eminently clear in the findings of the Outdoor Recreation Resources Review Commission.[35] In this work and some of the state studies which preceded and followed it, increasing attention is focused on state systems of open space as extensions of metropolitan systems.[36] These developments clearly indicate the broad scope involved in region-serving forms of recreation.

Techniques of analyzing both region-serving and local recreation needs are undergoing some much-needed overhaul. The advent of a market analysis type of approach involving a user and supplier view of recreation as variables in the conventional facility-oriented type of study has introduced changes in approach to estimating future requirements. In one approach an activities survey is contemplated as discussed in Chapter 6, with sampling surveys used to get at the expected intensity of activity among various user groups for various categories of activity.[37] A second paralleling investigation focuses on the supply side of the problem, both in terms of resources and facilities, with the plan derived on the basis of cost-benefit analysis. Other approaches direct attention to the program concept of

---

[34] William H. Whyte, Jr., *Securing Open Space for Urban America: Conservation Easements,* Technical Bulletin No. 36, Washington: Urban Land Institute, 1959.

[35] Outdoor Recreation Resources Review Commission, *Outdoor Recreation for America,* Washington: U.S. Government Printing Office, 1962.

[36] For example, see California Public Outdoor Recreation Plan Committee, *California Public Outdoor Recreation Plan,* Sacramento: The Committee, 1960.

[37] National Advisory Council on Regional Recreation Planning, *A User-Resource Recreation Planning Method,* Loomis, Calif.: The Council, May, 1959.

suppliers, with this being compared to user preferences to establish the outline of facility needs.

For preliminary planning, no special effort is made to quantify space needs. The problem is not "how much" but "where can space be found." Moreover, as we shall see presently, rule-of-thumb standards of space per unit of population are very rough, and to aggregate the standards of individual facilities into one general standard becomes meaningless. For inlying areas, the need is frequently a remedial one of acquiring space through renewal programs and a program of purchase. In outlying areas, where much space can be acquired by dedication as land goes into development, there is a premium on defining the outlines of an open space system, even though the perimeter lines of this system are not set down precisely. In general, the drainage corridors become the structural elements of an open space system, with these finger-like elements supplying connections between reservations of natural areas and spaces needed for various recreation uses of the kind taken up below. Of course, floodways and areas where drainage problems are likely to be expensive to solve can be brought under public control by including them in the general public open space system. Private open spaces of the kind involved in college campuses, medical centers, and other institutional areas constitute another element in an overall system of open space. But beyond these needs, the amount of land required for open space is still likely to remain open-ended, for as yet we have no basis for quantifying the need for "breathing spaces" in cities.

Recreational Uses

The region-serving recreational uses encompass a variety of facilities with divergent location needs. At one extreme are the spectator sports involving ball parks, public stadiums, boxing arenas, and other facilities for regularly scheduled sports events and the occasional exhibition matches. These require inlying or intermediate locations directly accessible to the transit and major traffic-handling routes. Also found in central locations are the downtown parks in or near the CBD. At the other extreme are country parks or large public reservations in the outlying reaches of the planning area that are developed for picnicking, hiking, nature walks, boating, and other forms of activities for family excursions and organized group outings. These facilities are usually accessible only by car or stage. In between, at the edges of the built-up portions of the urban area, are public and private golf courses, race tracks, fairgrounds, botanical gardens, zoos, and other large space users. These usually locate close enough to the built-up area so as to be near the end of public transportation routes and near major traffic radials.

The estimation of space requirements for these recreation areas and public open spaces employ two criteria, one based on population and the other based on site size. The population standard indicates the number of people served per facility, and thus, when used in relation to the forecast population of the planning area, provides a rough measure of the number of facilities required. When a minimum site-size standard is applied to the number of facilities thus derived, a crude estimate of the minimum acreage of space is obtained for each type of facility. Final space requirements are an upgraded version of these minimum needs, with higher standards, in effect, achieved in the course of fitting facilities to particular sites. Table 37 summarizes some of the commonly used standards. In addition to these rather specific types of facilities, most cities have a general system of park and open space. Within this system fall the central parks, the miscellaneous small sitting areas in the central business district, squares, monument sites, and various historical plots (with or without structures) that have some special local, state, or national significance.

As noted above, the general open space system as a whole is less amenable to quantitative analysis and ill-adapted to the use of space standards, the amount of space provided being more a subjective determination, considering such factors as the natural drainage patterns in the urban area, the character of the terrain, and the aggregate amount of land considered uneconomic to develop for other uses. In this respect, the financial ability of public agencies with maintenance functions is sometimes an important limiting factor. However, such maintenance costs must be considered in relation to potential expenses incurred by public agencies in dealing with

Table 37. General Standards for Region-Serving Recreational Facilities

Type of Facility	Population Standard	Minimum Site-Size Standard
Major natural parks	1 park/40,000	100 acres/park
Public golf course	1 hole/3,000 [a]	150 acres/18 holes
County fairgrounds	1/county seat	special [b]
Colosseums	1/metro. area	special [b]
Public stadiums	1 stadium/100,000	special [b]
Botanical garden	1/metro. area	special [b]
Zoo	1/metro. area	special [b]

[a] Sometimes the standard of 18 holes/30–50,000 is used.
[b] Site size estimated according to size of facility appropriate to size of region served, facilities desired, and parking and service areas needed.

drainage and other problems which develop when some of these areas are pressed into use. To circumvent the problem of these maintenance costs, in some urban areas low-lying or steep areas are acquired and left in woodland strips and city forest reserves where maintenance costs are minimal.

Educational, Cultural, and Medical Centers

As in the case of public service facilities, space requirements for colleges, museums, music or art centers, medical centers, and various kinds of institutions requiring substantial acreages are estimated on a case-by-case basis. For preliminary land use planning purposes, these requirements will usually be determined on the basis of interviews with administrative officials in charge of developmental programs for these institutions and their estimates of the expansion anticipated during the planning period. Where institutional personnel or their consultants have prepared within recent time estimates of long-range developmental needs of the institutions concerned, these may be used *in toto*, with little or no adjustment. Where estimates are obviously subjective approximations, they should be checked for their reasonableness and possibly modified according to experience drawn from studies elsewhere.

Most colleges maintain a master plan for the development of their campuses. The enrollment in many educational institutions is the population equivalent of a small city, and with the millions of dollars of investment that a university represents, it is to be expected that it would maintain a planning staff. From the viewpoint of the city in which it is located, competent campus planning will materially assist in relating the institution's plans with the general plans for the urban area as a whole. Encompassing some of the same general considerations involved in planning for the civic center grouping of structures, campus planning studies must delve into other factors, especially higher-education enrollment trends as they are distributed among the various private and public institutions in the region and how the local university or college may be expected to share in these future enrollment trends.

Another kind of institutional grouping of facilities is the modern-day medical center. In recent years, there has been an evident trend, particularly in large metropolitan areas, for hospital facilities to gravitate together to form distinct medical centers. Sometimes a foundation grant or state and federal funds have provided the means for establishing such centers, and usually the presence of one or more medical schools has formed the core for these centers.

Again, developmental studies by these institutions themselves will facilitate general planning in the urban area, at the same time assuring a far-sighted approach to their own expansion needs. Indeed, a number of the larger centers are now maintaining their own master plans with their own planning staffs. In the case of the smaller medical centers, the local planning agencies may furnish planning assistance.

Space Needs of Residential Communities

We come now to the final category of uses, the residential communities of the urban area. These are the largest users of space, consisting mainly of residential uses proper, but also including accessory community facilities. As brought out earlier, analyses of residential areas cannot be divorced from consideration of their related community facilities, the location and space requirements for local shopping centers, churches, schools, and local recreation areas being interrelated with considerations of density, location, and character of the residential developments they are serving. In order to take these relationships into account on a scale that is meaningful, space requirements are analyzed within the framework of localized planning districts.

Since the number and extent of new community facilities depend mainly upon estimates of the location and density of new residential development, this discussion of space requirements for residential communities begins with housing requirements, then takes up local shopping centers, schools, and recreation facilities in that order, and finally considers residential communities as a whole. Space requirements for churches are usually omitted at this generalized stage of planning, these needs being more appropriately considered in detailed comprehensive plan studies. In keeping with the generalized result desired, it should be noted that throughout, analyses are pitched to an "approximation" level of accuracy where subjective estimates and assumptions are introduced at various steps in the procedure in substitution for what would become objective determinations in the later detailed plan investigations. The general character of some of these later studies is indicated at the end of this section of the chapter.

Residential Space Requirements

The sequence of the analysis of residential area requirements falls into the following steps:

1. Organize data relative to the existing supply of dwelling units and density of development and summarize by planning districts.
2. Develop working assumptions as to future residential trends, and on the basis

of these assumptions, determine additions to total supply of dwelling units required and estimate how this total is to be allocated to assumed future housing types and residential density classes.

3. On the basis of the supply of vacant and renewal land suited to residential development and its approximate effective net holding capacity by planning district, make tentative allocation of additions to total dwelling unit stock for the several density classes to the various planning districts.

4. Summarize space requirements and population estimates by planning district.

The key unit of measurement normally employed in residential area analyses is the family,[38] but in this somewhat abbreviated approach the household[39] is used as a crude substitute term. Thus population data, being the original yardstick of growth, are translated into household data, which in turn can be expressed in terms of dwelling units, and through the medium of residential densities, dwelling units are ultimately converted to acreage equivalents, the end product desired in this analysis.

1. *Existing housing supply.* The first major step is one of organizing data concerning existing residential areas into a form suitable for such an analysis. This involves first a summary of the existing stock of dwelling units, a summary of existing acreages in residential use, and a summary of prevailing net densities—all by planning district. For control purposes, planning districts are grouped into central city districts and fringe area districts, with subtotals developed for each of these portions of the planning area. Dwelling unit counts come from punch cards or land use field sheets (see Figure 26, 27, or 28A); acreages are read off the tabular summary of land uses; and net densities are computed from these two series of data. Table 38 illustrates the form of the summary, using five classes of housing types. These housing types correspond to residential classes used in the land use survey, the original selection of classes having been made with this type of analysis in mind. The selection of housing types in the first instance is governed by what is typical to a particular urban area. Usually large metropolitan areas will have a greater variety than small urban areas. Thus the selection of land use classes and consequently the format of Table 38 must be developed in terms of predominant housing types typical of the urban area under study. Where there is reason to believe new housing types will be introduced into the local housing market during the planning period, additional types will appear in the later stages of the analysis.

Another summary developed at the outset sets forth the trends in con-

---

[38] For purposes of the 1960 census, "a family consists of two or more persons in the same household who are related to each other by blood, marriage or adoption; all persons living in one household who are related to each other are regarded as one family."

[39] In the 1960 census, "a household consists of all persons who occupy a housing unit. . . . These persons include any lodgers, foster children, wards, and resident employees who shared the living quarters of the household head."

Table 38. Current Stock of Dwelling Units, Acreage in Residential Use, and Net Densities in Urban Area by Housing Type, 19xx

Planning District	Single-Family			Two-Family			Row Housing		
	DU's	Acres	Density	DU's	Acres	Density	DU's	Acres	Density
1	xx	xx	xx	xx	xx	xx	xx	xx	xx
2	xx	xx	xx	xx	xx	xx	xx	xx	xx
etc.	xx	xx	xx	xx	xx	xx	xx	xx	xx
Subtotal central city	xx	xx	xx	xx	xx	xx	xx	xx	xx
10	xx	xx	xx	xx	xx	xx	xx	xx	xx
11	xx	xx	xx	xx	xx	xx	xx	xx	xx
etc.	xx	xx	xx	xx	xx	xx	xx	xx	xx
Subtotal fringe area	xx	xx	xx	xx	xx	xx	xx	xx	xx
Planning area total	xx	xx	xx	xx	xx	xx	xx	xx	xx

version and new construction activity. Table 39 illustrates the form used in this summary. The table is compiled from building permit records, usually for the past five- or ten-year period. Reading horizontally, it shows the relative emphasis between conversion and new construction in any planning district, and within the new construction category, the relative emphasis between the various housing types. Reading vertically and used in conjunction with a map of planning districts, the table indicates the sectors of the urban area where conversion activity is most pronounced and which areas appear to be preferred ones for new construction. By reference to this summary and annual building permit plots (prepared in map form as discussed in Chapter 7), it is possible to establish the important directions of residential expansion.

2. *Estimates of future need.* The second step develops and applies working assumptions relative to future residential area requirements. Attention is first focused on procedures for estimating the total number of new dwelling units needed by the end of the planning period, either by conversion or from new construction, and on procedures for approximating the distribution of new construction both as to housing types and as to classes of residential density. The end product of the first series of assumptions is a tabular summary such as that presented in Table 40. Involved here are assumptions as to (1) changes in household size during the planning period, (2) losses in the existing stock of dwelling units, and (3) changes in the vacancy rate.

Garden Apts.			Multistory Apts.			Total		
DU's	Acres	Density	DU's	Acres	Density	DU's	Acres	Density
xx	xx	xx	xx	xx	xx	xx	xx	xx
xx	xx	xx	xx	xx	xx	xx	xx	xx
xx	xx	xx	xx	xx	xx	xx	xx	xx
—	—	—	—	—	—	—	—	—
xx	xx	xx	xx	xx	xx	xx	xx	xx
xx	xx	xx	xx	xx	xx	xx	xx	xx
xx	xx	xx	xx	xx	xx	xx	xx	xx
xx	xx	xx	xx	xx	xx	xx	xx	xx
—	—	—	—	—	—	—	—	—
xx	xx	xx	xx	xx	xx	xx	xx	xx
—	—	—	—	—	—	—	—	—
xx	xx	xx	xx	xx	xx	xx	xx	xx

a. *Household-size assumptions.* As already pointed out, household size is a key element in making the transition from population estimates to dwelling unit requirements. On the basis of a study of trends in the change in average household size, assumptions are made as to the average size of household by the end of the planning period. These assumptions are presumed to reflect changes (1) arising out of net population increases, and (2) developing from shifts in living patterns within the surviving population such as changes relative to family size, doubled-up living conditions, and so on. By applying the present average household size to the present population and the assumed future household size to the estimated future population, the difference between these two results provides a crude unadjusted estimate of the total new dwelling unit requirements as shown in Row 1 of Table 40. In this connection, it is useful for control purposes to develop separate assumptions for central city and fringe area planning districts.

b. *Assumptions on DU losses.* Estimates of losses in the current stock of dwelling units by the end of the planning period are covered under three categories: DU's eliminated by highway and public renewal programs, DU's eliminated by other use invasions, and DU's lost by fire and from other catastrophes. Besides DU's in the path of planned expressways, the first category includes all dwelling units in clearance areas as defined by techniques discussed earlier, all substandard structures in rehabilitation

Table 39. Recent Trends in Distribution of New Additions to Housing Stock, 19xx to 19xx

| Planning District | Total Number DU's Added | Per Cent in Conversions | Per Cent in New Construction by Housing Type | | | | |
			Single-Family	Two-Family	Row Housing	Garden Apts.	Multistory Apts.
1	xxx	xx	xx	xx	xx	xx	xx
2	xxx	xx	xx	xx	xx	xx	xx
etc.	xxx	xx	xx	xx	xx	xx	xx
	—	—	—	—	—	—	—
Subtotal central city	xxx	xx	xx	xx	xx	xx	xx
10	xxx	xx	xx	xx	xx	xx	xx
11	xxx	xx	xx	xx	xx	xx	xx
etc.	xxx	xx	xx	xx	xx	xx	xx
	—	—	—	—	—	—	—
Subtotal fringe area	xxx	xx	xx	xx	xx	xx	xx
	—	—	—	—	—	—	—
Planning area total	xxx	xx	xx	xx	xx	xx	xx

areas, and finally an assumed allowance of the present stock of standard housing that is judged likely to fall into the substandard category by the end of the planning period. The latter assumptions are usually based on local observations as to past rates of deterioration (rough comparisons between the last two Censuses of Housing) and the anticipated effectiveness of local rehabilitation and conservation programs during the planning period. Either by actual count or by estimate, these losses are recorded for the appropriate planning district in Table 41.

Losses by use invasion occur principally in central areas, and these can be tallied up from previous studies of the CBD. This estimate can then be adjusted upward to cover any losses tentatively identified in previous space need analyses in manufacturing, wholesale, and other use areas. By actual count or by estimate, losses from this source are recorded for appropriate planning districts in Table 41.

Assumptions relating to the third category of losses, those attributed to fires or other catastrophes, are based on local observations of past rates of loss, adjusted downward for anticipated improvements in fire-fighting potential, and the expected effectiveness of local renewal programs and code enforcement activities during the planning period. Distribution of these losses by planning districts as summarized in Table 41 is based on observations as to concentrations of fire calls during the past and expecta-

Table 40. Derivation of Total New Dwelling Unit Requirements, 19xx

	Number of Dwelling Units	
Sequence of Steps	Central City	Fringe Areas
1. Crude unadjusted estimate of new DU's needed	xx	xx
2. Plus net losses in current stock of DU'S	xx	xx
Losses by public renewal programs	xx	xx
Losses by use invasions	xx	xx
Assumed catastrophe losses	xx	xx
3. Plus allowance for vacancy rate[a]	xx	xx
Total: Adjusted crude estimate of new	—	—
DU's needed	xx	xx
Assumed conversions	xx	xx
Assumed new construction	xx	xx

[a] Vacancy rate applied to total of new DU's (Row 1 entries) *and* current stock of DU's (obtained from last column of Table 38).

tions as to how renewal programs and other similar measures will alter these concentrations in the future. The left-hand plate in Figure 34 shows the way the pattern of DU losses can be represented in land areas.

c. *Vacancy rate assumptions.* Estimates of dwelling unit replacements to cover these three categories of losses are tallied by planning district as shown in Table 41 and summarized in Row 2 of Table 40. The final entry made in Table 40, Row 3, increases the cumulative total to make allowance for a normal vacancy ratio. This ratio should be applied to the sum of the Row 1 entry and the current stock of dwelling units (see Table 38). Although a 5 per cent vacancy ratio has been in common usage in estimating future requirements in the past, this rule-of-thumb figure may not be suited to all situations. In this respect, special seasonal studies may be desirable in urban areas having significance as resort centers.

d. *Conversion–new construction assumptions.* With all three segments of need for new dwelling units covered, results are totaled as indicated in Table 40, yielding an adjusted crude estimate of total new dwelling unit requirements. The final working assumption to be made in this phase of the analysis is the expected allocation of this total between conversions and new construction by the end of the planning period. This brings the analysis to the point of considering the second series of assumptions, namely, those concerned with the distribution of the total need for new dwelling units by housing and density types.

The working assumptions relative to housing and density types assist in making the transition from dwelling unit requirements to space requirements. Thus, having arrived at estimates of the total additional units re-

Table 41. Estimated Distribution of Dwelling Unit Losses by Planning District, 19xx

Planning District	Current Stock DU's	DU's Removed by Type of Loss				DU's Remaining by 19xx
		Renewal	Invasion	Catastrophe	Total	
1	xxx	x	x	x	x	xx
2	xxx	x	x	x	x	xx
etc.	xxx	x	x	x	x	xx
	—	–	–	–	–	—
Subtotal central city	xxx	x	x	x	x	xx
10	xxx	x	x	x	x	xx
11	xxx	x	x	x	x	xx
etc.	xxx	x	x	x	x	xx
	—	–	–	–	–	—
Subtotal fringe area	xxx	x	x	x	x	xx
	—	–	–	–	–	—
Planning area total	xxx	x	x	x	x	xx

quired during the planning period, we are first concerned with assumptions as to how this total can be expected to break down into housing types. Although some types of housing market analyses (see the discussion at the end of the chapter) attempt to establish consumer preferences in this respect, for the generalized result required in this analysis, assumptions are usually based on trends in the crude distribution characteristics reflected in recent additions to the housing stock. These trends can be approximated by analyzing building permits on an annual or five-year basis for past increments of time and observing changes in the proportions devoted to each housing type (see Table 39). On the basis of these observed trends, assumptions are made relative to the future distribution of housing types. As a check on the reasonableness of such assumptions, figures in Table 38 can be converted to percentages and the distribution of the present stock of dwelling units among housing types can be compared with that proposed for future additions to the housing supply.

e. *Residential density assumptions.* The final set of assumptions are concerned with the further breakdown of housing types into density types. However, before this breakdown can be made, decisions must be reached concerning a classification of "density types," a term used here to represent *the range of assumed densities (in terms of dwelling units per acre) at which development in the future will take place.* Assumptions in this respect are generally based on locally adopted "density standards," here used to represent *a classification of proposed maximum permissible residential densities.* Both the average assumed densities and the adopted standards as to maximum permissible densities can be expressed in "net" and "gross" terms.[40]

Net residential density standards have a very specific and direct application in the development of the zoning ordinance in implementation of the land use plan. They are used in setting up the various density districts within categories of land to be zoned for residential use. *Gross residential density standards* are also sometimes used in zoning ordinances in provisions relative to group housing developments. Gross residential density standards should be distinguished from *neighborhood density standards* which are sometimes used in the so-called "community development districts," special districts recognized in zoning ordinances for the integrated development of entire residential communities.[41]

On the other hand, land use planning procedures employ what in effect amounts to higher-order "standards." The various types of *assumed average net residential densities* are primarily significant in estimating space needs for developed or partially developed areas, and as brought out later in this section of the chapter, after consideration of local shopping, school, and recreation space requirements, the various *assumed average neighborhood* densities become significant yardsticks in estimating space requirements in areas presently undeveloped or in large clearance areas made available under public renewal programs.

The net residential density standards employed in any urban area are usually a local adaptation of generally recognized national standards considered to be consistent with sound principles of healthful housing. Table 42 presents general standards recommended by the Committee on the Hygiene of Housing of the American Public Health Association.[42] This range of net densities is commonly used as a guide in examining net densities presently existing in the urban area of interest (derived as shown in Table 38) for purposes of developing local standards as to maximum permissible densities for future development.

These standards will not be concerned alone with the higher-order densities possible in open land portions of the fringe areas. The range of

---

[40] *Net residential density* refers to dwelling units per acre of land actually in use or proposed to be used for residential purposes, and *gross residential density* is computed on the basis of net residential land area plus traversing streets, alleys, and drives, and one-half of bounding streets and one-quarter of bounding street intersections.

[41] *Neighborhood density* refers to dwelling units per acre of land area in use or proposed for development as a neighborhood area including residential land, areas for local shopping, school, and public open spaces, and land taken up in streets.

[42] Committee on the Hygiene of Housing, American Public Health Association, *Planning the Neighborhood,* Chicago: Public Administration Service, 1960.

Table 42. Net Residential Density Standards[a]

| | DU's per Net Acre | |
Dwelling Unit Type	Desirable	Maximum
One- and two-family		
1-family detached	5	7
1-family semidetached		
or	10	12
2-family detached		
1-family attached (row)		
or	16	19
2-family semidetached		
Multifamily		
2-story	25	30
3-story	40	45
6-story	65	75
9-story	75	85
13-story	85	95

[a] Committee on the Hygiene of Housing, American Public Health Association, *Planning the Neighborhood*, Chicago: Public Administration Service, 1960, p. 39.

standards adopted must recognize that for inlying renewal areas designated for clearance, lower-order densities must usually be provided for. As another practical consideration, the range of proposed net densities must usually recognize what can be expected to emerge in any large vacant areas already subdivided but as yet undeveloped. These will often be of a lower order than standards adopted for open land areas. Of course, if the subdivision pattern imposed on the land is below general standards to a serious extent, it would be a function of the land use plan to propose higher-order local standards, with specific implementing recommendations for any necessary steps to achieve replanning.

As would be expected, illustrations of locally adopted net residential density standards exhibit considerable variation. Presented here for illustrative purposes are standards adopted, respectively, for the city of Philadelphia,[43] for the Roanoke Valley Region,[44] and for the Baltimore Regional Planning Council's "Metrotown" project:[45]

[43] Philadelphia City Planning Commission, *Comprehensive Plan for the City of Philadelphia.*
[44] The Roanoke Valley Regional Planning Commission, *A Land Use Plan for the Roanoke Valley Region.*
[45] Baltimore Regional Planning Council, "Metrotowns for the Baltimore Region—a Pattern Emerges," supporting data for Planning Report No. 2, Baltimore: Maryland State Planning Department, June, 1962, processed.

Dwelling Units per Net Acre	Housing Type
Under 20	Single-family detached, single-family twin house, single-family row house, multifamily very low density (e.g., garden apts.)
20 – 39	Duplex twin house, single-family row house, multifamily low density (e.g., high-rise apt. with low land coverage)
40 – 59	Duplex row house, pre-1920 single-family row house, multifamily medium density
60 & over	High-rise apts., multifamily row house

Dwelling Units per Net Acre	Housing Type
1 – 6	Single-family
8 – 10	Two-family, row house
10 – 20	Two- and three-story apts.
20 – 40	Multistory apts.

Dwelling Units per Net Acre	Housing Type
1 – 5	Single family
10 – 14	Row house
15 – 20	Garden apts.
25 – 35	High-rise apts.

f. *Allocation assumptions by type and density.* Once standards have been established, and from these, assumptions made as to average net densities at which future development will occur, it is then possible to extend the breakdown by housing types to a more detailed form, recognizing the assumed density types. This involves making assumptions as to how the estimated new construction dwelling units obtained in Table 40 will be distributed to various density and housing types. For lower-order densities (that is, densities of lower standard), generally the percentage allocation will be guided by observations as to the supply of subdivided land and renewal land which originally influenced the choice of these density classes. For higher-order densities, assumed allocations will usually be based on observed recent trends of the rates at which land has gone into develop-

Table 43. Allocation of Total New Constrúction Dwelling Units by Housing and Density Types and Derivation of Total Acreage Requirements, 19xx[a]

Density Type	Housing Types	Assumed Av. No. DU's/Net Acre	Total Requirements DU's	Net Acreage
Density A	xxxxxxxxxxxxx	x	xxx	xx
Density B	xxxxxxxxxxxxx	x	xxx	xx
Density C	xxxxxxxxxxxxx	x	xxx	xx
Density D	xxxxxxxxxxxxx	x	xxx	xx
Density E	xxxxxxxxxxxxx	x	xxx	xx
Density F	xxxxxxxxxxxxx	x	xxx	xx
Etc.	xxxxxxxxxxxxx	x	xxx	xx
Planning area total	—	—	xxx	xx

[a] This same general tabular format is used for separate summaries of central city and fringe areas.

ment in lot sizes reasonably similar to those included in the upper-order selections of residential densities. To illustrate, let us say we are dealing with four density types: Density A, low-density, single-family detached houses; Density B, medium-density, single-family detached houses; Density C, either garden apartments or low-density town houses (row houses); and Density D, multistory apartments. The step involved here is development of assumptions as to how the new dwelling units will be distributed. In considèration of the existing pattern of densities and housing types in Table 38 and how recent trends are deviating from this pattern as determined from building permit data over the past five or ten years, it might be assumed that 20 per cent of new dwelling units built in the planning period would be Density A, 35 per cent Density B, 20 per cent Density C, and 25 per cent Density D.

The results of the foregoing analyses thus yield a tabular presentation such as that shown in Table 43. It should be noted that this table summarizes requirements only for new construction, conversions being excluded from this part of the analysis on the assumption that for the most part they will not involve additional land. This is in extension of the work already completed and summarized in Table 40 and prepares the way for the next step concerned with the allocations of total dwelling unit requirements to the individual planning districts. Table 43 can be used as a prototype for separate tables, one on the central city and another on the fringe area subtotals.

3. *Fitting space needs to land supply.* The third major step in the sequence to the procedure in analyzing residential space requirements is one of establishing *approximate effective net holding capacities* of the various planning districts and making a tentative allocation of total dwelling unit

requirements to planning districts which is within the ceilings indicated by these holding capacities. The *holding capacity* of a planning district is the number of dwelling units the vacant and renewal land in the planning district will accommodate according to a prescribed pattern of residential densities. The *net* holding capacity excludes allowance for streets, and the *effective* net holding capacity excludes areas unavailable for development due to whims of property owners, legal entanglements, and so on. Holding capacities are *approximate* at this stage of the analysis since space requirements for community facilities and resulting reductions in effective net holding capacities are still to be determined. As in analyses of all the preceding classes of land use, only a tentative allocation of dwelling units is made here, since all location decisions are subject to review and possible revision in the design phase of land use planning procedures.

a. *Holding capacity analyses.* To determine approximate effective net holding capacities, two steps are involved. In the first, a tentative generalized pattern of residential densities is developed, showing how net density standards would be applied to the urban area as a whole, considering locational requirements previously developed, the pattern of existing densities in built-up areas, and the use capabilities of vacant and renewal land as previously determined. In Philadelphia, for example, the "receiving areas" would include sections of the city earmarked for future residential use in the left-hand plate of Figure 34 and the areas designated for reconstruction in the right-hand plate, with Figure 35 representing the prescribed density pattern.

The second step focuses on the vacant and renewal areas in this pattern of residential densities. Using assumed average net density figures (in place of the net density standard figures), approximate net holding capacities are computed planning district by planning district and tabulated by density type. These figures are then adjusted downward district by district by crude percentage correction factors appropriate to each district to convert them into effective net holding capacities. For planning districts in built-up or partially developed portions of the urban area, these deduction percentages are based on prevailing practices with respect to purchase of double lots and what is known concerning the unavailability of vacant tracts of land in the planning district. For planning districts in open country, correction factors are approximated on the basis of those derived for nearby developed or developing areas which have a character similar to that contemplated in these planning districts. Although reasonably appropriate for the generalized results of preliminary land use planning, these subjective methods are of course superseded by special investigations in comprehensive plan analyses of residential requirements. The result of the foregoing steps is a tabular summary such as that presented in

Figure 34. Philadelphia's Residential Land Use and Treatment Plans. Shown in the left-hand plate are the areas to be removed, retained, or added to the residential land use pattern during the planning period. Designated in the right-hand plate are the forms of treatment recommended in order to bring residential areas into a pattern of development and quality set for the period 1960 to 1980. (*Source:* Philadelphia City Planning Commission, *Comprehensive Plan for the City of Philadelphia*, 1960.)

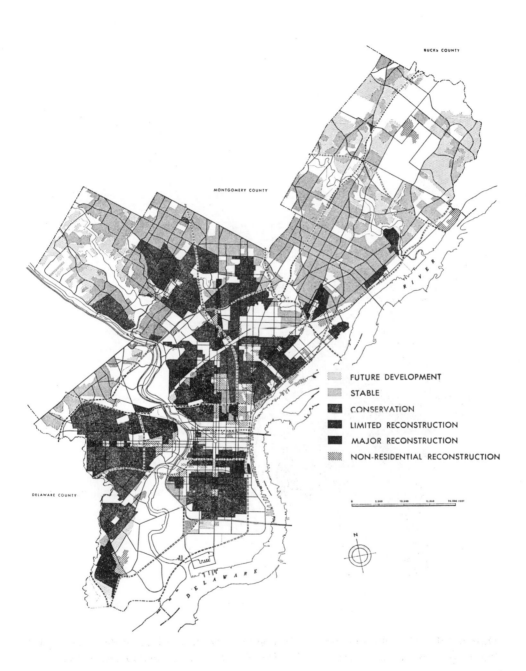

FUTURE DEVELOPMENT
STABLE
CONSERVATION
LIMITED RECONSTRUCTION
MAJOR RECONSTRUCTION
NON-RESIDENTIAL RECONSTRUCTION

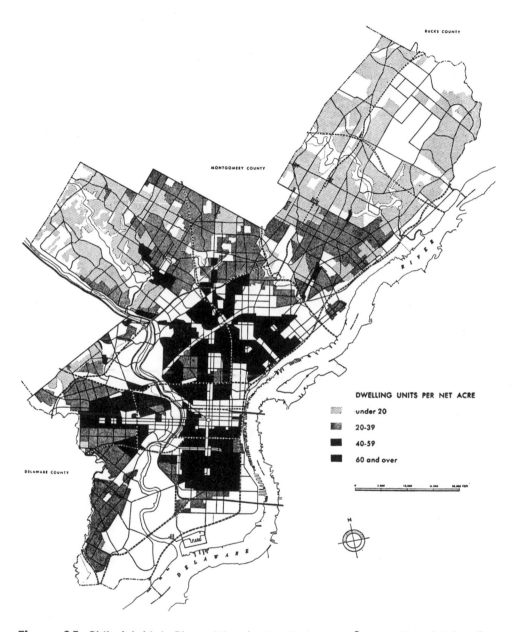

Figure 35. Philadelphia's Plan of Residential Densities. (*Source:* Philadelphia City Planning Commission, *Comprehensive Plan for the City of Philadelphia*, 1960.)

Table 44. Approximate Effective Net Holding Capacity of Vacant-Renewal Land Suited for Residential Development, by Planning District, 19xx

Planning District	Number of Dwelling Units by Density Type							
	A	B	C	D	E	F	Etc.	Total
1	xx	xx	xx	xx	xx	xx	xx	xxx
2	xx	xx	xx	xx	xx	xx	xx	xxx
etc.	xx	xx	xx	xx	xx	xx	xx	xxx
Subtotal central city	xx	xx	xx	xx	xx	xx	xx	xxx
10	xx	xx	xx	xx	xx	xx	xx	xxx
11	xx	xx	xx	xx	xx	xx	xx	xxx
etc.	xx	xx	xx	xx	xx	xx	xx	xxx
Subtotal fringe area	xx	xx	xx	xx	xx	xx	xx	xxx
Planning area total	xx	xx	xx	xx	xx	xx	xx	xxx

Table 44 and an overlay or key map identifying by density types the vacant and renewal land to which planning district holding capacities refer.

The holding capacity total for the planning area as derived in Table 44 is usually considerably in excess of total dwelling unit requirements as derived in Table 43. Of course, if the planning area holding capacity is under the estimated dwelling unit total requirements, the planning area must be enlarged according to procedures previously described.

b. *Estimating distribution of new DU's.* The final operation in this third major step of the procedure is one of distributing new dwelling unit requirements to the various planning districts within the holding capacity ceilings shown in Table 44. This is a "cut and fill" process of allocating dwelling units to planning districts by density types within the limits of the controlling density-type quotas set forth in Table 43. For the various density classes, preference is given first to planning districts with land previously determined as prime for residential use, which are situated in the directions where there appears to be the greatest preference for building new homes. Location criteria as developed in Chapter 10 and the preliminary thoroughfare study (being developed concurrently with the land use plan) may indicate other sectors of the urban area which should receive emphasis in this allocation process. Other considerations are the rate at which scattered vacant lots in the older areas can be expected to fill in and

Table 45. Total New Dwelling Unit Requirements by Density Type Tentatively Distributed Among Planning Districts, 19xx

Planning District	Total New DU's [a]	No. New DU's by Conversion [a]	No. DU's from New Construction by Density Type							
			A	B	C	D	E	F	Etc.	Total [a]
1	xxxx	xx	xx	xx	xx	xx	xx	xx	xx	xxx
2	xxxx	xx	xx	xx	xx	xx	xx	xx	xx	xxx
etc.	xxxx	xx	xx	xx	xx	xx	xx	xx	xx	xxx
Subtotal central city	xxxx	xx	xx	xx	xx	xx	xx	xx	xx	xxx
10	xxxx	xx	xx	xx	xx	xx	xx	xx	xx	xxx
11	xxxx	xx	xx	xx	xx	xx	xx	xx	xx	xxx
etc.	xxxx	xx	xx	xx	xx	xx	xx	xx	xx	xxx
Subtotal fringe area	xxxx	xx	xx	xx	xx	xx	xx	xx	xx	xxx
Planning area total	xxxx	xx	xx	xx	xx	xx	xx	xx	xx	xxx

[a] Total and subtotals match up with those at the foot of Table 40.

the extent to which condemned or destroyed units will be replaced on their original sites. These factors have a bearing on the distribution of new units.

Along with these positive factors, certain limiting factors should be considered in the allocation process. For example, planning districts falling in general areas which cannot be economically served by water, sewer, and other utility lines would be de-emphasized. Similarly, it would be important to recognize unfavorable soil conditions in areas which are likely to remain beyond the public sewer service area and which therefore would depend upon septic tanks for sewage disposal. The land use plan must recognize these and other similar factors, and through its implementing recommendations it actually exerts some control in seeing that these limiting factors are respected.

Results of this allocation process as finally balanced against the requirements in Table 43 and kept within the ceilings of Table 44 are summarized in a form such as shown in Table 45. It should be noted that the table includes a column on conversions. While not directly necessary in the derivation of residential space requirements, estimates of the distribution of conversions among planning districts during the planning period are made as part of this process so that population distribution data can be computed

Table 46. New Residential Space Requirements by Density Type Tentatively Distributed Among Planning Districts, 19xx

Planning District	Net Addition in Residential Land by Density Type (acres)							
	A	B	C	D	E	F	Etc.	Total
1	xx	xx	xx	xx	xx	xx	xx	xx
2	xx	xx	xx	xx	xx	xx	xx	xx
etc.	xx	xx	xx	xx	xx	xx	xx	xx
Subtotal central city	xx	xx	xx	xx	xx	xx	xx	xx
10	xx	xx	xx	xx	xx	xx	xx	xx
11	xx	xx	xx	xx	xx	xx	xx	xx
etc.	xx	xx	xx	xx	xx	xx	xx	xx
Subtotal fringe area	xx	xx	xx	xx	xx	xx	xx	xx
Planning area total	xx	xx	xx	xx	xx	xx	xx	xx

for purposes of community facility analyses. Allocation of conversions is made on the basis of the previously prepared map showing the proposed pattern of maximum permitted residential densities and considering those planning districts where the pressures for conversion are apt to be greatest, principally those containing the large, old, outmoded homes frequently found ringing the central business district.

4. *Summary of space needs and population.* The fourth and final step in the analysis of residential area requirements summarizes tentative new space needs, and according to the assumed average household size, determines the tentative distribution of the total population by the end of the planning period. In this connection, it should be noted that the population distribution estimates thus derived provide a more refined result than that obtained by methods described in Chapter 5. Table 46 represents the form of the summary showing how total acreage requirements developed in Table 43 are distributed by planning district. Table 47 indicates the form in which the future population by planning district is summarized. The results of the analyses discussed in the preceding pages take the form of a plan for residential land use (Figure 34, left) and the densities at which development is to take place (Figure 35), and a plan for the treatment of various residential areas in order to bring them to prescribed standards (Figure 34, right).

Table 47. Approximating the Distribution of Total Planning Area Population by Planning District, 19xx

Planning District	Current			By End of Planning Period				
	Pop. 1	DU's 2	House-hold Size 3	Existing DU's Remaining by 19xx 4	DU's Added by 19xx 5	Total DU's by 19xx 6	House-hold Size 7	Pop. 8
1	x	x	x	x	x	x	x	x
2	x	x	x	x	x	x	x	x
etc.	x	x	x	x	x	x	x	x
	—	—	—	—	—	—	—	—
Subtotal central city	x	x	x	x	x	x	x	x
10	x	x	x	x	x	x	x	x
11	x	x	x	x	x	x	x	x
etc.	x	x	x	x	x	x	x	x
	—	—	—	—	—	—	—	—
Subtotal fringe area	x	x	x	x	x	x	x	x
Planning area total	x	x	x	x	x	x	x	x

Explanation: Columns 1 through 3 show the derivation of the existing household sizes by planning district. Column 1 figures are estimated by methods described in Chapter 5, and Column 2 is a summary of the dwelling unit count appearing in Table 38 as obtained from the land use survey. Approximations of the household sizes by the end of the planning period are derived in Columns 4 through 7. Column 4 comes from Table 41 and Column 5 from Table 45, with Column 6 representing the sum of entries in these two columns. Using previously assumed future household sizes for the central city and fringe area and using Column 3 as a guide, household sizes of the future are approximated, first on a proportional basis and then adjusted on a subjective basis, considering the previously derived distribution of housing types and expectations as to the planning districts which will attract families with children, those which will attract childless couples, and so on. Estimates of population by planning district appearing in Column 8 are finally computed from entries in Columns 6 and 7. Obviously this whole process is an extremely crude one, but it may be considered sufficiently accurate for the generalized character of the result desired.

Local Business Space Requirements

As previously noted, it is not practicable to include in a preliminary land use planning analysis the detailed kind of investigation of retail space requirements involved in purchasing power and similar studies. Moreover, for the generalized result desired in a preliminary land use plan, this level of detail is not warranted, particularly when it is considered that the space required is very nominal in comparison with that for other land use categories.

Estimating Standards

Fairly crude rule-of-thumb procedures are usually employed in the preliminary planning stage in estimating space requirements of local retail

Table 48. Crude Standards for Estimating Space Requirements of Neighborhood and Community Shopping Centers

Selected Neighborhood Population Sizes in Residential Communities of 30–50,000	Acres of Combined Community-Neighborhood Shopping Area per 1,000 Population		
	Parking Ratios [a]		
	2 :1	3 :1	4 :1
5,000	0.7	0.9	1.1
2,500	0.8	1.0	1.3
1,000	1.1	1.5	1.8

[a] Parking ratio is here defined as the square feet of parking space for every square foot of ground area covered by store buildings.

business areas. They begin with estimates of total space requirements for combined community and neighborhood facilities. These estimates are made on the basis of local adaptations of empirically derived general standards such as those summarized in Table 48. In adapting such yardsticks to local needs, it should be borne in mind that detailed test applications of general standards to a particular locality may show that variable standards should be developed for neighborhoods and communities of different density characteristics. Thus a suburban residential development of acreage plots may have a different order of standard than one in densely developed apartment areas.

Using some such locally adopted standards of shopping space per 1,000 population served, crude estimates of the total shopping space required are developed community by community for each assemblage of planning districts which are considered to approximate a residential community. When such a standard is applied to existing population figures, it is common to find that in many residential communities by these standards local business is overexpanded. Often the business is scattered and interspersed with residences. If there is still an oversupply when the standard is applied to the forecast population, subtractions are indicated for these communities.[46] In other residential communities, additions to existing retail business acreage will be indicated.

---

[46] It might be observed parenthetically that it is an important function of the land use plan to identify the major centers to be retained, and, by omission, the areas and the scattered establishments which are proposed to be retired. The nonconforming use provisions of a zoning ordinance developed on the basis of the land use plan, if sufficiently stringent and if enforced, over a period of time can assist scattered businesses in becoming re-established in centers. From the standpoint of the poorly located businesses, the land use plan provides a guide to finding relocation sites in expanding areas where businesses, under modern zoning provisions, are assured strategic locations with ample room for off-street parking and loading areas and other essential requirements of the modern shopping center.

Space Needs by Facility Type

The first step thus provides a gross indication of space needs by residential communities. The succeeding steps use these gross estimates as guides in deriving more refined and superseding estimates. The second step divides the combined standard into its two components. On the basis of observed local trends in the existing distribution of local retail space between community shopping centers and local neighborhood outlets, the combined yardstick is split into separate yardsticks for each of these two functional types of shopping facilities. If a system of residential communities has been identified within the framework of planning districts, the yardstick for community shopping centers is sometimes applied to the estimated future population of these community areas to obtain guides on a residential community level. In some urban areas where residential communities are not identified as intermediate analytical areas, the community shopping center yardstick is applied on an urban-wide basis. Similarly, using the neighborhood portion of the original yardstick and applying it on a planning district basis, space requirement guides are obtained at the localized level. The estimates of future population by planning district as summarized in Table 47 are used in this analysis.

Trial Distribution Scheme

The third and final step first examines within the framework of location criteria previously developed the existing pattern of shopping centers and develops a tentative scheme of strategic sites for retention, for expansion, and for the development of entire new centers. Then, using the foregoing yardsticks as general ceilings, estimates of space requirements for each site are derived. Finally, these estimates are summarized on a planning district basis for community shopping centers, neighborhood facilities, and a combined total in a form such as that indicated in Table 49. This analysis cannot go into the details of store types for each site. Although practice in approximating site sizes varies, one method is to select typical inlying, midtown, and outlying community and neighborhood centers presently existing, analyze the facilities for the range of services provided and the space allotted, and derive typical site sizes which would approximate space needs for each type of center in these typical locations. At sites in fully developed areas, parking space is usually the principal space need. The provision of off-street parking lots and the amount of space allowed must be considered in terms of such practicalities as land values, the appeal and risk involved to public and private agencies available to undertake the development and management of such facilities, the prevailing and prob-

Table 49. New Space Requirements for Local Business Centers by Planning District, 19xx

Planning District	Net Reduction in Space (acres)	Net Additions in Space (acres)								
		Community Shopping Centers			Neighborhood Facilities			All Local Business Facilities		
		Invasion	V & R[a]	Total	Invasion	V & R	Total	Invasion	V & R	Total
1	xx	x	x	x	x	x	x	x	x	x
2	xx	x	x	x	x	x	x	x	x	x
etc.	xx	x	x	x	x	x	x	x	x	x
	—	–	–	–	–	–	–	–	–	–
Subtotal central city	xx	x	x	x	x	x	x	x	x	x
10	xx	x	x	x	x	x	x	x	x	x
11	xx	x	x	x	x	x	x	x	x	x
etc.	xx	x	x	x	x	x	x	x	x	x
	—	–	–	–	–	–	–	–	–	–
Subtotal fringe area	xx	x	x	x	x	x	x	x	x	x
	—	–	–	–	–	–	–	–	–	–
Planning area total	xx	x	x	x	x	x	x	x	x	x

[a] V & R is an abbreviation for "vacant and renewal land."

able future character of on-street parking restrictions, and so on. At developing midtown and outlying sites, off-street parking requirements in a new or revised zoning ordinance can be anticipated, using higher-order space allowances. In outlying undeveloped areas, space allowances can approach those of planned shopping centers with the highest standards of off-street parking and loading spaces and the provision of planted areas.

The final result of this analysis as summarized in Table 49 indicates tentative proposals for the amount of land to be retired from local business use in its present location and for the amount of land to be added to each planning district for community shopping centers and for neighborhood facilities. Accompanying such a table as part of the working materials of this analysis would be a key map identifying actual locations of additions and reductions. Obviously, some planning districts will have both additions and subtractions. Because community shopping centers serve areas sometimes covering as many as five and six planning districts, entries in the table for these facilities will appear only for planning districts in which these centers happen to be located. In some instances, space requirements allowed for some community and neighborhood facilities will be split among two or three planning districts where district boundaries pass through sites of these facilities. It should be noted, too, that the V & R column in the summary of net additions for all facilities contains the data required in analyses of gross residential densities taken up later in the chapter. This entire analysis of local business space requirements is, of course, tentative and may be subject to revision in the final design phase of the land use planning procedure. In this connection, net additions in retail space may involve invasion of land previously counted as part of the residential land supply, and net reductions in retail space may have the reverse effect. These are illustrative of some of the "cut and fill" adjustments which must be made in the final design phase.

School Space Requirements

Although involving different measurement units, the basic method used in estimating space needs for schools is very similar to that employed in estimating space needs for local business areas. This method involves first a determination of the number of facilities needed, and then on the basis of estimates of space needed for each facility, space requirements are assigned to the appropriate planning districts in which each such facility is located. As in the space analyses for other land use classes, crude approximation techniques are employed. The implications for the location and distribution of schools that educational objectives and policies have in such matters as planning for school integration or in relating the school to community life are taken up in the later more detailed stages of planning.

Study of Existing School Plant

For purposes of the preliminary land use plan, space requirements are derived in the following sequence of steps. First, pertinent data concerning the present school system or systems in the urban area and long-range school policies are assembled. This involves preparing summary tabulations of past enrollments for each school; totals for each administrative school jurisdiction falling within the planning area, public and parochial (or increments thereof, where a school board's jurisdiction is partially within the planning area); school capacities as measured by the number of classrooms of standard size (generally 30 square feet per pupil, with a maximum of 25 to 30 pupils per classroom); school site sizes in acres; and presently prevailing and proposed changes in school board policies with respect to the organization of the system or systems (that is, 6–3–3, 8–4, or other breakdown of grade organization) and the community use of schools and recreation facilities.

Estimating Future Enrollments

The second major step is one of estimating future total enrollments in the planning area according to the anticipated typical future grade organizations of the systems involved, and approximating the distribution of this future school population by planning district. The ratio method for estimating future total enrollments examines all school systems as if they were a single system, and, according to the typical grade organization, develops historical series for past decades showing the percentages, for example, that elementary, junior high, and senior high school age groups in the population are of the total population at each census enumeration. These percentage series are then extrapolated and applied to the population estimate forecast for the end of the planning period as discussed in Chapter 5 to yield crude estimates of the future school-age composition of the population.[47] Two additional percentage series are then developed, the second being required only where there is a parochial system involved in the urban area: (1) the proportion of each census-enumerated school-age group enrolled in each level of the grade organization, and (2) the proportion of enrolled children in each level of the school system enrolled in public schools. Each percentage series is arranged in a time sequence and extrapolated, and the resulting crude estimates of future proportions applied to the above derived estimates of school-age population. The results are a series of estimates of future total enrollment broken down as to elementary, junior high, and senior high school levels (assuming here a 6–3–3 system) and by public and parochial systems (assuming both systems are present).

The next operation is one of distributing planning area totals to the various communities and planning districts for each type of school and each school system. This distribution is made on a crude basis following proportions in the way the future total population is distributed by planning districts as previously summarized in Table 47. The resulting crude allocation of total future enrollment to planning districts by type of school and for each separate school system (where this situation exists) is usually subject

---

[47] A much cruder ratio technique sometimes used to approximate the total school population is based on the average number of school children per dwelling unit in, say, the elementary, the junior high, and the senior high school levels. Using school enrollment data from decennial census years in relation to census counts of dwelling units as a source of reference, a set of ratios of school children per dwelling unit for central areas and fringe areas is assumed for the future. Estimates on enrollment are then derived by applying these ratios to dwelling unit figures to subtotals in Column 6 of Table 47. In fact, a crude distribution to planning districts can also be made.

Table 50. General Standards for School Site Sizes

Type of School[a]	Minimum (acres)	Desirable Minimum (acres)	Preferred Range (acres)
Elementary	5	5 + 1 per 100 ultimate enrollment	10– 25
Junior high	10	10 + 1 per 100 ultimate enrollment	25– 50
Senior high	20	20 + 1 per 100 ultimate enrollment	40–100

[a] To establish the number of schools of each type required, enrollment size standards commonly used are: elementary schools—350-400 students; junior high schools—700-1,500 students; and senior high schools—1,000-2,000 students.

to further adjustment. For planning districts in fringe area locations where the land is open or where residential development is just commencing, by reference to household-size data in Table 47, crude upward adjustments are made, recognizing that the pattern of the proportion of children attending school to total population which will emerge here will be above average, tending to correspond with recent experience in this respect in existing new developments. Such upward adjustments for peripheral areas of course will involve compensating downward adjustments in the inlying planning districts, probably in conversion areas, and in planning districts with large numbers of small apartment accommodations. Again, household-size data in Table 47 will provide guides for these adjustments. Obviously, data developed by such crude techniques will have limited significance for school-building programming until they can be substantiated by the more detailed studies mentioned below at the end of this section of the chapter. However, for generalized land use planning purposes they are sufficiently accurate to indicate general locations where concentrations of school children may be expected in the future, and thus where school sites should be reserved.

Trial Scheme of School Sites

In the third major step, the existing school locations are examined in terms of approximations as to the future concentrations of school-age population and the location requirements previously developed, and, considering the general age and adequacy of existing school buildings, the adequacy of existing school sites, and the availability of vacant or renewal land for new sites, a tentative scheme of school sites is developed for the urban area for each school type and each school system. Such a scheme would give particular attention to new sites and those existing sites which by standards cited below require additional land or, in other words, special attention to locations where additional land will be needed. At the same time, locations should be noted where schools are likely to be abandoned

Table 51. New Space Requirements for Schools by Planning District, 19xx

| Planning District | Net Additions in Space (acres) | | | | | | | | | | | |
| | Elementary | | | Junior High | | | Senior High | | | All Schools | | |
	Invasion	V & R[a]	Total	Invasion	V & R	Total	Invasion	V & R	Total	Invasion	V & R	Total
1	x	x	x	x	x	x	x	x	x	x	x	x
2	x	x	x	x	x	x	x	x	x	x	x	x
etc.	x	x	x	x	x	x	x	x	x	x	x	x
	—	—	—	—	—	—	—	—	—	—	—	—
Subtotal central city	x	x	x	x	x	x	x	x	x	x	x	x
10	x	x	x	x	x	x	x	x	x	x	x	x
11	x	x	x	x	x	x	x	x	x	x	x	x
etc.	x	x	x	x	x	x	x	x	x	x	x	x
	—	—	—	—	—	—	—	—	—	—	—	—
Subtotal fringe area	x	x	x	x	x	x	x	x	x	x	x	x
	—	—	—	—	—	—	—	—	—	—	—	—
Planning area total	x	x	x	x	x	x	x	x	x	x	x	x

[a] V & R is an abbreviation for "vacant and renewal land."

and where land in these sites may be expected to become available for other uses. In developing this tentative scheme, comments of local school authorities would be invited and drawn upon to the fullest practicable extent, and, of course, what advanced planning that has been undertaken by these authorities or their consultants would be taken into consideration.

Summary of Space Needs

The fourth and final step is the development of the summary of new space requirements by planning districts. On the basis of such generally recognized "preferred" standards as those reproduced in Table 50, local site-size standards are adopted and applied. Space requirements are then compiled on a planning district basis for each type of school for all systems of schools as presented in Table 51. Since junior and senior high schools serve communities which will encompass a number of planning districts, entries in these columns in Table 51 will appear only for the planning districts in which these schools happen to be located. In small urban areas, usually under 100,000 population, there may be only one consolidated high school. Some sites may be split among two or three districts if they

happen to be located on district lines. As in the previous analyses, the
V & R column in the summary for "all schools" will be of particular interest
in the later discussions of gross residential densities.

Local Recreation Space Requirements

As noted earlier in discussions of local requirements, recreation facilities
serving residential communities are usually classified according to general
age groups served and according to whether they are active or passive.
For active recreation facilities, space requirements are developed on the
basis of two criteria: (1) a population yardstick to indicate the total acreage required for each type of area, and (2) a minimum site-size criterion.
A population yardstick is also used as a general guide in estimating space
requirements for passive recreation areas. Since passive recreation areas are
often integrated into an urban-wide system of public open space as previously discussed, such a yardstick is often simply a means of checking
space allotments already made to insure that each planning district measures up to minimum standards.

Recreation Area Standards

Generally recognized crude standards for local recreation facilities are reproduced in Table 52. Even such crude standards may not fit the conditions
of all urban areas, and, where warranted, local adaptations should be developed. In more detailed studies of recreation space requirements in extension of those developed for the preliminary land use plan, variations in
these standards would be developed according to density classes of residential development.[48]

Obviously, an important consideration in the application of such standards is the pattern of school sites and the recreation facilities provided in
these areas. Thus some of the space requirements for playground areas will
be satisfied by facilities on elementary school sites, and recreation center
or playfield space needs, at junior and senior high school sites. While there
may be presently unreconciled conflicts in school board and recreation commission policies with respect to joint use of recreation facilities, the probabilities are that in the long run, cost considerations will dictate integrated
planning of active public recreation facilities and school site facilities. At
the same time it should be remembered that location criteria, population
yardsticks, and site-size considerations may dictate the provision of active

[48] See detailed standards of the Committee on the Hygiene of Housing, *Planning the Neighborhood,* pp. 48–49.

Table 52. General Estimating Standards for Local Recreation Areas

Facility or Area	Population Standard	Site-Size Standard
Playground	1 acre/800 population	5–10 acres
Local parks	1 acre/1,000 population [a]	2 or more acres
Recreation center	1 acre/800 population	15–20 acres
or playfield	1 acre/800 population	10–30 acres

[a] Varies according to residential densities ranging from 2 acres per 1,000 population in areas of multi-family dwellings down to three-quarters of an acre per 1,000 population in single-family developments.

recreation areas in addition to or separate from what may be available at school sites.

Trial Scheme of Recreation Areas

Once local recreation standards have been established, space requirements are estimated in the following manner. Referring to the general urban-wide pattern of open spaces and the system of existing and proposed school sites previously developed, a tentative schematic plan of recreation sites is developed for each type of facility. In this study scheme, attention is given to the availability of surplus public lands, abandoned school sites, and tax title lands. Considered, too, are the ideas and previous proposals of recreation and park officials or their consultants. The final result of this process is a scheme of sites with areas dimensioned according to the locally adopted standards of desirable (as opposed to minimum) site size and balanced off against gross requirements as determined by population standards. With acreages compiled by planning district, the result is summarized in tabular form as shown in Table 53. Comments made concerning procedures in tabulating school data apply equally well here, namely, that in the case of facilities serving a larger residential community, such as playfields and recreation centers, Table 53 will show entries only for those planning districts in which the facilities happen to be located. Again, the V & R data under "all facilities" have special significance for the analysis of gross residential densities which follows.

Space for Residential Communities as a Whole

This subsection on residential community space requirements serves two functions. First, it directs attention to any revisions in net residential space requirements which may be necessitated by the results of the subsequent

Table 53. New Requirements for Local Recreation Areas by Planning District, 19xx

Planning District	Net Additions in Local Recreation Space (acres)											
	Local Parks			Playgrounds			Playf'ds — Rec. Ctrs.			All Facilities		
	Invasion	V & R[a]	Total	Invasion	V & R	Total	Invasion	V & R	Total	Invasion	V & R	Total
1	x	x	x	x	x	x	x	x	x	x	x	x
2	x	x	x	x	x	x	x	x	x	x	x	x
etc.	x	x	x	x	x	x	x	x	x	x	x	x
	—	—	—	—	—	—	—	—	—	—	—	—
Subtotal central city	x	x	x	x	x	x	x	x	x	x	x	x
10	x	x	x	x	x	x	x	x	x	x	x	x
11	x	x	x	x	x	x	x	x	x	x	x	x
etc.	x	x	x	x	x	x	x	x	x	x	x	x
	—	—	—	—	—	—	—	—	—	—	—	—
Subtotal fringe area	x	x	x	x	x	x	x	x	x	x	x	x
	—	—	—	—	—	—	—	—	—	—	—	—
Planning area total	x	x	x	x	x	x	x	x	x	x	x	x

[a] V & R is an abbreviation for "vacant and renewal land."

analyses of community facility requirements and the pre-emption of land for these purposes that may have been tentatively included as residential land in the first place. Second, it focuses attention on effective gross holding capacity and gross residential density concepts which have special significance in estimating space requirements in the presently undeveloped planning districts or in districts with large clearance areas becoming available under public renewal programs.

Final Adjustments in Net Space Needs

The data developed in terms of net effective holding capacities in the analysis of residential areas will continue to serve an important purpose in developed and partially developed planning districts where streets are in place or dedicated, for in these areas, estimates of space needs based on gross data do not apply. Thus on the basis of the space requirement summaries appearing in Tables 49, 51, and 53, a summary such as that shown in Table 54 is prepared, recapitulating space requirements for community facilities and giving the amount of vacant and renewal land remaining for residential use in each planning district after deducting the total land ab-

Table 54. Allocations of Residentially Suited Supply of Vacant-Renewal Land to Local Community Facility Uses by Planning District, 19xx

Planning District	Total V & R [a] Land Suitable for Residential Communities	Space Rqts. of Community Facilities from V & R Supply of Land				V & R Land Remaining for Residential Use
		Local Bus.	Schools	Recreation	Total	
1	xx	x	x	x	x	xx
2	xx	x	x	x	x	xx
etc.	xx	x	x	x	x	xx
	—	—	—	—	—	—
Subtotal central city	xx	x	x	x	x	xx
10	xx	x	x	x	x	xx
11	xx	x	x	x	x	xx
etc.	xx	x	x	x	x	xx
	—	—	—	—	—	—
Subtotal fringe area	xx	x	x	x	x	xx
	—	—	—	—	—	—
Planning area total	xx	x	x	x	x	xx

[a] V & R is an abbreviation for "vacant and renewal land."

sorbed by these community facilities. Then a new Table 44 of final effective net holding capacities is prepared. These revisions, in turn, may involve revisions in the distribution of dwelling units among planning districts (see Table 45) and in the distribution of acreage requirements by planning district (see Table 46). While it is possible that these revisions will involve several repeated trial computations extending into revisions of community facility estimates of space needs in order to balance off the supply of land with the combined space needs of all relevant uses, it is more probable that adjustments will be relatively minor since community facility space needs make up only a very nominal part of the total.

Estimating Gross Space Needs

The final matter of concern is the development of estimates of space requirements for entire residential communities which may be expected to develop in outlying planning districts during the planning period. These requirements are analyzed in terms of effective gross holding capacities and gross residential densities. These data are prepared primarily for planning districts with large amounts of open land or containing large areas earmarked for clearance and redevelopment as residential communities. The

Table 55. Derivation of Gross Space Requirements for Entirely New Residential Communities in Selected Planning Districts

Planning District	Net Acreage Requirements by Use Class									Gross Acreage Rqts.
	Residential Use by Density Type							Community Facilities	Allowance for Streets	
	A	B	C	D	E	F	Etc.			
X	x	x	x	x	x	x	x	x	x	xx
Y	x	x	x	x	x	x	x	x	x	xx
Z	x	x	x	x	x	x	x	x	x	xx

procedure is relatively simple. The figures in the last column of Table 54 are adjusted downward for the appropriate planning districts by an amount which it is estimated will accommodate needed streets. This adjustment is crudely approximated on the basis of observed existing proportions of total land area devoted to streets in presently built-up planning districts as recorded in the summary of existing land uses, and on the basis of subjective allowances for the character of the terrain in each planning district of interest. In the more detailed analyses of residential communities, special adjustments for each class of residential density are recommended. Such detail is not warranted in the broad-gauge analyses employed in developing the preliminary land use plan.

With an adjustment made in the supply of vacant and renewal land available for residential use to allow for streets, procedures then follow those previously outlined. A tabular summary of effective gross holding capacities is prepared for the appropriate planning districts following the format of Table 44. Next a table similar to Table 45 is developed, showing for the planning districts of interest any changes in the distribution of dwelling unit requirements by density type, considering changes in the holding capacity ceilings developing as a result of a shift from a net to a gross presentation of data. The final step is the summary of space requirements for the appropriate planning districts as shown in Table 55.

From Preliminary to Refined Studies

The foregoing procedures for the analysis of residential communities are especially designed for preliminary planning. While the basic framework in later more detailed studies is similar, at certain points in the procedures, specialized investigations can be introduced to sharpen the analyses, substituting more precise estimating techniques for the approximation approaches employed in selected stages of the work described above. Thus, in residential area studies, a housing market analysis would be a "must"; in. the study of recreation area needs, user surveys would be introduced enabling analyses to take more direct account of "consumer" preferences; in school plant investigations, a more reliable forecasting technique would be introduced, and more detailed studies of the existing school plant would be made; in shopping center analyses, a detailed survey of existing floor space in local business use and a purchasing power and family expenditures study would be undertaken (see references to these studies in an earlier section of this chapter); and studies of church space needs would be introduced.[49] These are a few of the kinds of studies which can be undertaken in detailing the first preliminary planning analyses. Two examples are taken up below to indicate the general character of work carrying preliminary planning analyses a step further—one relating to housing market analysis and the other to school plant planning. Undoubtedly, as research is conducted into various aspects of land use planning procedures for residential communities, some elements in the above framework will be superseded by improved methods and techniques in both the preliminary and later stages of land use planning. To indicate the general character of these more detailed studies at the present stage of research development, the first two areas of investigation cited above will be briefly alluded to in the following paragraphs.

Housing Market Analysis

In a monograph on theory and methods of housing market analysis, Rapkin, Winnick, and Blank define this kind of a study as "a process that attempts to identify and measure the forces that produce change in the size and utilization of the housing inventory and thus influence the distribution of dwelling units among the population." [50] Thus it is essentially an analysis of supply and demand conditions in the housing market. Broadly, supply is concerned with "how much of the product will be made available at different prices when costs (of various kinds) and the organization of the industry are taken into account," and demand, with "how much of the product the public will buy, given its income, tastes, and the price of the product (relative to the prices of other goods)." [51]

---

[49] For a useful reference on church planning needs, see Robert C. Hoover and Everett L. Perry, *Church and City Planning*, Survey Guide 2, New York: Bureau of Research and Survey, National Council of the Churches of Christ in the U.S.A., November, 1955.

[50] Chester Rapkin, Louis Winnick, and David M. Blank, *Housing Market Analysis, a Study of Theory and Methods*, a Housing and Home Finance Agency research monograph, Washington: U.S. Government Printing Office, December, 1953, p. 1.

[51] Louis Winnick, "Housing Market Analysis," *Journal of Housing*, December, 1955, p. 432.

The procedure outlined in the above framework for the analysis of residential areas is essentially aimed at determining existing and long-range housing need as opposed to housing demand. The most important elements missing in this framework are, first, an analysis of the housing inventory by rent and price categories compared with the rent-paying and purchase ability of the population under study, and, second, a study of choice factors which affect demand, given rents and prices that match up with the financial abilities and desires of this population to take up housing at these rentals and prices. While the above framework introduced assumptions as to choice, to be firmly based, these assumptions must be geared to market forces.

Now obviously, market analyses have their greatest utility in terms of short-run eventualities. Over long-run periods, there are a great many intangibles in the matter of tastes, income levels, family sizes, and other factors which are difficult to anticipate. Yet if assumptions concerning the future can be framed in terms of an intimate knowledge of the workings of the present housing market, long-range planning proposals affecting the future market are more likely to prove practicable than had market factors been entirely ignored. The residential areas portion of the land use plan is a long-range proposal which seeks to fulfill future housing needs, but is attuned as closely as possible to realistic market factors. Thus the housing market analysis provides valuable insights into the economic factors likely to influence proposals based purely on social need. Properly evaluated and introduced into the studies for residential land use planning, these factors can be used in framing more studied assumptions, setting more detailed developmental specifications, and preparing a plan that is reasonably possible of attainment and yet does not compromise the important social objectives sought in the plan.

Recent work on the structure of the market by Grigsby provides important new insights into the complexities of the market process.[52] We cannot go into this important aspect of housing analysis, nor can we go into the methods of surveying the market. Survey techniques are adequately described elsewhere and are beyond the scope of this discussion.[53] On the supply side, they involve surveys of a somewhat different order than the studies heretofore described, although some of the basic types of data will obviously be similar. On the demand side, a whole new array of investigations are introduced, including sampling studies which delve into both the future housing intentions of people as well as their past behavior in the selection of housing. Finally, it should be noted that the

---

[52] William G. Grigsby, *Housing Markets and Public Policy*, Philadelphia: University of Pennsylvania Press, 1963.
[53] See Rapkin, Winnick, and Blank, *Housing Market Analysis*.

whole market analysis process is extremely complex and requires the skills of persons trained or experienced in this specialty.

School Plant Planning

Another illustration of the character of the more detailed work to be carried out in comprehensive planning studies is found in school plant planning analyses. In preliminary land use planning, investigations go only into sufficient detail to permit the identification of a general pattern of school sites as they relate to other space-using facilities in residential communities. Although school officials may be and usually are consulted at this first stage of planning, the generalized character of these first studies is such as to be more fitted to the needs of general planning than to the work of the school board itself. The more detailed studies in extension of these first investigations, therefore, aim not only to provide more studied general planning information with which to develop the comprehensive plan, but to supply the school board with a service in which it has confidence as a basis for programming school plant needs. Essentially, this means that the planning agency is functioning in a service capacity and that, even though the planning agency conducts the studies, the school plant plan which emerges must for all purposes be the school board's plan.

On the surface of it, such an approach may appear to be simply a matter of "changing hats," that is, writing in the name of the school board on the face of school planning reports as sponsor or cosponsor. But it goes more deeply than this. It involves an appreciation of a schoolman's point of view, and, more specifically, a full understanding of educational objectives and school board policies as they impinge on school plant planning. For the city planner, long-range planning is primarily tied up in physical needs of the school plant; for the school administrator, long-range planning includes, as well, future curriculum considerations, future personnel requirements, and future budget needs for these as well as for the school plant.

There are a number of basic policy matters which impinge on school plant planning. Among them is the organization of the school system and the probabilities of change in the future, say from an 8–4 to a 6–3–3 grade system, or from a 6–3–3 to a 6–3–3–2 system in which a junior college program is introduced into the traditional 12-grade organization. Another policy consideration concerns the community use of school facilities, not only in school-sponsored adult education programs, but in programs sponsored by other agencies or groups, for example, the recreation commission, or drama, music, and other similar civic groups. Still another policy matter relates to pupil transportation and the use of school buses or special transit passes to extend the attendance areas of schools beyond the traditional walking distance service radii. A related consideration is the basis for the establishment of attendance areas of the individual schools and the policy with respect to the admission of pupils from beyond the school district as a whole in the light of integration objectives for the school system.

Though seemingly less tangibly connected with school plant planning than such administrative policy considerations, there are educational objectives which must be taken into account. Indeed, as self-evident as it seems, the basic objectives relating to the scope of the program, the curriculum content, and the methods of education are the most fundamental determinants of the character of the school plant. They can dictate variations in the approach to school planning. This places a premium on an approach in which the school authorities share in the planning process. Finally, as a practical matter it must be recognized that the school plant plan is effectuated by the school authorities. Thus, if they can be persuaded to spare time from their day-to-day administrative burdens to participate in the planning process at critical points along the way, there is greater likelihood that the plan will be carried out.

Again, it is noted that considerations of the methods and techniques employed in these more detailed studies of space requirements are beyond the scope of the present discussion. Survival methods of estimating future enrollments are well covered elsewhere,[54] and the specific requirements of the elementary and secondary school plants and their sites have been treated in detail in specialized publications.[55] These more exacting kinds of studies, predicated on the above kinds of guiding considerations, however, clearly fall within the comprehensive planning stage of the progressive planning approach.

---

[54] See Planning Advisory Service, *Planning for School Capacities and Locations,* Information Report No. 36, Chicago: American Society of Planning Officials, March, 1952.

[55] See James L. Taylor, *School Sites—Selection, Development, and Utilization,* a Department of Health, Education, and Welfare monograph, Washington: U.S. Government Printing Office, 1958; see also National Council on Schoolhouse Construction, *Guide for Planning School Plants,* Nashville: W. D. McClurkin, Peabody College, 1958; and Planning Advisory Service, "School Site Selection," Information Report No. 175, Chicago: American Society of Planning Officials, August, 1963.

Chapter 12

The Land Use Plan

Implicit in the theoretical formulations of Part I and in the procedural sequence which has been unfolding in the chapters of Parts II and III is an emphasis on plan*ning*, and more particularly on land use plan*ning*. Though there has been this emphasis on process, to have utility, plan*ning* must produce some tangible and concrete results in the form of plans, in this case a land use or land development plan. Up to this point in Part III, we have been concerned with the analysis of location and space requirements as investigative steps in the development of the land use plan. Particular attention has been given to these studies as they apply to the preliminary planning stage in what has been identified as a "progressive process." It will be recalled that this process begins with goal formulation and the establishment of general policy directions for the long pull, with growth projections carried to the horizon year. Once these policy guidelines are set, according to the rationale of this process, analyses advance through at least two successive cycles from approximation to more precise analytical forms, with each cycle moving into more detailed areas of policy review.

Figure 36 indicates the general sequence to these cycles. Chapter 11 has been concerned with preliminary investigations involved in the first of these two analytical cycles. The more generalized approach was selected for emphasis in this volume in order to present the basic rationale in its simplest, most elemental form. If the process is understood in this rudimentary form, it should be possible for the analyst to extend these techniques into more elaborate forms. These may involve "hand" or machine methods of processing data and the use of more exacting techniques of analysis referred to in the preceding chapters. With the aid of high-speed computers, they may draw upon mathematical models to systematize the analytical steps. As indicated in the lower portion of Figure 36, where models are employed, analyses are generally performed in the framework of two major systems—one focusing on land use and the other on transportation, each with a series of subsystems feeding results from one to the other.

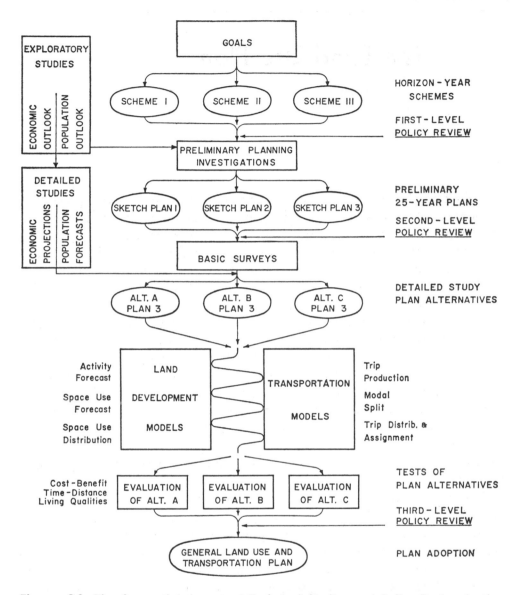

Figure 36. The Sequential Aspect of Technical Studies and Policy Review in the "Progressive Planning Approach." As indicated in the right-hand column, this representation of the approach involves cycles of planning, each involving more detailed and exacting forms of analysis than the preceding one. Plans are presented in the form of alternatives, with one emerging from each level of policy review and providing the basis for consideration of alternative policies at the next more detailed stage of analysis. The general land use and transportation plan is the end product of this sequence. As noted earlier, this is not a straight-line but rather a circular sequence, and so, with the adoption of this plan, a new sequence is set in motion, perhaps at the first or perhaps at the second level above.

In this concluding chapter, the first section relates to steps taken in bringing a land use plan into equilibrium and readying it for second-level policy review. The final section aims to prepare the way for the next steps in the progressive approach and provide an introduction to the use of models, an option open to a planning agency at the most detailed level of analysis. Thus, in one sense, this chapter terminates one cycle in the land use planning process, but in another, it indicates the scope of more advanced approaches that may follow.

Finalizing Design Considerations

We now turn to the steps involved in firming up the sketch plans which have been emerging from the analyses outlined in Part III. We wish to examine each for its sufficiency as a balanced and scaled representation of the metropolitan area in terms of the goals set at the outset and the policies assumed at the beginning of the analysis. As a result of following steps outlined in Chapter 10 in applying location principles and standards, the *parti* of each sketch plan has been set down in pursuance of the general policy orientation emerging from the policy review of horizon-year schemes. In following procedures in Chapter 11, space requirements for the 20- to 25-year period ahead have been dimensioned into areas prime for development and appropriate to each *parti*. So at this juncture we have a first sketch showing in general how each *parti* would take form on the ground based on the assumption that development will proceed in a sequence similar to the one followed in Chapter 11 in making trial applications of space requirements.[1] The finalizing design phase of land use planning remains. The task now is to evaluate each scheme as it has emerged from the process of scaling-in land uses and finally to translate it into a well-articulated scheme for land development in harmony with the particular generalized scheme for transportation introduced in the *parti* as a policy "given."

---

[1] It should be noted that this general sequence roughly corresponds to the sequence in the chain of land development decisions as they occur in the real world. Thus, as suggested in the author's conceptual framework set forth in Chapter 2, decisions affecting centers of employment (industrial areas, wholesale districts, and region-serving business centers) along with certain public decisions tend to influence decisions in the use of land for residential communities. But, as noted in Chapter 2, our knowledge of the "queuing order" of these decisions is imperfect, and as research begins to shed more light on the feedback effect of one kind of decision on another, we may need to modify the general sequence outlined in Chapter 11. In this connection it is of interest to note that the same kind of postulation with respect to sequence is involved in "hooking up" models in a systems approach.

Evaluation of Schemes

The design criteria used in evaluating each scheme in its present stage of development fall into two groups—those of a general nature applicable to all schemes, and those applicable primarily to one particular scheme. Foremost in the first category is a re-examination of the structural elements of the design—a check-out on such questions as: Is there a basic logic to the organization of the spaces and interconnecting transportation systems (Chapter 2)? Does the plan follow logically from analyses of anticipated future interaction needs of residents, firms, and institutions in both the activity component (Chapter 6) and the movement component (Chapter 8)? Having satisfied ourselves that each scheme meets basic structural criteria, next we examine each for its sufficiency in fulfilling the stated land use planning goals. Here the plan is evaluated in terms of such criteria as these: Does the plan reflect full consideration of the needed and desired environmental qualities set forth in goal statements? Does it reflect balanced consideration of resident, firm, and institutional needs? Are public costs of carrying out the plan realistic in terms of foreseeable revenues and the long-term debt structure? Does the plan consider the preferences of residents in relation to their willingness to pay for qualities desired? Does it provide imaginative choices to the various segments of the population? To what extent are the metropolitan area's visual resources creatively considered in the design?

In addition to the foregoing criteria, which apply to all schemes, there are checks to be made to establish that the policy assumptions that go with each particular scheme are reflected in its design concept. Among the policy assumptions that are likely to be involved, there are three which have particular importance in the evaluation of the design—assumptions relating to focal points of activity, to transportation elements, and to intensity of development. To illustrate, let us assume that the horizon-year review stage of land use planning reflects a general preference for some form of the nucleated pattern of development, a form which combines features of both rapid transit and expressway systems of transportation, and one which favors generally a compact pattern of development. Given this general policy emphasis and given certain more detailed policy positions posed as alternatives in setting a course in the general direction chosen, the task here is to determine whether the scheme which goes with each policy position is an imaginative and a reasonable representation of the development that would occur under that combination of policies.

The whole process of design conception beginning with the *parti* and extending through to this final stage of synthesis is a creative one and is not reducible to a formula. The design criteria we have been enumerating supply discipline to the execution of a design, but they cannot be put into any formula to produce a design. By the same token there are no absolutes of evaluation which can measure the imaginative qualities of design once it is executed.[2] While there is no measured test of the imaginativeness of the design, there are some approaches for testing out policies to determine whether they are likely to produce the scheme in question. As we shall see in the final section of this chapter, these involve the use of models as a tool of design. Far from intruding on the design function, the use of models frees up this all-important central concern of planning. It enables the planner to test out a much wider range of design alternatives than ever before, and in this sense it promises to usher in a whole new era in planning design.

For purposes of the preliminary planning stage of land use planning, a subjective check-out of the policy implications of each scheme is adequate and is generally consistent with the character of analytical procedures followed in this stage. In a subjective approach, we are essentially making an examination of each policy assumption as it is reflected in the design execution and gauging how successfully the design is in handling each policy in relation to the mix of policies as a whole. To carry our illustration further, under the first of the three policy areas, conceivably one scheme might be developed on the basis of the CBD continuing as the focal point of the metropolitan area but with strong satellite centers developing as semiautonomous centers of activity, perhaps in the form of a series of regional centers of employment or shopping (new ones or suburban CBD's) or a center of transportation (as in a metropolitan airport complex). For this illustrative policy assumption, we must satisfy ourselves that the design execution reflects, both in structure and in form (two-dimensionally and three-dimensionally), a dominant focal point and a series of logically positioned subfocal points of activity.

The second illustrative policy area, the one relating to transportation systems, is of course closely associated with the first. Historically transportation systems have been oriented toward the central city CBD and therefore have a long history of reinforcing the prominence of this focal point in the metropolitan area. Indeed, other satellite centers which already exist in the surrounding region may owe some of their prominence to similar

---

[2] However, the Lynch-Rodwin typology of design elements discussed in Chapter 2 and their suggestions for cross-classifying these elements in their original article are useful in organizing the factors to be taken into account in evaluating the design qualities of the scheme. See Kevin Lynch and Lloyd Rodwin, "A Theory of Urban Form," *Journal of the American Institute of Planners*, November, 1958.

historical advantages in transportation. In earlier periods of growth these subcenters have frequently originated as intersections of outlying circumferentials with radials or as points of transfer from a local subsystem of transportation to a main-line commuter or rapid transit system leading to the central city CBD. Very often the transportation policy assumptions will involve some major surgery to enable realignment of movements to new subcenters or to permit revitalization and growth in existing subcenters. Here we must satisfy ourselves that the transportation networks shown in the scheme adequately interconnect residential communities, the central city CBD, and the selected subcenters of activity, at the same time achieving the balance between transit and automotive modes of transportation set forth in the policy assumptions determined at the outset.

The third policy area, which relates to intensity of development, is concerned with the degree of spread or concentration to be sought in various aggregated systems of use areas. At the metropolitan scale, these assumptions relate to the differentiation to be introduced among clusters of uses —for example, between residential communities or between industrial concentrations and residential communities. At the submetropolitan scale, they relate to the heterogeneity or homogeneity of development within, say, a residential community or the CBD. At the metropolitan scale, we are concerned with a means for defining the limits of use aggregations. In much the same way that transportation networks assist in defining and developing the focal points of the metropolitan area plan, the open space pattern (public and private) is an important means of differentiating between clusters of uses surrounding these focal points—in effect introducing breaks between cluster systems. The juxtaposition of use systems with differing degrees of compaction at the submetropolitan scale provides another means of introducing breaks in the metropolitan area pattern.

At the submetropolitan scale, differentiation in intensity of development is established in part by varying residential or employee densities as they may be related to land areas directly or by floor area ratios. Under modern performance standards, it is now possible to introduce some measure of heterogeneity in use patterns. Street systems may also be important variables in this respect. Indeed, the choices in density, use combinations, and street layout constitute a matrix of variables which regulate the intensity of development at the submetropolitan scale.

In this policy area, at both the metropolitan and submetropolitan scales, there are important related policy areas subsumed—policies relative to the extension of water and sewer facilities and service levels provided, school location and school bus service policies, density policies as reflected in zoning and subdivision regulations, and so on. Here again in this third policy area, we must satisfy ourselves that the scheme reflects the assumptions made at the outset.

Revision and Synthesis

Having checked the sufficiency of each alternative scheme by means of such design criteria at both the general and particular level, we move into the final stage of revision and synthesis. This is a stage of reconciling conflicts in location and making compensatory adjustments in the whole matrix of relationships. Since these usually involve the resolution of conflicts between transportation and land use and inconsistencies among use relationships, it may be helpful to discuss briefly the way in which the planner goes about achieving synthesis in both areas of concern.

Transportation and Land Use

Usually the planner begins with the focal points of activity and then expands his scope to the full metropolitan area. In our illustrative case above, he would therefore start with the CBD. In the central area of the city the basic circulation principles call for a mechanism which separates and distributes traffic bound for the CBD and collects and channels to outlying destinations traffic leaving the CBD. In medium- and small-size urban areas, this involves the development of an inner loop surrounding the CBD somewhat on the order of a giant traffic circle. This loop serves as an interchange between radial routes converging on the downtown area and permits drivers to select their points of entrance into the CBD without the necessity of entering the CBD's internal street system. In large metropolitan areas, this involves differential levels of traffic service—one handling the relatively high-speed in-out and through movements on expressways radial to the CBD, and the other handling at relatively slow speeds the distribution and collection of traffic coming off or entering the expressway system. The "in" portion of the traffic must be deccelerated and distributed to destinations in the CBD, and the "out" portion must be collected and accelerated to make the transition into expressway speeds from conventional street systems. Essentially the basic requirement of the large metropolitan area is a multisystem of circulation—an expressway system with its complex of ramps feeding into the inner loop which in turn feeds into access streets.

Once the traffic is brought to the CBD, terminals are needed close to major destinations. In principle, the all-day, low-price parking areas fringe the inner loop, providing a quick means of siphoning off traffic at inbound times of the day to keep it from penetrating the CBD itself. At outbound times, traffic is fed from these parking terminals directly onto the loop and eventually to the radials which drain the CBD. Closer in at the edges of the CBD are the higher-price parking lots for short-term parkers.

The land use plan for the CBD both influences and is influenced by the location of the inner loop (and any auxiliary expressway loop that may be warranted). CBD land use planning studies establish the general location of the loop, but thoroughfare planning studies set the location in greater detail, considering such factors as future desire lines of traffic (in turn influenced by the CBD plan), the selection of streets available from the existing street pattern that are adaptable and feasible for inclusion in such an inner loop, the engineering problems posed in connecting the inner loop to the expressway system, the conflicts posed by railroads and transit, and so on.

The size of the CBD, of course, is influenced by the policy preconditions relative to satellite centers and modes of transportation. Less space will be required in the CBD where subcenters are designed to absorb new growth, and less space will be required in a strong transit-oriented scheme, since less parking space would be provided and less capacity would be required in the downtown street system.

Having checked each scheme's central area, we turn our attention to the outlying areas. Concentric to the inner loop, there are intermediate and outer loop systems of crosstown streets or parkways supplying interconnections between industrial areas, wholesale districts, and various residential communities in the urban area. Intersecting these crosstown streets are the major radials: the expressways and major thoroughfares which radiate outward from the CBD to outlying residential areas and employment centers.

Here again, land use planning considerations influence and are influenced by thoroughfare planning requirements. The intersections of major radial and circumferential streets are the strategic locations for satellite region-serving business centers and for community shopping centers. In some such centers, a perimeter loop with its own web system of radials and circumferentials, subordinate to but integrated with the larger metropolitan web system, may be required. The design of this subordinate system of major streets must be closely coordinated with the design of the business center and surrounding residential areas. Similarly, outlying employment centers such as organized industrial districts may be the focal points for other subordinate web systems of radial and crosstown routes which must also be related to surrounding use areas and to the larger metropolitan system of major streets. Finally and fundamental in residential community design, every effort is made to locate the metropolitan and more localized radials and circumferentials so that they bound rather than penetrate or

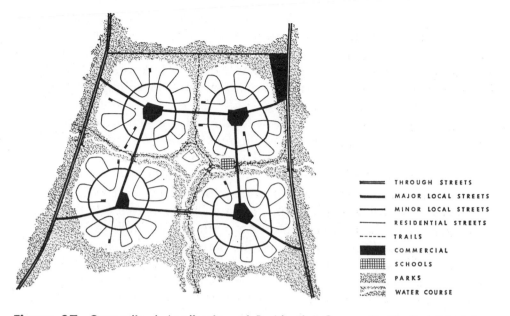

Figure 37. Generalized Application of Residential Community Design Principles. (*Source:* Philadelphia City Planning Commission, *Preliminary Far Northeast Physical Development Plan*, January, 1955.)

truncate any particular system of neighborhoods that compose each residential community. This general principle is illustrated in Figure 37. It should be noted that within residential communities there are various lower-order major streets, one supplying interconnections between neighborhood centers, and still another supplying a means of collecting or distributing traffic within each neighborhood or sometimes bounding the neighborhood. All these various subordinate systems of major streets, whether they serve business centers, industrial areas, or residential communities, obviously must be fitted to the use areas they serve and to the surrounding pattern of uses.

Use Relationships

Related to the foregoing considerations are the interrelationships intrinsic to uses themselves—relationships between industrial areas and residential communities, between region-serving recreational, educational, and cultural areas and residential communities or business centers, and so on. The basic principles for these relationships have been set forth in the location requirements discussed in Chapter 10. But there remains the task of checking the trial pattern of uses developed in the sequence of analyses in Chapter 11. This involves not only tests for compatibility, but also checks to insure that proposals for the use of vacant and renewal areas are, in fact, the best use of these areas. Even though the vacant land classification system employed in the first instance would tend to preclude basic miscalculations, it is necessary to establish that the peculiar sequence followed in Chapter 11 in the analysis of major use categories has not introduced any distortions in the use relationships.

In checking out use relationships we make tests for such basic elements as the convenience between use areas, the relationship of prevailing winds to industrial and residential areas, or the way in which glare from business areas or the noise and gasoline fumes from traffic in business or employment centers may interfere with the amenities of residential communities, and so on. Also involved at this juncture are checks to ascertain the general compatibility of the trial pattern of uses with the structure of land values, and tests to establish whether in the particular locations selected the densities proposed for residential areas and the intensity of development proposed in commercial and industrial areas yield a favorable cost-revenue relationship. These elements plus the aesthetic considerations in the use of natural and man-made visual assets intrinsic to the setting of the city and the arrangements of use areas in this setting, citizen attitudes and preferences on such things as differential densities within any single residential area, the siting of industry under performance standards in areas traditionally closed to industry—these considerations all enter into the summary re-examination of use relationships.

Preparing the Plan

On the basis of these design considerations, the earlier trial scheme for the location and distribution of future land uses can be shaped up into its final version, what we have termed here the preliminary sketch plan. The creative aspects of this final synthesizing process of design, as noted above, are not readily described in words, but it may assist in picturing the rudiments of this process to summarize briefly its mechanics and the form in which the results are presented.

Design of the Plan

The design of the plan is the culmination of repeated tests and retests of alternative arrangements in the pattern of uses, considering location and space needs previously specified and the density and intensity of development prescribed in the course of deriving these needs. The scope of these tests will of course be guided by the above kinds of design considerations.

Overlays are used in the testing process. Over the trial scheme of uses cumulatively derived is inserted an overlay of the trial thoroughfare scheme called for under the policy assumption which goes with this particular plan alternative. Next, an annotated overlay is prepared, identifying the conflicts in transportation and land use and the inconsistencies or awkward elements in use relationships. In general, tests of conflicts with transportation systems begin with the CBD and are carried from there to outlying sections of the urban area. Concurrently or separately, according to the preferences of the land use planner, the workability of use relationships are established in both their localized and their broad patterns.

The overlay with annotations of conflicts and other problems then becomes the reference work for the design analyses. By other overlays, different solutions to each problem are tested in sketch form. Where a solution has implications for other aspects of the plan not previously noted on the reference overlay, special additional adjustments which go with that particular solution may become involved. Thus each problem is studied individually and finally in combination until a scheme emerges with all elements in balance and harmony. With a decision reached on each scheme, the final task of the operation is the recapitulation of the summary of space allocation adjusted to the final version of each preliminary sketch plan.

Plan Presentation

The general scope and content of the report on the land use plan was outlined in Chapter 9. Of primary concern here is the tangible form that the map presentation takes as a means of visualizing the alternate schemes emerging as end products of the design process. A number of factors dictate the form and detail employed in the presentation, principal among them being the size of the urban area and the purpose to be served by the presentation. Generally the land use plan is a combined presentation of the principal elements of the thoroughfare network and the pattern of proposed uses, supplying a visual explanation as to how various major functional use areas are to be tied together by thoroughfares and developed in balanced relationship to one another. However, some planning agencies prefer to show the elements separately.

To provide a fully meaningful picture of use relationships, the presentation must show the entire metropolitan area pattern of proposed uses. While the official presentation of a plan prepared for adoption may be restricted to the incorporated area, the studies incident to the plan will have taken the entire urban area into the scope of investigations. Generally, the use patterns shown on the map include as many of the major use categories employed in analytical procedures as the scale of the presentation will per-

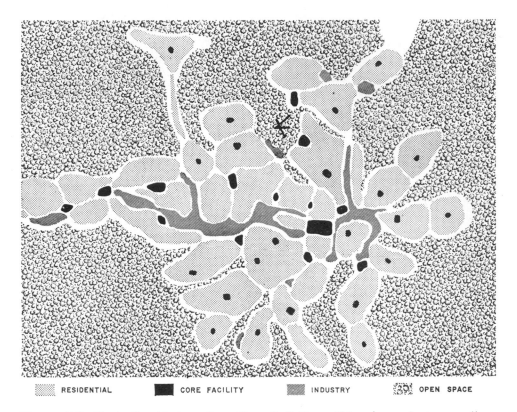

RESIDENTIAL   CORE FACILITY   INDUSTRY   OPEN SPACE

Figure 38. Illustrative Horizon-Year Growth Pattern. This scheme features a "corridor" plan for extending residential communities in the growth period to the year 2000. The corridors will carry the utility systems and a relatively high-order, free-moving, transportation system for automobile and express bus modes of moving people. (*Source:* The Roanoke Valley Regional Planning Commission, *A Land Use Plan for the Roanoke Valley Region*, Roanoke: Department of City Planning, June, 1963.)

mit. Very often in large metropolitan areas two presentations are necessary —one which shows the entire metropolitan area in generalized patterns, and another which shows the detailed categories by small subareas on a larger scale.

Sometimes in presenting the plan it is helpful to show the design concept featured in the horizon-year scheme in order to convey the underlying ideas featured in the 20- to 25-year plan. Thus, the Roanoke Valley Regional Land Use Plan (Figure 39) features a cellular pattern of residential communities developed in a "corridor" scheme proposed as a policy emphasis in the horizon-year growth pattern (Figure 38). Complementing the corridor concept is a regional open space concept growing out of the land forms of this valley.

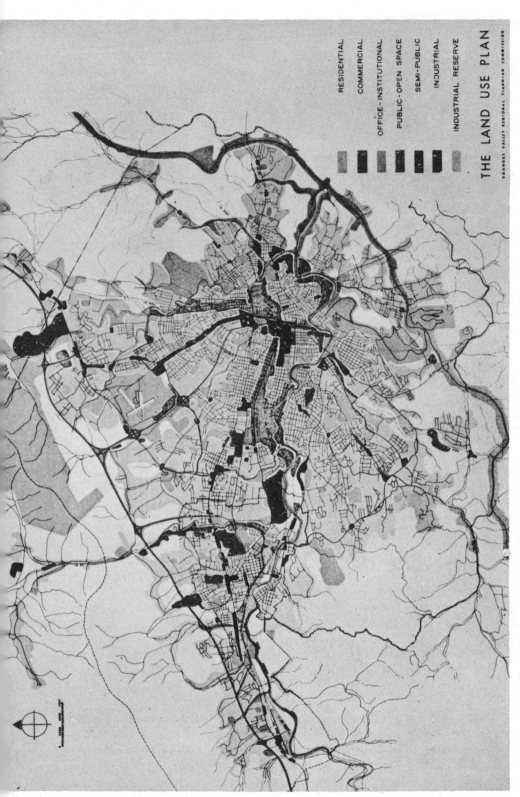

RESIDENTIAL

COMMERCIAL

OFFICE - INSTITUTIONAL

PUBLIC - OPEN SPACE

SEMI-PUBLIC

INDUSTRIAL

INDUSTRIAL RESERVE

THE LAND USE PLAN

ROANOKE VALLEY REGIONAL PLANNING COMMISSION

Figure 39. Illustrative Land Use Plan. Shown here are the results of analyses of the kind set forth in Chapters 10 and 11. Using the basic design concept presented in Figure 38, a *parti* is developed on the basis of location requirements, and after space requirements are scaled in, a fully articulated general scheme of the kind shown here eventually takes form as a preliminary proposal. (*Source:* The Roanoke Valley Regional Planning Commission, *A Land Use Plan for the Roanoke Valley Region,* Roanoke: Department of City Planning, June, 1963.)

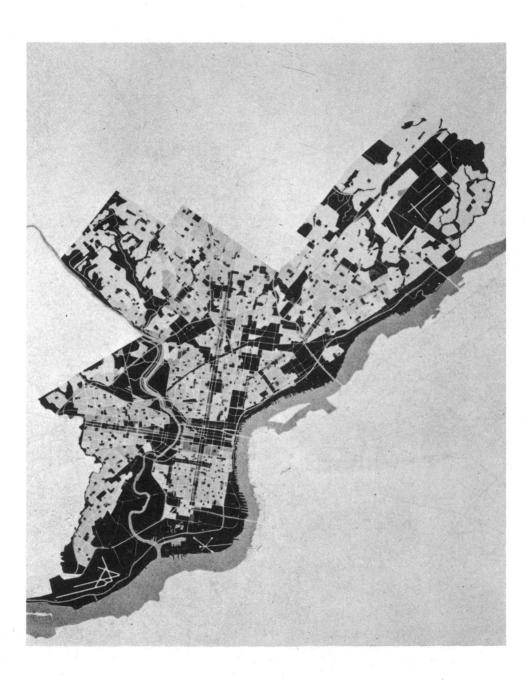

Figure 40. The Philadelphia Comprehensive Plan, 1960. Although the detail of this plate is difficult to interpret, it demonstrates the degree of detail involved when planning proposals have reached the stage in the planning process where they are set down in the form of a comprehensive plan. (*Source:* Philadelphia City Planning Commission, *Comprehensive Plan for the City of Philadelphia*, 1960.)

Figure 40 shows the land development proposals contained in the Philadelphia Comprehensive Plan. Proposals appear here in much greater detail than those shown in Figure 39 partly because they have reached the comprehensive plan stage of the planning process and partly because of the differing circumstances involved in presenting a plan for an area which is already largely developed. As a plan prepared for official actions of one governmental unit in a large metropolitan area, it presents proposals only for its own area of jurisdiction. Separate plates present transportation and other elements of the plan. For example, proposals for renewal and the proposed pattern of residential densities are shown in Figures 34 and 35, respectively.

Plan Evaluation

Once alternative schemes have been brought into balance in a form such as that illustrated in Figure 39, the final step in the preliminary planning cycle preparatory to policy review and eventual decision on a single scheme is an evaluation of the relative merits of each scheme on at least three bases: cost-benefit, time-distance, and the living quality considerations of each. In making investigations for these evaluations, the degree of detail is kept commensurate with the kind of detail employed in the analytical techniques as described in Chapter 11. Thus, in evaluating cost implications of each scheme, generally no attempt is made to develop absolute dollar costs. Rather, a relative measure of cost is devised for various elements in the plan as a means of documenting a generally subjective review of the pros and cons of each scheme. However, as indicated in the lower section of Figure 36, more rigorous tests are made at the comprehensive planning stage of the progressive process.

There are no standard substitute techniques for cost-benefit analysis, but there are some rough tests that can be used to get at the relative differences between alternatives. Thus, cost aspects can be inferred from estimates of lineal feet of each class of street, sewer outfall, and water main involved in each scheme, with comparisons expressed in the per cent that one scheme exceeds another in lineal footage required.[3] To evaluate the tax revenue implications of alternative planning schemes is more difficult. One study evaluated plan alternatives in this respect by projecting recent levels of local expenditures and taxable property valuations as they would be applied to each scheme, using results of correlation and multiple regression analyses

---

[3] For an example of this type of analysis applied to alternative sketch plans of the Research Triangle Region of North Carolina, see Pearson H. Stewart and Ray R. Lester, "Considerations Relevant to Potential Development of the Triangle Area," Raleigh: Research Triangle Regional Planning Commission, September, 1960, processed.

of economic and income data as projection indices.[4] From this analysis estimates were made of the possible effects that each scheme would have on the tax structure and future tax rates of the metropolitan area municipalities.

In addition to a purely dollars-and-cents basis of evaluation, there are other bases on which decisions are made. One involves essentially an evaluation of accessibility (or convenience); another, livability (or amenity). In the first, we evaluate the relative advantages of one scheme over another in terms of time-distance. Differences in this respect are in part a function of the design execution itself. For purposes of preliminary plans, differences can be compared by constructing "iso-time" lines around each major focal point of the scheme and conclusions reached concerning the relative advantages of one scheme over another in general terms. In the more advanced stages of planning, transportation models can be used to evaluate differences.

The third basis of evaluation is more difficult to set down in procedural terms. The living qualities inhering to a design are generally not amenable to objective measurement. Conceivably a design jury might apply Lynch's criteria of imageability (see Chapter 7) and arrive at a consensus as to the relative merits of each scheme in a perceptual sense. Similarly the jury might systematically check each scheme against the dominant livability preferences established from attitude studies (see Chapters 6 and 7). However, commonly the pros and cons are subjectively summarized in very general terms. It may be some time before tools become available to assist in the evaluation of these aspects of a plan.

Perspectives of Land Use Planning

We have been viewing the land use planning process in a technical perspective. Although excluded from the scope of this book, there are other important perspectives which warrant at least passing mention as they relate to the technical aspects of the process. These final observations concern citizen and official perspectives of land use planning.

Citizen Perspectives

It may be observed that the citizen's view of land use planning traditionally has been vague, if indeed he has recognized it as a process at all. Generally, it touches him either in a *fait accompli* situation such as "that new sub-

---

[4] Capitol Region Planning Agency, *Municipal Taxation and Regional Development*, Hartford: Capitol Region Planning Agency, March, 1963.

division down the street" or "the slum clearance project on the north side," or in connection with some zoning issue that affects him or a friend. He is thus aware of land use planning in an effectuation context, either in connection with a developmental or a regulatory measure, and usually only in an isolated segment of the whole and in one section of the city. It might be noted too that other aspects of city planning are frequently viewed by the citizen in this same kind of fuzzy perspective.

Partly because of the lack of understanding of the nature and purposes of city planning and the consequent public apathy to planning proposals, and partly because of a genuine interest in bringing planning decisions closer to the ultimate consumers of planning, city planners today are devoting increasing attention to civic relations. While older approaches were based largely on promotion through eye-catching reports and newspaper articles, much more positive and broadly conceived civic relations programs are being undertaken today. The objectives of these programs are generally threefold:

1. To develop an *understanding* among citizens and the organized private interests in the community of the principal physical problems and needs of the area and the role of urban planning in dealing with them and generally bringing about a more livable environment.
2. To cultivate the practice among civic leaders and civic organizations of *sharing in the planning* from the earliest study stages through the later review stages.
3. To provide media for *reporting* on planning studies and recommendations so that civic action programs have the benefit of studied analysis of the community's problems and needs.

In some of the more advanced approaches, the civic relations program is as carefully scheduled and timed as the technical program, with very specific civic relations activities keyed into particular stages of the technical program.[5]

Much can be gained by tying the land use planning process into the civic relations program. General citizen advisory committees have been extremely effective in goal-definition assignments and in exercising review functions at strategic points in the course of land use planning studies, and special advisory committees composed of technical people have provided invaluable guidance on special technical problems. In a number of communities such groups as the Jaycee's and various women's service organizations have proved to be of valuable assistance in carrying out some types of surveys. These ways of bringing people into the land use planning proc-

---

[5] For a discussion of a systematic programmed approach in the use of this and other implementation techniques, see the author's "Taking Stock of Techniques for Shaping Urban Growth," *Journal of the American Institute of Planners*, May, 1963.

ess not only facilitate the work but broaden the base of participation and assist in achieving more widespread understanding of the full scope and purpose of land use planning.

Thus, under such a civic relations program, by the time the preliminary plan alternatives are developed, more widespread response and more intelligent reactions can be anticipated. Review is accomplished through study committees of chamber of commerce, merchant association, real estate, homebuilder, and other special interest groups as well as through orientation meetings with civic clubs, neighborhood organizations, and similar general-interest groups. Thus, element by element the plan can be given careful review, the cumulative result of which is a picture of both the workable and unworkable features of the plan as viewed by these participating groups. The results of these review sessions become important reference sources in the work ahead in the refinement and revision of the preliminary land use plan.

Official Perspectives

What are the perspectives of the official groups in the urban area—the city council and the administrative officials of the one or more municipalities that may be involved? Obviously, they have a direct stake in the product of the land use planning process. If features of the plan are carried out as proposed, not only are many of the community facilities built and maintained by the city, but the whole pattern of development as effectuated through zoning, subdivision, urban renewal, and other public measures affects the cost-revenue balance that develops and thus the basic long-run municipal finance outlook as we have noted. Yet the way the land use process is viewed by the council, the mayor or city manager, and the various department heads is dependent upon the confidence these officials have in the planning agency, which, in turn, is largely a function of human relations.

The perspective of city officials thus can vary from one urban center to another. Some city councils are well versed in the basic purposes and principles of land use planning and have confidence in the land use plan as a guide to many of the decisions they must make, and some city councils have never heard of the land use plan or, if they have, it is vaguely recalled as a bit of "legal fluff" in the wording of planning and zoning enabling legislation. While mayors and city managers have more opportunity to become conversant with the general elements of the process, their confidence in land use planning tends to be a function of the extent to which the process gives attention to cost considerations, local developmental policies, and similar factors, and the extent to which it supplies answers to present-day problems they are facing. While department heads are less apt to take a broad view of land use planning and will generally be concerned with proposals that directly affect their primary functions, astute relations with these officials can contribute immeasurably to the effective implementation of the land use plan.

While coverage of the many complex elements of political behavior involved in keeping the land use planning process attuned to the broader governmental processes is beyond the scope of this discussion, it is evident that in the conduct, scheduling, and timing of land use planning studies, the city planner must be both sensitive to the necessities of maintaining effective rapport with all segments of the city hall family and appreciative of the contributions that each of these segments can make to the process. At the same time he must recognize and make use of the opportunities the land use planning process affords for bringing public officials into more studied contact with some of the most fundamental and critical problems of local government today. It is largely due to these needs that in recent time we see the progressive planning approach coming more and more into use, and we see a developing emphasis on integrating the technical sequence with the policy-review sequence in the planning process.

The Use of Models in Planning Analyses

In this final section of the chapter we turn our attention to land use models. As noted in Chapter 2, the use of models in planning has encountered skepticism, distrust, and sometimes vehement denunciation. These complaints stem in part from misunderstandings and in part from the struggle involved in overcoming a form of obsolescence in the field. When the first edition of this book came out, there were no models in use in the field, and there were no indications immediately discernible that these changes were in prospect. In the intervening seven years there has been an extraordinary change in progress. Conversion to new systems of data handling and data storage was a necessary first step. The development of the high-speed computer meant that these more efficient data-handling systems could be tied into analytical operations at tremendous savings of time. But even with the speed-up, operations were expensive and beyond the means of most planning agencies. However, fortuitously we have also been in a period of advance in theoretical research, some of it reaching a point at which models could be used effectively in exploring the more complex aspects of land development. So on the heels of these developments has come a flurry of experimentation in the use of mathematical models for planning needs.

Much of the work is still in the research and development stage. Thus some work is concerned with the methodological problems of formulating a systems approach to the study of urban processes,[6] and some is immersed in theoretical explanations of location behavior in the conventions of economic theory.[7] As noted earlier, the works of Artle, Lowry, Harris, and Huff provide illustrations of research being carried to a stage of empirical experimentation,[8] but much of the work at this level is still preoccupied with the very fundamental problem of identifying and observing the behavior of variables—in effect, isolating the essential elements which go into a model and testing the behavior of these variables in pilot investigations. Many of them are designed to study urban development rather than to simulate it.

Our concern here is with the use of models as tools for determining the implications for urban form of pursuing each of several possible policy orientations.[9] Referring to Figure 36, we have, say, three schemes, each purported to be a true representation of the policy combination favored in the policy review in the preceding preliminary planning stage. Essentially the variations in these schemes constitute policy choices of a more detailed order, and the model is used here to generate the pattern of development which can be expected from the policy combination emerging from the preliminary planning stage, compare each of the schemes with this "policy pattern," and establish the extent of deviation of each scheme within pre-established confidence limits. With these tests of the extent that the new policy choices depart from the original policy direction, and with cost-benefit, time-distance, and livability checks of each scheme, there is a basis for making a choice. It is possible that the planning agency would run through several tests of this nature, revising each scheme to achieve a more favorable correspondence with the original policy direction, or achieving a more favorable balance in cost-benefit, time-distance, and livability, or both. Or it is possible that, finding the results obtained from these

---

[6] For example, see William L. Garrison, "Toward a Simulation Model of Urban Growth and Development," Proceedings of the Symposium in Urban Geography, Lund, 1960, *Lund Studies in Geography,* Lund, Sweden: C. W. K. Gleerup, 1962.

[7] For example, see John F. Kain, A *Multiple Equation Model of Household Locational and Tripmaking Behavior,* Santa Monica: The RAND Corporation, April, 1962.

[8] Roland Artle, *Studies in the Structure of the Stockholm Economy,* Stockholm: The Business Research Institute at the Stockholm School of Economics, 1959; Ira S. Lowry, A *Model of Metropolis,* Santa Monica: The RAND Corporation, August, 1964; Britton Harris, "Experiments in Projection of Transportation and Land Use," *Traffic Quarterly,* April, 1962; and David L. Huff, *Determination of Intra-Urban Retail Trade Areas,* Los Angeles: Real Estate Research Program, Graduate School of Business Administration, University of California, 1962.

[9] An alternative use of this type of model would be as an aid to planning design. The question asked would be: Given this urban form, what policy combination is most apt to produce this pattern?

more exacting analyses of cost-benefit, time-distance, and livability to be out of focus with the intent of the original policy orientation, the "policy pattern" itself would be modified and a new set of schemes developed and tested in the above manner.

Clearly such a use of models is a powerful tool of planning design. Very soon we may expect most aspects of the analytical task to be linked up in a systems approach. Machine-programmed cost-benefit analyses and time-distance comparisons are already being made in the transportation field, and several joint planning and transportation studies have introduced experimental forms of land development and transportation models designed to function in tandem as suggested by Figure 36.

Requirements of a Model

In the usage here a "model" is a mathematical representation of a phenomenon previously conceptualized in verbal and logical form in theory.[10] For the needs of planning agencies, in place of using models designed to test theories, we seek a model designed to apply one or more aspects of a theory. Three of the criteria noted in Chapter 2 as a basis for evaluating the sufficiency of a theory can be reintroduced here as requirements we seek to satisfy in selecting a model: first, that the model must grow out of a logically consistent organizing concept; second, that it have some relation to a phenomenon or process as it actually occurs or functions in reality; and third, that it have a dynamic quality which is recursive (capable of repetitive applications, with each such iteration stabilized before proceeding to the next) and capable of taking into account feedback effects in the course of the stabilizing process—both land development feedback and transportation feedback.

The importance of the first requirement needs no laboring. The validity of a model is dependent on the validity of the underlying organizing concept, and the validity of this concept is of course dependent on a firm base in theory of the kind we can expect to develop from work summarized in Chapter 2. Essentially the organizing concept draws on some basic theoretical framework, usually seeking to represent in the operations of the model a process or phenomenon as it occurs in reality. Depending to some extent on the discipline in which the model originator is accustomed to working, land use models can be organized around the market concept from economics, around communications theory, around a theory of social action, and so on. For use as a planning tool in testing features of a land use plan, we require that the organizing concept be brought to focus on

---

[10] In the conventions of many fields, a model and a theory are used interchangeably.

the *development process.* This, of course, is essentially the process we have been following in simplified form in Part III.

This brings us directly into the second requirement—the importance of the model's bearing a close relation to reality. Here we seek a model that simulates the development process as it occurs in the real world. Thus a model designed to take account of the kinds of factors developers consider in selecting and developing subdivision sites and the kinds of factors households consider in renting or buying a home site is more attuned to the real-world development process than one which utilizes indices or past trends in rates of growth as gross indicators of the attractiveness of an area for development.

The third requirement—the dynamic aspect of the model—follows from the second. One very real-world characteristic of the development process is the evolutionary sequence in the way one land use influences the purchase of land and development of another use in the normal course of this process. For a model adequately to recognize linkage of this kind in the process, it is essential that it be recursive and operate in a manner so that development sequences can be simulated. Ideally a model would provide for a continuous flow of development, and simulate the growth and renewal of the urban area on a parcel-by-parcel basis. But because the state of the arts does not permit us to set parameters of the model with an accuracy commensurate to a lot-by-lot representation of the development process, and because we do not actually need this kind of detail in testing out the policy assumptions of a plan, we introduce breaks in the process and design the model to simulate development by larger aggregates of land use. Usually these breaks are introduced at uniform intervals, with the time spans set to correspond to the unit of time represented in the typical capital budget (five or six years). This time span sets the rhythm of inventory systems and data collection, enabling a "take-off period" in the operation of the model extending back in time at least 10 or 12 years. At each break in the system, we insert new parameters, start the system up, and generate an increment of growth. Thus each growth cycle corresponds with an iterative period in the operation of the model, with growth handled in small increments in five- or six-year steps at a time rather than in one giant step to the end of the planning period as was done in the preliminary planning stage.

For this dynamic aspect of the model to produce realistic results, it is necessary to give special study to the parameters. These are constants which bring the weight of each variable in the model into balance with every other variable during one particular iteration. They are estimated from a historical investigation over the immediate past, constituting what we referred to above as the "take-off period" of the development process.

If data inputs on variables are available for the past periods of time and fed into the model, mathematically it is possible to derive parameters for past periods of growth. Since relationships among variables will frequently change in the real world from one period of time to another, this type of analysis assists in arriving at plausible future values to parameters, considering the range of variation in each in the past and recent trends in its behavior. The user of a model must decide whether or not he will make assumptions concerning changes and introduce adjustments to parameters as iterations proceed. For short-period forecasts up to 10 or 12 years ahead, most users keep values constant and make the results contingent on "no change" in the relationships among variables in the forecast period. Of course, it is almost axiomatic that as the model generates development forward in time, the further forward the more subject the parameters are to error. For long-range forecasts where it is almost certain that changes in science and technology will alter relationships, the user will often introduce assumptions as to how parameters can be expected to change. Of course, as iterations are carried forward in time, there is not only the eventuality that parameters will change but also that new variables not presently incorporated in the model will become important. So the whole emphasis in estimating parameter values is a cautionary one: "If the parameters selected are correct and if these indeed are the important variables, this is likely to be the pattern of development."

The foregoing considerations do not cover the mathematical sufficiency and the conventions followed in the formulation of models. This, too, certainly is a requirement to be investigated by the user of models. In summarizing these requirements, we seek only to give a general insight into planning needs, and it is beyond the scope of a volume of this kind to go into the actual process of formulating a model in mathematical terms. Further, we leave it to the reader to apply these criteria. We now turn to a few examples of models.

Some Illustrative Models

At this stage in model development, there appear to be two general classes being tested and introduced into planning analyses. One draws upon indices of various kinds, using them as "forces" regulating the development process. The gravity model has frequently been used, and sometimes a multiple regression equation is used to provide a composite index of a variety of factors or forces significantly associated with growth or decline. The other class is based on a behavioral concept of development, with the model simulating the way in which households and firms reach location decisions. Here, depending on the particular organizing concept of the model and the designer's mathematical representation of the process, there is some variation in the variables used as noted below. In either class the model may be expressed in probabilistic form in the sense that it distributes growth on a randomizing basis, or it may be expressed in a deterministic form in the sense that it produces one and only one pattern of development. These distinctions will become clearer below.

Growth Index Models

In the present early stage of model development, this class of models has been used more generally than the other class. For purposes of illustration, we shall briefly review the work of Hansen and that of Lakshmanan and Fry.[11] In effect, Hansen uses the concept of accessibility as an organizing concept for distributing to specific sections of the metropolitan area a given aggregate estimate of residential growth. His basic concept calls for the distribution of new population to zones according to their respective development potentials and holding capacities relative to those of all other zones in the metropolitan area. To get at a zone's development potential, Hansen establishes what he calls its "development ratio," which is operationally defined as a function of accessibility to employment. In his formulation of the accessibility function he uses the gravity model. In its most elemental form, the model is presented in the traditional manner:

$$_1A_2 = \frac{S_2}{T^x_{1-2}}$$

where $_1A_2$ is a relative measure of the accessibility of Zone 1 to employment activity in Zone 2; S_2 is the size of employment activity in Zone 2; T_{1-2} is the travel distance between Zones 1 and 2; and x is an exponent describing the effect of travel time between zones. Applying this relationship to all employment zones, a composite measure of accessibility is obtained:

$$A_1 = \frac{S_2}{T^x_{1-2}} + \frac{S_3}{T^x_{1-3}} + \cdots + \frac{S_n}{T^x_{1-n}} \qquad (1)$$

Using existing employment (S) and distance (T) data, a value can be computed for x. Hansen suggests that the value of x varies very little from zone to zone if estimates are expressed in terms of time from portal to

[11] Walter G. Hansen, "How Accessibility Shapes Land Use," *Journal of the American Institute of Planners,* May, 1959; and Tiruvarur R. Lakshmanan and Margaret E. Fry, "An Approach to the Analysis of Intraurban Location," a paper presented at the annual meetings of the Southeastern Section, Regional Science Association, November, 1963.

portal. In Washington he found the value of x to be 2.7 for residential accessibility to employment areas.

Having established a measure of accessibility for each zone, he then proceeds to compute for each zone a development ratio (actual development divided by probable development). Using the exponent value from the Washington study, it is computed from this expression:

$$D_1 = kA_1^{2.7} \qquad (2)$$

where D_1 is the development ratio for Zone 1; A_1 is the accessibility to employment from Zone 1; and k is a constant of proportionality. Thus he draws on values obtained in Equation (1) to solve Equation (2).

Now, having devised a means of estimating a zone's accessibility to employment and from this its development ratio, Hansen proceeds to distribute household population to the metropolitan area, using a model expressed in the form of a proportion:

$$\frac{P_1}{P_t} = \frac{D_1 O_1}{D_1 O_1 + D_2 O_2 + \cdots + D_n O_n} \qquad (3)$$

where P_1 is the increase in residential population in Zone 1; P_t is the total increase in residential population for the entire metropolitan area; and O_1 is the developable land in Zone 1. Of course, Equation (3) can be transformed into the following estimating equation:

$$\frac{P_1}{P_t} = \frac{A_1^{2.7} O_1}{A_1^{2.7} O_1 + A_2^{2.7} O_2 + \cdots + A_n^{2.7} O_n} \qquad (4)$$

Such a formulation was found useful in small growing urban areas, but some kind of adaptation became necessary when the approach was applied to large metropolitan areas where the central city was an area of declining population, with only the outlying suburbs receiving growth.

This problem lead Lakshmanan and Fry to suggest a dual set of models, one for declining areas and one for growing areas. Using a linear form of multiple regression, they developed general estimating equations for each of the two situations. In their Baltimore study for the central city area such factors as age of district, the extent of nonwhite occupancy, and prestige were used as indices of change. The multiple regression equation took the following form:

$$\triangle P_c = b_1 AL_r + b_2 HP + b_3 NW + b_4 PRG + b_0 \qquad (1)$$

where $\triangle P_c$ is central city population change; AL_r is available vacant residential land in acres based on an assumed zoning policy; HP is percentage of new housing built in the decade previous to the beginning of the growth period; NW is percentage of nonwhite population in the central city; PRG is "prestige level" in the area (measured by income of families and unrelated individuals in the area); and b_1, b_2, b_3, and b_4 are the respective beta coefficients of these independent variables, and b_0 the residual.

For the suburban growth area, the form of the equation was:

$$\triangle P_s = b_1 AL_r + b_2 AC_w + b_3 SW + b_4 LV_a + b_5 PRG_a + b_0 \qquad (2)$$

where $\triangle P_s$ is suburban area population change; AC_w is an index of accessibility to work; SW is an index of sewer and water service (per cent of land with sewer and water service in area); and LV_a is "land value" (the product of the median value of homes and prevailing density of housing). Other factors were defined as above.

The factors in the first equation (1) were found to be significantly associated with population change in the central city area, and the factors in the second (2) were found to be significantly associated with population change in the suburban growth area.[12] On the basis of the statistical tests, these prediction equations were considered suitable in forecasting the distribution of a given estimate of the total population to residential areas in Baltimore. In effect, this constitutes a forecast of residential development.

Multiple regression techniques have also been used to estimate the distribution of other land uses. In his study of Stockholm, Artle distributed the total number of retail establishments of different categories (previously determined in his input-output analysis of the metropolitan area) to various zones in the urban area using size of resident population and size of working population in each zone as independent variables.[13] While strong relationships were found using this mix of variables, he suggests that the level of rent these establishments would be paying and some measure of time-distance should probably be included in the formulation. Lakshmanan and Fry's regression model for retail employment introduces the latter variable, using as a measure "accessibility to population" as a third independent variable.[14] In their Baltimore study, multiple regression techniques are also used to distribute service employment, construction-transportation-

---

[12] In tests of 29 central city districts of Baltimore, a multiple determination coefficient (R^2) of 0.88 was obtained and an F-ratio of 43.1 at the 0.001 level of significance; in the 13 suburban districts, an R^2 of 0.85 and F-value of 8.0 at the 0.025 level of significance were obtained. See Lakshmanan and Fry, *ibid.*

[13] Artle uses a probability distribution of establishments to construct his index of association (the quotient of the standard deviation of the distribution of establishments obtained by regression analysis and the standard deviation of the distribution obtained on a probability basis) and thus evaluate the results obtained. See Artle, *Studies in the Structure of the Stockholm Economy*, pp. 126–138.

[14] Lakshmanan and Fry, "An Approach to the Analysis of Intraurban Location."

wholesale employment, and government employment using other appropriate indices.

For the local-serving retail sector, the gravity model has been widely used. Suggesting it as an alternative to the simpler regression approach, Artle outlines a conceptual basis for the use of an income potential form of this model.[15] In this kind of application of the gravity model, income is used in the numerator, with the usual time or distance measure in the denominator. Such a model in effect says that the income of people living in any particular zone has a potential influence on all other zones, but with the influence declining with distance. Given a forecast of the aggregate income potential in each zone and viewing this income in terms of possible future demand and thus receipts for various categories of goods and services, Artle suggests that this model can be used to distribute to sections of the metropolitan area a total number of retail establishments of appropriate types which have been previously estimated from a study such as his input-output study. These would be the shops that come into being in response to this demand. He points out that to make such a model realistic, refinements would be required to give recognition to consumption patterns of various socio-economic groups, the distribution of purchases among local and nonlocal places, and the rent structure arising out of competition for sites. As Artle points out, under the regression approach we are theoretically implying that there will be no significant trade occurring between zones, whereas in the gravity model we are implying no barriers between zones from the viewpoint of site selection.[16]

Huff has developed and tested a probability form of the gravity model.[17] His is a consumer- rather than a producer-oriented model. He assumes a distribution of shopping centers, and asks: What is the probability that a consumer in a given zone will travel to a given shopping center? His type of model offers possibilities of checking the plausibility of a distribution of establishments obtained by regression techniques.

Behavioral Models

Up to this point in this summary of models, the reader may wonder whether such formulations as Artle's or Huff's are not really behavioral in character. The line of demarcation at best is a very general one. Certainly

---

[15] For a review of gravity and potential models and various applications, see Gerald A. P. Carrothers, "An Historical Review of the Gravity and Potential Concepts of Human Interaction," *Journal of the American Institute of Planners*, May, 1956.

[16] See Artle, *Studies in the Structure of the Stockholm Economy*, p. 138.

[17] See Huff, *Determination of Intra-Urban Retail Trade Areas*.

producer and consumer behavior as conceptualized in these two models in one sense make them behavioral in character. But if the position is taken that we seek to derive the form of the model from the process we are endeavoring to simulate, rather than fitting the process to a borrowed principle, then in this sense we are dealing in this section with a different class of model. In the gravity model and, to a greater extent, in the regression approach, we start from the empirical situation and endeavor to find some way to develop an organizing concept to explain or forecast a state we find we wish to predict. In the behavioral approach, we start with a conceptual framework and within this framework we focus on a particular organizing concept and come finally to the empirical problem involved.

Because the theoretical developments in urban spatial structure are still in a very formative stage, examples in this class of models are only just beginning to take shape. Since most are still in an experimental form and may therefore undergo further modification before an operational version emerges, only a general description of a few formulations which are in a more advanced stage of test will be given here. We shall illustrate with three economic models and one Monte Carlo–type model.

The three economic models provide two contrasting approaches, one being a macro-type model (the Pittsburgh model) in the sense of dealing with interactions of broad aggregates of activity and the other two being micro-type models (the Penn-Jersey Transportation Study model and the Southeastern Wisconsin Regional Planning Commission model) in the sense of simulating market processes in some detail. As developed by Lowry for the Pittsburgh Regional Economic Study, the Pittsburgh model actually consists of sets of models, the first of which distributes households on the basis of an assumed distribution of "basic" employment, and the second of which distributes retail employment of local-serving establishments on the basis of results generated in the first operation.[18]

The key feature in Lowry's model is his trip distribution indices computed from data assembled in the Pittsburgh Area Transportation Study. For the household model he constructs around each of 13 residential zones a set of 11 concentric rings of one mile radial width measured outward from the zone's centroid. Then using the transportation study trip data, he computes the percentage of all work trips originating in each zone which can be expected to find terminals in each successive ring outward, assuming employment opportunities of each ring are evenly distributed. In his analysis of these indices he shows how the trip distribution function varies with four major occupation groups.

---

[18] See Lowry, *A Model of Metropolis.*

Indices obtained in this fashion are applied to employment estimates at centers of "basic" employment to arrive at the residential distribution of this employment and its household equivalent in population, with the result forming various overlapping patterns of population densities generated from the different work centers. The second model is based on trip indices for four types of retail establishments and for various other use-related trips. Applying these indices to the new population generated in the first model, Lowry obtains a distribution of retail and other forms of local-serving employment developing to serve this population. For details of the approach, the mathematical formulations, and the progress of tests, the reader should consult Lowry's work.

As sketched out by Herbert and Stevens, the Penn-Jersey Transportation Study proposes a linear programming approach to distributing households in the metropolitan area.[19] They see households seeking to satisfy their housing needs and desires in the marketplace, with location decisions reached according to costs of obtaining the wanted items as measured against the household budget available. Assuming households will have full knowledge of the market, the model is designed to find optimum locations for households of various income levels.

The model seeks to give recognition to four location factors—a type of house, an amenity level, an accessibility combination, and a site size—with households locating to maximize their rent-paying ability and minimize their total land rent within certain constraints of the market (the holding capacity of zones and the given numbers of households in each group). This type of model requires a sampling survey of present households to establish preferences on housing type, amenity level (which presumably includes community facilities as well as qualities of attractiveness), and site size. Investigations of this kind would provide a basis for determining assumptions on future preferences. This information and data on the desired levels of accessibility could be obtained as part of the home interview operation customarily carried out in connection with transportation studies. Information on characteristics of sites to receive households conceivably could be obtained as part of a land use survey, or it could be approximated from interviews with real estate people and others familiar with the market. The reader interested in this approach should refer to Herbert and Stevens for the general mathematical statement and may want to keep informed on tests of the model when these are made and results are reported. Undoubtedly changes will emerge as the approach is made operational.

[19] John D. Herbert and Benjamin H. Stevens, "A Model for the Distribution of Residential Activity in Urban Areas," *Journal of Regional Science,* Fall, 1960.

Harris' description of the use of this kind of model in the framework of the total system of models Penn-Jersey has under consideration for their long-pull program of studies provides a good picture of the fundamental approach involved in integrating systems of land use models with the transportation models:[20]

The combined transportation and land use model which we have in mind will operate along the following lines. We will start in 1960 with the known distributions of residence and activity, and a functioning transportation system. For each five-year period we will introduce changes in the transportation system following some line of transportation development policy, and changes in other associated public policies. The transportation changes will be in the form of additions of links to the transportation system through highway or rail construction, the deleion of links, and changes in speeds through improvements or congestion. Other public policies will be introduced in such forms as zoning restraints on types of land development or the acquisition of lands for public parks and their removal from private development. Population and industrial and commercial growth over the five-year period will also be introduced. People and businesses will be given a propensity to move, and will select their best new locations according to accessibility and desirability of the various available areas. Areas may be available because they are now vacant or because the pressure for redevelopment is sufficient to cause a change in use. At the conclusion of the five-year period there will be a somewhat altered distribution of activity and residence, which will place different demands upon the transportation system and alter its performance. Thus at the end of one five-year iteration a new distribution of population and business is available to influence the next period of iteration, and the performance of the updated transportation system is known and spelled out in terms of time between districts, vehicle miles of travel, and so on.

The Wisconsin model is part of a larger systems-engineering approach being developed by the Southeastern Wisconsin Regional Planning Commission.[21] The overall approach involves the development and use of a regional economic simulation model and a land use simulation model, each with subsystems consisting of a linked set of submodels. The land use model is designed primarily as a tool for testing regional land use plans. From preliminary information on this work, the residential submodel focuses on consumer and producer interaction involved in the development process. Feeling that the linear programming approach is somewhat unrealistic in its "perfect knowledge" assumption and that the complex interplay of variables that impinge on decisions in the land development process cannot be reduced to profit optimization alone, Schlager seeks to focus more directly on how decisions are actually made, considering the kinds of factors known to land developers, contractors, and

---

[20] Harris, "Experiments in Projection of Transportation and Land Use," pp. 315–316.

[21] Kenneth J. Schlager, "A Report on Models of the Southeastern Wisconsin Regional Planning Commission," *Newsletter of the Transportation Planning Computer Program Exchange Group,* Vol. 1, No. 2, Washington: U.S. Bureau of Public Roads, October 15, 1963.

households when they actually make decisions.[22] The approach focuses on a sequence of decisions—first, the developer's decision to prepare land for residential use; next, the builder's decision on dwelling unit types; and finally, the decision of the household to rent or buy a dwelling unit. Each decision involves a range of variables which are introduced as the model passes through each stage in the development sequence. Since it is a recursive model, the manner in which each cycle of decisions modifies the market situation for the next cycle is taken into account in the next decision sequence. Here too the reader will need to consult reports as they are issued in the future to follow the development and uses of this simulation model.

The fourth is a residential model.[23] Developed by the author and his colleagues at the University of North Carolina, it draws on the conceptual view of the development process outlined in Chapter 2. It will be recalled that under this framework this process is set in motion by certain basic needs of human interaction, the particular nature of which can be defined in analyses of activity systems and movements of people and goods or substitute forms of communication between activity centers. The need that households, firms, and other activities have to interact and be in proximity to one another is seen to set in motion location decisions which, taken as a whole, constitute the development process in a metropolitan area.

The development process is thus seen as a flow of development decisions. This flow is viewed as having an internal order in the sense that some appear to be decisions of a strategic nature and lead the way to a whole series of other subsequent decisions. Mediating this development process are city hall and marketplace actions. In formulating the model, all strategic public decisions from city hall and the location decisions of large employers are "givens." Presented in alternatives, these are the policy preconditions assumed in each land development scheme. As presently designed, the model, then, seeks to simulate the market by distributing households to land determined to be suited for residential development. Rather than distributing households individually, for practical reasons they are distributed in aggregates, the size of the aggregate being dependent on the scale of the grid system used in the system of analysis areas.

A Monte Carlo approach has been developed by Donnelly to fit this conceptual framework.[24] Still in a test stage, under his computer program

[22] From an informal discussion with Kenneth J. Schlager, Chief Systems Engineer, Southeastern Wisconsin Regional Planning Commission, in December, 1963.

[23] F. Stuart Chapin, Jr., and Shirley F. Weiss, *Factors Influencing Land Development*, Chapel Hill: Institute for Research in Social Science, University of North Carolina, in cooperation with the U.S. Bureau of Public Roads, August, 1962.

[24] Thomas G. Donnelly, F. Stuart Chapin, Jr., and Shirley F. Weiss, *A Probabilistic Model for Residential Growth*, Chapel Hill: Institute for Research in Social Science, University of North Carolina, in cooperation with the U.S. Bureau of Public Roads, May, 1964.

a randomizing feature operates to distribute households in a probabilistic manner as opposed to the more common deterministic approach. Such a feature gives recognition to chance considerations and variables of location behavior we are unable to identify with our present knowledge.

The requirements for the operation of this model are threefold: first, land areas in the metropolitan grid suited to receive residential development need to have been identified by land capability analysis and the pattern of residential densities must have been prescribed by the plan; second, the relative pulling power for development of this pattern of "receiving areas" must have been established; and third, a prior analysis must have been completed establishing the extra pulling power that planned improvements of certain kinds would exert on residential development under policies assumed. Thus, under the first requirement each grid cell which is suited to receive development is identified and its holding capacity coded. Under the second requirement the land value of each such grid cell is coded. It is a premise in this simplified model that threshold levels of relative accessibility and amenity of each plot of land will be reflected in the value placed on the parcel in the market.

Under the third requirement, in establishing the relative effect that planned improvements would have on residential development, multiple regression analysis can be used to advantage. By ex post facto studies of the effect on development of different mixes of improvements and policies, the pulling power of such policy mixes can be calibrated relative to the base pulling power of unimproved land by following the relationships observed during the time span immediately preceding the "start" date for the operation of the model. With these values coded and an exogenously determined estimate of households available for distribution in each iterative period and ready for input, the Monte Carlo computer program can be set in motion to distribute households in each successive period.

Given a metropolitan area with its particular configuration of uses, community facilities, transportation systems, and pattern of vacant and open land, the computer inputs the structure of existing land values at the threshold date. The computer then consults the plan in skeletal form and notes the locations of strategic public improvements and employment centers expected to develop in the first growth period.[25] Land values are advanced in accordance with the expected effects the new improvements will have on the structure of land values. Having reassessed land for the effect these planned changes would have, the development process

---

[25] The skeletal features of the plan are the strategic public decisions taken as preconditions for a particular scheme. In the test city, these plan elements were the estimated expansion in employment at existing major centers or the creation of new centers, major highway extensions or widenings, sewer outfall extensions or the installation of important new lift stations, and new schools or important additions to existing schools at the elementary level.

is set in motion. To areas of pre-established densities with a pre-deter-mined attractiveness for development, household units available for this iterative period are distributed by a randomizing process. For the next growth period any changes in the land value rates assumed due to expected realignments in policies and any changes assumed due to technology or other considerations are introduced. The plan is consulted again and im-provements scheduled during this period noted; the land remaining for residential development is revalued again; and the development process set in motion again. So the process is continued through to the end of the planning period. The result is the pattern of probable residential develop-ment fitted to the skeletal elements of the plan as they were "built" segment by segment in successive iterative periods.

There are many ways in which such a model can be improved. For example, it can be designed to differentiate between newly developing areas and renewal areas; it can be modified to recognize distinctions between different socio-economic groups and between households in the rental and the sale markets; and it can be brought to focus on the market behavior of lending institutions, developers, and builders. The operations of the model itself need further study. For example, the time differential in the impact of different policies on the structure of land values needs further study. There could be a lag of as much as one iterative period from the time a strategic element of the plan is "built" and the time that the effect on land value is experienced. As noted above, amenities are assumed to be reflected in the value placed on the land. This may be a realistic assumption at the threshold of development, but in successive periods of growth some adjustments may need to be introduced to reflect feedback effects on amenities.

Though brief and selective, this review gives a little of the shape of things beginning to emerge in the use of models. It will be recalled that the purpose in discussing models in this final section was to indicate the kind of rigor and detail involved in the more advanced stages of the pro-gressive planning sequence. Not all urban centers will find it feasible to use ADP systems of data handling and models of the kind described above in developing a general land use and transportation plan. For urban areas under 100,000 population, refinements in preliminary planning techniques of the kind suggested in Chapter 11 will be sufficient. In larger urban areas and certainly in the major metropolitan areas, planning agencies cannot hope to cope with the demands on their time and provide the kind of staff work for policy formulation that will be increasingly their responsibility to provide unless they avail themselves of these tools of analysis. So this volume ends on a note which in effect becomes the introduction to a new one—one which will supply guidelines for this new form of systems analysis.

Index

National Committee on Urban Transportation, 343, 344
National Council on Schoolhouse Construction, 456n
National Planning Association, 120n, 123n, 167, 171n, 175-176
National Resources Committee, 130, 132
National Resources Planning Board, 351n
Navin, R. B., 322n
Neighborhood density concept, 429
Nuisances, control of, 46-47
    and land uses, 47, 299, 378-379

O-D surveys. *See* Transportation
Odum, H. W., 133
Office functions, employment in, 179
    space requirements of, 405-407
Official map. *See* Maps
O'Harrow, Dennis, 378
Open space, reservation of, 417-419
Outdoor Recreation Resources Review Commission, 120n, 167n, 171n, 175n, 418

Parking ratios, business areas, 407, 441
Parks, local, 375, 377, 448-449
    natural, 377, 420
    region-serving, 374, 419-421
    See also Open space
Pasma, T. K., 394n, 395n
Pearl, Raymond, 212
Penn-Jersey Transportation Study, 89, 340, 341, 484
Perloff, H. S., 121n, 127n
Perry, E. L., 453n
Perry, Josef, 215
Pfouts, R. W., 147-148
Philadelphia City Planning Commission, 315, 387, 388-389, 394, 410, 434-436, 465, 469
Pickard, J. P., 364n
Plan, capital improvements, 198
    comprehensive (master or general plan), 197-198, 270, 357, 362
    evaluation of, 380-381, 460-463, 469-470
    general land use and transportation, 357, 458
    horizon year, 198, 361-362, 458
    preliminary land use, defined, 270, 356-357, 458
    See also Land use plan
Planning Advisory Service. *See* American Society of Planning Officials

Planning area. *See* Area delineations
Planning districts. *See* Area delineations
Planning period, 197-198, 261
Playfields, 377, 449
Playgrounds, 375, 377, 449
Police stations, 416
Policies, defined, 349
    and effectuation of plan, 349, 362-363
    hierarchical aspect of, 349-351
    land development, 349-354, 380-382
    relating to CBD, 461-462, 463-464
    school, 455-456
    transportation, 350, 381, 461-462
    See also Land use planning
Policy review. *See* Progressive planning approach
Political climate, 60-62
Population, methods of measuring, 182
    sources of data, 182-183
    vital statistics, 183, 186
Population, current estimates, censal ratio methods, 189-190, 192-193
    composite methods, 191-192
    dwelling unit method, 193
    evaluation of methods, 194-196
    migration and natural increase method, 184-189
    regression method, 192
    vital statistics rate method, 190-191
Population characteristics, age composition, 214-215
    daytime-nighttime distribution, 43, 44, 217-218
    fertility ratio, 204
    household size, 216, 425
    income, 215-216
    migration, 199-200
    military, 188-189, 209-210
    residential distribution, 218-219, 440
    See also Models, residential
    school, 186-187, 445, 456
Population forecasts, by age groups, 203-205, 214-215
    considerations in developing, 196-203
    cohort-survival method, 203-205
    estimates based on employment forecasts, 210-211
    estimates based on forecasts for larger areas, 208-210
    evaluation of methods, 212-213
    mathematical and graphical methods, 211-212
    migration and natural increase method, 205-208